Why Do You Need this New Edition?

If you're wondering why you should buy this new edition of *Pathways: Writing Scenarios: Sentences and Paragraphs* here are 10 good reasons!

1 **The Writing-Reading Connection.** Good writing is directly connected to active reading. *Pathways* not only teaches you the skills you need to be a successful writer but also how to use reading to develop and improve your thinking and writing skills. You become not only a better writer but a better reader and overall student as well.

2 **Writing in Progress Exercises.** In each chapter, writing-in-progress exercises build upon each other and guide you through the *activity* of writing while simultaneously enhancing your writing skills.

3 **New Analyze It! Feature.** Starting in Chapter 2, you are asked to analyze a paragraph and apply the skills you have been learning in a chapter by completing an idea map, figuring out the meaning of vocabulary, or correcting sentence and grammar errors. This is a fun way to practice your skills and evaluate your progress.

4 **New Examine It! Feature.** In Chapter 14, "Using Methods of Organization," annotated paragraphs by professional writers and textbook authors are used to illustrate the different methods of organization. These paragraphs provide a quick snapshot of the major elements you need to include when you write a paragraph using a specific pattern of organization.

5 **All New ESL Guide.** If English is not your first language, this guide will help you to understand the grammar issues most important to good writing in an easy-to-follow format. Even for native speakers, grammar can be tough, so use this guide to improve your grasp of grammar basics.

6 **ESL Tips:** Throughout the text, ESL Tips appear in the margin to provide you with immediate definitions of unfamiliar vocabulary, explanations of idiomatic speech and cultural references, and cross references to "Reviewing the Basics" and the ESL guide for more detailed information.

7 **New Professional and Student Readings** cover current, high-interest topics including Internet dating, smoking, and body image. New student essays cover a range of topics including rebuilding after a hurricane, comparing best and worst jobs, learning English, and dating online and through Facebook.

8 **New Commonly Confused Words Section.** The new Part E in "Reviewing the Basics" includes a comprehensive list of the most commonly confused words with definitions and example sentences that will ensure you use these troublesome words correctly in your writing.

9 **Sticky Tabs:** A unique page of **sticky tabs** allows you to tab important information, flag new vocabulary, note when assignments are due, remind yourselves to follow up with the instructor, or to bookmark useful charts, summaries, and other information.

10 **MyWritingLab.** Now you can use *Pathways: Writing Scenarios* in combination with Pearson's unique **MyWritingLab** (www.mywritinglab.com). This online site contains diagnostic tests you can use to identify which skills you need to brush up on, 9,000 practice exercises to get up to speed, and a program that lets you track your progress as you move toward mastery of important writing skills.

If practice makes perfect, imagine what *better* practice can do . . .

MyWritingLab is an online learning system that provides better writing practice through progressive exercises. These exercises move students from literal comprehension to critical application to demonstration of their ability to write properly. With this better practice model, students develop the skills needed to become better writers!

When asked if they agreed with the following statements, here are how students responded:

97%
The MyWritingLab Student-user Satisfaction Level

"MyWritingLab helped me to improve my writing." **89%**

"MyWritingLab was fairly easy to use." **90%**

"MyWritingLab helped make me feel more confident about my writing ability." **83%**

"MyWritingLab helped me to better prepare for my next writing course." **86%**

"MyWritingLab helped me get a better grade." **82%**

"I wish I had a program like MyWritingLab in some of my other courses." **78%**

"I would recommend my instructor continue using MyWritingLab." **85%**

Student Success Story

"The first few weeks of my English class, my grades were at approximately 78%. Then I was introduced to MyWritingLab. I couldn't believe the increase in my test scores. My test scores had jumped from that low score of 78 all the way up to 100% (and every now and then a 99)."

—Exetta Windfield, *College of the Sequoias* (MyWritingLab student user)

TO PURCHASE AN ACCESS CODE, GO TO
WWW.MYWRITINGLAB.COM

PATHWAYS
WRITING SCENARIOS
SENTENCES AND PARAGRAPHS

Second Edition

KATHLEEN T. McWHORTER

Niagara County Community College

Longman

New York   San Francisco   Boston
London   Toronto   Sydney   Tokyo   Singapore   Madrid
Mexico City   Munich   Paris   Cape Town   Hong Kong   Montreal

Acquisitions Editor: Matthew Wright

Director of Development: Mary Ellen Curley

Development Editor: Gillian Cook

Marketing Manager: Thomas DeMarco

Senior Supplements Editor: Donna Campion

Senior Media Producer: Stefanie Liebman

Production Manager: Jacqueline A. Martin

Project Coordination, Text Design, and Electronic Page Makeup: Pre-PressPMG

Senior Cover Design Manager: Nancy Danany

Cover Image: © Photographer's Choice/Getty Images, Inc.

Photo Researcher: Jody Potter

Senior Manufacturing Buyer: Alfred C. Dorsey

Printer and Binder: Webcrafters, Inc.

Cover Printer: Phoenix Color Corporation, Hagerstown

For permission to use copyrighted material, grateful acknowledgment is made to the copyright holders on pp. 650–651, which are hereby made part of this copyright page.

Library of Congress Cataloging-in-Publication Data

McWhorter, Kathleen T.
    Pathways' writing scenarios : from sentences to paragraphs / Kathleen T. McWhorter. -- 2nd ed.
        p. cm.
    ISBN-13: 978-0-205-61776-0 (student ed.)
    ISBN-10: 0-205-61776-X (student ed.)
    ISBN-13: 978-0-205-63434-7 (aie)
    ISBN-10: 0-205-63434-6 (aie)
    1. English language—Rhetoric—Problems, exercises, etc. 2. English language—Sentences—Problems, exercises, etc. 3. English language—Paragraphs—Problems, exercises, etc. 4. Report writing—Problems, exercises, etc. 5. Critical thinking. 6. College readers. I. Title.

PE1417.M4565 2009
808'.0427--dc22   2008049761

Longman
is an imprint of

2 3 4 5 6 7 8 9 10—WC—12 11 10 09

ISBN-10: 0-205-61776-X (Student Edition)
ISBN-10: 0-205-63434-6 (Annotated Instructor's Edition)
ISBN-13: 978-0-205-61776-0 (Student Edition)
ISBN-13: 978-0-205-63434-7 (Annotated Instructor's Edition)

Brief Contents

Detailed Contents

PART V COMMON PARAGRAPH PROBLEMS AND HOW TO AVOID THEM 421

Preface

*P*athways: *Writing Scenarios*: *Sentences and Paragraphs* guides students toward effective writing through a unique and practical approach. It teaches fundamental sentence and paragraph writing skills by engaging student interest, keeping the focus on ideas rather than on rules, and stressing the interconnection of grammar and the writing process.

This book presents the study of grammar and the study of the "whole paper" as inseparable. Seven of *Pathways'* 18 chapters deal with grammar topics; in these chapters, students examine student essays, read and respond to ideas, and write and revise paragraphs. In Parts II through IV, students are encouraged to apply what they have learned about sentence-level correctness to their own writing as they explore the logical paragraph development and organization of ideas. The last two chapters of the book provide an introduction to essay writing, enabling students to make the transition from paragraphs to essays. This lively, integrated approach leads to greater student interest and better, more fully assimilated, writing skills.

Chapters 2–18 of *Pathways* all contain a brief, high-interest professional reading that sets up opportunities for writing and relates the chapter's lesson to the student's own work. These readings encourage students to think about, discuss, and consider their own experiences, and to respond to what they read by writing, strengthening their confidence in the value and worth of their ideas. Most chapters also include sample student essays that serve as realistic models of student writing. "A Multicultural Reader," Part VII, provides extra opportunities to explore the reading/writing connection. Through the readings and the accompanying apparatus, the text stresses that effective writing must evolve from student interest and experience.

Overview of the Text

Pathways features an integrated reading-writing approach, step-by-step instruction, and a supportive tone. It teaches students the fundamentals of sentence, paragraph, and essay writing through structured, sequential instruction, varied exercises that build upon each other, numerous examples of student writing, and the use of current, issue-oriented readings.

Sentence-level instruction is presented as integral to the clear expression of ideas; a handbook with exercises appears at the end of the text. The text also emphasizes both paragraph and essay writing skills. Each chapter offers paragraph- and essay-level writing assignment options, allowing instructors to move from paragraph to essay writing whenever their students are ready. The text emphasizes academic writing; most chapters contain student essays that are annotated to guide students in examining the aspects of writing taught in the chapter. For each student essay, the writer and the writing task are described and questions follow the reading to help students react to and evaluate it.

Features

The following features further distinguish *Pathways* from other developmental writing texts and make its approach unique:

■ **Visual Approach to Writing** Many students are visual learners; that is, they process information visually rather than verbally or by auditory means. Because many students are visual learners, they respond well to diagrams, charts, and maps. In *Pathways*, students learn to draw idea maps—visual representations of the content and organization of a paragraph or essay—in order to examine ideas. Students also learn to draw revision maps of their own writing as a means of evaluating the effectiveness of the content and its organization and to help them make necessary changes. Sections that feature idea or revision maps are labeled "Visualize It!"

■ **Emphasis on Reading Skills** Chapters 2 and 3 focus on reading skills. Chapter 2 presents strategies for active reading that include previewing, connecting to prior knowledge, reading to learn, and using idea maps to understand a reading, as well as how to approach difficult readings. Chapter 3 focuses on vocabulary development; topics include using a dictionary, using context and word parts to figure out unfamiliar words, using word mapping, and developing a system for learning new words. Reading skills are emphasized throughout the text using professional readings in each chapter that include literal and critical comprehension questions and vocabulary review.

■ **Paragraph Writing Scenarios** Each of Chapters 4–18 contains a set of writing assignments grouped into four categories: friends and family, classes and campus life, working students, and communities and cultures. These writing assignments give students the opportunity to apply chapter content while exploring a relevant theme.

■ **Emphasis on Grammar and Correctness** Seven chapters are devoted to grammar topics. Part VIII, "Reviewing the Basics," is a handbook written with the needs of ESL students in mind. It provides a simple, clear presentation of the forms and rules of grammar, plentifully illustrated with examples, and it includes ample exercises for review of skills. It is designed to help both ESL and developmental writers grasp the fundamentals of grammar, punctuation, and mechanics.

■ **ESL Guide for Nonnative Speakers of English** This guide offers a comprehensive review of grammar and usage topics of particular concern to students learning English as a second language.

■ **New Commonly Confused Words Section** The new Part E in "Reviewing the Basics" includes a comprehensive list of the most commonly confused words with definitions and example sentences that will ensure you use these troublesome words correctly in your writing.

■ **Interconnected Writing in Progress Exercises** These exercises build on each other throughout the course of each chapter, walking students through the different steps of the writing process from prewriting through drafting, writing using different modes, and revision.

■ **Emphasis on Student Success** The book begins with a lively introduction, "Writing Success Starts Here!" that focuses on the skills students need to be successful in their writing class and in college. The first section,

"Take Charge of Your Learning," identifies five behaviors that lead to success and offers concrete strategies for implementing them using sticky tabs (see p. 1). In the second section, "Use the Help Features in This Book," students are shown how they can benefit from various features throughout the book, including how to examine sample student essays and how to learn from reading professional essays. The third section, "Success Workshops," offers practical suggestions on time management, organizing a place to write, improving concentration, building a strong academic image, and learning from feedback.

■ **Reusable Sticky Tabs** The tabs described in the introduction are linked to key success strategies and demonstrate how students can implement each strategy. Tabs are included for marking important material to review ("Important: Review This" tab), checking with classmates and instructors ("Follow Up With" tab), connecting and applying skills ("Useful For" tab), keeping track of assignments ("Assignment Due" tab), and strengthening vocabulary ("Vocabulary" tab). These tabs encourage students to take responsibility for their own learning and become active learners.

■ **Student Essays** Chapters 1, 7, and 8 and all the chapters in Parts III through VI each contain a sample student essay that provides a model of the writing process and sets realistic, attainable expectations for students. Each essay is annotated and is followed by questions that guide students in evaluating the essay.

■ **High-Interest, Engaging Readings** Beginning with Chapter 2, each chapter includes an engaging professional reading around which prewriting, critical thinking, and writing assignments are structured. Readings touch on topics within the students' realm of interest and experience, such as credit card overuse, Internet dating, and military personnel returning from deployment. Each reading offers students a model for the writing skills taught in the particular chapter, as well as a source of ideas and a base for discussion and collaborative learning activities.

Organization of the Text

The text opens with an introduction, "Writing Success Starts Here!" that orients the student to the textbook's features, shows students how to take charge of their own learning using sticky tabs, and offers valuable writing success tips.

The text is organized into nine parts. **Part I, "Getting Started,"** opens with a chapter that establishes the importance of effective writing and provides an overview of the writing process, with an emphasis on prewriting techniques. This chapter also shows how a sample student paper develops through several stages from first draft to final version. Chapter 2, "The Reading-Writing Connection," discusses previewing, reading for meaning in both paragraphs and essays, handling difficult readings, annotating, drawing idea maps, and journal writing. Chapter 3, "Expanding Your Vocabulary," focuses on dictionary usage, context clues, word parts, idea maps, and systems for learning new words.

In **Part II, "Sentence Basics and Development,"** Chapter 4 covers sentence fragments, Chapter 5 examines run-on sentences and comma splices, Chapter 6 discusses sentence types, expansion, and combining, Chapter 7 details adjective and adverb usage, and Chapter 8 addresses modifiers.

In **Part III, "Common Sentence Problems and How to Avoid Them,"** common errors are discussed. Chapter 9 focuses on pronoun usage, shifts in person, number, and verb tense, misplaced and dangling modifiers, and parallelism. Chapter 10 is concerned with verb usage: verb tense, irregular verbs, subject-verb agreement errors, and active versus passive voice.

Part IV, "Paragraph Basics and Development," equips students with the tools for paragraph writing, and leads them sequentially though the writing process. Chapter 11 discusses topic selection, audience, methods of generating ideas (brainstorming, freewriting, and branching) and basic methods of organizing ideas (least/most, time sequence, and spatial arrangement). Chapter 12 concentrates on writing topic sentences, developing paragraphs using supporting details, and using revision maps to revise students' writing. Chapter 13 shows students how to develop a paragraph using specific details, how to arrange details in a paragraph, and how to use transitions. Chapter 14, "Using Methods of Organization" provides a brief introduction to the rhetorical modes of narration, description, example, definition, comparison and contrast, classification, process, cause and effect, and argument.

Part V, "Common Paragraph Problems and How to Avoid Them," focuses on the problems students often experience in paragraph writing. In Chapter 15, students learn to revise ineffective topic sentences and underdeveloped paragraphs. Five key questions guide students in revision and the use of revision maps in Chapter 16.

Part VI, "Essay Basics, Development, and Common Problems," offers introductory material on essay writing and revision. Chapter 17, "Essay Basics and Development," emphasizes writing effective thesis statements, supporting them with evidence, and crafting strong introductions and conclusions. Chapter 18, "Avoiding Common Problems in Essays," identifies five common problems and offers suggestions on how to correct them: a topic that is too broad, a topic that is too narrow, an ineffective thesis statement, an underdeveloped essay, and a disorganized essay.

Part VII, "A Multicultural Reader," contains five selections on a range of stimulating topics that represent a diverse range of authors. These readings offer instructors flexibility in choosing and assigning readings, and further represent the rhetorical modes. Selections are accompanied by the same apparatus as in-chapter professional readings, thereby allowing instructors to substitute those from the Multicultural Reader for in-chapter readings where appropriate.

Part VIII, "Reviewing the Basics," is a brief handbook with exercises. It reviews the principles of grammar, sentence structure, mechanics, punctuation, and spelling. ESL Tips are included to guide English-language learners in applying the content of the handbook.

Part IX, "ESL Guide for Nonnative Speakers of English," addresses grammer and usage concerns of English-language learners.

Chapter Format

■ **Write About It!** Each chapter opens with a photograph or other visual image that is intended to capture the student's attention, generate interest, and connect the topic of the chapter to the student's experience. This feature engages the student and gets the student writing immediately about chapter-related content.

■ **Direct Skill Instruction** The content of each chapter is presented in a simple, direct style, in short sections interspersed with opportunities to practice each skill.

■ **Visualize It!** Many chapters contain idea maps that show how to organize paragraphs and essays. The professional reading also contains a partially completed idea map for students to finish.

■ **Need to Know Boxes** Interspersed throughout chapters, these boxes summarize key content or review important terminology.

■ **Student Essays** Chapters 7–18 each feature an example of student writing presented as a model of a particular writing strategy. The writer and writing task are introduced, and each student essay is annotated and followed by evaluation questions.

■ **Analyze It!** This feature offers students an opportunity to interact with text using skills taught in the chapter. Students may be asked to correct errors, revise, outline, map, or evaluate.

■ **Paragraph Writing Scenarios** Appearing in Chapters 4–18, these sets of writing assignments are grouped into four themes: friends and family, classes and campus life, working students, and communities and cultures.

■ **Writing Success Tips** Each chapter contains a writing success tip that offers practical advice on topics such as keeping an error log, avoiding trite expressions, avoiding plagiarism, using nonsexist language, and writing a summary.

■ **Writing About a Reading** Chapters 2–18 each contain a professional reading to serve as a stimulus for writing. A consistent apparatus is used in each:

> *Thinking Before Reading* precedes each reading. It directs the student to preview the reading and contains several questions designed to activate the student's own knowledge and experience about the subject of the reading.

> *Marginal annotations* for each selection provide definitions of difficult or unusual terminology that is likely to be outside the student's realm of knowledge or experience.

> *Getting Ready to Write* consists of four activities that prepare students to write about the reading.

> - **Reviewing the Reading** checks the student's literal comprehension of the reading.

> - **Examining the Reading Using an Idea Map** encourages the student to analyze the content and organization of the reading by drawing or completing idea maps.

> - **Strengthening Your Vocabulary** reviews important words in the reading and reinforces the use of word mapping.

> - **Reacting to Ideas: Discussion and Journal Writing** offers the student a range of thought-provoking questions on which class discussions or collaborative learning activities may be built.

Writing About the Reading provides assignments that involve the student with ideas expressed in the reading and encourages writing about personal experiences related to the topic. Both paragraph-level and essay-level writing assignments are provided.

■ **Chapter Review and Practice** This section contains three activities designed to provide additional practice and help the student evaluate his or her mastery of chapter content:

Chapter Review Using a test format, this activity allows the student to test his or her recall of important chapter content.

Editing Practice Each chapter contains one or more paragraphs for editing and error correction.

Internet Activities These activities direct the student to various Web sites that focus on writing skills as well as MyWritingLab for additional practice and reinforcement of skills taught in the chapter.

Changes to the Second Edition

The goals of the revision of the text are to provide additional models of effective writing, to increase student interaction with those models, and to provide nonnative speakers with additional help in working through the book and in mastering English. The second edition features

■ **NEW ESL Tips** ESL students will find helpful tips and explanations of grammar usage, idiomatic expressions, cultural references, and vocabulary in marginal boxes throughout each chapter.

■ **NEW ESL Guide** Part IX has been added to the text. This ESL Guide offers additional grammar instruction on areas particularly troublesome to nonnative speakers of English.

■ **NEW Analyze It! feature** Each chapter contains an activity that requires students to interact with a paragraph of professional writing. Students may be asked to revise, edit, map, outline, or critique the writing sample. For example, students correct errors in Chapters 4 and 9, draw maps and write outlines in Chapter 14, and analyze sample brainstorming in Chapter 17.

■ **NEW Examine It! feature** Chapter 14 contains nine professionally written paragraphs that serve as models of the modes taught in the chapter. The paragraphs have been annotated to call attention to particular features of the mode.

■ **NEW Student Essays** Four new student essays have been added to the book. These essays demonstrate skills taught in the chapter and engage students with current topics: learning English, rebuilding a home destroyed by a hurricane, comparing best and worst jobs, and dating and MySpace.

■ **NEW Professional Readings** Four new professional readings have been added on the topics of online dating, learning Spanish, working-class smoking, and media and body image.

■ **NEW Exercises in Part VIII** All of the exercises in "Reviewing the Basics" have been replaced.

Book-Specific Ancillary Materials

■ **The Instructor's Manual/Test Bank (ISBN 0-321-41194-3)** This supplement is full of useful teaching suggestions and includes an introduction to the textbook, activities to engage students' interest, advice to new instructors, and additional writing assignments. The manual also offers suggestions for handling the professional readings, sample syllabi, overhead transparencies, and a full bank of test questions.

■ **Expanding Your Vocabulary by Kathleen McWhorter (ISBN: 0-205-64586-0)** This supplemental text provides additional instruction and practice in vocabulary. Topics covered include methods of vocabulary learning, contextual aids, word parts, connotative meanings, idioms, and euphemisms. The book also offers word lists representative of ten academic disciplines.

■ **The Pearson Longman Developmental Writing Package** Pearson Longman is pleased to offer a variety of support materials to help make teaching developmental writing easier for teachers and to help students excel in their course work. Visit http://www.pearsonhighered.com or contact your local Pearson sales representative for a detailed listing of the supplements package or for more information on pricing and how to create a package.

Acknowledgments

I appreciate the excellent ideas, suggestions, and advice of my colleagues who served as reviewers: Sharon Bone, Ivy Tech Community College-Central Indiana, Cheyenne Bonnell, Copper Mountain College, Frieda Campbell-Peltier, Portland Community College, Elissa Caruth, Oxnard College, Irene Caswell, Lander University, Laura Foster-Eason, Collin County Community College, Jean Garrett, Mt. San Antonio College, John Grosskopf, North Florida Community College, Janet Harclerode, Santa Monica College, Eric Hibbison, J. Sargeant Reynolds Community College, Melissa Michelson, Santa Monica College, Mary Nielsen, Dalton State College, Lisa Moreno, LA Trade Technical College, Tim Reding, Morehead State University, and Jim Schwartz, Wright State University.

The entire editorial staff with whom I have worked deserves praise and credit for its assistance throughout the writing and revision of this text. In particular, I wish to thank Matthew Wright, Acquisitions Editor, for his enthusiastic support throughout the project and Gillian Cook, Development Editor, whose knowledge of the field, creative energy, and organizational abilities kept me on target throughout the revision. I appreciate the willingness of the students to donate samples of their writing for the paragraph samples and student essays: Ebtisam Abusamak, Kally Bajier, Gentry Carlson, Darlene Gallando, Rachel Goodman, Kim Hyo-Joo, Anna Majerczyk, Maya Preswich, Fidel Sanchez, Ted Sawchuck, and Markella Tsoukalas. I also value the professional and creative efforts of Melissa Sacco and her team at Pre-PressPMG. I wish to thank Ethel Tiersky, ESL specialist, for her review of the manuscript and preparation of the ESL Tips and the ESL Guide for Nonnative Speakers of English. Finally, I thank my students, who continue to make teaching a challenging and rewarding profession.

KATHLEEN T. MCWHORTER

Introduction

Writing Success Starts Here!

Writing is an important part of your everyday life, your college career, and the workplace. In your everyday life, for example, you find yourself writing e-mail and filling out forms. In the classroom, you write exams and papers. On the job, you write e-mail, letters, and reports. It is important to be able to write clearly and correctly in each of these situations. Being able to write well is a valuable asset that greatly increases your potential for success.

In this introduction you will learn numerous strategies for becoming a better writer and a more successful student. Specifically, you will learn how to use the sticky tabs described below to take charge of your learning. You will also learn about other features in this book that will make improving your writing easier. Finally, you will complete several success workshops that will help you get off to the right start in college. Along the way, you will hear from real students. They will share practical advice that has helped them become successful students.

TABS: TAKE CHARGE OF YOUR LEARNING

Success in a writing course or in any college course, for that matter, involves taking responsibility for your own learning. Your writing instructor is your guide, but you are in charge. It is not enough to attend class and do your assignments. You have to decide what to learn and how to learn it. This section offers five methods for taking charge of your own learning. For each method, sticky tabs are provided to help you become an active learner.

Decide What Is Important to Learn

TAB: Important: Review This

As you work through this book, you will find a wide range of strategies, rules, samples, examples, steps, tables, checklists, and idea maps. Not everyone learns in the same way. For some students examples may be very useful, while for others a list of steps to follow may be more helpful. You should identify the most important and useful materials for you in each chapter and refer to

1

them often throughout the course. Use the sticky tabs "Important: Review This" to mark these sections. For example, one student realized that knowing how to correct a sentence fragment would help her, so she marked the Need to Know box, "How to Spot Fragments," on p. 112, with a tab. Then, every time she found a fragment in her writing, she used the tab to locate these revision suggestions.

Here is a partial list of items that students have found useful to tab:

- Idea maps—diagrams of how an essay is organized
- Revision checklists
- Annotated student essays
- Ideas for topics to write about
- Need to Know boxes
- Writing Success Tips
- ESL Tips

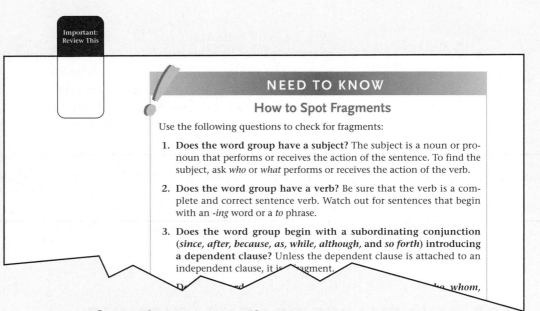

Important: Review This

NEED TO KNOW

How to Spot Fragments

Use the following questions to check for fragments:

1. **Does the word group have a subject?** The subject is a noun or pronoun that performs or receives the action of the sentence. To find the subject, ask *who* or *what* performs or receives the action of the verb.

2. **Does the word group have a verb?** Be sure that the verb is a complete and correct sentence verb. Watch out for sentences that begin with an *-ing* word or a *to* phrase.

3. **Does the word group begin with a subordinating conjunction (*since, after, because, as, while, although,* and *so forth*) introducing a dependent clause?** Unless the dependent clause is attached to an independent clause, it is a fragment.

D   rd   o *whom,*

Learn from Classmates and Instructors

TAB: Follow Up With

Follow Up With

You are never alone in a writing class. Your instructor is your most valuable resource. Work closely with your instructor by discussing topics, talking about writing problems, and seeking help with assignments. Do not be afraid to ask questions. When you find things you want to discuss with your instructor, use the "Follow Up With" tab. Write your instructor's name in the blank space, and use this tab to mark material you have a question about, so you can locate it easily and will remember to speak with your instructor about it. Tabs can be placed on print copies of your essays, class notes, or instructor handouts, as well as on textbook pages.

Your classmates are also valuable resources. They can offer support and friendly feedback. Get together with them informally to discuss assignments, compare notes, and react to one another's papers. Mark material you want to discuss with other students using the "Follow Up With" tab.

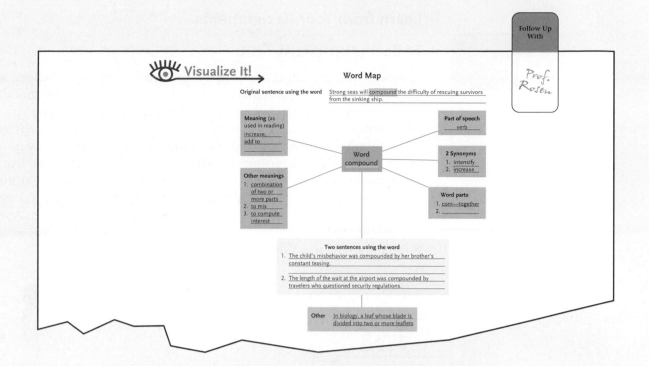

Connect and Apply Your Skills

TAB: Useful For

Your writing will improve when you consciously and deliberately connect skills to one another. This means that you have to use skills learned in one chapter as you complete assignments for a subsequent chapter. For example, you will need to use the vocabulary skills you learn in Chapter 3 when you read and write paragraphs or essays for the subsequent chapters in the book. Your writing will improve more quickly if you use the skills you learn regularly and frequently. Try to apply what you learned last week to what you are writing in your other classes, in your everyday writing, and in any writing you do at work. When you find something useful that applies to writing in other chapters or in other courses or situations, use the "Useful For" tab to mark it for future reference. For example, a nursing student was asked to write a short paper outlining new approaches to diabetes treatment using several sources. He found the suggestions for how to avoid plagiarism in Chapter 14 on p. 413 useful, so he tabbed the page.

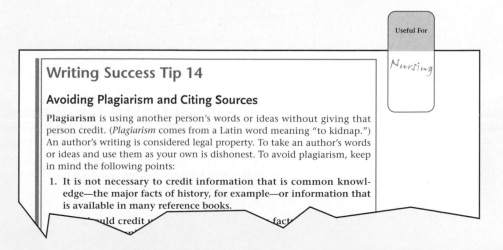

Writing Success Tip 14

Avoiding Plagiarism and Citing Sources

Plagiarism is using another person's words or ideas without giving that person credit. (*Plagiarism* comes from a Latin word meaning "to kidnap.") An author's writing is considered legal property. To take an author's words or ideas and use them as your own is dishonest. To avoid plagiarism, keep in mind the following points:

1. It is not necessary to credit information that is common knowledge—the major facts of history, for example—or information that is available in many reference books.

Learn from Your Assignments

TAB: Assignment Due

Assignment Due

Assignments, including reading assignments, writing exercises, and paragraph and essay assignments, are learning tools. Every assignment that your instructor gives is intended to teach you something. Make sure you complete all assignments carefully and completely. Mark each assignment given with the "Assignment Due" tab and fill in the date. Don't do any assignment just to get it done. Pay attention to what you are supposed to be learning. For reading assignments, highlight what is important and use the other tabs described above. For written assignments, be sure to submit neat, easy-to-read, well-labeled, and well-organized work. Keep copies of all the essays you write and be sure to keep returned, graded assignments as well. Study your instructor's comments to identify areas in which you can improve.

Assignment Due

Paragraph Writing Scenarios

1/12/09

Friends and Family

1. Write a paragraph that begins "The most important thing I learned from my mother is . . ." ✓ honesty? courage? perserverance?

2. Write about an event that stands out in the history of your family.

Classes and Campus Life

1. Which of the "Three R's" (Reading, Writing and Arithmetic) is the most difficult for you? What are you doing to make it easier?

2. Do you think race should be considered in awarding financial aid? Why or why not?

Working Students

1. Write a paragraph that begins "When I go to bed at night, I worry about . . ."

2. Write an imaginary job description that fits you perfectly.

Communities and Cultures

1. What is a typical weekend activity you enjoy doing with a group?

2. Write a paragraph about what you would miss most about your present community if you had to move away.

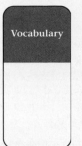

Vocabulary

Strengthen Your Vocabulary

TAB: Vocabulary

Words are the building blocks of language. To write clear sentences and effective paragraphs, you need to have a solid vocabulary with which to start. Everyone can improve his or her vocabulary, and one of the easiest ways to do so is by reading. Throughout the book you will be reading numerous student and professional essays. When you encounter a word you do not know, or one that you know but do not use in your own writing, tab it using the "Vocabulary" tab. If you can get a hint about the word's meaning from the context of the words around it, keep reading and check its meaning later. If you need the word's meaning in order to understand the sentence in which it appears, stop reading and look it up in a dictionary right away. When you find the word's meaning, record it in the margin of the page the word appears on, and later transfer the definition to a vocabulary log.

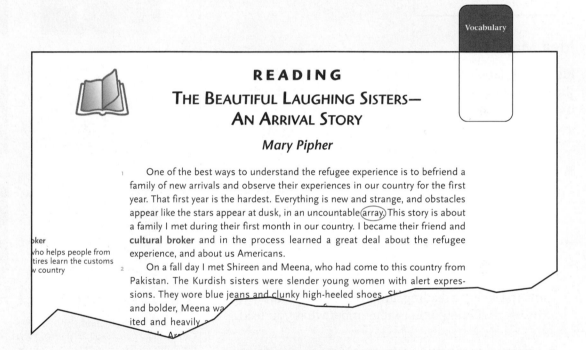

Vocabulary

READING

THE BEAUTIFUL LAUGHING SISTERS— AN ARRIVAL STORY

Mary Pipher

1   One of the best ways to understand the refugee experience is to befriend a family of new arrivals and observe their experiences in our country for the first year. That first year is the hardest. Everything is new and strange, and obstacles appear like the stars appear at dusk, in an uncountable array. This story is about a family I met during their first month in our country. I became their friend and **cultural broker** and in the process learned a great deal about the refugee experience, and about us Americans.

oker
who helps people from
ttires learn the customs
w country

2   On a fall day I met Shireen and Meena, who had come to this country from Pakistan. The Kurdish sisters were slender young women with alert expressions. They wore blue jeans and clunky high-heeled shoes. Sh___
and bolder, Meena wa___
ited and heavily ___

A Note About the Tabs You may run out of tabs before you finish the course. However, by then you will have built the habit of using them and can switch over to using sticky notes for the same purpose.

USE THE HELP FEATURES IN THIS BOOK

Although your instructor and your classmates are your most important sources for learning how to write well, this book also contains numerous features to help you become a successful writer.

In this chapter you will:

1. Look at writing as a way to express ideas.

2. Get an overview of the writing process.

3. Get some practical advice for starting to write.

Chapter Objectives

These lists of topics tell you what you should expect to learn in each chapter. If you know what you are supposed to learn before you begin, you will find that learning is easier and that you will remember more of what you read.

WRITE ABOUT IT!

Study the six photographs shown above one at a time (cover the o your hand as you look at them). What is happening in each? It i difficult to tell because there is so little information in each. Then, six photographs all together. Now it is clear what is happening. V tence that states the main point of the combined photograph.

Idea Maps

Idea maps, labeled "Visualize It!" are diagrams that show the content and organization of a piece of writing. You can use these maps in several ways:

- **To organize and guide your own writing.** Think of them as models you can follow.

- **To help you analyze a paragraph or essay you have written.** Drawing a map of your writing will help you identify problems in organization or spot ideas that do not belong in a paragraph or essay.

- **As an aid to understanding a professional reading that you have been assigned.** By filling in an idea map, you can assure yourself that you have understood the reading, and the process of drawing the map will help you to remember what you read.

Write About It!

Each chapter opens with a photograph or other visual image that is intended to capture your attention, generate interest, and connect the topic of the chapter to your own experience. This "Write About It!" feature also encourages you to start writing immediately about chapter-related content using a relevant topic.

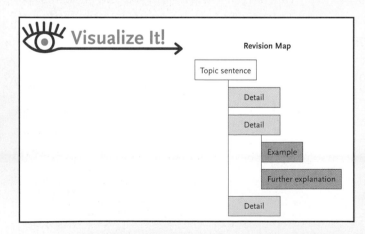

Student Writing Samples

Paragraphs and essays written by students appear throughout this book. They are realistic models of good writing, but they are not perfect. These pieces of student writing are included to illustrate particular writing techniques. Chapter 7, which discusses writing using adjectives and adverbs, for example, includes a student paragraph that demonstrates how to use these parts of speech to add interest and detail to sentences. Here are some suggestions for reading and learning from student writers:

■ **Read the piece of writing more than once.** Read it once to understand the writer's message. Read it again to examine the writing technique it illustrates.

■ **Read the piece to answer this question: What does this writer do that I can use in my own writing?**

■ **Highlight as you read.** Use an "Important: Review This" tab to mark words, sentences, or paragraphs that you want to study further or that you feel work particularly well.

A STUDENT ESSAY
The Student Writer and the Writing Task

The Writer
Kelly Bajier is a student at Avila University in Kansas City, Missouri, where she is majoring in nursing.

The Writing Task
Bajier wrote this essay for a writing class. Her instructor encouraged her to submit her essay to a writing contest sponsored by Longman Publishers, the publisher of this book. Bajier's essay was selected from among hundreds of essays as a good model essay. As you read, notice Bajier's use of clear and correct sentences throughout.

Rebuilding a Dream
Kelly Bajier

It only took one final strong gust of wind, filled with debris and bullet-like raindrops to finish the destruction of the home I knew and loved. My perfect beachfront home was a casualty to one of Mother Nature's most monstrous creations, otherwise known as a hurricane. My father had the house built almost fifteen years ago. I remember him overseeing the construction process as the carpenters and other workers slaved for hours each day. At last the work

background information about the home

NEED TO KNOW
Planning and Organizing

Planning and organizing contribute to successful writing. Be sure to

• focus on ideas, not general topics.

• use events, activities, physical surroundings, media, and people around you as sources of ideas.

• make sure your topic is manageable—neither too broad nor too narrow.

• choose a topic that is well suited to your audience.

Need to Know Boxes

In many chapters you will find boxes titled "Need to Know." Pay particular attention to these boxes because they present or summarize important information. They are a quick, speedy way to review information, so refer to them often. You may want to use your "Important: Review This" tabs to mark boxes that you find particularly valuable.

ESL Tips

ESL (English as a Second Language) boxes appear throughout the book. They are intended to help ESL students learn and apply chapter content by pointing out special concerns, differences among languages, and typical grammatical errors. Even if you are not an ESL student, many of these boxes will emphasize or clarify important points that can be helpful to you.

Allow Sufficient Time to Complete Your Assignments

Begin assignments well before they are due. You will need time to plan, organize, draft, revise, and proofread. Plan to let your drafts "sit" awhile—preferably a day—before you begin to revise. Necessary changes will become much more obvious after some time away from your work.

Take Breaks

If you get stuck and cannot think or write, take a break. Clear your mind by going for a walk, talking to a friend, or having a snack. Set a time limit for your break, though, so you return to work in a reasonable time. When you begin again, start by rereading what you have already written. If you still cannot make progress, use freewriting, brainstorming, and branching techniques (see pp. 20–21) to generate more ideas about your topic.

Use Full 8.5-by-11-Inch Sheets of Paper

By using standard-sized 8.5-by-11-inch paper, you will be able to see better how your ideas connect. Write on only one side of the paper so that you can

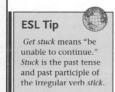

ESL Tip

Get stuck means "be unable to continue." *Stuck* is the past tense and past participle of the irregular verb *stick*.

Paragraph Writing Scenarios

This section offers four groups of writing assignments, categorized "Friends and Family," "Classes and Campus Life," "Working Students," and "Communities and Cultures." The writing assignments under each heading offer a wide range of interesting topics and provide an opportunity for you to apply what you have learned in the chapter by writing paragraphs on interesting and relevant topics.

Essay Writing Scenarios

Friends and Family

1. Describe a family item you would save in the event of a natural disaster. Whose was it, and why is it special to you?

2. Write an essay that begins "The best vacation my family ever took together was . . ."

Classes and Campus Life

1. Mark Twain wrote, "The person who *does* not read good books has no advantage over the person who *can't* read them." Write a short essay explaining what you think he meant.

2. Where do you do your best work, in class discussions or alone on a computer? Why?

Working Students

1. Explain which you'd prefer, a job in which you deal with people or with things.

2. Describe something you do in your daily life that you would never do at work.

Communities and Cultures

1. Community leaders can be elected officials or ordinary citizens. Write an essay about one person who makes (or has made) a difference in your community.

2. Describe one thing you did as a teenager to fit in with a particular group.

Writing Success Tip 18

Taking Writing Competency Tests

Some colleges require students to pass competency tests in writing. Competency tests are designed so that you will not be placed in courses that are too difficult or too easy. Think of them as readiness tests. Try your best, but don't be upset if you don't score at the required level. It is best to be certain you have the skills you need before tackling more difficult courses.

Preparing for Competency Tests

If your test requires that you write an essay, follow these suggestions:

1. **Study your error log** (see Writing Success Tip 4 on p. 116). If you haven't kept an error log, review papers your instructor has marked to identify your most common errors. Make a list of these common

---

Writing Success Tips

Near the end of each chapter you will find a "Writing Success Tip" that discusses a particular way to improve your writing. You may want to tab particularly useful tips or those that address problems you have experienced in your own writing.

Professional Essays

The professional essays in this book were written by expert writers and have been published in books, news magazines, and journals. A professional essay appears at the end of most chapters. By studying the work of professional writers, you can improve your own writing. As with the student writing samples, plan on reading each essay several times. Be sure to look for techniques the writer uses that you can use in your own writing. Both before and after each reading, you will find questions and activities intended to guide you in reading, examining, and writing about the reading. You should complete these, even if they are not assigned by your instructor, because doing so will help you to be better prepared to discuss and write about the reading.

READING
CAN I GET YOU SOME MANNERS WITH THAT?

So often it was the "professionals" who looked down on me who were lacking in social grace.

Christie Scotty

1   Like most people, I've long understood that I will be judged by my occupation. It's obvious that people care what others do for a living: head into any social setting and introductions of "Hi, my name is . . ." are quickly followed by the ubiquitous "And what do you do?" I long ago realized my profession is a **gauge** that people use to see how smart or talented I am. Recently, however, I was disappointed to see that it also decides how I'm treated as a person.

2   Last year I left a professional position as a small-town reporter and took a job waiting tables while I figured out what I wanted to do next. As someone paid to serve food to people, I had customers say and do things to me I suspect they'd never say or do to their most casual acquaintances. Some people would stare at the menu and mumble drink orders—"Bring me a water, extra lemon, no ice"—while refusing to meet my eyes. Some would interrupt me midsentence to say the air conditioning was too cold or the sun was too bright through the windows. One night a man talking on his cell phone waved me away, then beckoned me back with his finger a minute later, complaining he was ready to order and asking where I'd been.

gauge
a way to evaluate

Tab Your Way to Success

Use these tabs to mark important sections and pages of the book that you need to pay special attention to.

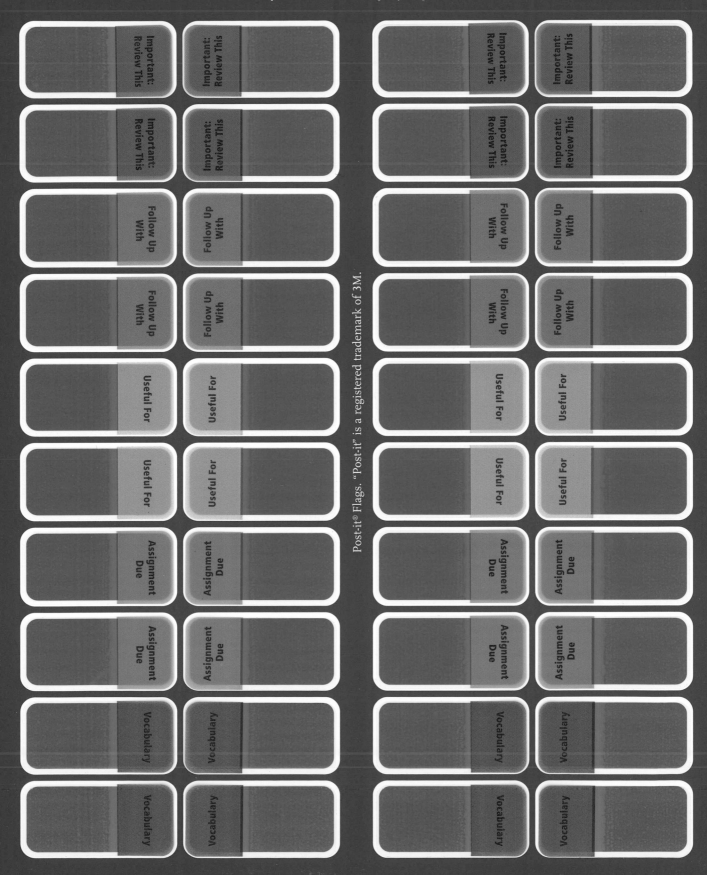

Post-it® Flags. "Post-it" is a registered trademark of 3M.

TAKE CHARGE OF YOUR LEARNING

These tabs offer you five ways to be successful in your writing course by taking charge of your own learning. Be sure to read Writing Success Starts Here! for additional information.

Important: Review This

Use this tab to identify the most important and useful materials for you in each chapter and refer to them often throughout the course. These may include strategies, rules, samples, examples, steps, tables, checklists, and idea maps.

Follow Up With

Your instructor is here to help you. When you find things you want to talk about with your instructor, use this tab. Write your instructor's name in the blank, and mark material you have questions about. Tabs can be placed on print copies of your essays, class notes, or instructor handouts, as well as on textbook pages. Your classmates are also valuable resources and you can use this tab to mark material you want to check with one of them.

Useful For

Use this tab when you find something useful that will apply to topics or assignments in other chapters. Also use it to mark sections that will help you in your other college courses.

Assignment Due

Assignments, including reading assignments, writing exercises, and paragraph and essay assignments, are learning tools. Mark each assignment given with the "Assignment Due" tab and fill in the date.

Vocabulary

When you meet a word you do not know, or one that you know but do not use in your own writing, tab it using this "Vocabulary" tab. If you can get a hint about the word's meaning from the words around it, keep reading and check its meaning later. If you need the word's meaning in order to understand the sentence in which it appears, stop reading, and look it up in a dictionary right away. When you find the word's meaning, record it in the margin of the page the word appears in, and later transfer the definition to a vocabulary log.

A Note about the Tabs: **You may run out of tabs before you finish the course. However, by then you will have built the habit of using them and can switch over to using Post-it notes for the same purpose.**

Visualize It!

Many people are visual learners; they process information more effectively when they see it presented in a map, diagram, photograph, or chart format. Throughout the text, idea maps are used to show the structure of paragraphs and the different ways ideas can be organized within them. Idea maps are also used to analyze ideas in paragraphs and to show how first drafts can be revised and improved. Look for the Visualize It! arrow!

Visualize It!

Model Idea Map for Example

Topic sentence

Example

Example

Example

Note: The number of examples will vary.

Idea Map for Annie's Paragraph on Superstition

Superstition affects many people on a daily basis.

Black cats are unlucky.

Walking under ladders bring bad luck.

Shoes on a bed means death.

Analyze It!

Practicing the skills you are learning is Important, as this is the way you make them part of your own writing process. Starting in Chapter 2, you are asked to analyze a paragraph and apply the skills you have been learned by completing an outline or idea map, figuring out the meaning of vocabulary, or correcting sentence and grammar errors.

Analyze It!

Directions: The following paragraph is correct except that it contains sentence fragments. Underline each fragment. Then revise the paragraph in the space provided by rewriting or combining sentences to eliminate fragments.

Social networks such as Facebook and MySpace appeal to college students for a variety of reasons. Social networks are a way of having conversations. Staying in touch with friends without the inconvenience of getting dressed and meeting them somewhere. Friends can join or drop out of a conversation whenever they want. Social networks also allow college students to meet new people and make new friends. Members can track who is friends with whom. Students may choose to share only portions of their profiles. To protect their privacy. Some students use social networks to form groups. Such as clubs, study groups, or special interest groups. Other students use networks to screen dates. And discover who is interested in dating or who is already taken.

Examine It!

In Chapter 14: Using Methods of Organization, annotated paragraphs by professional writers and textbook authors are used to illustrate the different methods of organization. These paragraphs provide a quick snapshot of the major elements you need to include when you write a paragraph using a specific pattern of organization.

Examine It!

about animals.

Directions: The following paragraph uses the narrative method of development. Study its annotations to discover how the writer supports the topic sentence and organizes her ideas.

Author establishes the importance of the narrative

Topic sentence

Description of events

Final comment reveals McPherson's mental state

I can't eat. I can't sleep. And I certainly can't study. I stare at a single paragraph for a quarter of an hour but can't absorb it. How can I, when behind the words, on the white background of the paper, I'm watching an endless loop of my parents' deaths? Watching as their cream-colored Buick flies through the guardrail and over the side of the bridge to avoid old Mr. McPherson's red truck? Old Mr. McPherson, who confessed as he was led from the scene that he wasn't entirely sure what side of the road he should have been on and thinks that maybe he hit the gas instead of the brake? Old Mr. McPherson, who showed up at church one legendary Easter without trousers?

—Gruen, *Water for Elephants*, p. 21

Chapter Review and Practice

Appearing at the end of every chapter, this section offers you some, or all, of the following ways to review what you learned in a particular chapter:

■ **The "Chapter Review" section provides a review of the skills taught in the chapter.** Use this to help you remember skills you want to apply in your own writing.

■ **The "Editing Practice" gives you an opportunity to identify and correct errors in the writing of others so that you learn to edit your own writing.** Pay particular attention to the types of errors you see and correct in these exercises. The errors shown are common ones, and you may find them in your own writing as well.

■ **The "Internet Activities" section directs you to Web sites, including the Web site for MyWritingLab, for additional instruction and/or practice of the skills taught in the chapter.** Use this section to extend and vary your use of the skills you learn in a chapter.

CHAPTER REVIEW AND PRACTICE

CHAPTER REVIEW

To review and check your recall of the chapter, match each term in Column A with its meaning in Column B and write the letter of the correct definition in the space provided.

COLUMN A	COLUMN B
_____ 1. Classification	a. focuses on similarities and differences
_____ 2. Definition	b. describes the order in which things are done or how they work
_____ 3. Process	c. takes a position on an issue
_____ 4. Narration	d. presents, supports an impression with sensory details
_____ 5. Description	e. makes a point by telling a story
_____ 6. Example	f. explains by giving situations that illustrate the topic sentence
_____ 7. Cause and effect	g. explains why things happen or explains what happens as a result of an action
_____ 8. Argument	h. explains a term by giving its class and distinguishing characteristics
_____ 9. Comparison and contrast	i. explains by dividing something into groups or categories

EDITING PRACTICE

The following informative paragraph comparing two types of skis is not organized logically. Revise this paragraph so that its main idea is developed logically.

> Cross-country skis and downhill skis are different in many aspects. Cross-country skis are intended for gliding over fairly level terrain. Unlike cross-country skis, downhill skis have steel edges and their bindings keep the entire boot

(continued)

SUCCESS WORKSHOPS

The following workshops are presented to help you become a more successful student. As you work through them, tab any information you want to refer to again.

Workshop #1: Manage Your Valuable Time

Many students say they do not have enough time to pay adequate attention to classes, studying, jobs, family, and friends. You can avoid or overcome this problem by managing your time effectively.

Veronica Evans-Johnson
Durham Technical College
Durham, NC
Veronica has been attending Durham Tech since 2000, first as a part-time student and recently as a full-time student. She is successfully working toward an associate's degree in business administration. She plans to transfer to Central University and prepare for a career in business administration.

Advice on Time Management: Dreams do come true. Always follow your heart. Never feel you're a failure. No matter what age you are, you can always go back to school. Once you've got an education, no one can steal it away from you. Set your goals high, write them down, and check them off as you go.

I take care of my family first in the evenings. Then I go to my room, close the door, and don't take calls. My family knows not to bother me. I have a laptop and I take it everywhere with me so if I have some free time I can get some [school] work done

How to Manage Your Time

- **Develop a weekly study plan.** Set aside time for reading assignments, writing and revising papers, reviewing what you have learned, and studying for exams. Identify specific times each week for working on each of your courses.

- **As a rule of thumb, reserve two study hours for each hour you spend in class.**

- **Work on difficult assignments first.** It is tempting to get the easy tasks out of the way first, but then you are left with the more challenging ones when you are tired. Work on difficult tasks, like brainstorming ideas for an essay, when your mind is fresh. When you are tired, do more routine tasks such as organizing lecture notes.

- **Schedule study for a particular course close to class time.** By studying close to class time, you will find it easier to relate what goes on in class to what you have been reading and writing about.

- **Include short breaks in your study time.** Studying for long, uninterrupted periods of time leads to fatigue. Taking periodic, short breaks refreshes you and helps you to focus when you resume working.

Try It Out!

Plan a weekly schedule using the tips provided. Try it for one week, evaluate what worked and what did not, and then revise it.

Workshop #2: Organize a Place to Read and Write

You will find that it is easier to read and write if you do so in the same place, as well as at the same time, each day.

Ryan Vidaurri
Montgomery College
Conroe, TX
After service in the military, Ryan has been attending Montgomery College and successfully working toward a degree in biotechnology. He plans to transfer to Texas A&M and earn a bachelor's degree in range-land management.

Advice on Where to Study: Our library has individual study rooms. I get in one of the back rooms without windows and cut myself off from all other distractions. There are also loads of picnic tables in back of the school in a wooded area and there are no distractions there; it's just a comfortable, peaceful environment. I have to be comfortable to study. If I'm too hot I can't study, or if I'm too cold or hungry.

Organizing a Place to Read and Write

- **Try to find a quiet area that you can reserve for reading and writing.** If possible, avoid areas used for other purposes, such as the dining room or kitchen table, because you'll have to move or clean up your materials frequently. If you live in a dorm, your desk is an ideal place to write, unless the dorm is too noisy. If it is, find a quiet place elsewhere on campus.

- **Use a table or desk.** Do not try to write on the arm of a comfortable chair. Choose a space where you can spread out your papers.

- **Eliminate distractions from your writing area.** Get rid of photos or stacks of bills to pay that may take your mind off your writing.

- **Be sure that the lighting is adequate and your chair is straight and not too comfortable.**

- **Collect and organize supplies.** You will need plenty of paper, pens, pencils, erasers, a ruler, a stapler, and so forth. If you write on a computer, keep spare CDs on hand.

- **Organize completed and returned papers, quizzes, class handouts, and other course materials in separate folders.**

Try It Out!

Choose one place at home (or in your dorm) and organize it. Write a list of supplies you need. Try using this location for one week. Do you notice a difference in your ability to get down to work and get things done?

Workshop #3: Build Your Concentration

No matter how intelligent you are, how serious you are, or what skills and talents you possess, reading and writing will be difficult and frustrating if you cannot keep your mind on the task at hand. Improving your concentration involves two tasks: eliminating distractions and building your attention span.

Dimitrus Loza
Portland Community College
Portland, OR
Dimitrus is a freshman at Portland Community College where she is studying for her bachelor's degree in law. When she graduates she plans to attend Texas Technical University and pursue a master's degree in law.

Advice on concentration and memorizing information: I have three puppies and I take them to the park and study while they play. It's very relaxing and I get fresh air, and I don't get overwhelmed the way I do inside. I take my books and a notepad, read through a chapter, and write down what's important. When it rains I visit a friend who has a gazebo. In the house it can feel chaotic and cooped up.

I never did well on tests when I was a freshman and sophomore in high school. I asked my family and friends how they studied and grabbed techniques from all of them. I had a lot of trouble memorizing, so I got into a drama class. It really helped me to memorize information and to be more confident. One thing I learned there was to read right before I go to sleep. I spend about 30–40 minutes going through my notes and everything I wrote down when I was studying, and in the morning I know it. That's how I study for tests.

Eliminating Distractions

- **Choose a place to study with minimal distractions.** Try it out and identify any distractions that occur. If you cannot eliminate them, find a different place to work.

- **Control noise levels.** Determine how much background noise you need or can tolerate, and choose a place best suited to those requirements.

- **Write down bothersome details.** When you think of an errand you need to do or a call you need to make, write it down on a separate notepad to follow up on later. Once you have written it down, you will be able to stop thinking about it.

- **Ask for cooperation.** Your family, friends, and roommates need to understand that you need to be by yourself in order to get your work done.

Focusing Your Attention

■ **Establish goals and time limits for each assignment.** Deadlines will keep you motivated, and you will be less likely to daydream.

■ **Use writing to keep mentally and physically active.** Highlighting, outlining, and note-taking will force you to keep your mind on what you are doing.

■ **Reward yourself.** Use rewards such as instant messaging with a friend or ordering a pizza when you complete an evening of study or a particularly challenging assignment.

Try It Out!

Place a check mark in front of three suggestions in the two preceding lists that may work for you. Choose three days this week and try to build one of these suggestions into your routine each day.

Workshop #4: Build a Strong Academic Image

It is important to present yourself as a serious student to your instructor and to other students. Your academic image is important because it lets your instructor know you are serious about the course and you are, therefore, someone it is worth spending extra time with if you need help. Image is also important in building trusting relationships with classmates.

Viola Degraffenreid
Copper Mountain College
Joshua Tree, CA
After four years in the U.S. Marine Corps, Viola is now a sophomore at Copper Mountain College where she is studying for her associate's degree. She plans to transfer to California State University, San Bernadino, to pursue a bachelor's degree in business.

   Advice on creating a strong academic image: To make a good impression I always sit at the front of the class, I ask questions, and I volunteer for class activities. For example, in a math class the professor might ask for someone to come up and explain how they work out a problem, and I'll volunteer to do it. I'm attentive in class. It lets the professor know I'm interested. If you sit in the front of the class you build a relationship with the professors, so if something happens and you're not there you have a rapport with them, and they know you're reliable and credible when you tell them why you couldn't come to class.

Building an Academic Image

Try the following quiz. It will help you evaluate and change your academic image, if needed.

Try It Out!

For each item, place a check mark in the column that best describes you. Highlight those items you marked "Sometimes" or "Never," and work on improving one item each day.

	Always	Sometimes	Never
1. I attend all my classes and explain necessary, lengthy absences to my instructors.			
2. I avoid talking with classmates during class time.			
3. I arrive at class before the instructor and never leave early.			
4. I ask and answer questions in class.			
5. I come to class prepared, bringing my textbook, writing materials, and any other pertinent course work.			
6. I sit in class with other serious students.			
7. I stay alert and show that I am interested.			
8. I make eye contact with the instructor during class.			
9. I make an effort to speak with my instructor before or after class.			
10. I turn in neat, carefully completed assignments.			

Workshop #5: Learn from Feedback

Feedback is information about your performance that you get from others. In a writing class, feedback may come from your instructor or from other students who read your work. Feedback from your instructor may be in oral or written form and can include written comments on papers, verbal responses to questions you ask in class, or grades for papers, quizzes, and exams.

It is easy to get angry or upset when you get negative feedback. Instead of feeling angry, consider feedback an opportunity to learn from your mistakes and improve as a writer. Get in the habit of asking for more feedback. Visit your instructor during office hours to discuss an assignment or to ask how to improve your performance.

Jonathan Fischer
New Jersey Institute of Technology
Newark, NJ
Jonathan successfully completed an associate's degree in civil engineering at Middlesex County College in May 2005. He has recently transferred to the New Jersey Institute of Technology to earn a bachelor's degree in construction management.

Advice on Getting Feedback: When I did badly on a test, I approached my teacher a week or two later. We were already doing new material. We met and made a plan. We started with the material on the test and went over it all and then caught up with the new material. He went step by step through everything, saying "this is good, you went wrong here," and then we went back over what I did to make sure I really understood. The only dummy is the one who doesn't go for help.

How to Learn from Feedback

■ **Writing Assignments:** What weaknesses did my instructor identify? How can I improve my paper? What errors in grammar, punctuation, and spelling did I make?

■ **Exams:** What type(s) of questions did I miss? What topics was I unsure of?

■ **Class Discussions:** What does the instructor think of my ideas? How can I improve my class participation?

Try It Out!

1. List three kinds of feedback you received today in your classes. Indicate what you learned from each.

   a. _____

   b. _____

   c. _____

2. List three questions you can ask your instructors to let them know you value and encourage feedback.

   a. _____

   b. _____

   c. _____

1

An Introduction to Writing

WRITE ABOUT IT!

In the photo above, the student at the computer is writing an assigned essay. Write a few sentences describing what that student might be feeling, using your own experiences with writing as a guide. What problems might he be facing? What things can he do well? What are his trouble spots?

For problems and trouble spots, did you identify problems such as not knowing what to write about, not knowing what to say, or problems catching and correcting spelling and grammar errors?

This book will address common writing problems and help you improve your writing. It will concentrate on writing as a means of expressing ideas. You will learn to plan, organize, and develop your ideas. You will learn to write sentences and paragraphs that express your ideas clearly and effectively. You will also learn how to avoid common problems writing paragraphs and sentences. Finally, after you have expressed your ideas, you will discover that grammar, punctuation, and spelling do have an important function in writing.

WRITING

What Writing Is and Is Not

The following list explains some correct and incorrect notions about writing:

Writing is ...

- following a step-by-step process of planning, drafting, and revising.
- thinking through and organizing ideas.
- explaining *your* ideas or experiences clearly and correctly.
- using precise, descriptive, and accurate vocabulary.
- constructing clear, understandable sentences.
- a skill that can be learned.

Writing is not ...

- being able to pick up a pen (or sit at a computer) and write something wonderful on your first try.
- developing new, earthshaking ideas no one has ever thought of before.
- being primarily concerned with grammatical correctness.
- showing off a large vocabulary.
- constructing long, complicated sentences.

EXERCISE 1-1

Directions: Suppose you are writing a letter to a toy manufacturer about a defective toy you purchased for your niece or nephew. You feel the toy is unsafe for toddlers. Describe, step by step, how you would go about writing this letter. (What is the first thing you would do? What would you do after that? And so forth.) You are not actually writing the letter in this exercise or listing what you would say. You are describing your writing *process*.

The Writing Process: An Overview

Writing, like many other skills, is not a single-step process. Think of the game of football, for instance. Football players do not simply put on uniforms and rush onto the field. Instead, they spend a great deal of time planning and developing offensive and defensive strategies, trying out new plays, improving existing plays, and practicing. Writing involves similar planning and preparation. It also involves testing ideas and working out the best way to express them. Writers often explore how their ideas might "play out" in several ways before settling upon one plan of action.

People have many individual techniques for writing, but all writing involves five basic steps, as shown in Table 1.1. You will learn more about each of these steps in later chapters.

TABLE 1-1

Steps in the Writing Process	Description of Steps
1. Generating ideas	Finding ideas to write about.
2. Organizing your ideas	Discovering ways to arrange your ideas logically.
3. Writing a first draft	Expressing your ideas in sentence and paragraph form without worrying about spelling, punctuation, capitalization, and grammar.
4. Revising	Rethinking your ideas and finding ways to make your writing clearer, more complete, and more interesting. Revising involves changing, adding, deleting, and rearranging your ideas and words to make your writing better.
5. Proofreading	Checking for errors in grammar, spelling, punctuation, and capitalization.

ESL Tip

A *draft* is a piece of writing that is not finished.

Revising is the process of rethinking your ideas. It involves adding ideas, deleting ideas, rearranging ideas, and changing the way you have expressed your thoughts.

NEED TO KNOW

The Writing Process

- Writing is a step-by-step process of explaining your ideas and experiences.

- Writing involves five basic steps: generating ideas, organizing your ideas, writing a first draft, revising, and proofreading.

Beginning Tips for Generating Ideas

Before you can write about a topic, you have to collect ideas to write about. Because many students need help with this right away, three helpful techniques are described here: (1) freewriting, (2) brainstorming, and (3) branching. These techniques are discussed in detail in Chapter 11. Here is a brief introduction to each.

Freewriting

What is freewriting? Freewriting is writing nonstop about a topic for a specified period of time.

How does freewriting work? You write whatever comes into your mind, and you do not stop to be concerned about correctness. After you have finished, you go back through your writing and pick out ideas that you might be able to use.

What does it look like? Here is a sample of freewriting done on the topic of owning a dog.

Sample Freewriting

I really wish I had a dog. I need some what's it called ... oh, yeah, unconditional love. Something that never gets mad at me, no matter what I do. Jumping up and happy whenever it sees me. Definitely loves me best. I could teach it tricks, like roll over and speak or dance with me. Maybe I could get on TV, like Letterman's Stupid Pet Tricks or Those Amazing Animals. What breeds are the smartest? I don't want one that's so big I can't lift it by myself. But I hate those yappy little ones that shiver all the time. I saw a woman walking one once in the winter. It had a little coat on that matched the woman's coat. I wouldn't do something that lame. How do you get them to be good guard dogs? Guess I'd have to pay for training. Ow. What else would I have to pay for; shots, neutering, bed, collar, vet bills? I can't afford that stuff, even if I get a mutt from the shelter. Can I take it to work? Ha! I can just see my boss's face when I walk in with a giant, slobbering Newfoundland! There goes that job. And how could I get home to walk it in between work and class? I only have half an hour. Guess I'd better wait.

Brainstorming

What is brainstorming? Brainstorming is making a list of everything you can think of that has to do with your topic.

How does brainstorming work? Try to stretch your imagination and think of everything related to your topic. Include facts, ideas, examples, questions, and feelings. When you have finished, read through what you have written and highlight usable ideas.

What does brainstorming look like? Here is a sample of brainstorming on the topic of fast food:

SAMPLE BRAINSTORMING ON FAST FOOD

Brands: Burger King, KFC, McDonald's, Wendy's, Pizza Hut, Taco Bell

Advertised on TV; famous

Lots of them across the country, in every city and town

Small menu, limited choices

Familiar; food is the same everywhere

Young or inexperienced workers

Boring to work there

Comfort food

Delicious but high in fat and calories

Hard to order only healthy food

Burgers, fries, pizza, chicken

Soft drinks

Sometimes lines are long

Cheap compared to restaurants

Can eat in car, on the run

Branching

What is branching? Branching is a way of using diagrams or drawings to generate ideas.

How does branching work? Begin by drawing a 2-inch oval in the middle of a page. Write your topic in that oval. Think of the oval as a tree trunk. Next, draw lines radiating out from the trunk, as branches would. Write an idea related to your topic at the end of each branch. When you have finished, highlight the ideas you find most useful.

What does branching look like? Here is a sample of branching done on the topic of religious holidays:

EXERCISE 1-2

Writing in Progress

Directions: Choose one of the following topics. Then try out two of the techniques described for generating ideas.

1. Identity theft

2. Internet communication

3. Telemarketing

4. Advertising ploys and gimmicks

5. Airport security

Beginning Tips for Organizing Your Ideas

Two common methods of organizing ideas are outlining and idea mapping. Understanding each of them will help you decide how to arrange the ideas that you have identified as useful, depending on the method you used to generate those ideas.

Outlining

What is outlining? Outlining is a method of listing the main points you will cover and their subpoints (details) in the order in which you will present them.

How does outlining work? To make an outline, you list the most important ideas on separate lines at the left margin of a sheet of paper, leaving space underneath each idea. In the space under each main idea, list the details that you will include to explain that main idea. Indent the list of details that fits under each of your most important ideas.

What does outlining look like? Here is a sample outline for a brief essay on the topic of a vacation in San Francisco:

Sample Outline for Paragraph on Favorite Places

> I. Chinatown
>   A. Restaurants and markets
>   1. Fortune cookie factory
>   2. Dim sum restaurants
>   B. Museums
>   1. Chinese Culture Center
>   2. Pacific Heritage Museum
>
> II. Fisherman's Wharf
>   A. Pier 39
>   1. Street performers
>   2. Sea lions sunning themselves
>   on the docks
>   B. Ghirardelli Square

Idea Mapping

What is idea mapping? An idea map is a drawing that shows the content and organization of a piece of writing.

How does idea mapping work? An idea map shows you how ideas are connected and can help you see which ideas are not relevant to the topic of your essay.

What does an idea map look like? Here is a sample idea map drawn for a paragraph on the topic of choosing an Internet password:

Visualize It! →

Idea Map

> It is important to choose Internet passwords carefully, using the following suggestions.
>
> Do not use common words or names.
>
> Do not use the same password in many places.
>
> Use both numbers and letters.
>
> Change your password frequently.
>
> Tell no one your password.

EXERCISE 1-3

Writing in Progress

Directions: For the topic you chose in Exercise 1-2, use outlining or idea mapping to organize your ideas.

Writing Paragraphs

A **paragraph** is a group of sentences, usually at least three or four, that expresses one main idea. Paragraphs may stand alone to express one thought, or they may be combined into essays. Paragraphs are one of the basic building blocks of writing, so it is important to learn to write them effectively.

A paragraph's one main idea is expressed in a single sentence called the **topic sentence**. The other sentences in the paragraph, called **supporting details**, explain or support the main idea. You can visualize a paragraph as follows:

Visualize It!

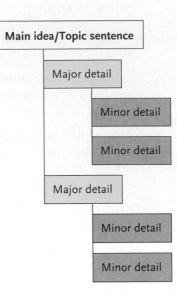

Here is a sample paragraph; its idea map appears on p. 25.

The Abkhasians (an agricultural people who live in a mountainous region of Georgia, a republic of the former Soviet Union) may be the longest-lived people on earth. Many claim to live past 100—some beyond 120 and even 130. Although it is difficult to document the accuracy of these claims, government records indicate that an extraordinary number of Abkhasians do live to a very old age. Three main factors appear to account for their long lives. The first is their diet, which consists of little meat, much fresh fruit, vegetables, garlic, goat cheese, cornmeal, buttermilk and wine. The second is their lifelong physical activity. They do slow down after age 80, but even after the age of 100 they still work about four hours a day. The third factor—a highly developed sense of community—goes to the very heart of the Abkhasian culture. From childhood, each individual is integrated into a primary group, and remains so throughout life. There is no such thing as a nursing home, nor do the elderly live alone.

—adapted from Henslin, *Sociology*, pp. 380–381

EXERCISE 1-4

Writing in Progress

Directions: Using one or more of the ideas you generated and organized in Exercises 1-2 and 1-3, write a paragraph about the topic you chose.

EXERCISE 1-5

Directions: Write a paragraph on one of the following topics. Be sure to begin with a sentence that states the one idea your paragraph is about.

1. Describe a space alien's fear or surprise when stepping out of a spaceship onto Earth. Explain what the alien sees or hears and how it reacts to what it sees.

2. Describe your reaction to your first day of college classes. Include specific examples to support your description.

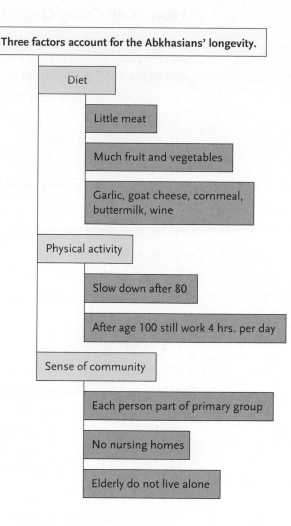

Three factors account for the Abkhasians' longevity.

Diet

Little meat

Much fruit and vegetables

Garlic, goat cheese, cornmeal, buttermilk, wine

Physical activity

Slow down after 80

After age 100 still work 4 hrs. per day

Sense of community

Each person part of primary group

No nursing homes

Elderly do not live alone

Writing Essays

An **essay**, which consists of three or more paragraphs, expresses and explains a series of related ideas, all of which support a larger, broader idea.

The emphasis of this text is on writing effective sentences and paragraphs. However, in some of your courses your instructors may ask you to write essays or take essay exams. Some writing instructors prefer that their students write essays right away. Other instructors prefer that their students begin by writing single paragraphs and then progress to essay writing. Regardless of when you begin writing essays, the following introduction to essay techniques will be useful to you. It will show you why good paragraph-writing skills are absolutely necessary for writing good essays.

What Is an Essay?

An **essay** is a group of paragraphs about one subject. It contains one key idea about the subject that is called the **thesis statement**. Each paragraph in the essay supports or explains some aspect of the thesis statement.

How Is an Essay Organized?

An essay follows a logical and direct plan: it introduces an idea (the thesis statement), explains it, and draws a conclusion. Therefore, an essay usually has at least three paragraphs:

1. Introductory paragraph
2. Body (one or more paragraphs)
3. Concluding paragraph

The Introductory Paragraph

Your **introductory paragraph** should accomplish three things:

1. It should establish the topic of the essay.
2. It should present the thesis statement of your essay in an appropriate way for your intended audience.
3. It should interest your audience in your essay.

The Body

The **body** of your essay should accomplish three things:

1. It should provide information that supports and explains your thesis statement.
2. It should present each main supporting point in a separate paragraph.
3. It should contain enough detailed information to make the main point of each paragraph understandable and believable.

The Concluding Paragraph

Your **concluding paragraph** should accomplish two things:

1. It should reemphasize but not restate your thesis statement.
2. It should draw your essay to a close.

You can visualize the organization of an essay using the following idea map:

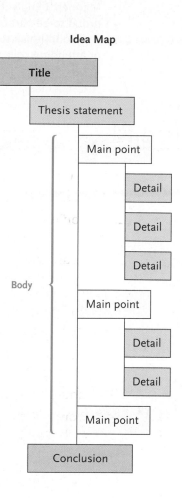

Idea Map

In the following sample essay, the marginal notes indicate the function of each paragraph. Read the essay and study the idea map that follows it.

A Sample Student Essay

Title: identifies the two topics

College and the Marine Corps

Introduction: topic is introduced

I have made two important decisions in my lifetime. They were to join the Marine Corps and to attend college. Each decision turned out to be the right one for me. Although the Marines and college are very different, each has had a similar effect on me.

Thesis statement

Description of Marine Corps

There was only one reason for joining the Marine Corps. I had to make money to go to college. I needed it, and they offered it. The Marine Corps was more difficult and challenging than I had thought it would be. Boot camp was horrible. Being deployed to Iraq was worse. Each day was filled with obstacles, physical as well as mental. Each day, however, I felt a strong sense of accomplishment in making it through the day. At the end of my tour of duty I was proud to call myself a Marine.

Description of college

College has turned out to be the same as the Marine Corps in many ways. I chose to attend college for one reason: to have a career. I am enrolled in the Operating Room Assistant program, and it is much more difficult than I imagined it to be. Biology and Medical Terminology are hard courses. There are many obstacles, such as unannounced quizzes, labs, and exams. However, each time I earn a passing grade, I feel the same sense of accomplishment that I felt in the Marines. I know that when I graduate and walk into an operating room, I will be proud to be part of the medical team.

Conclusion: draws essay to a close; looks ahead to the future

Soon I plan to make a decision just as important as joining the Marine Corps or attending college. Next spring, I am planning to get married to a person I met in the Marines. I hope it, too, will work out.

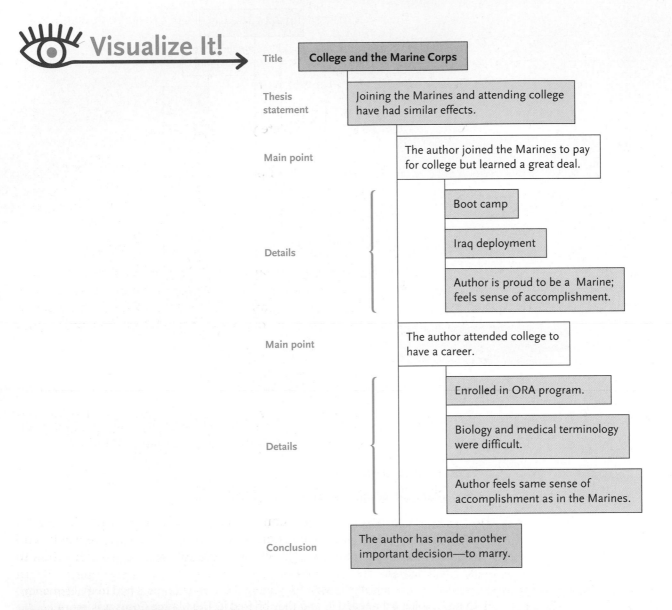

Visualize It!

Title	**College and the Marine Corps**
Thesis statement	Joining the Marines and attending college have had similar effects.
Main point	The author joined the Marines to pay for college but learned a great deal.
Details	Boot camp
	Iraq deployment
	Author is proud to be a Marine; feels sense of accomplishment.
Main point	The author attended college to have a career.
Details	Enrolled in ORA program.
	Biology and medical terminology were difficult.
	Author feels same sense of accomplishment as in the Marines.
Conclusion	The author has made another important decision—to marry.

EXERCISE 1-6
Writing in Progress

Directions: Using the ideas you generated in Exercise 1-2 but did not use to write a paragraph in Exercise 1-4, write a short essay. You may need to do additional brainstorming, freewriting, or branching to come up with enough ideas to write about.

Practical Advice for Getting Started

Writing is a skill that you can learn. Like any other skill, such as basketball, accounting, or cooking, writing takes practice. Be sure to focus your attention on new techniques suggested by your instructor as well as the ones given in each chapter of this book. To improve, you often need to be open to doing things differently. Approach writing positively; expect success. Don't hesitate to experiment.

Consider the following points as ways to get off to a successful start:

1. Think first, then write.
2. Plan on making changes.
3. Give yourself enough time to write.
4. Develop a routine.
5. Allow sufficient time to complete your assignments.
6. Take breaks.
7. Use full 8.5-by-11-inch sheets of paper.
8. Keep a journal.

Think First, Then Write

Writing is a thinking process: it is an expression of your thoughts. Don't expect to be able to pick up a pen or sit down at a computer and immediately produce a well-written paragraph or essay. Plan to spend time generating ideas and deciding how to organize them before you write your first draft.

Plan on Making Changes

Most writers revise (rethink, rewrite, change, add, and delete) numerous times before they are pleased with their work. For example, I revised this chapter of *Pathways* five times before I was satisfied with it.

Give Yourself Enough Time to Write

For most of us, writing does not come easily. It takes time to think, select a topic, generate ideas, organize them, draft a piece of writing, revise it, and proofread it. Reserve a block of time each day for writing. Use the time to read this book and to work on its writing exercises and assignments. Begin by reserving an hour per day. This may seem like a lot of time. However, most instructors expect you to spend at least two hours outside of class for every hour you spend in class. If your writing class meets for a total of three hours per week, then you should spend at least six hours per week working on writing.

Develop a Routine

Try to work at the same time each day. You will develop a routine that will be easy to follow. Be sure to work at peak periods of concentration. Don't write when you are tired, hungry, or likely to be interrupted.

Allow Sufficient Time to Complete Your Assignments

Begin assignments well before they are due. You will need time to plan, organize, draft, revise, and proofread. Plan to let your drafts "sit" awhile—preferably a day—before you begin to revise. Necessary changes will become much more obvious after some time away from your work.

Take Breaks

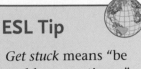

ESL Tip

Get stuck means "be unable to continue." *Stuck* is the past tense and past participle of the irregular verb *stick*.

If you get stuck and cannot think or write, take a break. Clear your mind by going for a walk, talking to a friend, or having a snack. Set a time limit for your break, though, so you return to work in a reasonable time. When you begin again, start by rereading what you have already written. If you still cannot make progress, use freewriting, brainstorming, and branching techniques (see pp. 20–21) to generate more ideas about your topic.

Use Full 8.5-by-11-Inch Sheets of Paper

By using standard-sized 8.5-by-11-inch paper, you will be able to see better how your ideas connect. Write on only one side of the paper so that you can spread out the sheets and track the development of your ideas.

Keep a Journal

A writing journal is an excellent way to improve your writing and keep track of your thoughts and ideas. A **writing journal** is a collection of your writing and reflections.

How to Keep a Writing Journal

1. Buy an 8.5-by-11-inch spiral-bound notebook. Use it exclusively for journal writing. Alternatively, you can use a computer file.

2. Reserve ten to fifteen minutes a day to write in your journal. Write every day, not just on days when a good idea strikes.

3. Write about whatever comes to mind. You might write about events that happened and your reactions to them, or describe feelings, impressions, or worries.

If you have trouble getting started, ask yourself some questions:

- What happened at school, work, or home?

- What world, national, or local events occurred?

- What am I worried about?

- What positive experience have I had lately? Maybe it was eating a good meal, making a new friend, or finding time to wash your car.

- What did I see today? Practice writing descriptions of beautiful, funny, interesting, or disturbing things you've noticed.

- What is the best or worst thing that happened today?
- Who did I talk to? What did I talk about? Record conversations as fully as you can.

Sample Journal Entries

The following student journal entries will give you a better picture of journal writing. They have been edited for easy reading. However, as you write, do not be concerned with neatness or correctness.

Jeffrey The best thing that happened today happened as soon as I got home from work. The phone rang. At first, I wasn't going to answer it because I was tired and in one of those moods when I wanted to be by myself. It rang so many times I decided to answer it. Am I glad I did! It was MaryAnn, a long-lost girlfriend whom I'd always regretted losing touch with. She said she had just moved back into the neighborhood, and …. I took it from there.

Malcolm This morning while walking across campus to my math class, I stopped for a few minutes under a chestnut tree. Perfect timing! I've always loved collecting chestnuts, and they were just beginning to fall. When I was a kid, I used to pick up lunch bags full of them. I never knew what to do with them once I had them. I just liked picking them up, I guess. I remember liking their cold, sleek, shiny smoothness and how good they felt in my hand. So I picked up a few, rubbed them together in my hand, and went off to class, happy that some things never change.

Allison This morning my new, seven-week-old puppy tore up the house. I went upstairs to get dressed, and I forgot to take her with me. She got into my houseplants. When I came down, there were dirt, moss, and leaves spread all through the living room and kitchen. I was furious until I looked at her. She sat in the middle of the mess, wagged her tail, and looked at me with *those* eyes. All of a sudden, all was forgiven.

Benefits of Journal Writing

When you write in your journal, you are practicing writing and becoming better at expressing your thoughts in writing. You can feel free to practice without pressure or fear of criticism. Besides practice, journal writing has other benefits:

1. Your journals will become a good source of ideas. When you have a paper assigned and must select your own topic, review your journal for ideas.

2. You may find that journal writing becomes a way to think through problems, release pent-up feelings, or keep an enjoyable record of life experiences. Journal writing is writing *for yourself*.

Peer Review

Not everything you write in a college writing class needs to be graded by your instructor. Instead, you can get valuable "peer review," or feedback, from other members of your class. Peers (classmates) can tell you what they like and what they think you need to do to improve your writing. You can also learn a lot from reading and commenting on the work of other students.

If your instructor wants you to choose your own reviewer, look for someone who is reliable, serious, and conscientious. It is not necessarily a good idea to work with close friends, since they may feel reluctant to give you honest criticism. With friends, it is also easy for conversation to drift away from

ESL Tip

The noun *peer* literally means "an equal." People who are at the same academic and professional level are peers.

A *peer review* is when a classmate or a colleague reviews your work. It usually includes a discussion of strengths and suggestions for improvement.

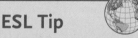

ESL Tip

A *conscientious* person makes every effort to do things carefully and correctly.

Reluctant means "not eager to do something."

In this paragraph, *criticism* means "telling about weaknesses or errors." It sometimes means "evaluating and pointing out strengths and weaknesses."

the task at hand. If you are on the giving end of peer review, take your job seriously. The following tips tell you how to use the peer review process.

Tips for the Writer

1. Prepare your draft in a readable form. Double-space your work; be sure to use full 8.5-by-11-inch sheets of paper. Use only one side of the paper.

2. Keep a copy of your paper for yourself, if possible.

3. When you receive your reviewer's comments, weigh them carefully, but do not feel you have to accept every suggestion that is made.

4. If you have questions or are uncertain about the advice your reviewer gave you, talk with your instructor.

Tips for the Reviewer

1. Read the draft through at least once before making any judgments.

2. Read the draft two or more times before you make specific comments.

3. As you read, keep in mind the writer's intended audience (see Chapter 11). The draft should be appropriate for the audience for whom it was intended.

4. Offer positive comments first. Say what the writer did well.

5. Use the Revision Checklists that appear at the end of Chapter 12 through 18 as a guide.

6. Avoid general comments. Don't just say that a sentence is unclear. Instead, explain what it lacks or how it could be improved, but do not make actual corrections for the writer.

EXERCISE 1-7
Writing in Progress

Directions: Use the paragraph you wrote in Exercise 1-4 or the short essay you wrote in Exercise 1-6 for peer review.

NEED TO KNOW

Peer Review

- You can get valuable help with your writing from class members by using peer review.

- You should weigh a reviewer's comments seriously but not feel obliged to accept every suggestion.

- As a reviewer, you should read the work several times and offer positive comments as well as specific suggestions for improvement.

Writing Success Tip 1

Participating in Your Writing Class

Your writing class is your primary source for improving your writing. While this book is helpful, too, it is your writing class—both the instructor and the other students—that will guide you through the book and help you learn from it. Use the following suggestions to get the most out of your writing class:

1. **Attend all classes.** Do not miss any classes, even if several absences are allowed.

2. **Come prepared to class.** Make sure you have read the assigned chapters and have done the assigned exercises. Many instructors will assign exercises but will not collect and grade them. Do them regardless of whether they count toward your grade.

3. **Determine the purpose of assigned exercises.** The exercises are intended to help you learn, so focus on what you are supposed to learn by completing them, rather than just doing them to get them done.

4. **Take notes in class.** When your instructor gives information or assignments, be sure to write them down. While what your instructor says may seem clear at the time, remembering it two weeks later may not be as simple as it seems.

5. **Ask questions in class.** Be sure to ask questions when there is something you do not understand. Probably other students are wondering the same thing, and they will be glad you asked.

6. **Participate in class discussions.** You will find the class more interesting if you get involved rather than just watch others get involved.

7. **Attend writing conferences.** Many instructors offer students the opportunity to meet with them individually to discuss specific writing assignments or overall course progress. Be sure to take advantage of this individualized instruction. Prepare for the conference by looking over recent writing assignments and listing questions you want to ask.

8. **Find a buddy.** Get to know at least one student in your class well. Exchange phone numbers and e-mail addresses. Work together and help each other. (See suggestions for peer review, p. 32.)

9. **Do not hesitate to ask for help.** If you are stuck on an assignment, ask either your buddy or your instructor to look at what you've done so far and make suggestions.

CHAPTER REVIEW AND PRACTICE

CHAPTER REVIEW

To review and check your recall of the chapter, match each term in Column A with its meaning in Column B and write the correct letter in the space provided in Column A.

COLUMN A

_i_ 1. Peer review

_d_ 2. Writing journal

_e_ 3. Writing

_a_ 4. Freewriting

_h_ 5. Brainstorming

_g_ 6. Branching

_b_ 7. Outlining

_j_ 8. Idea map

_f_ 9. Paragraph

_c_ 10. Essay

COLUMN B

a. writing nonstop about a topic for a specified period of time

b. listing points and subpoints you will cover in the order in which you will cover them

c. a group of paragraphs about one subject

d. a collection of your writing and reflections

e. a process of planning, drafting, and revising ideas

f. a group of sentences that express one main idea

g. using drawings and diagrams to generate ideas

h. generating ideas by making a list of everything that comes to mind on a topic

i. a process in which a classmate reads and comments on a student's writing

j. a diagram that shows both the content and organization of a planned piece of writing

INTERNET ACTIVITIES

1. Writer's Block

Sometimes it is hard to get started on a writing assignment. Read over and print out the tips on this site from Brigham Young University-Idaho for overcoming writer's block.

http://www.byui.edu/ WritingCenter/ webpages/ Writer's%20Block.htm

Mark any you have tried in the past with success. Then mark the ones you think might work for you in the years to come. Keep this list handy for future reference.

2. Peer Review Suggestions

Examine the ideas for the peer review of student papers at this Vanderbilt University Web site.

http://sitemason.vanderbilt.edu/site/liumxq/peerchecklist

Also visit this Web site of the University of Hawaii at Manoa.

http://mwp01.mwp.hawaii.edu/resources/wm7.htm

Compare the methods that are presented, especially the sample materials. What do you think would be the most valuable way to perform peer reviews? Explain your answer.

3. The Importance of College Writing

In an online guide, the writing center at the University of Maryland University College explains why there is so much emphasis on writing in college.

http://www.umuc.edu/prog/ugp/ewp_writingcenter/writinggde/chapter1 /chapter1-03.shtml

Read this section and summarize the information it presents about college writing.

4. MyWritingLab

Visit this site to get an overview of the writing process.

http://www.mywritinglab.com

Click on the Study Plan tab, then on "Getting Started," and then on "The Writing Process: An Overview."

2

The Reading-Writing Connection

In this chapter you will:

1. Explore the connection between reading and writing.

2. Learn to approach reading assignments more effectively.

3. Discover methods for writing about assigned readings.

WRITE ABOUT IT!

Although the people in the two photos seemingly have nothing to do with one another, they are connected. Write a sentence stating how are they connected.

The correspondents are interviewing a local citizen for newspaper and television reports; the person in the second photo is reading a news article that one of the correspondents wrote. Readers and writers are always connected in this way. In this chapter you will learn about the reading-writing connection. You will learn reading skills that will make an immediate, noticeable change in how well you understand and remember what you read. As you work through this chapter, you will see that there is a strong connection between reading and writing. Improving one skill often improves the other.

EXPLORING THE READING-WRITING CONNECTION

At first, reading and writing may seem like very different, even opposite, processes. A writer starts with a blank page or computer screen and creates and develops ideas, while a reader starts with a full page and reads someone else's ideas. Although reading and writing may seem very different, they are actually parts of the same communication process.

Writers begin with a message they want to communicate; readers attempt to understand that message through their own experiences, as shown in the photographs below.

The Writer

The Reader

Because reading and writing work together, improving one often improves the other. By learning to read more effectively, you'll become a better writer as well as a better reader. For example, as you learn more about writing paragraphs, you will be able to read them more easily. Similarly, as you learn more about how an essay is organized, you will find it easier to read essays and to organize your own ideas into essay form.

NEED TO KNOW

The Relationship Between Reading and Writing

- Reading and writing are parts of the same communication process.

- Writers begin with a message they want to communicate.

- Readers try to understand the message by connecting it to their own experiences.

This text uses readings to help you become a better writer. Every chapter concludes with a reading that illustrates the skills taught in the chapter and provides ideas for you to write about. This chapter offers strategies and skills for approaching reading assignments. It will "walk you through" a reading assignment, offering tips at each stage and suggesting what to do before, during, and after reading an assignment to strengthen your comprehension, help you remember more of what you read, and show you how to find ideas to write about.

Previewing Before Reading

Do you wish you could remember more of what you read? **Previewing** is a way of becoming familiar with what a reading is about and how it is organized *before* you read it. Previewing will make an assignment easier to read and remember, as well as make it more interesting. It will also help you discover what you already know about the topic before you begin reading.

Previewing is like looking at a map before you begin to drive in an unfamiliar city. It familiarizes you with the organization and content of a reading. It also allows you to connect what you learn to your own experiences. Then, when you read the selection, you are able to understand it more easily. Previewing is not time consuming. You can preview a brief selection in several minutes by following these basic steps:

1. **Read and think about the title of the selection**. What does it tell you about the subject? Does it offer any clues as to how the author feels about the subject or how the author will approach it? What do you already know about the subject?

2. **Check the author's name**. If it is familiar, what do you know about the author?

3. **Read the first paragraph**. Here the author often introduces the subject. Look for a statement of the main point of the entire reading. If the first paragraph is lengthy, read only the first few sentences.

4. **Read all boldface headings**. Headings divide the reading into sections and announce the topic of each section.

5. **Read the first sentence under each heading**. This sentence often states the main point of the section.

6. **If the reading lacks headings, read the first sentence of each of a few paragraphs on each page**. You will discover many of the main ideas of the article.

7. **Read the last paragraph**. Often this paragraph summarizes or concludes the reading. If the last paragraph is lengthy, read only the last few sentences.

The more you practice previewing and get in the habit of previewing, the more effectively it will work. Use the preview strategy for all your college textbooks, as well as for assigned chapters and readings in this book. You will notice in this book a section titled "Thinking Before Reading," which comes before each reading and reminds you to preview it.

Demonstration of Previewing

Now, preview the following reading, "Ways to Improve Your Memory." The portions you should preview have been highlighted. Preview this reading now, reading only the shaded portions.

READING

WAYS TO IMPROVE YOUR MEMORY

Saul M. Kassin

1 Before taking office, President Clinton invited five hundred business leaders to an economic summit in Little Rock. When it was over, many of the guests marveled at Clinton's ability to address them all by name. I have always been impressed by stories like this one—by stories of stage actors who memorize hundreds of lines in only one week of rehearsal, of people who fluently speak five languages, and of waiters who take dinner orders without a note pad. How can these accomplishments be explained?

2 Over the years, psychologists have stumbled upon a few rare individuals who seemed equipped with extraordinary "hardware" for memory. But often the actors, waiters, multilinguists, and others we encounter use memory tricks called mnemonics—in other words, they vary their memory's "software." Can you boost your recall capacity through the use of mnemonics? Can you improve your study skills as a result? At this point, let's step back and consider several ways you can improve your memory.

3 *Practice time:* To learn names, dates, vocabulary words, formulas, or the concepts in a textbook, you'll find that practice makes perfect. In general, the more time spent studying, the better. In fact, it pays to overlearn—that is, to review the material even after you think you have it mastered. It's also better to spread out your studying over time than to cram all at once. You will retain more information from four two-hour sessions than from one eight-hour marathon.

4 *Active thinking:* The sheer amount of practice time is important, but only if it's "quality time." Mindless drills may be helpful in the short run, but long-term retention requires that you think actively and deeply about material—about what it means and how it is linked to what you already know. Ask yourself critical questions about the material. Think about it in ways that relate to your own experiences. Talk about the material to a friend, thus forcing yourself to organize it in terms that can be understood.

5 *Organization of information:* Once you have information to be learned, organize it as in an outline. Start with a few broad categories, then divide these into more specific subcategories and sub-subcategories. This is how many experts chunk new information, and it works. Thus, when Andrea Halpern (1986) presented subjects with 54 popular song titles, she found that recall was greater when the titles were organized hierarchically than when they were scrambled. The implication for studying is clear: organize the material in your notes, preferably in the form of an outline—and make sure to review these notes later.

6 *Verbal mnemonics:* Sometimes the easiest way to remember a list of items is to use verbal mnemonics, or "memory tricks." Chances are, you have already used popular methods such as *rhymes* ("*i* before *e*, except after *c*" is my favorite; "thirty days hath September, April, June, and November" is another) and *acronyms* that reduce the amount of information to be stored (for example, *ROY G BIV* can be used to recall the colors of the light spectrum: *red, orange,*

yellow, green, *blue*, *indigo*, and *violet*). Relying on verbal mnemonics, advertisers create slogans to make their products memorable.

7   *Interference:* Because one learning experience can disrupt memory for another, it is wise to guard against the effects of interference. This problem is particularly common among college students, as material learned in one course can make it harder to retain that learned in another. To minimize the problem, follow two simple suggestions. First, study right before sleeping and review all the material right before the exam. Second, allocate an uninterrupted chunk of time to one course, and then do the same for your others as well. If you study psychology for a while, then move to biology, and then on to math and back to psychology, each course will disrupt your memory of the others—especially if the material is similar.

8   *Study environment:* Information is easier to recall when people are in the setting in which it was learned. That's why actors like to rehearse on the stage where they will later perform. So the next time you have an important exam to take, it may help to study in the room where the test will be administered.

9   These are just a few ways to improve your memory. Experiment with each to discover those that work for you.

—Kassin, *Psychology*

Although you may not realize it, you learned a great deal about improving your memory in the minute or two you spent previewing.

EXERCISE 2-1

Directions: Without referring to the above reading, "Ways to Improve Your Memory," make a list of ideas or suggestions you recall.

Connecting the Reading to Your Own Experience

Once you have previewed a reading, try to connect the topic to your own experience. Take a moment to recall what you already know or have read about the topic. This activity will make the reading more interesting and easier to write about. Here are a few suggestions to help you make connections:

1. **Ask questions and answer them.** Suppose you have just previewed a reading titled "Advertising: Institutionalized Lying." Ask questions such as: Do ads always lie? If not, why not? What do I already know about deceptive advertising?

2. **Brainstorm.** Jot down everything that comes to mind about the topic on a sheet of paper or a computer file. For example, if the topic of a reading is "The Generation Gap," write down ideas as they occur to you. You might list reasons for such a gap, try to define it, or mention names of families in which you have observed it. For more about brainstorming, see Chapter 11, p. 299.

3. **Think of examples.** Try to think of situations, people, or events that relate to the topic. For instance, suppose you have previewed a reading titled "Fashions, Fads, and Crazes." You might think of recent examples of each: pajamas as casual attire, iPods, or tattoos.

ESL Tip

A *generation* means the number of years that commonly separate parent and child (usually 20–30 years). A *gap* is a space between two things or people. The idiom *generation gap* refers to the difficulties that people of different generations often have in understanding each other's behavior, attitudes, and values.

Each of these techniques will help you identify ideas or experiences that you may share with the writer and that will help you focus your attention on the reading. In this book, the section titled "Thinking Before Reading," which comes before each reading, lists several questions that will help you make connections to your own experiences.

EXERCISE 2-2
Writing in Progress

Directions: Based on your preview of "Ways to Improve Your Memory," use one or more of the above techniques to connect the reading to your own experience. You might think of memory tricks you already use or things you find difficult (or easy) to remember.

Reading for Meaning

Reading is much more than moving your eyes across a line of print. To get the most out of a reading, you should search for, grasp, and react to the author's ideas. To do so, you'll need to know how essays and paragraphs are organized, how to develop strategies for dealing with difficult or confusing sentences or passages, and how to handle unfamiliar vocabulary.

What to Look for in Paragraphs

Paragraphs will be easier to understand and remember if you look for their three essential parts:

- **The topic** A paragraph is about one topic. This topic is discussed throughout the paragraph.

- **The main idea** A paragraph expresses one idea about its topic. Often this idea is expressed in a sentence called the **topic sentence**.

- **The supporting details** All the other sentences in the paragraph explain its main idea. Supporting details are facts that explain more about the main idea.

You can visualize a paragraph as follows:

Visualize It!

```
        ┌─────────────────┐
        │ Topic sentence  │
        └─────────────────┘
            ┌─────────────────┐
            │ Supporting detail │
            └─────────────────┘
            ┌─────────────────┐
            │ Supporting detail │
            └─────────────────┘
            ┌─────────────────┐
            │ Supporting detail │
            └─────────────────┘
            ┌─────────────────┐
            │ Supporting detail │
            └─────────────────┘
    ┌──────────────────────────────────┐
    │ Concluding or transitional sentence │
    └──────────────────────────────────┘
```

In the diagram on p. 41, the topic sentence appears first. The topic sentence is usually placed first in a paragraph, but it can appear anywhere in the paragraph. (You will learn much more about topic sentences and supporting details in Chapters 12 and 13.)

As you read, search for the topic sentence of each paragraph and notice how the other sentences in the paragraph explain it. This process will help you keep your mind on the reading and will direct your attention to the reading's key points. Try underlining or highlighting each topic sentence as you find it.

In this book you will find an exercise titled "Reviewing the Reading" following each reading. It is designed to help you check your understanding of the reading—both main ideas and details.

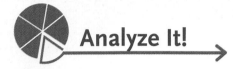 **Analyze It!**

Directions: Complete the idea map for the paragraph below. Notice how the writer states and then explains ideas.

Verbal mnemonics:

Sometimes the easiest way to remember a list of items is to use verbal mnemonics, or "memory tricks." Chances are, you have already used popular methods such as *rhymes* ("*i* before *e*, except after *c*" is my favorite; "thirty days hath September, April, June, and November" is another) and *acronyms* that reduce the amount of information to be stored (for example, *ROY G BIV* can be used to recall the colors of the light spectrum: *r*ed, *o*range, *y*ellow, *g*reen, *b*lue, *i*ndigo, and *v*iolet). Relying on verbal mnemonics, advertisers create slogans to make their products memorable.

Topic sentence: _____
_____.

Major detail: _____.

Minor detail: *i* before *e*, except after *c*

Minor detail: thirty days hath September, April, June, and November

Major detail: _____.

Minor detail: *ROY G BIV*

Conclusion: _____
_____
_____.

What to Look for in Essays

If you know what to look for as you read, you'll find reading an essay is easier, goes faster, and requires less rereading. When you read the essays in this book, be sure to pay attention to each of the following parts:

1. **The title** In some essays, the title announces the topic of the essay and may reveal the author's viewpoint. In others, the meaning of the title becomes clear only after you have read the essay.

2. **The introduction** The opening paragraph of an essay should interest you, announce the subject of the essay, and provide necessary background information on the subject.

3. **The author's main point** The main point is often called the *thesis statement*. It is the one big idea that the entire essay explains. Often it appears in the first paragraph, but it can be placed anywhere in the essay. Don't confuse the phrase *thesis statement* with *topic sentence*. The sentence that states the main idea of a paragraph is a topic sentence.

4. **Support and explanation** The body of the essay should explain, give reasons for, or offer support for the author's thesis. Each supporting paragraph should have a topic sentence that identifies the paragraph's main idea.

5. **The conclusion** The last paragraph brings the essay to a close. Often, it will restate the author's main point. It may also suggest directions for further thought.

Now, reread "Ways to Improve Your Memory," which has been marked here to identify each of the parts described above.

READING

WAYS TO IMPROVE YOUR MEMORY

Saul M. Kassin

Introduction

1   Before taking office, President Clinton invited five hundred business leaders to an economic summit in Little Rock. When it was over, many of the guests marveled at Clinton's ability to address them all by name. I have always been impressed by stories like this one—by stories of stage actors who memorize hundreds of lines in only one week of rehearsal, of people who fluently speak five languages, and of waiters who take dinner orders without a note pad. How can these accomplishments be explained?

Introduction continues

2   Over the years, psychologists have stumbled upon a few rare individuals who seemed equipped with extraordinary "hardware" for memory. But often the actors, waiters, multilinguists, and others we encounter use memory tricks called mnemonics—in other words, they vary their memory's "software." Can you boost your recall capacity through the use of mnemonics? Can you improve

Thesis statement

your study skills as a result? At this point, let's step back and consider several ways you can improve your memory.

Topic sentence: first way to improve memory

3   *Practice time:* To learn names, dates, vocabulary words, formulas, or the concepts in a textbook, you'll find that practice makes perfect. In general, the more time spent studying, the better. In fact, it pays to overlearn—that is, to review the material even after you think you have it mastered. It's also better to spread out your studying over time than to cram all at once. You will retain more information from four two-hour sessions than from one eight-hour marathon.

Topic sentence: second way

4   *Active thinking:* The sheer amount of practice time is important, but only if it's "quality time." Mindless drills may be helpful in the short run, but long-term retention requires that you think actively and deeply about material—about what it means and how it is linked to what you already know. Ask yourself

critical questions about the material. Think about it in ways that relate to your own experiences. Talk about the material to a friend, thus forcing yourself to organize it in terms that can be understood.

Topic sentence: third way 5

Organization of information: Once you have information to be learned, organize it as in an outline. Start with a few broad categories, then divide these into more specific subcategories and sub-subcategories. This is how many experts chunk new information, and it works. Thus, when Andrea Halpern (1986) presented subjects with 54 popular song titles, she found that recall was greater when the titles were organized hierarchically than when they were scrambled. The implication for studying is clear: organize the material in your notes, preferably in the form of an outline—and make sure to review these notes later.

Topic sentence: fourth way 6

Verbal mnemonics: Sometimes the easiest way to remember a list of items is to use verbal mnemonics, or "memory tricks." Chances are, you have already used popular methods such as *rhymes* ("*i* before *e*, except after *c*" is my favorite; "thirty days hath September, April, June, and November" is another) and *acronyms* that reduce the amount of information to be stored (for example, *ROY G BIV* can be used to recall the colors of the light spectrum: *red, orange, yellow, green, blue, indigo,* and *violet*). Relying on verbal mnemonics, advertisers create slogans to make their products memorable.

Topic sentence: fifth way 7

Interference: Because one learning experience can disrupt memory for another, it is wise to guard against the effects of interference. This problem is particularly common among college students, as material learned in one course can make it harder to retain that learned in another. To minimize the problem, follow two simple suggestions. First, study right before sleeping and review all the material right before the exam. Second, allocate an uninterrupted chunk of time to one course, and then do the same for your others as well. If you study psychology for a while, then move to biology, and then on to math and back to psychology, each course will disrupt your memory of the others—especially if the material is similar.

Topic sentence: sixth way 8

Study environment: Information is easier to recall when people are in the setting in which it was learned. That's why actors like to rehearse on the stage where they will later perform. So the next time you have an important exam to take, it may help to study in the room where the test will be administered.

Conclusion 9

These are just a few ways to improve your memory. Experiment with each to discover those that work for you.

How to Handle Difficult Readings

All of us, at one time or another, come across a piece of material that is difficult or confusing. An entire reading may be difficult, or just a paragraph or two within an otherwise comfortable reading may be troublesome. Don't give in to the temptation to skip over difficult parts or just give up. Instead, try to approach challenging readings using the methods in the box on page 45.

> ## Tips for Reading Difficult Material
>
> 1. **Analyze the time and place in which you are reading.** If you have been reading or studying for several hours, mental fatigue may be the source of the problem. If you are reading in a place with numerous distractions, lack of concentration may contribute to poor comprehension.
>
> 2. **Look up unfamiliar words.** Often, a few unfamiliar words can block understanding. Keep a dictionary handy and refer to it as needed.
>
> 3. **Do not hesitate to reread difficult or complicated sections.** In fact, sometimes several rereadings are appropriate and necessary.
>
> 4. **Rephrase each paragraph in your own words.** You might approach extremely complicated material sentence by sentence, expressing each idea in your own words.
>
> 5. **Read aloud sentences or sections that are particularly difficult.** Hearing ideas aloud often aids comprehension.
>
> 6. **Make a brief outline of the major points of the reading.** An outline will help you see the overall organization and progression of ideas.
>
> 7. **Slow down your reading rate if you feel you are beginning to lose comprehension.** On occasion, simply reading more slowly will boost your comprehension.
>
> 8. **Summarize.** Test your recall by summarizing each section after you read it.
>
> 9. **Work with a classmate.** Working through and discussing a reading with a classmate often will increase your understanding of it.

How to Record Your Thinking: Annotation

Annotation is a way of jotting down your ideas, reactions, opinions, and comments as you read. Think of annotation as recording your ideas about what you are reading. It is a personal way to brainstorm and "talk back" to the author—to question, challenge, agree, disagree, or comment. Annotations are particularly useful when you will be writing about what you have read.

You can also use annotation to mark key parts of the essay to clarify meaning. To clarify meaning, you might

- underline or highlight key ideas.

- place an asterisk (*) by key terms or definitions.

- number key items of supporting information.

- define unfamiliar words.

- paraphrase a complicated idea.

- bracket [ ] a useful example.

- mark useful summary statements with an asterisk.

- connect ideas with arrows.

- highlight statements that reveal the author's feelings or attitudes.

Here are some ways you might "talk back" to the author:

Ask questions.	Why would . . .?
Challenge the author's ideas.	If this is true, wouldn't . . .?
Look for inconsistencies.	But the author has already said that . . .
Add examples.	For instance . . .
Note exceptions.	This isn't true in the case of . . .
Disagree with the author.	How could . . .?
Make associations with other sources.	This is similar to . . .
Make judgments.	Good point . . .

Overall, you will find annotation useful for helping you understand and interact with an author's words and ideas. When you have to write an essay about a reading, you will understand the reading much better and thus be able to go right to the part you need to make your point. Here is a sample of the annotation one student did as she read "Ways to Improve Your Memory." Study it to see how she recorded her responses to and impressions of the reading.

But this takes time!

How will I know when I've mastered it?

How much time?

Practice time: To learn names, dates, vocabulary words, formulas, or the concepts in a textbook, you'll find that practice makes perfect. In general, the more time spent studying, the better. In fact, it pays to overlearn—that is, to review the material even after you think you have it mastered. It's also better to spread out your studying over time than to cram all at once. You will retain more information from four two-hour sessions than from one eight-hour marathon.

EXERCISE 2-3

Directions: Reread the following excerpt from "Ways to Improve Your Memory" and annotate it to reflect your thoughts about it and responses to it.

Active thinking: The sheer amount of practice time is important, but only if it's "quality time." Mindless drills may be helpful in the short run, but long-term retention requires that you think actively and deeply about material—about what it means and how it is linked to what you already know. Ask yourself critical questions about the material. Think about it in ways that relate to your own experiences. Talk about the material to a friend, thus forcing yourself to organize it in terms that can be understood.

Organization of information: Once you have information to be learned, organize it as in an outline. Start with a few broad categories, then divide these into more specific subcategories and sub-subcategories. This is how many experts chunk new information, and it works. Thus, when Andrea Halpern (1986) presented subjects with 54 popular song titles, she found that recall was greater when the titles were organized than when they were scrambled. The implication for studying is clear: organize the material in your notes, preferably in the form of an outline—and make sure to review these notes later.

Verbal mnemonics: Sometimes the easiest way to remember a list of names is to use verbal mnemonics, or "memory tricks." Chances are, you have already used popular methods such as *rhymes* ("*i* before *e*, except after *c*" is my favorite; "thirty days hath September, April, June, and November: is another) and *acronyms* that reduce the amount of information to be stored (for example, *ROY G BIV* can be used to recall the colors of the light spectrum: *red*, *orange*, *yellow*, *green*, *blue*, *indigo*, and *violet*). Relying on verbal mnemonics, advertisers create slogans to make their products memorable.

Using Idea Maps

Many students have difficulty remembering what they have read and find they have to reread frequently in order to write about a reading. One solution to this problem is to draw an idea map: a diagram that helps you both understand and remember how the writer's ideas relate to one another and how the essay is organized. Idea maps work because they force you to think about and analyze the relationships between ideas. They also are effective because they require you to express ideas from the reading in your own words; this activity increases your recall of those ideas.

Here is a sample idea map for the reading "Ways to Improve Your Memory." Notice that it includes all of the key ideas.

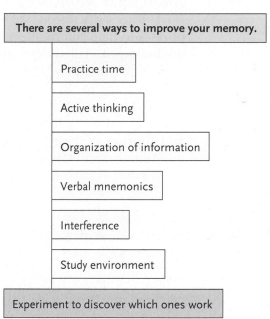

In each of the remaining chapters in this book you will find a section titled "Examining the Reading Using an Idea Map," in which you will find a partially completed idea map. By completing the idea map, you will learn more about the reading's content and organization. As you work through these chapters, you will gradually learn how to draw idea maps. As you go along, more and more boxes in the idea maps will be left for you to fill in.

Once you are comfortable using idea maps, do not hesitate to begin drawing your own for reading assignments in other courses. You will find that idea maps make a big difference in how much you can remember of what you read.

How to Write About a Reading

Once you have finished reading an essay, be sure you have understood what you have read. Define any unfamiliar words, and make sure you have found the author's thesis statement and key supporting ideas. In this book, you will find a set of questions following each reading. Called "Reviewing the Reading," these questions will help you check your understanding of the key points of the reading. To answer them, do not hesitate to refer to the reading frequently, especially to the parts you've highlighted and annotated. For certain questions, you may need to reread some of the material to clarify ideas or check details. Once you are confident that you have grasped the full meaning of the reading, you are ready to react to the reading's ideas through discussion and journal writing.

Class Discussion: An Opportunity to Explore Ideas

Class discussions are valuable sources of ideas to write about. By talking to classmates about a reading and listening to their ideas, you often discover ways to apply the reading to your own experience, uncover new ways of looking at ideas, or see relationships or connections you had not previously thought of. Be sure to get involved in the discussion. Don't just listen; you will learn more if you participate. By expressing your ideas orally, you will also be better prepared to express them in writing.

During a discussion, try to take only brief notes. Jot down key words and phrases to help you recall striking, new, or unusual ideas that develop in your discussions. Detailed notes are usually not a good idea because you spend all your time writing and don't participate in the discussion. When class is over, however, try to fill in your notes, recording ideas more completely and adding ideas as you recall them. Your instructor may begin class discussions with the questions listed in the section titled "Reacting to Ideas: Discussion and Journal Writing," which follows every reading. Be sure to read these questions before class and think about possible responses.

EXERCISE 2-4

Directions: If your instructor conducts a class discussion of the reading "Ways to Improve Your Memory," take brief notes during the discussion and fill them in when the class is over. Possible discussion questions are:

1. Are some types of material more difficult to memorize than others? Give some examples.

2. What positive (or negative) experiences have you had with memorizing information? When has your memory failed you or served you well?

3. Do you know anyone with extraordinary memory skills? Describe his or her skills.

Journal Writing: An Opportunity to Test Your Ideas

Responding to a reading by writing in your journal gives you a chance to explore ideas and experiment with ways of expressing them. Use the questions in the section titled "Reacting to Ideas: Discussion and Journal Writing" as starting points to help you discover your own ideas about the reading, as well as to clarify those of the author. Don't limit yourself to these specific questions; here are some general questions that may help you develop a response to a reading:

> ## Questions to Direct Your Thinking
>
> - Why did the author write the essay? What was his or her purpose?
> - For what audience was the essay written?
> - What issue, problem, concern, or question does the essay address?
> - What is the author's main point or position on that issue?
> - How well did the author explain and support the position?
> - Do you agree or disagree with the author's position? Why?
> - Do ideas in the essay apply or connect to your life? If so, how?
> - What, in your experience, is similar to or different from what the author describes in this essay?

EXERCISE 2-5

Directions: Select two or more techniques suggested in "Ways to Improve Your Memory." Write a journal entry in response to the following question: How can you apply these techniques to your studies?

Writing Assignments: Expressing Your Ideas

In this book, the section "Writing About the Reading" offers both paragraph and essay assignments on topics related to the reading. When your instructor gives you an assignment, use the following suggestions to help you produce a solid, well-written paper:

1. **Read the assignment several times before you begin.** Express in your own words what the assignment requires. If you have a choice of assignments, take a fair amount of time to choose. It is worthwhile to spend a few minutes thinking about and weighing possible topics. You don't want to work your way through a first draft and then realize that you don't have enough to say or you cannot work well with the topic.

2. **Try discussing the assignment with a classmate.** By talking about it, you can make sure you are on the right track, and you may discover new or additional ideas to write about. Also consider asking the classmate to react to your paper once you have a draft.

3. **Review your journal entries and notes of class discussions for possible topics or approaches to the assignment.** (Chapter 11, "Planning and Organizing," offers several strategies for discovering and selecting ideas to write about.)

4. **Don't be satisfied with the first draft that you write.** As you will discover in Chapter 12, "Drafting and Revising," you need to rethink and revise both what you have said and how you have said it.

Writing Success Tip 2

Organizing a Place and Time to Read and Write

You may find that you read and write more easily if you do so in the same place and at the same time each day. Use the following tips to organize a place and time to read and write:

ORGANIZING A PLACE TO READ AND WRITE

1. **If you live at home or in an apartment, try to find a quiet area that you can reserve for reading and writing.** If possible, avoid areas used for other purposes, such as the dining room or kitchen table, because you'll have to move or clean up your materials frequently. If you live in a dorm, your desk is an ideal place to write, unless the dorm is too noisy. If it is, find a quiet place elsewhere on campus.

2. **You'll need a table or desk; don't try to write on the arm of a comfortable chair.** Choose a space where you can spread out your papers.

3. **Eliminate distractions from your writing area.** Photos or stacks of bills to pay will take your mind off your writing.

4. **Be sure that lighting is adequate and your chair is straight and comfortable.**

5. **Collect and organize supplies: plenty of paper, pens, pencils, erasers, a stapler, white-out, and so forth.** If you write on a computer, keep spare disks on hand.

6. **Organize completed and returned papers, quizzes, class handouts, and other class materials in separate folders.**

7. **Keep a dictionary nearby, as well as any other reference materials recommended by your instructor—a thesaurus, for instance.** (See Chapter 3, p. 59 for advice on what type of dictionary to buy.)

8. **Use this place for reading, studying, and writing for your other courses, as well.**

ORGANIZING A TIME TO READ AND WRITE

1. **Reserve a block of time each day for reading this book and working on writing exercises and assignments.** Also reserve time for writing in your journal.

2. **For now, reserve an hour a day for writing.** This may seem like a lot of time, but most instructors expect you to spend a minimum of two hours outside of class for every hour you spend in class.

3. **Try to work at the same time each day.** You'll establish a routine that will be easy to follow.

4. **Choose a time during the day when you are at the peak of your concentration.** Don't try to write when you are tired or likely to be interrupted.

5. **Begin assignments well ahead of their due dates so that you have time to plan, organize, write, revise, and proofread.** It's best to leave a day or more between finishing your first draft and beginning to revise.

WRITING ABOUT A READING

THINKING BEFORE READING

The following reading first appeared in *Parade* magazine in March 2003. In "What Really Scares Us?" author David Ropeik explains some of the emotional factors behind our fears. Notice while you read how the essay is organized with main points and supporting details. Before you read:

1. Preview the reading, using the steps discussed on p. 38.

2. Connect the reading to your own experience by answering the following questions:

   a. What fears do you have? Why do you think these things frighten you?

   b. Are your fears mostly logical or emotional?

READING

WHAT REALLY SCARES US?

David Ropeik

1   The list of things to be afraid of seems to grow daily: terrorism, snipers, child abductions, and the West Nile virus. According to a number of public-opinion surveys, many people think it's more dangerous to be living now than it ever has been.

fly in the face of
challenge, defy

2   But those fears **fly in the face of** evidence that, in many ways, things are better than they've ever been. The average American life expectancy in 1900 was about 47 years. Now it's nearing 80. Diseases that plagued us—polio, smallpox, tuberculosis—have been all but eradicated in the U.S. In 1960, out of every 1000 babies born, 26 did not survive their first year. That number is now down to seven.

3   So why this disconnect between the facts and our fears? Well, it turns out that when it comes to the perception of risks, facts are only part of how we decide what to be afraid of and how afraid to be. Another huge factor—sometimes the most important factor—is our emotions.

4   Why do humans perceive risks this way if our highly advanced brain gives us the power to reason? It's because our brains are biologically built to fear first and think second. Which, in the end, is a pretty good strategy for survival.

5   Say you're walking through the woods and see a line on the ground, and you're not sure if it's a snake or a stick. The visual information goes to two parts of the brain. One is called the prefrontal cortex, behind your forehead. That's the area where we do a lot of our reasoning and thinking. The other area is called the amygdala, which is the brain's key emotion center.

6   Because of the way the brain is constructed, the information gets to the amygdala before it gets to the prefrontal cortex. So, before the reasoning part of the brain has had a chance to consider the facts, the fear center is saying, "Jump back, you dummy! It *could* be a snake!"

7   But how does the brain turn raw sensory information into fear? Apparently our brains have built-in patterns for interpreting sensory information that help us subconsciously filter incoming messages, making us more afraid of some things than others. Psychologists have identified many of the specific emotional characteristics of risks that are likely to make us more, or less, afraid.

Emotional Factors That Determine Our Fears

full-fledged
complete, total

8   **Control.** Imagine that you're driving down the highway, feeling pretty safe because you're behind the wheel. Now switch seats with your passenger. You're probably a little more nervous, maybe even turning into a **full-fledged** backseat driver. Not because the risk has gone up—the annual odds of being killed in a motor vehicle crash are 1 in 6700—but because you no longer are in control.

9   **Trust.** We trust certain sources more than others. We're less afraid when a trusted doctor or scientist, such as the head of the Centers for Disease Control and Prevention, explains **anthrax** than when a politician explains it.

anthrax
a serious infectious disease

10   **Newness.** When a risk first shows up, we treat it more like a snake until we've lived with it for a while and our experience lets us put the risk in perspective. We are more afraid of West Nile virus when it first shows up in our area than after it has been around for a few years. (Odds of dying from West Nile virus: 1 in 1,000,000.)

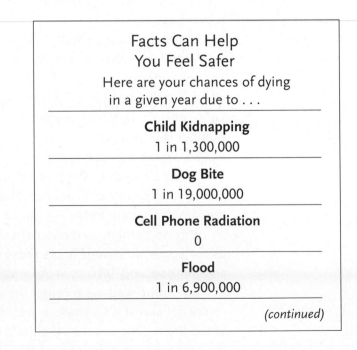

Facts Can Help
You Feel Safer
Here are your chances of dying
in a given year due to . . .

Child Kidnapping
1 in 1,300,000

Dog Bite
1 in 19,000,000

Cell Phone Radiation
0

Flood
1 in 6,900,000

(continued)

Flu
1 in 130,000
Lightning
1 in 3,000,000
Guns
1 in 28,000
Snake/Lizard/Spider
1 in 56,000,000

(Figures provided by David Ropeik
based on data from private and U.S. government
agencies. Odds are for the average American.
Individual risk may vary.)

11   **Choice**. We're more afraid of risks that are imposed on us than risks we take by choice. Imagine that you're driving along, talking on your cell phone. In the next lane, some other guy is driving and using *his* cell phone. Though both of you are in danger, the risk from the motorist next to you feels greater, because it's being imposed on you.

12   **Dread.** Things that can kill us in really awful ways seem riskier. We're more afraid of being eaten alive by a shark (odds, 1 in 281,000,000) or dying in a plane crash (1 in 9,000,000) than of dying from heart disease (1 in 300).

13   **Me or them.** If the risk is to you, it's worse than if that same risk only threatens somebody else. We're *all* worried about terrorism, now that we know it can happen here too, to us. A one in a million risk is too high if we think *we* could be that "one."

14   **Is it hard to understand?** The more complicated a risk is, the less we can understand it—and the more we treat it like a snake, just to be safe. For example, we're concerned about ionizing (nuclear) radiation, but we're not worried about infrared radiation, which we know simply as heat.

15   **Natural or manmade?** If it's natural, we're less afraid than if it's manmade. We're more frightened of nuclear power accidents (odds, 1 in 200,000) than of solar radiation. Yet sun exposure causes an estimated 1.3 million new cases of skin cancer in America per year, 7800 of which are fatal.

16   Several of these factors are often at work on the same risk at the same time, some making us more afraid and some less. The effect of these factors changes over time. Also, individual fears vary based on individual circumstances. For instance, women fear breast cancer more than men, while men fear prostate cancer more than women.

17   While it's understandable that we perceive risks this way, it also can be dangerous. Some people, afraid to fly because they lack control or because the risk or terrorism is new and feels high, choose instead to drive—a much bigger risk. It may make them *feel* safer, but overreacting this way raises their risks.

18   Underreacting can be dangerous too. People who aren't concerned about the risk of the sun—because it's natural and because of that nice glowing tan—raise their cancer risk by not taking the danger of sun exposure seriously enough to slap on sunscreen or wear a hat.

19   In the end, the best way to reduce the danger of any given risk is to arm yourself with some basic facts from a reliable, neutral source, so the rational side of your perceptions can hold its own in the contest against your natural emotions. The better you can do at keeping your perception of risks closer in line with what the risks actually are, the happier *and safer* you'll be.

GETTING READY TO WRITE

Reviewing the Reading

1. Name some of the things we fear these days. What sorts of things were concerns for us in the past?

2. Explain how the brain deals with a potential threat.

3. Identify the eight emotional factors that determine how fearful we are of something.

4. Why is the chart included in the reading?

5. Why is it dangerous to overreact and misperceive the level of risk in a particular situation?

6. What advice does the author have for us for dealing with our fears?

Examining the Reading Using an Idea Map

Review the reading by completing the missing parts of the idea map shown on the following page.

Strengthening Your Vocabulary

Using the word's context, word parts, or a dictionary, write a brief definition of each of the following words or phrases as it is used in the reading.

1. eradicated (paragraph 2) _____

2. disconnect (paragraph 3) _____

3. subconsciously (paragraph 7) _____

_____

4. imposed (paragraph 11) _____

5. arm (paragraph 19) _____

6. rational (paragraph 19) _____

ESL Tip

Don't confuse the word part *over-* with *over* as a complete word. *Over-* usually means "too much" (as in *overcook*). However, it can also mean "above" or "in addition to" (as in *overtime*).

The word part *mis-* means "bad" or "wrong." To *misperceive* is to interpret what you see incorrectly.

 Visualize It!

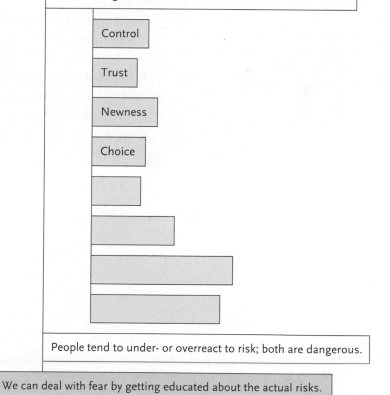

What Really Scares Us?

There is a discrepancy between our perception of risk and the actual risk involved; emotions are involved.

Humans have many fears.

Present fears: terrorism, snipers, child kidnappings, West Nile virus

Our brains deal with fear in a certain way.

Visual information goes to the prefrontal cortex.

The emotional center reacts first before the information is processed.

There are eight emotional factors that determine our fears.

Control

Trust

Newness

Choice

People tend to under- or overreact to risk; both are dangerous.

We can deal with fear by getting educated about the actual risks.

Reacting to Ideas: Discussion and Journal Writing

Get ready to write about the reading by discussing the following:

1. Discuss a current public fear. How justified is the public in being frightened?
2. Discuss whether television and newspaper reporting encourage fear in their audiences.
3. Write a journal entry about a time when you felt scared. Which of the eight factors were involved?
4. Discuss whether knowing the statistics behind risky situations is helpful.

WRITING ABOUT THE READING

Paragraph Options

1. Ropeik points out that what we fear now is different from what we feared in the past. Write a paragraph about something in the very recent past that was a big concern that we do not worry so much about today.
2. Some fears are timeless. Write a paragraph about something that many humans have always feared.
3. One of the emotional factors is control. Write a paragraph that describes a time when you felt frightened because you were not in control.

Essay Options

4. Survey some friends and family members about their greatest fears. Organize them into categories. Use the information to write an essay about some of the specific fears people have today.
5. Think about your daily routine. Write an essay describing some of the dangers you face every day. Explain how you assess the risk in your life.
6. Choose a scary situation and write an essay that gives advice and information to help lessen someone's fears of this situation.

CHAPTER REVIEW AND PRACTICE

CHAPTER REVIEW

To review and check your recall of the chapter, match each term in Column A with its meaning in Column B.

COLUMN A		COLUMN B
_f_	1. Topic	a. a way of recording your reactions to a reading in its margins
_c_	2. Previewing	b. a diagram that shows the content and organization of an essay or reading
_g_	3. Thesis statement	c. a method of becoming familiar with a reading before you actually begin reading
_h_	4. Main idea	d. a way of exploring your own ideas and experimenting with them before you begin to write an essay
_a_	5. Annotating	e. the facts that explain the main idea of a paragraph
_B_	6. Idea map	f. the one thing a paragraph or essay is about
_e_	7. Supporting details	g. the main point of an essay
_D_	8. Journal writing	h. the one point a paragraph makes about its topic

INTERNET ACTIVITIES

1. Reading Toward Writing

This online handout from the Writing Center at the University of North Carolina, Chapel Hill, provides many suggestions for connecting reading and writing. Print this list and try these techniques for your next reading assignment. Make notes about what worked best for you.

http://www.unc.edu/depts/wcweb/handouts/readingwriting.html

2. Making an Idea Map

Use these instructions from the Substantial Writing Component Resource Office at the University of Texas at Austin to create an idea map on a topic that is of current interest on your campus.

http://www.utexas.edu/cola/progs/wac/highschool/worksheets/hsideamapwksht/

Expanding Your Vocabulary

*In this chapter
you will:*

1. Learn to use a
dictionary effectively.

2. Learn to use context
to figure out unfamil-
iar words.

3. Learn to use word
parts to figure out
meanings.

4. Learn to use word
mapping to expand
your vocabulary.

5. Develop a system for
learning new words.

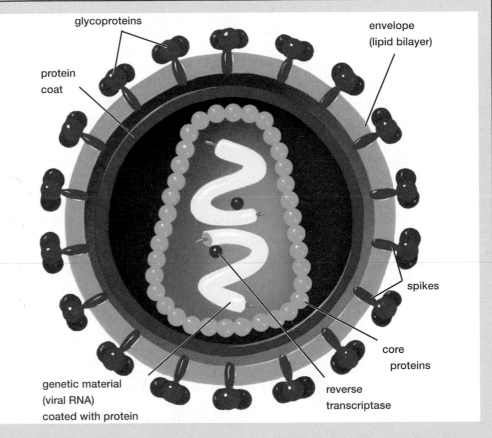

glycoproteins

envelope
(lipid bilayer)

protein
coat

spikes

core
proteins

genetic material
(viral RNA)
coated with protein

reverse
transcriptase

WRITE ABOUT IT!

The labels that accompanies the photograph above contains several unfamiliar words. Write a list of ways you can figure out their meanings. In this
chapter you will learn numerous strategies for figuring out and learning
unfamiliar words.

VOCABULARY

Why Improve Your Vocabulary?

Your vocabulary is one of your most valuable assets. Because words are the basic building blocks of language, you need a strong vocabulary to express yourself clearly in both speech and writing. A strong vocabulary identifies you as an effective communicator—an important skill both in college and in the workplace. Further, a solid vocabulary is the mark of an educated person—someone who is able to think, write, read critically, and speak effectively. Vocabulary building is well worth your while, and will pay off hundreds of times both in college and on the job. Let's get started!

Get the Right Tools

Building your vocabulary is much easier if you have the right tools to help you. Be sure you have a dictionary, and consider purchasing a thesaurus.

Buying and Using a Dictionary

Every writer needs a dictionary, not only to check spellings, but also to check meanings and the appropriate usages of words. You should have a desk or collegiate dictionary plus a pocket dictionary that you can carry with you to classes. Widely used dictionaries include:

The American Heritage Dictionary of the English Language

Webster's New Collegiate Dictionary

Webster's New World Dictionary of the American Language

Several dictionaries are available online. One of the most widely used is Merriam-Webster's (http://www.m-w.com). This site features an audio component that allows you to hear how a word is pronounced. You might also refer to http://www.dictonary.com. This site allows you to view and compare entries from several different dictionaries for a given word.

If you have difficulty with spelling, a misspeller's dictionary is another valuable reference. It can help you locate correct spellings easily. Two commonly used online dictionaries are *Webster's New World Misspeller's Dictionary* and *How to Spell It: A Handbook of Commonly Misspelled Words*.

Here is a brief review of the information a dictionary entry contains. As you read, refer to the sample dictionary entry shown on the next page.

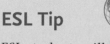

ESL Tip

ESL students will find an ESL dictionary extremely helpful for speaking and writing. Written for the nonnative speaker of English, it gives definitions in the simplest language possible, contains sample sentences to show how words are used, explains the differences between easily confused words, contains lots of labeled pictures, and offers many additional features. For students ready to write paragraphs and essays, the *Longman Advanced American Dictionary* is a good choice. (There are also ESL dictionaries for British English and for both American and British English.)

Pronunciation

Parts of speech

Verb forms

Restrictive meanings

Word history

◆ drink (drĭngk) *v.* drank (drăngk), drunk (drŭngk), drink•ing, drinks —*tr.* **1.** To take into the mouth and swallow (a liquid). **2.** To swallow the liquid contents of (a vessel): *drank a cup of tea.* **3.** To take in or soak up; absorb: *drank the fresh air; spongy earth that drank up the rain.* **4.** To take in eagerly through the senses or intellect: *drank in the beauty of the day.* **5a.** To give or make (a toast). **b.** To toast (a person or an occasion, for example): *We'll drink to your health.* **6.** To bring to a specific state by drinking alcoholic liquors: *drank our sorrows away.* —*intr.* **1.** To swallow liquid: *drank noisily; drink from a goblet.* **2.** To imbibe alcoholic liquors: *They only drink socially.* **3.** To salute a person or an occasion with a toast: *We will drink to your continued success.* ❖*n.* **1.** A liquid that is fit for drinking; a beverage. **2.** An amount of liquid swallowed: *took a long drink from the fountain.* **3.** An alcoholic beverage, such as a cocktail or highball. **4.** Excessive or habitual indulgence in alcoholic liquor. **5.** *Chiefly Southern U.S.* See **soft drink.** See Regional Note at **tonic. 6.** *Slang* A body of water; the sea: *The hatch cover slid off the boat and into the drink.* [Middle English, *drinken,* from Old English *drincan.* See **dhreg-** in Appendix I.]

American Heritage Dictionary of the English Language

1. **Pronunciation** The pronunciation of the word is given in parentheses. Symbols are used to indicate the sounds letters make within specific words. Refer to the pronunciation key printed on each page or on alternate pages of your dictionary.

2. **Grammatical information** The part of speech is indicated, as well as information about different forms the word may take. Most dictionaries include

   - principal forms of verbs (both regular and irregular).
   - plural forms of irregular nouns.
   - comparative and superlative forms of adjectives and adverbs.

3. **Meanings** Meanings are numbered and are usually grouped by the part of speech they represent.

4. **Restrictive meanings** Meanings that are limited to special situations are labeled. Some examples are:

   - *Slang*—casual language used only in conversation.
   - *Biol.*—words used in specialized fields, in this case biology.
   - *Regional*—words used only in certain parts of the United States.

5. **Synonyms** Words with similar meanings may be listed.

6. **Word history** The origin of the word (its etymology) is described. (Not all dictionaries include this feature.)

Beyond definitions, a dictionary contains a wealth of other information as well. For example, in the *American Heritage Dictionary*, Third Edition, you can find the history of the word *vampire*, the population of Vancouver, and an explanation of the New England expression "Vum!" Consider your dictionary a helpful and valuable resource that can assist you in expressing your ideas more clearly and correctly.

EXERCISE 3-1

Directions: Use a dictionary to answer each of the following questions:

Word: *reconstitute*

1. What is one definition of this word?

   _____

2. What part of speech is this word?

   _____

3. Write your own sentence using this word.

   _____

word: *launch*

1. What is one definition of this word?

   _____

2. What part of speech is this word?

   _____

3. Write your own sentence using this word.

   _____

word: *console*

1. What is one definition of this word?

   _____

2. What part of speech is this word?

   _____

3. Write your own sentence using this word.

   _____

EXERCISE 3-2

Directions: Use a dictionary to answer the following questions:

1. What does the abbreviation *obs.* mean?

   _____

2. What does the symbol *c.* stand for?

   _____

3. How many meanings are listed for the word *fall*?

   _____

4. How is the word *phylloxera* pronounced? (Record its phonetic spelling.)

_____

5. What is the plural spelling of *addendum*?

_____

6. Can the word *protest* be used other than as a verb? If so, how?

_____

7. The word *prime* can mean first or original. List some of its other meanings.

_____

8. What does the French expression *savoir faire* mean?

_____

9. List three synonyms for the word *fault*.

_____

10. List several words that are formed using the word *dream*.

_____

Finding the Right Meaning in a Dictionary Entry

Most words have more than one meaning. When you look up the meaning of a new word, you must choose the meaning that best fits the way the word is used in the context of the sentence. The following sample entry for the word *green* contains many meanings for the word.

Meanings grouped by parts of speech

7 Nouns

12 Adjectives

1 Verb

Many different meanings

Type of vegetable

Part of golf course

Unripe fruit

Inexperienced person

green (grēn) *n.* **1.** The hue of that portion of the visible spectrum lying between yellow and blue, evoked in the human observer by radiant energy with wavelengths of approximately 490 to 570 nanometers; any of a group of colors that may vary in lightness and saturation and whose hue is that of the emerald or somewhat less yellow that that of growing grass; one of the additive or light primaries; one of the psychological primary hues. **2.** Something green in color. **3. greens** Green growth or foliage, especially: **a.** The branches and leaves of plants used for decoration. **b.** Leafy plants or plant parts eaten as vegetables. **4.** A grassy lawn or plot, especially: **a.** A grassy area located usually at the center of a city or town and set aside for common use; a common. **b.** *Sports* A putting green. **5. greens** A green uniform: " A young...sergeant in dress greens" (Nelson DeMille). **6.** *Slang* Money. **7. Green** A supporter of a social and political movement that espouses global environmental protection, bioregionalism, social responsibility, and nonviolence. ❖*adj.* **green•er, green•est 1.** Of the color green. **2.** Abounding in or covered with green growth or foliage: *the green woods.* **3.** Made with green or leafy vegetables: *a green salad.* **4.** Characterized by mild or temperate weather: *a green climate.* **5.** Youthful; vigorous: *at the green age of 18.* **6.** Not mature or ripe; young: *green tomatoes.* **7.** Brand-new; fresh. **8.** Not yet fully processed, especially: **a.** Not aged: *green wood.* **b.** Not cured or tanned: *green pelts.* **9.** Lacking training or experience. See synonyms at **young. 10a.** Lacking sophistication or worldly experience; naive. **b.** Easily duped or deceived; gullible. **11.** Having a sickly or unhealthy pallor indicative of nausea or jealousy, for example. **12a.** Beneficial to the environment: *green recycling policies.* **b.** Favoring or supporting environmentalism: *green legislators who strengthened pollution controls.* ❖*tr. & intr. v.* **greened, green•ing, greens** To make or become green.
—*idiom:* **green around** (or **about) the gills** Pale or sickly in appearance. [Middle English *grene,* from Old English *grēne,* see **ghrē-** in Appendix I. N., sense 7, translation of German *(die) Grünen,* (the) Greens, from *grün,* green.] —**green'ly** *adv.* —**green'ness** *n.*

American Heritage Dictionary of the English Language

The meanings are grouped by part of speech and are numbered consecutively in each group. Generally, the most common meanings of the word are listed first, with more specialized, less common meanings appearing toward the end of the entry. Now find the meaning that fits the use of the word *green* in the following sentence:

> The local veterans' organization held its annual fund-raising picnic on the village **green**.

In this sentence, *green* refers to "a common or park in the center of a town or village." Since this is a specialized meaning of the word, it appears toward the end of the entry.

Here are a few suggestions for choosing the correct meaning from among those listed in an entry:

1. **If you are familiar with the parts of speech, try to use these to locate the correct meaning.** For instance, if you are looking up the meaning of a word that names a person, place, or thing, you can save time by reading only those entries given after *n.* (noun).

2. **For most types of college reading, you can skip definitions that give slang and colloquial (abbreviated as colloq.) meanings.** Colloquial meanings refer to informal or conversational language.

3. **If you are not sure of the part of speech, read each meaning until you find a definition that seems correct.** Skip over restrictive meanings that are inappropriate.

4. **Test your choice by substituting the meaning in the sentence with which you are working.** Substitute the definition for the word and see whether it makes sense in the context of the sentence.

Suppose you are looking up the word *oblique* to find its meaning in this sentence:

> My sister's **oblique** answers to my questions made me suspicious.

Oblique is used in the above sentence as an adjective. Looking at the entries listed after *adj.* (adjective), you can skip over the definition under the heading *Mathematics*, as it wouldn't apply here: Definition 4a (indirect or evasive) best fits the way *oblique* is used in the sentence.

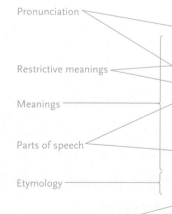

Pronunciation

Restrictive meanings

Meanings

Parts of speech

Etymology

Spelling of other forms of the entry word

o•blique (ō-blēk', ə-blēk') *adj.* **1a.** Having a slanting or sloping direction, course or position; inclined. **b.** *Mathematics* Designating geometric lines or planes that are neither parallel nor perpendicular. **2.** *Botany* Having sides of unequal length or form: *an oblique leaf.* **3.** *Anatomy* Situated in a slanting position; not transverse or longitudinal: *oblique muscles or ligaments.* **4a.** Indirect or evasive: *oblique political maneuvers.* **b.** Devious, misleading, or dishonest: *gave oblique answers to the questions.* **5.** Not direct in descent; collateral. **6.** *Grammar* Designating any noun case except the nominative or the vocative. ❖*n.* **1.** An oblique thing, such as a line, direction, or muscle. **2.** *Nautical* The act of changing course by less than 90°. ❖*adv.* (ō-blĭk', ə-blĭk') At an angle of 45°. [Middle English, from Old French, from Latin *oblīquus.*] —o•blique'ly *adv.* —o•blique'ness *n.*

ESL Tip

A bilingual dictionary (that translates from your native language to English and vice versa) is handy. However, these dictionaries sometimes contain errors and often do not give all the different meanings that a word may have in English. This type of dictionary is useful but not sufficient for academic writing. You should also have an ESL dictionary with a vocabulary of at least 80,000 words and, later, a standard desk-size college dictionary.

EXERCISE 3-3

Directions: The following words have two or more meanings. Look them up in your dictionary and write two sentences with different meanings for each word.

1. culture

   _____

   _____

2. perch

   _____

   _____

3. surge

   _____

   _____

4. extend

   _____

   _____

5. irregular

   _____

   _____

EXERCISE 3-4

Directions: Use the dictionary to help you find an appropriate meaning for the boldfaced word in each of the following sentences:

1. The last contestant did not have a **ghost** of a chance.

   _____

2. The race car driver won the first **heat**.

   _____

3. The police took all possible **measures** to protect the witness.

   _____

4. The orchestra played the first **movement** of the symphony.

   _____

5. The plane stalled on the **apron**.

   _____

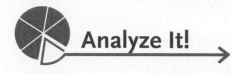

Analyze It!

Directions: Read the paragraph on the left, taken from a college textbook. Use context, word parts, and a dictionary, if necessary, to figure out the meanings of the words listed on the right. Write the meanings in the space provided.

Human communication, in one way or another, inevitably involves the body in sending and receiving messages. Beyond the mechanics of speaking, hearing, gesturing, and seeing, the body itself can function as a "text" that conveys messages. The full range of body language includes eye movements, posture, walking style, the way of standing and sitting, cultural inscriptions on the body such as tattoos and hairstyles, and accessories such as dress, shoes, and jewelry. Body language follows patterns and rules just as verbal language does. Like verbal language, the rules and meanings are learned, often unconsciously. Without learning the rules and meanings, one will commit communication errors, which are sometimes funny and sometimes serious.

inevitably _____

_____

mechanics _____

_____

body language _____

_____

accessories _____

_____

unconsciously _____

_____

Using a Thesaurus

A thesaurus is a dictionary of synonyms. It groups together words with similar meanings. A thesaurus is particularly useful when you want to do the following:

- Locate the precise or exact word to fit a particular situation. (Example: Replace "a *boring* movie" with "an *uneventful* movie.")
- Find an appropriate descriptive word. (Example: Choose from among the following words to describe *happiness*: *delight, pleasure, joy, glee.*)
- Replace an overused or unclear word. (Example: Replace "a *good* television program" with "a *thrilling* or *refreshing* television program.")
- Convey a more specific shade of meaning. (Example: Use one of the following words to describe *walking*: *swagger, strut, stroll.*)

Suppose you are looking for a more precise word for the phrase *will tell us about* in the following sentence:

In class today, our chemistry instructor **will tell us about** our next assignment.

The thesaurus lists the following synonyms for "tell" or "explain":

> 10 **explain, explicate, expound,** exposit; **give the meaning,** tell the meaning of; **spell out,** unfold; **account for,** give reason for; **clarify, elucidate,** clear up; **make clear,** make plain; **simplify,** popularize; **illuminate,** enlighten, **shed** or **throw light upon;** rationalize, euhemerize, demythologize, allegorize; tell or show how, show the way; **demonstrate, show, illustrate,** exemplify; decipher, crack, unlock, find the key to, unravel, **solve;** explain oneself; explain away.
> 11 **comment upon,** commentate, remark upon; **annotate,** gloss; **edit,** make an edition.
> 12 **translate, render,** transcribe, transliterate, put or turn into, transfuse the sense of; construe; English.
> 13 **paraphrase, rephrase, reword, restate,** rehash; give a free or loose translation.

The American Heritage College Thesaurus

Read the above entry and underline words or phrases that you think would be more descriptive than *tell about.* You might underline words and phrases such as *comment upon, illustrate, demonstrate,* and *spell out.*

The most widely used thesaurus is *Roget's Thesaurus.* Inexpensive paperback editions are available in most bookstores.

When you first consult a thesaurus, you will need to familiarize yourself with its format and learn how to use it. The following is a step-by-step approach:

1. **Locate the word you are trying to replace in the index.** Following the word, you will find the number(s) of the section(s) in the main part of the thesaurus that list(s) the synonyms of that word.

2. **Turn to those sections, scanning each list and jotting down all the words you think might work as synonyms.**

3. **Test each of the words you selected in the sentence in which you will use it.** The word should fit the context of the sentence.

4. **Select the word that best expresses what you are trying to say.**

5. **Choose only words whose shades of meaning you know.** Check unfamiliar words in a dictionary before using them. Remember, misusing a word is often a more serious error than choosing an overused or general word.

EXERCISE 3-5

Directions: Using a thesaurus, replace the boldfaced word or phrase in each of the following sentences with a more precise or descriptive word. Write the word in the space provided. Rephrase the sentence, if necessary.

1. Although the movie was **good,** it lasted only an hour and 20 minutes.

   _____

2. The judge **looked at** the criminal as she pronounced the sentence.

   _____

3. The accident victim was awarded a **big** cash settlement.

   _____

4. The lottery winner was **happy** to win the $100,000 prize, but he was surprised to learn that a sizable portion had already been deducted for taxes.

_____

5. On the first day of class, the instructor **talked to** the class about course requirements.

_____

Use Context Clues to Figure Out Unfamiliar Words

Context refers to the words around a given word. Often you can use context to figure out a word you do not know. Try it in the following sentence:

> **Phobias,** such as a fear of heights, water, or confined spaces, are difficult to overcome.

From the clues in the rest of the sentence, you can figure out that *phobias* are fears of specific objects or situations. Such clues are called **context clues.** There are five types of context clues that can help you figure out a word you do not know: definition, synonym, example, contrast, and inference. These are summarized in the Need to Know box shown on the following page.

Context clues do not always appear in the same sentence as the unknown word. They may appear anywhere in the passage, or in an earlier or later sentence. So if you cannot find a clue immediately, look before and after the word. Here is an example:

> Betsy took a *break* from teaching in order to serve in the Peace Corps. Despite the **hiatus,** Betsy's school was delighted to rehire her when she returned.

Notice that the clue for the word *hiatus, break,* appears in the sentence before the one containing the word you want to define.

EXERCISE 3-6

Directions: Using the definition or synonym clues in each sentence, write a brief definition of each boldfaced word in the following sentences:

1. After taking a course in **genealogy**, Don was able to create a record of his family's history dating back to the eighteenth century.

_____

2. Louie's **dossier** is a record of his credentials, including college transcripts and letters of recommendation.

_____

3. There was a **consensus**—or unified opinion—among the students that the exam was difficult.

_____

4. After each course heading there was a **synopsis**, or summary, of the content and requirements for the course.

_____

5. When preparing job application letters, Serena develops one standard letter or **prototype**. Then she changes that letter to fit the specific jobs for which she is applying.

_____

NEED TO KNOW

Five Useful Types of Context Clues

Type of Context Clue	How It Works	Examples
Definition	Writers often define a word after using it. Words such as _means_, _refers to_, and _can be defined as_ provide an obvious clue that the word's meaning is to follow. Sometimes writers use dashes, parentheses, or commas to separate a definition from the rest of the sentence.	**Corona** refers to <u>the outermost part of the sun's atmosphere.</u> <u>Broad flat noodles</u> that are served covered with sauce or butter are called **fettuccine.** The judge's **candor**—<u>his sharp, open frankness</u>—shocked the jury. **Audition,** <u>the process of hearing,</u> begins when a sound wave reaches the outer ear.
Synonym	Rather than formally define a word, some writers include a word or brief phrase that is close in meaning to a word you may not know.	The main character in the movie was an **amalgam,** <u>or combination,</u> of several real people the author met during the war.
Example	Writers often include examples to help explain a word. From the examples, you can often figure out what the unknown word means.	**Toxic** materials, such as <u>arsenic, asbestos, pesticides, and lead,</u> can cause bodily damage. (You can figure out that _toxic_ means "poisonous.") Many **pharmaceuticals,** including <u>morphine and penicillin,</u> are not readily available in some countries. (You can figure out that _pharmaceuticals_ are drugs.)
Contrast	Sometimes a writer gives a word that is opposite in meaning of a word you don't know. From the opposite meaning, you can figure out the unknown word's meaning. (Hint: watch for words such as _but_, _however_, _though_, _whereas_.)	Uncle Sal was quite **portly,** <u>but his wife was very thin.</u> (The opposite of _thin_ is _fat_, so you know that _portly_ means "fat.") The professor **advocates** the testing of cosmetics on animals, <u>but many of her students oppose it.</u> (The opposite of _oppose_ is _favor_, so you know that _advocates_ means "favors.")
Inference	Often your own logic or reasoning skills can lead you to the meaning of an unknown word.	Bob is quite **versatile:** <u>he is a good student, a top athlete, an excellent auto mechanic, and a gourmet cook.</u> (Because Bob excels at many activities, you can reason that _versatile_ means "capable of doing many things.") <u>On hot, humid afternoons,</u> I often feel **languid.** (From your experience you may know that you feel drowsy or sluggish on hot afternoons, so you can figure out that, _languid_ means "lacking energy.")

EXERCISE 3-7

Directions: Using the example clues in each sentence, write a brief definition of each boldfaced word in the following sentences:

1. **Histrionics**, such as wild laughter or excessive body movements, are usually inappropriate in business settings.

   _____

2. Jerry's child was **reticent** in every respect; she would not speak, refused to answer questions, and avoided looking at anyone.

   _____

3. Most **condiments**, such as pepper, mustard, and catsup, are used to improve the flavor of foods.

   _____

4. Dogs, cats, parakeets, and other **sociable** pets can provide senior citizens with companionship.

   _____

5. Paul's grandmother is a **sagacious** businesswoman; once she turned a small ice cream shop into a popular restaurant and sold it for a huge profit.

   _____

EXERCISE 3-8

Directions: Using the contrast clues in each sentence, write a brief definition of each boldfaced word or phrase in the following sentences:

1. Freshmen are often **naive** about college at first, but by their second semester they are usually quite sophisticated in the ways of their new school.

   _____

2. Although most members of the class agreed with the instructor's evaluation of the film, several strongly **objected**.

   _____

3. Little Jill hid shyly behind her mother when she met new people, yet her brother Matthew was very **gregarious**.

   _____

4. The child remained **demure** while the teacher scolded, but became violently angry afterward.

   _____

5. Some city dwellers are **affluent**; others live in or near poverty.

   _____

EXERCISE 3-9

Directions: Using logic and your own reasoning skills, choose the correct definition of each boldfaced word in the following sentences:

_____ 1. To **compel** Clare to hand over her wallet, the mugger said he had a gun.

    a. discourage   c. force

    b. entice   d. imagine

_____ 2. Student journalists are taught how to be **concise** when writing in a limited space.

    a. peaceful   c. proper

    b. clear and brief   d. wordy

_____ 3. There should be more **drastic** penalties to stop people from littering.

    a. dirty   c. extreme

    b. suitable   d. dangerous

_____ 4. To **fortify** his diet while weightlifting, Monty took 12 vitamins a day.

    a. suggest   c. avoid

    b. strengthen   d. approve of

_____ 5. On our wedding anniversary, my husband and I **reminisced** about how we first met.

    a. sang   c. argued

    b. remembered   d. forgot

EXERCISE 3-10

Directions: Read the following passage and then circle the answer that best defines each boldfaced word appearing in the text.

Worms and _viruses_ are rather unpleasant terms that have entered the **jargon** of the computer industry to describe some of the ways that computer systems can be invaded.

A worm can be defined as a program that transfers itself from computer to computer over a network and plants itself as a separate file on the target computer's disks. One worm was **injected** into an electronic mail network where it multiplied uncontrollably and clogged the memories of thousands of computers until they could no longer function.

A virus is a set of illicit instructions that passes itself on to other programs or documents with which it comes in contact. It can change or delete files, display words or obscene messages, or produce bizarre screen effects. In its most **vindictive** form, a virus can slowly **sabotage** a computer system and remain undetected for months, contaminating data or wiping out an entire hard drive. A virus can be dealt with using a vaccine, or antivirus, which is a computer program that stops the virus from spreading and often **eradicates** it.

—adapted from Capron, *Computers: Tools for an Information Age*

_____ **1.** jargon

    a. language   c. confusion

    b. system   d. security

_____ **2.** injected

    a. avoided   c. removed

    b. introduced   d. discussed

_____ **3.** vindictive

    a. creative   c. harmful

    b. simple   d. typical

_____ **4.** sabotage

    a. prevent   c. transfer

    b. destroy   d. produce

_____ **5.** eradicates

    a. eliminates   c. repeats

    b. allows   d. produces

Pay Attention to Word Parts

Suppose that you came across the following sentence in a human anatomy textbook:

Trichromatic plates are used frequently in the text to illustrate the position of body organs.

If you did not know the meaning of *trichromatic*, how could you determine it? There are no clues in the sentence context. One solution is to look up the word in a dictionary. An easier and faster way is to break the word into parts and analyze the meaning of each part. Many words in the English language are made up of word parts called **prefixes**, **roots**, and **suffixes**. These word parts have specific meanings that, when added together, can help you determine the meaning of the word as a whole.

The word *trichromatic* can be divided into three parts: its prefix, root, and suffix.

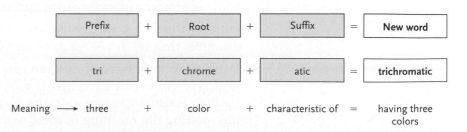

You can see from this analysis that *trichromatic* means "having three colors."

Here are a few other examples of words that you can figure out by using prefixes, roots, and suffixes:

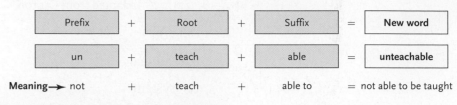

The parents thought their child was **unteachable**.

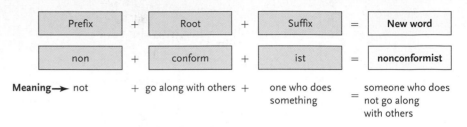

The student was a **nonconformist**.

The first step in using the prefix-root-suffix method is to become familiar with the most commonly used word parts. The prefixes and roots listed in Table 3-1 and Table 3-2 (see p. 74 and p. 76) will give you a good start in determining the meanings of thousands of words without looking them up in the dictionary. For instance, more than 10,000 words can begin with the prefix *non-*. Not all these words are listed in a collegiate dictionary, but they would appear in an unabridged dictionary. Another common prefix, *pseudo-*, is used in more than 400 words. A small amount of time spent learning word parts can yield a large payoff in new words learned.

Before you begin to use word parts to figure out new words, here are a few things you need to know:

1. **In most cases, a word is built upon at least one root.**

2. **Words can have more than one prefix, root, or suffix.**

    a. Words can be made up of two or more roots (geo/logy).

    b. Some words have two prefixes (in/sub/ordination).

    c. Some words have two suffixes (beauti/ful/ly).

3. **Words do not always have a prefix and a suffix.**

    a. Some words have neither a prefix nor a suffix (read).

    b. Others have a suffix but no prefix (read/ing).

    c. Others have a prefix but no suffix (pre/read).

4. **The spelling of roots may change as they are combined with suffixes.** Some common variations are included in Table 3-3 on p. 78.

5. **Different prefixes, roots, or suffixes may have the same meaning.** For example, the prefixes *bi-*, *di-*, and *duo-* all mean "two."

6. **Word parts may have more than one meaning.** A dictionary listing that begins or ends with a hyphen is a word part, not a complete word. The hyphen is usually not used in the spelling of the word. Be careful when interpreting the meaning of these word parts. Many have more than one meaning. For example, *ex-* means "former" (as in *ex-president*), but it can also mean "out" or "outside" (as in *exit* or *exterior*).

7. **Use a dictionary to find out which prefix to use.** Several word parts mean "not" and make the word they precede mean the opposite of its original meaning. For example, the following are some common negative prefixes: *in-* (*incomplete*), *im-* (*impossible*), *un-* (*unbearable*), *non-* (*nonsense*), *il-* (*illegal*), *ir-* (*irregular*), and *dis-* (*disobey*). Which one should you use? In many cases, the correct prefix is determined by the word's part of speech (such as *dis-* before a verb) and the first letter of the base word. Base words beginning with *m* or *p* usually use *im-*, words beginning with *l* usually use *il-*, and most words beginning with *r-* use *ir-* as their negative prefixes. If you're not sure which prefix to use, consult a dictionary.

8. **Sometimes you may identify a group of letters as a prefix or root but find that it does not carry the meaning of that prefix or root.** For example, the letters *mis* in the word *missile* are part of the root and are not the prefix *mis-*, which means "wrong or bad."

Prefixes

Prefixes appear at the beginnings of many English words. They alter the meaning of the root to which they are connected. For example, if you add the prefix *re-* to the word *test*, the word *retest* is formed, meaning to test again. If *pre-* is added to the word *test*, the word *pretest* is formed, meaning a test given before something else. If the prefix *post-* is added, the word *posttest* is formed, meaning a test given after something else. In Table 3-1, 40 common prefixes are grouped according to meaning.

EXERCISE 3-11

Directions: Use the list of common prefixes in Table 3-1 (p. 74) to determine the meaning of each of the following words. Write a brief definition or synonym for each. If you are unfamiliar with the root, you may need to check a dictionary.

1. interoffice

   _____

2. supernatural

   _____

3. nonsense

   _____

4. introspection

   _____

5. prearrange

   _____

6. reset

   _____

7. subtopic

_____

8. transmit

_____

9. multidimensional

_____

10. imperfect

_____

TABLE 3-1   COMMON PREFIXES

Prefix	Meaning	Sample Word
Prefixes referring to amount or number		
mono/uni	one	monocle/unicycle
bi/di/du	two	bimonthly/divorce/duet
tri	three	triangle
quad	four	quadrant
quint/pent	five	quintet/pentagon
deci	ten	decimal
centi	hundred	centigrade
milli	thousand	milligram
micro	small	microscope
multi/poly	many	multipurpose/polygon
semi	half	semicircle
equi	equal	equidistant
Prefixes meaning "not" (negative)		
a	not	asymmetrical
anti	against	antiwar
contra	against, opposite	contradict
dis	apart, away, not	disagree
in/il/ir/im	not	incorrect/illogical/irreversible/impossible
mis	wrongly	misunderstand
non	not	nonfiction
pseudo	false	pseudoscientific
un	not	unpopular
Prefixes giving direction, location, or placement		
ab	away	absent
ad	toward	adhesive
ante/pre	before	antecedent/premarital
circum/peri	around	circumference/perimeter
com/col/con	with, together	compile/collide/convene
de	away, from	depart
dia	through	diameter
ex/extra	from, out of, former	ex-wife/extramarital
hyper	over, excessive	hyperactive
inter	between	interpersonal
intro/intra	within, into, in	introduction
post	after	posttest
re	back, again	review
retro	backward	retrospect
sub	under, below	submarine
super	above, extra	supercharge
tele	far	telescope
trans	across, over	transcontinental

EXERCISE 3-12

Directions: Read each of the following sentences. Use your knowledge of prefixes to fill in the blanks and complete the words.

1. A person who speaks two languages is _____ **lingual**.

2. A letter or number written beneath a line of print is called a _____ **script**.

3. The new sweater had a snag, and I returned it to the store because it was _____ **perfect**.

4. The flood damage was permanent and _____ **reversible**.

5. I was not given the correct date and time; I was _____ **informed**.

6. People who speak several different languages are _____ **lingual**.

7. A musical _____ **lude** was played between the events in the ceremony.

8. I decided the magazine was uninteresting, so I _____ **continued** my subscription.

9. Merchandise that does not pass factory inspection is considered _____ **standard** and is sold at a discount.

10. The tuition refund policy approved this week will apply to last year's tuition as well; the policy will be _____ **active** to January 1 of last year.

11. The elements were _____ **acting** with each other when they began to bubble and their temperature rose.

12. _____ **ceptives** are widely used to prevent unwanted pregnancies.

13. All of the waitresses were required to wear the restaurant's _____ **form**.

14. The _____ **viewer** asked the presidential candidates unexpected questions about important issues.

15. The draperies were _____ **colored** from long exposure to the sun.

EXERCISE 3-13

Directions: Working with a classmate, list as many words as you can think of for two of the following prefixes: **multi-, mis-, trans-, com-, inter-**. Then share your lists with the class.

Roots

Roots carry the basic or core meaning of a word. Hundreds of root words are used to build other words in the English language. Twenty of the most common and most useful are listed in Table 3-2 on p. 76. Knowledge of the meanings of these roots will enable you to unlock the meanings of many words. For example, if you knew that the root *dic/dict* means "tell or say," then you would have a clue to the meanings of such words as *dictate* (to speak while someone writes down your words), *diction* (wording or manner of speaking), or *dictionary* (a book that "tells" what words mean).

TABLE 3-2   TWENTY COMMON ROOTS

Common Root	Meaning	Sample Word
aud/audit	hear	audible
bio	life	biology
cap	take, seize	captive
cede	go	precede
chron(o)	time	chronology
cred	believe	incredible
dict/dic	tell, say	predict
duc/duct	lead	introduce
graph	write	autograph
mit/mis(s)	send	permit/dismiss
path	feeling	sympathy
photo	light	photosensitive
port	carry	transport
scrib/script	write	inscription
sen/sent	feel	insensitive
spec/spic/spect	look, see	retrospect
sym/syn	same, together	synonym
ven/vent	come	convention
vert/vers	turn	invert
voc	call	vocation

EXERCISE 3-14

Directions: Complete each of the following sentences using one of the words listed below. Not all of the words will be used.

apathetic	dictated	graphic	scriptures	tendon
captivated	extensive	phonics	spectators	verdict
deduce	extraterrestrial	prescribed	synchronized	visualize

1. The jury brought in its _____ after one hour of deliberation.
2. Religious or holy writings are called _____.
3. The _____ watching the football game were tense.
4. The doctor _____ two types of medication.
5. The criminal appeared _____ when the judge pronounced his sentence.
6. The runners _____ their watches before beginning the race.

7. The textbook contained numerous _____ aids, including maps, charts, and diagrams.

8. The district manager _____ a new policy on business expenses.

9. Through his attention-grabbing performance, he _____ the audience.

10. By putting together the clues, the detective was finally able to _____ who committed the crime.

EXERCISE 3-15

Directions: List two words for each of the following roots: *dict/dic; spec/spic/spect; cred; photo; scrib/script.*

_____

_____

_____

Suffixes

Suffixes are word endings that often change the part of speech of a word. For example, adding the suffix *y* to the noun *cloud* forms the adjective *cloudy*. Accompanying the change in part of speech is a shift in meaning (*cloudy* means "resembling clouds; overcast with clouds; dimmed or dulled as if by clouds").

Often, several different words can be formed from a single root word by adding different suffixes.

EXAMPLES

Root: class
root + suffix = class/ify, class/ification, class/ic

Root: right
root + suffix = right/ly, right/ful, right/ist, right/eous

If you know the meaning of the root word and the ways in which different suffixes affect the meaning of the root word, you will be able to figure out a word's meaning when a suffix is added. A list of common suffixes and their meanings appears in Table 3-3 on p. 78.

You can expand your vocabulary by learning the variations in meaning that occur when suffixes are added to words you already know. When you find a word that you do not know, look for the root. Then, using the sentence in which the word appears, figure out what the word means with the suffix added. Occasionally you may find that the spelling of the root word has been changed. For instance, a final *e* may be dropped, a final consonant may be doubled, or a final *y* may be changed to *i*. Consider the possibility of such changes when trying to identify the root word.

EXAMPLES

The article was a **compilation** of facts.
root + suffix

compil(e) + -ation = compilation (something that has been compiled, or put together into an orderly form)

We were concerned with the **legality** of our decision to change addresses.
root + suffix
legal + -ity = legality (pertaining to legal matters)

The couple **happily** announced their engagement.
root + suffix
happ(y) + -(i)ly = happily (in a pleased or contented way)

TABLE 3-3 COMMON SUFFIXES	
Suffix	**Sample Word**
Suffixes that refer to a state, condition, or quality	
able	touchable
ance	assistance
ation	confrontation
ence	reference
ible	tangible
ion	discussion
ity	superiority
ive	permissive
ment	amazement
ness	kindness
ous	jealous
ty	loyalty
y	creamy
Suffixes that mean "one who"	
an	Italian
ant	participant
ee	referee
eer	engineer
ent	resident
er	teacher
ist	activist
or	advisor
Suffixes that mean "pertaining to or referring to"	
al	autumnal
hood	brotherhood
ship	friendship
ward	homeward

EXERCISE 3-16

Directions: On a sheet of paper, for each suffix shown in Table 3-3, write another example of a word you know that contains that suffix.

EXERCISE 3-17

Directions: For each of the words listed below, add a suffix so that the word will complete the sentence. Write the new word in the space provided. Check a dictionary if you are unsure of the spelling.

1. **converse**

   Our phone _____ lasted ten minutes.

2. **assist**

   The medical _____ labeled the patient's blood samples.

3. **qualify**

   The job applicant outlined his _____ to the interviewer.

4. **intern**

   The doctor completed her _____ at Memorial Medical Center.

5. **eat**

   We did not realize that the blossoms of the plant could be _____.

6. **audio**

   She spoke so softly that her voice was not _____.

7. **season**

   It is usually very dry in July, but this year it has rained constantly. The weather isn't very _____.

8. **permit**

   The professor granted her _____ to miss class.

9. **instruct**

   The lecture on Freud was very _____.

10. **remember**

    The wealthy businessman donated the building in _____ of his deceased father.

11. **mortal**

    The _____ rate in Ethiopia is very high.

12. **president**

    The _____ race held many surprises.

13. **feminine**

    She called herself a _____, although she never actively supported the movement for equal rights for women.

14. **hazard**

    The presence of toxic waste in the lake is _____ to health.

15. **destine**

    The young man felt it was his _____ to become a priest.

EXERCISE 3-18

Directions: For each word listed below, write as many new words as you can create by adding suffixes.

1. compare _____

2. adapt _____

3. right _____

4. identify _____

5. will _____

6. prefer _____

7. notice _____

8. like _____

9. pay _____

10. promote _____

How to Use Word Parts

Think of roots as being at the root or core of a word's meaning. There are many more roots than are listed in Table 3-2. You already know many of these, because they are used in everyday speech. Think of prefixes as word parts that are added before the root to qualify or change its meaning. Think of suffixes as add-ons that make the word fit grammatically into the sentence in which it is used.

When you come upon a word you do not know, keep the following pointers in mind:

1. **First, look for the root.** Think of this as looking for a word inside a larger word. Often a letter or two will be missing.

   EXAMPLES

   un/<u>utter</u>/able   <u>defens</u>/ible

   inter/<u>colleg</u>/iate   re/<u>popular</u>/ize

   post/<u>operat</u>/ive   non/<u>adapt</u>/able

   im/<u>measur</u>/ability   non/<u>commit</u>/tal

2. **If you do not recognize the root, then you will probably not be able to figure out the word.** The next step is to check its meaning in a dictionary.

3. **If you did recognize the root word, look for a prefix.** If there is one, determine how it changes the meaning of the word.

   EXAMPLES

   un/utterable   un- = not

   post/operative   post- = after

4. **Locate the suffix.** Determine how it further adds to or changes the meaning of the root word.

EXAMPLES

unutter/able   -able = able to

postoperat/ive   -ive = state or condition

5. **Next, try out the meaning in the sentence in which the word was used.** Substitute your meaning for the word and see whether the sentence makes sense.

EXAMPLES

Some of the victim's thoughts were **unutterable** at the time of the crime.

unutterable = that which cannot be spoken

My sister was worried about the cost of **postoperative** care.

postoperative = state or condition after an operation

EXERCISE 3-19

Directions: Use the steps listed previously to determine the meaning of each boldfaced word. Underline the root in each word and then write a brief definition of the word that fits its use in the sentence.

1. The doctor felt the results of the X-rays were **indisputable**.

   _____

2. The **dissimilarity** among the three brothers was surprising.

   _____

3. The **extortionist** demanded two payments of $10,000 each.

   _____

4. It is **permissible** to camp in most state parks.

   _____

5. The student had **retentive** abilities.

   _____

6. The **traumatic** event changed the child's attitude toward animals.

   _____

7. We were surprised by her **insincerity**.

   _____

8. The child's **hypersensitivity** worried his parents.

_____

9. The English instructor told Peter that he had written a **creditable** paper.

_____

10. The rock group's agent hoped to **repopularize** their first hit song.

_____

EXERCISE 3-20

Directions: Read each of the following paragraphs and determine the meaning of each boldfaced word. Write a brief definition for each in the space provided.

A. Exercising in hot weather can create stress on the circulatory system due to the high **production** of body heat. In hot weather the **distention** of blood vessels in the skin **diverts** increased quantities of blood to the body surfaces, where heat is released. As the body heats, skin heat evaporates the sweat, cooling the skin and the blood **circulating** near the skin.

—Curtis, Byer, and Shainberg, _Living Well: Health in Your Own Hands_

1. production _____

2. distention _____

3. diverts _____

4. circulating _____

B. In addition to being **irreversible**, interpersonal communication is also **unrepeatable**. The reason is simple: Everyone and everything are constantly changing. As a result, you can never **recapture** the exact same situation, frame of mind, or relationship that defined a previous interpersonal act. For example, you can never repeat meeting someone for the first time, comforting a grieving friend, or resolving a specific conflict.

—DeVito, _Building Interpersonal Communication Skills_

1. irreversible _____

2. unrepeatable _____

3. recapture _____

C. People with positive emotional **wellness** can function **independently**. They can think for themselves, make decisions, plan their lives, and follow through with their plans. **Conversely**, people who have difficulty making decisions are often immature and **insecure**. They are afraid to face the consequences of the decisions they make, so they make as few decisions as possible. Growth involves making **mistakes** as well as achieving success. Our mistakes are best viewed as learning experiences. We must take some risks in order to live our lives most fully.

—Curtis, Byer, and Shainberg, _Living Well: Health in Your Own Hands_

1. wellness _____

2. independently _____

3. conversely _____

4. insecure _____

5. mistakes _____

D. We could probably greatly reduce the risks associated with nuclear power by simply exercising more care and common sense. There are a **multitude** of published accounts that attest to our carelessness, however. For example, it has been revealed that the Diablo Canyon nuclear power plant in California was built on an earthquake fault line. Of course it was girded for that risk. **Incredibly**, however, the blueprints were somehow **reversed** and the earthquake supports were put in backwards. Furthermore, the mistake was not noticed for four years. At the Comanche Peak Plant in Texas, supports were **constructed** 45 degrees out of line. At the Marble Hill in Indiana, the concrete surrounding the core was found to be full of air bubbles. At the WNP-2 plant in Washington state, the concrete contained air bubbles and pockets of water as well as shields that had been **incorrectly** welded. At the San Onofre plant in California, a 420-ton reactor vessel was installed backwards and the error was not detected for months.

—Wallace, *Biology: The World of Life*

1. multitude _____

2. incredibly _____

3. reversed _____

4. constructed _____

5. incorrectly _____

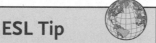

ESL Tip

English has many idiomatic phrasal verbs. Often, the meaning is quite different from the one-word verb. When an airplane *takes off*, it isn't taking anything. Many phrasal verbs that begin with *get* are not about getting anything. (Check the meanings of *get by with*, *get through*, *get up*, *get into*, and *get lost* if you don't know them already). An ESL dictionary or a dictionary of phrasal verbs will help you understand these expressions.

Learn Idioms

An <u>idiom</u> is a phrase that has a meaning other than the common meaning of the words in the phrase. For example, the phrase *turn over a new leaf* is not about the leaves on a tree. It means to "start fresh" or "begin over again in a new way." You can locate idioms in a dictionary by looking up the key words in the phrase. To find the meaning of the idiom *as the crow flies*, look up the entry for *crow*. Idioms are usually identified by the label "—idiom," followed by the complete phrase and its meaning.

If you need more help figuring out idioms, consult a handbook or dictionary of American idioms, such as *Webster's New World American Idioms Handbook*. It is usually best not to use idioms in your own writing. Many are overused and will not express your ideas in a clear or concise way.

EXERCISE 3-21

Directions: Explain the meaning of each of the following idioms:

1. to keep tabs on _____

_____

2. to steal someone's thunder _____

_____

_____

3. in the dark _____

4. to bite the bullet _____

_____

5. to make no bones about _____

_____

Use Word Mapping to Expand Your Vocabulary

Word mapping is a visual method of expanding your vocabulary. It involves examining a word in detail by considering its meanings, synonyms (words similar in meaning), antonyms (words opposite in meaning), part(s) of speech, word parts, and usages. A word map is a form of word study. By the time you have completed the map, you will find that you have learned the word and are ready to use it in your speech and writing. On the next page is a sample map for the word *compound*.

 Visualize It!

Word Map

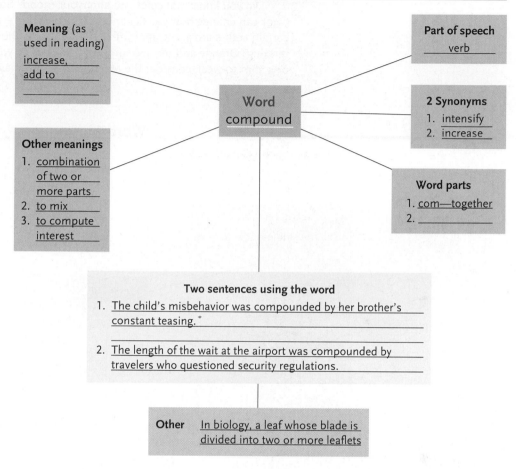

Original sentence using the word   Strong seas will compound the difficulty of rescuing survivors from the sinking ship.

Meaning (as used in reading)
increase,
add to

Other meanings
1. combination of two or more parts
2. to mix
3. to compute interest

Word
compound

Part of speech
verb

2 Synonyms
1. intensify
2. increase

Word parts
1. com—together
2. _____

Two sentences using the word
1. The child's misbehavior was compounded by her brother's constant teasing.
2. The length of the wait at the airport was compounded by travelers who questioned security regulations.

Other   In biology, a leaf whose blade is divided into two or more leaflets

Use the following steps in completing a word map:

1. **When you find a word you don't know, locate the entry for the word in a dictionary.** Write the sentence in which the word appeared at the top of the map. Figure out which meaning fits the context and write it in the box labeled "Meaning (as used in the reading)." Fill in the word's part of speech based on how it is used in context.

2. **Study the dictionary entry to discover other meanings of the word.** Put them in the map in the box labeled "Other Meanings."

3. **Find or think of two synonyms (words similar in meaning).** You might need to use a thesaurus for this.

4. **Write two sentences using the word.**

5. **Analyze the word's parts. Identify any prefixes, roots, and suffixes.** Write the word part and its meaning in the space provided.

6. **In the box labeled "Other" include any other interesting information about the word.** You might include antonyms, restrictive meanings, or word history.

EXERCISE 3-22

Directions: Using a dictionary, complete a word map for one of the underlined words in the paragraph below.

Did you know that color can <u>alter</u> your mood? Some researchers believe that color can change how you act and feel. Numerous experiments demonstrate that certain colors are <u>associated</u> with certain moods. Blues and pinks are soothing and relaxing. Orange and red are <u>stimulating</u>. Whether you are choosing paint for a wall or a shirt to wear, consider the reaction the color may create in those who see it.

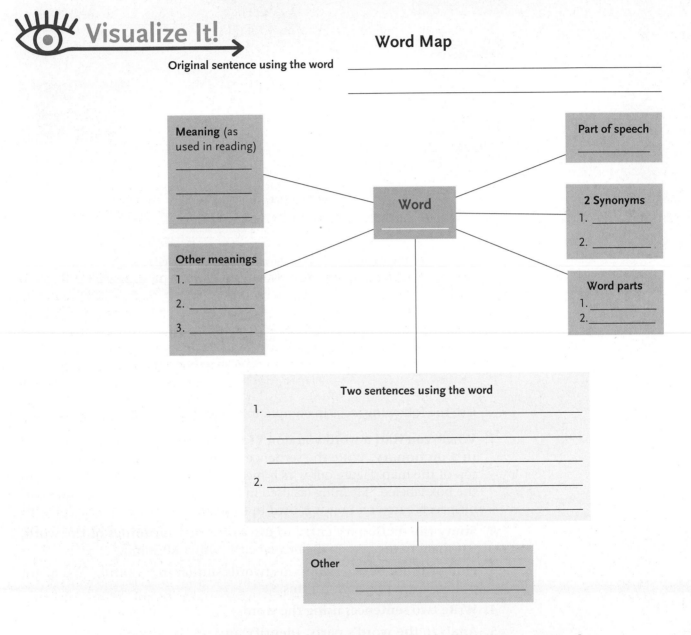

Develop a System for Learning New Words

Here are two effective ways to organize and learn specialized or technical vocabulary for each of your courses.

The Vocabulary Card System

Once you have identified and marked new terminology, both in your lecture notes and in your textbook, the next step is to organize the words for study and review. One of the most efficient and practical ways to accomplish this is the vocabulary card system. Use a 3-by-5-inch index card for each new term. Record the word on the front and its meaning on the back. If the word is particularly difficult, you might also include a guide to its pronunciation. Underneath the correct spelling of the word, indicate in syllables how the word sounds. For the word *eutrophication* (a term used in chemistry to mean "overnourishment"), you could indicate its pronunciation as "you-tro-fi-kay'-shun." On the back of the card, along with the meaning, you might want to include an example to help you remember the term more easily. A sample vocabulary card, front and back, is shown below.

Sample Vocabulary Card

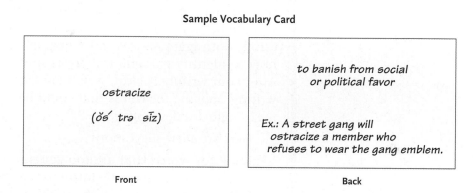

Front   Back

Use these cards for study, for review, and for testing yourself. Go through your pack of cards once, looking at the front and trying to recall the meaning on the back. Then reverse the procedure; look at the meanings and see whether you can recall the terms. As you go through the pack in this way, sort the cards into two piles: words you know and words you don't know. The next time you review the cards, use only cards in the "don't know" pile for review. This sorting procedure will help you avoid wasting time reviewing words you have already learned. Continue to review the cards until you are satisfied that you have learned each new term. To avoid forgetting a word, review the entire pack of cards periodically.

The Computerized Vocabulary File

Using a word processing program, create a computer file for each of your courses. Daily or weekly, review both textbook chapters and lecture notes and enter specialized and technical terms that you need to learn. Use a two-column or table format, entering the word in one column and its meaning in the other. You might subdivide or code your file by textbook chapter so that you can review easily when exams or quizzes on particular chapters are announced.

Your files can be used in several different ways. If you alphabetize the words, you will have created a glossary that will serve as a handy reference. Keep a print copy handy as you read new chapters and review lecture notes. When studying the words in your file, try scrambling the words to avoid learning them in a fixed order.

Writing Success Tip 3

Improving Your Writing Vocabulary

When you are planning and drafting a paragraph or essay, you should be concerned with expressing your ideas—not the words you use to express them. However, after you have written several drafts and are confident that you have expressed your ideas clearly and in an organized way, then you can begin to polish your essay. First, you want to be sure to remove all errors, both grammatical and typographical. (You will learn more about how to identify grammatical errors in upcoming sections of the book.) After your writing is clear, well organized, and correct, then reread your writing, looking for words that could be replaced with a more accurate, meaningful, or descriptive word.

Here are a few suggestions:

- **Look for words that are too general.** Words such as *good, great*, and *wonderful* give very little information other than to express a positive feeling. Replace them with words that give more information. If you are writing about a "wonderful dinner," say what was wonderful about it. Was it well prepared? Did if offer unique tastes? Was the time with your family enjoyable?

- **Look for overused words.** Words such as *awesome, wonderful*, and *boring* are used so frequently that they are no longer descriptive. Replace them with words that are unique and interesting.

    EXAMPLE

    Not Descriptive: The gown my sister wore for her wedding was awesome.

    More Descriptive: The gown my sister wore for her wedding was white lace studded with pearls, and it gave her an elegant and romantic look.

WRITING ABOUT A READING

THINKING BEFORE READING

The following reading describes the benefits and problems of caffeine consumption. As you read, you will find several unfamiliar words. Use the skills you learned in this chapter to figure out their meanings. Before you read:

1. Preview the reading using the steps listed in Chapter 2, p. 38.

2. After you have previewed the reading, connect the reading to your own experience by answering the following questions:

   a. How much caffeine do you consume each day? What benefits or problems do you notice as a result?

   b. What foods or drinks, other than coffee, contain caffeine?

READING

THE BUZZ ON CAFFEINE

Jeffrey Cluger

fatigue
physical exhaustion

1   It's hard to find much wrong with a drug that can battle **fatigue** and improve creativity and could even help prevent Parkinson's disease and diabetes. It's also hard to find much right with a drug that elevates blood pressure, aggravates stress, causes insomnia and leads to addiction. When both drugs are the same thing, it's hard to know what to think.

2   That's the rap—and the rep—associated with caffeine, the recreational chemical of choice for nearly 60% of Americans. But what of the received wisdom is true? Is caffeine a **scourge**, a **tonic**, a little bit of both?

scourge
instrument of punishment

tonic
substance that refreshes and restores

3   One thing's for certain: we sure love the stuff. There are 167 million coffee drinkers in the U.S. and they consumed nearly 6.3 billion gal. last year alone. The average drinker admits to 3–4 cups a day, although the National Coffee Association is studiously vague about what constitutes a cup deliberately, perhaps, in an era in which a large Starbucks sloshes in at a whopping 20 oz. On top of our coffee, we poured down 2.4 billion gal. of tea in 2003, not all of which was gentle herbals. Biggest of all are carbonated soft drinks, 70% of which are caffeinated. Americans consumed a stunning 15.3 billion gal. in 2003, or 574 cans for every man, woman, and child.

4   The good news is that not only does all the caffeine not necessarily hurt but in some ways it may help. Java's famous energy jolt is no illusion, improving performance on tasks and helping people stay alert. That, however, requires drinking caffeine the right way, and most people don't, loading up first thing in the morning and then crashing by the afternoon when the chemical with a half-life of up to six hours is leaving the system.

Jeffrey Kluger, "The Buzz on Caffeine," *Time* Magazine, December 14, 2004. Copyright TIME, Inc. Reprinted by permission. TIME is a registered trademark of Time, Inc. All rights reserved.

cognitive
mental

5   Better, says sleep researcher James Wyatt of Rush University Medical Center in Chicago, to consume a little caffeine in the morning and continue to take it in very small doses throughout the day. That should evenly block the uptake of adenosine, a neurotransmitter-like chemical that helps trigger sleep. In a recent study, Wyatt and others tested that theory, comparing a group of volunteers taking low, steady caffeine doses with subjects who got none at all. The caffeinated group indeed performed better on **cognitive** tests, with no late day crash (though p.m. caffeine may not do much for your ability to sleep when you want to.)

epidemiology
study of diseases that spread rapidly and widely

6   In another area of study entirely, some research suggests that caffeine may help prevent Parkinson's disease and Type 2 diabetes. Using data gathered for an 18-year health survey of 125,000 men and women, Meir Stampfer, professor of nutrition **epidemiology** at the Harvard School of Public Health, found that coffee drinkers had lower incidences of both diseases, though the benefit was a bit less pronounced for Parkinson's. He concedes that the work is preliminary, particularly in light of other studies that show caffeine worsens diabetes in people who already have it. But he is convinced that further studies of possible therapeutic effects may lead to treatments. "Our findings point to more research," he says, "[to] figure out why caffeine is working this way."

fabled
imaginary, told in stories

opiate
causing or producing sleep

7   A tougher question concerns caffeine's **fabled** ability to lift mood. Studies since the 1980s have looked into its effect on **opiate** centers of the brain hoping for a treatment for depression or alcoholism. But is the high also hype? Certainly, among people new to caffeine, the buzz is real. A caffeine novice can get a kick from as little as 20 mg. of caffeine—the equivalent of 1.5 oz. of strong drip coffee. But the average coffee drinker may consume upwards of 300 mg. a day, often with no discernible effect on mood. Reason: the body quickly **habituates** to the chemical and requires ever-higher doses to feel anything at all.

habituates
becomes used to through frequent repetition

8   "Physical dependence can occur in three days," says Roland Griffiths, a professor of psychiatry and neuroscience at Johns Hopkins University School of Medicine. "Habituation to some of the (stimulating) effects may happen even more rapidly." What passes for a lift, Griffiths warns, may be nothing more than relief from symptoms of caffeine withdrawal such as **lethargy** and headache which begin after overnight abstinence. The discomfort is probably caused by adenosine-starved brain receptors overreacting when the caffeine is removed and the brain chemical starts flowing again.

lethargy
feeling drowsy or sluggish

9   What's more, as users chase the caffeine buzz, their intake climbs sometimes to 1,200 mg a day or more, leading to jitteriness and sleeplessness. Blood pressure may become elevated, and although the increase is not always dramatic, it can be dangerous for people at risk for hypertension or other cardiovascular problems.

10   The key—no surprise—is moderation. If you're experiencing all the bad and none of the good of caffeine, cut back. Mixing caffeinated drinks with decaf can make for a comparatively painless detox. When a 20 oz. latte can set you back nearly $4, there's more than one reason to keep the joe under control.

With reporting by Paul Cuadro/Chapel Hill, N.C., and Charlotte Faltemayer/ New York

GETTING READY TO WRITE

Reviewing the Reading

1. In what way must caffeine be consumed to get the maximum benefits for an energy boost?

2. What is the danger of consuming caffeine in the evening?

3. What research still needs to be done about the effects of caffeine?

4. Why do caffeine drinkers need more and more caffeine to get the same effects?

5. What are the symptoms of caffeine withdrawal? How can you reduce the amount of caffeine you consume without experiencing withdrawal symptoms?

Examining the Reading Using an Idea Map

Review the reading by completing the missing parts of the idea map shown below.

Visualize It!

Idea Map

The Buzz on Caffeine

Caffeine is both good and bad for us.

Benefit 1: improves performance and alertness

Problem 1: physical dependence

Moderation is the key.

Strengthening Your Vocabulary

Part A: Using the word's context, word parts, or a dictionary, write a brief definition of each of the following words or phrases as it is used in the reading.

1. aggravates (paragraph 1) _to make worse, or annoy_

2. constitutes (paragraph 3) _to establish, makeup or to compose_

3. concedes (paragraph 6) _to admit as true or acknowledge_

4. therapeutic (paragraph 6) _serving to cure or heal, persieve_

5. novice (paragraph 7) _____

6. abstinence (paragraph 8) _____

Part B: Choose one of the words above and draw a word map (see p. 84) of it.

Reacting to Ideas: Discussion and Journal Writing

Get ready to write about the reading by discussing the following:

1. Why do you think the National Coffee Association is unclear about how much coffee is in a cup?

2. Do you agree or disagree that caffeine should be considered a "recreational chemical" (paragraph 2)?

3. The writer uses several casual or informal words—*buzz*, *rep*, *rap*, and *detox*. How does the use of these words change the essay or your perception of the author?

WRITING ABOUT THE READING

Paragraph Options

1. Write a paragraph describing your caffeine consumption and analyzing its effects on you.

2. Write a paragraph describing a food preference or addiction you have. (You might write about a comfort food, or a favorite snack, for example.) Describe the food, explain why you like it, and describe how it makes you feel.

Essay Option

3. Since both caffeine and alcohol are considered recreational chemicals, what is the difference between them? Write an essay analyzing the differences between the two chemicals. You might consider reasons for their consumption, their effects, addictions to them, or the types of caffeine and alcohol available to consumers.

CHAPTER REVIEW AND PRACTICE

CHAPTER REVIEW

To review and check your recall of the chapter, select the word or phrase from the box below that best completes each of the following sentences. Keep in mind that three of the words will not be used.

vocabulary log	roots	definition	synonym
etymology	suffixes	thesaurus	prefixes
restrictive	idiom	context	

1. Dictionary meanings that are limited to a special situations are called ___restrictive___ meanings.

2. ___etymology___ is the study of a word's history.

3. A dictionary of synonyms is called a ___thesaurus___.

4. The words, phrases, and sentences around an unknown word are its ___context___.

5. The beginnings of words that change the meaning of the root word to which they are attached are called ___prefixes___.

6. The endings of words that change the meaning of the root word to which they are attached are called ___suffixes___.

7. A(n) ___idiom___ is a phrase that has a meaning other than the common meaning of the words in the phrase.

8. A(n) ___vocabulary log___ is a method of organizing words you want to learn.

INTERNET ACTIVITIES

Using Context Clues

Review the types of context clues used for learning the meaning of unfamiliar words. Write your own sentence for each type of clue.

http://www.nj.devry.edu/esc/vocab.htm

Learn a Word a Day

Sign up to receive a word a day in your e-mail or read a newsletter about words at this interesting language-lovers' Web site. Use the new words in your writing and speech as soon as possible.

http://www.wordsmith.org/awad/index.html

4

Complete Sentences Versus Fragments

In this chapter you will learn to:

1. Write complete sentences.

2. Avoid sentence fragments.

Helping Mary, Bill and Stan live their American Dream

Everybody has a dream. Theirs happens to be crawling on their hands and knees through flames and heat approaching 200 degrees.

For over 50 years, our retirement and savings products have helped those who worked in the not-for-profit world turn their dreams into reality.

401(k)
403(b)
457
ANNUITIES
TDA
RETIREMENT PLANS
LIFE INSURANCE

Individuals and groups, companies and partnerships – big and small – receive the same quality service and care. The same freedom of choice. The same retirement and savings products offering a variety of investment options. All without front-end charges, withdrawal fees or transfer charges, from a local salaried consultant you get to know by name and who has a personal and professional interest in the financial well being of those we serve. For more information call us at **1-800-468-3785** or visit our web site at *www.mutualofamerica.com*

People like Mary, Bill and Stan work hard for us, the least we can do is the same for them.

MUTUAL OF AMERICA
the spirit of America

320 Park Avenue, New York, NY 10022-6839 1 800 468-3785 www.mutualofamerica.com Mutual of America Life Insurance Company is a Registered Broker/Dealer
*For complete information on our variable accumulation annuity products, including all charges and expenses, please refer to the applicable prospectuses which can be obtained from Mutual of America by calling 1-800-468-3785 and should be read carefully before investing.

WRITE ABOUT IT!

When you read the caption under the picture in the advertisement—"Helping Mary, Bill and Stan live their American dream"—does it make sense? No doubt your answer is yes. Write a sentence stating the message it communicates about Mutual of America. From the caption, the picture, and the accompanying text, you know that the company is selling retirement plans.

Now suppose you saw the caption alone, without the accompanying photograph and text. Would it make sense? Would you understand the message of the advertisement? Probably not. You do not know *who* is helping Mary, Bill, and Stan. The caption is a sentence fragment. A fragment is an incomplete sentence. It lacks a subject. It does have a verb—helping. How can you make the caption into a complete sentence? You must add a subject. Here are a few ways to make the caption a complete sentence:

ESL Tip

Remember that in English every sentence must have a subject and a verb. The usual word order in **statements** is to put the subject before the verb:

      subject   verb

The clowns are coming!

However, occasionally, the verb is put first:

  verb   subject   verb   subject

Here come the clowns! There are ten clowns!

The usual **question pattern** has the helping verb before the subject and the main verb after.

helping verb   subject   main verb

Why are ten clowns getting into that little tiny car?

FRAGMENT   Helping Mary, Bill and Stan live their American dream.

                                   subject   verb

COMPLETE SENTENCE   Mutual of America is helping Mary, Bill, and Stan live their American dream.

The new version now makes sense even without the photograph. This version has a subject and a verb and expresses a complete thought. In this chapter you will learn to identify fragments and correct them.

WRITING

What Is a Fragment?

A **fragment** is an incomplete sentence that lacks either a subject, a verb, or both. Following are a few more statements taken from magazine ads. Each is a sentence fragment because each lacks a subject and a verb and does not express a complete thought. As you read the fragments, notice how difficult they are to understand. Try to guess what product each sentence fragment describes. Correct answers appear at the bottom of p. 97.

FRAGMENT	PRODUCT
1. "Comfort, warmth, quiet"	1. _____
2. "Because you and your family deserve the very best"	2. _____ _____
3. "Bye-bye, Crocodile"	3. _____
4. "Introducing color so rich you can feel it"	4. _____

Because advertisers use pictures to complete their messages, they do not have to worry about the confusing nature of sentence fragments. Also, no one requires writers of ads to use complete sentences. Your instructors, however, expect you to write sentences that are complete and correct. You will, therefore, need to know how to spot and correct sentence fragments. To do so, you need to understand three sentence elements:

1. subjects
2. verbs
3. dependent clauses (also called subordinate clauses)

Subjects

The **subject** of a sentence is usually a **noun**. (For a review of nouns, see Part VIII, "Reviewing the Basics," p. 551.)

The <u>Babylonians</u> wrote the first advertisements.

The <u>advertisements</u> were inscribed on bricks.

The <u>kings</u> conducted advertising campaigns for themselves.

NEED TO KNOW

Subjects, Verbs, and Sentence Fragments

- The **subject** of a sentence tells you who or what the sentence is about—who or what does or receives the action of the verb.

- A **verb** expresses action or state of being. Sometimes a verb consists of only one word. (The doorbell *rang*.) Often, however, the main verb has a helping verb. (The guest *had arrived*.)

SUBJECT	VERB
Heat	rises.
Joyce	laughed.
Weeds	grow.
Opportunities	exist.

- A **sentence fragment** is not a complete idea because it lacks either a subject or a verb, or both. It needs to be connected to a nearby sentence, or to be expanded into a new sentence.

The subject of a sentence can also be a **pronoun**, a word that refers to, or substitutes for, a noun. For example, *I, you, he, she, it, they,* and *we* are all familiar pronouns. (For a review of pronouns, see Part VIII, p. 553.)

Early <u>advertisements</u> were straightforward. <u>They</u> carried the names of temples.

The <u>wall</u> was built. <u>It</u> was seen by thousands of people.

The subject of a sentence can also be a group of words:

<u>Inscribing the bricks</u> was a difficult task.

<u>Uncovering the bricks</u> was a surprise.

<u>To build the brick wall</u> was a time-consuming task.

Compound Subjects

Some sentences contain two or more subjects joined together with a coordinating conjunction (*and, but, or, nor, for, so,* or *yet*). The subjects that are linked together form a **compound subject.**

compound subject

<u>Carter's Little Liver Pills</u> and <u>Ivory Soap</u> are examples of early brand-name advertising.

Note that when there are two subjects, there is no comma before the *and*. When there is a series of subjects, however, commas appear after each subject except the last.

compound subject

<u>Calendars</u>, <u>toys</u>, <u>posters</u>, and <u>clocks</u> carried advertisements for early brand-name products.

Distinguishing Subjects from Prepositional Phrases

Do not mistake a noun in a prepositional phrase for the subject of a sentence. The subject of a sentence is *never* in a prepositional phrase. A **prepositional phrase** is a group of words that begins with a preposition (such as *after, in, of*). A prepositional phrase usually ends with a noun or pronoun that tells what or whom is the object of the preposition.

preposition   noun that is object of preposition

<u>on</u> the house

preposition   noun that is object of preposition

<u>from</u> my instructor

Here are a few more prepositional phrases using common prepositions. (For a review of prepositions and more examples, see Part VIII, p. 568.)

<u>across</u> the lawn	<u>until</u> last night
<u>throughout</u> history	<u>to</u> Maria
<u>before</u> the judge	<u>between</u> friends

ESL Tip

Be sure to use a plural verb with a compound subject even if each of the two nouns or pronouns is singular.

<u>The library and the gym</u> <u>are</u> at the northern end of campus.

Answers to sentence fragments on page 96: (1) BMW car; (2) Alpha SH (sinus-headache medication); (3) Lubriderm (dry-skin lotion); (4) Cover Girl lipstick.

ESL Tip

In this sentence, the singular noun, *idea*, is the subject, so the simple present tense verb is also singular: <u>disturbs</u>. (An *-s* ending on a noun is plural, but an *-s* ending on a verb makes it singular.) For more information about subjects that take third-person singular verbs, see the ESL Guide, A.1, "Verbs: Ways to Write About the Present" (p. 623).

Remember, the noun within a prepositional phrase is *never* the subject of a sentence.

PREPOSITIONAL PHRASE   subject

Beneath the chair, the <u>cat</u> dozed.

subject   PREPOSITIONAL PHRASE

The <u>students</u> in the art class painted a mural.

PREPOSITIONAL PHRASE   subject

Inside the house, the <u>temperature</u> was 75 degrees.

It is especially easy to mistake the noun in the prepositional phrase for the subject of the sentence when the prepositional phrase comes between the subject and verb.

subject   PREPOSITIONAL PHRASE

The <u>idea</u> of killing animals disturbs Brian.

EXERCISE 4-1

Directions: Circle each prepositional phrase. Then underline the subject in each of the following sentences:

EXAMPLE   The <u>superintendent</u> (of our school) was quoted (in the newspaper.)

1. A crowd of teenagers had purchased tickets for the concert.

2. Rows of birds perched on the telephone wires in the cornfields.

3. The strap on my backpack was tattered.

4. Trash from the festival covered the grounds inside the park.

5. Patches of blue sky are visible above the horizon.

EXERCISE 4-2

Directions: Write a sentence using each of the following words as subjects. Then circle any prepositional phrases in your sentence.

EXAMPLE   sister   My sister has the best sense (of humor.)

1. history _____

2. movie actresses _____

3. dancing _____

4. telephone calls _____

5. studying _____

Fragments Without a Subject

A common sentence-writing error is to write a sentence without a subject. The result is a sentence fragment. Writers often make this mistake when they think the subject of a previous sentence or a noun in a previous sentence applies to the next sentence as well.

COMPLETE SENTENCE   FRAGMENT

Marge lost her keys on Tuesday. And found them on Wednesday.

[The missing subject is *Marge*.]

COMPLETE SENTENCE   FRAGMENT

The instructor canceled class. But did not postpone the quiz.

[The missing subject is *instructor*.]

COMPLETE SENTENCE

Relieved that it had stopped raining, Teresa rushed into the mall.

Then remembered her car window was open.

FRAGMENT

[The missing subject is *Teresa*.]

You can revise a fragment that lacks a subject in two ways:

1. **Add a subject, often a pronoun referring to the subject of the preceding sentence.**

   FRAGMENT   And found them on Wednesday.

   subject

   REVISED   <u>She</u> found them on Wednesday.

   FRAGMENT   Then remembered her car window was open.

   subject

   REVISED   Then <u>she</u> remembered her car window was open.

2. **Connect the fragment to the previous sentence.**

   FRAGMENT   And found them on Wednesday.

   subject verb   verb

   REVISED   Marge lost her keys on Tuesday and found them on Wednesday.

FRAGMENT   But did not postpone the quiz.

REVISED   The instructor canceled class but did not postpone the quiz.

Each of these sentences now has a subject and a compound verb (see Part VIII, p. 575).

EXERCISE 4-3

Directions: Each of the following items consists of a complete sentence followed by a sentence fragment that lacks a subject. Make each fragment into a complete sentence by adding a subject. You may need to take out words, add new ones, capitalize words, or make them lowercase as you revise.

EXAMPLE   Bert threw the basketball. ~~And~~ He cheered when it went in the hoop.

1. The president waved as he left the building. Then got in the car and drove away.

2. The novel was complex. Was also long and drawn out.

3. The scissors were not very sharp. Were old and rusty, you see.

4. Hundreds of students waited to get into the bookstore. Milled around until the manager unlocked the door.

5. My roommate Tonya is an excellent skater. Gets teased sometimes about her name.

6. The computer printed out the list of names. Then beeped loudly.

7. Fans crowded the stadium. And cheered after each touchdown.

8. Many guests arrived early for the wedding. Unfortunately, were not seated until ten o'clock.

9. The delivery man put the large package down. Then rang the doorbell.

10. The big black dog sat obediently. But growled nonetheless.

EXERCISE 4-4

Writing in Progress

Directions: Write a paragraph describing an advertisement you have seen or heard recently. Explain to whom the advertisement appeals and why. After you have finished revising and proofreading your paragraph, underline the subject of each sentence. Exchange papers with a peer reviewer, and see if you agree on the choices of subjects. Discuss any differences of opinion with another peer reviewer or with your instructor. Save your paper. You will need it for another exercise in this chapter.

Verbs

A **verb** is a word or word group that indicates what the subject does or what happens to the subject. Most verbs express action or a state of being, for example, *run, invent, build, know, be.* (For a review of verbs, see Part VIII, p. 556.)

Advertising <u>is</u> bland without a slogan.

Slogans <u>promote</u> a specific product.

Sometimes a verb consists of only one word.

The announcer <u>speaks</u>.

Often, however, the main verb is accompanied by one or more **helping (auxiliary) verbs** such as *will, can,* and forms of *be, have,* or *do.* (For a review of helping verbs, see Part VIII, p. 557.)

helping verb   main verb

The announcer <u>will</u> <u>speak</u>.

helping verb   main verb

The announcer <u>will be</u> <u>speaking</u>.

helping verb   main verb

The first trademark <u>was</u> <u>registered</u> in 1870.

helping verb   main verb

<u>Do</u> any companies <u>use</u> animals as trademarks?

helping verb main verb

The lion <u>has</u> <u>been</u> MGM's trademark for a long time.

Compound Verbs

Some sentences have two or more verbs joined together with a coordinating conjunction (such as *and, or,* or *but*).

subject   compound verb

The "Uncle Sam Wants You" poster <u>stirred</u> patriotism and <u>increased</u> enlistments.

coordinating conjunction

compound verb

The posters <u>appeared</u> on billboards and <u>hung</u> on buildings.

coordinating conjunction

EXERCISE 4-5

Directions: Underline the verb(s), including any helping verb(s), in each of the following sentences:

EXAMPLE

The lectures in psychology <u>have been focusing</u> on instinctive behavior lately.

1. Preschools teach children social and academic skills.

2. Exercise clubs offer instruction and provide companionship.

3. Millions of people have watched soap operas.

4. Essay exams are given in many college classes.

5. The audience will be surprised by the play's ending.

Fragments Without Complete Verbs

Fragments often occur when word groups begin with words ending in *-ing* or with phrases beginning with the word *to*. These words and phrases are verb forms and may look like verbs, but they cannot function as verbs in sentences.

"-ing" Fragments

Note the *-ing* word in the fragment below:

FRAGMENT   <u>Walking</u> across campus after lunch.

In this word group, *walking* has no subject. Who is walking? Now let's add a subject and see what happens:

Allison <u>walking</u> across campus after lunch.

The word group still is not a complete sentence; the verb form *walking* cannot be used alone as a sentence verb. You can make the word group a complete sentence by adding a helping verb (for example, *is, was, has been*) or by using a different verb form (*walked* or *walks*).

helping verb added

REVISED   Allison <u>was</u> <u>walking</u> across campus after lunch.

verb form changed to present tense

REVISED   Allison <u>walks</u> across campus after lunch.

Now the word group is a complete sentence.

You can correct fragments beginning with *-ing* words in four ways:

1. **Add a subject and change the verb form to a sentence verb.**

FRAGMENT

FRAGMENT   Morris was patient. Waiting in line at the bank.

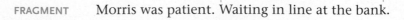

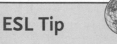

ESL Tip

The simple present tense is used for repeated action. "Allison <u>walks</u> across campus after lunch" means she does this regularly. On the other hand, "Allison is walking" (present continuous tense) means right now or at some stated future time (perhaps tomorrow). To read more about these tenses, see the ESL Guide, A.1, "Ways to Write About the Present" (p. 623).

subject   verb changed to past tense

REVISED   Morris was patient. <u>He</u> <u>waited</u> in line at the bank.

2. **Add a subject and a form of *be* (such as *am, are, will be, has been, is, was, were*) as a helping verb.**

FRAGMENT

FRAGMENT   Juan was bored. Listening to his sister complain about her boyfriend.

subject   form of *be*   main verb

REVISED   Juan was bored. <u>He</u> <u>was</u> <u>listening</u> to his sister complain about her boyfriend.

3. **Connect the fragment to the sentence that comes before or after it.**

FRAGMENT

FRAGMENT   Mark finished lunch. Picking up his tray. Then he left the cafeteria.

modifies *he*

REVISED   Mark finished lunch. Picking up his tray, he left the cafeteria.

4. **If the *-ing* word is *being*, change its form to another form of *be (am, are, is, was, were)*.**

FRAGMENT

FRAGMENT   Sally failed the math quiz. Her mistakes being careless errors.

verb form changed

REVISED   Sally failed the math quiz. Her mistakes <u>were</u> careless errors.

Fragments with *To* Phrases

A phrase beginning with *to* cannot be the verb of the sentence. When it stands alone, it is a sentence fragment.

FRAGMENT   To review for the psychology test

This word group lacks a subject and a sentence verb. To make a complete sentence, you need to add a subject and a sentence verb.

subject   verb

REVISED   <u>Jeff</u> <u>plans</u> to review for the psychology test.

You can revise fragments that begin with *to* in two ways:

1. **Add a subject and a sentence verb.**

   FRAGMENT   To reach my goal.

   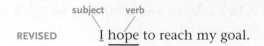

   REVISED   I hope to reach my goal.

2. **Connect the *to* phrase to a nearby sentence.**

   FRAGMENT   To earn the highest grade. Libby studied eight hours.

   REVISED   To earn the highest grade, Libby studied eight hours.

EXERCISE 4-6

Directions: Each of the following word groups is a fragment. Revise each to form a complete sentence.

EXAMPLE

FRAGMENT   Walking along the waterfront.

COMPLETE SENTENCE   Andrea was walking along the waterfront.

1. Photographing the wedding.

   _____

2. To have a family.

   _____

3. Hanging up the suit in the closet.

   _____

4. Deciding what to have for dinner.

   _____

5. To attend the awards ceremony.

   _____

6. Writing the speech.

   _____

7. To sketch a diagram.

   _____

8. To quit her job.

   _____

9. Making the paper less repetitious.

   _____

10. Being old and in disrepair.

    _____

EXERCISE 4-7
Writing in Progress

Directions: Go back to the paragraph you wrote in Exercise 4-4, and circle the verb or verbs in each sentence. Exchange papers with a peer reviewer, and check each other's work.

Clauses: An Overview

A sentence must not only contain a subject and a verb; *it must also express a complete thought.* That is, a sentence should not leave a question in your mind or leave an idea unfinished. To spot and avoid sentence fragments in your writing, you must be able to recognize the difference between independent and dependent (or subordinate) clauses. A **clause** is a group of related words that contains a subject and its verb. There are two types of clauses, independent and dependent. An **independent clause** expresses a complete thought and can stand alone as a complete sentence. A **dependent** (or **subordinate**) **clause** does not express a complete thought. When a dependent clause stands alone, it is a fragment.

Independent Clauses

An **independent clause** has a subject and a verb and can stand alone as a complete and correct sentence. It expresses a complete thought.

COMPLETE THOUGHT

INDEPENDENT CLAUSE

subject   verb

Advertising was not halted during World War II.

COMPLETE THOUGHT

INDEPENDENT CLAUSE

subject   verb

Advertisers prominently displayed brand names.

COMPLETE THOUGHT

INDEPENDENT CLAUSE

subject   verb

Produce will be in short supply because the heavy storms damaged newly planted crops.

Dependent (or Subordinate) Clauses

A **dependent clause** has a subject and a verb but cannot stand alone as a complete and correct sentence. It does not express a complete thought. A dependent clause makes sense only when it is joined to an independent clause. When a dependent clause stands alone, it is a **dependent clause fragment.** A dependent clause fragment leaves an unanswered question in your mind.

INCOMPLETE THOUGHT

DEPENDENT CLAUSE FRAGMENT

subject   verb

After World War II ended. [What happened after World War II ended?]

INCOMPLETE THOUGHT

DEPENDENT CLAUSE FRAGMENT

subject   verb

If new products are developed. [What happens if new products are developed?]

INCOMPLETE THOUGHT

DEPENDENT CLAUSE FRAGMENT

subject   verb

When magazine circulation increased. [What happened when circulation increased?]

How can you spot dependent clauses? A dependent clause often begins with a word or group of words called a **subordinating conjunction.**

Subordinating conjunctions signal dependent clauses. When you see a clause beginning with one of these words, as shown in the Need to Know box on p. 108, make sure the clause is attached to an independent clause. A subordinating conjunction explains the relationship between the dependent clause and the independent clause to which it is joined.

DEPENDENT CLAUSE   INDEPENDENT CLAUSE

After World War II ended, advertising became more glamorous.

subordinating
conjunction

INDEPENDENT CLAUSE   DEPENDENT CLAUSE

There will be new advertising campaigns if new products are developed.

subordinating
conjunction

DEPENDENT CLAUSE	INDEPENDENT CLAUSE

When magazine circulation increased, magazines became a popular new advertising medium.

subordinating
conjunction

EXERCISE 4-8

Directions: Decide whether the following clauses are independent or dependent. Write "I" for independent or "D" for dependent before each clause.

_____ 1. While Arturo was driving to school.

_____ 2. *Sesame Street* is a children's educational television program.

_____ 3. Samantha keeps a diary of her family's holiday celebrations.

_____ 4. Because Aretha had a craving for chocolate.

_____ 5. Exercise can help to relieve stress.

_____ 6. When Peter realized he would be able to meet the deadline.

_____ 7. A snowstorm crippled the eastern seaboard states on New Year's Eve.

_____ 8. Unless my uncle decides to visit us during spring break.

_____ 9. Long-distance telephone rates are less expensive during the evening than during the day.

_____ 10. As long as Jacqueline is living at home.

Correcting Dependent Clause Fragments

You can correct a dependent clause fragment in two ways:

1. **Join the dependent clause to an independent clause to make the dependent clause fragment part of a complete sentence.**

FRAGMENT	Although competition increased.
COMPLETE SENTENCE	Although competition increased, the sales staff was still getting new customers.
FRAGMENT	Because market research expanded.
COMPLETE SENTENCE	The company added new accounts because market research expanded.

FRAGMENT	Although statistics and market research have become part of advertising.
COMPLETE SENTENCE	Although statistics and market research have become part of advertising, consumers' tastes remain somewhat unpredictable.

ESL Tip

Some of these words and phrases have more than one meaning (for example, *as, as long as, once, since,* and *while*). Check your dictionary if necessary. Also, see the ESL Guide, E, "Transitional Words and Phrases" (p. 642) for examples and explanations of subordinating conjunctions.

NEED TO KNOW

Subordinating Conjunctions

A clause beginning with a subordinate conjunction is a dependent clause. It cannot stand alone. It must be connected to an independent clause. Here is a list of common subordinating conjunctions:

after	if	though
although	inasmuch as	unless
as	in case	until
as far as	in order that	when
as if	in order to	whenever
as long as	now that	where
as soon as	once	whereas
as though	provided that	wherever
because	rather than	whether
before	since	while
during	so that	
even if	than	
even though	that	

2. **Take away the subordinating conjunction, and the dependent clause fragment becomes an independent clause that can stand alone as a complete sentence.**

FRAGMENT	Although competition increased.
COMPLETE SENTENCE	Competition increased.
FRAGMENT	Because market research expanded.
COMPLETE SENTENCE	Market research expanded.
FRAGMENT	Although statistics and market research have become part of advertising.
COMPLETE SENTENCE	Statistics and market research have become part of advertising.

Note: When you join a dependent clause to an independent clause, you need to think about punctuation:

1. **If the *dependent* clause comes first, follow it with a comma.** The comma separates the dependent clause from the independent clause and helps you know where the independent clause begins.

	DEPENDENT CLAUSE	INDEPENDENT CLAUSE
COMMA NEEDED	After World War II ended,	humor and sex were used in commercials.

2. **If the *independent,* clause comes first, do *not* use a comma between the two clauses.**

	INDEPENDENT CLAUSE	
NO COMMA NEEDED	Humor and sex were used in commercials	after World War II ended.
		DEPENDENT CLAUSE

EXERCISE 4-9

Directions: Make each of these dependent clause fragments into a sentence by adding an independent clause before or after the fragment. Add or remove punctuation if necessary.

EXAMPLE   After we got to the beach/, we put on sunscreen.

1. Since the surgery was expensive.

   _____

2. As long as my boss allows me.

   _____

3. Because I want to be a journalist.

   _____

4. Until the roof is repaired.

   _____

5. Once I returned the library books.

   _____

6. So that I do not miss class.

   _____

7. Provided that Marietta gets the loan.

   _____

8. Unless you would rather go to the movies.

   _____

9. If the thunderstorm comes during the barbecue.

_____

10. Although we visited Pittsburgh last summer.

_____

Dependent Clauses Beginning with Relative Pronouns

Dependent clauses also may begin with **relative pronouns.** (For more information on relative pronouns, see Part VIII, p. 554.)

Relative Pronouns

RELATIVE PRONOUNS THAT REFER TO PEOPLE

who	whom	whose
whoever	whomever	

RELATIVE PRONOUNS THAT REFER TO THINGS

that	whichever
which	whatever

The relative pronoun that begins a dependent clause connects the dependent clause to a noun or pronoun in the independent clause. However, the verb in the dependent clause is _never_ the main verb of the sentence. The independent clause has its own verb, the main verb of the sentence, and expresses a complete thought.

The following sentence fragments each consist of a noun followed by a dependent clause beginning with a relative pronoun. They are not complete sentences because the noun does not have a verb and the fragment does not express a complete thought.

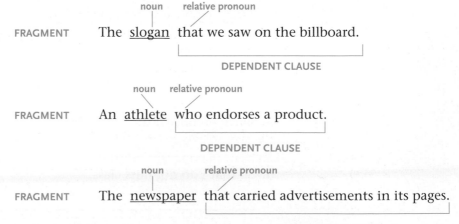

FRAGMENT   The <u>slogan</u> that we saw on the billboard.
noun   relative pronoun   DEPENDENT CLAUSE

FRAGMENT   An <u>athlete</u> who endorses a product.
noun   relative pronoun   DEPENDENT CLAUSE

FRAGMENT   The <u>newspaper</u> that carried advertisements in its pages.
noun   relative pronoun   DEPENDENT CLAUSE

You can correct this type of fragment by adding a verb to make the noun the subject of an independent clause. Often the independent clause will be split, and the dependent clause will appear between its parts.

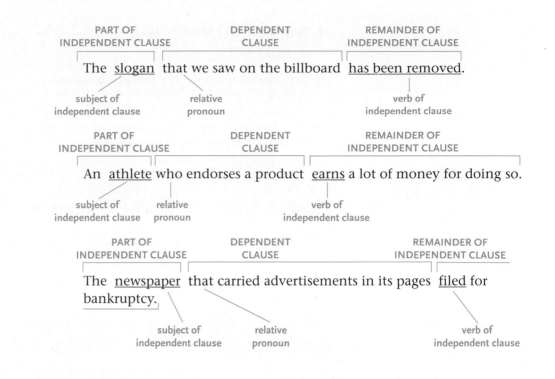

EXERCISE 4-10

Directions: Make each of these fragments into a complete sentence. Add words, phrases or clauses, and punctuation as needed.

EXAMPLE   The usher who was available <u>led us to our seats.</u>

1. The radio that Trevor had purchased last night.

   _____

2. The official who had signed the peace treaty.

   _____

3. The athlete who won the tennis tournament.

   _____

4. Mark, whose nose had been broken in a fight.

   _____

5. The advice that his lawyer gave him.

   _____

6. The student who needed the scholarship the most.

   _____

7. The answering machine that is in the kitchen.

   _____

8. Sarah, whom I knew in high school.

_____

9. The problems that the professor assigned.

_____

10. The men who signed the Declaration of Independence.

_____

How to Spot and Revise Fragments: A Brief Review

Now that you have learned to identify subjects, verbs, and dependent clauses, you will be able to spot and correct fragments. The Need to Know box provides a brief review.

NEED TO KNOW

How to Spot Fragments

Use the following questions to check for fragments:

1. **Does the word group have a subject?** The subject is a noun or pronoun that performs or receives the action of the sentence. To find the subject, ask *who* or *what* performs or receives the action of the verb.

2. **Does the word group have a verb?** Be sure that the verb is a complete and correct sentence verb. Watch out for sentences that begin with an *-ing* word or a *to* phrase.

3. **Does the word group begin with a subordinating conjunction** (*since, after, because, as, while, although,* **and** *so forth*) **introducing a dependent clause?** Unless the dependent clause is attached to an independent clause, it is a fragment.

4. **Does the word group begin with a relative pronoun** (*who, whom, whose, whoever, whomever, that, which, whatever*) **introducing a dependent clause?** Unless the dependent clause forms a question, is part of an independent clause, or is attached to an independent clause, it is a fragment.

NEED TO KNOW

How to Revise Fragments

Once you spot a fragment in your writing, correct it in one of the following ways:

1. **Add a subject if one is missing.**

   FRAGMENT   Appeared on television ten times during the game.

   REVISED   The advertisement for Pepsi appeared on television ten times during the game.

2. **Add a verb if one is missing.** Add a helping verb if one is needed, or change the verb form.

   FRAGMENT   An action-packed commercial with rap music.

   REVISED   An action-packed commercial with rap music advertised a new soft drink.

3. **Combine the fragment with an independent clause to make a complete sentence.**

   FRAGMENT   Because advertising is expensive.

   REVISED   Because advertising is expensive, companies are making shorter commercials.

4. **Remove the subordinating conjunction or relative pronoun so the group of words can stand alone as a sentence.**

   FRAGMENT   Since viewers can "zap" out commercials on video-recorders.

   REVISED   Viewers can "zap" out commercials on video-recorders.

EXERCISE 4-11

Directions: Make each of the following sentence fragments a complete sentence by combining it with an independent clause, removing the subordinating conjunction or relative pronoun, or adding the missing subject or verb.

EXAMPLE

FRAGMENT   Many environmentalists are concerned about the spotted owl. Which is almost extinct.

COMPLETE SENTENCE   Many environmentalists are concerned about the spotted owl, which is almost extinct.

1. Renting a DVD of the movie *Titanic*.

_____

_____

2. Spices that had been imported from India.

_____

_____

3. The police officer walked to Jerome's van. To give him a ticket.

_____

_____

4. My English professor, with the cup of tea he brought to each class.

_____

_____

5. After the table was refinished.

_____

_____

6. Roberto memorized his lines. For the performance tomorrow night.

_____

_____

7. A tricycle with big wheels, painted red.

_____

_____

8. On the shelf an antique crock used for storing lard.

_____

_____

9. Because I always wanted to learn to speak Spanish.

_____

_____

10. Looking for the lost keys. I was late for class.

_____

_____

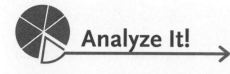 **Analyze It!**

Directions: The following paragraph is correct except that it contains sentence fragments. Underline each fragment. Then revise the paragraph in the space provided by rewriting or combining sentences to eliminate fragments.

Social networks such as Facebook and MySpace appeal to college students for a variety of reasons. Social networks are a way of having conversations. Staying in touch with friends without the inconvenience of getting dressed and meeting them somewhere. Friends can join or drop out of a conversation whenever they want. Social networks also allow college students to meet new people and make new friends. Members can track who is friends with whom. Students may choose to share only portions of their profiles. To protect their privacy. Some students use social networks to form groups. Such as clubs, study groups, or special interest groups. Other students use networks to screen dates. And discover who is interested in dating or who is already taken.

EXERCISE 4-12

Writing in Progress

Directions: Review the paragraph you wrote for Exercise 4-4, checking for sentence fragments. If you find a fragment, revise it.

Paragraph Writing Scenarios

Friends and Family

1. Choose a close friend and write a paragraph that explains the characteristics that make him or her a good friend.

2. Write a paragraph that begins with the topic sentence: "There are three main ways to ruin a friendship."

Classes and Campus Life

1. Choose one of your courses and a particular class session for that course. Explain what you learned from that class session. Discuss how you can use what you learned.

2. Which of your classes do you expect to be the most difficult or challenging? Write a paragraph explaining your reasons.

Working Students

1. Write a paragraph on the value of work. Other than a paycheck, what are its benefits?

2. Write a paragraph describing the perfect or ideal job. If you could choose any job you wanted, what would you pick?

Communities and Cultures

1. Everyone belongs to various communities. A community is a group of people who share a common goal or purpose. Clubs, colleges, ethnic groups, and religious groups are all communities. Employees working in the same business form a community, as do members of a sports team or diners in a restaurant. Choose one of your classes and write a paragraph describing why it is a community. That is, explain what you share or have in common with other students.

2. Choose a community (see #1 for a definition of community), other than your classes, that you belong to. Write a paragraph explaining your common goals or purposes.

Writing Success Tip 4

Keeping an Error Log

Most writers make certain types of errors and not others. The first step in improving your writing is to discover what errors you make. Then you can work on correcting them. An error log is an easy way to identify the types of errors you make. To make an error log, follow these simple steps:

1. **Organize a section of your journal, create a computer file, or use a sheet of paper to create an error log using the following format:**

Sample Error Log

ASSIGNMENT	TYPES OF ERRORS				
	Sentences		Grammar	Punctuation	Misspelled Words
	run-on	fragments			
1					
2					
3					

2. **Whenever your instructor returns a corrected paper, spend time reviewing your errors.**

3. **If you do not understand why something is marked as an error, ask your instructor to explain it.**

4. **Fill in your error log by listing each error you made.** Be as specific as possible. Group your errors into four categories: sentences, grammar,

punctuation, and misspelled words. (See the sample error log below.) Add a paragraph-development or essay-development category if you are writing essays.

5. **After you have filled in the errors for several assignments, look for a pattern in your errors.** The student who produced the following log needs to concentrate on run-on sentences, subject-verb agreement, verb tenses, and commas.

6. **Not all instructors mark all errors on every paper.** Some mark more serious errors when they first start correcting your papers. Once you have corrected those errors, your instructor may mark different types of errors.

Sample Error Log

ASSIGNMENT	TYPES OF ERRORS				
	Sentences		Grammar	Punctuation	Misspelled Words
	run-on	fragments			
1	one	one	subject-verb agreement verb tense pronoun ref.	comma	favorite relies knowledge
2	two	—	verb tense	comma quotation	chemicals majority especially
3	one	—	subject-verb agreement verb tense pronoun ref.	comma semicolon	necessary hoping definitely
4					
5					
6					

WRITING ABOUT A READING

THINKING BEFORE READING

In the following reading, a young woman tells how a scar on her face affected her life. As you read, notice that the writer uses clear, complete sentences.

1. Preview the reading, using the steps listed in Chapter 2, p. 38.

2. After you have done your preview, connect the reading to your own experience by answering the following questions:

    a. Do you know or have you heard of a person who has dealt with and overcome a physical handicap or deformity?

    b. What actions or events have strengthened your character or your opinion of yourself?

READING

SCARS

The mark on my face made me who I am.

Cynthia Audet

1   Growing up, I had a scar on my face—a perfect arrow in the center of my cheek, pointing at my left eye. I got it when I was 3, long before I knew that scars were a bad thing, especially for a girl. I knew only that my scar brought me attention and tenderness and candy.

2   As I got older I began to take pride in my scar, in part to stop bullies from taunting me, but mainly to counter the **assumption** that I should feel embarrassed. It's true, I was embarrassed the first couple of times someone pointed at my cheek and asked, "What's that?" or called me Scarface. But the more I heard how unfortunate my scar was, the more I found myself liking it.

3   When I turned 15, my parents—on the advice of a plastic surgeon—decided it was time to operate on what was now a thick, shiny red scar.

4   "But I don't mind the scar, really," I told my father as he drove me home from the local mall, explaining that I would have the surgery during my summer vacation. "I don't need surgery." It had been years since I'd been teased. And my friends, along with my boyfriend at the time, felt as I did—that my scar was unique and almost pretty in its own way. After so many years, it was a part of me.

5   "You do need surgery," my father said, his eyes on the road, his lips tight.

6   "But I like it," I told him. "I don't want to get rid of it."

7   "You need surgery," he said again and he lowered his voice. "It's a **deformity**."

8   I don't know what hurt more that day: hearing my father call my scar a deformity or realizing that it didn't matter to him how I felt about it.

9   I did have plastic surgery that summer. They cut out the left side of the arrow, leaving a thinner, zigzag scar that blended into the lines of my face when I smiled. The following summer they did the same to the right side of the arrow. Finally, when I was 18, the surgeon sanded my cheek smooth.

10   In my late 20s, I took a long look at my scar, something I hadn't done in years. It was still visible in the right light, but no one asked me about it anymore. I examined the small step-like pattern and the way it made my cheek dimple when I smiled. As I leaned in awkwardly toward the mirror, I felt a sudden sadness.

11   There was something powerful about my scar and the defiant, proud person I became because of it. I have never been quite so strong since they cut it out.

assumption
something believed to be true without proof

deformity
something badly formed or ugly

GETTING READY TO WRITE

Reviewing the Reading

1. Why did Cynthia like her scar?
2. In what way did the scar help Cynthia build character and strength?

3. Why was Cynthia upset when her father called her scar a deformity and said she must have surgery?

4. How did removal of the scar change Cynthia's life?

Examining the Reading Using an Idea Map

Review the reading by completing the missing parts of the idea map shown below.

Visualize It! →

Idea Map

Title	**Scars**
Thesis statement	The girl's scar gave her power, pride, and defiance.

Cynthia got her scar at age 3. It drew attention to her.

_____ .

Parents took Cynthia to a plastic surgeon.

Father says Cynthia needs surgery.

_____ .

Plastic surgery is done.

_____
_____ .

Conclusion	Cynthia is not as strong since her scar was removed.

Strengthening Your Vocabulary

Part A: Using the word's context, word parts, or a dictionary, write a brief definition of each of the following words or phrases as it is used in the reading.

1. taunting (paragraph 2) _____

2. unfortunate (paragraph 2) _____

3. unique (paragraph 4) _____

4. visible (paragraph 10) _____

5. defiant (paragraph 11) _____

Part B: Choose one of the words above and draw a word map (see p. 84) of it.

Reacting to Ideas: Discussion and Journal Writing

Get ready to write about the reading by discussing the following:

1. Do you agree with Cynthia's father that the scar was a deformity and needed to be removed?

2. Why do you think the father wanted the scar removed, although Cynthia did not? What were his concerns or reasons?

3. Discuss alternative ways the father could have persuaded Cynthia to have plastic surgery.

WRITING ABOUT THE READING

Paragraph Options

1. Cynthia's life was changed by the removal of her scar. Write a paragraph describing an event that changed your life.

2. Write a paragraph explaining a situation in which your views or wishes were at odds with those of your parents, a close friend, or your spouse. Explain how the conflict was resolved.

Essay Option

3. Write an essay explaining an event, action, or decision that strengthened you and made you feel more powerful or more in control of your life.

4. Cynthia felt a "sudden sadness" as she looked in the mirror. Write an essay describing a sadness, sudden or otherwise, that you have experienced. Explain its cause and its effect on you and whether you have overcome it.

5. Rewrite the essay with a different ending. Perhaps Cynthia did not have the surgery and now regrets it, or perhaps she is now happy that she did have the surgery.

CHAPTER REVIEW AND PRACTICE

CHAPTER REVIEW

To review and check your recall of the chapter, match each term in Column A with its meaning in Column B and write the letter of the correct meaning in the space provided.

COLUMN A	COLUMN B
_____ 1. subject	a. words that express a complete thought and can stand alone as a sentence

h	2. verb	b.	words such as *who, whom, which, that*
g	3. sentence fragment	c.	words such as *if, as, unless, while*
f	4. prepositional phrase	d.	words that have a subject and verb but do not form a complete and correct sentence
a	5. independent clause	e.	group of words that contains both a subject and a verb
i	6. compound subject	f.	group of words that begins with a preposition
D	7. dependent clause	g.	incomplete sentence that lacks a subject, a verb, or both
C	8. subordinating conjunctions	h.	word or group of words that indicates what the subject does or what happened to the subject
E	9. clause	i.	two or more subjects for the same verb
B	10. relative pronouns	j.	part of a sentence that tells you who or what the sentence is about

EDITING PRACTICE

The following paragraph contains numerous fragments. Highlight each fragment and then revise each to eliminate the fragment.

More than 300 million cubic miles. That's how much water covers our planet. However, 97 percent being salty. Which leaves 3 percent fresh water. Three-quarters of that fresh water is in icecaps. And in glaciers. Sixteen thousand gallons. That's how much water the average person drinks in a lifetime. Each family of four, using more than 300 gallons per day. Although the world's demand for water has more than doubled since 1960. There is still a sufficient supply to take care of humanity's needs. However, regular water shortages in certain parts

(continued)

of the world. Because the pattern of rainfall throughout the world is uneven. For instance, 400 inches of rain per year in some parts of India, but no rain for several years in other parts of the world.

INTERNET ACTIVITIES

1. Repairing Sentence Fragments

Practice what you have learned about sentence fragments with this online quiz from Capital Community College.

http://grammar.ccc.commnet.edu/grammar/quizzes/fragment_fixing.htm

2. Revising Student Errors

Complete this exercise from Purdue University that uses sentence fragments from student papers.

http://grammar.ccc.commnet.edu/grammar/quizzes/fragment_fixing.htm

3. MyWritingLab

Visit this site to get more help with identifying and correcting fragments.

http://www.mywritinglab.com

Click on the Study Plan tab, then on "Sentence Basics and Development," and then on "What Is a Fragment."

5

Run-On Sentences and Comma Splices

In this chapter you will learn to:

1. Recognize and correct run-on sentences.

2. Recognize and correct comma splices.

WRITE ABOUT IT!

Study the paragraph below. Why is it difficult to read?

Tattoos are a popular but permanent form of body decoration tattoos similar to body painting used by primitive societies in fact the word tattoo comes from the Tahitian word *ta-tu* they are used to communicate things about the wearer to those who view them a tattoo may used to identify the person wearing the tattoo as part of a group they have recently become popular within a wide range of age groups people getting tattoos are cautioned to be sure to choose a safe, clean tattoo parlor and be sure that sterile procedures are used people considering a tattoo should realize that it is permanent and that they may not want a given tattoo when they are older or in a different social situation.

Did you have trouble reading this paragraph? Why? Write a sentence explaining your difficulty.

Most likely you said that the paragraph lacked punctuation. You could not see where one idea ended and another began. A similar confusion can occur in writing. If you run sentences together, you run the risk of confusing your readers. In this chapter you will learn how to avoid this problem. Specifically, you will learn to use punctuation to connect or distinguish separate ideas within a sentence.

WRITING

The Function of Punctuation

All punctuation serves one primary purpose—to separate. Periods, question marks, and exclamation points separate complete sentences from one another. Think of these punctuation marks as *between*-sentence separators. All other punctuation marks—commas, colons, semicolons, hyphens, dashes, quotation marks, and parentheses—separate parts *within* a sentence. To correct and avoid run-on sentences and comma splices, you need a good grasp of both between-sentence and within-sentence punctuation.

Between-Sentence Punctuation

The period, question mark, and exclamation point all mark the end of a sentence. Each has a different function.

BETWEEN-SENTENCE PUNCTUATION

Punctuation	Function	Example
Period (.)	Marks the end of a statement or command	The lecture is about to begin. Please be seated.
Question mark (?)	Marks the end of a direct question	Are you ready?
Exclamation point (!)	Marks the end of statements of excitement or strong emotion	We are late! I won an award!

ESL Tip

Punctuation marks vary from language to language. Here are a few examples:

- In Spanish, a question is preceded by an inverted English question mark and then followed by a regular question mark.

- In Ethiopian languages, the comma resembles the English colon.

- In Japanese, the comma is shaped like a tear drop and points toward the bottom right.

Be sure to follow English punctuation rules when writing in English.

Within-Sentence Punctuation

Commas, colons, semicolons, hyphens, dashes, quotation marks, and parentheses all separate parts of a sentence from one another. For a complete review of how and when to use each, refer to Part VIII, "Reviewing the Basics," pp. 591–593.

The **comma** is the most commonly used within-sentence punctuation mark and also the most commonly misused. The comma separates parts of a sentence from one another. In this chapter, we'll be concerned with just one type of separation: the separation of two complete thoughts. *Note:* Some instructors refer to a complete thought as an independent clause. An independent clause has a subject and a verb and can stand alone as a sentence. (For a review of independent clauses, see Chapter 4, p. 105.)

The comma can be used to separate two complete thoughts within a sentence *if and only if* it is used along with one of the coordinating conjunctions (*and, but, for, nor, or, so, yet*). Coordinating conjunctions are words that link and relate equally important parts of a sentence. The comma is not a strong enough separator to be used between complete thoughts without one of the coordinating conjunctions.

I work now for a big company, but I am hoping someday to take over my father's business.

I am undecided about a career, so I am majoring in liberal arts.

When you do not insert punctuation and a coordinating conjunction between two complete thoughts, you create an error called a **run-on sentence**. (This is sometimes called a **fused sentence** because two sentences are incorrectly fused, or joined together.) When you use *only* a comma to separate two complete thoughts, you make an error called a **comma splice**.

Run-On Sentences

When you do not separate two complete thoughts (two independent clauses) with the necessary punctuation, the two clauses run together and form a run-on sentence.

How to Recognize Run-On Sentences

1. **Read each sentence aloud.** Listen for a break or change in your voice midway through the sentence. Your voice automatically pauses or slows down at the end of a complete thought. If you hear a break but have no punctuation at that break, you may have a run-on sentence. Try reading

the following run-on sentences aloud. Place a slash mark (/) where you hear a pause.

RUN-ON   The library has a copy machine it is very conveniently located.

RUN-ON   The Career Planning Center on campus is helpful one of the counselors suggested I take a career-planning course.

RUN-ON   My major is nursing I do enjoy working with people.

Did you mark the sentences as follows?

The library has a copy machine/it is very conveniently located.

The Career Planning Center on campus is helpful/one of the counselors suggested I take a career-planning course.

My major is nursing/I do enjoy working with people.

The pause indicates the need for punctuation.

2. **Look for sentences that contain two complete thoughts (independent clauses) without punctuation to separate them.**

complete thought (independent clause)

RUN-ON   Houseplants are pleasant additions to a home or office they add color and variety.

complete thought (independent clause)

complete thought
(independent clause)   complete thought
(independent clause)

RUN-ON   My sister decided to wear black I chose red.

complete thought
(independent clause)

RUN-ON   Having a garage sale is a good way to make money it unclutters the house, too.

complete thought
(independent clause)

complete thought
(independent clause)   complete thought
(independent clause)

RUN-ON   We bought a portable phone then we had to connect the base unit into our phone line.

3. **Look for long sentences.** Not every long sentence is a run-on, but run-ons do tend to occur more frequently in longer sentences than in shorter ones.

RUN-ON   Choosing a mate is one of the most important decisions you will ever make unless you make the right choice, you may be unhappy.

RUN-ON   I plan to work in a day-care center some days taking care of my own kids is enough to make me question my career choice.

ESL Tip

Then cannot be used to connect two independent clauses even if it is preceded by a comma. When using *then* as a connector, write the sentence one of these ways:

- We adopted a dog, **and then** we adopted four cats.

- We adopted a dog; **then**, we adopted four cats.

- We adopted a dog **and then** four cats.

EXERCISE 5-1

Directions: Read each sentence aloud. Place a check mark in the blank before each sentence that is a run-on. Use a slash mark to show where punctuation is needed. Not all of these sentences are run-ons.

_____ 1. Parking spaces on campus are limited often I must park far away and walk.

_____ 2. Before exercising, you should always stretch and warm up to prevent injury.

_____ 3. Theodore's car wouldn't start fortunately Phil was able to use jumper cables to help him get it started.

_____ 4. The skydiver jumped from the plane when she had fallen far enough she released her parachute.

_____ 5. Radio stations usually have a morning disc jockey whose job is to wake people and cheer them up on their way to work.

_____ 6. It continued to rain until the river overflowed many people had to be evacuated from their homes.

_____ 7. Calla bought a bathrobe for her brother as a birthday gift it was gray with burgundy stripes.

_____ 8. The rooms in the maternity section of the hospital have colorful flowered wallpaper they are cheerful and pleasant.

_____ 9. Because my cousin went to nursing school and then to law school, she is going to practice medical malpractice law.

_____ 10. We rented _Rocky_ to watch on the DVD player later we practiced boxing moves.

How to Correct Run-On Sentences

1. **Create two separate sentences.** Split the two complete thoughts into two separate sentences. End the first thought with a _period_ (or a _question mark_ or an _exclamation point_ if one is needed). Begin the second thought with a capital letter.

	Complete thought. Complete thought.
RUN-ON	Many students do not have a specific career goal they do have some general career directions in mind.
CORRECT	Many students do not have a specific career goal. They do have some general career directions in mind.
RUN-ON	Some students choose courses without studying degree requirements these students may make unwise choices.
CORRECT	Some students choose courses without studying degree requirements. These students may make unwise choices.

RUN-ON   Some people love their jobs they are delighted that someone is willing to pay them to do what they enjoy.

CORRECT   Some people love their jobs. They are delighted that someone is willing to pay them to do what they enjoy.

RUN-ON   Some people hate their jobs going back to school may be a good idea in these cases.

CORRECT   Some people hate their jobs. Going back to school may be a good idea in these cases.

The separation method is a good choice if the two thoughts are not closely related or if joining the two thoughts correctly (by one of the methods described next) creates an extremely long sentence.

2. **Use a semicolon.** Use a **semicolon** (;) to connect two complete thoughts that will remain parts of the same sentence.

> Complete thought   ;   complete thought.

RUN-ON   Our psychology instructor is demanding he expects the best from all his students.

CORRECT   Our psychology instructor is demanding; he expects the best from all his students.

RUN-ON   Sunshine is enjoyable it puts people in a good mood.

CORRECT   Sunshine is enjoyable; it puts people in a good mood.

RUN-ON   A course in nutrition may be useful it may help you make wise food choices.

CORRECT   A course in nutrition may be useful; it may help you make wise food choices.

Use this method when your two complete thoughts are closely related and the relationship between them is clear and obvious.

EXERCISE 5-2

Writing in Progress

Directions: Revise the run-on sentences you identified in Exercise 5-1 by creating two separate sentences in each case.

EXERCISE 5-3

Directions: Place a check mark in the blank before each sentence that is a run-on. Correct each run-on by using a semicolon. Not all of these sentences are run-ons.

_____ 1. The economic summit meeting was held in Britain many diplomats attended.

_____ 2. I especially enjoy poetry by Emily Dickinson her poems are intense, concise, and revealing.

_____ 3. The Use and Abuse of Drugs is a popular course because the material is geared for nonscience majors.

_____ 4. The food festival offered a wide selection of food everything from hot dogs to elegant desserts was available.

_____ 5. Since the flight was turbulent, the flight attendant suggested that we remain in our seats.

_____ 6. The bowling alley was not crowded most of the lanes were open.

_____ 7. Swimming is an excellent form of exercise it gives you a good aerobic workout.

_____ 8. When the space shuttle landed, the astronauts cheered.

_____ 9. The two-lane highway is being expanded to four lanes even that improvement is not expected to solve the traffic congestion problems.

_____ 10. Before visiting Israel, Carolyn read several guidebooks they helped her plan her trip.

NEED TO KNOW

How to Use Coordinating Conjunctions

There are seven coordinating conjunctions. Choose the one that shows the right relationship between the two complete thoughts in a sentence.

COORDINATING CONJUNCTION	MEANING	EXAMPLE
and	added to, in addition, along with	Budgeting is important, *and* it is time well spent.
but	just the opposite, on the other hand	I had planned to visit Chicago, *but* I changed my mind.
for	since, because	Sarah is taking math, *for* she is a chemistry major.
nor	and not, or not, not either	Sam cannot choose a career, *nor* can he decide upon a major.
or	either	I will major in liberal arts, *or* I will declare myself "undecided."
so	as a result, consequently	Yolanda enjoys mathematics, *so* she is considering it as a career.
yet	but, despite, nevertheless	I plan to become a computer programmer, *yet* a change is still possible.

ESL Tip

Yet means "up to this time," but it is also a contrast word, a synonym for *but*. Note that *nor* requires inverted (or question) word order:

I don't like taking final exams, nor do I enjoy taking midterm exams.

3. **Use a comma and a coordinating conjunction.** Use a **comma** and a **coordinating conjunction** to separate two complete thoughts placed within one sentence.

Note: When you separate two complete thoughts by using a coordinating conjunction, you must also use a comma.

The seven coordinating conjunctions are listed below:

Complete thought	, and	complete thought.
	, but	
	, for	
	, nor	
	, or	
	, so	
	, yet	

When you use a coordinating conjunction to separate two complete thoughts, be sure to use the right one. Since each coordinating conjunction has a particular meaning, you should choose the one that shows the right relationship between the two thoughts. For example, the conjunction *and* indicates the ideas are equally important and similar. The words *but* and *yet* indicate that one idea is contrary to or in opposition to the other. *For* and *so* emphasize cause-effect connections. *Or* and *nor* indicate choice.

The following examples show how to use a comma and a coordinating conjunction to correct a run-on sentence:

RUN-ON   Interests change and develop throughout life you may have a different set of interests 20 years from now.

comma and conjunction *so* used to show cause-effect relationship

CORRECT   Interests change and develop throughout life, so you may have a different set of interests 20 years from now.

RUN-ON   Take courses in a variety of disciplines you may discover new interests.

comma and conjunction *for* used to show cause-effect relationship

CORRECT   Take courses in a variety of disciplines, for you may discover new interests.

RUN-ON   Alexis thought she was not interested in biology by taking a biology course, she discovered it was her favorite subject.

comma and conjunction *but* used to show contrast

CORRECT   Alexis thought she was not interested in biology, but, by taking a biology course, she discovered it was her favorite subject.

RUN-ON   The weather forecast threatened severe thunderstorms just as the day ended, the sky began to cloud over.

comma and conjunction and *used to show addition*

CORRECT   The weather forecast threatened severe thunderstorms, and just as the day ended, the sky began to cloud over.

This method of correcting run-ons allows you to indicate to your reader how your two ideas are connected. Use this method for correcting run-on sentences when you want to explain the relationship between the two thoughts.

EXERCISE 5-4

Directions: Correct each of the following run-on sentences by using a comma and a coordinating conjunction. Think about the relationship between two thoughts, and then choose the best coordinating conjunction. (These are the coordinating conjunctions you should use: *and, but, for, nor, or, so, yet.*)

EXAMPLE   I thought I had left for class in plenty of time ,but I was two minutes late.

1. Jameel got up half an hour late he missed the bus.

2. My creative-writing teacher wrote a book our library did not have a copy.

3. Ford is an interesting first name we did not choose it for our son.

4. Smoking cigarettes is not healthy it can cause lung cancer.

5. My paycheck was ready to be picked up I forgot to get it.

6. The window faces north the room gets little sun.

7. I may order Chinese food for dinner I may bake a chicken.

8. Miranda had planned to write her term paper about World War I she switched her topic to the Roaring Twenties.

9. The journalist arrived at the fire she began to take notes.

10. The table is wobbly we keep a matchbook under one leg to stabilize it.

4. **Make one thought dependent.** Make one thought dependent by making it a dependent clause. A **dependent clause** depends on an independent clause for its meaning. It cannot stand alone because it does not express a complete thought. In a sentence, a dependent clause must always be linked to an independent clause, which expresses a complete thought. By itself, a dependent clause always leaves a question in your mind; the question is answered by the independent clause to which it is joined.

dependent clause raises a question

Because I missed the bus   [What happened?]

independent clause answers the question

Because I missed the bus, I was late for class.

dependent clause raises a question

When I got my exam back   [What did you do?]

independent clause answers the question

When I got my exam back, I celebrated.

Did you notice that each dependent clause began with a word that made it dependent? In the above sentences, the words that make the clauses dependent are *Because* and *When.* These words are called **subordinating conjunctions.** Subordinating conjunctions let you know that the sense of the clause that follows them depends on another idea, an idea you will find in the independent clause of the sentence. Some common subordinating conjunctions are *after, although, before, if, since,* and *unless.* (For a more complete list of subordinating conjunctions, see p. 108.)

You can correct a run-on sentence by changing one of the complete thoughts into a dependent clause and joining the ideas in the two clauses with a subordinating conjunction. This method places more emphasis on the idea expressed in the complete thought (independent clause) and less emphasis on the idea in the dependent clause.

RUN-ON   Aptitudes are built-in strengths they are important in career planning.

dependent clause

subordinating conjunction | comma | complete thought (independent clause)

CORRECT   <u>Because</u> aptitudes are built-in strengths, they are important in career planning.

RUN-ON   Emotional involvement can interfere with job performance be sure to keep work and friends and family separate.

dependent clause

subordinating conjunction

CORRECT   <u>Since</u> emotional involvement can interfere with job performance, be sure to keep work and family and friends separate.

comma   complete thought (independent clause)

Note: A dependent clause can appear before or after an independent clause. If the dependent clause appears first, it must be followed by a comma, as in the examples above. No comma is needed when the complete thought comes first.

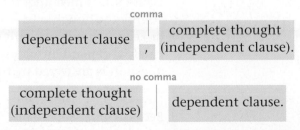

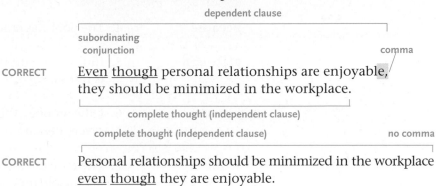

RUN-ON   Personal relationships are enjoyable they should be minimized in the workplace.

CORRECT   Even though personal relationships are enjoyable, they should be minimized in the workplace.

CORRECT   Personal relationships should be minimized in the workplace even though they are enjoyable.

NEED TO KNOW

How to Correct Run-On Sentences

You can correct run-on sentences in four ways:

Method 1 Separate the two complete thoughts into two sentences.

Method 2 Separate the two complete thoughts with a semicolon.

Method 3 Join the two complete thoughts with a comma and co-ordinating conjunction (*and, but, for, nor, or, so, yet*).

Method 4 Make one thought dependent upon the other by using a subordinating conjunction (see the list on p. 108).

EXERCISE 5-5

Directions: In each of the following run-on sentences, make one thought dependent on the other by using the subordinating conjunction in boldface. Don't forget to use a comma if the dependent clause comes first.

EXAMPLE

until   We called the plumber we were without water.

SUBORDINATING
CONJUNCTION:

even though   1. David wants a leather jacket it is very expensive.

so that   2. Margery runs ten miles every day she can try out for the cross-country squad in the spring.

when	3. The television program ended Gail read a book to her son.
because	4. The pool was crowded it was 95 degrees that day.
although	5. Industry is curbing pollution our water supply still is not safe.
because	6. I always obey the speed limit speeding carries a severe penalty in my state.
while	7. The crowd fell silent the trapeze artist attempted a quadruple flip.
since	8. The Cold War with the USSR is over, there are greater opportunities for cultural exchange.
as	9. The storm approached I stocked up on batteries.
whenever	10. The moon is full our dog is restless.

EXERCISE 5-6

Directions: Write five sentences, each of which has two complete thoughts. Then revise each sentence so that it has one dependent clause and one complete thought (independent clause). Use a comma, if needed, to separate the two clauses. You may want to refer to the list of subordinating conjunctions on p. 108.

Comma Splices

Like run-ons, comma splices are serious sentence errors that can confuse and annoy your readers. Also, like run-ons, they are easy to correct once you know what to look for. In fact, they are corrected in the same way that run-ons are. A comma splice occurs when you use *only* a comma to separate two complete thoughts. A comma alone is not sufficient to divide the two thoughts. A stronger, clearer separation is necessary. You can visualize a comma splice this way:

COMMA SPLICE	Complete thought , complete thought.
COMMA SPLICE	Spatial aptitude is the ability to understand and visualize objects in physical space, it is an important skill for engineers and designers.
COMMA SPLICE	Some people have strong mechanical ability, they often prefer hands-on tasks.
COMMA SPLICE	Verbal reasoning is important to many careers, it is the ability to think through problems.

How to Recognize Comma Splices

To avoid comma splices, you have to make sure that you do not place *only a comma* between two complete thoughts. To test a sentence to see if you have written a comma splice, take the sentence apart at the comma. If the part before the comma is a complete thought and the part after the comma is a complete thought, then you need to check whether the second clause starts with a coordinating conjunction (*and, but, for, nor, or, so, yet,*). If you do not have a coordinating conjunction to separate the two complete thoughts, then you have a comma splice.

How to Correct Comma Splices

To correct comma splices, use any one of the four methods you used to correct run-ons:

1. **Separate the thoughts into two complete sentences, deleting the comma.**

   Complete thought.   Complete thought.

2. **Separate the two thoughts with a semicolon, deleting the comma.**

   Complete thought ; complete thought.

3. **Separate the two thoughts by adding a coordinating conjunction after the comma.**

   Complete thought   , and   complete thought.
                       , but
                       , for
                       , nor
                       , or
                       , so
                       , yet

4. **Make one thought dependent on the other by using a subordinating conjunction to separate the two thoughts.** (For a complete list of subordinating conjunctions, see p. 108.)

   Subordinating conjunction   dependent clause , independent clause.

   Independent clause   subordinating conjunction   dependent clause.

NEED TO KNOW

How to Correct Comma Splices

Correct comma splices the same way you correct run-on sentences:

Method 1   Separate the two complete thoughts into two sentences.

Method 2   Separate the two complete thoughts with a semicolon.

Method 3   Join the two complete thoughts with a comma and a coordinating conjunction (*and, but, for, nor, or, so, yet*).

Method 4   Make one thought dependent upon the other by using a subordinating conjunction. (See the list on p. 108.)

EXERCISE 5-7

Directions: Some of the following sentences have comma splices. Correct each comma splice by using one of the four methods described in this chapter. Write "OK" in the blank before each sentence that is correct.

_____ 1. The stained glass window is beautiful, it has been in the church since 1880.

_____ 2. Replacing the spark plugs was simple, replacing the radiator was not.

_____ 3. School buses lined up in front of the school, three o'clock was dismissal time.

_____ 4. The gymnast practiced her balance-beam routine, she did not make a single mistake.

_____ 5. A huge branch fell on the driveway. it just missed my car.

_____ 6. The receptionist answered the phone, she put the caller on hold.

_____ 7. The couple dressed up as Raggedy Ann and Andy for Halloween, but their red-yarn wigs kept falling off.

_____ 8. Bill left his notebook in the cafeteria. he was confused later when he was unable to find the notebook.

_____ 9. The strawberries were red and sweet, the blueberries were not ripe yet.

_____ 10. There had been a severe drought, so the waterfall dried up.

EXERCISE 5-8

Directions: In the blanks, identify each sentence as a run-on sentence (RO), a comma splice (CS), or a correct sentence (C). Then correct the faulty sentences using one of the four methods.

EXAMPLE   _CS_   ^when t^ The children chased the ball into the street, cars screeched to a halt.

_____ 1. Inez packed for the camping trip she remembered everything except insect repellant.

_____ 2. A limousine drove through our neighborhood, everybody wondered who was in it.

_____ 3. The defendant pleaded not guilty the judge ordered him to pay the parking fine.

_____ 4. Before a big game, Louis, who is a quarterback, eats a lot of pasta and bread he says it gives him energy.

_____ 5. Four of my best friends from high school have decided to go to law school, I have decided to become a legal secretary.

_____ 6. Felicia did not know what to buy her parents for their anniversary, so she went to a lot of stores she finally decided to buy them a camera.

_____ 7. After living in a dorm room for three years, Jason found an apartment the rent was very high, so he had to get a job to pay for it.

_____ 8. The cherry tree had to be cut down it stood right where the new addition was going to be built.

_____ 9. Amanda worked every night for a month on the needlepoint pillow that she was making for her grandmother.

_____ 10. Driving around in the dark, we finally realized we were lost, Dwight went into a convenience store to ask for directions.

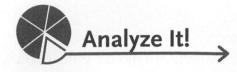

Analyze It!

Directions: Find and correct the run-on sentences and comma splices in the following paragraph. You should find two run-ons and three comma splices.

If you work in an office with cubicles—small partitioned workspaces—make sure to observe cubicle etiquette. Most cubicles are composed of three chest-high partitions, the fourth side is an open entryway. Cubicle etiquette is designed to minimize invasions of personal space for example as you walk past a cubicle, resist the temptation to peer down at the person. If you need to talk to a cubicle occupant, do not startle the person by entering abruptly or speaking loudly. Similarly, do not silently lurk in the entryway if the person's back is turned, speak quietly to announce your presence. Try to keep cubicle conversations or phone calls brief, in deference to your coworkers in adjacent cubicles. Finally, remember that odors as well as noise can "pollute" the cubicle environment. don't even think about eating leftover garlic pasta at your desk!

Paragraph Writing Scenarios

Friends and Family

1. Choose someone close to you. Make a list of how that person looks; his or her eyes, skin, hair, clothing, etc. Now write a paragraph describing that person in detail, using the items from your list. Make sure you write complete sentences and avoid run-on sentences.

2. Write a paragraph that begins with the topic sentence: "If I could change one thing about. . . ." Describe what you might change about one of your relatives.

Classes and Campus Life

1. Choose an assignment from one of your courses. Explain what you have been asked to do for that assignment. Discuss three steps you will take in order to complete the assignment.

2. Write a paragraph that explains why you chose to apply to your college. Describe any other colleges that you considered as well.

Working Students

1. Write a paragraph on the kind of work you do. Is it boring or fun; easy or hard? How did you find this job?

2. Write a paragraph describing someone else's job at the same place. Would you rather have that job than the one you currently have? Why or why not?

Communities and Cultures

1. Think about American culture. Write a paragraph describing one thing from another culture that has become part of everyday life in America. It could be a food Americans like, a popular style of dress or music, or words from a language other than English that most Americans would know.

2. Listen to the broadcast of a game, tournament, or other athletic competition. Make a list of dependent clauses the announcer uses in calling the play. Now turn these clauses into complete sentences that describe what is happening in the game.

Writing Success Tip 5

Proofreading Tips

Proofreading is checking for errors. Think of proofreading as giving your work an important final polish. Carefully study what you have written, and be concerned with correctness. Use Part VIII, "Reviewing the Basics," as a reference for checking points of grammar, punctuation, and mechanics. Check each paragraph for just one kind of error at a time so you can focus on that error.

1. **Check for errors you commonly make by consulting your error log.** (See Writing Success Tip 4, "Keeping an Error Log," on p. 116.) Read your paragraph through once for each type of error.

2. **Check your paragraph through once, looking just at the verbs to be sure you have used a consistent tense.**

3. **Read your paragraph through once to check whether you have used pronouns correctly.**

4. **Read your paragraph again, checking for subject-verb agreement.** Each time you spot a singular subject, be sure you have used a singular verb. Each time you spot a plural subject, check to be certain you have used a plural verb.

5. **Read your paragraph another time for mechanics.** Check capitalization and punctuation.

6. **To spot spelling errors, read your paragraph backward, from the last word to the first word.** This process removes you from the flow of ideas so you can focus on spotting errors. Check your dictionary for the spelling of any questionable words.

7. **Read each sentence aloud, slowly and deliberately.** Reading aloud will help you catch missing words, endings you have left off verbs, or missing plural endings.

8. **Check for errors again as you rewrite or type your paragraph in final form.** Prepare your final draft when you are fresh; if you are tired, you might introduce new mistakes.

WRITING ABOUT A READING

THINKING BEFORE READING

This reading about student debt, "Back to School: Students Must Be Prepared to Use Debt Wisely," originally appeared on August 20, 2003, in the business publication *Card News*. In it, the author explains the essentials of credit cards and debt management. Before you read:

1. Preview the reading, using the steps discussed in Chapter 2, p. 38.
2. Connect the reading to your own experience by answering the following questions:

   a. Do you think most college students are in debt?

   b. Do you prefer to use a credit or a debit card?

READING

BACK TO SCHOOL: STUDENTS MUST BE PREPARED TO USE DEBT WISELY

1   With an average credit card debt of $3,000, graduating college students appear to be following the current consumer trend towards deeper debt, according to a national student loan survey conducted by Nellie Mae Corp. According to the report, in 2002 students who used credit cards to finance part of their undergraduate education left college with a $3,400 credit card balance, compared to an average balance of $1,600 for most students. The study showed that those who used credit cards to pay for part of their education had an average undergraduate education loan debt of $21,200. This is approximately 20 percent more than the average undergraduate education loan debt of $17,700 based on those who did not rely on credit cards.

debt reduction
lowering the amount of money owed

2   Given this increase in student debt, American Credit Counselors (ACC), a nonprofit organization that provides quality credit counseling, **debt reduction** and financial education services, has outlined several money management survival tips to help college students maneuver through the decision-making maze when considering the use of credit cards. "Credit cards can be helpful for students who can afford them and use them for their intended purpose, such as an emergency situation," says Virginia Garretson, President of ACC.

paramount
of the highest importance

"What is **paramount** when using credit is understanding how best to manage credit and debt."

3   The credit-counseling group encourages students to remember the following tips before they sign:

4   ■ Credit card purchases are loans to pay for products and services. When signing for a credit card, the customer agrees to repay the loan according to the creditor's rules, which come with conditions such as "pay late and pay more." A customer's record of payment is reported to the three major credit bureaus and this payment history becomes the basis for determining credit scores.

5   ■ A 30-day free Internet account or free T-shirt or cap may not be a bargain if you have to sign up for a credit card with an annual fee, monthly fees and high interest rates. **Solicitations** like these can lead to multiple credit card accounts that can easily overextend a college student's budget. Think twice about these quick offers and read all of the fine print on the credit applications.

solicitations
requests, usually asking people to buy a product or service

6   ■ Know the difference between a credit card and debit card. While both may carry the Visa or MasterCard logos, they're considerably different. With a credit card, customers borrow the money from a third party to buy now and pay later. A debit card transaction removes funds directly from customers' bank accounts, so they buy now and pay now.

7   ■ Read the **fine print** in the marketing material or contract that explains the interest rate and penalty rates that may apply. For example, a zero percent interest rate during an introductory period may easily rise as high as 20 percent or more, once the period ends. Know the length of time before an introductory rate expires and avoid late payments and high balances, which could cause a spike in the interest rate.

fine print
details

8   ■ Review whether an annual fee, monthly fees and penalty fees (late and over-the-limit) are associated with a card account. If an account has a high balance, adding a monthly or annual fee could result in balances beyond the allowable limit for the card, which could result in additional penalty fees averaging $30.00 per billing cycle until the account is brought within spending limits.

9 ■ Be selective with purchases and keep a low debt level: Be selective with credit card use and be sure to save room for unplanned necessities and emergencies like a book that was added to a course agenda, uncovered medical expenses, an automobile repair or last minute emergency travel. After charges have been made, balances should be paid off as quickly as possible; doing so will cost less money in the long run. For example, if $1,000 is charged on a credit card with an annual percentage rate of 17 percent and a minimum payment of $25 is made, it will take 5 years (60 months) to pay off the loan. Ultimately, almost $500 will be paid in interest alone. By increasing payments to $50, it would take 24 months to pay it off with just over $180 in interest charges.

10 ■ Avoid becoming a victim of identity theft: Students should obtain credit reports at least once a year to verify that the information reported is accurate. Avoid exposing credit cards, social security numbers and other personal information to others. If a credit card is lost or stolen, report it to the credit card company right away and ask for a written list of the latest charges to verify authorized purchases. **Unauthorized** charges should be disputed in writing.

unauthorized
charges not made by the card owner

11 Overall, students should apply for credit judiciously and be sure to use their credit cards cautiously and wisely.

GETTING READY TO WRITE

Reviewing the Reading

1. What is contributing to the increase in the debt held by today's students?
2. What is ACC? What services does this organization provide?
3. What sorts of dangers can lie in the "fine print" of credit card agreements?
4. Explain the difference between a credit card and a debit card.
5. Describe the best way to use a credit card.
6. How can a person avoid identity theft?

Examining the Reading Using an Idea Map

Review the reading by completing the missing parts of the idea map shown on the next page.

Strengthening Your Vocabulary

Part A: Using the word's context, word parts, or a dictionary, write a brief definition of each of the following words or phrases as it is used in the reading.

1. maneuver (paragraph 2) _____

2. overextend (paragraph 5) _____

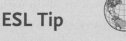

ESL Tip

Fine print refers to very small writing in a legal document. The idea is that the person signing the document may not notice it.

3. spike (paragraph 7) _____

4. verify (paragraph 10) _____

5. disputed (paragraph 10) _____

Part B: Choose one of the words above and draw a word map (see p. 84) of it.

Visualize It!

Back to School: Students Must Be Prepared to Use Debt Wisely

Thesis — Students are incurring more and more debt.

Nellie Mae Corp. conducted a survey of college student debt.

Graduating college students have an average of $3,000 in credit card debt.

_____
_____.

There are important issues to understand about the use and terms of credit cards.

Credit card buying is borrowing and must be paid back according to certain rules.

_____
_____.

Credit cards and debit cards are not the same.

_____
_____.

Keep track of annual, monthly, and penalty fees.

_____
_____.

_____.

Students should use credit cards cautiously and wisely and consult trained counselors, if needed.

Reacting to Ideas: Discussion and Journal Writing

Get ready to write about the reading by discussing the following:

1. Discuss college costs. What percentage of your budget goes for tuition? Why do tuition costs increase?

2. What are the unexpected costs of attending school?

3. Discuss ways in which college students can save money.

4. Write a journal entry about an experience you have had with a bank. Did you find the personnel helpful and friendly? Were the policies reasonable?

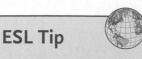

ESL Tip

Don't confuse *personnel* (stressed on the last syllable) with *personal* (stressed on the first syllable). *Personnel* are people who work in a particular place of business. The word is always plural, so it's used with a plural verb.

WRITING ABOUT THE READING

Paragraph Options

1. Write a paragraph about fun activities for college students that do not cost money.

2. The ACC states that credit cards should be used for emergencies. Write a paragraph about an emergency situation in which a credit card would be or has been useful.

3. Discuss the tactics that credit card companies use to entice new customers and keep the old customers using their cards.

Essay Options

4. Write an essay aimed at prospective students that offers advice on budgeting and managing money while in college.

5. Write an essay that explains where your money goes each month. Conclude with some ideas for saving money.

6. Identity theft is mentioned as a problem for college students with credit cards. Write an essay that defines it and discusses ways in which identify theft can occur and how people can protect themselves.

■

CHAPTER REVIEW AND PRACTICE

CHAPTER REVIEW

To review and check your recall of the chapter, select the word or term from the box below that best completes each of the following sentences. Keep in mind that three of the words or terms will not be used.

separate sentences	comma splice	exclamation point
comma	period	complete thoughts
semicolon	joined	dependent
coordinating conjunction	subordinating	comma splice
dependent clause		

1. A comma is used to separate two _____.

2. A run-on sentence occurs when two complete thoughts are not correctly _____.

3. A(n) _____ occurs when two complete thoughts are separated only by a comma.

4. One way to correct a run-on sentence is to use a _____ to connect the two complete thoughts.

5. Another way to correct a run-on sentence is to create two _____.

6. A third way to correct a run-on sentence is to join the two complete thoughts with a _____ and a coordinating conjunction.

7. A fourth way to correct a run-on sentence is to make one thought _____ on the other by using a subordinating conjunction.

8. A comma splice can be corrected by adding a _____.

9. A _____ cannot stand alone as a sentence.

10. A(n) _____ conjunction is used to join an independent clause and a dependent clause.

EDITING PRACTICE

Revise the following paragraphs, correcting the run-on sentences and comma splices.

1. As in so many other undertakings, the Greeks were ahead of their time in mapmaking their maps showed the world as round rather than flat, the Greeks also developed a system of longitude and latitude for identifying locations. The Romans were excellent administrators and military strategists therefore, it was no surprise that they made worthy road maps and military maps. The most famous mapmaker of ancient times was Claudius Ptolemy of Alexandria, Egypt, he created a comprehensive map of the world.

2. It seems there is a problem on the Internet with certain types of messages that people post. There are people who argue that anyone has the right to say anything on the Internet people do have the right of free speech, but the line should be drawn when it comes to hate messages. It is immoral—and should be illegal—to make remarks that are racist, sexist, and anti-Semitic. After all, these verbal attacks are no longer tolerated in the classroom or in the workplace, why should the Internet be different? The problem with the Internet is that there seem to be no established rules of etiquette among users, maybe there should be some guidelines about what people can and cannot say on the Internet. Why should people be subjected to hate-filled speech in order to preserve the right of free speech?

ESL Tip

Anti-Semitic is an adjective referring to comments or behavior that insult and/or injure people of the Jewish religion. (The noun is *anti-Semitism*.) *Etiquette* refers to the rules of good manners in a particular culture, to polite, socially acceptable behavior.

INTERNET ACTIVITIES

1. Sentence Construction Practice

Try this online quiz from Utah Valley State College.

http://www.uvsc.edu/owl/info/tests/run_frag.html

2. Run-Ons and Splices

Review this well-illustrated information on run-on sentences and comma splices from St. Cloud State. Then find an article in a magazine or newspaper. Identify and fix any problem sentences. Identify the complex sentences that are already in correct form. Make note of the techniques most commonly used.

http://www.uvsc.edu/owl/info/tests/run_frag.html

3. MyWritingLab

Visit this site to get more help with identifying and correcting run-on sentences. Click on the Study Plan tab, then on "Sentence Basics and Development," and then on "Run-on Sentences."

http://www.mywritinglab.com

6

Combining and Expanding Your Ideas

In this chapter you will learn to:

1. Combine ideas to create more effective sentences.

2. Show relationships among ideas.

WRITE ABOUT IT!

Study the six photographs shown above one at a time (cover the others with your hand as you look at them). What is happening in each? It is probably difficult to tell because there is so little information in each. Then, look at the six photographs all together. Now it is clear what is happening. Write a sentence that states the main point of the combined photograph.

The six photographs seen separately are difficult to understand because each contains so little information, and it is unclear if and how each is related to the other. A similar uncertainty can occur in writing when a writer uses too many very short sentences in a paragraph in which the relationship between them is unclear.

In this chapter, you will learn to combine your ideas to make your sentences more effective as well as more interesting. You will also learn how to use sentence arrangement to show the relationships and the logical connections between and among ideas.

WRITING

Understanding Independent and Dependent Clauses

If you are financially independent, you alone accept full responsibility for your finances. If you are financially dependent, you depend on someone else to pay your living expenses. Clauses, too, are either independent or dependent. (A clause is a group of words that contains a subject and a verb.) Clauses either stand alone and accept responsibility for their own meaning, or they depend on another clause to complete their meaning. Independent clauses can stand alone as sentences. Dependent clauses can never stand alone because they are not complete sentences. The key to combining and expanding your ideas is to recognize this difference between independent and dependent clauses.

The various combinations of independent and dependent clauses shown in the Need to Know box on the next page allow you to link your ideas to one another.

Combining Ideas of Equal Importance

Many times, ideas are of equal importance. For example, in the following sentence, it is just as important to know that the writer never has enough time as it is to know that she always rushes.

I never have enough time, so I always rush from task to task.

Complete thoughts (independent clauses) of equal importance are combined by using a technique called **coordination**. *Co-* means "together." *Coordinate* means "to work together." When you want two complete thoughts to work together equally, you can combine them into a single sentence by using coordination.

Method 1: Use a Comma and a Coordinating Conjunction

The most common way to join ideas is by using a comma and a coordinating conjunction. Use a semicolon only when the two ideas are *very* closely related and the connection between the ideas is clear and obvious. In this section, we will concentrate on using a comma and a coordinating conjunction.

NEED TO KNOW

Independent and Dependent Clauses

Sentences are made up of various combinations of independent and dependent clauses. Here are the possible combinations:

1. **Simple sentence** A simple sentence has one independent clause and no dependent clauses.

   independent clause

   Richard hurried to his car.

2. **Compound sentence** A compound sentence has two or more independent clauses and no dependent clauses.

   independent clause   independent clause

   Richard hurried to his car, but he was already late for work.

3. **Complex sentence** A complex sentence has one independent clause and one or more dependent clauses.

   independent clause   dependent clause

   Richard hurried to his car because he was late for work.

4. **Compound-complex sentence** A compound-complex sentence has two or more independent clauses and one or more dependent clauses.

   dependent clause   independent clause

   As Richard hurried to his car, he knew he would be late for work, but he hoped that he would not be docked an hour's pay.

   independent clause   dependent clause

The following two sentences contain equally important ideas:

Samatha works 20 hours per week.

Samatha manages to find time to study.

You can combine these ideas into one sentence by using a comma and a coordinating conjunction.

   idea 1   comma conjunction   idea 2

Samatha works 20 hours per week, but she manages to find time to study.

As we saw in the section on correcting run-ons (see Chapter 5, p. 127), a **coordinating conjunction** joins clauses and adds meaning to a sentence. A coordinating conjunction indicates how the ideas are related. Here is a brief review of the meaning of each coordinating conjunction and the relationship it expresses:

COORDINATING CONJUNCTION	MEANING	RELATIONSHIP
and	in addition	The two ideas are added together.
but	in contrast	The two ideas are opposite.
for	because	The idea that follows for is the cause of the idea in the other clause.
nor, or	not either, either	The ideas are choices or alternatives.
so	as a result	The second idea is the result of the first.
yet	in contrast	The two ideas are opposite.

Note: Do *not* use the words *also, plus*, and *then* to join complete thoughts. They are *not* coordinating conjunctions.

NEED TO KNOW

How to Join Independent Clauses

There are two basic ways to join two ideas that are equally important:

Method 1. Separate them by using a **comma** and a **coordinating conjunction** (*and, but, for, nor, or, so, yet*).

Complete thought , coordinating conjunction complete thought.

Method 2. Separate them by using a **semicolon.**

Complete thought ; complete thought.

Here are a few more examples:

SIMPLE SENTENCES	Time is valuable. I try to use it wisely.
COMBINED SENTENCE	Time is valuable, so I try to use it wisely.
SIMPLE SENTENCES	Many students try to set priorities for work and study. Many students see immediate results.
COMBINED SENTENCE	Many students try to set priorities for work and study, and they see immediate results.
SIMPLE SENTENCES	I tried keeping lists of things to do. My friend showed me a better system.
COMBINED SENTENCE	I tried keeping lists of things to do, but my friend showed me a better system.

ESL Tip

Sample Sentences Using Coordinating Conjunctions

COORDINATING CONJUNCTION	SAMPLE SENTENCE
and	The sky darkened, <u>and</u> it began to rain.
but	I thought it would rain, <u>but</u> the sun shone instead.
for	Be sure to study both the textbook chapter and your lecture notes, <u>for</u> the instructor may test on both.
nor	You cannot smoke in the lecture hall, <u>nor</u> are you allowed to consume food.
or	In sociology, you can take the written final exam, <u>or</u> you can make an oral presentation instead.
so	I was early for class, <u>so</u> I reread my notes from the previous class.
yet	My brother promised to call, <u>yet</u> I have not heard from him.

EXERCISE 6-1

Directions: For each of the following sentences, add the coordinating conjunction that best expresses the relationship between the two complete thoughts.

EXAMPLE   I never learned to manage my time, _____*so*_____ I am planning to attend a time-management workshop.

1. I might study math, _____ I might review for my history exam.

2. The average person spends 56 hours a week sleeping, _____ the average person spends seven hours a week eating dinner.

3. Watching television is tempting, _____ I usually shut the set off before I start studying.

4. I do not feel like typing, _____ do I feel like reviewing math.

5. I am never sure of what to work on first, _____ I waste a lot of time deciding.

6. A schedule for studying is easy to follow, _____ it eliminates the need to decide what to study.

7. My cousin has a study routine, _____ she never breaks it.

8. Frank studies his hardest subject first, _____ then he takes a break.

9. I know I should not procrastinate, _____ I sometimes postpone an unpleasant task until the next day.

10. I had planned to study after work, _____ my exam was postponed.

EXERCISE 6-2

Directions: Complete each of the following sentences by adding a second complete thought. Use the coordinating conjunction shown in bold. Be sure to insert a comma before the coordinating conjunction.

EXAMPLE   I feel torn between studying and spending time with friends, **but** _I usually choose to study._

1. My psychology class was canceled, **so** _____
2. I waste time doing unimportant tasks, **and** _____
3. The phone used to be a constant source of interruption, **but** _____

4. I had extra time to study this weekend, **for** _____

5. I had hoped to finish reading my biology chapter, **but** _____

6. Every Saturday I study psychology, **or** _____
7. I had planned to finish work early, **yet** _____

8. I can choose a topic to write about, **or** _____
9. I had hoped to do many errands this weekend, **but** _____

10. I tried to study and watch television at the same time, **but** _____

EXERCISE 6-3

Directions: Combine each of the following pairs of sentences by using a comma and a coordinating conjunction (*and, but, for, nor, or, so, yet*). Change punctuation, capitalization, and words as necessary.

EXAMPLE   a. I have a free hour between my first and second classes.
          b. I use that free hour to review my biology notes.

I have a free hour between my first and second classes, so I use that hour to review my biology notes.

1. **a.** Some tasks are more enjoyable than others.

   b. We tend to put off unpleasant tasks.

   _____

   _____

2. **a.** Many people think it is impossible to do two things at once.

   b. Busy students soon learn to combine routine activities.

   _____

   _____

ESL Tip

To *prioritize* means to "decide what needs to be done immediately or soon and what can be postponed until more important things are done."

3. **a.** Marita prioritizes her courses.

   b. Marita allots specific blocks of study time for each.

   _____

   _____

4. **a.** Marcus may try to schedule his study sessions so they are several hours apart.

   b. Marcus may adjust the length of his study sessions.

   _____

   _____

5. **a.** Sherry studies late at night.

   b. Sherry does not accomplish as much as she expects to.

   _____

   _____

6. **a.** Marguerite studies without breaks.

   b. Marguerite admits she frequently loses her concentration.

   _____

   _____

7. **a.** Alfonso studies two hours for every hour he spends in class.

   b. Alfonso earns high grades.

   _____

   _____

8. a. Deadlines are frustrating.

   b. Deadlines force you to make hasty decisions.

_____

_____

9. a. Juan thought he was organized.

   b. Juan discovered he was not.

_____

_____

10. a. Monica sets goals for each course.

   b. Monica usually attains her goals.

_____

_____

Method 2: Use a Semicolon

A semicolon can be used alone or with a transitional word or phrase to join independent clauses. These transitional words and phrases are called **conjunctive adverbs.** Conjunctive adverbs are adverbs that *join*.

Independent clause ; therefore, independent clause.

                 ; however,

                 ; consequently,

independent clause   independent clause

            semicolon   conjunctive adverb

I had hoped to earn a good grade; however, I never expected an A.

independent clause   independent clause

         semicolon   conjunctive adverb

I lost my wallet; consequently, I had to cancel two credit cards.

As you can see in these examples, a comma follows the conjunctive adverb.

Use this method when the relationship between the two ideas is clear and requires no explanation. Be careful to choose the correct conjunctive adverb. Here is a list of conjunctive adverbs and their meanings:

CONJUNCTIVE ADVERB	MEANING	EXAMPLE
therefore, consequently, thus, hence	cause and effect	I am planning to become a nurse; <u>consequently</u>, I'm taking a lot of science courses.
however, nevertheless, nonetheless, conversely	differences or contrast	We had planned to go bowling; <u>however</u>, we went to hear music instead.
furthermore, moreover, also	addition; a continuation of the same idea	To save money I am packing my lunch; <u>also</u>, I am walking to school instead of taking the bus.
similarly, likewise	similarity	I left class as soon as I finished the exam; <u>likewise</u>, other students left.
then, subsequently, next	sequence in time	I walked home; <u>then</u> I massaged my aching feet.

Note: If you join two independent clauses with only a comma and fail to use a coordinating conjunction or semicolon, you will produce a comma splice. If you join two independent clauses without using a punctuation mark and a coordinating conjunction, you will produce a run-on sentence.

ESL Tip

These words mean the same as *and*: *also, besides, furthermore*, and *in addition*. These mean the same as *but*: *however, nevertheless, on the other hand*, and *still*. These mean the same as *so* when it is used to introduce a result: *therefore, consequently*, and *as a result. Otherwise* and *unless* usually mean *if not*. Use a dictionary to check the meanings of any other conjunctive adverbs you don't understand. For examples of some of these words in sentences, see the ESL Guide, E., "Transitional Words and Phrases." (p. 642).

NEED TO KNOW

How to Use Conjunctive Adverbs

Use a conjunctive adverb to join two equal ideas. Remember to put a semicolon before the conjunctive adverb and a comma after it. Here is a list of common conjunctive adverbs:

also	in addition	otherwise
as a result	instead	similarly
besides	likewise	still
consequently	meanwhile	then
finally	nevertheless	therefore
further	next	thus
furthermore	now	undoubtedly
however	on the other hand	

EXERCISE 6-4

Directions: Complete each of the following sentences by adding a coordinating conjunction or a conjunctive adverb and the appropriate punctuation.

> EXAMPLE   Teresa vacationed in Denver last year ___*; similarly,*___ Jan will go to Denver this year.

1. Our professor did not complete the lecture _____ did he give an assignment for the next class.

2. A first-aid kit was in her backpack _____ the hiker was able to treat her cut knee.

3. The opening act performed at the concert _____ the headline band took the stage.

4. I always put a light on when I leave the house _____ I often turn on a radio to deter burglars.

5. Sue politely asked to borrow my car _____ she thanked me when she returned it.

6. My roommate went to the library _____ I had the apartment to myself.

7. Steve and Todd will go to a baseball game _____ they will go to a movie.

8. Cheryl looks like her father _____ her hair is darker and curlier than his.

9. Maureen took a job at a bookstore _____ she was offered a job at a museum.

10. Our neighbors bought a barbecue grill _____ we decided to buy one.

EXERCISE 6-5

Directions: Write five compound sentences about how you study for tests or how you spend your weekends. Each sentence should contain two complete thoughts. Join the thoughts by using a comma and a coordinating conjunction. Use a different coordinating conjunction in each sentence.

EXERCISE 6-6

Directions: Write a paragraph evaluating how well you manage your time. Use at least two compound sentences.

Combining Ideas of Unequal Importance

Consider the following two simple sentences:

Pete studies during peak periods of attention.

Pete accomplishes a great deal.

Reading these sentences, you may suspect that Pete accomplishes a great deal *because* he studies during peak periods of attention. With the sentences separated, however, that cause-and-effect relationship is only a guess. Combining the two sentences makes the relationship between the ideas clear.

Because Pete studies during peak periods of attention, he accomplishes a great deal.

The combined sentence makes it clear that one event is the cause of another.

Let's look at another pair of sentences:

Yolanda analyzed her time commitments for the week.

Yolanda developed a study plan for the week.

You may suspect that Yolanda developed the study plan *after* analyzing her time commitments. Combining the sentences makes the connection in time clear.

After Yolanda analyzed her time commitments for the week, she developed a study plan.

In each of these examples, the two complete thoughts were combined so that one idea depended on the other. This process of combining ideas so that one idea is dependent on another is called **subordination.** *Sub-* means "below." Think of subordination as a way of combining an idea of lesser or lower importance with an idea of greater importance.

Ideas of unequal importance can be combined by making the less important idea depend on the more important one. Notice how, in the following sentence, the part before the comma doesn't make sense without the part after the comma.

While Malcolm was waiting for the bus, he studied psychology.

If you read only the first half of the sentence, you'll find yourself waiting for the idea to be completed, wondering what happened while Malcolm was waiting. The word *while* (a subordinating conjunction) makes the meaning of the first half of the sentence incomplete by itself. Thus, the first half of the sentence is a **dependent clause.** It depends on the rest of the sentence to complete its thought. A dependent clause never can be a complete sentence. It must always be joined to an *independent* clause to make a complete thought. The dependent clause can go at the beginning, in the middle, or at the end of a sentence.

Review the following list for other words that are commonly used to begin dependent clauses. Such words are called **subordinating conjunctions.** Use these words to indicate how a less important idea (a dependent clause) relates to another, more important idea (an independent clause).

ESL Tip

The word *after* is placed before the *earlier* idea. This sentence means that she analyzed her commitment first and then made a plan.

ESL Tip

For sample sentences using some of these words and phrases, see the ESL Guide, E., "Transitional Words and Phrases" (p. 642). Note that *while* can mean either "at the same time" or "but." *Since* can mean "from a stated past time" or "because." *Whether* means "if." *So* and *so that* are discussed in the ESL Guide, E.2, E.4, and E.5. (pp. 644–646).

SUBORDINATING CONJUNCTION	MEANING	EXAMPLE
before, after, while, during, until, when, once	time	*When* you set time limits, you are working toward a goal.
because, since, so that	cause or effect	*Because* I felt rushed, I made careless errors.
whether, if, unless, even if	condition	*If* I finish studying before nine o'clock, I will read more of my mystery novel.
as, as far as, as soon as, as long as, as if, as though, although, even though, even if, in order to	circumstance	*Even if* I try to concentrate, I still am easily distracted.

Note: Relative pronouns (*who, whom, whose, that, which, whoever, whomever, whichever*) can also be used to show relationships and to join a dependent clause with an independent clause. The topic of relative pronouns is covered in detail in Chapter 8, p. 213.

When you combine a dependent clause with an independent clause, use a comma to separate the clauses if the dependent clause comes *first* in the sentence.

Dependent clause , independent clause.

| dependent clause | comma | independent clause |

When I follow a study schedule, I accomplish more.

When the dependent clause comes in the *middle* of the sentence, set it off with a *pair* of commas.

First part of independent clause , dependent clause , remainder of independent clause.

| subject of independent clause | dependent clause | remainder of independent clause |
| comma | | comma |

Malcolm , while he was waiting for a ride , studied psychology.

If the dependent clause comes at the end of the sentence, do not use a comma to separate it from the rest of the sentence.

Independent clause   dependent clause.

| independent clause | no comma | dependent clause |

I accomplish more when I follow a study schedule.

EXERCISE 6-7

Directions: For each of the following sentences, add a subordinating conjunction that makes the relationship between the two ideas clear. Try to use as many different subordinating conjunctions as possible.

EXAMPLE _____When_____ I finish studying, I am mentally exhausted.

1. _____ math requires peak concentration, I always study it first.

2. _____ Terry starts to lose concentration, he takes a short break.

3. Julia never stops in the middle of an assignment _____ she is too tired to finish.

4. _____ she likes to wake up slowly, Shannon sets her alarm for ten minutes before she needs to get up.

5. _____ Maria took a five-minute study break, she felt more energetic.

6. Alan worked on his math homework _____ he did the laundry.

7. _____ Jason increases his study time, he may not earn the grades he hopes to receive.

8. _____ Marsha completes an assignment, she crosses it off her "To do" list.

9. _____ Robert did not know when he wasted time, he kept a log of his activities for three days.

10. _____ noises and conversation do not interfere with my concentration, I wear a headset with soft music playing.

EXERCISE 6-8

Directions: Make each of the following sentences complete by adding a complete thought. Be sure the meaning fits the subordinating conjunction used in the sentence.

EXAMPLE _____I edited my essay_____ while the ideas were fresh in my mind.

1. _____
   after I finished studying.

2. Because my job is part time, _____
   _____

3. Once I finish college, _____
   _____

4. _____
   while I was studying.

5. If you schedule blocks of study time, _____

_____

6. _____

unless I carry a pocket calendar.

7. Although English is my favorite subject, _____

_____

8. _____

as far as I can tell.

9. Even if I finish by eight o'clock, _____

_____

10. As soon as I decide what to do, _____

_____

EXERCISE 6-9

Directions: Combine each of the following pairs of sentences by using a subordinating conjunction and a comma. Change punctuation, capitalization, and words as necessary. You may wish to refer to the list of subordinating conjunctions on p. 108.

EXAMPLE **a.** Ann is taking voice lessons.

b. Ann always sings scales in the shower.

Because Ann is taking voice lessons, she always sings scales in the shower.

1. **a.** Christine has a six-month-old child.

b. She must study while the baby sleeps.

_____

_____

2. **a.** George jots stray thoughts on a notepad to clear them from his mind.

b. George can concentrate through a fire drill.

_____

_____

3. **a.** Gary finished a difficult biology assignment.

   b. He rewarded himself by ordering a pizza.

   _____

   _____

4. **a.** It takes Anthony 45 minutes to drive to school.

   b. Anthony tape-records lectures and listens while he drives.

   _____

   _____

5. **a.** Molly felt disorganized.

   b. Molly made a priority list of assignments and due dates.

   _____

   _____

6. **a.** Juanita walked from her history class to her math class.

   b. She observed the brilliant fall foliage.

   _____

   _____

7. **a.** Kevin skipped meals and ate junk food.

   b. Kevin signed up for a cooking class.

   _____

   _____

8. **a.** Barbara joined the soccer team.

   b. Barbara became the first woman to do so.

   _____

   _____

9. **a.** John ate dinner on Saturday night.

   b. John reviewed his plans for the week with his less-than-fascinated date.

   _____

   _____

10. **a.** Frank waited for his history class to begin.

    b. He wondered if he was in the right room.

_____

_____

EXERCISE 6-10

Directions: Write ten complex sentences on a subject that interests you. Each must contain one dependent clause and one independent clause. Use a comma to separate the clauses when the dependent clause comes first. Use two commas to set off a dependent clause in the middle of the sentence. You do not need a comma when the dependent clause comes last.

EXERCISE 6-11

Directions: Write a paragraph on one of the following topics. Include at least two complex sentences.

1. Renting videos
2. Catalog shopping
3. Visiting the dentist or doctor
4. Advantages or disadvantages of credit cards
5. A favorite possession or a favorite piece of clothing

Writing Compound-Complex Sentences

A compound-complex sentence is made up of two or more independent clauses and one or more dependent clauses. This type of sentence is often used to express complicated relationships. Look at the following examples of compound-complex sentences. Here, a dependent clause is followed by two independent clauses:

dependent clause   independent clause

Even though Marsha needed to be better organized, she avoided weekly study plans, and she ended up wasting valuable time.

independent clause

Here, an independent clause containing a dependent clause is followed by a second independent clause with a dependent clause:

first part of   dependent   remainder of
independent clause   clause   independent clause

The new students who had just arrived wanted a tour of the town; Lamar told them that he had no time.

independent clause   dependent clause

Here, the sentence is made up of a dependent clause, an independent clause containing a dependent clause, and another independent clause:

independent clause

dependent clause   dependent clause

Although Amanda changed her work schedule, she found **that she still needed more time to study,** and she ended up quitting her job.

independent clause

The key to writing effective and correct compound-complex sentences is to link each clause to the one that follows it in the correct way. The rules you have already learned in this chapter apply. For example, if you have two independent clauses followed by a dependent clause, link the two independent clauses as you would in a compound sentence by using a comma and a coordinating conjunction. Then link the second independent clause to the dependent clause by using a subordinating conjunction.

independent clause   independent clause   dependent clause

I got up early, and **I left the house before rush hour** because I wanted to be on time for my interview.

EXERCISE 6-12

Directions: Each of the following sentences is made up of at least three clauses. Read each sentence, and then make it correct by adding the necessary subordinating and/or coordinating conjunctions in the blanks.

EXAMPLES ____Because____ they both got home from work late, Ted

grilled hamburgers ____While____ Alexa made a salad.

1. _____ Sarah's sociology class required class discussion of the readings, she scheduled time to review sociology before each class meeting _____ she would have the material fresh in her mind.

2. Although making a "To do" list takes time, Jill found that the list actually saved her time, _____ she accomplished more when she sat down to study.

3. _____ Terry's history lecture was over, he reviewed his notes, _____ when he discovered any gaps, he was usually able to recall the information.

4. Many students have discovered that distributing their studying over several evenings is more effective than studying in one large block of time _____ it gives them several exposures to the material, _____ they feel less pressured.

5. We have tickets for the concert, _____ we may not go _____ Jeff has a bad cold.

EXERCISE 6-13

Directions: Write a compound-complex sentence. Then label its dependent and independent clauses.

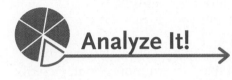

Analyze It!

Directions: The following paragraph consists of simple sentences and lacks details. Revise the paragraph by expanding or combining sentences. Write your revised paragraph in the space at the right.

Cell phones cause many problems. Cell phones are a nuisance. They ring all the time. They often ring when I am busy doing something important. They are a distraction. They interrupt me when I am studing. They interrupt me at work. Cell phones are sometimes a safety hazard. I see people talking on their cell phones while doing other things. They are not paying attention. And then there is the social aspect. Cell phones disrupt conversations with friends. My cell phone rings when I am out with friends. I have to ignore them to answer the phone. I try to enjoy dinner in a restaurant. People around me are talking on their cell phones.

Paragraph Writing Scenarios

Friends and Family

1. Choose a casual acquaintance and write a paragraph about what makes you want to know him or her better.

2. Write a paragraph that begins with the topic sentence: "I really hated the way. . . ."

Classes and Campus Life

1. Describe the way you feel before an exam. Explain the difference in how you feel when you are prepared and when you're not.

2. Write a paragraph describing the things you have to carry with you throughout a day on campus.

Working Students

1. Write a paragraph on one thing a working student could do to manage his or her time better. Is there something that you do to stay organized that might work for others?

2. Write a paragraph describing the shoes (or other apparel) you wear to work. Do you choose them for looks or comfort?

Communities and Cultures

1. Choose a culture or country whose people you find particularly interesting or one that you would like to learn more about. Describe what makes this culture or country interesting to you.

2. Describe a family ritual that you know—or guess—came from another country. Who in your family is the one who keeps the ritual going?

Writing Success Tip 6

Writing with a Computer

Today, many students use a computer when they write. Drafting, revising, and correcting errors are all easier and less time consuming when done on a computer. Here are a few tips for getting started:

1. **Investigate computer availability on your campus.** Many colleges have computer labs or writing labs with computers available for your use and with assistants present to help you. Find times when the labs are not crowded so you can concentrate more easily.

2. **Save your work frequently.** You can instruct the computer to make a permanent copy of what you are writing at any time by using a "save" command. Save your work often—every ten or 15 minutes—if you are not sure whether your computer is doing so automatically. This practice will prevent your work from being accidentally erased by a power failure or a mistaken command.

3. **Work with printed copy.** At various stages in the writing process, you may find it easier to work with printed copy than with what appears on the screen. Most screens display only about 20 lines of print at a time. Therefore, when you are evaluating the overall organization of a lengthy paragraph or essay, it may be easier for you to see the flow of your ideas on a printed copy of your work.

4. **Use, but do not rely on, a spell-check program.** Most word processing programs come with a built-in spell-check program. Spell-checkers have a vocabulary of common words and can identify any misspellings of these words; some can give you the correct spelling as well. Spell-checkers are not 100 percent accurate, however, so you should still always look for misspellings. Also, spell-checkers only confirm that a word exists; they do not indicate whether you have used it correctly.

5. **Create file folders in which to keep all your writing for each course you are taking.** Retain these files until the semester is over, or longer.

6. **Consider saving your files on a CD.** If your hard drive crashes, you may lose all your work, including papers you are currently working on. Save your important files on a CD or other back-up system.

WRITING ABOUT A READING

THINKING BEFORE READING

David Bardeen's "Not Close Enough for Comfort" first appeared in the *New York Times Magazine* on February 29, 2004. The author focuses on a simple encounter that is at the center of a complex situation. Notice how he uses references to past events and encounters with other people to develop his story. Before you read:

1. Preview the reading, using the steps discussed in Chapter 2, p. 38.

2. Connect the reading to your own experience by answering the following questions:

   a. What is your relationship with your siblings or other family members? To whom are you closest?

   b. Have you ever had to reveal a secret? What was that like?

READING

NOT CLOSE ENOUGH FOR COMFORT

David P. Bardeen

1   I had wanted to tell Will I was gay since I was 12. As twins, we shared everything back then: clothes, gadgets, thoughts, secrets. Everything except this. So when we met for lunch more than a year ago, I thought that finally coming out to him would close the distance that had grown between us. When we were kids, we created our own language, whispering to each other as our bewildered parents looked on. Now, at 28, we had never been further apart.

2   I asked him about his recent trip. He asked me about work. Short questions. One-word answers. Then an awkward pause.

3   Will was one of the last to know. Partly it was his fault. He is hard to **pin down** for brunch or a drink, and this was not the sort of conversation I wanted to have

pin down

get someone to commit to something

over the phone. I had actually been trying to tell him for more than a month, but he kept canceling at the last minute—a friend was in town, he'd met a girl.

4   But part of me was relieved. This was the talk I had feared the most. Coming out is, in an unforgiving sense, an admission of fraud. Fraud against yourself primarily, but also fraud against your family and friends. So, once I resolved to tell my secret, I confessed to my most recent "victims" first. I told my friends from law school—those I had met just a few years earlier and deceived the least—then I worked back through college to the handful of high-school friends I still keep in touch with.

5   Keeping my sexuality from my parents had always seemed permissible, so our sit-down chat did not stress me out as much as it might have. We all mislead our parents. "I'm too sick for school today." "No, I wasn't drinking." "Yes, Mom, I'm fine. Don't worry about me." That deception is understood and, in some sense, expected. But twins expect complete transparency, however romantic the notion.

6   Although our lives unfolded along parallel tracks—we went to college together, both moved to New York and had many of the same friends—Will and I quietly drifted apart. When he moved abroad for a year, we lost touch almost entirely. Our mother and father didn't think this was strange because, like many parents of twins, they wanted us to follow **divergent** paths. But friends were baffled when we began to rely on third parties for updates on each other's lives. "How's Will?" someone would ask. "You tell me," I would respond. One mutual friend, sick of playing the intermediary, once sent me an e-mail message with a carbon copy to Will. "Dave, meet Will, your twin," it said. "Will, let me introduce you to Dave."

divergent
differing, going in opposite directions

7   Now, here we were, at lunch, just the two of us. "There's something I've been meaning to tell you," I said. "I'm gay." I looked at him closely, at the edges of his mouth, the wrinkles around his eyes, for some hint of what he was thinking.

8   "O.K.," he said evenly.

9   "I've been meaning to tell you for a while," I said.

10   "Uh-huh." He asked me a few questions but seemed slightly uneasy, as if he wasn't sure he wanted to hear the answers. Do Mom and Dad know? Are you seeing anyone? How long have you known you were gay? I hesitated.

11   I've known since I was young, and to some degree, I thought Will had always known. How else to explain my adolescent **melancholy**, my withdrawal, the silence when the subject changed to girls, sex, and who was hot. As a teenager I watched, as if from a distance, as my **demeanor** went from outspoken to sullen. I had assumed, in the self-centered way kids often do, that everyone noticed this change—and that my brother had guessed the reason. To be fair, he asked me once in our 20's, after I had ended yet another brief relationship with a woman. "Of course I'm not gay," I told him, as if the notion were absurd.

melancholy
dejection, sadness

demeanor
outward behavior

12   "How long have you known?" he asked again.

13   "About 15 years," I said. Will looked away.

14   Food arrived. We ate and talked about other things. Mom, Dad, the mayor and the weather. We asked for the check and agreed to get together again soon. No big questions, no heart to heart. Just **disclosure**, explanation, follow-up,

disclosure
the revealing of secret information

conclusion. But what could I expect? I had shut him out for so long that I suppose ultimately he gave up. Telling my brother I was gay hadn't made us close, as I had naively hoped it would; instead it underscored just how much we had strayed apart.

15   As we left the restaurant, I felt the urge to apologize, not for being gay, of course, but for the years I'd kept him in the dark, for his being among the last to know. He hailed a cab. It stopped. He stepped inside, the door still open.

16   "I'm sorry," I said.

17   He smiled. "No, I think it's great."

18   It was a nice gesture—supportive. I think he misunderstood.

19   A year later, we are still only creeping toward the intimacy everyone expects us to have. Although we live three blocks away from each other, I can't say we see each other every week or even every two weeks. But with any luck, next year, I'll be the one updating our mutual friends on Will's life.

GETTING READY TO WRITE

Reviewing the Reading

1. Who are Will and Dave? What is special about their relationship?

2. How has the relationship between Will and Dave changed over the years? Give examples.

3. When did Dave realize that he was gay? How long did it take him to start telling people?

4. How did Dave decide which people to tell first? What was his experience like in telling his parents?

5. What was Will's reaction to the news that Dave is gay?

6. How does Dave think his relationship with Will will change?

Examining the Reading Using an Idea Map

Review the reading by completing the missing parts of the idea map shown on the next page.

Strengthening Your Vocabulary

Part A: Using the word's context, word parts, or a dictionary, write a brief definition of each of the following words or phrases as it is used in the reading.

1. bewildered (paragraph 1) _____

2. fraud (paragraph 4) _____

3. permissible (paragraph 5) _____

4. transparency (paragraph 5) _____

5. intermediary (paragraph 6) _____

6. sullen (paragraph 11) _____

7. naively (paragraph 14) _____

Part B: Choose one of the words above and draw a word map (see p. 84) of it.

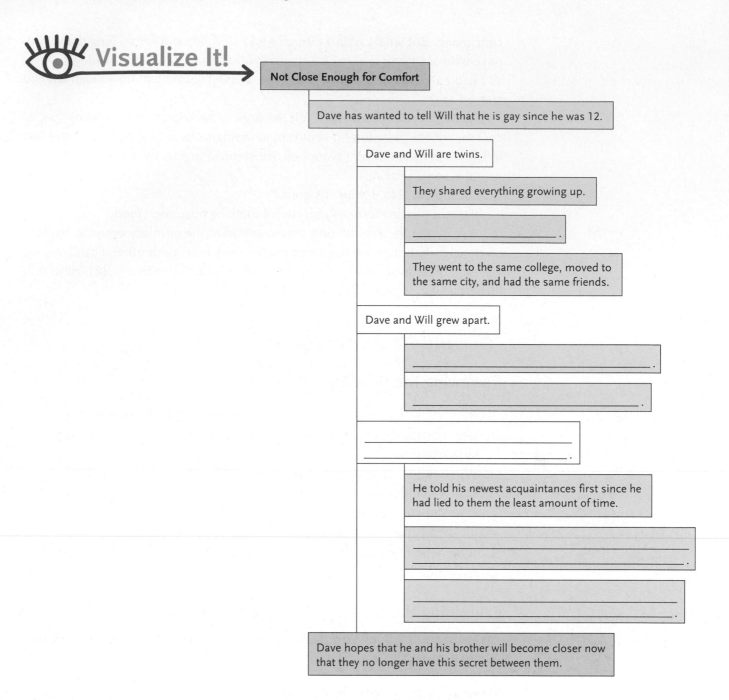

Visualize It!

Not Close Enough for Comfort

Dave has wanted to tell Will that he is gay since he was 12.

Dave and Will are twins.

They shared everything growing up.

_____ .

They went to the same college, moved to the same city, and had the same friends.

Dave and Will grew apart.

_____ .

_____ .

_____
_____ .

He told his newest acquaintances first since he had lied to them the least amount of time.

_____
_____
_____ .

_____
_____ .

Dave hopes that he and his brother will become closer now that they no longer have this secret between them.

Reacting to Ideas: Discussion and Journal Writing

Get ready to write about the reading by discussing the following:

1. Why do people have a hard time telling others about their sexual preference?

2. Discuss the relevance of research that investigates whether sexual preference is genetic or chosen.

3. In what ways has our society become more tolerant of gays and lesbians? What issues are we still debating?

4. Write about a time that you felt persecuted for just being yourself.

5. Bardeen uses both short sentences and more complex ones. Find and highlight several examples of each. Why does he vary his sentence length and complexity?

WRITING ABOUT THE READING

Paragraph Options

1. Write a paragraph about a secret you tried to keep, but could not.

2. The author states that "We all mislead our parents." Write a paragraph expressing your opinion on this statement.

3. Explain why Dave's parents would want their sons to follow "divergent paths."

Essay Options

4. Write an essay from the point of view of one of the other people in the reading, expressing your reaction to Dave's news. Feel free to make up details to fill out your essay.

5. Write an essay that provides instructions and advice to someone who has something difficult to tell others.

6. Will misunderstood Dave's apology. Write an essay in which a misunderstanding occurred due to the lack of clear communication. Give specific examples.

CHAPTER REVIEW AND PRACTICE

CHAPTER REVIEW

To review and check your recall of the chapter, match each term in Column A with its meaning in Column B and write its letter in the space provided.

COLUMN A	COLUMN B
_____ 1. Independent clause	a. a sentence containing one dependent and one independent clause
_____ 2. dependent clause	b. a word used to begin dependent clauses
_____ 3. conjunctive adverb	c. a group of words containing a subject and verb that can stand alone in a sentence
_____ 4. coordinating conjunction	d. a sentence containing one independent clause

(continued)

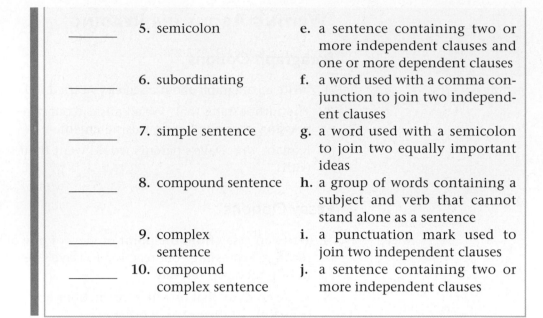

_____   5. semicolon

_____   6. subordinating

_____   7. simple sentence

_____   8. compound sentence

_____   9. complex sentence

_____   10. compound complex sentence

e. a sentence containing two or more independent clauses and one or more dependent clauses

f. a word used with a comma conjunction to join two independent clauses

g. a word used with a semicolon to join two equally important ideas

h. a group of words containing a subject and verb that cannot stand alone as a sentence

i. a punctuation mark used to join two independent clauses

j. a sentence containing two or more independent clauses

EDITING PRACTICE

The following student paragraph has had all errors corrected, but it consists mainly of simple sentences and lacks details. Revise it by expanding or combining the sentences.

Many people are homeless. Our country has a problem. Now is the time for the government to take action on the problem of homelessness. The media have focused a great deal of attention on the homeless. This has been happening for the past several years. Many college campuses have been holding "sleepouts." These call attention to the problems of the homeless. Religious groups have been trying to help. They have been opening shelters for them. Still, this is not enough. The problem is only getting worse. The government needs to be pushed to do something about this problem now. Students should write their government officials. Religious groups should put pressure on members of Congress. They should urge them to act upon the problems of the homeless. Concerned citizens should become involved now. This problem is a disgrace to our country.

INTERNET ACTIVITIES

1. Combining Sentences

Edmonds Community College created this handout on combining sentences. Create your own handout in the same style using a different set of sentences.

http://www.edcc.edu/lsc/Handouts/3--Combining_Sentences.php

2. Sentence Patterns

Try this online sentence pattern tutorial from CUNY Write Site (be sure to click on the "Next Step" link when you are ready to move on).

http://www.writesite.cuny.edu/grammar/hotspots/sentence/patterns/

Jot down notes on any information that might be new or especially helpful.

3. MyWritingLab

Visit this site to get more help with combining and expanding your ideas.

http://www.mywritinglab.com

Click on the Study Plan tab, then on "Sentence Basics and Development," and then on "Combining and Expanding Your Ideas."

7 Using Adjectives and Adverbs to Describe

In this chapter you will learn to:

1. Use adjectives to add descriptive detail.

2. Use adverbs to describe actions more vividly.

WRITE ABOUT IT!

Study the photo above and then write a few sentences that describe it in detail.

Some of the words you wrote are probably adjectives—words that describe a noun or pronoun. In this chapter you will learn to use adjectives and adverbs. Adverbs are words that describe verbs or other adverbs. You will see how they are essential to effective communication and how to use them to make your sentences lively and interesting.

WRITING

Using Adjectives to Describe

Adjectives describe nouns and pronouns. Notice that the following sample student paragraph uses very few adjectives.

Sample Paragraph

The congregation had just finished singing a hymn as the minister stepped up to the pulpit. Just as the man asked the congregation to pray, a boy screamed. The grandmother tried to calm the child as she placed a hand over the lips of the child. The child obviously didn't enjoy this because he bit her hand. The minister continued with the prayer and tried to ignore the cries of the boy. Somehow the boy slipped away from the grip of the grandmother and ran down the aisle to the front of the church. The minister walked down from the pulpit and picked up the child. "Lord," he said as he continued the prayer, "help all the children of this world and bless all of the grandmothers, ministers, and members of the congregation who have to put up with them! Amen." With that he ended the service.

This paragraph, which contains no adjectives, gives the bare bones of an interesting story, but how well does it enable you to visualize the people involved? Adjectives give you details about the nouns and pronouns they modify. They can add four kinds of information to your writing:

WHICH?	the <u>young</u> man, the <u>largest</u> stove
WHOSE?	<u>Sam's</u> application, <u>my</u> mug
WHAT KIND?	the <u>job</u> interviewer, the <u>traffic</u> helicopter
HOW MANY?	<u>thirty</u> résumés, <u>no</u> cookies

Thus, we say that adjectives *describe* and *identify* (which? whose?), *qualify* (what kind?), or *limit* (how many?) nouns and pronouns. (For more on adjectives, see Part VIII, "Reviewing the Basics," p. 562.) The following revised version of the above paragraph uses adjectives (underlined) to add interesting and important information.

Revised Paragraph

The congregation had just finished singing a <u>sacred</u> hymn as the <u>tall</u>, <u>young</u> minister stepped up to the <u>well-lit</u> pulpit. Just as the man asked the <u>reverent</u> congregation to pray, a <u>red-headed, four-year-old</u> boy screamed. His <u>embarrassed</u> grandmother tried to calm the <u>angry</u> child as she placed a <u>firm</u> hand over his <u>quivering</u> lips. The <u>squirming</u> child obviously didn't enjoy this because he bit his <u>grandmother's</u> hand. The <u>calm</u> minister continued with the prayer and tried to ignore the <u>little</u> boy's <u>loud, shrill</u> cries. Somehow, the <u>determined, tearful</u> boy slipped away from his grandmother's <u>firm</u> grip and ran down the <u>long center</u> aisle to the front of the church. The <u>patient</u> minister walked down from the pulpit and picked up the <u>screaming</u> child. "Lord," he said as he continued the prayer, "help all the children of this world and bless all of the <u>loving</u> grandmothers, <u>patient</u> ministers, and <u>long-suffering</u> members of the congregation who have to put up with them! Amen." With that he ended the service.

EXERCISE 7-1

Directions: *The Adjective Contest:* The time limit for this exercise is three minutes. List as many positive adjectives as you can that describe one of your instructors. This is your chance to flatter an instructor! Exchange lists with a partner, verify that each word listed is an adjective, and count the words on the list. The winner is the student who has listed the most positive adjectives.

"The face of the pear-shaped man reminded me of the mashed turnips that Aunt Mildred used to serve alongside the Thanksgiving turkey. As he got out of the strawberry-hued car, his immense fists looked like two slabs of slightly gnawed ham. He waddled over to the counter and snarled at me under his lasagna-laden breath, 'Something, my little bonbon, is fishy in Denmark.' Slowly, I lowered my grilled cheese sandwich . . ."

Using Adjectives Correctly

To use adjectives effectively, you must also use them correctly. Keep the following points in mind:

1. **Adjectives are usually placed in front of the word they describe.**

   the <u>wet</u> raincoat

   the <u>purple</u> dragon

2. **An adjective can follow a <u>linking verb</u>, such as** *be*, *seem*, **or** *feel*. A linking verb expresses a state of being.

   Serafina seems <u>sleepy</u>. [*Sleepy* describes Serafina.]

   the room was <u>warm</u>. [*Warm* describes the room.]

3. **Several adjectives can describe the same noun or pronoun.**

   <u>George's</u> <u>three</u> <u>biology</u> assignments

   the <u>worn</u>, <u>ragged</u> <u>denim</u> jacket

4. **When two or more adjectives describe the same noun or pronoun, there are specific rules concerning when to use a comma between the adjectives.**

   - First, *never* place a comma between an adjective and the noun or pronoun it describes.

no comma

a soft-spoken, understanding counselor

no comma

an interesting, appealing job

- *Do* place a comma between two adjectives when each describes the same noun (or pronoun) separately.

comma

a soft-spoken, understanding counselor

- *Do not* place a comma between two adjectives when the adjective closest to the noun (or pronoun) describes the noun and the other adjective describes the combination of those two words.

no comma

a worn English dictionary

no comma

a broken glass bottle

no comma

an accurate job description

Use the following test to decide whether you need to place a comma between two adjectives: if the word *and* makes sense when placed between the two adjectives, a comma is needed.

MAKES SENSE	a soft-spoken <u>and</u> understanding counselor
USE A COMMA	a soft-spoken, understanding counselor
DOES NOT MAKE SENSE	a new <u>and</u> Mexican restaurant
DO NOT USE A COMMA	a new Mexican restaurant

EXERCISE 7-2

Directions: Add commas to each of the following phrases, if needed.

EXAMPLE   the lazy, sleepy pot-bellied pig

1. an elderly California senator

2. the gentle quiet waves

3. a folded used newspaper

4. the dedicated cancer specialist

5. the sharp cat's claw

6. valuable family photographs

7. a weathered twisted pine tree

8. excited happy children

9. brown leather wallet

10. worthless costume jewelry

Using Adjectives to Expand Sentences

Adjectives are powerful words. They can create vivid pictures and impressions in the mind of your reader. Consider the following sentence:

EXAMPLE   The applicant greeted the interviewer.

This sentence has two nouns: *applicant* and *interviewer*. Without adjectives, however, what do we know about them or the situation? With adjectives, the same sentence becomes more informative.

REVISED   The <u>eager</u>, <u>excited</u> applicant greeted the <u>friendly</u>, <u>welcoming</u> <u>job</u> interviewer.

REVISED   The <u>nervous</u>, <u>insecure</u> applicant greeted the <u>cool</u>, <u>polished</u> <u>job</u> interviewer.

Now can you imagine the people and the situation each sentence describes? Let's take another sentence and expand it several ways by using adjectives.

EXAMPLE   The building houses the lab.

REVISED   The <u>ivy-covered</u> <u>brick</u> building houses the <u>well-equipped</u>, <u>up-to-date</u> <u>biology</u> lab.

REVISED   The <u>dilapidated</u>, <u>unpainted</u> building houses the <u>time-worn</u>, <u>outdated</u> <u>biology</u> lab.

As you can see from the examples above, you can drastically alter and expand your meaning by using adjectives. Think of adjectives as words that allow you to choose details that create the impression you want to convey.

NEED TO KNOW

Adjectives

- **Adjectives** describe nouns and pronouns.

- An **adjective** is usually placed before the word it describes.

- An **adjective** can follow a linking verb.

- Use **adjectives** to add interest and detail to your sentences.

EXERCISE 7-3

Directions: Expand and revise each of the following sentences in two different ways by adding adjectives. Each of your two revisions should create a different impression. Underline your adjectives.

EXAMPLE	The interviewer asked Julie a question.
REVISED	The <u>skillful</u> interviewer asked Julie an <u>indirect</u> question.
REVISED	The <u>young</u>, <u>inexperienced</u> interviewer asked Julie a <u>personal</u> question.

1. Mr. Lindgren's parrot was able to speak several words.

   a. _____

   b. _____

2. The department store made sales.

   a. _____

   b. _____

3. The Wildlife Rehabilitation Center sponsored an exhibit.

   a. _____

   b. _____

   _____

4. A professor published an article on campus reform.

   a. _____

   _____

   b. _____

   _____

5. The chef prepared a dish.

   a. _____

   b. _____

6. The diner serves food throughout the night.

   a. _____

   b. _____

7. The disc jockey plays music.

   a. _____

   b. _____

8. The book was read by each member of the club.

   a. _____

   b. _____

9. The newspaper lay on the table.

a. _____

b. _____

10. The teacher calmed the child by showing her books.

a. _____

b. _____

EXERCISE 7-4

Directions: Rewrite the following paragraph by adding adjectives. You can also add new phrases and sentences anywhere in the paragraph—beginning, middle, or end—as long as they have adjectives in them. Underline the adjectives.

> I had been looking forward to my vacation for months. I was going to lie on the beach all day and dance all night. I didn't get off to a good start. On the flight to Miami, I had the middle seat between a big man and a mother with a baby. Then we sat on the ground for two hours because of fog. It was hot and noisy. When we did get off the ground, the flight was very bumpy. Finally we got to Miami. I waited and waited for my suitcase. Needless to say, it didn't arrive. I could just picture all my new clothes sitting in some other city. Actually, though, all I needed for my week in Miami was a raincoat, because it rained every day. I didn't need my party clothes either because the first morning, I slipped getting out of the shower and sprained my ankle. I need a vacation from my vacation.

EXERCISE 7-5

Directions: Write a paragraph on one of the following topics. After you have written your first draft, revise your paragraph by adding adjectives. Underline your adjectives.

1. A full- or part-time job you held

2. A trip you took

3. A valued possession

4. Searching for _____

5. Interviewing for _____

Using Adverbs to Describe

Adverbs describe, qualify, or limit verbs, adjectives, or other adverbs. The following paragraph uses no adverbs:

Sample Paragraph

> The old door opened on its rusty hinges. A young woman entered the attic. She searched for the box of costumes. She saw a carton on the shelf across the room. She lifted the box and undid its dusty strings. She opened it. She began laughing. A huge chicken costume was in the box!

Did this paragraph give you enough details to visualize the scene? Imagine you are directing this scene in a movie: How would the rusty door hinges sound? How would the young woman walk when she entered the attic? Where would she look for the costumes? Adverbs give you details about the verbs, adjectives, and other adverbs they modify.

Adverbs can add five kinds of information to your writing:

HOW?	He announced his intentions <u>cautiously</u>.
WHEN?	We will leave <u>tomorrow</u>.
WHERE?	We searched <u>everywhere</u>.
HOW OFTEN?	I exercise <u>daily</u>.
TO WHAT EXTENT?	The caller was <u>very</u> polite.

The following revised version of the above paragraph uses adverbs to add details that let you visualize the scene more fully:

Revised Paragraph

The old door opened <u>creakily</u> on its rusty hinges. A young woman <u>quickly</u> entered the attic. She searched <u>everywhere</u> for the box of costumes. <u>Finally</u>, she saw a carton on the shelf across the room. <u>Gingerly</u>, she lifted the box down and undid its dusty strings. <u>Very carefully</u>, she opened it. She began laughing <u>gleefully</u>. A huge chicken costume was in the box!

From this revision, you can see that adverbs help bring actions alive.

EXERCISE 7-6

Directions: *The Adverb Contest:* The time limit for this exercise is ten minutes. Expand the "attic" paragraph above, and see how many more adverbs you can add. You can add new phrases and sentences anywhere in the present paragraph—beginning, middle, or end—as long as they have adverbs in them. Underline your adverbs, and exchange your expanded story with a partner to verify how many adverbs you have added. The winner is the student who has added the most adverbs.

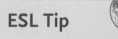

ESL Tip

Some words (such as *hard* and *fast*) can be adjectives or adverbs. *Note: Hardly* is not about something being difficult or the opposite of *soft. Hardly* means "almost not at all."

Using Adverbs Correctly

To use adverbs effectively, you must also use them correctly. Keep the following points in mind:

1. **Many <u>adverbs</u> end in *-ly*.** Some do not, however, such as *often, now, always*, and *not*. To determine whether a word is an adverb, look at how it functions in your sentence.

2. Adverbs can modify verbs, adjectives, or other adverbs.

- Here is an adverb describing a verb (a verb expresses action or state of being):

verb

Clara <u>patiently</u> waited for the appointment.

verb

The building crumbled <u>quickly</u>.

verb

The winning team <u>proudly</u> watched the videotape of the playoff game.

- Here is an adverb describing an adjective (an adjective modifies a noun or pronoun):

adjective

An <u>extremely</u> long interview is tiring.

adjective

The reporters asked <u>briskly</u> efficient questions.

adjective

<u>Microscopically</u> small plankton live in the ocean.

- Here is an adverb describing another adverb:

adverb

Read a want ad <u>very</u> carefully.

adverb

Microscopes allow one to view an object <u>more</u> closely.

adverb

The automated door opened <u>quite</u> easily.

3. Adverbs <u>can be placed</u> almost anywhere in a sentence. Three common placements are:

AT THE BEGINNING OF THE SENTENCE	<u>Briefly</u>, Mark explained.
IN FRONT OF THE VERB	Mark <u>briefly</u> explained.
AFTER THE VERB	Mark explained <u>briefly</u>.

4. Adverbs should be followed by a comma only when they begin a sentence.

comma

Slowly, Jim walked into the reception area.

comma

Cautiously, he asked to see Mr. Stoneface.

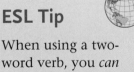

ESL Tip

When using a two-word verb, you *can place the adverb* between the two words:

He <u>has often driven</u> to New York.

I <u>will carefully finish</u> this work.

When adverbs are used elsewhere in a sentence, they are *not* set off by commas.

no comma   no comma

Jim walked slowly into the reception area.

no comma   no comma

He cautiously asked to see Mr. Stoneface.

Using Adverbs to Expand Sentences

Like adjectives, adverbs are powerful words. Adverbs can create a more complete impression of the action within a sentence. Consider the following sentence and its two revisions:

EXAMPLE	The car runs.
REVISED	The car runs <u>smoothly</u>.
REVISED	The car runs <u>haltingly</u>.

In one revised sentence, the car runs well; in the other revision, the car barely runs at all. Notice how adverbs, like adjectives, let you change the meaning of a sentence.

In the following examples, adverbs provide extra details about the action:

EXAMPLE	The president prepared his <u>State of the Union address</u>.
	adverb adverb adverb
REVISED	The president <u>very</u> <u>carefully</u> and <u>thoroughly</u> prepared his State of the Union address.
EXAMPLE	The swim team accepted the gold medal.
	adverb adverb
REVISED	<u>Proudly</u> and <u>excitedly</u>, the swim team accepted the gold medal.

Like adjectives, adverbs allow you to choose details that expand your sentences and refine your meaning.

ESL Tip

The *State of the Union address* is a speech given annually by the U.S. president. It is delivered before Congress and televised worldwide. It tells about the state (the condition) of the union (the United States) and includes the president's suggestions for new laws that the president wants Congress to pass.

NEED TO KNOW

Adverbs

- **Adverbs** qualify or limit verbs, adjectives, or other adverbs.
- Many adverbs end in -*ly,* but some do not.
- Use a comma after an adverb only when the adverb begins the sentence.
- Use adverbs to qualify and expand your ideas.

EXERCISE 7-7

Directions: Expand and revise each of the following sentences in two different ways by adding adverbs. Each revision should create a different impression. Underline your adverbs.

EXAMPLE   The employment agency lists hundreds of management positions.

REVISED   The employment agency <u>usually</u> lists hundreds of management positions.

REVISED   The employment agency <u>seldom</u> lists hundreds of management positions.

1. The gymnast performed his routine.

    a. _____

    b. _____

2. The chemistry experiment was completed.

    a. _____

    b. _____

3. Botanists study newly discovered plant life.

    a. _____

    b. _____

4. The furniture in our office breaks.

    a. _____

    b. _____

5. The businesspeople in my office use cell phones.

    a. _____

    b. _____

6. The professor will post the exam grades.

    a. _____

    b. _____

7. Mirrors should be handled carefully.

    a. _____

    b. _____

8. Many people lived through the Depression.

    a. _____

    b. _____

9. Seatbelts have saved thousands of lives.

a. _____

b. _____

10. The boat left the dock.

a. _____

b. _____

EXERCISE 7-8

Directions: Write a paragraph on one of the following topics. After you have written your first draft, revise your paragraph by adding adverbs. Underline your adverbs.

1. A long-lasting or vivid memory

2. The lack of privacy in apartments

3. How to make a(n) _____

4. Learning to _____

5. How to avoid _____

EXERCISE 7-9

Directions: Rewrite the following paragraph by adding adjectives and adverbs. You can also add phrases and sentences anywhere in the beginning, middle, or end of the paragraph, as long as they have adjectives and adverbs in them. Underline the adjectives, and circle the adverbs.

Every family has someone who's eccentric—someone who's lovable but strange. In my family, that's Aunt Irma. Aunt Irma lives in an apartment filled with souvenirs from her many trips. She has souvenirs of all kinds—big and small—from everywhere in the world. If you want to sit down at Aunt Irma's, you have to move a souvenir, and probably what you're sitting on is a souvenir, too. Aunt Irma also has unusual eating habits. She eats only soup and sandwiches. She always makes her own soups and they are unusual. The sandwiches are strange, too. You'll never see one on a menu. Aunt Irma is also an exercise nut. She has several sets of weights in different rooms. She runs in place whenever she watches TV. Finally, Aunt Irma has a distinctive way of dressing. I have seen her wear some really strange outfits. But she is lovable and, when all's said and done, what would we do without Aunt Irma stories?

Using Adjectives and Adverbs to Compare

Adjectives and adverbs modify, describe, explain, qualify, or restrict the words they modify. **Adjectives** modify nouns and pronouns. **Adverbs** modify verbs, adjectives, and other adverbs; adverbs can also modify phrases, clauses, or whole sentences.

ADJECTIVES   the <u>red</u> car; the <u>quiet</u> one

ADVERBS   <u>quickly</u> finish; <u>only</u> four reasons; <u>very</u> angrily

Comparison of Adjectives and Adverbs

1. **Positive** adjectives and adverbs modify but do not involve any comparison: *green, bright, lively.*

2. **Comparative** adjectives and adverbs compare two persons, things, actions, or ideas.

    COMPARATIVE ADJECTIVE   Michael is <u>taller</u> than Bob.

    COMPARATIVE ADVERB   Antonio reacted <u>more calmly</u> than Robert.

    Here is how to form comparative adjectives and adverbs. (Consult your dictionary if you are unsure of the form of a particular word.)

    - **If the adjective or adverb has one syllable, add *-er*. For some two-syllable words, also add *-er*.**

    cold → colder   slow → slower   narrow → narrower

    - **For most words of two or more syllables, place the word *more* in front of the word.**

    reasonable → more reasonable   interestingly → more interestingly

    - **For two-syllable adjectives ending in -*y*, change the -*y* to -*i* and add -*er*.**

    drowsy → drowsier   lazy → lazier

3. **Superlative** adjectives and adverbs compare more than two persons, things, actions, or ideas.

    SUPERLATIVE ADJECTIVE   Michael is the <u>tallest</u> member of the team.

    SUPERLATIVE ADVERB   Of everyone in the class, she studied the <u>most diligently</u> for the test.

    Here is how to form superlative adjectives and adverbs:

    - **Add -*est* to one-syllable adjectives and adverbs and to some two-syllable words.**

    cold → coldest   slow → slowest   narrow → narrowest

    - **For most words of two or more syllables, place the word *most* in front of the word.**

    reasonable → most reasonable   interestingly → most interestingly

    - **For two-syllable adjectives ending in -*y*, change the -*y* to -*i* and add -*est*.**

    drowsy → drowsiest   lazy → laziest

EXERCISE 7-10

Directions: Fill in the blank with the comparative form of the adjective or adverb given.

1. seriously   Mary was injured _____ than Tom.
2. lively   I feel a lot _____ than I did yesterday.
3. pretty   This bouquet of flowers is _____ than that one.
4. interesting   My biology teacher is _____ than my history teacher.
5. softly   Speak _____, or you'll wake the baby.

EXERCISE 7-11

Directions: Fill in the blank with the superlative form of the adjective or adverb given.

1. beautiful   It was the _____ wedding I'd ever seen.
2. slow   I always get in the _____ checkout line at the grocery store.
3. early   This is the _____ Jana has ever arrived.
4. difficult   That is the _____ trick the magician performs.
5. loud   It was by far the _____ band that played last Saturday.

Irregular Adjectives and Adverbs

Some adjectives and adverbs form their comparative and superlative forms in irregular ways.

POSITIVE	COMPARATIVE	SUPERLATIVE
Adjectives		
good	better	best
bad	worse	worst
little	littler, less	littlest, least
Adverbs		
well	better	best
badly	worse	worst
Adjectives and Adverbs		
many	more	most
some	more	most
much	more	most

ESL Tip

Littler and *littlest* are used to describe size. *Less* and *least* describe amounts.

Joe is the littlest boy in his class.
I have less money than I had last week.

EXERCISE 7-12

Directions: Fill in the blanks with the correct positive, comparative, or superlative form of the adjective or adverb given.

1. good   Bob's barbecue sauce is _____ than Shawna's, but I think Leo's recipe is _____ of all.

2. little   Please give me just a _____ piece of pie. You can give me even _____ ice cream.

3. well   I don't feel _____ today, but I'm still _____ than I was yesterday.

4. much   I have _____ homework this semester than last semester. Of all my classes, I get the _____ homework in math.

5. bad   It rained _____ on Thursday than on Friday, but it rained the _____ on Saturday.

Common Mistakes to Avoid

1. **Do not use adjectives to modify verbs, other adjectives, or adverbs.**

   INCORRECT   Peter and Mary take each other <u>serious</u>.

   CORRECT   Peter and Mary take each other <u>seriously</u>. [Modifies the verb *take*.]

2. **Do not use the adjectives *good* and *bad* when you should use the adverbs *well* and *badly*.**

   INCORRECT   Juan did <u>good</u> on the exam.

   CORRECT   Juan did <u>well</u> on the exam. [Modifies the verb *did*.]

3. **Do not use the adjectives *real* and *sure* when you should use the adverbs *really* and *surely*.**

   INCORRECT   Jan scored <u>real</u> on the exam.

   CORRECT   Jan scored <u>really</u> well on the exam. [Modifies the verb *well*.]

   INCORRECT   I <u>sure</u> was surprised to win the lottery.

   CORRECT   I <u>surely</u> was surprised to win the lottery. [Modifies the verb *was surprised*.]

4. **Do not use *more* or *most* with the *-er* or *-est* form of an adjective or adverb.** Use one form or the other, according to the rules above.

   INCORRECT   That was the <u>most tastiest</u> dinner I've ever eaten.

   CORRECT   That was the <u>tastiest</u> dinner I've ever eaten.

5. **Avoid double negatives—that is, two negatives in the same clause.**

   INCORRECT   He did <u>not</u> want <u>nothing</u> in the refrigerator.

   CORRECT   He did <u>not</u> want <u>anything</u> in the refrigerator.

6. **When using the comparative and superlative forms of adverbs, do not create an incomplete comparison.**

   INCORRECT   The heater works more <u>efficiently</u>. [More efficiently than what?]

   CORRECT   The heater works <u>more efficiently than it did before we had it repaired</u>.

7. **Do not use the comparative or superlative form for adjectives and adverbs that have no degree.** It is incorrect to write, for example, *more square, most perfect, more equally,* or *most unique.* Do not use a comparative or superlative form for any of the following adjectives and adverbs:

ADJECTIVES				
complete	equal	infinite	pregnant	unique
dead	eternal	invisible	square	universal
empty	favorite	matchless	supreme	vertical
endless	impossible	parallel	unanimous	whole

ADVERBS		
endlessly	infinitely	uniquely
equally	invisibly	universally
eternally	perpendicularly	
impossibly	straight	

EXERCISE 7-13

Directions: Revise each of the following sentences so that all adjectives and adverbs are used correctly.

   EXAMPLE   I answered the question polite~~ly~~.

1. Michael's apartment was more expensive.

2. When I heard the man and woman sing the duet, I decided that the woman sang best.

3. Our local movie reviewer said that the film's theme song sounded badly.

4. The roller coaster was excitinger than the merry-go-round.

5. *The Scarlet Letter* is more good than *War and Peace.*

6. Susan sure gave a rousing speech.

7. Last week's storm seemed worse than a tornado.

8. Some women thought that the Equal Rights Amendment would guarantee that women would be treated more equally.

9. Taking the interstate is the more fast route to the outlet mall.

10. Professor Reed had the better lecture style of all my instructors.

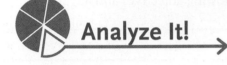

Analyze It!

Directions: Revise the following paragraph by adding adjective and adverbs. You can also add phrases and sentences anywhere in the beginning, middle, or end of the paragraph, as long as they have adjectives or adverbs in them. Underline the adjectives, and circle the adverbs.

When I think back on all my college professors, one stands out as the best. His name was Thomas P. Meyerson, but he was known as Professor M. His lectures were legendary; every student seemed to have at least one story about Professor M's teaching style. I was fortunate to take the last American history class he taught before retiring. At that time, he still had a full head of hair and a moustache with waxed tips. He always wore a suit and tie, with a handkerchief spilling from his pocket. For a lecture on the Revolution, he donned the type of hat worn during that period. For a lecture on Abraham Lincoln, he showed up wearing a stovepipe hat. During a presentation about Civil War battles, he flourished a sword. His lectures were not only entertaining but also educational, as his voice and teaching style brought the past to life, leaving me with images as well as knowledge.

A STUDENT ESSAY
The Student Writer and the Writing Task

The Student Writer

Gentry Carlson is a student at Itasca College in Grand Rapids, Minnesota. When Carlson graduated from high school, he joined the Marines. After four years of service, he worked as an automation technician and decided to attend college to pursue a career in forestry.

The Writing Task

For his writing class, Carlson was asked to write an essay describing a memorable experience. As you read, note how he uses adjectives and adverbs to make his essay engaging and interesting. In the first two paragraphs the adjectives are underlined and the adverbs are circled.

The Longest Day
Gentry Carlson

Thesis statement	1 My <u>first</u> day in <u>Marine</u> <u>boot</u> camp is a day I'll never forget. From fear of the unknown to the <u>ridiculous</u> antics of the drill instructors, it was an experience I don't believe I want to go through again.
Carlson builds suspense	2 The very <u>first</u> moment while quietly waiting at the <u>San Diego</u> airport was an <u>eerie</u> feeling in itself. All of us <u>Marine Corps</u> recruits were patiently waiting for something to happen, but what? We all waited in fear of the unknown. Then, all of a sudden, I could hear <u>squeaky</u> <u>air</u> brakes. Those <u>air</u> brakes belonged to <u>three</u> <u>large</u> <u>white</u> <u>school</u> buses that had U.S. Marine Corps etched on the side. The time had come; this is what we'd been waiting for.
Series of events begins *Suspense builds again*	3 It was night; we sat quietly as the buses drove us to our new home, where we would live for the next three months. Our fears increased as we rolled into the Marine Corps recruit depot in San Diego. The bus stopped. Again, we all waited for the next thing to happen. All of a sudden, the door flew open; we had entered the life of a Marine Corps recruit.
Series of events continues	4 A dark-complexioned man with razor-sharp creases in his shirt and pants appeared before us. He told us in a commanding tone to quickly, but safely, exit the bus and to find a yellow set of footprints. Upon his command, we all hurriedly exited the bus. After loads of mass confusion, we managed to find our set of yellow footprints. The senior drill instructor proceeded to tell us our agenda for the night.
Next event *Details add interest*	5 The agenda he spoke of was not the most appealing. First, we had to sit in a room for about three hours in a time of amnesty, to get rid of anything that's not allowed in boot camp, including cigarettes, candy, lighters, watches, and pictures of our girlfriends. Next, we were given our first military haircut. We lined up in a long line; there were about 120 of us. All of us stood heel to toe with each other, staring at the back of the head of the guy in front of us. Moving, talking, or flinching were all prohibited. I was near the front of the line, so I did not have a long wait. I sat down in the chair; within 60 seconds, I was sheared to the scalp. I had an urge to feel my shaved head, but I did not, due to the fact that a number of the recruits already got chewed out for doing it. Our next stop was supply.
Next event *Details make situation seem real*	6 Once again, we were lined up heel to toe, staring into the back of the head of the guy in front of us as we waited to receive our military issue. Quickly, we shuffled through the line as we yelled out our sizes for everything from our socks up to our cover (Marine Corps jargon for hat). Most of the gear we received was one or two sizes too large. Finally, we got to take a break; we all sat (very quietly) in this large room, trying our best to stay awake. We had no idea what day it was, what time it was; most of us had to be thinking, what the hell am I doing this for? I want to go home!
Next event	7 Finally, the last phase of the day was upon us; it was time to shuffle on to sick bay and get a few shots. Of course, like always, we all formed a long line again, heel to toe, staring at the shaved head in front of us. We went through

what seemed to be a gauntlet of shots. One shot in the left arm, one in the right, then two to three more in the left, a couple more in the right, and more and more. Either a needle gun or regular needle was the weapon of choice. Meanwhile, every now and then, someone would pass out; I thought that was hilarious. Finally, to top it all off (or to bottom it all off), we all received one in each cheek of our behinds!

Conclusion   8   After the shots, we headed back to the barracks, each of us praying that we could hit the rack. We were all in such disarray. They shaved us, shot us, and dressed us in white T-shirts, camouflage pants, and tennis shoes, and made us act and look like idiots. This was a long day that I will never forget because it took almost three days to complete.

EXAMINING STUDENT WRITING

1. Underline all the adjectives used in the remainder of the essay.

2. Circle all the adverbs in the remainder of the essay.

3. Try reading the essay by skipping over all the adjectives and adverbs you underlined and circled. How does the essay change?

4. How did Carlson organize his essay?

5. Evaluate the amount of background information Carlson gives at the opening of his essay. Is more needed?

6. Carlson builds suspense throughout the essay. How is this useful?

Paragraph Writing Scenarios

Friends and Family

1. Every family has its own rituals, things they do together over and over again. Write a paragraph on one ritual your family has. It can be the way you practice your religion, share a weekly meal, or celebrate a particular holiday.

2. Write a paragraph that begins with the topic sentence: "My ideal day with my family would be . . ."

Classes and Campus Life

1. Think of one task you have trouble with in school. Write a paragraph about what makes it difficult.

2. Do you procrastinate or get right to work on your assignments? Write a paragraph that describes the way you approach homework.

Working Students

1. Write a paragraph on what makes good customer service. What personality traits do you have that would make you a good or a poor customer service representative?

2. Write a paragraph describing what you wear to work. Even if it's as simple as a T-shirt and jeans, use plenty of details.

Communities and Cultures

1. Choose a hobby, activity, or interest that introduced you into a new community. What else, if anything, did you have in common with the members of this group?

2. Describe an article of clothing or a fashion trend that came out of a particular culture and is now worn by people of all different cultures.

Writing Success Tip 7

Spelling Tips

How can you improve your spelling? The following practical tips will help:

1. **Don't worry about spelling as you write your first draft.** Checking a word in a dictionary at this point will interrupt your flow of ideas. If you don't know how a word is spelled, spell it the way it sounds. Circle or underline the word so you remember to check it later.

2. **Develop a spelling awareness.** Your spelling will improve just by being aware that spelling is important. When you encounter a new word, notice how it is spelled and practice writing it.

3. **Pronounce words you are having difficulty spelling.** Pronounce each syllable distinctly.

4. **Keep a list of words you commonly misspell.** You can make this list part of your error log. (See Writing Success Tip 4, "Keeping an Error Log," in Chapter 4 on p. 116.) or part of your writing journal. Every time you catch an error or find a misspelled word on a returned paper, add it to your list.

5. **Study your list.** Ask a friend to quiz you on the list. Eliminate words from the list after you have passed several such quizzes.

6. **Review basic spelling rules.** Your college library or learning lab may have manuals, workbooks, or computer programs that review basic rules and provide guided practice. Also see Part VIII, p. 607, for more information on spelling rules.

7. **Have a dictionary readily available when you write.** See Chapter 3, "Buying and Using a Dictionary," p. 59, for more information on using a dictionary in your writing.

8. **Use the spell-checker on your computer.** If you are writing on a computer that has a spell-check program, get into the habit of using this feature. However, do not rely on a spell-check program to catch all of your errors.

9. **Read your final draft through once just for spelling errors.** Before you hand in an assignment, check any spellings you are not sure of.

WRITING ABOUT A READING

THINKING BEFORE READING

This reading, "The Homecoming and Then the Hard Part" by Anthony Swofford, originally appeared in *Newsweek* on May 31, 2004. The author, who is a veteran, attempts to explain a soldier's behavior when he comes home on leave from military duty. As you read, be aware of the conflicts between the soldier's two lives. Before you read:

1. Preview the reading, using the steps discussed in Chapter 2, p. 38.

2. Connect the reading to your own experience by answering the following questions:

    a. Do you know someone who has served in the military? What experiences did they tell you about freely? What experiences were more difficult for them to discuss?

    b. What does it mean to "support our troops"?

READING

THE HOMECOMING AND THEN THE HARD PART

How do you return to the real world when only other soldiers can understand how you've changed?

Anthony Swofford

A Soldier's Story: He'll tell about the movie star who appeared for a photo op. He won't tell about watching his squad leader get hit in the chest with an RPG.

philosophical
relating to the study of the deep questions and larger issues of life

spit-and-polish
a military term meaning very clean and organized

1   In my mother's house there hangs a photo of the two of us taken days after my return from the 1991 gulf war. In the photo, we're both smiling and my mother is crying as I remove a yellow ribbon from a tree in her front yard. The ribbon meant everything to her—my safety and my life, my past and my future, a notice to the world that she had a son at war—and nothing to me.

2   Ribbons, flags and parades help convince families and the citizenry that our cause is just and that the price paid by the few—death, heinous injury, a long-term psychological disorder—is worth the gain for us all. The soldier appreciates these gestures but knows that flags and ribbons will not save his life.

3   When the soldier returns on leave, there are many homecomings. He is back in this physical and **philosophical** space, America: the republic he fought for, ideally. He returns to base, a **spit-and-polish** space where he must shave daily and shine his boots to glass—chores that have no meaning after combat. And he returns home.

4   Those who greet him at his homecoming party will have no idea what he has endured. Family and friends must remember that no matter how many

hours of war coverage they've watched, how many newspaper articles they've read or how many photos of injured and dead soldiers they've turned away from in shock, their soldier has lived this war, and he has a reel of these events playing constantly in his head.

5   Because scenes of combat are constantly available to the soldier does not mean that he is prepared to transfer his horror to his loved ones. Instead, he'll tell stories about the time the movie star or politician appeared for a photo op, his first hot shower in 40 days or the Iraqi children he played soccer with. He won't tell about watching his squad leader get hit in the chest with an **RPG**, or the day the **Humvee** in front of his detonated a roadside bomb killing three men from his company. He won't mention the dead Iraqi children.

6   The soldier will visit friends from high school. They'll ask him what he really saw, now that his mom isn't around. He'll tell them that he was afraid of death, and they won't know how to respond because they've never had to consider dying in combat. The chasm between the men will be obvious. After the high-school friends depart, the soldier will call one of his platoon mates who is also on leave and attempting to make sense of a changed world, a changed self.

7   The soldier will sleep restlessly. After a year or longer of sleeping on the desert floor or a cot, a mattress will feel dangerously comfortable. He's used to sleeping with a rifle or pistol: he'll reach for it at night and awake with a start when it isn't there. He'll walk the neighborhood at 3 in the morning. He'll welcome the smell of his mother's breakfast. She shouldn't be surprised when he devours it in two minutes and then leaves for a run. Early-morning exercise is a part of his military schedule, and the solace and fatigue it brings will help him cope with his new reality.

8   It's likely the soldier will return from leave early. After a week, the parties will be over and he'll have grown tired of the questions: How many Iraqis did you kill? Did your unit get Saddam? He'll call his platoon mates to find out if they, too, are bored and miss each other and if they'd like to meet back at base sooner rather than later.

9   This will be the soldier's most important return. He'll be living among the soldiers he served with, people who won't ask how many Iraqis he killed because they know and don't care whether the number is zero or five. He'll be safe.

10   And now the government that spent years and thousands of dollars preparing the soldier for war should take responsibility for his physical and mental health. The post-war saga of physically and psychologically injured American soldiers is nearly always a **bureaucratic sinkhole**. In "Home to War," author Gerald Nicosia narrates the embarrassing treatment Vietnam vets received from the Veterans Administration. **Agent Orange** and posttraumatic-stress disorder killed and paralyzed veterans for many years before the VA began to treat them. Currently, veterans of the first gulf war are battling to receive benefits for the multiple ailments known as gulf-war syndrome.

11   The soldier's family must give him time—allow him to share his experiences at his leisure, or never. But the government must act immediately on his return from battle. This responsibility is not just to the soldier, but to his family and the citizens in whose names he fought.

RPG
rocket-propelled grenade

Humvee
High Mobility Multipurpose Wheeled Vehicle; a military vehicle

bureaucratic sinkhole
a time-consuming, frustrating tangle of governmental rules and regulations

Agent Orange
code name for a herbicide that was sprayed on the jungles of Vietnam by the U.S. military during the Vietnam Conflict

GETTING READY TO WRITE

Reviewing the Reading

1. What do yellow ribbons mean to people on the home front? To the soldiers?
2. Describe a soldier's experience when he comes home on leave.
3. Why are homecomings difficult for those who have experienced combat?
4. Why might a soldier want to return to his platoon mates early?
5. How can we help those who are returning from war?
6. What does the author think the government and family members should do to help soldiers who return from combat?

Examining the Reading Using an Idea Map

Review the reading by completing the missing parts of the idea map shown on the next page.

Strengthening Your Vocabulary

Part A: Using the word's context, word parts, or a dictionary, write a brief definition of each of the following words or phrases as it is used in the reading.

1. heinous (paragraph 2) _____
2. photo op (paragraph 5) _____
3. detonated (paragraph 5) _____
4. chasm (paragraph 6) _____
5. devours (paragraph 7) _____
6. solace (paragraph 7) _____
7. saga (paragraph 10) _____
8. narrates (paragraph 10) _____

Part B: Choose one of the words above and draw a word map (see p. 84) of it.

Reacting to Ideas: Discussion and Journal Writing

Get ready to write about the reading by discussing the following:

1. How has war changed over time? How has it remained the same?
2. Write about a time when you felt out of place because people didn't understand an experience that you had.
3. Write about your feelings toward our government's military policies.
4. Discuss whether our government should be responsible for the mental and physical health care of veterans.

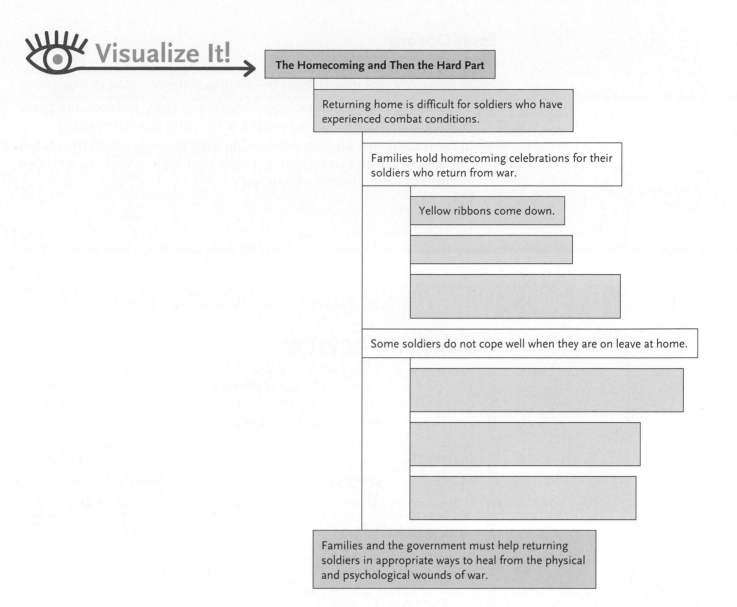

Visualize It!

The Homecoming and Then the Hard Part

Returning home is difficult for soldiers who have experienced combat conditions.

Families hold homecoming celebrations for their soldiers who return from war.

Yellow ribbons come down.

Some soldiers do not cope well when they are on leave at home.

Families and the government must help returning soldiers in appropriate ways to heal from the physical and psychological wounds of war.

WRITING ABOUT THE READING

Paragraph Options

1. Swofford states that soldiers know yellow ribbons won't save their lives. Write a paragraph about what skills will save their lives.

2. Write a paragraph about a life-changing experience you had that was difficult to explain to others.

3. The author writes that the soldier will "be safe" when he is back with his platoon mates. Write a paragraph explaining the meaning of this statement.

Essay Options

1. Write an essay that explains how a traumatic event changed your life. Be sure to include details about the event and the resulting changes.

2. Some people believe that violence only creates more violence, not peace or stability. Write an essay supporting or rejecting this statement.

3. In the reading, the soldier's relationship with his high school friends has changed. Write an essay describing how your high school or childhood friendships have changed over time.

CHAPTER REVIEW AND PRACTICE

CHAPTER REVIEW

To review and check your recall of the chapter, select the word or phrase from the box below that best completes each of the sentences that follow. Keep in mind that eight of the words will not be used.

in front of	is	is not	*-ly*	end	comparative
adverb	adjective	after	*-ing*	superlative	verbs
begin	lazier	more	lazy	laziest	nouns

1. A(n) _____ is a word that describes a verb, another adjective, or another adverb.

2. A(n) _____ is a word that describes a noun or pronoun.

3. Adjectives usually appear _____ the words they describe.

4. A comma _____ placed between two adjectives that describe the same noun separately.

5. Many adverbs end in _____.

6. Adverbs should be followed by a comma only when they _____ a sentence.

7. _____ adjectives compare two or more things.

8. _____ adjectives compare three or more things.

9. The comparative form of the word *lazy* is _____.

10. The words *good* and *bad* should be used to describe _____.

EDITING PRACTICE

The following student paragraph is correct in every aspect except for the use of adverbs and adjectives. Revise it so that all adverb and adjective problems are corrected.

> I am a very impatient person, and my impatience interferes with how easy I can get through a day. For example, when I decide to buy something, such as a new CD, I have to have it right away—that day. I usually drop everything and quick run to the store. Of course, I shortchange myself on studying, and that hurts my grades. My impatience hurts me, too, when I'm waiting for someone, which I hate to do. If my friend Jerome and I agree to meet at noon to work on his car, I get real annoyed if he's even five minutes late. Then I usually end up speaking nasty or sarcastic, saying, "Well, where were *you?*" which I regret later. Perhaps I am the more impatient when I'm behind the steering wheel. If I get behind a slow driver, I get annoyed quick and start honking and beeping my horn. I know this might fluster the other driver, and afterwards I feel guiltily. I've tried talking to myself to calm down. Sometimes it works, so I sure hope I'm overcoming this bad trait.

INTERNET ACTIVITIES

1. Adjectives and Adverbs

Practice putting adjectives and adverbs in order with these fun "magnetic" quizzes from Capital Community College.

http://www.ccc.comment.edu/writing/magnetX.htm

http://grammar.ccc.commnet.edu/grammar/quizzes/magnets/adv_magnets.htm

2. Describing with Adverbs and Adjectives

Pick two images from the Illustrated London News Picture Library.

http://www.ilnpictures.co.uk/default.asp

Write about one image using adjectives and write about the other image using adverbs. For example, you could describe the image you select or create a story about it.

3. MyWritingLab

Visit this site to get more help with using adjectives and adverbs.

http://www.mywritinglab.com

Click on the Study Plan tab, then on "Sentence Basics and Development," and then on "Using Adjectives" and "Using Adverbs."

8

Using Modifiers to Add Detail

In this chapter you will learn to add detail by using:

1. Prepositional phrases.

2. *-ing* phrases.

3. *Who*, *which*, and *that* relative clauses.

WRITE ABOUT IT!

Compare the two images above. Write a sentence explaining how they differ.

These two images demonstrate what a paragraph looks like without words and phrases that add detail. A paragraph is just a skeleton, as is the first photograph, without words and phrases that explain or change the meaning. In this chapter you will learn to use **modifiers**—words that change or limit the meaning of another word or word group.

WRITING

To further understand the value of modifiers, read this sample paragraph and the revised paragraph that follows it:

Sample Paragraph

Eyes produce tears. Tears wash the eye. Tears clean away dust and germs. People cry sometimes when happy, sad, or in pain. No one knows why. The eye also waters if something touches it or if the person has a cold or other infection. Used tear fluid drains away. It goes to a chamber in the nose. Crying produces a runny nose.

Did this paragraph seem choppy and underdeveloped to you? Now read the revised paragraph below. To add information and improve flow, the writer has used modifiers, such as prepositional phrases, *-ing* phrases, and relative clauses, which are underlined.

Revised Paragraph

Eyes produce tears in the lachrymal glands behind the upper eyelids. Cleaning away dust and germs with every blink, tears wash the eye. For reasons not well understood, people who are happy, sad, or in pain sometimes produce extra tears, which flood down their cheeks. The eye also waters if something touches it or if the person has a cold or other infection. Used tear fluid drains away through two tiny holes in the eyelids near the nose, entering small tubes that are called the tear ducts. These ducts empty into a chamber in the nose. This fact explains why someone who is having a good cry will often get a runny nose as well.

This chapter will help you learn to write more interesting, effective sentences by using three types of modifiers: prepositional phrases, *-ing* phrases, and *who, which,* and *that* relative clauses.

Using Prepositional Phrases to Add Detail

A **preposition** links its object (a noun or pronoun) to the rest of the sentence. Prepositions often show relationships of *time, place, direction,* or *manner.*

TIME	Let's study after class.
PLACE	Meet me behind Hayes Hall.
DIRECTION	Who's that coming toward us?
MANNER	I acted according to my principles.

Prepositions show other relationships as well, usually variations on *time, place, direction,* or *manner.*

DURATION	We walked until dark.
REASON	They were late because of the snow.
RELATION	She looks like her sister.
QUALIFICATION	Everyone attended except Suzanna.
ORIGIN	In the beginning, I thought I couldn't write.
DESTINATION	We're going to the Grand Canyon in May.
LOCATION	The book is in my car.

Become familiar with the following common prepositions. They will help you link your ideas and make your sentences more varied and interesting.

COMMON PREPOSITIONS			
about	beneath	in spite of	round
above	beside	instead of	since
according to	between	into	through
across	beyond	like	throughout
after	by	near	till
against	concerning	next to	to
along	despite	of	toward
along with	down	off	under
among	during	on	underneath
around	except	onto	unlike
as	except for	out	until
aside from	excepting	out of	up
at	for	outside	upon
because of	from	over	with
before	in	past	within
behind	in addition to	regarding	without
below	inside		

A **prepositional phrase** consists of a preposition and the object of the preposition (a noun or pronoun). It may also include words that modify the object.

preposition   object of preposition   preposition   modifier   object of preposition
Sam sat beside me.   Turn left at the red barn.

You can add a prepositional phrase to a sentence to describe a noun, pronoun, verb, or adjective.

PREPOSITIONAL PHRASE DESCRIBING A ...

noun
NOUN   The man <u>with the suitcase</u> boarded the train.

pronoun
PRONOUN   Both <u>of the skaters</u> wore red.

verb
VERB   I swam <u>in the ocean</u>.

adjective
ADJECTIVE   I was pleased <u>with my exam grade</u>.

Using Prepositional Phrases to Expand Sentences

Now let's look at how you can use prepositional phrases to add detail to your sentences and expand them:

BASIC SENTENCE	I met an old friend.
ADDITIONAL DETAIL	My old friend was <u>from California</u>. [location]
	We met <u>at a quiet restaurant</u>. [place]
	We met <u>on Saturday night</u>. [time]
EXPANDED SENTENCE	On Saturday night, I met an old friend from California at a quiet restaurant.
BASIC SENTENCE	Molly got a job.
ADDITIONAL DETAIL	Her job is <u>at the bakery</u>. [place]
	The bakery is <u>on Seventh Street</u>. [place]
	She got the job <u>on Monday</u>. [time]
EXPANDED SENTENCE	On Monday, Molly got a job at the bakery on Seventh Street.

Punctuating Prepositional Phrases

To use prepositional phrases effectively, you must also punctuate them correctly. Keep the following points in mind:

1. **A preposition is never separated from its object by a comma.**

   comma
   |
   INCORRECT   <u>According to</u>, the newspaper

   no comma
   |
   CORRECT   According to the newspaper

2. **A prepositional phrase is never a complete sentence.** It lacks both a subject and a verb. Be sure you do not punctuate a prepositional phrase as a sentence. Doing so creates a fragment.

   INCORRECT   We went for a walk. <u>Along the road</u>.

   CORRECT   We went for a walk <u>along the road</u>.

3. **A prepositional phrase that introduces a sentence is set apart from the rest of the sentence by a comma, unless the prepositional phrase is very short (two or three words).**

   comma
   |
   <u>According to my sister and my cousin</u>, the party lasted until midnight.

   no comma
   |
   <u>On Tuesday</u> I missed class.

4. **When a prepositional phrase interrupts a sentence and is not essential to the meaning of the sentence, it is set apart from the sentence with commas.**

   comma   comma
   | |
   The president, <u>unlike those before him</u>, intends to establish new policies.

EXERCISE 8-1

Directions: Underline each prepositional phrase. Add punctuation if it is needed.

EXAMPLE   The mayor according to the television news report has approved the proposed school budget.

The mayor, <u>according to the television news report</u>, has approved the proposed school budget.

1. The family walked toward the museum.

2. Throughout the film the man next to me kept sneezing.

3. A tree branch crashed to the ground and slid down the hill.

4. Over the past few years the sculptor has created many works.

5. Barbara bought an iPod instead of a CD player with her bonus check.

6. After dinner Dominic gave me a gift.

7. Over the phone the salesman tried to convince me to buy his product.

8. The dog and the squirrel ran around the tree.

9. We were busy talking and drove past the restaurant.

10. Firemen broke into the building and rescued seven people.

EXERCISE 8-2

Directions: Expand each of the following basic sentences by using prepositional phrases to add additional detail. Your new sentence should have only one subject and one verb. Add punctuation if it is needed. Underline the prepositional phrases.

EXAMPLE

BASIC SENTENCE   I ordered a pizza.

ADDITIONAL DETAIL   I ordered it from Mazia's.

I ordered it with mushrooms and anchovies.

I ordered it before noon.

EXPANDED SENTENCE   <u>Before noon</u> I ordered a pizza <u>with mushrooms and anchovies from Mazia's.</u>

1. BASIC SENTENCE   Maria plays the drums.

ADDITIONAL DETAIL   She plays in a band.

The band plays at the Rathskeller.

She plays on weekends.

EXPANDED SENTENCE

_____

_____

_____

2. BASIC SENTENCE   The construction crew is building a skyscraper.

ADDITIONAL DETAIL   They are building it next to a church.

They are building it on Ivy Street.

EXPANDED SENTENCE

_____

_____

_____

3. BASIC SENTENCE   The folders should be organized and filed.

ADDITIONAL DETAIL   They should be organized by subject.

The folders are beside the phone.

They should be filed under "Marketing Ideas."

EXPANDED SENTENCE

_____

_____

_____

4. BASIC SENTENCE   Jason will buy a house.

ADDITIONAL DETAIL   The house is in Williamsville.

He will buy it as an investment.

The house has a two-car garage.

EXPANDED SENTENCE

_____

_____

_____

5. BASIC SENTENCE   The library is a popular place.

ADDITIONAL DETAIL   It is popular for socializing.

The library is in the Humanities Building.

Many students study there during the exam period.

EXPANDED SENTENCE

_____

_____

_____

6. BASIC SENTENCE   The vice president was honored.

ADDITIONAL DETAIL   He was honored for his volunteer work.

He was honored after the staff meeting.

He volunteered throughout his career.

EXPANDED SENTENCE

_____

_____

_____

7. BASIC SENTENCE   Tamara joined a sorority.

ADDITIONAL DETAIL   She joined along with her friend Marion.

This was unlike her sister Shara.

She joined despite her busy schedule.

EXPANDED SENTENCE   _____

_____

_____

8. BASIC SENTENCE   The movie is playing at the theater.

ADDITIONAL DETAIL   The theater is behind the mall.

The movie is about dinosaurs.

It is playing during the afternoon only.

EXPANDED SENTENCE   _____

_____

_____

9. BASIC SENTENCE   Women are waiting to get married.

ADDITIONAL DETAIL   They are waiting until they are older and have careers.

This is happening throughout the country.

This is true according to a recent survey.

EXPANDED SENTENCE   _____

_____

_____

10. BASIC SENTENCE   The museum is famous.

ADDITIONAL DETAIL   The museum is outside the city.

It is famous for its Monet paintings.

It is famous despite its out-of-the-way location.

EXPANDED SENTENCE   _____

_____

_____

EXERCISE 8-3

Directions: Expand each of the following sentences by adding at least two prepositional phrases anywhere in the sentence. Underline your prepositional phrases.

EXAMPLE

BASIC SENTENCE   Jack rented an apartment.

EXPANDED SENTENCE   Jack rented an apartment <u>with a beautiful view</u> <u>of the waterfront</u>.

1. The bank was recently taken over.

   _____

   _____

2. The grocery store closed permanently.

   _____

   _____

3. The publisher uses only recycled paper.

   _____

   _____

4. The children heard a story.

   _____

   _____

5. Lightning struck the old oak tree.

   _____

   _____

6. The tanker spilled oil.

   _____

   _____

7. Alaskan brown bears catch salmon.

   _____

   _____

8. The road was being paved.

   _____

   _____

9. The Bach sonata was played.

_____

_____

10. The show dog won a ribbon.

_____

_____

EXERCISE 8-4
Writing in Progress

Directions: Write a paragraph on one of the following topics. After you have written your first draft, make sure your paragraph includes at least five prepositional phrases. Underline these phrases.

1. When the unexpected happened
2. Something simple that became difficult
3. A lost and never-found item
4. Signs of laziness
5. A phobia (fear) of _____

Using -*ing* Phrases to Add Detail

Another way to add detail to your writing is to use -*ing* phrases to expand your sentences. An -*ing* phrase begins with the -*ing* verb form (*running, calling*) and functions as an adjective—that is, it modifies a noun or pronoun.

Walking slowly, the couple held hands.

Sitting on the sofa, Sally watched a video.

The phrase *walking slowly* describes the couple. The phrase *sitting on the sofa* describes Sally.

You can also use -*ing* phrases to combine ideas from two sentences into a single sentence.

TWO SENTENCES	Matt grilled a steak.
	He was standing on the patio.
COMBINED	Standing on the patio, Matt grilled a steak.
TWO SENTENCES	The couple discovered an injured pelican.
	The couple searched for sea shells.
COMBINED	Searching for sea shells, the couple discovered an injured pelican.
TWO SENTENCES	The photographer slipped off his stepstool.
	He fell two feet.
COMBINED	The photographer slipped off his stepstool, falling two feet.

Punctuating *-ing* Phrases

Remember the following rules for punctuating *-ing* phrases:

1. **A comma must follow an *-ing* phrase that appears at the beginning of the sentence.** Its purpose is to separate the *-ing* phrase from the independent thought that follows.

   comma

   Driving home, I saw a shooting star.

2. **If the *-ing* phrase appears at the end of the sentence, a comma separates the *-ing* phrase from the independent thought that comes before the phrase.**

   comma

   I explored the flooded basement, wishing I had worn my boots.

3. **When the *-ing* phrase interrupts a sentence and is not essential to the meaning of the sentence, it is set apart from the sentence with commas.**

   ESSENTIAL   The cows munching grass were facing us; the other cows were facing the other way.

                      comma   comma

   NOT ESSENTIAL   The cows, munching grass, all stood with their backs to the wind.

EXERCISE 8-5

Directions: Combine each pair of sentences into a single sentence that begins with an *-ing* phrase. Underline each *-ing* phrase.

EXAMPLE

TWO SENTENCES   Art wished it would stop raining.

                  Art was walking home without a raincoat.

COMBINED   <u>Walking home without a raincoat</u>, Art wished it would stop raining.

1. **a.** Kedra did not listen to the lecture.

   b. Kedra was thinking about her essay.

   COMBINED _____

   _____

2. **a.** Kenyon was driving to the bookstore.

   b. Kenyon was singing to himself.

   COMBINED _____

3. **a.** The plumber entered the house.

   b. The plumber carried a toolbox.

   COMBINED   _____

   _____

4. **a.** The baby was crying for her mother.

   b. The baby was standing in her crib.

   COMBINED   _____

   _____

5. **a.** The press secretary held a press conference.

   b. The press secretary was wearing a navy pin-striped suit.

   COMBINED   _____

   _____

EXERCISE 8-6

Directions: Expand each of the following sentences by adding an *-ing* phrase. You may add your *-ing* phrase at the beginning, in the middle, or at the end of the sentence. Underline each *-ing* phrase.

EXAMPLE   The man stood on a ladder.

EXPANDED SENTENCE   <u>Painting his garage</u>, the man stood on a ladder.

1. The programmer sat at her desk.

   _____

2. The doctor walked through the hospital.

   _____

3. Rafael climbed the tree.

   _____

4. The teenagers walked through the mall.

   _____

5. The instructor returned the exams.

   _____

6. Ellen waited for a bus.

   _____

7. The clerk bagged the groceries.

   _____

8. The movie star accepted the award.

_____

9. They spent a quiet evening.

_____

10. The kitten was curled up on the sofa.

_____

EXERCISE 8-7

Writing in Progress

Directions: Review the paragraph you wrote for Exercise 8-4. Double-underline any *-ing* phrases. If you have not used any *-ing* phrases, revise your paragraph to include at least one.

Using *Who*, *Which*, and *That* Relative Clauses to Add Detail

> **ESL Tip**
>
> For more explanations and examples of sentences with *relative clauses*, see the ESL Guide, D.2., "Relative (Adjective) Clauses" (p. 640).

A **clause** is a group of words that has a subject and a verb. Clauses that begin with the pronoun *who, which,* or *that* are called **relative** (or **adjective**) **clauses** because they relate one idea to another. The pronoun

who refers to people.

which refers to things.

that refers to people or things.

Relative clauses add variety to your writing, as well as interesting detail. Here are a few examples of relative clauses used to expand sentences by adding detail:

BASIC SENTENCE	My sister is a football fan.
ADDITIONAL DETAIL	She is ten years old.
EXPANDED SENTENCE	My sister, <u>who is ten years old</u>, is a football fan.
BASIC SENTENCE	My favorite movie is *The Return of the King*.
ADDITIONAL DETAIL	I saw *The Return of the King* ten times.
EXPANDED SENTENCE	My favorite movie is *The Return of the King*, <u>which I've seen ten times</u>.
BASIC SENTENCE	I own a large van.
ADDITIONAL DETAIL	The van can haul camping equipment.
EXPANDED SENTENCE	I own a large van <u>that can haul camping equipment</u>.

ESL Tip
Using Relative Pronouns

Be sure to use relative pronouns, not personal pronouns, to introduce a clause that explains a noun.

INCORRECT Laptop computers, <u>they</u> are convenient to use and easy to carry, are costly.

CORRECT Laptop computers, <u>which</u> are convenient to use and easy to carry, are costly.

Placement of Relative Clauses

Who, which, and *that* clauses usually come directly after the words they relate to or modify.

My math instructor, <u>who lives in Baltimore</u>, has a British accent.

Mickey's, <u>which serves 32 varieties of coffee</u>, is part of a national chain.

Punctuating Relative Clauses

Note the following guidelines for punctuating relative clauses:

1. **A relative clause is never a sentence by itself.** Alone, a relative clause is a fragment. It must be combined with a complete sentence.

FRAGMENT	That has two fireplaces.
REVISED	The house <u>that has two fireplaces</u> is for sale.
FRAGMENT	Who lives next door.
REVISED	The woman <u>who lives next door</u> is a plumber.
SENTENCE + FRAGMENT	I needed my notebook. Which I left at home.
REVISED	I needed my notebook, <u>which I left at home</u>.

2. **If the relative clause is essential to the meaning of the sentence, no punctuation is needed.**

   Pens <u>that have refillable cartridges</u> are expensive.

   The sentence above states that not all pens are expensive. Only those pens that have refillable cartridges are expensive. Here the relative clause is essential to the meaning of the sentence, so no commas are needed. Essential relative clauses always use the word "that."

3. **If the relative clause is *not* essential to the meaning of the sentence, then it should be separated from the remainder of the sentence by commas.** To discover whether the clause is essential, try reading the sentence without the clause. If the basic meaning does not change, the clause is not essential. Nonessential clauses use the word "which" for things and "who" for a person or people.

   My car, <u>which is a Nissan</u>, has over 100,000 miles on it.

   In this sentence, the additional information that the car is a Nissan does not change the basic meaning of the sentence.

   People <u>who talk constantly</u> are annoying.

   In this sentence, the clause is essential: only people who talk constantly are annoying.

> **NEED TO KNOW**
>
> ## Modifiers
>
> - Use *prepositional phrases* to show relationships of time, place, direction, or manner.
>
> - Use *-ing phrases* to describe or modify a noun or pronoun.
>
> - Use *relative clauses* (*who, which,* and *that*) to add detail by showing relationships.
>
> - Be sure to check the punctuation of each of these phrases and clauses.

EXERCISE 8-8

Directions: Underline each relative clause. Add punctuation if it is needed. Circle the word to which each clause relates.

EXAMPLE   My bicycle which I rode all summer needs repair.

REVISED   My (bicycle), which I rode all summer, needs repair.

1. An apartment that has three bedrooms is expensive.

2. The tape that I handed you has a concert recorded on it.

3. Becky who has been there before said the food is terrific.

4. Trees that lose their leaves are called deciduous.

5. Animals that live both on land and in water are called amphibians.

6. The fence which was put up to keep rabbits out of the garden is becoming rusted.

7. My car which I bought at an auction is seven years old.

8. The professor asked a question of Michael who had not done the reading.

9. Bettina reconditions outboard motors which she buys at marinas.

10. Brady who visited France last year speaks six languages fluently.

EXERCISE 8-9

Directions: Combine each pair of sentences into a single sentence that has a relative clause. Underline the relative clause and circle the word to which each clause relates.

EXAMPLE

TWO SENTENCES   **a.** Sam lives in New Orleans

b. Sam travels around the country demonstrating computer software.

COMBINED   (Sam,) who lives in New Orleans, travels around the country demonstrating computer software.

1. **a.** The trunk was old.

   b. The trunk contained antique clothing.

   COMBINED _____

   _____

2. **a.** The coins were valuable.

   b. The coins had sunk on a boat hundreds of years ago.

   COMBINED _____

   _____

3. **a.** The students attended the Garth Brooks concert.

   b. The students enjoy country and western music.

   COMBINED _____

   _____

4. **a.** Einstein stated the theory of relativity.

   b. Einstein was a very humorous man.

   COMBINED _____

   _____

5. **a.** The truck had a flat tire.

   b. The truck was going to the repair shop.

   COMBINED _____

   _____

6. **a.** The wreath was hung on the door.

   b. The wreath was made of dried flowers and leaves.

   COMBINED _____

   _____

7. a. An appointment book was found on the desk.

b. The appointment book was filled with writing.

COMBINED   _____

_____

8. a. Roberto was hired as an accountant.

b. Roberto has a degree from this college.

COMBINED   _____

_____

9. a. The pool sold for 300 dollars.

b. The pool had a tear in its lining.

COMBINED   _____

_____

10. a. Test questions should be approached systematically.

b. Some test questions are multiple choice.

COMBINED   _____

_____

EXERCISE 8-10

Writing in Progress

Directions: Review the paragraph you wrote for Exercise 8-4. Bracket any relative clauses. If you have not included any relative clauses, revise your paragraph to include at least one.

EXERCISE 8-11

Directions: Expand each of the following sentences by adding a relative clause. Underline all relative clauses and set off unessential ones with commas.

EXAMPLE   Mr. Schmidt had a heart attack.

EXPANDED SENTENCE   Mr. Schmidt, <u>who had always been healthy</u>, had a heart attack.

1. "The Three Little Pigs" is a popular children's story.

_____

_____

2. Our dog is afraid to climb the spiral staircase.

_____

_____

3. A paper plate lay in the garbage.

_____

_____

4. The stereo was too loud.

_____

_____

5. I picked up my screwdriver and tightened the screw.

_____

_____

6. The student called the Records Office.

_____

_____

7. The wineglass shattered.

_____

_____

8. The lottery jackpot is one million dollars.

_____

_____

9. Jackie stepped on the thistle.

_____

_____

10. The train crossed the bridge.

_____

_____

EXERCISE 8-12

Directions: Expand the following sentences by adding prepositional phrases, *-ing* phrases, and relative clauses. Underline the phrases and clauses that you add.

EXAMPLE   The sportscaster reported the game.

EXPANDED   The sportscaster, <u>who was wearing a really wild tie</u>, reported the game <u>with great enthusiasm</u>.

1. Randall will graduate.

   _____

   _____

2. The race began.

   _____

   _____

3. The Smiths are remodeling.

   _____

   _____

4. Hillary walked alone.

   _____

   _____

5. Manuel repairs appliances.

   _____

   _____

6. The motorcycle was loud.

   _____

   _____

7. My term paper is due on Tuesday.

   _____

   _____

8. I opened my umbrella.

   _____

   _____

9. Austin built a garage.

   _____

   _____

10. Lucas climbs mountains.

   _____

   _____

EXERCISE 8-13

Directions: Write a paragraph describing what you think is happening in the photograph below. To make your writing vivid, use adjectives and adverbs, prepositional phrases, -*ing* phrases, and relative clauses.

 Analyze It!

Directions: Revise the following paragraph by adding modifiers in each space provided.

Going to the dentist terrified me until I discovered an effective strategy for _____. I dreaded dental work so much that _____. At the dentist's office, I would sit nervously in the waiting room, _____. Minutes seemed like hours as I flipped through old magazine, trying to _____. _____, I would smile weakly at the receptionist, who _____ _____. When I finally sat in the dentist's chair, I would literally tremble with fear throughout _____. Recently, a friend suggested that music might calm my fear of the dentist, so I took my MP3 player and headphones to _____. In the waiting room, I put on my headphones and listened to _____. Right away I could feel some of the tension leaving my body. In the dentist's chair, I switched to mellow jazz and was amazed that _____ _____. _____, the dentist even commented on how relaxed I was. When the drilling started, I flinched but soon discovered that the drill was no match for the music of _____.

A STUDENT ESSAY
The Student Writer and the Writing Task

The Student Writer

Kim Hyo-Joo is a student at Our Lady of the Lake University in San Antonio, Texas, and is majoring in psychology.

The Writing Task

Hyo-Joo wrote this essay for a writing class. Her instructor encouraged her to enter her essay in a writing contest sponsored by Longman Publishers, the publisher of this book. Hyo-Joo's essay was selected from among hundreds of essays as a good model essay. As you read, notice Hyo-Joo's use of modifiers—prepositional phrases, adjectives and adverbs, relative clauses, and -*ing* phrases.

English, Friend or Foe?

Kim Hyo-Joo

Thesis statement

I love writing. Frankly, I much prefer writing to talking. I am delighted every time I think up new and striking expressions. However, it is frustrating to me that it is difficult for me to write well in English. I love the delicate shades of meaning that languages have based on their own cultures and traditions, and I do not know many of the delicate meanings of English words. When I try to write something in English, I struggle to find the most appropriate vocabulary, but I am not always convinced that I have made the best choice. On the one hand, this problem makes me feel down, but on the other hand, I think it is unavoidable because I cannot make English my mother tongue. It is also an important reason why I cannot love English. I like to play with words by using and rearranging them, but in English I cannot have this kind of fun.

Hyo-Joo explains why writing is difficult

Topic sentence

Details about learning English

To tell the truth, there is another reason why I hate and fear English. All throughout my school days in Korea, my English scores were low. English was always my weakest point, and most English words were obscure code words to me. I had no interest and felt no necessity to learn English. English was just a subject that I had to memorize. I actually had English phobia. I used to have headaches when I even opened a book related to English. When I was a high school student, I decided that I would never read any more English after graduation. In my university, the Catholic University of Korea, however, some English courses were required and I received bad grades again. My major is psychology, so I had to read many textbooks written in English. I could not avoid English.

Topic sentence

Details about the trip

When I took a trip to Japan, I realized my attitude toward English was wrong. The trip to Japan sparked my interest in foreign cultures and languages. I realized that if I wanted to grow mentally and broaden my experience, it was essential to learn foreign languages, especially English. I came to realize that foreign languages are not just a means for making friends without barriers. As a result, I decided to study English in America. By becoming an exchange student, I started to study English again, but with a new mental attitude and without headaches.

Topic sentence

Details about her college experience

At the beginning of my first semester in an English-speaking college, Our Lady of the Lake University, I was out of my mind with frustration. It was so difficult to understand what teachers and friends were saying, so sometimes I could not do my assignments or prepare for my tests. I sometimes felt down because of my poor English. I wish I had realized earlier that it was important to learn English. Why didn't it occur to me that if I wanted to experience culture, life, classes, etc., I should make a stronger effort to learn English before I came to the United States?

Topic sentence

Details about people she has met

Many classes were admirable; my instructors were helpful, and I met many nice and kind people. In Korea I had many large-scale classes. However, here most classes are small-scale, and professors are never authoritative. I can feel their consideration for me. If I were more proficient in English, I could learn more from their teaching. Many people are also very kind. I am often surprised at their intimate conversations with me. Korean people seldom talk to strangers. I am a talkative person, but I am irritated that I can express in English only some of the things I want to say. In addition, I want to enjoy college to the fullest, but the anxiety that my poor English will cause problems makes me waver.

Topic sentence

Details reasons

Up until now, English was only a school subject to me. I only studied English to earn high scores on exams. Now, I want to be proficient in English in order to expand my world, not just for the high scores on exams. Countries where English is spoken were just foreign countries to me in the old days, but now, if I make English mine, these countries can be included in my world. I will be able to understand people's thoughts and their culture and communicate with them.

Conclusion: Hyo-Joo offers final positive outlook

I know learning English will not be easy for me, as a matter of course. I believe it will be easier than in the past, because I have a new attitude. I really want to talk confidently to others who live in a foreign country, listen to them, and communicate. Through this, my world will extend and my mental vision will broaden.

EXAMINING STUDENT WRITING

1. Highlight at least two examples each of prepositional phrases and relative clauses.

2. Hyo-Joo uses a wide range of adjectives. Highlight several examples.

3. How did Hyo-Joo organize the essay?

4. What types of supporting information does Hyo-Joo use to promote her thesis?

5. Evaluate the introduction and conclusion. What does each accomplish?

Paragraph Writing Scenarios

Friends and Family

1. Think of something you recently discussed with a friend about which you had very different opinions. Write a paragraph explaining how your viewpoints differed.

2. Write a paragraph about a movie you have seen. Begin with the topic sentence: "My friend (name of friend) has to see (include name of movie)." Describe what you think your friend would like about this film.

Classes and Campus Life

1. Different awards and scholarships are given to students for excellence in various fields of study and activities. Describe something you do very well and what an award for that specialty might be called.

2. Write a paragraph about what you do—or wish you did—to stay in shape. If your campus has a gym, explain what you use it for.

Working Students

1. Write a paragraph on one authority figure at school or work whom you admire. What are the qualities that person has that make him or her a good leader?

2. Make a list of chores you don't ever seem to have the time to do. Which one would you like to get done the most? Why?

Communities and Cultures

1. Describe your family's attitude toward education. How is your own attitude different? How is it the same?

2. Write a paragraph that begins with the phrase "I have always wanted to visit . . ." Pick a country you've never been to, and explain why you'd like to go there.

Writing Success Tip 8

Avoiding Slang Expressions

Slang refers to informal, casual expressions used by specific groups to identify themselves as a group. Teenagers, for example, have numerous slang expressions that create an in-group feeling. Slang changes rapidly and is not widely understood by those outside its group of origin. People generally use slang when they are certain the person they are speaking to will understand it or when they want to make an outsider feel even more like an outsider.

Slang can interfere with effective communication. If your reader is unfamiliar with the slang you are using, confusion or misunderstanding can occur. Also, the use of slang suggests a casualness or familiarity that may be inappropriate for your reader.

In each of the following examples, the Standard English version provides more complete and detailed information.

SLANG	I told Joe to *call the shots*.
STANDARD ENGLISH	I told Joe to select a movie and check the times.
SLANG	I *rattled my sister's cage* about our weekend trip.
STANDARD ENGLISH	I urged my sister to finalize the plans for our weekend trip.
SLANG	I was *up* for the job interview.
STANDARD ENGLISH	I was optimistic about and prepared for the job interview.

Sometimes it is difficult to know whether a word you commonly use in speech is considered slang. If you are uncertain of a word or phrase, check your dictionary. If you do not find the term in your dictionary, do not use it. If the word is listed, but its definition is preceded by the label *Slang* or the abbreviation *Sl.*, you will know the word is inappropriate to use in formal writing.

WRITING ABOUT A READING

THINKING BEFORE READING

In the following reading, "Before and After," Lance Armstrong, a champion cyclist who has won the Tour de France (an endurance bicycle race) seven times, describes how having cancer changed his life. This piece first appeared in his book *It's Not About the Bike,* an autobiography published in 2000. Notice how the personal testimony and details provide an intimate portrayal of Armstrong's struggle. Also pay attention to his use of modifiers.

1. Preview the reading, using the steps discussed in Chapter 2, p. 38.

2. Connect the reading to your own experience by answering the following questions:

   a. Why do people compete in endurance races? Would you consider competing?

   b. What other people have you heard about or know who have struggled with cancer?

READING

BEFORE AND AFTER

Lance Armstrong

1   I want to die at a hundred years old with an American flag on my back and the star of Texas on my helmet, after screaming down an Alpine descent on a bicycle at 75 miles per hour. I want to cross one last finish line as my stud wife and my ten children applaud, and then I want to lie down in a field of those famous French sunflowers and gracefully expire, the perfect contradiction to my once-anticipated poignant early demise.

2   A slow death is not for me. I don't do anything slow, not even breathe. I do everything at a fast cadence: eat fast, sleep fast. It makes me crazy when my wife, Kristin, drives our car, because she brakes at all the yellow caution lights, while I squirm impatiently in the passenger seat.

3   "Come on, don't be a skirt," I tell her.

4   "Lance," she says, "marry a man."

5   I've spent my life racing my bike, from the back roads of Austin, Texas, to the **Champs-Elysées**, and I always figured if I died an untimely death, it would be because some rancher in his Dodge 4x4 ran me headfirst into a ditch. Believe me, it could happen. Cyclists fight an ongoing war with guys in big trucks, and so many vehicles have hit me, so many times, in so many countries, I've lost count. I've learned how to take out my own stitches: all you need is a pair of fingernail clippers and a strong stomach.

6   If you saw my body underneath my racing jersey, you'd know what I'm talking about. I've got marbled scars on both arms and discolored marks up and

Champs-Elysées
a famous avenue in Paris where the Tour de France bike race usually ends

down my legs, which I keep clean shaven. Maybe that's why trucks are always trying to run me over; they see my sissy-boy calves and decide not to brake. But cyclists have to shave, because when the gravel gets into your skin, it's easier to clean and bandage if you have no hair.

7   One minute you're pedaling along a highway, and the next minute, *boom*, you're facedown in the dirt. A blast of hot air hits you, you taste the acrid, oily exhaust in the roof of your mouth, and all you can do is wave a fist at the disappearing taillights.

8   Cancer was like that. It was like being run off the road by a truck, and I've got the scars to prove it. There's a puckered wound in my upper chest just above my heart, which is where the catheter was implanted. A surgical line runs from the right side of my groin into my upper thigh, where they cut out my testicle. But the real prizes are two deep half-moons in my scalp, as if I was kicked twice in the head by a horse. Those are the leftovers from brain surgery.

9   When I was 25, I got testicular cancer and nearly died. I was given less than a 40 percent chance of surviving, and frankly, some of my doctors were just being kind when they gave me those odds. Death is not exactly cocktail-party conversation, I know, and neither is cancer, or brain surgery, or matters below the waist. But I'm not here to make polite conversation. I want to tell the truth. I'm sure you'd like to hear about how Lance Armstrong became a Great American and an Inspiration To Us All, how he won the Tour de France, the 2,290-mile road race that's considered the single most grueling sporting event on the face of the earth. You want to hear about faith and mystery, and my miraculous comeback, and how I joined towering figures like Greg LeMond and Miguel Indurain in the record book. You want to hear about my lyrical climb through the Alps and my heroic conquering of the Pyrenees, and how it *felt*. But the tour was the least of the story.

10   Some of it is not easy to tell or comfortable to hear. I'm asking you now, at the outset, to put aside your ideas about heroes and miracles, because I'm not storybook material. This is not Disneyland, or Hollywood. I'll give you an example: I've read that I *flew* up the hills and mountains of France. But you don't fly up a hill. You struggle slowly and painfully up a hill, and maybe, if you work very hard, you get to the top ahead of everybody else.

11   Cancer is like that, too. Good, strong people get cancer, and they do all the right things to beat it, and they still die. That is the essential truth that you learn. People die. And after you learn it, all other matters seem irrelevant. They just seem small.

constitution

the physical makeup or nature of a person

12   I don't know why I'm still alive. I can only guess. I have a tough **constitution**, and my profession taught me how to compete against long odds and big obstacles. I like to train hard and I like to race hard. That helped, it was a good start, but it certainly wasn't the determining factor. I can't help feeling that my survival was more a matter of blind luck.

13   When I was 16, I was invited to undergo testing at a place in Dallas called the Cooper Clinic, a prestigious research lab and birthplace of the aerobic exercise revolution. A doctor there measured my VO_2 max, which is a gauge of how much oxygen you can take in and use, and he says that my numbers are still the highest they've ever come across. Also, I produced less lactic acid than most people. Lactic acid is the chemical your body generates when it's winded and fatigued—it's what makes your lungs burn and your legs ache.

14 Basically, I can endure more physical stress than most people can, and I don't get as tired while I'm doing it. So I figure maybe that helped me live. I was lucky—I was born with an above-average capacity for breathing. But even so, I was in a desperate, sick fog much of the time.

15 My illness was humbling and starkly revealing, and it forced me to survey my life with an unforgiving eye. There are some shameful episodes in it: instances of meanness, unfinished tasks, weakness, and regrets. I had to ask myself, "If I live, who is it that I intend to be?" I found that I had a lot of growing to do as a man.

16 I won't kid you. There are two Lance Armstrongs, precancer, and post. Everybody's favorite question is "How did cancer change you?" The real question is how didn't it change me? I left my house on October 2, 1996, as one person and came home another. I was a world-class athlete with a mansion on a riverbank, keys to a Porsche, and a self-made fortune in the bank. I was one of the top riders in the world and my career was moving along a perfect arc of success. I returned a different person, literally. In a way, the old me did die, and I was given a second life. Even my body is different, because during the chemotherapy I lost all the muscle I had ever built up, and when I recovered, it didn't come back in the same way.

17 The truth is that cancer was the best thing that ever happened to me. I don't know why I got the illness, but it did wonders for me, and I wouldn't want to walk away from it. Why would I want to change, even for a day, the most important and shaping event in my life?

18 People die. That truth is so disheartening that at times I can't bear to articulate it. Why should we go on, you might ask? Why don't we all just stop and lie down where we are? But there is another truth, too. People live. It's an equal and opposing truth. People live, and in the most remarkable ways. When I was sick, I saw more beauty and triumph and truth in a single day than I ever did in a bike race—but they were *human* moments, not miraculous ones. I met a guy in a fraying sweatsuit who turned out to be a brilliant surgeon. I became friends with a harassed and overscheduled nurse named LaTrice, who gave me such care that it could only be the result of the deepest sympathetic affinity. I saw children with no eyelashes or eyebrows, their hair burned away by chemo, who fought with the hearts of **Indurains**.

19 I still don't completely understand it.

20 All I can do is tell you what happened.

Indurains

Miguel Indurain, Spanish cyclist who won the Tour de France five times in succession

GETTING READY TO WRITE

Reviewing the Reading

1. How does Armstrong see himself dying? Why does he think this is an appropriate death?

2. Summarize the main events in Armstrong's life as revealed in the reading.

3. Why does Armstrong have so many scars? Why do you think he feels it is important to describe all these scars?

4. Describe Armstrong's attitude toward his cancer. How does he get this across in the reading?

5. Where did Armstrong go when he was 16? How does this information relate to his struggle with cancer?

6. What conclusions did Armstrong come to about life and death as a result of his experience with cancer?

Examining the Reading Using an Idea Map

Review the reading by completing the missing parts of the idea map shown below.

Visualize It!

> **Before and After**
>
> Armstrong's battle with cancer gave him strength and courage.
>
> > Lance Armstrong lives his life fast.
> >
> > > He rides his bike fast.
> > >
> > >
> > >
> > > He would like to die at an old age after riding down a mountain fast.
> >
> > He has experienced a great deal of pain because of biking.
> >
> >
> >
> >
> >
> >
> > He has experienced a great deal of pain because of cancer.
> >
> > He got testicular cancer when he was 25 years old.
> >
> > He struggled to overcome his disease just as he struggles to win races.
> >
> >
> >
> >
> >
> > Surviving cancer changed Armstrong.
> >
> >
> >
> >
> >
> > > He had to find meaning in human moments and simple triumphs.
>
> He concludes that he doesn't completely understand the human struggle for life in the face of death.

Strengthening Your Vocabulary

Part A: Using the word's context, word parts, or a dictionary, write a brief definition of each of the following words or phrases as it is used in the reading.

1. poignant (paragraph 1) _____

2. cadence (paragraph 2) _____

3. acrid (paragraph 7) _____

4. starkly (paragraph 15) _____

5. disheartening (paragraph 18) _____

6. articulate (paragraph 18) _____

7. affinity (paragraph 18) _____

Part B: Choose one of the words above and draw a word map (see p. 84) of it.

Reacting to Ideas: Discussion and Journal Writing

Get ready to write about the reading by discussing the following:

1. Discuss your thoughts on Lance Armstrong and his experiences and accomplishments.

2. Write about another sports figure who has overcome disease, tragedy, or other difficult circumstances to succeed.

3. Discuss the differences between biographies and autobiographies.

4. Cancer kills millions of people each year. Discuss the things you can do to minimize your risk of developing cancer. What risk factors can you not control?

5. Write a journal entry about the worst physical injury you have sustained.

WRITING ABOUT THE READING

Paragraph Options

1. Write a paragraph about one thing you want to accomplish during your life.

2. Write a paragraph describing a time that you struggled to overcome an unfortunate circumstance.

3. Armstrong describes drivers who he feels purposely drove him off the road. Write a paragraph about someone who purposely hurt you.

Essay Options

4. Write an essay that could be a part of your own autobiography. Choose any event or experience to develop fully into an explanation of who you are.

5. Armstrong states that cancer was the best thing that ever happened to him. Write an essay examining how a negative experience has had a positive outcome for you.

6. Many people who excel at one thing began focusing on that thing at a young age. Write an essay about the pros and cons of concentrating on one sport or activity as a youth.

CHAPTER REVIEW AND PRACTICE

CHAPTER REVIEW

To review and check your recall of the chapter, match each term in Column A with its meaning in Column B and write the correct letter in the space provided.

COLUMN A

_____ 1. modifiers

_____ 2. prepositions

_____ 3. prepositional phrase

_____ 4. *-ing* phrase

_____ 5. clause

_____ 6. relative clause

COLUMN B

a. group of words that contains both a subject and a verb

b. clause that begins with *who*, *which*, or *that*

c. group of words containing a preposition and the object of the preposition

d. group of words that begins with the *-ing* verb form and modifies a noun or pronoun

e. words that show relationships of time, place, direction, or manner

f. words that change or limit the meaning of other words

EDITING PRACTICE

Revise the following student paragraph by supplying adjectives and adverbs, and by adding prepositional phrases, *-ing* phrases, or relative clauses.

My grandmother lives in an antiques-filled house. She is picky about her furniture. Because of this, nobody puts his or her feet on chairs or sits on beds. When we were little, one of my cousins used to think he could ignore her rules. We would sleep over at Gram's often. Each time, Eric would turn off the lights and swan dive into the bed. This would shove the mattress sideways. It would knock nearly every slat out of place. Of course, Gram noticed and always asked him to stop being so rough on the bed. Anyone else would have changed his or her ways, but Eric thought he was different. My grandmother decided that he needed a lesson. During the next sleepover, when everyone was in bed, we heard a crash from Eric's room. We rushed to his room. When we got there, we were surprised to see Eric and the mattress flat on the floor! Gram had fine-tuned the slats in her bed. She taught Eric a lesson. He now restricts his diving to beaches and pools.

INTERNET ACTIVITIES

1. Comma Placement

Practice comma placement with this exercise from the Online Writing Lab at Purdue University.

http://owl.english.purdue.edu/handouts/interact/g_commaEX1.html

2. Clauses

Work through these two online relative clause exercises from a professor at Youngstown State University.

http://www.cc.ysu.edu/~tacopela/Relative-Clauses-intro-ex.htm

http://www.cc.ysu.edu/~tacopela/Relative-Clauses1-ex.htm

3. MyWritingLab

Visit this site to get more help with using modifiers.

http://www.mywritinglab.com

Click on the Study Plan tab, then on "Sentence Basics and Development," and then on "ESL Concerns: Modifiers."

9

Revising Confusing and Inconsistent Sentences

In this chapter you will learn to:

1. Use pronouns clearly and correctly.

2. Avoid shifts in person, number, and verb tense.

3. Avoid misplaced and dangling modifiers.

4. Use parallelism.

WRITE ABOUT IT!

The ad above shows an inconsistent set of circumstances. Write a sentence explaining why the situation shown is inconsistent.

The situation shown in the photo does not "seem right." Inconsistencies in your writing can also make it seem "not right" or confusing. Here are a few examples from a book titled *Anguished English* by Richard Lederer that show how errors create confusion and sometimes unintentional humor.

1. We do not tear your clothing with machinery. We do it carefully by hand.

2. Have several very old dresses from grandmother in beautiful condition.

3. Tired of cleaning yourself? Let me do it.

Sometimes sentence errors create unintentional humor, as in Lederer's examples. Most often, though, they distract or confuse your reader. They may also convey the impression that you have not taken time to check and polish your work. In this chapter you will learn to avoid several common types of sentence errors.

WRITING

Using Pronouns Clearly and Correctly

A **pronoun** is a word that substitutes for, or refers to, a noun or another pronoun. *I, you, he, she, it, we, they, his, mine, yours, who,* and *whom* are all examples of pronouns. The noun or pronoun to which a pronoun refers is called the pronoun's **antecedent**. To use pronouns correctly, you need to make sure that the antecedent of the pronoun (your pronoun reference) is clear to your reader and that the pronoun and antecedent agree in number (singular or plural) and in gender.

> ### ESL Tip
>
> For more information about pronouns, see the ESL Guide, C., "Pronouns" (p. 636).

Pronoun Reference

If your pronoun reference is unclear, your sentence may be confusing and difficult to follow. Note the confusing nature of the following sentences:

> The aerobics instructor told the student that *she* made a mistake. [Who made the mistake?]

> *They* told Kevin that he was eligible for a Visa card. [Who told Kevin?]

> Aaron bought a bowling ball at the garage sale *that* he enjoyed. [Did Aaron enjoy the garage sale or the bowling ball?]

The following suggestions will help you make sure that all your pronoun references are clear:

1. **Make sure there is only one possible *antecedent* for each pronoun.** The antecedent (the word to which the pronoun refers) comes before the pronoun (*ante-* means "before") in the sentence. The reader should not be left wondering what the antecedent of any given pronoun is.

   UNCLEAR   The father told the child that *he* was sunburned.

   REVISED   The father told the child, "I am sunburned."

2. **Avoid using vague pronouns that lack an antecedent.** *They* and *it* are often mistakenly used this way.

   UNCLEAR   *They* told me my loan application needs a cosigner.

   REVISED   The loan officer told me my loan application needs a cosigner.

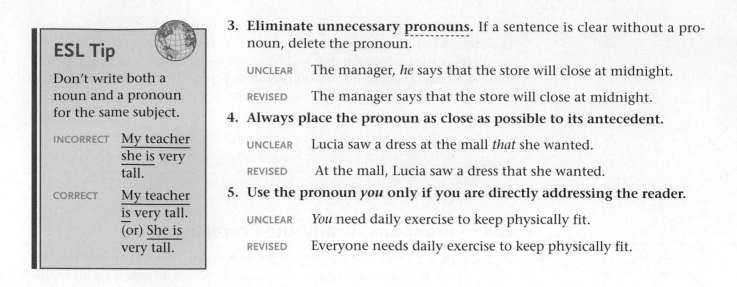

ESL Tip

Don't write both a noun and a pronoun for the same subject.

INCORRECT   <u>My teacher</u> <u>she</u> is very tall.

CORRECT   <u>My teacher</u> is very tall. (or) <u>She</u> is very tall.

3. **Eliminate unnecessary <u>pronouns</u>.** If a sentence is clear without a pronoun, delete the pronoun.

UNCLEAR   The manager, *he* says that the store will close at midnight.

REVISED   The manager says that the store will close at midnight.

4. **Always place the pronoun as close as possible to its antecedent.**

UNCLEAR   Lucia saw a dress at the mall *that* she wanted.

REVISED   At the mall, Lucia saw a dress that she wanted.

5. **Use the pronoun *you* only if you are directly addressing the reader.**

UNCLEAR   *You* need daily exercise to keep physically fit.

REVISED   Everyone needs daily exercise to keep physically fit.

EXERCISE 9-1

Directions: Revise each of the following sentences to correct problems in pronoun reference.

EXAMPLE   The glass, it filled to the rim.

1. you should try to be honest at all times.

2. When I bought the shirt, I told him that I would pay with my credit card.

3. Bert told Rob, he had received an A in the course.

4. James talked with Bill because he did not know anyone else at the party.

5. The teachers told the school board members, that they needed more preparation time.

6. The board of directors, they decided that the company would have to declare bankruptcy.

7. The gallery owner hung a painting on the wall that was blue.

8. They sent our grades at the end of the semester.

9. The Constitution says you have the right to bear arms.

10. They filled the parking lot on Sunday.

EXERCISE 9-2

Directions: Revise each of the following sentences to correct problems in pronoun reference. If a sentence contains no errors, write *Correct* beside it.

EXAMPLE   ~~It~~ said that the grades would be posted on Tuesday. *The professor's note*

_____ 1. On the bulletin board it says there will be a fire drill today.

_____ 2. Laverne and Louise they pooled their money to buy a new CD player.

_____ 3. They said on the news that the naval base will be shut down.

_____ 4. The street that was recently widened is where I used to live.

_____ 5. Ivan sat on the couch in the living room that he bought yesterday.

_____ 6. "Sarah," the tutor advised, "you should underline in your textbooks for better comprehension."

_____ 7. Christina handed Maggie the plate she had bought at the flea market.

_____ 8. Bridget found the cake mix in the aisle with the baking supplies that she needed for tonight's dessert.

_____ 9. Rick told Larry, "he was right.

_____ 10. It said in the letter that my payment was late.

EXERCISE 9-3

Writing in Progress

Directions: Write a paragraph on one of the following topics. After you have written your first draft, reread it to be certain your pronoun references are clear. Make corrections if needed.

1. A recent clothing fad
2. Advice columns
3. Horoscopes
4. Remembering names
5. An extreme weather condition (heat wave, storm, blizzard, flood) that you lived through

Pronoun-Antecedent Agreement

A pronoun must "agree" with its antecedent—that is, a pronoun must have the same number (singular or plural) as the noun or pronoun it refers to or replaces. Singular nouns and pronouns refer to one person, place, or thing; plural nouns and pronouns refer to more than one.

Always check your sentences for pronoun-antecedent agreement.

	plural singular
UNCLEAR	The dogs are in its kennels.
CLEAR	The dogs are in their kennels.

	plural singular
UNCLEAR	Marcia and Megan called all her friends about the party.
CLEAR	Marcia and Megan called all their friends about the party.

Use the following guidelines to make sure the pronouns you use agree with their antecedents:

1. **Use singular pronouns with singular nouns.**

singular noun   singular pronoun

Teresa sold her bicycle.

2. **Use plural pronouns with plural nouns.**

plural noun   plural pronoun

The neighbors always shovel their walks when it snows.

3. **Use a plural pronoun to refer to a compound antecedent joined by *and*, unless both parts of the compound refer to the same person, place, or thing.**

plural antecedent   plural pronoun

Mark and Keith bought their concert tickets.

singular antecedent   singular pronoun

The pitcher and team captain broke her ankle.

4. **When antecedents are joined by *or, nor, either. . . or, neither. . . nor, not. . . but,* or *not only. . . but also,* the pronoun agrees in number with the nearer antecedent.**

plural noun   plural pronoun

Either the professor or the students will present their views.

Note: When one antecedent is singular and the other is plural, avoid awkwardness by placing the plural antecedent second in the sentence.

AWKWARD	Neither the salespersons nor the manager has received his check.
REVISED	Neither the manager nor the salespersons have received their checks.

5. **Avoid using *he, him,* or *his* to refer to general, singular words such as *child, person, everyone.*** These words exclude females. Use *he or she, him or her,* or *his or hers,* or rewrite your sentence to use a plural antecedent and a plural pronoun that do not indicate gender.

INCORRECT	A person should not deceive his friends.
REVISED	A person should not deceive his or her friends.
BETTER	People should not deceive their friends.

6. **With collective nouns (words that refer to a group of people, such as *army, class, congregation, audience*), use a singular pronoun to refer to the noun when the group acts as a unit.**

The <u>audience</u> showed <u>its</u> approval by applauding.

The <u>team</u> chose <u>its</u> captain.

Use a plural pronoun to refer to the noun when each member of the group acts individually.

The <u>family</u> exchanged <u>their</u> gifts.

The <u>team</u> changed <u>their</u> uniforms.

To avoid using a plural verb or pronoun after a collective noun, write "the members of the team," which gives you a plural subject (members).

EXERCISE 9-4

Directions: Revise each of the following sentences to correct errors in pronoun-antecedent agreement.

EXAMPLE   Usually when a driver has been caught speeding, ~~they~~ ^{he or she} readily admit_s the mistake.

1. Each gas station in town raised their prices in the past week.

2. Neither the waitress nor the hostess received their paycheck from the restaurant.

3. The committee put his or her signatures on the document.

4. An infant recognizes their parents within the first few weeks of life.

5. The Harris family lives by his or her own rules.

6. Lonnie and Jack should put his ideas together and come up with a plan of action.

7. An employee taking an unpaid leave of absence may choose to make their own health-insurance payments.

8. The amount of time a student spends researching a topic depends, in part, on their familiarity with the topic.

9. Alex and Susana lost her way while driving through the suburbs of Philadelphia.

10. Neither the attorney nor the protesters were willing to expose himself to public criticism.

Agreement with Indefinite Pronouns

Indefinite pronouns (such as *some, everyone, any, each*) are pronouns without specific antecedents. They refer to people, places, or things in general. When an indefinite pronoun is an antecedent for another pronoun, mistakes in pronoun agreement often result. Use the following guidelines to make your pronouns agree with indefinite pronoun antecedents:

ESL Tip

Everybody, everyone, and *everything* refer to a group of people or things, but these words are grammatically singular, so use a singular verb with them:

When there's a snowstorm, <u>everyone gets</u> to class late.

1. **Use singular pronouns to refer to indefinite pronouns that are singular in meaning.**

another	either	nobody	other
anybody	everybody	no one	somebody
anyone	everyone	nothing	someone
anything	everything	one	something
each	neither		

singular antecedent   singular pronoun

<u>Someone</u> left <u>his</u> dress shirt in the locker room.

singular antecedent   singular compound pronoun

<u>Everyone</u> in the office must pick up <u>his or her</u> paycheck.

   Note: To avoid the awkwardness of *his or her,* use plural antecedents and pronouns.

plural antecedent   plural pronoun

Office <u>workers</u> must pick up <u>their</u> paychecks.

2. **Use a plural pronoun to refer to indefinite pronouns that are plural in meaning.**

both	few	many	more	several

plural antecedent   plural pronoun

<u>Both</u> of the policemen said that as far as <u>they</u> could tell, no traffic violations had occurred.

3. **The indefinite pronouns *all, any, more, most,* and *some* can be singular or plural, depending on how they are used.** If the indefinite pronoun refers to something that cannot be counted, use a singular pronoun to refer to it. If the indefinite pronoun refers to two or more of something that can be counted, use a plural pronoun to refer to it.

<u>Most</u> of the students feel <u>they</u> can succeed.

<u>Most</u> of the air on airplanes is recycled repeatedly, so <u>it</u> becomes stale.

NEED TO KNOW

Pronouns

- **Pronouns** substitute for, or refer to, nouns or other pronouns.

- The noun or pronoun to which a pronoun refers is called its **antecedent**.

- Make sure that it is always clear to which noun or pronoun a pronoun refers.

- A pronoun must agree with its antecedent in number (singular or plural) and gender. Singular nouns and pronouns refer to one thing; plural nouns and pronouns refer to more than one.

- **Indefinite pronouns** are pronouns without specific antecedents. Follow the rules given in this chapter to make indefinite pronouns agree with their antecedents.

EXERCISE 9-5

Directions: Revise each of the following sentences to correct errors in pronoun-antecedent agreement.

EXAMPLE	No one could remember their student number.
REVISED	No one could remember his or her student number.
BETTER	The students could not remember their student numbers.

1. Someone left their jacket in the car.

2. Everything Todd said was true, but I did not like the way he said them.

3. In my math class, everyone works at their own pace.

4. When someone exercises, they should drink plenty of liquids.

5. No one should be forced into a curriculum that they do not want.

6. No one will receive their exam grades before Friday.

7. Many of the club members do not pay his or her dues on time.

8. Both of the cooks used her own secret recipes.

9. No one was successful on their first attempt to run the race in less than two hours.

10. Each of the workers brought their own tools.

EXERCISE 9-6

Directions: Revise the sentences below that contain agreement errors. If a sentence contains no errors, write *Correct* beside it.

EXAMPLE   Somebody dropped ~~their~~ ring down the drain.
(handwritten above: his or her)

_____ 1. Many of the residents of the neighborhood have had their homes tested for radon.

_____ 2. Each college instructor established their own grading policies.

_____ 3. The apples fell from its tree.

_____ 4. Anyone may enter their painting in the contest.

_____ 5. All the engines manufactured at the plant have their vehicle identification numbers stamped on them.

_____ 6. No one requested that the clerk gift wrap their package.

_____ 7. Either Professor Judith Marcos or her assistant, Maria, graded the exams, writing their comments in the margins.

_____ 8. James or his parents sails the boat every weekend.

_____ 9. Most classes were not canceled because of the snowstorm; it met as regularly scheduled.

_____ 10. Not only Ricky but also the Carters will take his children to Disneyland this summer.

EXERCISE 9-7

Writing in Progress

Directions: Reread the paragraph you wrote for Exercise 9-3 to be certain that there are no errors in pronoun-antecedent agreement. Revise as needed.

Avoiding Shifts in Person, Number, and Verb Tense

The parts of a sentence should be consistent. Shifts in person, number, or verb tense within a sentence make it confusing and difficult to read.

Shifts in Person

Person is the grammatical term used to identify the speaker or writer (**first person:** *I, we*), the person spoken to (**second person:** *you*), and the person or thing spoken about (**third person:** *he, she, it, they,* or any noun, such as *Joan, children*). Be sure to refer to yourself, your audience (or readers), and people you are writing about in a consistent way throughout your sentence or paragraph.

In the following paragraph, note how the writer shifts back and forth when addressing her audience:

A <u>person</u> should know how to cook. <u>You</u> can save a lot of money if <u>you</u> make your own meals instead of eating out. <u>One</u> can also eat more healthily at home if <u>one</u> cooks according to principles of good nutrition.

Here the writer shifts from sentence to sentence, first using the indefinite phrase *a person,* then the more personal *you,* then the more formal *one.*

In the next paragraph, the writer shifts when referring to himself.

> Arizona has many advantages for year-round living, so I am hoping to move there when I graduate. One reason I want to live in Arizona is that you never need to shovel snow.

In this paragraph, the writer shifts from the direct and personal *I* to the indirect and more general *you.*

To avoid making shifts in references to yourself and others, decide before you begin to write how you will refer to yourself, to your audience, and to those about whom you are writing. Base your decision on whether you want your paragraph to be direct and personal or more formal. In academic writing, most instructors prefer that you avoid using the personal pronoun *I* and try to write in a more formal style.

PERSONAL	I want to live in Florida for a number of reasons.
MORE FORMAL	Living in Florida is attractive for a number of reasons.
PERSONAL	I have difficulty balancing school and a part-time job.
MORE FORMAL	Balancing school and a part-time job is difficult.

Shifts in Number

Number distinguishes between singular and plural. A pronoun must agree in number with its antecedent. Related nouns within a sentence must also agree in number.

SHIFT	All the women wore a dress.
CONSISTENT	All the women wore dresses.

EXERCISE 9-8

Directions: Revise each of the following sentences to correct shifts in person or number.

EXAMPLE   I perform better on exams if the professor doesn't hover over ~~you.~~ *me*

1. Each student has to plan their schedules for the semester.

2. Eva said she doesn't want to go to the wedding because you have to bring a gift.

3. In some states, continuing education is required for doctors or lawyers; after you pass the board or bar exam, you are required to take a specified number of credits per year in brush-up courses.

4. Construction workers must wear a hard hat.

5. I swim with a life vest on because you could drown without it.

6. A good friend is always there when you need them most.

7. The first and second relay racers discussed his strategies.

8. I always tell yourself to think before acting.

9. Patients often expect their doctors to have all the answers, but you should realize doctors are not miracle workers.

10. Each giraffe stretched their neck to reach the leaves in the trees.

Shifts in Verb Tense

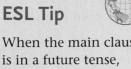

ESL Tip

When the main clause is in a future tense, the verb in the dependent time clause is put in the present tense even though the entire sentence is about the future.

Use the same verb tense (past, present, future, etc.) throughout a sentence and paragraph unless meaning requires you to make a shift.

REQUIRED SHIFT

$\overset{\text{present}}{\text{rises}}$ ... $\overset{\text{future}}{\text{will go}}$

After the moon rises, we will go for a moonlight swim.

Incorrect shifts in verb tense can make a sentence confusing. One of the most common incorrect shifts is between present and past tenses.

INCORRECT

$\overset{\text{past}}{\text{joined}}$ ... $\overset{\text{present}}{\text{seems}}$

After Marguerite joined the food co-op, she seems healthier.

CORRECT

$\overset{\text{past}}{\text{joined}}$ ... $\overset{\text{past}}{\text{seemed}}$

After Marguerite joined the food co-op, she seemed healthier.

NEED TO KNOW

Shifts in Person, Number, and Verb Tense

- *Person* is a term used to identify the speaker or writer (**first person:** *I, we*), the person spoken to (**second person:** *you*), and the person or thing spoken about (**third person:** *he, she, it, they,* or any noun, such as *desk* or *Robert*).

- Be sure to use a consistent person throughout a piece of writing.

- **Number** distinguishes between singular and plural. A pronoun must agree in number with its antecedent.

- **Verb tense** is the form of a verb that indicates whether the action or state of being that the verb tells about occurs in the past, present, or future. Unless there is a specific reason to switch tenses, be sure to use a consistent tense throughout a piece of writing.

EXERCISE 9-9

Directions: Revise each of the following sentences to correct shifts in verb tense.

    EXAMPLE   I ~~was waiting~~ *waited* for the hailstorm to end, and then I dashed into the restaurant.

1. In the morning, the factory workers punch in, but have not punched out at night.

2. José looked muscular; then he joined a gym and looks even more so.

3. I run two miles, and then I rested.

4. Quinne called me but hangs up on my answering machine.

5. Until I took physics, I will not understand the laws of aerodynamics.

6. While the rain fell, the campers take shelter in their tent.

7. Because the moon will be full, the tide was high.

8. Katie drives me to work, and I worked until 9:30 p.m.

9. Richard went to the mall because he need to buy a suit for his job interview.

10. The speaker stands at the podium and cleared his throat.

EXERCISE 9-10

Directions: Revise each of the following sentences to correct errors in shift of person, number, or verb tense. If a sentence contains no errors, write *Correct* beside it.

    EXAMPLE   Boats along the river were tied to their ~~dock.~~ *docks*

_____ 1. When people receive a gift, you should be gracious and polite.

_____ 2. When we arrived at the inn, the lights are on and a fire is burning in the fireplace.

_____ 3. Before Trey drove to the cabin, he packs a picnic lunch.

_____ 4. The artist paints portraits and weaves baskets.

_____ 5. The lobsterman goes out on his boat each day and will check his lobster traps.

_____ 6. All the cars Honest Bob sells have a new transmission.

_____ 7. Rosa ran the 100-meter race and throws the discus at the track meet.

_____ 8. Public schools in Florida an have air-conditioning system.

_____ 9. Office workers sat on the benches downtown and are eating their lunches outside.

_____ 10. Before a scuba diver go underwater, you must check and recheck your breathing equipment.

EXERCISE 9-11
Writing in Progress

Directions: Reread the paragraph you wrote for Exercise 9-3. Check for shifts in person, number, and verb tense. Revise as needed.

Avoiding Misplaced and Dangling Modifiers

A **modifier** is a word, phrase, or clause that describes, qualifies, or limits the meaning of another word. Modifiers that are not correctly placed can confuse your reader.

Types of Modifiers

The following list will help you review the main types of modifiers:

1. **Adjectives modify nouns and pronouns.**

    It is an interesting photograph.

    She is very kind.

2. **Adverbs modify verbs, adjectives, or other adverbs.**

    I walked quickly.

    The cake tasted very good.

    The flowers are very beautifully arranged.

3. **Prepositional phrases modify nouns, adjectives, verbs, or adverbs.**

    The woman in the green dress is stunning.

    They walked into the store to buy milk.

4. **-ing phrases modify nouns or pronouns.**

    Waiting for the bus, Joe studied his history notes.

5. **Dependent clauses modify nouns, adjectives, verbs, or adverbs.** (A dependent clause has a subject and verb but is incomplete in meaning.)

After I left campus, I went shopping.

I left because classes were canceled.

The kitten that I found in the bushes was frightened.

Misplaced Modifiers

Placement of a modifier in a sentence affects meaning:

I need <u>only</u> to buy Marcos a gift.

<u>Only</u> I need to buy Marcos a gift.

I need to buy <u>only</u> Marcos a gift.

If a modifier is placed so that it does not convey the meaning you intend, it is called a **misplaced modifier.** Misplaced modifiers can make a sentence confusing.

MISPLACED	Anthony found a necklace at the mall <u>that sparkled and glittered</u>. [Which sparkled and glittered—the mall or the necklace?]
MISPLACED	The president announced that the club picnic would be held on August 2 <u>at the beginning of the meeting</u>. [Is the picnic being held at the beginning of the meeting on August 2, or did the president make the announcement at the beginning of the meeting?]

You can avoid a misplaced modifier if you make sure that the modifier immediately precedes or follows the word it modifies.

CORRECT	Anthony found a necklace <u>that sparkled and glittered</u> at the mall.
CORRECT	The club president announced <u>at the beginning of the meeting</u> that the picnic would be held on August 2.

Dangling Modifiers

Dangling modifiers are words or phrases that do not clearly describe or explain any part of the sentence. Dangling modifiers create confusion and sometimes unintentional humor. To avoid dangling modifiers, make sure that each modifying phrase or clause has a clear antecedent.

DANGLING	<u>Uncertain of which street to follow</u>, the <u>map</u> indicated we should turn left. [The opening modifier suggests that the map was uncertain of which street to follow.]
CORRECT	<u>Uncertain of which street to follow</u>, <u>we</u> checked a map, which indicated we should turn left.

DANGLING   My <u>shoes</u> got wet <u>walking across the street</u>. [The modifier suggests that the shoes were walking across the street by themselves.]

CORRECT   My <u>shoes</u> got wet <u>as I crossed the street</u>.

DANGLING   <u>To pass the test</u>, careful review is essential. [Who will pass the test?]

CORRECT   <u>To pass the test</u>, I must review carefully.

There are two common ways to revise dangling modifiers.

1. **Add a word or words that the modifier clearly describes.** Place the new material immediately after the modifier, and rearrange other parts of the sentence as necessary.

   DANGLING   <u>While walking in the garden</u>, <u>gunfire</u> sounded. [The opening modifier implies that the gunfire was walking in the garden.]

   CORRECT   <u>While walking in the garden</u>, <u>Carol</u> heard gunfire.

2. **Change the dangling modifier to a dependent clause.** You may need to change the verb form in the modifier.

   DANGLING   <u>While watching television</u>, the cake burned.

   CORRECT   <u>While Pat was watching television</u>, the cake burned.

NEED TO KNOW

Misplaced and Dangling Modifiers

- A **modifier** is a word, phrase, or clause that describes, qualifies, or limits the meaning of another word.

- A **misplaced modifier** is placed so that it does not convey the intended meaning.

- To avoid misplaced modifiers, be sure that you place the modifier immediately before or after the word it modifies.

- A **dangling modifier** is a word or phrase that does not clearly describe or explain any part of the sentence.

- To revise a dangling modifier you can add a word or words that the modifier clearly describes, or change the dangling modifier to a dependent clause.

EXERCISE 9-12

Directions: Revise each of the following sentences to correct misplaced or dangling modifiers.

EXAMPLE   Jerome mailed a bill at the post office that was long overdue.

REVISED   At the post office, Jerome mailed a bill that was long overdue.

1. Running at top speed, dirt was kicked up by the horse.

_____

_____

2. Swimming to shore, my arms got tired.

_____

_____

3. The helmet on the soldier's head with a red circle represented his nationality.

_____

_____

4. In order to answer your phone, the receiver must be lifted.

_____

_____

5. Walking up the stairs, the book dropped and tumbled down.

_____

_____

6. Twenty-five band members picked their instruments up from chairs that were gleaming and began to play.

_____

_____

7. Laughing, the cat chased the girl.

_____

_____

8. When skating, skate blades must be kept sharp.

_____

_____

9. The ball bounced off the roof that was round and red.

_____

10. Ducking, the snowball hit Andy on the head.

_____

_____

EXERCISE 9-13

Directions: Revise each of the following sentences to correct misplaced or dangling modifiers.

EXAMPLE   Deciding which flavor of ice cream to order, another customer cut in front of Roger.

REVISED   While Roger was deciding which flavor of ice cream to order, another customer cut in front of him.

1. Tricia saw an animal at the zoo that had black fur and long claws.

_____

_____

2. Before answering the door, the phone rang.

_____

_____

3. I could see large snowflakes falling from the bedroom window.

_____

_____

4. Honking, Felicia walked in front of the car.

_____

_____

5. After leaving the classroom, the door automatically locked.

_____

_____

6. Applauding and cheering, the band returned for an encore.

_____

_____

7. The waiter brought a birthday cake to our table that had 24 candles.

_____

_____

8. Books lined the library shelves about every imaginable subject.

_____

_____

9. While sobbing, the sad movie ended and the lights came on.

_____

_____

10. Turning the page, the book's binding cracked.

_____

_____

_____

EXERCISE 9-14

Writing in Progress

Directions: Reread the paragraph you wrote for Exercise 9-3. Check for dangling or misplaced modifiers. Revise as needed.

Using Parallelism

Study the following pairs of sentences. Which sentence in each pair reads more smoothly?

Pair 1
1. Seth, a long-distance biker, enjoys swimming and drag races cars.
2. Seth enjoys long-distance biking, swimming, and drag racing.

Pair 2
3. The dog was large, had a beautiful coat, and it was friendly.
4. The dog was large, beautiful, and friendly.

Do sentences 2 and 4 sound better than 1 and 3? Sentences 2 and 4 have balance. Similar words have similar grammatical form. In sentence 2, _biking, swimming,_ and _drag racing_ are all nouns ending _-ing_. In sentence 4, _large, beautiful,_ a _friendly_ are all adjectives. The method of balancing similar elements within a sentence is called **parallelism.** Parallelism makes your writing smooth and makes your ideas easier to follow.

EXERCISE 9-15

Directions: In each group of words, circle the element that is not parallel.

EXAMPLE   walking, running, (to jog,) dancing

1. intelligent, successful, responsibly, mature

2. happily, quickly, hurriedly, hungry

3. wrote, answering, worked, typed

4. to fly, parachutes, to skydive, to drive

5. were painting, drew, were carving, were coloring

6. sat in the sun, played cards, scuba diving, ate lobster

7. thoughtful, honestly, humorous, quick-tempered

8. rewrote my résumé, arranging interviews, buying a new suit, getting a haircut

9. buy stamps, cash check, dry cleaning, return library books

10. eating sensibly, eight hours of sleep, exercising, drinking a lot of water

What Should Be Parallel?

When you write, be sure to keep each of the following elements parallel:

1. **Nouns in a series**

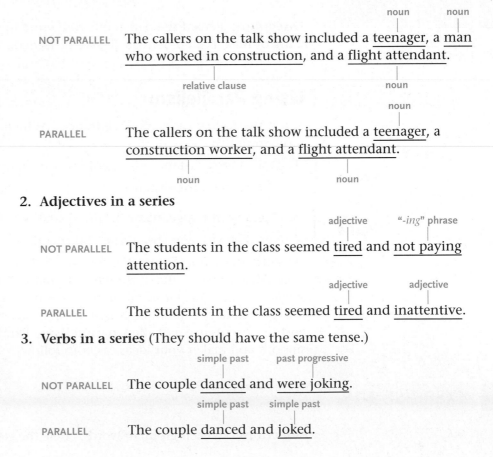

NOT PARALLEL The callers on the talk show included a teenager, a man who worked in construction, and a flight attendant.

PARALLEL The callers on the talk show included a teenager, a construction worker, and a flight attendant.

2. **Adjectives in a series**

NOT PARALLEL The students in the class seemed tired and not paying attention.

PARALLEL The students in the class seemed tired and inattentive.

3. **Verbs in a series** (They should have the same tense.)

NOT PARALLEL The couple danced and were joking.

PARALLEL The couple danced and joked.

4. Clauses within sentences

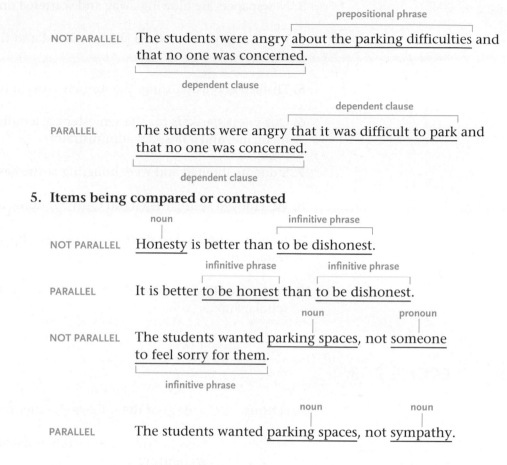

NOT PARALLEL   The students were angry about the parking difficulties and that no one was concerned.

PARALLEL   The students were angry that it was difficult to park and that no one was concerned.

5. Items being compared or contrasted

NOT PARALLEL   Honesty is better than to be dishonest.

PARALLEL   It is better to be honest than to be dishonest.

NOT PARALLEL   The students wanted parking spaces, not someone to feel sorry for them.

PARALLEL   The students wanted parking spaces, not sympathy.

NEED TO KNOW

Parallelism

- **Parallelism** is a method of balancing similar elements within a sentence.

- The following elements of a sentence should be parallel: nouns in a series, adjectives in a series, verbs in a series, clauses within a sentence, and items being compared or contrasted.

EXERCISE 9-16

Directions: Revise each of the following sentences to correct errors in parallel structure.

EXAMPLE   The instructor ~~was demanding~~ *demanded hard work* and insisted on high standards.

1. Accuracy is more important than being speedy.

2. The teller counted and recounts the money.

3. Newspapers are blowing away and scattered on the sidewalk.

4. Judith was pleased when she graduated and that she received an honors diploma.

5. Thrilled and exhausting, the runners crossed the finish line.

6. Our guest speakers for the semester are a radiologist, a student studying medicine, and a hospital administrator.

7. Students shouted and were hollering at the basketball game.

8. We enjoyed seeing the Grand Canyon, riding a mule, and photography.

9. Laughing and relaxed, the co-workers enjoyed lunch at the Mexican restaurant.

10. Professor Higuera is well known for his humor, clear lecturing, and scholarship.

EXERCISE 9-17

Directions: Revise each of the following sentences to achieve parallelism.

EXAMPLE   Rosa has decided to study nursing instead of ~~going into~~ accounting.

1. The priest baptized the baby and congratulates the new parents.

2. We ordered a platter of fried clams, a platter of corn on the cob, and fried shrimp.

3. Lucy entered the dance contest, but the dance was watched by June from the side.

4. Léon purchased the ratchet set at the garage sale and buying the drill bits there, too.

5. The exterminator told Brandon the house needed to be fumigated and spraying to eliminate the termites.

6. The bus swerved and hit the dump truck, which swerves and hit the station wagon, which swerved and hit the bicycle.

7. Channel 2 covered the bank robbery, but a python that had escaped from the zoo was reported by Channel 7.

8. Sal was born when Nixon was president, and Johnson was president when Rob was born.

9. The pediatrician spent the morning with sore throats, answering questions about immunizations, and treating bumps and bruises.

10. Belinda prefers to study in the library, but her brother Marcus studies at home.

EXERCISE 9-18

Writing in Progress

Directions: Reread the paragraph you wrote for Exercise 9-3. Correct any sentences that lack parallelism.

EXERCISE 9-19

Directions: Now that you have learned about common errors that produce confusing or inconsistent sentences, turn back to the humorous sentences used to introduce the chapter on p. 231. Identify each error, and revise the sentence so it conveys the intended meaning.

EXERCISE 9-20

Directions: Revise this student paragraph by correcting all instances of misplaced or dangling modifiers, shifts in verb tense, and faulty parallelism.

Robert Burns said that the dog is "man's best friend." To a large extent, this statement may be more true than you think. What makes dogs so special to humans is their unending loyalty and that they love unconditionally. Dogs have been known to cross the entire United States to return home. Unlike people, dogs never made fun of you or criticize you. They never throw fits, and they seem happy always to see you. This may not necessarily be true of your family, friends, and those who live near you. A dog never lies to you, never betrays your confidences, and never stayed angry with you for more than five minutes. Best of all, he or she never expects more than the basics from you of food and shelter and a simple pat on the head in return for his or her devotion. The world would be a better place if people could only be more like their dogs.

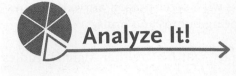

Analyze It!

Directions: Revise any sentences in the paragraph that contain errors in pronoun reference, shifts in person, number, or verb tense, or dangling or misplaced modifiers.

In 1994 the Smithsonian Institution received the largest single cash donation in their history; the Mashantucket Pequots presented a 10-million-dollar gift to the Smithsonian to help build the National Museum of the American Indian. That small Connecticut tribe wanted to share the riches from their giant casino and bingo complex. The Pequot tribe owns the Mashantucket Pequot Museum and Research Center, located in Connecticut, in addition to supporting the National Museum of the American Indian; it serves as a major resource on American Native histories and cultures. The Pequots have given donations to many other causes; for example, it gave two million dollars to the Special Olympics World Games held in New Haven, Connecticut, in 1995.

Most of the money for the National Museum of the American Indian came from the federal government, but private organizations and individuals also donated hir or her share of the construction costs. It says on the museum's website that the facility was designed in consultation with Native peoples. The museum opened their doors on the National Mall in Washington, D.C., on September 2004.

Adapted from the *Cape Cod Times*, October 25, 1994

A STUDENT ESSAY
The Student Writer and the Writing Task

The Writer

Kelly Bajier is a student at Avila University in Kansas City, Missouri, where she is majoring in nursing.

The Writing Task

Bajier wrote this essay for a writing class. Her instructor encouraged her

to submit her essay to a writing contest sponsored by Longman Publishers, the publisher of this book. Bajier's essay was selected from among hundreds of essays as a good model essay. As you read, notice Bajier's use of clear and correct sentences throughout.

Rebuilding a Dream
Kelly Bajier

Background information about the home

It only took one final strong gust of wind, filled with debris and bullet-like raindrops to finish the destruction of the home I knew and loved. My perfect beachfront home was a casualty to one of Mother Nature's most monstrous creations, otherwise known as a hurricane. My father had the house built almost fifteen years ago. I remember him overseeing the construction process as the carpenters and other workers slaved for hours each day. At last the work had been completed. The result was a dream vacation house. The first time I set foot in the brand new entry foyer, I trembled with excitement. I could only imagine the magical moments that would take place over the next years of my life. Some of my most vivid and life-changing memories took place in that house. The first summer ever spent in that house was the most memorable because everywhere I went I had a new adventure waiting for me. I explored the beach for miles. I would run up into the dunes, and my mom would later have to come searching for me to tell me that dinner was ready. After the hurricane destroyed the house, it was up to me and my brother to rebuild it.

Thesis statement

Topic sentence

Details

After the hurricane, the house was just one big pile of soggy wood. My first task was to clean up the debris, with the help of my brother, David, and plan the rebuilding process. We carried all of the pieces that we could over to a nearby Dumpster. Then we had to break down some of the larger pieces that were still held together by a few screws here and there. Within a couple of months, we had the lot almost completely cleaned up. All that remained of the house was its foundation. David had someone come out to inspect the lot to make sure that it was still buildable. To our delight, it was. First, we had blueprints drawn. Then we ordered wood. The journey had begun and I was on my way to rebuilding the house.

Topic sentence

Details

Every day for the next three months, I got up at seven thirty in the morning and picked up where I left off the night before. My hands were burning with exhaustion. Not to mention, I have the world's worst farmer's tan on my shoulders and legs. After five months of hard work, the frame was finally built. Then, I could actually start building the house. I had to get all of the technical work done before I could go any further with the building process. I got the roof done, followed by the siding. Finally, it actually began to look like a house. At the end, I got to decorate it.

Topic sentence

Details

The final result was a four-bedroom, two-and-a-half-bath masterpiece. It has all the latest luxuries: a Jacuzzi tub, heated wood floors, and a new alarm system. Every room has its own theme. The kitchen, of course, has the beach theme. The bathrooms all have the same concept of soft and inviting pastels. The master bedroom is my favorite. It has a tribal theme. The blinds are made of bamboo and the bedspread is made of the most intriguing material that is cold and silky to the touch. It has little gold beads imbedded throughout the entire surface. The other three bedrooms are simple. One has a sailboat theme; another has a train theme. The last one has an Indian-like theme, with maroon complimented by gold and various shades of green. This house truly is a dream come true.

Conclusion: Bajier reflects on the rebuilding process.

A year ago to this day, I stood staring at a pile of trash. After months and months of hard work, I could finally stand back and survey my creation. I stood on the beach facing my new home. The steady waves of wind caressed my face as they made their way past me. The sun's rays beat down on my shoulders and upper back and sent a wave of warmth racing through my entire body. All I could hear was the screeching of seagulls as they glided through the air, surfing in the wind. Clear skies blanketed the ocean for what seemed like forever. All I could think about was how grateful I was for this moment. As a cluster of emotions ran through me, I realized that this was it. My heart and soul belonged in this peaceful place that I called home—my rebuilt home.

EXAMINING STUDENT WRITING

1. Evaluate Bajier's thesis statement and its placement. How could the statement be strengthened.

2. How does Bajier organize her essay?

3. Evaluate the types of details that Bajier includes. Highlight several places where her details help you visualize the situation.

4. Evaluate Bajier's conclusion. Why is it effective?

Paragraph Writing Scenarios

Friends and Family

1. Think of a relative you were close to as a child. Write a paragraph about a time you did something together that made you laugh.

2. Write a paragraph that begins "I thought (choose a person) was my friend, but . . ."

Classes and Campus Life

1. Think of a place on campus where you usually have to wait in line. Write a paragraph about that place, what you are waiting for, and how you feel about lines.

2. Some instructors allow food and drinks in class; others don't. Write a paragraph expressing your opinion on whether or not you should be allowed to eat in class.

Working Students

1. Write a paragraph about the worst day in your week. What makes this day more difficult than the others?

2. Write a paragraph describing the perfect day off.

Communities and Cultures

1. Think of a country you've never seen but would like to visit. Write a paragraph explaining why you would like to go there. Use your imagination and plenty of details to describe what appeals to you about this country.

2. Transportation varies from place to place. Bus or plane passengers, for example, form a community. Write a paragraph about a kind of transportation you use on a regular basis. What behaviors do you share with other passengers or drivers?

Writing Success Tip 9

Avoiding Trite Expressions

Trite expressions, also known as **clichés**, are tired words and phrases that have been used so often they have become stale. They hurt your writing by making it seem lazy and bland.

The following list of trite expressions probably includes some you hear and use frequently:

add insult to injury	heavy as lead
all work and no play	hit the nail on the head
better late than never	ladder of success
beyond a shadow of a doubt	singing the blues
a drop in the bucket	strong as an ox
easier said than done	tried and true
face the music	work like a dog

Trite expressions like these take the place of original, specific, meaningful descriptions in your writing. When you use a trite expression, you have lost a chance to convey a fresh, precise impression. Meaning suffers. Notice, in the sets of sentences below, that the revised version gives you much more precise and complete information.

TRITE	I worked like a dog to finish my term paper.
REVISED	I worked until midnight every night last week to finish my term paper.

TRITE	He smokes like a chimney.
REVISED	He smokes two packs of Camel cigarettes a day.

TRITE	My favorite restaurant is a hop, skip, and a jump from my apartment.
REVISED	My favorite restaurant is a safe, easy, five-minute walk from my apartment, all downhill.

TRITE	I huffed and puffed into work thinking "better late than never," but I knew I would have to face the music.
REVISED	I jogged to work and was only a half hour late, but I knew I would get an angry lecture from my manager.

Whenever you find yourself using a trite expression, stop and take the time to reword it into an original, detailed description.

WRITING ABOUT A READING

THINKING BEFORE READING

In April 2004, Francis Bok spoke at the University of Washington about his experiences as a slave in Africa. This reading from the *Seattle Times* reports on Bok's past and present struggles. As you read, pay attention to the details. They provide important information, making the report fuller and more complete. Also notice that the author uses clear, correct, and consistent sentences throughout.

1. Preview the reading, using the steps discussed in Chapter 2, p. 38.

2. Connect the reading to your own experience by answering the following questions:

   a. Do you know of places in the world where slavery still exists?

   b. When and why was slavery eliminated in the United States?

READING

SUDANESE DESCRIBES HOW HE BECAME A SLAVE AT 7

Lornet Turnbull

1   On a day in May 1986 when all Francis Bok could think about was playing with his friends, the south Sudanese boy was rounded up in a slave raid, strapped to a donkey and taken to north Sudan. All around him in his village's market that day, he said, adults and children were slaughtered at a level of violence Bok had never seen. He was 7 years old.

2   With a simple, matter-of-fact delivery, Bok, now 23, recounted the story of his capture and subsequent escape to about 75 people at the University of Washington's HUB Auditorium this week. Bok's story is of a twentieth-century slave who eventually escaped and lived to tell the world. His **memoir**, "Escape from Slavery," has been described as the modern-day counterpart to that of Frederick Douglass, the nineteenth-century slave-turned-**abolitionist**.

memoir
autobiography

abolitionist
one who believes in getting rid of slavery

bondage
slavery

3   Bok told of spending the next 10 years in **bondage**, being beaten repeatedly, forced to eat garbage and to sleep alongside the animals he tended. When he first arrived at his new home, "the whole family came out to meet me and started beating me; even the children were whipping me with sticks," he said. "I was confused why they didn't care about a 7-year-old boy when they had children my age. They called me 'abeed' (Arabic for black slave)." Much later, when he'd learned Arabic, Bok says, he asked his master why the family was so mean. "He said to me, 'Because you are an animal.'"

4   Now an activist with the Boston-based American Anti-Slavery Group, Bok is part of a growing campaign to shed light on slavery, which exists in many parts of the world. The United Nations estimates 27 million men, women and children are forced to labor with no pay under the threat of violence. Bok's enslavement "is not an isolated incident," said Dennis Bennett, a founder of Servant's Heart, a New York-based Christian aid organization. "This is still going on."

5   Sudan, south of Egypt, is the largest country in Africa. Arab Muslims living in the north have been locked in a civil war with black Africans in the rural south and Nuba Mountains since 1986. The Islamic-controlled government of Sudan has come under fire globally for ignoring the Arab militia that has attacked, captured and enslaved black tribespeople. A few manage to escape. But more commonly, Arab rescuers operating a Sudanese version of the Underground Railroad have brought more to freedom. Since the war began, more than 2 million south Sudanese have been killed and 4 million displaced, Bennett said. About 100,000 remain in bondage.

6   Bok, some say, is lucky. He remembers clearly the day in May 1986 when his mother called him from playing to go to the market to sell milk and beans. "I didn't know that my life would change so drastically in only a few hours," he said. In a slave raid at the market that day, he and other children were rounded up and transported to the north where they were given to Arab families as slaves. He overheard someone talking about gunshots but paid them no mind. "I looked behind me and people with guns started shooting people in the market. I'd never witnessed such violence. Never seen a dead person."

7   For 10 years at the north Sudanese home of Giema Abdullah, Bok said, he tended the animals, sleeping with them, eating with them. Beatings, he said, were a daily ritual. When he was 17, with the assistance of an Arab man, he managed to get to the capital of Khartoum. From there he made his way to Egypt, a way station of sorts for many South Sudanese trying to get to the West. In August 1999, he arrived in Fargo, N.D., where a family was willing to sponsor him.

8   Initially he resisted efforts of American Anti-Slavery's president, Charles Jacobs, to bring him on board: "I didn't want to talk about what happened to me," he said. "I was in America now." But on his first visit to the organization's headquarters, he saw the images of enslaved children. "In those little boys, I saw myself," he said.

9   At the UW on Tuesday, he urged Americans to discover the truth about slavery and to "shame the U.S. government into shaming the government of Sudan" to bring about change. Bok said he's been threatened by the Sudanese government for speaking out. "They say if they catch me, they'll kill me. I say, 'So be it.' I won't abandon my people. What good is my freedom if my people are still being enslaved, still dying? We can abolish slavery once again."

GETTING READY TO WRITE

Reviewing the Reading

1. Describe the events that led to Bok's enslavement.

2. What was Bok's life as a slave like?

3. Explain the circumstances in Sudan that contribute to the slave trade there.

4. What does Bok want to accomplish now through telling his story?

5. How does the author conclude the reading? How does this make you feel?

Examining the Reading Using an Idea Map

Review the reading by completing the missing parts of the idea map shown on the following page.

Strengthening Your Vocabulary

Part A: Using the word's context, word parts, or a dictionary, write a brief definition of each of the following words or phrases as it is used in the reading.

1. subsequent (paragraph 2) _____

2. counterpart (paragraph 2) _____

3. enslavement (paragraph 4) _____

4. displaced (paragraph 5) _____

5. ritual (paragraph 7) _____

Part B: Choose one of the words above and draw a word map (see p. 84) of it.

Reacting to Ideas: Discussion and Journal Writing

Get ready to write about the reading by discussing the following:

1. Discuss your reaction to Bok's ordeal.

2. Discuss the side effects of war.

3. Bok spoke at a university about his experiences. Discuss a recent speaker who visited your campus or community. What issues did he or she address?

4. Write a journal entry about a time when you were forced to do something you did not want to do.

Visualize It!

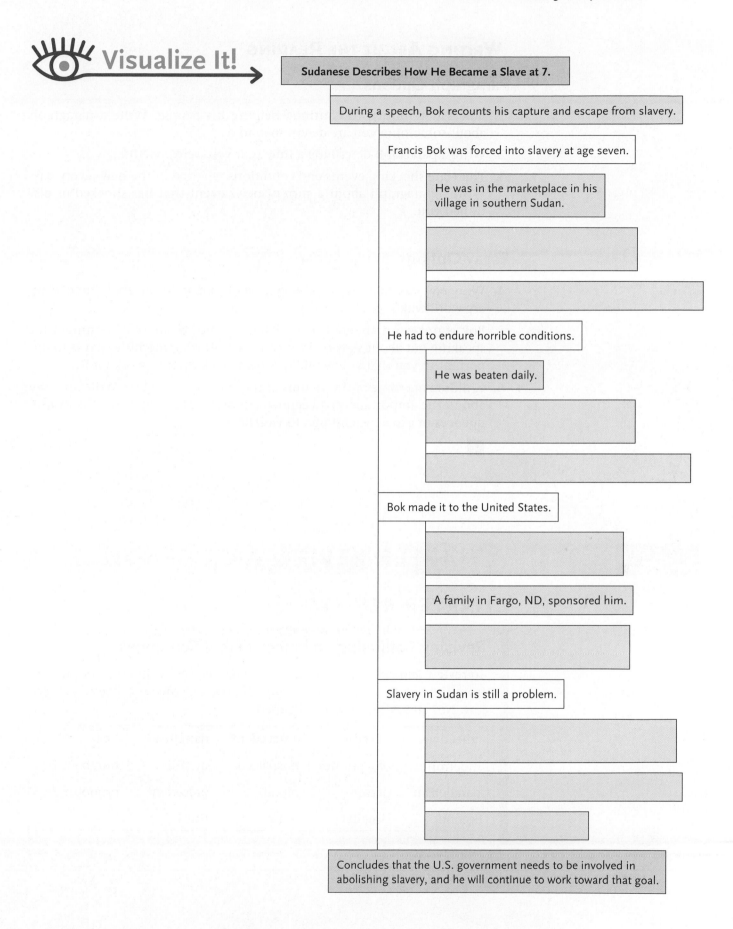

Sudanese Describes How He Became a Slave at 7.

During a speech, Bok recounts his capture and escape from slavery.

Francis Bok was forced into slavery at age seven.

He was in the marketplace in his village in southern Sudan.

He had to endure horrible conditions.

He was beaten daily.

Bok made it to the United States.

A family in Fargo, ND, sponsored him.

Slavery in Sudan is still a problem.

Concludes that the U.S. government needs to be involved in abolishing slavery, and he will continue to work toward that goal.

WRITING ABOUT THE READING

Paragraph Options

1. Bok is determined to continue helping his people. Write a paragraph about something you are determined to do.

2. Write a paragraph describing a time that you were a victim.

3. There are shocking events and conditions reported in the news every day. Write a paragraph about a current news event that has shocked or disturbed you.

Essay Options

4. Write an essay that urges our government to help in the abolition of slavery worldwide. Use Bok's story for evidence.

5. Bok is not worried about being killed by the Sudanese government for speaking out about slavery. Write an essay about something that is so important to you that you would face death to keep it or work for it.

6. Children are some of the victims of the Sudanese civil war. Write an essay about the importance of keeping children safe. What are the consequences of exposing children to violence?

■

CHAPTER REVIEW AND PRACTICE

CHAPTER REVIEW

Revising Confusing and Inconsistent Sentences

To review and check your recall of the chapter, select the word or phrase from the box below that best completes each of the sentences that follow. Not all of the words will be used.

adjectives	adverbs	antecedent	dangling	first
indefinite	-ing phrases	misplaced	modifier	number
parallelism	person	plural	precedent	pronoun
second	singular	tense	third	

1. A(n) _____ must always come before the pronoun to which it refers.

2. A pronoun and its antecedent must agree in _____. They must both be either singular or plural.

3. *Any*, *each*, *everyone*, and *some* are examples of _____ pronouns.

4. The grammatical term used to identify the speaker or writer is _____.

5. Verb _____ indicates past, present, or future.

6. A _____ is a word, phrase, or clause that describes, qualifies, or limits the meaning of another word.

7. _____ and *-ing* phrases modify nouns and pronouns.

8. A _____ modifier is a modifier that has been placed in a sentence where its meaning is unclear.

9. A _____ modifier is a word or phrase that does not clearly describe or explain any part of the sentence it is in.

10. _____ is a method of balancing a series of nouns, verbs, or adjectives in a sentence.

 **EDITING PRACTICE**

Revise the following paragraph so that all words or phrases in a series, independent clauses joined by a coordinating conjunction, and items being compared are parallel. Write your corrections above the lines.

> The first practical pair of roller skates was made in Belgium in 1759 and is designed like ice skates. The skates had two wheels instead of being made with four wheels as they are today. The wheels were aligned down the center of the skate, but were containing no ball bearings. The skates had a life of their own. Without ball bearings, they resisted turning, then were turning abruptly, and then refuse to stop. Finally, they jammed to a halt on their own. Until 1884, when ball bearings were introduced, roller-skating was unpopular, difficult, and it was
>
> *(continued)*

dangerous for people to do. However, when skating technology improved, roller-skates began to compete with ice-skating. Later, an American made roller skates with sets of wheels placed side-by-side rather than by placing them behind one another, and that design lasted until recently. Since 1980, however, many companies have been manufacturing skates based on the older design. In other words, in-line skates are back, and more and more people are discovering Rollerblading joys and that it benefits their health.

INTERNET ACTIVITIES

1. Pronoun Practice

Complete this pronoun quiz from the Online Writing Lab at Utah Valley State College.

> http://grammar.ccc.commnet.edu/grammar/cgi-shl/quiz.pl/
> pronouns_add1.htm

2. Dangling Modifiers

Print out this flowchart for identifying dangling modifiers that was put together by the Academic Center of University of Houston–Victoria. Use it to identify dangling modifiers in your reading and writing.

> http://www.uhv.edu/ac/grammar/pdf/danglingmodifiersflowchart.pdf

3. MyWritingLab

Visit this site to get more help with revising confusing and inconsistent sentences.

> http://www.mywritinglab.com

Click on the Study Plan tab, then on "Sentence Basics and Development," and then on "Using Parallelism," "Using Pronouns Clearly and Correctly," "Pronoun-Antecedent Agreement," "Using Consistent Verb Tense and Active Voice," and "Avoiding Misplaced and Dangling Modifiers."

10 Using Verbs Correctly

"Then she goes, 'I gotta go,' and I go, 'Okay,' and she goes, 'Later,' and I go, 'Go already!'"

WRITE ABOUT IT!

Have you ever stopped to listen to the way people misuse verbs? Write a sentence evaluating this teenager's use of language.

Did you notice that, in this sentence, the speaker has used "go" instead of more interesting and descriptive verbs like "yelled," "retorted," "said," "replied," "snorted," or "exclaimed"? Verbs are words that express action. Using them correctly is essential to good writing and can make the difference between something that is dull or difficult to read and something that is interesting or fun to read. In this chapter you will focus on forming verb tenses with regular and irregular verbs.

WRITING

Using Verb Tenses Correctly

The primary function of verbs is to express action or a condition. However, verbs also indicate time. <u>Verb tenses</u> tell us whether an action takes place in the present, past, or future.

The three basic verb tenses are the **simple present**, **simple past**, and **simple future.** There are also nine other verb tenses in English. To review these tenses, see Part VIII, "Reviewing the Basics," p. 558. Using verb tenses consistently (avoiding shifts in tense) is discussed in Chapter 9, on p. 240.

There are two types of verbs: *regular* and *irregular.* The forms of **regular verbs** follow a standard pattern of endings; the forms of **irregular verbs** do not. The English language contains many more regular verbs than irregular verbs.

The Simple Present Tense

The **present tense** indicates action that is occurring at the time of speaking or describes regular, habitual action.

| HABITUAL ACTION | Maria works hard. |
| ACTION AT TIME OF SPEAKING | I see a rabbit on the lawn. |

In the **simple present tense**, the verb for first person (*I* or *we*), second person (*you*) or third person plural (*they*) is the same as the infinitive; no ending is added. The verb for third person singular subjects (noun or pronoun) must end in *-s*.

To most third person singular infinitive verbs, just add *-s.* If the verb ends in *-s, -sh, -ch, -x,* or *-z,* add *-es* to make the third person singular form. If the verb ends in a consonant plus *-y,* change the *y* to *i,* and then add *-es* (*I hurry, he hurries*). If the verb ends in a vowel plus *-y,* just add *-s.* (*I stay, he stays*).

Third person singular subjects include the pronouns *he, she,* and *it* and all singular nouns (*a desk, the tall man*). In addition, uncountable nouns (*money, music, homework,* abstractions such as *beauty* and *happiness,* liquids, and so on) are followed by third person singular verbs. (*Water is essential for life.*) Singular collective nouns, such as *family, orchestra, team,* and *class,* also usually take a third person singular verb since they refer to one group.

SIMPLE PRESENT TENSE

Singular		Plural	
Subject	*Verb*	*Subject*	*Verb*
I	like	we	like
you	like	you	like
he, she, it	likes	they	like
Sam	likes	Sam and Brenda	like

In speech we often use nonstandard verb forms, and these are perfectly acceptable in informal conversation. However, these nonstandard forms are *not* used in college writing or in career writing.

In the examples on the next page, note the nonstandard forms of the verb *lift* and the way these forms differ from the correct, standard forms that you should use in your writing.

ESL Tip

For a review of all 12 *verb tenses* (how to form them and when to use them), see the ESL Guide A., "Verbs" (p. 623).

NONSTANDARD PRESENT	STANDARD PRESENT
Singular	*Singular*
I lifts	I lift
you lifts	you lift
she (he) lift	she (he) lifts
Plural	*Plural*
we lifts	we lift
you lifts	you lift
they lifts	they lift

EXERCISE 10-1

Directions: The sentences below are in the simple present tense. First, under-line the subject or subjects in each sentence. Then, circle the correct verb form.

EXAMPLE   <u>Sal</u> (pick, (picks)) apples.

1. Planes (take, takes) off from the runway every five minutes.

2. I (enjoy, enjoys) sailing.

3. She (own, owns) a pet bird.

4. We (climb, climbs) the ladder to paint the house.

5. Engines (roar, roars) as the race begins.

6. They always (answer, answers) the phone on the first ring.

7. That elephant (walk, walks) very slowly.

8. You (speak, speaks) Spanish fluently.

9. He (say, says) his name is Luis.

10. Dinosaur movies (scare, scares) me.

EXERCISE 10-2

Directions: For each of the following verbs, write a sentence using the simple present tense. Use a noun or *he, she, it,* or *they* as the subject of the sentence.

EXAMPLE   prefer   *Art prefers to sit in the front of the bus.*

1. call   _____

2. request   _____

3. laugh _____

4. grow _____

5. hide _____

ESL Tip
Subject Pronouns

Remember, in English you must include the subject pronoun with the verb. In some languages you do not need to do this because the verb ending indicates the person (first, second, or third) and number (singular or plural) of the sentence's subject.

EXAMPLE <u>He</u> goes to the store.

For more information about these words called modal auxillaries or modals, see the ESL Guide A.2. Verbs: Modal auxillaries (p. 627).

The Simple Past Tense

The **past tense** refers to action that was completed in the past. To form the **simple past tense** of regular verbs, add *-d* or *-ed* to the verb. Note that with the simple past tense, the verb form does not change with person or number.

SIMPLE PAST TENSE

Singular		Plural	
Subject	*Verb*	*Subject*	*Verb*
I	worked	we	worked
you	worked	you	worked
he, she, it	worked	they	worked
Sam	worked	Sam and Brenda	worked

ESL Tip

Occasionally, *shall* (rather than *will*) is used as the first person helping verb in the *simple future* and *future continuous* tenses. It may be used in these situations

TALKING ABOUT A SERIOUS MATTER   Our country shall win this war no matter how long it takes!

MAKING A SUGGESTION OR AN OFFER   <u>Shall</u> we be going now? <u>Shall</u> I get you some tea?

In nonstandard English, the *-d* or *-ed* is often dropped. You may hear "Last night I work all night" instead of "Last night I work*ed* all night." In written English, be sure to include the *-d* or *-ed* ending.

The Simple Future Tense

The **future tense** refers to action that *will* happen in the future. Form the **simple future tense** by adding the helping verb *will* before the verb. Note that the verb form does not change with person or number.

SIMPLE FUTURE TENSE

Singular		Plural	
Subject	*Verb*	*Subject*	*Verb*
I	will work	we	will work
you	will work	you	will work
he, she, it	will work	they	will work
Sam	will work	Sam and Brenda	will work

NEED TO KNOW

Verb Tense

- **Verb tense** indicates whether an action takes place in the present, past, or future.

- There are three basic verb tenses: **simple present**, **simple past**, and **simple future**.

- The **simple present tense** is used to describe regular, habitual action or can be used for nonaction verbs. It can also indicate action that is occurring at the time of speaking: The ending of a simple present tense verb must agree with the subject of the verb.

- The **simple past tense** refers to action that was completed in the past. For regular verbs, the simple past tense is formed by adding -d or -ed.

- The **simple future tense** refers to action that will happen in the future. The simple future tense is formed by adding the helping verb *will* before the verb.

EXERCISE 10-3

Directions: For each of the following verbs, write a sentence using the simple past tense and one using the simple future tense.

EXAMPLE   overcook   The chef overcooked my steak.
I know he will overcook my steak.

1. dance   _____

_____

2. hunt   _____

_____

3. joke   _____

_____

4. watch   _____

_____

5. photograph   _____

_____

EXERCISE 10-4
Writing in Progress

Directions: Write a paragraph on one of the following topics, using either the simple past tense or the simple future tense.

1. Selecting a movie to rent

2. Cleaning the attic or garage

3. Selecting courses for next semester

4. Buying groceries

5. Caring for a three-year-old child

Using Irregular Verbs Correctly

Errors in verb tense can occur easily with irregular verbs. Irregular verbs do not form the simple past tense according to the pattern we have studied. A regular verb forms the simple past tense by adding -*d* or -*ed*. An irregular verb forms the simple past tense by changing its spelling internally (for example, "I feed" becomes "I fed") or by not changing at all (for example, "I cut" remains "I cut").

Three Troublesome Irregular Verbs

The verbs *be, do,* and *have* can be especially troublesome. You should master the correct forms of these verbs in both the present tenses and the past tenses since they are used so often.

1. Irregular Verb: Be

	Present	*Past*
Singular	I am	I was
	you are	you were
	he, she, it is	he, she, it was
Plural	we are	we were
	you are	you were
	they are	they were

- It is nonstandard to use *be* for all present tense forms.

INCORRECT	I <u>be</u> finished.
CORRECT	I <u>am</u> finished.

INCORRECT	They <u>be</u> surprised.
CORRECT	They <u>are</u> surprised.

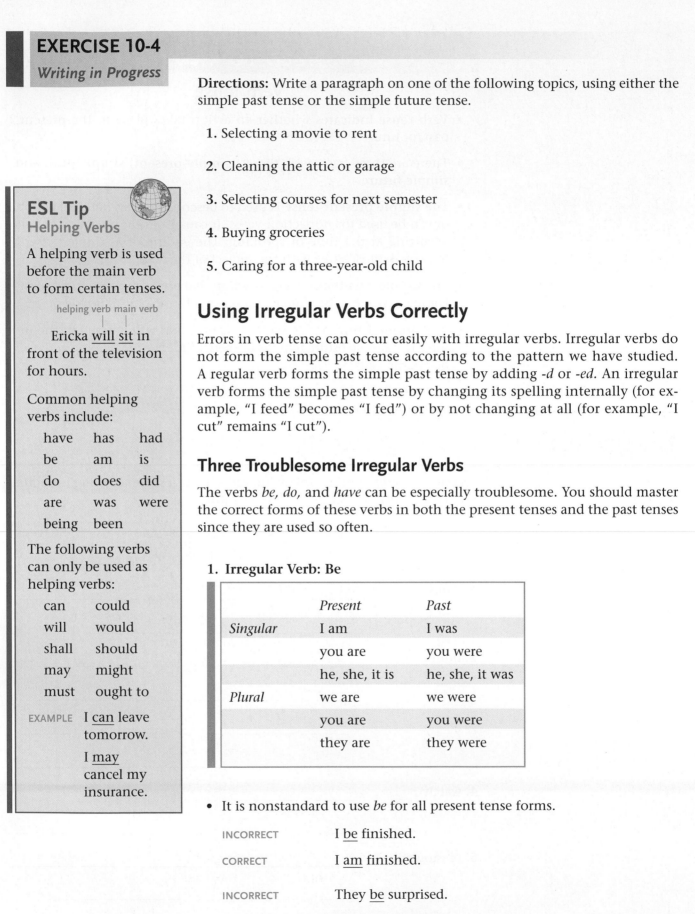

ESL Tip
Helping Verbs

A helping verb is used before the main verb to form certain tenses.

helping verb main verb

Ericka <u>will</u> <u>sit</u> in front of the television for hours.

Common helping verbs include:

have	has	had
be	am	is
do	does	did
are	was	were
being	been	

The following verbs can only be used as helping verbs:

can	could
will	would
shall	should
may	might
must	ought to

EXAMPLE I <u>can</u> leave tomorrow.

I <u>may</u> cancel my insurance.

- Another error is to use *was* instead of *were* for plural past tenses or with <u>*you*</u>.

INCORRECT	We <u>was</u> late.
CORRECT	We <u>were</u> late.

INCORRECT	<u>You</u> <u>was</u> wrong.
CORRECT	You <u>were</u> wrong.

- Note that the verb *to be* never takes an object.

2. Irregular Verb: Do

	Present	Past
Singular	I do	I did
	you do	you did
	he, she, it <u>does</u>	he, she, it did
Plural	we do	we did
	you do	you did
	they do	they did

- A common error is to use *does* instead of *do* for present plural forms.

INCORRECT	We <u>does</u> our best.
CORRECT	We <u>do</u> our best.

INCORRECT	They <u>doesn't</u> know the answer.
CORRECT	They <u>don't</u> know the answer.

- Another error is to use *done* instead of *did* for past plural forms.

INCORRECT	We <u>done</u> everything. You <u>done</u> finish.
CORRECT	We <u>did</u> everything. You <u>did</u> finish.

3. Irregular Verb: Have

	Present	Past
Singular	I have	I had
	you have	you had
	he, she, it has	he, she, it had
Plural	we have	we had
	you have	you had
	they have	they had

- A common, nonstandard form uses *has* instead of *have* for the present plural.

  INCORRECT   We <u>has</u> enough. They <u>has</u> a good reason.

  CORRECT   We <u>have</u> enough. They <u>have</u> a good reason.

- Another error occurs in the past singular.

  INCORRECT   I <u>has</u> nothing to give you. You <u>has</u> a bad day.

  CORRECT   I <u>had</u> nothing to give you. You <u>had</u> a bad day.

EXERCISE 10-5

Directions: Circle the correct, standard form of the verb in each of the following sentences.

EXAMPLE   Last April Anne (was, were) in Nevada.

1. After I watched the news, I (does, did) my homework.

2. You (be, were) lucky to win the raffle.

3. The electrician (have, has) enough time to complete the job.

4. When I am reading about the Civil War, I (am, be) captivated.

5. All the waitresses I know (have, has) sore feet.

6. We (was, were) at the grocery store yesterday.

7. He (do, does) his studying at the library.

8. We (did, done) the jigsaw puzzle while it rained.

9. Alice Walker (be, is) a favorite author of mine.

10. You (was, were) in the audience when the trophy was awarded.

EXERCISE 10-6

Directions: Write a sentence for each irregular verb shown below. Try to write several sentences that ask questions.

EXAMPLE   am <u>I am going to the Bulls game tonight.</u>

                 be <u>Will you be at home tonight?</u>

1. do   _____

   does _____

2. was   _____

   were   _____

3. is   _____

   be   _____

4. do   _____

   did   _____

5. am   _____

   was   _____

EXERCISE 10-7

Directions: Write sentences for each pair of irregular verbs shown below. Use a plural pronoun (*we, you, they*) or a plural noun.

EXAMPLE   be <u>We will be at my dad's house.</u>

    were <u>They were happy to see us.</u>

1. do   _____

   did   _____

2. are   _____

   be   _____

3. have   _____

   had   _____

4. are   _____

   were   _____

5. be   _____

   were   _____

EXERCISE 10-8

Directions: Read the following student paragraph and correct all verb errors.

Sometimes first impressions of people is very inaccurate and can lead to problems. My brother, Larry, learn this the hard way. When he was 17, Larry and I was driving to the mall. Larry decided to pick up a hitchhiker because he looks safe and trustworthy. After the man got in the car, we notice that he was wearing a knife. A few miles later, the man suddenly tell us to take him to Canada. So my brother said we'd have to stop for gas and explained that he did not have any money. The man get out of the car to pump the gas. When he goes up to the attendant to pay for the gas, we took off. We do not stop until we reach the police station, where we tell the officer in charge what happens. The police caught the man several miles from the gas station. He be serving time in prison for burglary and had escaped over the weekend. Later, Larry said, "I was lucky that my first impression were not my last!"

Other Irregular Verbs

Among the other verbs that form the past tense in irregular ways are *become (became)*, *drive (drove)*, *hide (hid)*, *stand (stood)*, and *wear (wore)*. For a list of the past-tense forms of other common irregular verbs, see Part VIII, p. 558. If you have a question about the form of a verb, consult this list or your dictionary.

Confusing Pairs of Irregular Verbs

Two particularly confusing pairs of irregular verbs are *lie/lay* and *sit/set*.

Lie/Lay

Lie means to recline. *Lay* means to put something down. The past tense of *lie* is *lay*. The past tense of *lay* is *laid*.

SIMPLE PRESENT	SIMPLE PAST
Command the dog to <u>lie</u> down.	The dog <u>lay</u> down.
<u>Lay</u> the boards over here.	The carpenter <u>laid</u> the boards over there.

Sit/Set

Sit means to be seated. *Set* means to put something down. The past tense of *sit* is *sat*. The past tense of *set* is *set*.

SIMPLE PRESENT	SIMPLE PAST
Please <u>sit</u> over here.	We <u>sat</u> over here.
<u>Set</u> the books on the table.	He <u>set</u> the books on the table.

NEED TO KNOW

Irregular Verbs

- An **irregular verb** does not form the simple past tense with *-d* or *-ed*.

- Three particularly troublesome irregular verbs are *be, do,* and *have*.

- Two confusing pairs of verbs are *lie/lay* and *sit/set*. Each has a unique meaning.

EXERCISE 10-9

Directions: Circle the correct verb in each of the following sentences.

EXAMPLE   Eric plans to (lay, (lie)) in bed all day.

1. The chef (sat, set) the mixer on "high" to beat the eggs.

2. I prefer to (lie, lay) on the hammock rather than on a chaise.

3. The students (sit, set) in rows to take the exam.

4. After putting up the wallboard, James (lay, laid) the hammer on the floor.

5. Bags of grain (set, sat) on the truck.

6. I'm going to (lie, lay) down and take a short nap.

7. Because we came late, we (sat, set) in the last row.

8. The kitten (lay, laid) asleep in the laundry basket.

9. Bob (sat, set) the groceries on the counter.

10. Completely exhausted, Shawna (lay, laid) on the sofa.

Avoiding Subject-Verb Agreement Errors

A subject and its verb must agree (be consistent) in person (first, second, third) and in number (singular, plural). (For more on pronoun forms, see p. 553; for more on verb forms in all persons and number, see p. 557.)

The most common problems with subject-verb agreement occur with third-person present tense verbs, which are formed for most verbs by adding -*s* or -*es*. (For the present tense and past tense forms of certain irregular verbs, see p. 558.)

Agreement Rules

1. **Use the present tense ending -*s* or -*es* if a verb's subject is third-person singular.** For first and second person, no ending is added.

Singular Subject	Verb	Singular Subject	Verb
I	talk	it	talks
you	talk	Sally	talks
he	talks	a boy	talks
she	talks		

2. **For a plural subject (more than one person, place, thing, or idea), use a plural form of the verb.**

Plural Subject	Verb	Plural Subject	Verb
We	talk	Sally and James	talk
you	talk	boys	talk
they	talk		

Common Errors

The following circumstances often lead to errors in subject-verb agreement:

1. **Third-person singular** A common error is to omit the -*s* or -*es* in a third-person singular verb in the present tense. The subjects *he, she,* and *it,* or a noun that could be replaced with *he, she,* or *it,* all take a third-person singular verb.

INCORRECT   She act like a professional.

CORRECT   She acts like a professional.

INCORRECT   Professor Simmons pace while he lectures.

CORRECT   Professor Simmons paces while he lectures.

2. **Verbs before their subjects** When a verb comes before its subject, as in sentences beginning with *Here* or *There,* it is easy to make an agreement

error. *Here* and *there* are never subjects of a sentence and do not determine the correct form of the verb. Look for the subject *after* the verb and, depending on its number, choose a singular or plural verb.

singular verb   singular subject

There <u>is</u> a <u>pebble</u> in my shoe.

plural verb   plural subject

There <u>are</u> two <u>pebbles</u> in my shoe.

3. **Words between the subject and its verb** Words, phrases, and clauses coming between the subject and its verb do not change the fact that the verb must agree with the subject. To check that the verb is correct, mentally remove everything between the subject and its verb and make sure that the verb agrees in number with its subject.

singular subject   singular verb

A <u>list</u> of course offerings <u>is posted</u> on the bulletin board.

plural subject   plural verb

<u>Details</u> of the accident <u>were not released</u>.

Note: Phrases beginning with prepositions such as *along with, together with, as well as,* and *in addition to* are not part of the subject and should not be considered in determining the number of the verb.

singular subject   singular verb

The <u>stereo</u>, together with the radios, televisions, and lights, <u>goes</u> dead during electrical storms.

Note: Using contractions such as *here's* and *there's* leads to mistakes because you cannot "hear" the mistake. "Here's two pens" may not sound incorrect, but "Here is two pens" does.

4. **Compound subjects** Two or more subjects joined by the coordinating conjunction *and* require a plural verb, even if one or both of the subjects are singular.

INCORRECT   <u>Anita</u> and <u>Mark</u> <u>plays</u> cards.

CORRECT   <u>Anita</u> and <u>Mark</u> <u>play</u> cards.

When a compound subject is joined by the conjunctions *or, nor, either . . . or, neither . . . nor, not . . . but,* or *not only . . . but also,* the verb should agree with the subject nearer to it.

<u>Neither</u> the <u>book</u> <u>nor</u> the <u>article</u> <u>was</u> helpful to my research.

<u>Sarah</u> <u>or</u> the <u>boys</u> <u>are</u> coming tomorrow.

> ## NEED TO KNOW
> ### Subject-Verb Agreement
>
> - A **subject** of a sentence must agree (be consistent) with the **verb** in person (first, second, or third) and in number (singular or plural).
>
> - Watch for errors when using the third-person singular, placing verbs before their subjects, using compound subjects, and adding words, phrases, or clauses between the subject and the verb.

EXERCISE 10-10

Directions: Circle the verb that correctly completes each sentence.

EXAMPLE   The newspapers (is, (are)) on the desk.

1. The hubcaps that fell off the car (was, were) expensive to replace.

2. The conductor and orchestra members (ride, rides) a bus to their concerts.

3. A Little League team (practice, practices) across the street each Tuesday.

4. Here (is, are) the computer disk I borrowed.

5. Not only the news reporters but also the weather forecaster (are broadcasting, is broadcasting) live from the circus tonight.

6. Nobody older than 12 (ride, rides) the merry-go-round.

7. The discussion panel (offer, offers) its separate opinions after the debate.

8. Terry's green shorts (hang, hangs) in his gym locker.

9. Several of the cookies (taste, tastes) stale.

10. A mime usually (wear, wears) all-black or all-white clothing.

EXERCISE 10-11

Directions: Circle the verb that correctly completes each sentence.

EXAMPLE   Everybody (like, (likes)) doughnuts for breakfast.

1. Physics (is, are) a required course for an engineering degree.

2. Most of my courses last semester (was, were) in the morning.

3. The orchestra members who (is, are) carrying their instruments will be able to board the plane first.

4. Suzanne (sing, sings) a touching version of "America the Beautiful."

5. Here (is, are) the performers who juggle plates.

6. Kin Lee and his parents (travel, travels) to Ohio tomorrow.

7. A box of old and valuable stamps (is, are) in the safe-deposit box at the bank.

8. The family (sit, sits) together in church each week.

9. Judith and Erin (arrive, arrives) at the train station at eleven o'clock.

10. Directions for the recipe (is, are) on the box.

EXERCISE 10-12

Directions: Revise any sentences that contain errors in subject-verb agreement.

Los Angeles have some very interesting and unusual buildings. There is the Victorian houses on Carroll Avenue, for example. The gingerbread-style trim and other ornate architectural features makes those houses attractive to tourists and photographers. The Bradbury Building and the Oviatt Building was both part of the nineteenth-century skyline. They was restored as office buildings that now houses twentieth-century businesses. Some of the architecture in Los Angeles seem to disguise a building's function. One of the most startling sights are a building that look like a huge ship.

Using Active Instead of Passive Voice

When a verb is in the active voice, the subject performs the action of the verb.

                                   subject   active-voice verb

ACTIVE VOICE   Mr. Holt opened his briefcase.

When a verb is in the **passive voice**, the subject is the receiver of the action of the verb.

                                   subject   passive-voice verb

PASSIVE VOICE   The briefcase was opened.

ESL Tip

For more information about forms and uses of the *passive voice,* see the ESL Guide A.4, "Verbs: Passive Voice" (p. 630).

This passive-voice sentence does not name the person who opened the briefcase. Passive-voice sentences seem indirect, as if the writer were purposefully avoiding giving information the reader might need or want.

PASSIVE VOICE   The fingerprints <u>had been</u> carefully <u>wiped</u> away.

PASSIVE VOICE   The vase <u>had been broken</u>.

Both active and passive voices are grammatically correct. However, the active voice is usually more effective because it is simpler, more informative, and more direct. Use the active rather than the passive voice unless

1. **you do not know who or what performs the action of the verb.**

   PASSIVE   The broken window <u>had been wiped</u> clean of fingerprints.

2. **you want to emphasize the object of the action rather than who or what performs the action.**

   PASSIVE   The poem "The Chicago Defender Sends a Man to Little Rock" by Gwendolyn Brooks <u>was discussed</u> in class. [Here, exactly who discussed the poem is less important than what poem was discussed.]

As a general rule, try to avoid writing passive-voice sentences. Get in the habit of putting the subject—the person or thing performing the action—at the beginning of each sentence. If you do this, you will usually avoid the passive voice.

NEED TO KNOW

Active and Passive Voices

- When a verb is in the **active voice**, the subject performs the action.

- When a verb is in the **passive voice**, the subject receives the action.

- Because the active voice is straightforward and direct, use it unless you do not know who or what performed the action or want to emphasize the object of the action rather than who or what performed it.

EXERCISE 10-13

Directions: Revise each of the following sentences by changing the verb from passive to active voice.

EXAMPLE   The china cups and saucers were painted carefully by Lois and her friends.

REVISED   <u>Lois and her friends carefully painted the china cups and saucers.</u>

1. *Goodnight Moon* was read by the mother to her daughter.

_____

2. The maple tree was trimmed by the telephone company.

_____

3. The vacuum cleaner was repaired by Mr. Fernandez.

_____

4. Many bags of flour were donated by the fraternity.

_____

5. Six quarts of strawberries were made into jam by Alice.

_____

6. Cornrows were braided into Pam's hair by Felicia.

_____

7. Tanya was driven to Weston City by Janice.

_____

8. The transmission was repaired by Mike.

_____

9. Potholes were filled by the city employees.

_____

10. Grapes were pressed into juice by the winemaker.

_____

EXERCISE 10-14

Directions: Revise each of the following sentences by changing the verb from passive to active voice

EXAMPLE   The patient was operated on by an experienced surgeon.

REVISED   _An experienced surgeon operated on the patient._

1. The coin collection was inherited by Roderick from his grandfather.

_____

2. A large bunch of roses was cut by my sister.

_____

3. The president's advisers were relied on by the president.

_____

4. Ice cream was served to the children at the birthday party by one of the adults.

_____

5. Tools were packed in a box by Terry.

_____

6. Scuba-diving equipment was handed to the students by the licensed instructor.

_____

7. Alaska was visited by my parents last fall.

_____

8. A large rock bass was caught by James.

_____

9. The newspaper was delivered by a 12-year-old girl on her bike.

_____

10. Trash was collected and disposed of by the picnickers before they left for home.

_____

EXERCISE 10-15

Writing in Progress

Directions: Reread the paragraph you wrote in Exercise 10-4. Check for subject-verb agreement errors and for sentences you wrote in the passive voice. Revise as necessary.

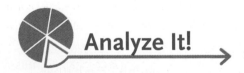 **Analyze It!**

Directions: Revise the following paragraph by correcting all verb usage errors.

The summer I turned ten, I learned the difference between being alone and being lonely. Growing up in a large family, I never had much time to myself, but that summer I visit my aunt for three weeks. She lived in the country, and I was the only kid for miles around. At first, I had felt lonely without my brothers and sisters, but then I discover the boulders in the woods. The jumble of huge rocks was endlessly fascinating. Some days I was an explorer, moving from one rock to another, surveying the countryside from the tallest boulder. Some days, I retired to my secret fort, tucked in a shadowy crevice. I furnished my rocky fort with an old cushion to set on and a cigar box for collecting treasures. On sunny mornings, before the air has lost its early chill, I laid on the flattest boulder, its smooth surface warming my skinny arms and legs. The boulders were my audience when I read aloud the stories I had wrote. I remember many things about my time alone in the woods that summer, but I don't recall ever feeling lonely.

A STUDENT ESSAY

The Writer

Rachel Goodman successfully completed her associate's degree at Middlesex County College in Edison, New Jersey, in May 2005, and transferred to Westchester University in Pennsylvania where she enrolled in the Elementary Education program, planning to become an elementary school English teacher.

The Writing Task

For a writing class, she was asked to write an essay about a place or places that have influenced her life. As you read, notice that she uses correct and consistent verbs throughout.

Title: identifies the subject of the essay

The Places in My Life
Rachel Goodman

Identifies the places she will discuss

Thesis statement

Place 1

Topic sentence

Topic sentence

Place 2

Topic sentence

I am a product of certain places in my life. For me, a place is the location of an event. Some of the most important places in my life have been a workplace, my grandparents' home in Florida, and the house my parents own. Each of these places has helped to shape the person I am today and who I will be in the future.

The workplace that had the biggest effect on me was a distribution company called Direct Fastening. I was in the twelfth grade and had never experienced a place like this before. Direct Fastening is a distributor of tools and building equipment. Every day at 1:00 P.M., Monday through Friday, I'd push aside the heavy glass doors and walk in. I'd say "hey" to the owner, Bill, who was usually behind the front counter, on the phone. Next, I'd hang up my coat and walk into the small room that served as the office. The phone would ring every two minutes, and I'd have to grab it and find the man it was for in the back room.

The back room, which took up the majority of the space, was as messy and chaotic as the office. All around me men were cursing, smoking cigarettes, and talking about women in ways that embarrassed me, as if they were playthings instead of human beings. I realized how uncomfortable I was being the only teenaged girl in this place and decided to never again put myself in a place filled with big, scruffy, rude, middle-aged men.

When my grandparents were alive, I looked forward to visits with them in their home in Fort Lauderdale, Florida. I went about once a year, when I was between the ages of one and twelve. Sometimes I took the three-hour plane ride all by myself. They lived in a beautiful white condominium where lots of other little old people lived. When I walked in, there were little silver bells that chimed magically as I opened the door. The guest room had a beautiful bathroom of white tile and flowered wallpaper that smelled of strawberry soap and coconut shampoo. It felt very luxurious, like an expensive hotel. But the best part of the condo was my grandparents' closet. It smelled wonderful, like my grandmother's Chantilly perfume. I would spend hours in there, trying on her old-fashioned, pastel-colored dresses and nightgowns. I knew that when I came to this place I would receive unconditional love. It was impossible to be unhappy there. My visits to that pretty, good-smelling place were the best times of my life.

Place 3

My immediate family's place, on the other hand, has been changeable. We've lived in four different houses. Finally we are settled into something permanent. The house we're in now is by far the best. There has been very little screaming and arguing in this house, but plenty of laughter and singing.

Topic sentence

Whenever I think of home, I appreciate how lucky I am to have such a loving and supportive family. I know I can turn to them when times are hard, something some of my friends don't have. This house, this place, is the one that suits me the best.

Conclusion: She reflects on the importance of place

There are many places that can influence a person's life. Each of the places I've described has helped shape my personality. I know that as I make other changes, places—where I am when important things happen—will influence who I become.

Examining Student Writing

1. Do you think it was effective for Goodman to write about three places instead of choosing just one? Did her choice to use three places strengthen her essay?

2. What is the benefit of identifying the three places in the first paragraph?

3. Evaluate Goodman's introduction and conclusion. How could she improve them?

4. The places Goodman discusses do not seem to be in any particular order. Suggest alternative ways Goodman could have organized her essay.

Paragraph Writing Scenarios

Friends and Family

1. Think of a family member who works very hard. Write a paragraph about the kind of dream vacation you would treat this person to if you could.

2. Write a paragraph about a pet owned by someone you know. Use details to describe what makes this animal special, cute, annoying, sweet, or unusual.

Classes and Campus Life

1. Some people are "morning people." Others would describe themselves as "night people." Write a paragraph about your own daily energy levels—when you're the most awake and ready to go and when you're the most sluggish. Include information about what

are your ideal times for going to sleep and waking up. Explain how this fits with your college class schedule.

2. Some campuses are sprawling, stately, or spacious places. Others are crammed into cement corners of urban neighborhoods. Write a paragraph that describes the physical place and atmosphere of your school's campus. Use details and plenty of descriptive words to "paint a picture" for your reader.

Working Students

1. Some employers are hesitant about hiring students, while others particularly like having students work for them. Write a paragraph about what you think might make an employer nervous about hiring a student. What would you say about yourself to overcome that employer's fears?

2. A job application asks for references. Choose someone you would use as a reference and write a paragraph describing what you think they would say about you.

Communities and Cultures

1. When we say "culture" we are usually talking about a way of life. Some people identify more closely with the traditional culture of their ancestors, while others follow the trends and fashions of popular culture. Write a paragraph describing which influences you more, the customs, religion, dress, foods, arts, or language of your traditional culture, or the fashions, music, trends, and news from the TV, movies, magazines, or newspapers of popular culture.

2. People migrate from all over the world to the United States in search of the "American dream." To some, this means religious freedom. To others, it means the search for fame and fortune. Write a paragraph describing your idea of the "American dream."

Writing Success Tip 10

Eliminating Wordiness and Redundancy

Wordiness results when you use more words than necessary to convey a message:

> The rushed and pressured <u>nature</u> of nursing <u>is due to the fact that</u> hospitals lack adequate staff.

This sentence can be shortened:

> Nurses are rushed and pressured because hospitals lack adequate staff.

(continued)

To eliminate wordiness:

1. **Look for words that do not add meaning, and eliminate them.** You may need to rearrange the words in your sentence, as in the above example.

2. **Eliminate empty words and phrases and make substitutions.**

WORDY PHRASE	SUBSTITUTE
spell out in detail	detail, explain
the only difference being that	except
it is clear that	clearly
in the vicinity of	near
on the grounds that	because
at this point in time	now

3. **Use strong verbs that carry full meaning.** Replace weak verbs such as *is, has, makes.*

   WEAK VERB   The workers <u>made</u> slow progress.

   REVISED   The workers <u>progressed</u> slowly.

4. **Avoid saying the same thing twice in two different ways (redundancy).**

REDUNDANT	CLEAR
square in shape	square [square is a shape]
mental attitude	attitude [the only type of attitude is a mental one]
the year of 1999	1999 [1999 is a year]

WRITING ABOUT A READING

THINKING BEFORE READING

This article by nurse Paul Duke first appeared in *Newsweek* on February 2, 2004. The author describes the working conditions of emergency room nurses. Notice how he develops his points and leads the reader to his final conclusions. Also notice how he uses verbs correctly and follows a consistent tense.

1. Preview the reading, using the steps discussed in Chapter 2, p. 38.

2. Connect the reading to your own experience by answering the following questions:

   a. Is nursing a profession you would consider?

   b. What type of service have you or those you know received in an emergency room?

READING

IF ER NURSES CRASH, WILL PATIENTS FOLLOW?

I'm so overworked that I go home at night praying I haven't made a mistake that might hurt someone.

Paul Duke

1   I was sprinting down the hall when a patient waiting to be seen by a doctor asked me for a blanket. She was in her mid-70s, cold, scared and without any family or friends nearby. Did I have time to get her that blanket, or even stop to say a few words to let her know she wasn't alone? No, I didn't.

2   As an emergency-room nurse, I'm constantly forced to shuffle the needs of the sick and injured. At that particular moment, half of my 12 patients were screaming for pain medication, most of the others needed to be rushed off to tests, and one was desperately trying not to die on me.

3   Was that blanket important in the grand scheme of things? Not really. She wasn't going to die without it. So it got tossed on the back burner, along with my compassion.

4   I often find myself hopping from task to task just to keep everyone alive. By the end of the shift, I often wonder, did I kill anyone today? I go home tired and beaten down, praying like mad that I didn't make any mistakes that hurt anyone.

LIFE OR DEATH: The charge nurse told me to keep the five sickest patients alive, and get to the rest when I could.

5   For five years I have worked in one of the busiest emergency rooms in southeastern Michigan. For the last two, I have picked up overtime by working in four other hospitals, including the busiest emergency room in inner-city Detroit. No matter where I am, I experience the same problem—too many patients, not enough staff.

6   When I started emergency-room nursing five years ago, I would typically have four or five patients. I could spend a few minutes chatting with them and answering their questions. Let's face it, when you are in a drafty emergency room in just a flimsy paper gown and your underwear, it is nice to have someone actually talk to you. It's a scary experience to get poked and prodded in various parts of your anatomy.

7   But now on an average day I have 10 to 12 patients. Once I even had 22. On that night I was feeling swamped, so I went to the charge nurse for help. She was as busy as I was, so she told me to take the five sickest patients and keep them alive, and get to the rest when I could. Now, here's a question: do you want to be one of the five sickest who get attention right away, or one of the others who have to wait maybe seven, eight or even 10 hours before someone gets to you?

8   That night I staggered home grateful that nobody had died. But I wondered, do I really want to do this job? I love the emergency room, but I was so damn frustrated. Was it just me?

9   I did an informal survey of the emergency rooms where I work. Every nurse I spoke to said the patient load had at least doubled in the last three years. None of them expected the situation to get better soon.

10   Troubling, but hardly scientific, so I did a little digging for some real statistics. According to the Centers for Disease Control and Prevention, from 1997 through 2000 the annual number of emergency-room visits went from 95 million to 108 million, while the number of ERs decreased. So who picked up the slack? The staff at emergency rooms, like mine, that are still standing.

11   The journal Nursing 2003 reports that approximately three out of 10 R.N.s believe their hospital has enough nurses to provide excellent care. Not exactly what you want to hear from the people responsible for your loved one's health.

12   The future doesn't look any brighter. Studies show that by 2010, 40 percent of all registered nurses will be over 50. That's when most of us are getting ready to cut back our hours or switch from direct patient care to chart review. By 2020 there will be an estimated shortfall of 808,400 nurses, partly because many will have retired or become so dissatisfied that they've quit, but also because fewer people are entering the profession. Yet the number of Americans older than 65 is expected to double from 35 million to 70 million over the next two decades. As someone who knows just how often the elderly visit ERs due to heart attacks, strokes, and falls, I see trouble ahead.

13   Don't get me wrong—my colleagues are some of the hardest-working and most professional nurses you will find. But when you're given 20 patients when you should have six, well, you're only so good.

14   After all this you, must wonder why I don't quit. The truth is, I love nursing. It's what I am good at. I love the challenge of not knowing what will come crashing through the doors. Emergency-room nurses rise to the occasion. But we are being steamrolled, stretched thin and beaten down, and the best of us are frustrated.

15   At the end of my 18-hour shift I got that little old lady her blanket and spent a few minutes talking to her. She took my hand, smiled and said thank you.

16   I'm frustrated, but I'll be back.

GETTING READY TO WRITE

Reviewing the Reading

1. Describe Duke's working conditions.

2. What does the author worry about in his own job? How does he deal with these worries?

3. Summarize the nursing crisis that Duke anticipates.

4. What details does Duke include that make the report effective?

5. Why does Duke include statistics and research findings?

6. What conclusions does the author make? How do these make you feel?

Examining the Reading Using an Idea Map

Review the reading by completing the missing parts of the idea map shown below.

Strengthening Your Vocabulary

Part A: Using the word's context, word parts, or a dictionary, write a brief definition of each of the following words or phrases as it is used in the reading.

1. shuffle (paragraph 2) _____

2. desperately (paragraph 2) _____

3. compassion (paragraph 3) _____

4. flimsy (paragraph 6) _____

5. slack (paragraph 10) _____

Part B: Choose one of the words above and draw a word map (see p. 84) of it.

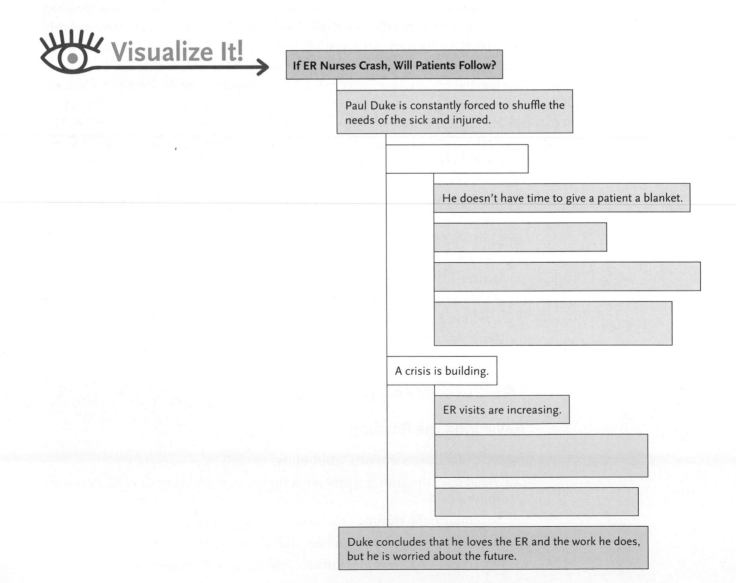

Visualize It!

If ER Nurses Crash, Will Patients Follow?

Paul Duke is constantly forced to shuffle the needs of the sick and injured.

He doesn't have time to give a patient a blanket.

A crisis is building.

ER visits are increasing.

Duke concludes that he loves the ER and the work he does, but he is worried about the future.

Reacting to Ideas: Discussion and Journal Writing

Get ready to write about the reading by discussing the following:

1. What personal qualities make Duke a good nurse?

2. Consider the potential crisis that Duke predicts. What are some of the possible solutions?

3. Discuss the treatment and service that you have received from the medical profession.

4. Write a journal entry about a time that you felt overworked at school or a job.

WRITING ABOUT THE READING

Paragraph Options

1. Duke wanted to help all his patients to the best of his abilities, but sometimes he just could not. Write a paragraph about a time when someone asked for your help, but you could not or did not give it.

2. Write a paragraph explaining whether you agree or disagree with the charge nurse's direction that Duke concentrate on keeping five patients alive.

3. Duke worries about doing things on the job that might hurt someone. Write a paragraph about a responsibility that you have (or had) that involves the well-being of others.

Essay Options

4. Identify another occupation whose members are overworked or highly stressed. Write an essay that compares and contrasts the working conditions of this occupation with that of nursing.

5. Write an essay that describes the ER experience from a patient's point of view using information from the reading. For example, you could be the 70-year-old woman who wants a blanket. Feel free to invent details.

6. Duke's job is stressful, yet he enjoys it. Write an essay about job stress. Identify its causes, and explain whether you feel it is beneficial or harmful.

CHAPTER REVIEW AND PRACTICE

CHAPTER REVIEW

Using Verbs Correctly

To review and check your recall of the chapter, match each term in Column A with its meaning in Column B. Write the letter in the space provided.

COLUMN A	COLUMN B
_____ 1. simple present	**a.** using more words than necessary to convey a message
_____ 2. simple past	**b.** the verb tense used for action that is happening at the time of the writing
_____ 3. compound subjects	**c.** the subject performs the action of the verb
_____ 4. irregular verbs	**d.** verb tense indicating action that has already been completed
_____ 5. subject-verb agreement error	**e.** verbs whose endings do not follow a standard pattern
_____ 6. active voice	**f.** when the subject receives the action of the verb
_____ 7. passive voice	**g.** when the subject and verb in a sentence are not consistent in person or number
_____ 8. wordiness	**h.** two or more subjects joined by a conjunction and requiring a plural verb

EDITING PRACTICE

The following student paragraph has been revised to correct all errors except for those in subject-verb agreement and shifts in person and number. Complete the revision by correcting all such problems.

Now that the fascination with exercise has been in full swing for a decade, the public are starting to get tired of our nation's overemphasis on fitness. It seems as though every time you turn on the TV or pick up a newspaper or talk with a friend, all we hear about is how we don't exercise enough. The benefits of exercise is clear, but do we really need to have them repeated to us in sermonlike fashion every time we turn around? Each of us are at a point now where we are made to feel almost guilty if we haven't joined a health club or, at the very least, participated in some heavy-duty exercise every day. It may be time you realized that there's better ways to get exercise than these. Americans might be better off just exercising in a more natural way. Taking a walk or playing a sport usually fit in better with our daily routines and isn't so strenuous. It could even be that our obsession with extreme forms of exercise may be less healthy than not exercising at all.

INTERNET ACTIVITIES

1. Verb Quiz

Try these additional online quizzes on subject-verb agreement from Capital Community College.

http://grammar.ccc.commnet.edu/GRAMMAR/cgi-shl/quiz.pl/sv_agr_quiz.htm

http://grammar.ccc.commnet.edu/GRAMMAR/quizzes/svagr2.htm

2. Active vs. Passive Voice

Active voice is especially important in business writing. Read over this information from Spaulding Associates, and use it to identify and correct passive constructions in a business article.

http://www.spauldingassociates.com/ActivePassive.htm

3. MyWritingLab

Visit this site to get more help with verbs.

http://www.mywritinglab.com

Click on the Study Plan tab, then on "Common Sentence Problems and How to Avoid Them," and then on "Using Verb Tense Correctly" and "Using Regular and Irregular Verbs Correctly."

11

Planning and Organizing

WRITE ABOUT IT!

Imagine for a moment that this is your kitchen, and you have only one hour to prepare a meal for someone important. It could be your boss, your future in-laws, or someone else you want to impress. Write a sentence describing how you would feel about this task, explaining whether you could pull it together in time and whether it would be as good as you'd like it to be.

You would probably have trouble preparing a meal in an hour because the kitchen is disorganized. Planning and organization are important in writing as well as in meal preparation. First, you have to choose a topic, just as you have to choose a main dish. Next, you have to plan and organize the details you'll write about, just as you have to plan a menu and organize the order in which you prepare each item. Plan properly, and you'll have a delicious meal. Organize well, and you won't be looking for the onions while the garlic burns.

Finally, planning and organizing your paragraph or paper will help to ensure its success, just as planning and organizing the details of your dinner will help to impress your guests. In this chapter you will learn to choose a topic, consider your audience, and generate and organize ideas.

WRITING

Choosing a Topic

Many times, your instructor will assign a topic to write about. Other times, however, instructors will ask you to write a paragraph or essay on a topic of your own choice. The topic you choose often determines how successful your writing will be. The following tips will help you choose a workable topic:

1. **Look for an idea, not just for a topic.** An idea makes a point or states an opinion about a topic. For example, instead of deciding to write about children, start with an idea: "Children often reflect their parents' attitudes." Or, "Children need their own personal space." Or, instead of trying to write about computers, start with the idea that computers are becoming more and more important in everyone's life. Start with an idea!

2. **Look for familiar topics and ideas.** It is easier to think of ideas about topics that you know a lot about. Therefore, examine your own experiences and areas of knowledge.

3. **Look for topics and ideas that interest you.** What subjects or problems grab your attention? What current events or issues spark your interest? You will feel more like writing and will write more successfully if you focus on something interesting and important to you.

4. **Keep an ongoing list of topics.** If a topic doesn't work for one assignment, it may be right for another.

Sources of Ideas

As long as you are aware of, and interacting with, the world around you, you will have ideas to write about. Never think that your ideas are unimportant or worthless. You can develop very simple, ordinary ideas into interesting, effective paragraphs and essays. Here is a list of some good sources of ideas:

SOURCES OF IDEAS	WHAT TO LOOK FOR
daily or weekly activities	likes, dislikes, problems; best, worst, unexpected, exciting events
your physical surroundings	surprising, beautiful, ugly, unusual objects or places
local, national, or world events	memorable, shocking, surprising, interesting, tragic, happy, or amusing occurrences
people (family, friends)	predictable or unpredictable behavior, personalities, actions, histories, insights gained from acquaintances
television or other media	news events, documentaries, trends in programming or advertising, likes, dislikes

"Write about dogs!"

EXERCISE 11-1
Writing in Progress

Directions: Make a list of five to ten topics or ideas that you know about and are interested in.

_____

_____

_____

_____

_____

_____

_____

_____

_____

Choosing a Manageable Topic

If your topic is either too broad or too narrow, you will have difficulty writing an effective paragraph or essay about it. If it is too broad, you will have too much to say. If your topic is too narrow, you won't have enough to say. Some warning signals for each situation are as follows:

A TOPIC MAY BE TOO BROAD IF	A TOPIC MAY BE TOO NARROW IF
• you don't know where to start writing.	• you end up repeating ideas.
• you don't know where to stop.	• your paragraph is too short and you have nothing to add.
• you feel as if you are going in circles.	• you find yourself focusing again and again on small details.
• the topic seems overwhelming.	• the topic seems unimportant.

Narrowing a Topic

If your topic is too broad, try to divide it into smaller topics. Just as a large house can be divided into apartments, so a large topic can be divided into smaller, more manageable topics.

Suppose you were asked to write a paragraph about a perfect vacation. Let's say you chose New York City as your destination and decided to write a paragraph about your choice. Most likely you would not be able to cover the reasons for your choice in a single paragraph. Because the topic is too broad, you need to divide it into smaller parts. Try to think in terms of ideas, not topics, as shown in the following diagram:

TOPIC   IDEAS

Reasons for visiting New York City ⟵ Many museums.

Historic sights are numerous.

Times Square is exciting.

Instead of writing about all of your reasons, you could limit your paragraph to any one of the above reasons.

The diagram below gives you a few other examples of ways to divide large topics into smaller, more manageable ones. Remember to think in terms of *ideas*.

TOPIC   IDEAS

1. parades ⟵ Parades are festive, happy occasions.

Parades are often patriotic.

Parades attract crowds.

2. campus newspaper ⟵ There are many types of articles.

Advertisements fill the paper.

Announcements are usually important.

3. compliments ⟵ There are many types of compliments.

Giving compliments is an art.

Accepting compliments is often awkward.

A **topic** is a thing, a person, or an object. Parades, newspapers, and compliments are things. An **idea** makes a statement about a topic. The statement "Parades are festive, happy occasions" makes a point about parades.

For each topic you consider, think to yourself, "What are the various angles on this subject?" This will help you find *ideas* about the topic. Sometimes more than one narrowing is necessary. Note that the divisions for topics 2 and 3 above are still *topics,* not *ideas,* and that some of them are still too broad to be covered in a single paragraph. For example, in topic 2, "advertisements" (one division of "campus newspaper") is still a topic, not an idea, and is still very broad. The diagram below shows how you can narrow this topic down still further using ideas.

Local businesses   pizza shops
offer coupons   bookstores
and discounts.

campus ⎯⎯ advertisements ⟵ National advertisers   music ads
newspaper   target youthful   soda ads
                               markets.

Newspaper relies   classified ads
on ads for income. ⟵ regular accounts

In the diagram above, the first narrowing of the topic "advertisements" yields ideas about the topic (for example, "National advertisers target youthful markets"). Note that each idea is further broken down into examples that support the idea (for instance, "soda ads" and "music ads" are examples of ads that target youthful markets). You'll be working more with supporting your ideas in Chapter 13.

EXERCISE 11-2

Directions: Divide each of the following topics into at least three smaller topics or ideas. Then, choose one division and narrow it further until you've produced an idea that seems manageable to cover in one paragraph.

1. Child-care problems
2. The importance of holidays
3. The value of friends

Keeping Your Reader in Mind

Whenever you speak, you are addressing a specific person or group of people. You usually have some knowledge about whom you are addressing. You may know your listeners personally—for example, friends or family. At other times, you may know your listeners in a more distant way. According to your level of familiarity with your listeners and your knowledge about them, you automatically adjust both what you say and how you say it. You speak differently with friends than with your instructors, for example. Suppose the following people made the following comments to you. What would you say to each person? Write your response in the space provided.

PERSON	COMMENT	YOUR RESPONSE
Parent or guardian	"Don't you think you should take a course in psychology?"	
Employer	"Have you taken a psychology course yet? If not, you should."	
College instructor	"I advise you to register for a psychology course."	
Close friend	"Why don't you take a psych. class?"	

Now analyze your responses. Did you choose different words? Did you express and arrange your ideas differently? Did your tone change? Were some responses casual and others more formal?

Your reaction to each person was different because you took into account who the speaker was as well as what each one said. In writing, your readers are your listeners. They are called your **audience**. As you write, keep your audience in mind. What you write about and how you explain your ideas must match the needs of your audience. Through your language and word choice, as well as through the details you include in your paragraphs, you can communicate effectively with your audience.

Remember, your audience cannot see you when you write. Listeners can understand what you say by seeing your gestures, posture, and facial expressions and hearing your tone of voice and emphasis. When you write, all these nonverbal clues are missing, so you must make up for them. You need to be clear, direct, and specific to be sure you communicate your intended meaning.

EXERCISE 11-3

Directions: Select two people from the list below. For each, write an explanation of why you decided to attend college.

1. Your best friend

2. Your English instructor

3. Your employer

Do not label which explanation is for which person. In class, exchange papers with a classmate. Ask your classmate to identify the intended audience of each explanation. When you've finished, discuss how the two pieces of writing differ. Then, decide whether each piece of writing is appropriate for its intended audience.

Generating Ideas

Once you have a topic and an audience in mind, the next step is to generate ideas that you can use to write about that topic. This section describes three techniques for generating ideas.

1. **Brainstorming**

2. **Freewriting**

3. **Branching**

You can use these techniques for both essay and paragraph writing, and they can help you narrow your topic if it is too broad or expand it if it is too narrow. If you are writing an essay, these techniques will help you break your general topic down into paragraphs. In paragraph writing, you can use these techniques for generating details that will fill out your paragraphs and support your main ideas.

Brainstorming

For **brainstorming**, make a list of everything you know about your topic. Include facts, ideas, examples, questions, or feelings. Do not stop to decide if your ideas are good or bad; write down *all* of them. Concentrate on generating *ideas,* not topics. Don't worry about grammar or correctness. Give yourself a time limit. You can brainstorm alone or with another person. After you finish brainstorming, read through your list and mark usable ideas. If you have trouble putting ideas down on paper, consider tape-recording your ideas or discussing ideas with a friend or classmate. The following is a list of ideas a student came up with while brainstorming on the topic of radio talk shows.

SAMPLE BRAINSTORMING

Radio Talk Shows

lots of them

some focus on sports

some deal with issues of the day

some hosts are rude

don't let callers finish talking

some crazy callers, though!

some lack knowledge

some get angry

can learn a lot

get other viewpoints

sometimes hosts get too opinionated

fun to listen to

some topics too controversial

overkill on some issues

The topic of radio talk shows is too broad for a single paragraph. This student's brainstorming produced several paragraph-sized ideas:

characteristics of callers

characteristics of hosts

characteristics of topics covered on radio talk shows

EXERCISE 11-4
Writing in Progress

Directions: Select a topic you listed in Exercise 11-1, or choose one of the following topics. Brainstorm for about five minutes. When you finish, review your work and mark ideas you could use in writing a paragraph.

1. Your dream vacation
2. Physical-education courses
3. Street gangs
4. Photographs
5. Magazines

Freewriting

Freewriting is a way to generate ideas on a topic by writing nonstop for a specified period. Here's how it works:

1. **Write whatever comes to your mind, regardless of whether it is about the topic.** If you cannot think of anything to write, rewrite your last interesting phrase or idea until a new idea comes to mind.

2. **Don't worry about complete sentences, grammar, punctuation, or spelling.** Just record ideas as they come to mind. Don't even worry about whether they make sense.

3. **The most important things are to keep writing and to write fast.**

4. **Give yourself a time limit: three to five minutes is reasonable.**

5. **After you have finished, underline or highlight ideas that might be usable in your paragraph.**

A sample of student freewriting on the topic of visiting the zoo is shown below.

Sample Freewriting

Pat and I went to the zoo Sunday. Great weather. Sunny. Warm. Warm . . . warm . . . warm . . . Oh! I know what I want to say. I didn't have as much fun as I thought I would. I used to love to go to the zoo as a kid. My parents would take us and we'd have a picnic. But I still could get cotton candy at the refreshment stand. It was a really big treat. My dad would carry me on his shoulders and my mother would be pushing my baby brother in the stroller. I loved the giraffes with their long necks and spots. And the tigers. But this time the animals looked so sad. The tiger was in an enclosed area, and he'd worn a path around the edges. He paces constantly. It was awful.

Notice that this sample contains numerous errors, including sentence fragments; this student was focusing on ideas, not correctness. Notice, too, that the student repeats the word *warm,* probably because she was stuck and needed to get her ideas flowing.

This freewriting contains two possible topics:

a childhood memory of the zoo

the quality of life for animals in a zoo

Once you have selected a topic, it may be helpful to freewrite again to generate more ideas.

EXERCISE 11-5

Directions: Freewrite for five minutes each on two of the following topics. Be sure to write without stopping. When you finish, underline or highlight any ideas that might be usable in writing a paragraph on that topic.

1. Movies
2. Cigarette smoke
3. Common sense
4. Bad motorists
5. Hitchhikers

Branching

Branching uses freestyle diagrams to generate ideas. Branching begins with a trunk—that is, with a general topic. Related ideas branch out from the trunk like limbs on a tree. As on a tree, branches also can originate from other branches. To do branching, just follow these simple steps:

1. **Write your general topic in the center of a full sheet of 8.5-by-11-inch paper.** Draw a circle around the topic.
2. **As you think of ideas related to the topic, write them down around the central circle.** Draw a line connecting each idea to the central circle. In the following diagram, a student has used branching to generate ideas on the topic of homeless people.

First Branching Diagram

3. **Now begin to think of ideas that relate to the branches.** Write them down near the appropriate branch. You don't need to work with each branch. Choose only one or two to develop further. You may need to use separate sheets of paper to give yourself room to develop each branch, as in the second branching diagram shown on the next page. Here the student chose to develop further the idea of shelters for the homeless.

4. **Continue to draw branches until you are satisfied you have enough for the assignment at hand.** The student who made the second branching diagram decided to write about one of the experiences she had when she volunteered to serve food in a shelter for the homeless.

Second Branching Diagram

EXERCISE 11-6

Directions: Use branching to develop two of the following topics:

1. Car-safety devices
2. Noise
3. Borrowing money
4. Sales tax
5. Convenience food stores

Choosing a Technique That Works

Now that you have tried these techniques, you may have a sense that one of them works best for you.

However, don't judge the techniques too quickly. Try each of them three or four times. As you continue working with them, another preference may develop. You will also find that for certain topics, one technique may work better than another. For example, suppose you are writing a paragraph about snowmobiling. You may find that freewriting about it does not yield as many fresh ideas as branching. If you're describing a close friend, you may find that branching doesn't work as well as brainstorming or freewriting.

Identifying Usable Ideas

Brainstorming, freewriting, and branching each produce a large assortment of ideas. Your job is to decide which ideas are useful for the writing assignment at hand. Don't feel as if you have to use them all. Sometimes you might select just one idea and develop it further by doing a second freewriting, branching, or brainstorming. For example, suppose you brainstormed on the topic of radio talk shows and selected from your brainstorming list the subtopic of sports talk shows; then you might generate more ideas about sports talk shows by further brainstorming. Your goal is to produce ideas that you can use to develop a paragraph on your selected topic.

NEED TO KNOW

Techniques for Generating Ideas

TECHNIQUE	DESCRIPTION
Brainstorming	1. List all ideas about your topic.
	2. Use words and phrases.
	3. Give yourself a time limit.
Freewriting	1. Write nonstop about your topic.
	2. Write whatever comes to mind.
	3. Give yourself a time limit.
Branching	1. Write down and circle your topic in the middle of your page.
	2. As you think of related ideas, write them down around the center circle. Connect with lines.
	3. Draw additional branches as needed.

EXERCISE 11-7

Directions: Select one of the topics listed below. Try brainstorming, freewriting, and branching to generate ideas on it. When you have finished, mark the usable ideas in each method and compare your results. Then answer the questions below.

1. The value of exercise
2. Dressing stylishly
3. Choosing an apartment
4. Managing money
5. Amusement parks

1. Which technique worked best this time? Why?

_____

_____

2. Which technique was least successful this time? Why?

_____

_____

Organizing Your Ideas

After you have developed usable ideas to include in your paragraph or essay, the next step is to decide how to organize them. Ideas should flow logically from one to another. There are many ways to group or arrange ideas in both paragraphs and essays so that they are clear and easy to follow. The list below describes three of the most common types of organization:

1. **Least/most arrangement** Arrange your ideas from most to least or least to most, according to some standard. For example, you might arrange ideas from most to least important, likeable, interesting, controversial, serious, or familiar.

2. **Time sequence** Arrange events in the order in which they happened. Whatever happened first is placed first in the paragraph. Whatever occurred last is placed last. A time-sequence organization would be good to use if, for example, you wanted to describe events at a surprise party. This type of organization is also what you would use to describe a process, such as how to change a flat tire.

3. **Spatial arrangement** Arrange descriptions of persons, places, or things according to their positions in space. You could describe your topic from outside to inside, right to left, or top to bottom. For example, you might use a left-to-right organization to describe your psychology classroom, or you might use a front-to-back organization to describe your friend's pickup truck.

These methods of organization are discussed in more detail in Chapter 14.

NEED TO KNOW

Planning and Organizing

Planning and organizing contribute to successful writing. Be sure to

- focus on ideas, not general topics.

- use events, activities, physical surroundings, media, and people around you as sources of ideas.

- make sure your topic is manageable—neither too broad nor too narrow.

- choose a topic that is well suited to your audience.

- use brainstorming, freewriting, and branching to generate ideas.

- organize your ideas using a logical method. Three common methods are least/most arrangements, time sequence, and spatial arrangement.

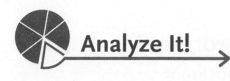 **Analyze It!**

Directions: The following is one student's freewriting on the topic of summer camps. Study the freewriting and in the space provided, list possible topics that could be used for a short essay.

The other day my son asked if he could go to summer camp. His friend is going to the YMCA sleep-away camp for two weeks next summer. I didn't know what to say. He's only 8, for crying out loud! I didn't go to camp until I was 10, and man, was I homesick. I cried myself to sleep every night the first week. I guess I'm glad he's curious about it. Adventurous spirit. Unlike me as a kid. Although, come to think of it, camp did build my confidence. And maybe improved my social skills. I loved canoeing and roasting marshmallows around the campfire. Oh, and we played some great pranks! But I got a wicked case of swimmer's ear. I'd be a wreck worrying that my kid might get hurt. He may be ready for sleep-away camp, but I'm not sure I'm ready to let him go. He likes sleeping over at friend's houses. How much does the Y camp cost anyway? I've heard good things about the staff. How DO you decide if your kid's ready? Wonder if there's financial aid available . . .

A STUDENT ESSAY

The Writer

Ebtisam Abusamak is attending Central Piedmont Community College in Charlotte, North Carolina, where she is majoring in Business Administration.

The Writing Task

For her writing class, she was asked to write an essay defining a label that is

often applied to people, and to examine whether it applies to her. Abusamak decided to write about conformity—going along with the crowd. As you read, be sure to notice how she carefully defines the term and then uses examples to evaluate whether or not the term applies to her.

Am I a Conformist?
Ebtisam Abusamak

Title in form of question catches interest

Introduction

1   If you ask children who they would like to be when they grow up, they will probably mention a superhero, like Batman or Spiderman; a famous athlete like Michael Jordan or Serena Williams; or a show business celebrity like Halle Berry or Leonardo DiCaprio. That's because there is something about those people that is unique. They are not conformists. They don't try to blend into the crowd; they stand out.

Writer explains concepts of self-expression and conformity

2   Given a choice, I think most people would rather be known as "special" than for how well they fit in. That's what self-expression is all about. Some people are naturally expressive. They might dye their hair because a certain color makes them feel better about themselves. They might wear only athletic shorts because they love sports and are always ready to play. But there are other people who will dye their hair or put on baggie shorts not because they're more comfortable, but because *someone else is doing it*. These are the conformists. When someone does something for themselves, something that feels totally right, that is self-expression. On the other hand, when someone does something because other people or groups are doing it and they want to fit in, that is conforming. So which am I, a unique individual or a conformist?

Examples

Thesis statement

Topic sentence

3   To be honest, I would have to say that the ways in which I express myself are not always unique. I could point out several ways in which I appear to be conforming to popular trends. For instance, my clothes; I wear clothes that are trendy, like Boho skirts and Juicy tees. However, I won't wear shirts that are cropped even though it's in fashion because it would make me feel self-conscious. And I don't buy super-high heels because they're uncomfortable.

Examples

Topic sentence

4   Then there is the way I talk. I use expressions that I hear on TV and from young people around me. I do say "Get outta here" instead of "Are you kidding?" and I know I say "like" too much. Am I deliberately trying to be cool or am I just expressing myself in a way that is natural? As I begin to analyze my behavior, I realize that I'm trying to do both. On some subconscious level, I am sure I'm making some choices in order to be accepted, but for the most part, I make choices based on who I am and what feels right.

Topic sentence

5   I'll probably never go the route of extreme expression just to be different. I won't get my face pierced in five different places just to let the world know I'm outside the mainstream. In fact, with so many people piercing themselves all over these days, I'm not even sure it *is* outside the mainstream anymore. And that's where the conflict between self-expression and conformity lies.

Topic sentence

6   I hope I never become like some people who choose to do something just to be different, like wear huge jeans that fall below their waist, get tattooed, or blare rap music from their cars. The problem is, once that music or clothing style becomes popular, other people start to imitate it. Soon, everyone around them is wearing jeans that fall down and listening to loud rap and suddenly they're not unique, they're like . . . well, they're like everyone else. In deliberately trying to be outsiders, they've actually become the very thing they hate—conformists.

Conclusion 7

She answers the question posed in the title.

It is natural to be affected by what's around you. However, the best choices a person can make come from one's self. I try to remember that and make choices based on what feels right for me. I'm not interested in being like everyone else, but I don't choose to be "different" for the sake of being different. I know that as long as I remain true to myself, I will be someone unique and special.

EXAMINING STUDENT WRITING

1. Abusamak's thesis statement is in a question format. Do you think this is effective? Reword it so it is a statement and not a question.

2. Abusamak uses plenty of examples throughout the essay. What purpose do they serve? How would the essay change if they were not included?

3. Evaluate Abusamak's introduction. Is it too long? Could it be shorter?

4. What suggestions could you give Abusamak for improving her essay?

Paragraph Writing Scenarios

Friends and Family

1. Choose a friend, and write a paragraph about how you met.

2. Think of someone you consider old-fashioned. Write a paragraph about the things this person does or says that are not contemporary or up-to-date.

Classes and Campus Life

1. Imagine that you are filling out a financial aid application. Write a paragraph explaining why you need an extra $1,000 this semester.

2. Write a paragraph about whether you would prefer to live at home with your family, on your own in an apartment or house, or in a dorm.

Working Students

1. You need a day off to prepare for an exam. Write a letter to your boss explaining why this test is so important. Include a suggestion for how you might make up the missed hours.

2. Write a paragraph describing the perfect job.

Communities and Cultures

1. Think of a place you like to go—other than school, work, or home—where you feel like you belong. Write a paragraph about what it is about this place that makes you comfortable.

2. Many Americans originally came from all over the world. Choose a friend or relative, living or deceased, and write a paragraph about where they came from and why they emigrated to this country.

> ## Writing Success Tip 11
>
> ### Using the Computer to Generate Ideas
>
> 1. **Use a computer in the same way you brainstorm or freewrite on paper.** Sometimes just using a different medium makes a difference.
> 2. **Try brainstorming or freewriting with your screen switched off (just turn down the brightness).** This frees you to write without looking at what you've already written and criticizing it.
> 3. **You can also branch on the computer.** Put your general topic in large print. Put your first set of branches in bold. Then go back and add more branches in regular type.
> 4. **Try talking about your topic with a friend on the Internet.**
> 5. **Make a list of questions that start with *Who*, *What*, *When*, *Where*, *Why*, and *How*, and answer them.**

WRITING ABOUT A READING

THINKING BEFORE READING

Christie Scotty's article first appeared in *Newsweek* on October 18, 2004. The author discusses the ways in which people are treated, based on their professions. Notice how Scotty begins with a thesis and provides evidence to support it.

1. Preview the readings, using the steps discussed in Chapter 2, p. 38.
2. Connect the reading to your own experience by answering the following questions:

   a. How have you been treated by the people you interact with at work?

   b. How do you treat people in the service industry when they are helping you?

READING

CAN I GET YOU SOME MANNERS WITH THAT?

So often it was the "professionals" who looked down on me who were lacking in social grace.

Christie Scotty

1   Like most people, I've long understood that I will be judged by my occupation. It's obvious that people care what others do for a living: head into any social setting and introductions of "Hi, my name is . . ." are quickly followed by the ubiquitous "And what do you do?" I long ago realized my profession is a **gauge** that people use to see how smart or talented I am. Recently, however, I was disappointed to see that it also decides how I'm treated as a person.

gauge
a way to evaluate

2   Last year I left a professional position as a small-town reporter and took a job waiting tables while I figured out what I wanted to do next. As someone paid to serve food to people, I had customers say and do things to me I suspect they'd never say or do to their most casual acquaintances. Some people would stare at the menu and mumble drink orders—"Bring me a water, extra lemon, no ice"—while refusing to meet my eyes. Some would interrupt me midsentence to say the air conditioning was too cold or the sun was too bright through the windows. One night a man talking on his cell phone waved me away, then beckoned me back with his finger a minute later, complaining he was ready to order and asking where I'd been.

peon
someone who works in servitude; a slave

3   I had waited tables during summers in college and was treated like a **peon** by plenty of people. But at 19 years old, I sort of believed I deserved inferior treatment from professional adults who didn't blink at handing over $24 for a seven-ounce fillet. Besides, people responded to me differently after I told them I was in college. Customers would joke that one day I'd be sitting at their table, waiting to be served. They could imagine me as their college-age daughter or future co-worker.

4   Once I graduated I took a job at a community newspaper. From my first day, I heard a respectful tone from most everyone who called me, whether they were readers or someone I was hoping to interview. I assumed this was the way the professional world worked—cordially.

5   I soon found out differently. I sat several feet away from an advertising sales representative with a similar name. Our calls would often get mixed up and someone asking for Kristen would be transferred to Christie. The mistake was immediately evident. Perhaps it was because their relationship centered on "gimme," perhaps it was because money was involved, but people used a tone with Kristen that they never used with me.

6   "I called yesterday and you still haven't faxed—"

7   "Hi, this is so-and-so over at the real-estate office. I need—"

8   "I just got into the office and I don't like—"

*AND **MAKE IT SNAPPY**: It seemed that many customers didn't get the difference between server and servant.*

make it snappy
hurry up, do it faster

9   "Hi, Kristen. Why did—"

10   I was just a fledgling reporter, but the governor's press secretary returned my calls far more politely than Kristen's accounts did hers, even though she had worked with many of her clients for years.

11   My job title made people chat me up and express their concerns and complaints with courtesy. I came to expect friendliness from perfect strangers. So it was a shock to return to the restaurant industry. Sure, the majority of customers were pleasant, some even a delight to wait on, but all too often someone shattered that scene.

12   I often saw my co-workers storm into the kitchen in tears or with a mouthful of expletives after a customer had interrupted, degraded or ignored them. In the eight months I worked there, I heard my friends muttering phrases like "You just don't treat people like that!" on an almost daily basis.

13   It's no secret that there's a lot to put up with when waiting tables, and fortunately, much of it can be easily forgotten when you pocket the tips. The service industry, by definition, exists to cater to others' needs. Still, it seemed that many of my customers didn't get the difference between *server* and *servant*.

14   Some days I tried to force good manners. When a customer said hello but continued staring at his menu without glancing up at me, I'd make it a point to say, "Hi, my name is Christie," and then pause and wait for him to make eye contact. I'd stand silent an awkwardly long time waiting for a little respect. It was my way of saying "I am a person, too."

15   I knew I wouldn't wait tables forever, so most days I just shook my head and laughed, pitying the people whose lives were so miserable they treated strangers shabbily in order to feel better about themselves.

16   Three months ago I left the restaurant world and took an office job where some **modicum** of civility exists. I'm now applying to graduate school, which means someday I'll return to a profession where people need to be nice to me in order to get what they want. I think I'll take them to dinner first, and see how they treat someone whose only job is to serve them.

modicum
a small amount

GETTING READY TO WRITE

Reviewing the Reading

1. What types of behavior did Scotty encounter from her customers at the restaurant?

2. How does her recent experience as a server compare to her experience as a server during her college days?

3. What types of behavior did the author encounter as a reporter?

4. How was Scotty's experience different from her co-worker, Kristen's?

5. How did Scotty try to force good manners?

Examining the Reading Using an Idea Map

Review the reading by completing the missing parts of the idea map shown on the next page.

Strengthening Your Vocabulary

Part A: Using the word's context, word parts, or a dictionary, write a brief definition of each of the following words as it is used in the reading.

1. ubiquitous (paragraph 1) _____

2. inferior (paragraph 3) _____

3. cordially (paragraph 4) _____

4. fledgling (paragraph 10) _____

5. expletives (paragraph 12) _____

6. degraded (paragraph 12) _____

Part B: Choose one of the words above and draw a word map (see p. 84) of it.

Reacting to Ideas: Discussion and Journal Writing

Get ready to write about the reading by discussing the following:

1. What are some characteristics of jobs in the service industry?

2. Write a journal entry about a time when you were treated poorly by a customer or as a customer.

3. Write a journal entry about one job you would like to have. How would you deal with the people around you?

Visualize It!

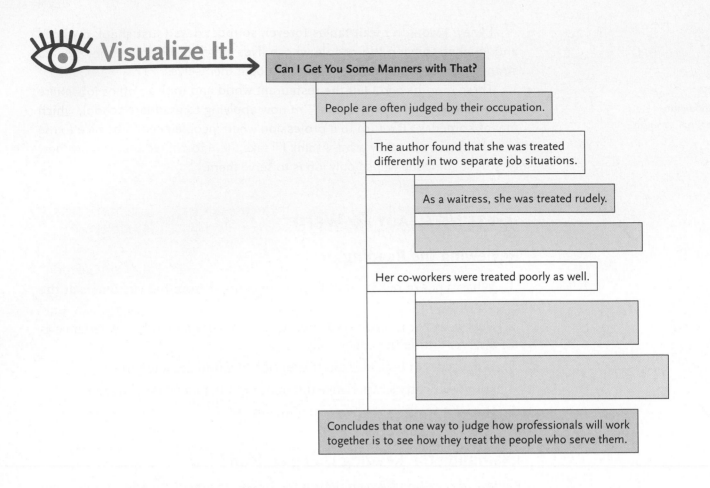

Can I Get You Some Manners with That?

People are often judged by their occupation.

The author found that she was treated differently in two separate job situations.

As a waitress, she was treated rudely.

Her co-workers were treated poorly as well.

Concludes that one way to judge how professionals will work together is to see how they treat the people who serve them.

WRITING ABOUT THE READING

Paragraph Options

1. Write a paragraph about the best or worst restaurant experience you have had.

2. Write a paragraph about a positive experience you had with someone in the service industry.

3. Scotty states that sometimes she tried to "force good manners." Write a paragraph explaining whether you think this is possible. Why or why not?

Essay Options

4. Write an essay about changing manners in our society. Explain whether you feel people are becoming ruder. Support your position with examples.

5. Write an essay defining what good manners are and giving examples. You could also describe situations in which good manners are especially important.

6. Spend some time in a restaurant or café. Observe the ways in which customers and servers interact. Write an essay describing what you saw and how it compares to the experiences of the author, Christie Scotty.

CHAPTER REVIEW AND PRACTICE

CHAPTER REVIEW

To review and check your recall of the chapter, select the word or phrase from the box below that best completes each of the sentences that follow. Keep in mind that four of the words will not be used.

agreeing	audience	brainstorming	branching	broad
diagram	freewriting	idea	least/most	manageable
narrow	reader	spatial	time sequence	

1. A(n) _____ topic is one that is neither too broad nor too narrow.

2. If you don't know where to start or stop writing, your topic may be too _____.

3. If you end up repeating ideas, your topic may be too _____.

4. If your topic seems overwhelming, making a _____ can help.

5. When you write, you should adjust both what you say and how you say it, depending on the _____ you have in mind.

6. _____ consists of making a list of everything you can think of about your topic.

7. Writing nonstop about anything that comes to your mind for a period of time is called _____.

8. Making diagrams with your topic in the center is called _____.

9. Arranging ideas in the order in which they happened is called _____.

10. Arranging descriptions of persons, places, or things according to their position is called _____ arrangement.

EDITING PRACTICE

The following paragraph describing how fog forms is confusing because it is disorganized. Revise it so that it reflects a time-sequence arrangement of the details.

> Fog is caused by the natural movement of air from one place to another. When this moist air that was picked up over warm water moves to cool land, or from warmer to cooler water, it cools down. As these warm winds pass over the water, they pick up moisture. When these water molecules condense into a liquid near the ground, fog forms. Warm winds pass over the ocean or another large body of water. As the moist air cools down, the molecules in the water move more slowly and begin to stick together rather than to bounce off each other when they collide.

INTERNET ACTIVITIES

1. Choosing a Subject

Read through this information about developing a topic from the Paradigm Online Writing Assistant.

http://www.powa.org/discovering/choosing-your-subject.html

Complete the activities that the author provides.

2. Finding a Topic

Read over this information from the UCLA Library about narrowing and broadening your topic:

http://www2.library.ucla.edu/libraries/college/11605_11640.cfm

Use the focusing worksheets to develop five potential topics for a paper.

3. MyWritingLab

Visit this site to get more help with planning and organizing paragraphs.

http://www.mywritinglab.com

Click on the Study Plan tab and then on "Getting Started with Paragraph Writing," and then on "Developing and Organizing a Paragraph."

12

Drafting and Revising

*In this chapter
you will learn to:*

1. Choose a manageable topic.

2. Write topic sentences.

3. Develop paragraphs using supporting details.

4. Revise paragraphs.

WRITE ABOUT IT!

Study the advertisement above. Write a sentence that states what message the advertisement conveys.

Advertisements often begin with a general announcement that catches your interest and suggests what the ad is about. This is called a *headline statement*.

315

In the ad shown on the preceding page, the headline, "Be faithful to your spouse—Play around with your salad" catches your attention and suggests the message the ad is trying to convey. The remainder of the ad, called the *body copy,* offers more information about the headline. Ads often end with either a *close* or a *tagline* intended to create a final, lasting impression or to urge action.

Paragraphs follow a similar structure. First, a paragraph must have a sentence that is similar to a headline statement. This sentence identifies the topic of the paragraph, indicates a main point (idea) about the topic, and catches the reader's interest. This sentence is called a **topic sentence**. Writers often place the topic sentence at the beginning of the paragraph. Paragraphs must also have details that support and explain the topic sentence. Finally, like ads, paragraphs need to draw to a close. Usually one or more sentences serve this function. The conclusion of a paragraph makes a strong statement. It leaves the reader with a summary of the paragraph's main point or a point related to what has come before.

In this chapter you will learn how to write topic sentences and develop details to support them. You will also learn how to revise paragraphs to make them more effective.

WRITING

Choosing a Manageable Topic

The topic you choose for a paragraph must not be too broad or too narrow. It must be the right size to cover in a single paragraph. If you choose a topic that is too broad, you will have too much to say. Your paragraph will wander and seem unfocused. If you choose a topic that is too narrow (too small), you will not have enough to say. Your paragraph will seem skimpy.

Suppose you want to write a paragraph about pollution. You write the following topic sentence:

Pollution is everywhere.

Clearly, the topic of global pollution is too broad to cover in a single paragraph. Pollution has numerous types, causes, effects, and potential solutions. Would you write about causes? If so, could you write about all possible causes in one paragraph? What about effects? Are you concerned with immediate effects? Long-term effects? You can see that the topic of widespread global pollution is not a manageable one for a single paragraph. You could make this topic more manageable by limiting it to a specific pollutant, an immediate source or effect, and a particular place. Your revised topic sentence might read:

Fuel emissions from poorly maintained cars greatly increase air pollution in the United States.

This topic may still prove too broad to cover in a single paragraph. You could narrow it further by limiting the topic to a particular city in the United States, or even a particular type of fuel emission.

Shown below are a few more examples of topics that are too broad. Each has been revised to be more specific.

TOO BROAD	Water conservation
REVISED	Lawn-watering restrictions
TOO BROAD	Effects of water shortages
REVISED	Sinkholes caused by water shortages
TOO BROAD	Crop irrigation
REVISED	A system for allocating water for crop irrigation in the San Joaquin Valley

If your topic is too narrow, you will run out of things to say in your paragraph. You also run the risk of straying from your topic as you search for ideas to include. Suppose you want to write a paragraph about environmental waste. You write the following topic sentence:

Each year Americans discard 2 billion disposable razors.

This sentence is too specific. It could work as a detail, but it is too narrow to be a topic sentence. To turn this statement into a good topic sentence, try to make your topic more general. Your revised topic sentence could be

Each year Americans strain their landfills with convenient but environmentally damaging products.

You then could develop a paragraph such as the following:

Sample Paragraph

Each year Americans strain their landfills with convenient but environmentally damaging products. For example, Americans discard billions of disposable razors. Disposable diapers are another popular product. Parents use mountains of them on their children instead of washable cloth diapers. Milk, which used to come in reusable glass bottles, is now sold mainly in plastic or cardboard cartons that can only be used once. Other items, such as Styrofoam cups, aluminum cans, disposable cameras, and ballpoint pens, add to the solid-waste problem in this country. Eventually people will need to realize it's not OK to "use it once, then throw it away."

Here are a few other examples of topic sentences that are too narrow. Each has been revised to be less specific.

TOO NARROW	Americans discard 250 million used tires per year.
REVISED	Several companies are tackling the problem of what to do with used tires.
TOO NARROW	Less than 4 percent of plastics are recycled.
REVISED	Consumers need to take recycling more seriously.
TOO NARROW	Americans in some states are paid five cents per can to recycle aluminum cans.
REVISED	Money motivates many consumers to recycle.

EXERCISE 12-1

Directions: For each of the following pairs of topic sentences, place a check mark in the blank before the sentence that is more effective (neither too broad nor too narrow):

1. _____ **a.** Power tools can be dangerous.

   _____ **b.** To avoid injury, users of power saws should follow several safety precautions.

2. _____ **a.** A Barbie doll from the 1950s recently sold for $3,000.

   _____ **b.** Barbie dolls from the 1950s are valued by collectors.

3. _____ **a.** Parachuting is a sport.

   _____ **b.** Parachuting is a sport that requires skill and self-confidence.

4. _____ **a.** Learning keyboarding skills requires regular practice.

   _____ **b.** Learning a new skill is difficult.

5. _____ **a.** Children's toys should be fun.

   _____ **b.** A toy should stimulate a child's imagination.

EXERCISE 12-2

Writing in Progress

Directions: Choose three of the following topics and narrow each one to a topic manageable in a single paragraph. Use branching (p. 301) to help you.

1. Packaging of products
2. The value of parks and "green spaces"
3. Garbage
4. Water pollution or conservation
5. Building environmental awareness
6. Recycling

Writing Topic Sentences

An effective **topic sentence** must

1. identify what the paragraph is about (the topic).
2. make a point (an idea) about that topic.

Suppose your topic is acid rain. You could make a number of different points about acid rain. Each of the following is a possible topic sentence:

1. Acid rain has caused conflict between the United States and Canada.
2. Acid rain could be reduced by controlling factory emissions.
3. Acid rain has adversely affected the populations of fish in our lakes.

Each of the sentences identifies acid rain as the topic, but each expresses a different point about acid rain. Each would lead to a different paragraph and be supported by different details.

Think of your topic sentence as a headline; it states what your paragraph will contain. You can also think of a topic sentence as a promise. Your topic sentence promises your reader what you will deliver in the paragraph.

What does each of the following topic sentences promise the reader?

1. There are three basic ways to dispose of sewage sludge.

2. Each year we discard valuable raw materials into landfills.

3. Many people do not understand how easy composting is.

Sentence 1 promises to explain three ways to dispose of sewage sludge. Sentence 2 promises to tell what valuable resources we discard. Sentence 3 promises to explain how easy composting is.

Your topic sentence must be a clear and direct statement of what the paragraph will be about. Use the following suggestions to write effective topic sentences:

1. **Be sure your topic sentence is a complete thought**. If your sentence is a fragment, run-on sentence, or comma splice, your meaning will be unclear or incomplete.

FRAGMENT	People who don't throw their litter in the bin.
RUN-ON SENTENCE	The audience was captivated by the speaker no one spoke or moved.
COMMA SPLICE	Many children's games copy adult behavior, playing nurse or doctor is an example.

   Chapter 4 and Chapter 5 discuss how to spot and correct these errors.

2. **Place your topic sentence first in the paragraph**. You *may* place your topic sentence anywhere in the paragraph, but you will find it easier to develop your paragraph around the topic sentence if you put it first.

3. **Avoid direct announcements or statements of intent**. Avoid sentences that sound like formal announcements, such as the following examples:

ANNOUNCEMENT	In this paragraph I will show that the average American is unaware of the dangers of smog.
REVISED	The average American is unaware of the dangers of smog.
ANNOUNCEMENT	This paragraph will explain why carbon monoxide is a dangerous air pollutant.
REVISED	There are three primary reasons why carbon monoxide is a dangerous air pollutant.

EXERCISE 12-3
Writing in Progress

Directions: Write a topic sentence for each of the three topics that you selected in Exercise 12-2.

Developing the Paragraph

Once you've written a preliminary topic sentence, your next step is to include the details that support your sentence. Just as an advertiser provides facts and information that support the headline, so must you provide details that support your topic sentence. Let's look at another advertisement—this time an advertisement for a flea medication.

In this ad shown below, the headline announces the subject—eating Mini Bonio dog food. Now study the body copy. What kinds of information are provided? Notice that only information that supports the headline is included: all the details provide information about the benefits and varieties of Spiller's Mini Bonio dog food. These are called **relevant details.** *Relevant* means that the details directly relate to or explain the headline. The ad does not mention. Notice, too, that a reasonable number of facts are included—enough to make the headline believable and convincing. In other words, a **sufficient** number of **details** are provided to make the headline effective. When you select details to support a topic sentence, they must also be *relevant* and *sufficient.* You must provide a sufficient number of details to make your topic sentence understandable and convincing. However, a detail that is interesting and true must be left out if it does not support the topic sentence.

To grow up big and strong like his Dad he should eat Mini Bonio too.

Like Father, like Son, like Mini Bonio a lot. That's because it's been specially made for smaller dogs and puppies. It's also enriched with calcium and minerals for healthy teeth and bones.

And if that's not enough there are four

Spillers takes the biscuit.

other nutritious biscuits in the Spillers range – Mini Chops, Cheese Crunches, Bonio and Shapes.

But even with Mini Bonio he may never grow up to be a Great Dane but he will grow up to be a great Sausage Dog.

Choosing Relevant Details

Relevant details directly support the topic sentence. The following paragraph contains two details that do not support the topic sentence, which is shaded. Can you spot them?

Sample Paragraph

(1) Corporations are beginning to recognize the importance of recycling. (2) Our landfills are getting too full, and we are running out of room for our garbage. (3) Many companies are selling products with reusable containers. (4) Tide laundry soap and Jergens hand cream, for example, sell refills. (5) It bothers me that some manufacturers charge the same or even more, for refills as for the original containers. (6) I believe all cities and towns should have recycling bins to make it easy for individuals to recycle. (7) By recycling tin, glass, plastic, and paper, companies can save valuable natural resources. (8) Some corporations recycle plastic and paper bags to conserve energy and natural resources. (9) Through these methods, corporations are helping to save our environment.

Sentence 5 is not relevant because what companies charge for reusable containers does not relate to the importance of recycling. Sentence 6 is not relevant because it is about towns and individuals, not corporations.

EXERCISE 12-4

Directions: Each of the topic sentences listed below is followed by a set of details. Place check marks in the blanks before those statements that are relevant supporting details.

1. TOPIC SENTENCE People should take safety precautions when outside temperatures reach 95 degrees or above.

   DETAILS

   _____ a. It is important to drink plenty of fluids.

   _____ b. If you are exposed to extreme cold or dampness, you should take precautions.

   _____ c. To prevent heat exhaustion, reduce physical activity.

   _____ d. Infants and elderly people are particularly at risk for heat exhaustion.

2. TOPIC SENTENCE Cuba is one of the last nations with a communist government.

   DETAILS

   _____ a. Cuba is an island nation and thus is able to keep out other political philosophies and opponents of communism.

   _____ b. Cuba earns high revenues from cigar sales despite the U.S. boycott against Cuba.

_____ **c.** Fidel Castro was not chosen by the Cuban people.

_____ **d.** The movement to overthrow communism in Cuba is centered in Miami and thus is not very effective within Cuba itself.

3. TOPIC SENTENCE Freedom of speech, the first amendment to the United States Constitution, does not give everyone the right to say anything at any time.

DETAILS _____ **a.** The Constitution also protects freedom of religion.

_____ **b.** Freedom of speech is a right that citizens of most Western countries take for granted.

_____ **c.** Freedom of speech is restricted by slander and libel laws, which prohibit speaking or publishing harmful, deliberate lies about people.

_____ **d.** Citizens may sue if they feel their freedom of speech has been unfairly restricted.

4. TOPIC SENTENCE Family violence against women is a growing problem that is difficult to control or prevent.

DETAILS _____ **a.** Abusive partners will often ignore restraining orders.

_____ **b.** Violence shown on television may encourage violence at home.

_____ **c.** New laws make it easier for observers of child abuse to report the violence.

_____ **d.** Battered women frequently do not tell anyone that they have been battered because they are ashamed.

_____ **e.** Violence against the elderly is increasing at a dramatic rate.

Including Sufficient Details

Including **sufficient details** means including _enough_ details to make your topic sentence believable and convincing. Your details should be as exact and specific as possible. The following paragraph lacks sufficient detail:

Sample Paragraph

Recycling has a lot of positive sides. When you recycle, you receive money if you return used containers. When you recycle, you clean up the earth, and you also save the environment. Less waste and more space are our goals.

Notice that the paragraph is very general. It does not describe any specific benefits of recycling, nor does it explain how recycling saves the environment or creates more space.

A revised version is shown below. Notice the addition of numerous details and the more focused topic sentence.

Revised Paragraph

Recycling offers benefits for consumers and manufacturers, as well as for the environment. Consumers benefit from recycling in several ways. Recycling generates revenue, which should, in the long run, reduce costs of products. Soda bottles and cans returned to the store produce immediate return for cash. Manufacturers benefit, too, since their costs are reduced. Most important, however, are benefits to the environment. Recycling reduces landfills. It also produces cleaner air by reducing manufacturing. Finally, recycling paper saves trees.

If you have difficulty thinking of enough details to include in a paragraph, try brainstorming, freewriting, or branching. Also, try to draft a more focused topic sentence, as the writer did in the paragraph above. You may then find it easier to develop supporting details. If you are still unable to generate additional details, your topic may be too narrow or you may need to do some additional reading or research on your topic. If you use information from printed sources, be sure to give the author credit by using a citation. Indicate the author, title, place of publication, publisher, and year.

ESL Tip

The word *draft* can be a noun or a verb.

NOUN   I wrote the first <u>draft</u> of my paper.

VERB   I <u>drafted</u> a revision two days later.

NEED TO KNOW

Drafting Paragraphs

To draft effective paragraphs, be sure to

- choose a manageable **topic.** Your topic should be neither too broad nor too narrow.

- write a clear **topic sentence.** Your topic sentence should identify the topic and make a point about that topic.

- develop your paragraph by providing **relevant** and **sufficient details.** Relevant details are those that directly support the topic. Including sufficient details means providing enough details to make your topic sentence believable and convincing.

EXERCISE 12-5

Writing in Progress

Directions: Write a paragraph developing one of the topic sentences you wrote in Exercise 12-3. Then, check to see if you can improve your topic sentence by making it more focused. Make the necessary changes. Finally, be sure you have included relevant and sufficient details in the rest of your paragraph.

Revising Paragraphs

Did you know that it takes an advertising agency months to develop and write a successful ad? Copy writers and editors work through many drafts until they decide on a final version of the ad. Often, too, an agency may test an ad on a sample group of consumers. Then, working from consumer responses, the agency makes further changes in the ad.

To produce an effective paragraph, you will need to revise and test your work. Revision is a process of examining and rethinking your ideas. It involves adding text, deleting text, and changing both *what* you have said and *how* you have said it.

When to Revise

It is usually best, after writing a draft of a paragraph, to wait a day before beginning to revise it. You will have a fresh outlook on your topic and will find that it is easier to see what you need to change.

How to Revise

Sometimes it is difficult to know how to improve your own writing. Simply rereading your own work may not help you discover flaws, weaknesses, or needed changes. This section presents two aids to revision that will help you identify what and how to revise: (1) a **revision map** and (2) a **revision checklist**.

Using Revision Maps

A **revision map** is a visual display of the ideas in your paragraph or essay. It is similar to an idea map (see p. 325). While an idea map shows how ideas in someone else's writing are related, a revision map will show you how ideas in your writing fit together. A revision map will also help you identify ideas that do not fit and those that need further explanation.

To draw a revision map of a paragraph, follow these steps:

1. **Write a shortened topic sentence at the top of your paper, as in the sample revision map on p. 325.** Be sure your topic sentence has both a subject and a verb and expresses an *idea*. Do *not* simply write the topic of your paragraph.

2. **Work through your paragraph sentence by sentence.** On your revision map, underneath the topic sentence, list each detail that directly supports the topic sentence.

3. **If you spot a detail that is an example or a further explanation of a detail already listed, write it underneath the first detail and indent it.**

4. **If you spot a detail that does not seem to support anything you've written, write it to the right of your list, as in the sample revision map.**

The diagram that follows is a sample revision map.

Visualize It!

Revision Map

| Topic sentence | | Unrelated details |

- Detail
- Detail
  - Example
  - Further explanation
- Detail

Unrelated details

1. _____

2. _____

3. _____

The following paragraph is a first draft written by a student named Eric. His revision map follows the paragraph.

Sample First Draft

Pizza is a surprisingly nutritious food. It has cheese, tomato sauce, and crust. Each of these is part of a basic food group. However, nutritionists now talk about the food pyramid instead of food groups. Toppings such as mushrooms and peppers also add to its nutritional value. Pepperoni, sausage, and anchovies provide protein. Pizza is high in calories, though, and everyone is counting calories. But pizza does provide a wide variety of nutrients from vegetables, dairy products, meats, and carbohydrates. And the best part is that it is tasty, as well as nutritious.

Visualize It!

Sample Revision Map

Pizza is nutritious.

- Cheese, sauce, crust are all in food groups.
- Toppings add nutrition.
- Pepperoni, sausage, anchovies add protein.
- It has a wide variety of nutrients.
  - It has vegetables, dairy, meat, and carbohydrates.
- It's tasty as well as nutritious.

Unrelated details

1. Nutritionists talk about pyramid
2. Pizza high in calories

Eric's map is a picture of his paragraph. The map reduces his ideas to a brief, skeletonlike form that allows him to concentrate on the ideas themselves. He is not distracted by other revision matters, such as wording, spelling, and punctuation, which come later in the revision process. The map showed Eric that two of his details—the ones about the food pyramid and the number of calories—do not belong in the paragraph.

EXERCISE 12-6

Directions: Draw a revision map of the sample paragraph on p. 325.

EXERCISE 12-7

Writing in Progress

Directions: Draw a revision map of the paragraph you wrote in Exercise 12-5.

Using the Revision Checklist

Focused questions can help you evaluate a piece of writing. The revision checklist is a list of questions in checklist form to help you look closely and critically at your writing and to identify parts that need improvement. It will also help you confirm that you have mastered certain skills. The revision checklist is divided into two parts: paragraph development and sentence development. The sentence development section covers what you learned in Chapter 4 through Chapter 10. As you learn more about writing paragraphs in later chapters, we will add items to the paragraph development section.

Revision Checklist

Paragraph Development

1. Is the topic manageable (neither too broad nor too narrow)?
2. Is the paragraph written with the reader in mind?
3. Does the topic sentence identify the topic?
4. Does the topic sentence make a point about the topic?
5. Does each sentence support the topic sentence?
6. Is there sufficient detail?
7. Is there a sentence at the end that brings the paragraph to a close?

Sentence Development

8. Are there any sentence fragments, run-on sentences, or comma splices?
9. Are ideas combined to produce more effective sentences?
10. Are adjectives and adverbs used to make the sentences vivid and interesting?
11. Are prepositional phrases like *-ing* phrases, and relative clauses used to add detail?
12. Are pronouns used correctly and consistently?

Now let's apply the questions from the paragraph development section of the checklist to a sample student paragraph. Read the paragraph and then answer the questions in the revision checklist that follows.

Sample Paragraph

The world is experiencing a steady decline in water quality and availability. About 75 percent of the world's rural population and 20 percent of its urban population have no ready access to uncontaminated water. Many states have a limited water supply, and others waste water. Bans on lawn sprinkling and laws restricting water use would help solve the problem. Building more reservoirs would also help.

Revision Checklist

Paragraph Development

1. Is the topic manageable (neither too broad nor too narrow)?

   _____

2. Is the paragraph written with the reader in mind?

   _____

3. Does the topic sentence identify the topic? (What is you're the topic?)

   _____

4. Does the topic sentence make a point about the topic? (What is the point?)

   _____

5. Does each sentence support the topic sentence? (List any that do not.)

   _____

6. Is sufficient detail included?

   _____

7. Is there a sentence at the end that brings the paragraph to a close? (What is it?)

   _____

The topic of the paragraph above—water quality and availability throughout the world—is too broad. Water quality and water availability are two separate topics, and both vary greatly throughout the world. To revise this paragraph the writer first narrowed the topic to one idea. Choosing the topic of increasing water availability in the United States, he wrote this revised paragraph:

Revised Paragraph

There are several easy-to-take actions that could increase water availability in the United States. First, lawn-sprinkling bans would reduce nonessential use of water in areas in which water is in short supply. Second, laws limiting the total amount of water a household could use would require people to cut down on their water use at home. Increasing the cost of water to households is a third way to restrict its use. Each of these actions could produce an immediate increase in water availability.

NEED TO KNOW

Revising Paragraphs

Revision is a process of examining and rethinking your ideas. It involves adding text, deleting text, and changing both what you say and how you say it. To know what to revise, do the following:

1. Draw a **revision map.** A revision map is similar to an idea map. It shows how your ideas relate to one another.

2. Use a **revision checklist.** The revision checklist offers focused questions that will help you evaluate your writing.

EXERCISE 12-8

Writing in Progress

Directions: Apply all the questions in the revision checklist—about both sentences and paragraphs—to the paragraph you wrote in Exercise 12-5.

 **Analyze It!**

Directions: In the following paragraph, underline the topic sentence. Then cross out sentences that contain unrelated details that do not support the topic sentence.

If you are a diner who loves to eat a little bit of everything, you should definitely sample the Spanish-based cuisine known as tapas. Tapas originated in Spain as small snacks—olives, almonds, cubes of cheese, slices of ham—eaten while drinking beer or wine in a neighborhood bar during the early evening. According to one legend. Alfonso, the king of Castile, acquired the habit of eating small snacks with wine when he was recovering from an illness, and he later advocated the practice for his subjects. Alfonso was a tyrant and not well-liked. Today, many diners order a selection of tapas for lunch or dinner rather than eating them only as cocktail appetizers. These diners are obviously not concerned with costs or calories Some tapas consist of toasted bread with toppings such as grilled anchovies, smoked ham, or marinated tomatoes. Other tapas are fried and served with sauces: for example, Patatas Brava consists of fried potatoes in a spicy sauce, and Albondigas are meatballs in garlic-tomato sauce. Spanish cuisine is known for delicious stews and soups as well as tapas If your taste buds are bored, and you want more variety, try some tapas!

Writing in Progress: Three Versions

This essay by Tracy Burgio illustrates the process of discovering and narrowing a topic, writing a first draft, and revising. As you read through Burgio's drafts, pay particular attention to the changes she makes.

Topic Selection

Beach

Illuminations

Holiday Inn Grand Island, modeling

Pleasure Island—Planet Hollywood

View from the window

Dinner at Grand Floridian Beach Resort

(Washington, D.C.)

Wash., D.C., changing of the guard

Narrowing a Topic

Washington, D.C.

Capitol

Lincoln Memorial

Visit to White House

(Vietnam Memorial) —— why it was created

(my reaction to it)

response of others

construction and location

The Mall

Smithsonian Museum

Georgetown University

First Draft Showing Revisions

Emotional

The ∧ Wall

Tracy Burgio

This is one of the trips that I went on, that I'll never forget. The place was
the Vietnam Memorial in
∧ Washington, D.C., about 6:30 P.M. and the sun was going down. ~~That means~~ *so there*
∧ *was a beautiful sunset*
~~that the sunset was beautiful~~.

I was standing at the beginning of the wall of the Vietnam Memorial. It
was the perfect time to be there, because all of a sudden, I felt very emotional
being so close to
~~next to~~ the Memorial. The Washington Monument is there, and after that, ~~its~~ *is*
the Capital. Straight in front of the Vietnam Memorial is the Lincoln Memorial.

The way that the sunset was going down, it lit up the whole sky, and the colors were just beautiful from reflecting on the memorials, and the Capitol.

What colors?—add

As I started walking passed the wall, ~~I had a very strange feeling~~ *certain things started to change*. The wall became larger and larger, *and taller than me and seemed as if it were 20-25 feet tall.* I felt very emotional. I couldn't get over how big the wall became. ~~On~~ *As I looked at* the wall, they had all the names of all the men who had died in the Vietnam War. As soon as *I* ~~you~~ start*ed* to look at all the names, *and felt as if I were going to cry. I felt sorry for all the men who* *I* ~~you~~ automatically became emotional *died in the Vietnam War.* A lady standing next to me was crying *as* ~~and~~ she put flowers in front of the wall on the ground. I *realized* ~~decided~~ that it was okay to be emotional at that time and at that place. After a

In what way?

little while, I wanted to touch the wall, to see what it was like, ~~and my friend took a picture of me.~~ *and as soon as I did, I had more feelings about it. It felt very smooth, and the names were engraved on the wall.*

What did it feel like?

Finally I finished walking and the wall became smaller and smaller, as it was in the beginning, which was a little higher above my ankles.

I realized that I'm never going to forget that moment in my life. The scenery was beautiful and the moment was sad, but the view was spectacular. It's something that *I won't* ~~you don't~~ want to forget, in fact *I will* ~~you will want to~~ treasure it!

Second Draft Showing Revisions

The Emotional Wall

Tracy Burgio

~~This is one of the trips that I went on that~~ *my trip to* I'll never forget. ~~The place was~~ the Vietnam Memorial in Washington, D.C. *It was* about 6:30 P.M. and the sun was going down, so there was a beautiful sunset! It was the perfect time to be ~~their~~ *there* because exactly right behind the memorial, the Washington Monument *is* ~~is there~~, and after that is the Capitol. Straight in front of the Vietnam Memorial is the Lincoln Memorial. The ~~way that the~~ sunset ~~was going down~~ *it* lit up the whole sky, and the colors were just beautiful, the way they reflected on the memorials and the Capitol. *Such as* pink, purple, yellow, and green.

As I started walking ~~passed~~ *past* the wall, ~~certain things started to change.~~ The wall became larger and larger, probably 20 to 25 feet taller than ~~me and the width would be about 30 inches.~~ *I am.* All of a sudden, I felt very emotional. I couldn't get over how big the wall became. As I looked on the wall, *I saw* ~~were~~ all the names of all the men *and women* who had died in the Vietnam War. As soon as I started to look at it, I automatically became emotional. *a* ~~As~~ if I were going to cry, because I felt very sorry for the men and women who died in the war. A lady standing next to me was crying as she put flowers in front of the wall ~~on the ground~~ *on the ground*. I realized that it was okay to be emotional at that time and that place. After a little while, I wanted to touch the wall, to see what it was like, and as soon as I did, I had more feelings about it. It felt very smooth and the names were engraved on the wall. Finally, as I finished walking and the wall became smaller and smaller as it was in the beginning which was a little higher above my ankles. when I first saw it.

I realized that I'm never going to forget that moment in my life. The scenery was beautiful and the moment was sad, but the view was spectacular. It's something that I won't want to forget, in fact I will always treasure it!

Final Draft

The Emotional Wall

Tracy Burgio

I'll never forget my trip to the Vietnam Memorial in Washington, D.C. It was about 6:30 P.M., and the sun was going down, so there was a beautiful sunset! It was the perfect time to be there because exactly right behind the memorial is the Washington Monument, and after that is the Capitol. Straight in front of the Vietnam Memorial is the Lincoln Memorial. The sun lit up the whole sky, and the colors were just beautiful; they reflected on the memorials and the Capitol, pink, purple, yellow, and green.

As I started walking past the wall, it became larger and larger, probably 20 to 25 feet taller than I am. I couldn't get over how big the wall became. As I looked at the wall, I saw the names of all the men and women who had died in the Vietnam War. As soon as I started to look at them, I automatically became emotional, as if I were going to cry. I felt very sorry for the men and women who died in the war. A lady standing next to me was crying as she put flowers on the ground in front of the wall. I realized that it was okay to be emotional at that time and that place.

After a little while, I wanted to touch the wall, to see what it was like, and, as soon as I did, I had more feelings about it. It felt very smooth, and the names were engraved on the wall. Finally, as I finished walking, the wall became smaller and smaller as it was when I first saw it.

I'm never going to forget that moment in my life. The scenery was beautiful, the view was spectacular, but the moment was sad. In fact, I will always treasure it!

Examining Student Writing

1. Evaluate the structure and content of the essay.
   a. Does the essay follow a logical plan? Describe its organization.
   b. What is Burgio's thesis?
   c. In what ways does she support her thesis?
   d. Evaluate the effectiveness of the title, introduction, and conclusion.
2. Study the changes Burgio made in her revisions. What kinds of changes did she make?
3. What further revisions would you suggest?

A STUDENT ESSAY

The Writer

Rachel Goodman successfully completed her associate's degree at Middlesex County College in Edison, New Jersey, in May 2005, and has transferred to Westchester University in Pennsylvania where she is enrolled in the Elementary Education program. She plans to become an elementary school English teacher.

The Writing Task

Rachel Goodman was taking a media course and studying advertising. Her instructor asked students to write a paper analyzing the appeal of advertising. Goodman chose to focus on the images, slogans, and jingles that help to sell products. As you read, be sure to notice how effectively she uses examples.

Title suggests a formula

Beautiful Words + Beautiful Images = One Beautiful Advertisement

Rachel Goodman

Introduction: opening with a question creates interest

What's the best way to sell a burger? You could use pictures of a family eating, laughing, and having a great time. You could write a catchy jingle people can't get out of their minds. Advertising is everywhere. It is in newspapers, magazines, and movies. It is on radio, television, and sides of buses. We are bombarded by the message that life will be better if we just use the advertised product. The best ads use simple pictures and words to make us feel good. An enormous amount of time and money goes into creating these ads.

Thesis statement

Companies pay advertising agencies thousands of dollars to come up with that one image, slogan, or jingle that will keep their products in the public's mind and make them loyal to their brands.

Topic sentence

One example is Oil of Olay. Whoever thought of the line "Love the skin you're in" was smart. It is simple and appeals to the emotions, sending the message that using Oil of Olay will make you feel better. It rhymes "in" with "skin," which makes it easy to remember and identifies the product as being good for the skin. In print, Olay places its products against a sky blue background, which gives the ads a pure and clean look—just the way you'd like your skin to feel.

Topic sentence

Another company that uses rhyme to sell their products is COVERGIRL.

"Be here. Be sheer. Let your energy show.
Sheer Rubies, Sheer Orchid, Pink Bliss, Orange Glow."

The word "sheer" is repeated, reinforcing the message that the makeup is light and natural looking. "Rubies" and "Orchid" stand for beauty and "Bliss" and "Glow" make ordinary colors sound more appealing. In print ads, COVER-GIRL uses purple as a background color for a dramatic look, a good choice for their main customers, teenage girls.

Topic sentence

Advertisers also use emotion to sell something as ordinary as fabric softener. In Purex ads the pictures and words use nature to reinforce a theme of purity.

Example

Nature is a smart tool to use when promoting something that is supposed to be clean and fresh. Calling the scent "After the Rain" or "Mountain Breeze" gives the impression that your clothes will smell and feel as if they were dried outside and are, therefore, more fresh and pure. The company also reinforces the message by using lots of white in their ads, including the word "Pure" as part of the brand name, and showing an innocent little girl on the product label.

Topic sentence

Pictures are worth a thousand words in advertising. If you see golden arches, you immediately think McDonald's. If you see a picture of a muscular bald man in a bright white T-shirt, you think Mr. Clean. Extra gum probably

Example

chose a stop sign for their print ads to make people flipping through magazines stop and look.

Topic sentence

And then there are logos. These are images that are used exclusively to identify a product. Think of the Coke logo, the swooping white lettering of

Example

"Coca Cola" on a bright red background. It probably was chosen because it gives Coke a youthful, energetic look, and the color red was picked because red can stimulate hunger and thirst.

Conclusion: Notice the use of questions.

The next time you go out to buy something, think about what made you decide to pick that particular brand. Is it because of the way it is advertised? Do you think you will feel or look better if you buy that product? Are you able to easily pick out that brand from a shelf of similar products? Can you hum the theme song? If the answer is yes, then the advertising has done its job!

EXAMINING STUDENT WRITING

1. How does Goodman move from one paragraph to another? Highlight transitional words and phrases that signal she is moving to a different topic.

2. Evaluate Goodman's introduction. What other ways could she have introduced her topic while building interest?

3. Examine Goodman's thesis statement. How accurately does it suggest the topics Goodman will cover in her essay?

4. What current ads could be used as examples in Goodman's essay?

Paragraph Writing Scenarios

Friends and Family

1. Write a paragraph describing an ancestor or relative you've never met, but about whom you've heard a lot. Include things others have said about this person that make him or her sound interesting.

2. Every family has its own idea of success. Write a paragraph about something you've done or could do to make your family proud of you.

Classes and Campus Life

1. You have an important assignment due tomorrow, but classes may be canceled because of the weather. Write a paragraph about how you will spend the evening, preparing for classes or hoping for a storm.

2. A book you need from the library has been out for weeks. Write a paragraph explaining how you will solve the problem.

Working Students

1. Imagine you are going to a job interview. Write a paragraph describing specific strengths you have that will enable you to handle both school and work.

2. Describe in a paragraph something you do to pass the time when work is slow.

Communities and Cultures

1. Some people do best as part of a team, and others prefer to do things alone. Write a paragraph describing one thing you'd rather do on your own and another in which you'd rather be part of a group or team.

2. Society has become very casual, with people wearing jeans in most places. Write a paragraph describing one place where you think jeans or other casual clothes are inappropriate.

ESL Tip

Nonsexist statements do not favor one sex over the other, nor do they ignore or insult either men or women. In general, writers are expected to use nonsexist language.

Writing Success Tip 12

Using Nonsexist Language

The words you choose when you write or speak can be unintentionally sexist. By using certain expressions and personal pronouns, you might make unfair references to males or females, or you may fail to include both sexes in a particular group.

SEXIST	A student will get good grades if *he* knows how to take lecture notes. (This statement fails to recognize that some students are women.)
NONSEXIST	A student will get good grades if *he* or *she* knows how to take lecture notes.
	or
	Students will get good grades if *they* know how to take lecture notes.
SEXIST	The *girl* at the customer service desk was helpful and efficient. (The term *girl* implies childishness or immaturity.)
NONSEXIST	The *woman* at the customer service desk was helpful and efficient.
	or
	The *customer service representative* was helpful and efficient.
SEXIST	The *male nurse* gave my grandmother the prescribed medication. (This statement makes an unnecessary distinction between male and female nurses.)
NONSEXIST	The nurse gave my grandmother the prescribed medication.

Here are a few guidelines to follow in avoiding sexist language:

1. **When referring to people in general, use "he or she" rather than "he."**

SEXIST	A writer should proofread *his* paper.
NONSEXIST	A writer should proofread *his or her* paper.

2. **When "he or she" seems awkward or wordy, rewrite your sentence using plural nouns and pronouns.**

NONSEXIST	*Writers* should proofread *their* papers.

3. **Avoid using the words "man" or "mankind" to refer to people in general; avoid occupational terms ending in *-man*.**

SEXIST	NONSEXIST
Any man who gives ...	Anyone who gives…
policeman	police officer
salesman	salesperson

4. **Avoid expressions that make unfair or negative references to men or women.**

SEXIST	NONSEXIST
career gal	career woman
my old man	my husband

5. **Refer to a woman by her own name, not by her husband's name.**

SEXIST	Mrs. Samuel Goldstein was named Educator of the Year.
NONSEXIST	Rita Goldstein was named Educator of the Year.

WRITING ABOUT A READING

THINKING BEFORE READING

The following reading, "Finding a Mate: Not the Same as It Used to Be," is taken from a textbook by James M. Henslin titled *Sociology: A Down-to-Earth Approach to Core Concepts*. As you read this selection, notice how the author uses examples to illustrate his thesis.

1. Preview the reading, using the steps discussed in Chapter 2, p. 38.

2. Connect the reading to your own experience by answering the following questions:

   a. How did your parents meet?

   b. What do you think is the best way to find a mate?

READING

FINDING A MATE:
NOT THE SAME AS IT USED TO BE

James M. Henslin

1   THINGS HAVEN'T CHANGED ENTIRELY. Boys and girls still get interested in each other at their neighborhood schools, and men and women still meet at college. Friends still serve as matchmakers and introduce friends, hoping they might click. People still meet at churches and bars, at the mall and at work.

2   But technology is bringing about some fundamental changes.

3   Among traditional people—Jews, Arabs, and in the villages of China and India—for centuries matchmakers have brought couples together. They carefully match a prospective couple by background—or by the position of the stars, whatever their tradition dictates—arranging marriages to please the families of the bride and groom, and, hopefully, the couple, too.

4   In China, this process is being changed by technology. Matchmakers use computerized records—age, sex, education, personal interests, and, increasingly significant, education and earnings—to identify compatibility and predict lifelong happiness.

5   But parents aren't leaving the process up to technology. They want their input, too. In one park in Beijing, hundreds of mothers and fathers gather twice a week to try to find spouses for their adult children. They bring photos of their children and share them with one another, talking up their kid's virtues while evaluating the sales pitch they get from the other parents. Some of the parents even sit on the grass, next to handwritten ads they've written about their children.

6   Closer to home, Americans are turning more and more to the Internet. Numerous sites advertise that they offer thousands of potential companions, lovers, or spouses. For a low monthly fee, you, too, can meet the person of your dreams.

7   The photos are fascinating in their variety. Some seem to be lovely people, attractive and vivacious, and one wonders why they are posting their photos and personal information online. Do they have some secret flaw that they need

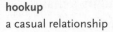

hookup
a casual relationship

to do this? Others seem okay, although perhaps, a bit needy. Then there are the pitiful, and one wonders if they will ever find a mate, or even a **hookup**, for that matter. Some are desperate, begging for someone—anyone—to make contact with them: women who try for sexy poses, exposing too much flesh, suggesting the promise of at least a good time; and men who try their best to look like hulks, their muscular presence promising the same.

8   The Internet dating sites are not filled with losers, although there are plenty of them. A lot of regular, ordinary people post their profiles, too. And some do so successfully. More and more, Internet postings are losing their stigma, and couples are finding mates via electronic matchmaking.

9   A frustrating aspect of these sites is that the "thousands of eligible propects" that they tout are spread over the nation. You might find that a person who piques your interest lives in another part of the country. You can do a search for your area, but there are likely to be few from it.

10   Not to worry. Technology comes to the rescue.

11   The latest is dating on demand. You sit at home, turn on your TV, and search for your partner. Your local cable company has already done all the hard work. They have hosted singles events at bars and malls and helped singles make three-to-five minute tapes talking about themselves and what they are looking for in a mate.

12   You can view the videos free—which is often more interesting than watching retuns of old TV shows. But if you get interested, for a small fee—again—you have the opportunity to contact the individuals who have caught your interest.

13   Now all you need is to get a private detective service—also available by on-line contact, for another fee—to see if this engaging person is already married, has a dozen kids, has been sued for paternity or child support, or is a child molester or a rapist.

14   Hmm, maybe the old village matchmaker wasn't such a bad idea, after all.

GETTING READY TO WRITE

Reviewing the Reading

1. List six criteria that matchmakers in China use to identify compatibility and predict happiness.

2. According to the author, what aspect of Internet dating sites is frustrating?

3. Explain how "dating on demand" works.

4. How does the author view electronic dating? Is he enthusiastic or skeptical about how technology has changed the process of finding a mate?

5. What is the purpose of the cartoon included with the selection?

Examining the Reading Using an Idea Map

Review the reading by completing the missing parts of the idea map shown below.

Finding a Mate: Not the Same as It Used to Be

Technology is changing how people go about _____ _____.

Traditional people—Jews, Arabs, those in villages of China and India—have relied for centuries on _____.

In China, technology is changing the matchmaking process.

Computerized records base compatibility on:
- _____
- _____
- _____
- _____
- _____
- _____

In America, people are also turning to technology to find a mate.

Internet dating sites offer:
- Wide variety of people
- _____
- _____

Dating on demand:
- Cable TV company helps singles make tapes of themselves
- _____
- _____
- _____
- _____

Author concludes with comment about the new ways of finding a mate versus the old.

Strengthening Your Vocabulary

Part A: Using the word's context, word parts, or a dictionary, write a brief definition of each of the following words as it is used in the reading.

1. prospective (paragraph 3) _____
2. compatibility (paragraph 4) _____
3. vivacious (paragraph 7) _____
4. stigma (paragraph 8) _____
5. tout (paragraph 9) _____
6. piques (paragraph 9) _____

Part B: Choose one of the words above and draw a word map (see p. 84) of it.

Reacting to Ideas: Discussion and Journal Writing

Get ready to write about the reading by discussing the following:

1. What do you think of the traditional methods of matchmaking described in this selection? How might technology improve upon these methods?
2. Evaluate the criteria that matchmakers use in China to identify compatibility and predict happiness. What traits would you add to the list? Which ones would you remove?
3. Would you trust the description of a person you met online? Why or why not? If you became interested in a person you met online, would you use a detective service to look into his or her background?

WRITING ABOUT THE READING

Paragraph Options

1. Write a paragraph describing how you first met a person who is important in your life.
2. If you are single, have you considered using an electronic dating site? Write a paragraph explaining why or why not.
3. Do you agree that Internet dating sites are losing their stigma? Write a paragraph explaining your answer.

Essay Options

4. Imagine the scene described in paragraph 5, with hundreds of parents trying to make matches for their children in a park in Beijing. If your parents were there, what would they say about you in their "sales pitch" to other parents? Write an essay explaining how you think your parents would describe you. In addition, try writing an ad that your parents might write about you.

5. What can you tell from the reading about the author's attitude toward Internet dating? Write an essay examining the ways the author reveals his feelings toward the subject. Include in your essay specific examples from the selection that show he is sympathetic, suspicious, disapproving, etc. Also, explain how the selection would be different if it were entirely objective. How does the author's tone add or detract from the reading?

6. What if you were to make a tape for a dating-on-demand video? Write an essay describing what you would want to include about yourself and the person you are hoping to meet.

Revision Checklist

Paragraph Development

1. Is the topic manageable (neither too broad nor too narrow)?
2. Is the paragraph written with the reader in mind?
3. Does the topic sentence identify the topic?
4. Does the topic sentence make a point about the topic?
5. Does each sentence support the topic sentence?
6. Is there sufficient detail?
7. Is there a sentence at the end that brings the paragraph to a close?

Sentence Development

8. Are there any sentence fragments, run-on sentences, or comma splices?
9. Are ideas combined to produce more effective sentences?
10. Are adjectives and adverbs used to make the sentences vivid and interesting?
11. Are relative clauses and prepositional phrases like *-ing* phrases used to add detail?
12. Are pronouns used correctly and consistently?

CHAPTER REVIEW AND PRACTICE

CHAPTER REVIEW

To review and check your recall of the chapter, match each term in Column A with its meaning in Column B, and write its letter in the space provided.

COLUMN A

_____ 1. topic sentence

_____ 2. revision map

_____ 3. sufficient

_____ 4. revision checklist

_____ 5. relevant details

_____ 6. topic

_____ 7. revision

COLUMN B

a. details directly related to or defining the topic

b. process of examining and rethinking written ideas and making changes by rewriting

c. the subject of a paragraph

d. states the main point or idea of a paragraph

e. enough

f. questions to use in evaluating your writing

g. a visual display of ideas

EDITING PRACTICE

Paragraph 1

The following student paragraph begins with a topic sentence that is too broad. Revise this topic sentence to make it more specific.

College is different from high school. In high school, there were almost no papers assigned. When we were given writing assignments, we were not expected to type them on a computer. It was acceptable to write papers using pencil and paper. My instructors at college not only expect me to type my papers, but to write papers that provide objective support for an opinion. During my first semester, I spent nearly all of my time at the library trying to figure out how to write an objective paper instead of a paper with just my opinion. It didn't take me

(continued)

long to figure out that the requirements for college papers are very different from those assigned in high school. Furthermore, my high school teachers would take class time to help students review for exams and even small tests. As a result, I did very little studying on my own. In addition, most high school tests were objective tests, and essay questions were found only on final exams. College instructors expect students to prepare themselves for exams, and only rarely are these exams objective ones. It was a real struggle for me to learn how to prepare for college exams and to write good essays, but now that I have two semesters' experience, I think I am on the right track.

Paragraph 2

The following paragraph is a description of a bedroom. It is a weak description because it lacks detail. Revise it by adding details that help the reader to visualize this room.

My favorite room in the house is my bedroom. My room is a shade of blue that contrasts with its white drapes and bedspread. The bed and dressers are made of pine. Plants hang in the windows. The room is always quiet because it is in the back of the house and overlooks the yard.

 **INTERNET ACTIVITIES**

1. Revising

Print out this checklist for revising writing from the George Mason University Writing Center.

http://www.gmu.edu/departments/writingcenter/handouts/check.html

Use it to check your own or a peer's essay.

2. Using Appropriate Language

Review this information on using appropriate language in your writing.

> http://owl.english.purdue.edu/owl/printable/608/

Notice that there are many issues that you need to pay attention to. Check how well your favorite news Web site is doing with these.

3. MyWritingLab

Visit this site to get more help with drafting and revising paragraphs.

> http://www.mywritinglab.com

Click on the Study Plan tab, then on "Paragraph Basics and Development," and then on "Writing Topic Sentences," "Revising Paragraphs," and "Editing Paragraphs."

13

Developing, Arranging, and Connecting Details

In this chapter you will learn to:

1. Develop specific details.

2. Arrange details in a paragraph.

3. Use transitions to connect details.

"It was a dark and stormy night. Rain fell in torrents, soaking through the thin cardboard that passed for a roof in the old mansion. Alone in the attic, Sarah sobbed, imagining her mother dancing while she shivered in the cold."

WRITE ABOUT IT!

The caption below the photograph presents one possible description of what is happening in the house. Write an alternative scenario for what could be happening in the photo. Be as detailed as possible.

What would horror stories or mysteries be without carefully arranged details like those in the caption above and the one you wrote?. They would be boring, for one thing. Imagine how quickly you'd lose interest if this story began, "Sarah's mother went out and left her home with a babysitter. But then

344

the babysitter's boyfriend called, so she left, and it was raining and Sarah got scared." Maybe "Sarah" *was* scared, but it's doubtful that you, the reader, feel any tension.

Details—how things happen and when they happen—are what drive a story. The way you arrange details is called **time sequence**. Words and phrases that lead readers from one step in a story to the next are called **transitions**. Your writing will improve as you learn to use details and arrange them well. In this chapter you will learn how to develop details and arrange them using time-sequence, spatial, and least/most arrangements to make your paragraphs clear, lively, and interesting. You will also learn how to use transitions to connect your details.

WRITING

Developing a Paragraph Using Specific Details

Read the following pairs of statements. For each pair, place a check mark in the blank before the statement that is more vivid and that contains more information.

1. _____ **a.** Professor Valquez gives a lot of homework.

   _____ **b.** Professor Valquez assigns 20 problems during each class and requires us to read two chapters per week.

2. _____ **a.** In Korea, people calculate age differently.

   _____ **b.** In Korea, people are considered to be one year old at birth.

3. _____ **a.** It was really hot Tuesday.

   _____ **b.** On Tuesday the temperature in New Haven reached 97 degrees.

These pairs of sentences illustrate the difference between vague statements and specific statements. Statement a in each pair conveys little information and also lacks interest and appeal. Statement b offers specific, detailed information and, as a result, is more interesting.

As you generate ideas and draft paragraphs, try to include as many specific details as possible. These details (called **supporting details** because they support your topic sentence) make your writing more interesting and your ideas more convincing.

The sample paragraph below lacks detail. Compare it with the revised paragraph that follows it. Notice how the revision has produced a much more lively, informative, and convincing paragraph.

Sample Paragraph

Being a waiter or waitress is a more complicated job than most people think. First of all, you must have a friendly personality. You must be able to maintain a smile no matter what your inner feelings may be. Proper attire and good hygiene are also essential. You have to be good at memorizing what your customers want and make sure each order is made to their specifications. If you are friendly, neat, and attentive to your customers, you will be successful.

ESL Tip

Concrete is the opposite of *abstract.* Something concrete can be experienced through the senses (by seeing, hearing, tasting, etc.). In contrast, abstractions are ideas, not physical things.

Specific is the opposite of *general.* There are many levels of specificity. For example, *beverage* is more specific than *liquid; coffee* is more specific than *beverage; Joe's black coffee* is even more specific.

Revised Paragraph

Being a waitress is a more complicated job than the average customer thinks. First of all, a friendly, outgoing personality is important. No one wants to be greeted by a waitress who has an angry, indifferent, or "I'm bored with this job" expression on her face. A waitress should try to smile, regardless of the circumstances. When a screaming child hurls a plate of french fries across the table, smile and wipe up the ketchup. Proper attire and good hygiene are important, too. A waitress in a dirty dress and with hair hanging down into the food does not please customers. Finally, attentiveness to customers' orders is important. Be certain that each person gets the correct order and that the food is prepared according to his or her specifications. Pay particular attention when serving salads and steaks, since different dressings and degrees of rareness are easily confused. Following these suggestions will lead to happy customers as well as larger tips.

In this revision, the writer added examples, included more descriptive words, and made all details more concrete and specific.

Here are a few suggestions for how to include more specific details:

1. **Add names, numbers, times, and places.**

VAGUE	I bought a used car.
MORE SPECIFIC	Yesterday afternoon I bought a red, two-door 1996 Toyota Tercel at the new "Toy-a-Rama" dealership.

2. **Add more facts and explanation.**

VAGUE	My fax machine works well.
MORE SPECIFIC	My fax machine allows me to send letters and documents through a phone line in seconds and at minimal cost.

3. **Use examples.**

VAGUE	Dogs learn their owners' habits.
MORE SPECIFIC	As soon as I reach for my wire garden basket, my golden retriever knows this means I'm going outside, and he rushes to the back door.

4. **Draw from your personal experience.**

VAGUE	People sometimes eat to calm down.
MORE SPECIFIC	My sister relaxes every evening with a bowl of popcorn.

Depending on your topic, you may need to do research to get more specific details. Dictionaries, encyclopedias, and magazine articles are often good sources. Think of research as interesting detective work and a chance to learn. For example, if you are writing a paragraph about the safety of air bags in cars, you may need to locate some current facts and statistics. Your college library and the Internet will be two good sources; a car dealership and a mechanic may be two others. (Refer to Writing Success Tip 14, "Avoiding Plagiarism and Citing Sources (p. 413)," to learn more about telling your reader where you got your information.)

EXERCISE 13-1

Directions: Revise each of the following statements to make it more specific.

EXAMPLE   Biology is a difficult course.

Biology involves memorizing scientific terms and learning some of life's complex processes.

1. I rode the train.

_____

_____

2. Pizza is easy to prepare.

_____

_____

3. The Fourth of July is a holiday.

_____

_____

4. I bought a lawnmower.

_____

_____

5. The van broke down.

_____

_____

EXERCISE 13-2

Directions: Write a paragraph on one of the following topics. Develop a topic sentence that expresses one main point about the topic. Then develop your paragraph using specific details.

1. Your favorite food (or junk food)
2. How pets help people
3. Why shopping is (or is not) fun
4. A sport (or hobby) you would like to take up
5. An annoying habit

Methods of Arranging Details

Your paragraph can have many good details in it, but if they are arranged in a jumbled fashion, your writing will lack impact. You must arrange your details logically within each paragraph. Let us look at three common ways of arranging details:

1. Time-sequence arrangement

2. Spatial arrangement

3. Least/most arrangement

Time-Sequence Arrangement

When you are describing an event or series of events, it is often easiest to arrange them in the order in which they happened. This arrangement is called **time sequence**. The following time-sequence map will help you visualize this arrangement of details.

Visualize It! →

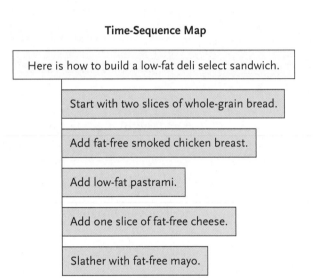

Time-Sequence Map

> Here is how to build a low-fat deli select sandwich.
>> Start with two slices of whole-grain bread.
>> Add fat-free smoked chicken breast.
>> Add low-fat pastrami.
>> Add one slice of fat-free cheese.
>> Slather with fat-free mayo.

You can also use time sequence to explain how events happened or to tell a story. For example, you can explain how you ended up living in Cleveland or tell a story about a haunted house. This is called a narrative and is discussed in more detail in Chapter 14, p. 368. In the following sample paragraph, the student has arranged details in time sequence. Read the paragraph and then fill in the blanks in the time-sequence map that follows it.

Sample Time-Sequence Paragraph

Driving a standard-shift vehicle is easy if you follow these steps. First, push the clutch pedal down. The clutch is the pedal on the left. Then start the car. Next, move the gearshift into first gear. On most cars this is the straight-up position. Next, give the car some gas, and slowly release the clutch pedal until you start moving. Finally, be ready to shift into higher gears—second, third, and so on. A diagram of where to find each gear usually appears on the gearshift knob. With practice, you will learn to start up smoothly and shift without the car making grinding noises or lurching.

 Visualize It!

Time-Sequence Map

Driving a standard-shift vehicle is easy.

Make sure clutch pedal is pushed in.

Practice.

Time-Sequence Transitions

Look again at the sample paragraph. Notice that transitions are used to lead you from one step to another. Try to pick them out; underline those that you find. Did you underline *first, then, next,* and *finally*? Using transitions like those listed below will help you to link details in a time-sequence paragraph.

> **NEED TO KNOW**
>
> **Common Time-Sequence Transitions**
>
> | first | next | before |
> |---|---|---|
> | second | during | now |
> | third | at the same time | later |
> | in the beginning | following | at last |
> | then | after | finally |

EXERCISE 13-3

Directions: Arrange in time sequence the supporting-detail sentences that follow the topic sentence below. Place a "1" in the blank before the detail that should appear first in the paragraph, a "2" before the detail that should appear second, and so on.

TOPIC SENTENCE   Registration for college classes requires planning and patience.

SUPPORTING-DETAIL SENTENCES

_____ a. Find out which of the courses that you need are being offered that particular semester.

_____ b. Study your degree requirements, and figure out which courses you need to take before you can take others.

_____ c. Then start working out a schedule.

_____ d. For example, a math course may have to be taken before an accounting or a science course.

_____ e. Then, when you register, if one course or section is closed, you will have others in mind that will work with your schedule.

_____ f. Select alternative courses that you can take if all sections of one of your first-choice courses are closed.

EXERCISE 13-4

Directions: Write a paragraph on one of the following topics. First, write a topic sentence that identifies your topic and expresses your main point about it. Then arrange your supporting-detail sentences in order. Be sure to use transitions to connect your ideas. When you have finished, draw a time-sequence map of your paragraph (see p. 349 for a model). Use your map to check that you have included sufficient details and that you have presented your details in the correct sequence.

1. Making up for lost time
2. Closing (or beginning) a chapter of your life
3. Getting more (or less) out of an experience than you expected
4. Having an adventure
5. Having an experience that made you feel like saying, "Look who's talking!"

ESL Tip

Look who's talking means the speaker doesn't think the person who expressed a criticism had a right to do so because of his or her own behavior (for example, if someone who's smoking a cigarette complains that the room is too smoky).

Spatial Arrangement

Suppose you are asked to describe a car you have just purchased. You want your reader, who has never seen the car, to visualize it. How would you organize your description? You could describe the car from bottom to top or from top to bottom, or from front to back. This method of presentation is called **spatial arrangement.** For other objects, you might arrange your details from inside to outside, from near to far, or from east to west. Notice how, in the following paragraph, the details are arranged from top to bottom.

Sample Spatial-Arrangement Paragraph

My dream house will have a three-level outdoor deck that will be ideal for relaxing on after a hard day's work. The top level of the deck will be connected by sliding glass doors to the family room. On this level there will be a hot tub, a large picnic table with benches, and a comfortable padded chaise. On the middle level there will be a suntanning area, a hammock, and two built-in planters for a mini-herb garden. The lowest level, which will meet the lawn, will have a built-in stone barbeque pit for big cookouts and a gas grill for everyday use.

Can you visualize the deck?

Spatial-Arrangement Transitions

In spatial-arrangement paragraphs, transitions are particularly important since they often reveal placement or position of objects or parts. Using transitions like those listed in the Need to Know box below will help you to link details in a spatial-arrangement paragraph.

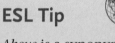

ESL Tip

Above is a synonym for *over*, and *below* is similar to *under* (or *beneath*). In some sentences, you can use either word in each pair, but sometimes you can't. When an object is *under* or *over* something, it is usually close to it. (In fact, the two objects may be touching.) Note: *Behind* means "in back of."

NEED TO KNOW

Common Spatial-Arrangement Transitions

above	next to	nearby
below	inside	on the other side
beside	outside	beneath
in front of	behind	to the west (or other direction)

EXERCISE 13-5

Directions: Use spatial arrangement to order the supporting-detail sentences that follow the topic sentence below. Place a "1" in the blank before the detail that should appear first in the paragraph, a "2" before the detail that should appear second, and so on.

TOPIC SENTENCE   My beautiful cousin Audry always looks as if she has dressed quickly and given her appearance little thought.

SUPPORTING-DETAIL SENTENCES

_____ **a.** She usually wears an oversized, baggy sweater, either black or blue-black, with the sleeves pushed up.

_____ **b.** Black slip-on sandals complete the look; she wears them in every season.

_____ **c.** On her feet she wears mismatched socks.

_____ **d.** Her short, reddish hair is usually wind-blown, hanging every which way from her face.

_____ **e.** She puts her makeup on unevenly, if at all.

_____ **f.** The sweater covers most of her casual, rumpled skirt.

EXERCISE 13-6

Directions: Write a paragraph on one of the following topics. First, write a topic sentence that identifies your topic and expresses your main point about it. Then, use spatial arrangement to develop your supporting details.

1. The room you are in now

2. The building where you live

3. A photograph or painting that you like

4. Your dream car

5. Your favorite chair or place

Least/Most Arrangement

Another method of arranging details is to present them in order from least to most or most to least, according to some quality or characteristic. For example, you might choose least to most important, serious, frightening, or humorous. In writing a paragraph explaining your reasons for attending college, you might arrange details from most to least important. In writing about an exciting evening, you might arrange your details from most to least exciting.

As you read the following paragraph, note how the writer has arranged details in a logical way.

Sample Least/Most Paragraph

This week has been filled with good news. One night when balancing my checkbook, I discovered a $155 error in my checking account—in my favor, for once! I was even happier when I finally found a buyer for my Chevy Blazer that I had been trying to sell all winter. Then my boss told me he was submitting my name for a 50-cent hourly raise; I certainly didn't expect that. Best of all, I learned that I'd been accepted into the Radiology curriculum for next fall.

In this paragraph, the details are arranged from least to most important.

Least/Most Transitions

In least/most paragraphs, transitions help your reader to follow your train of thought. Using transitions like those listed in the Need to Know box on the next page will help you link details in a least/most paragraph.

ESL Tip

English has many idioms with *under* and *over*. For example, *above all* means "most important."

Moreover and *in addition* mean "and." They are more formal ways to connect similar ideas.

NEED TO KNOW

Common Least/Most Transitions

most important	particularly important	moreover
above all	even more	in addition
especially	best of all	not only . . . but also

EXERCISE 13-7

Directions: Write a paragraph on one of the following topics. First, write a topic sentence that identifies your topic and expresses your main point about it. Then use a least/most arrangement to order your details. When you have finished, draw a map of your paragraph. Use your map to check that you have included sufficient details and that you have arranged your details in least/most order.

1. Your reasons for choosing the college you are attending
2. Changes in your life since you began college
3. Three commercials you saw on television recently
4. Why you like a certain book or movie
5. Good (or bad) things that have happened to you recently

EXERCISE 13-8

Directions: Write a topic sentence for each of the following topics. Then indicate what method (time sequence, spatial, or least/most) you would use to arrange supporting details.

TOPIC	relationship with a friend
TOPIC SENTENCE	Whenever George and I get together, he always takes over the conversation.
METHOD OF ARRANGEMENT	Time sequence

1. TOPIC   animals that have humanlike behaviors

    TOPIC SENTENCE _____

    METHOD OF ARRANGEMENT _____

2. TOPIC   a difficulty that I faced

    TOPIC SENTENCE _____

    METHOD OF ARRANGEMENT _____

3. TOPIC   feeling under pressure

   TOPIC SENTENCE   _____

   _____

   METHOD OF   _____
   ARRANGEMENT

4. TOPIC   a favorite dinner menu

   TOPIC SENTENCE   _____

   _____

   METHOD OF   _____
   ARRANGEMENT

5. TOPIC   an exciting sporting event

   TOPIC SENTENCE   _____

   _____

   METHOD OF   _____
   ARRANGEMENT

EXERCISE 13-9

Directions: Find several magazine or newspaper ads. Working in a group, identify the method of arrangement of the advertising copy.

NEED TO KNOW

Developing, Arranging, and Connecting Details

Be sure to use interesting and lively **details** to support your topic sentence.

- Choose details that are specific and concrete.

- Within your paragraphs, arrange **details** in a **logical order.** Three techniques for arranging **details** are

  - **time-sequence arrangement;** information is presented in the order in which it happened.

  - **spatial arrangement;** descriptive details are arranged according to their position in space.

  - **least/most arrangement;** ideas are arranged from least to most or most to least according to some quality or characteristic.

- Use **transitions** to help your reader move easily from one key detail to the next.

Analyze It!

Directions: The following paragraph lacks concrete details to make it interesting and informative. Revise the paragraph by adding details to help readers visualize the writer's shopping experience.

If I go grocery shopping before supper, without taking a list of items that I really need, the results can be disastrous. Because I'm hungry, everything looks good, and I tend to overload my cart. The problem starts in the produce department. Perhaps I need bananas and broccoli. After placing these items in my cart, I find myself adding a lot of other fruits and vegetables. Then I go to the fish department, where I get two kinds of fish instead of one. I proceed to the cereal aisle and put three boxes in my cart. On the way to get yogurt, I end up buying ice cream. "This has got to stop!" I say to myself, but myself does not listen.

A STUDENT ESSAY

The Writer

The following essay was written by Maya Prestwich, a student at Northwestern University, in Evanston, Illinois.

The Writing Task

Prestwich submitted an essay to her college newspaper, the *Daily Northwestern*, where it was published. This essay is a good example of the use of concrete details to support a thesis. As you read, highlight particularly informative or interesting details.

Title: suggests main point of the essay

Halloween: Fun Without Cultural Guilt
Maya Prestwich

Introduction: tells story of three children—essay opens with details

1   What are you gonna be?" That's the question circulating around school yards this week. I overheard a group of children talking about Halloween costumes as I walked by the school three blocks from my house.

2   The lone girl of the group was going as a ballerina, and the boys were fighting it out over who could be Batman. All feelings about feminism and gender

stereotypes aside, the whole scene made me smile. I'd forgotten how much children love Halloween and how much I love it, too. Years of being immersed in campus life had left me feeling as if Halloween really was just another day, but moving off-campus has allowed me to rediscover it.

Thesis statement

3   What is it about Halloween that seems to put everyone in a happier, more adventurous mood? There's that feeling in the air (beneath the chill), a festive feeling, a primitive feeling, a pagan feeling. October 31 is really the only time when we allow ourselves to freely embrace that aspect of our humanity.

Topic sentence

4   It's also a very rare chance for everyone, children and adults, to reinvent themselves a little. School teachers get to be witches, little boys and girls can be superheroes. Country farm girls who listen to Garth Brooks pretend to be punk rock fans, and for one night, I can pretend to be a confident, indifferent, dangerous black cat. It seems sort of ridiculous on the surface, but it's impor-

Interesting details

tant to me to have this day when coloring outside the lines is acceptable. I believe it is crucial that we help our children learn that doing things they wouldn't normally do can be fun and exhilarating and liberating.

Topic sentence

5   For grown-ups, and us almost-grown-ups, it's important to remember on Halloween that you can change what you are "going to be" if you know you made the wrong decision. Being a cat or a ghost or a globe or a Power Ranger is a decision I would agonize over for a full month, but it was still just a decision. A different costume could easily be thrown together or an old one dragged out of the closet, and I could take the evening in a different direction.

Topic sentence

6   Similarly, all of those big adult things that we agonize over, what career to choose, which job to go for, whom to marry, are still just decisions. Reinventing yourself, changing your life is not quite as simple as changing your costume, but it's not quite as difficult as we make it out to be, either.

Topic sentence

7   There's another pretty spiffy thing about Halloween, and that's the way that it unifies us, Catholic, Jewish, or unaffiliated, rich or middle class, city or country, believers in one god, believers in many gods, believers in no gods. We can share this one holiday without having to go through sensitivity training. Every kid gets dressed up and hopes for a good haul, everyone who can leaves the porch light on and answers the doorbell bearing Tootsie Rolls, and every mom decides that a crime wave is going to hit their small town and participates in the ritual "inspecting of the candy."

Good use of detail

Conclusion: refers back to the title

8   Halloween is freer of culture clash than even Independence or Columbus days. Face it, it is a really awesome holiday, a day for fun and spontaneity without any of the ramifications of cultural guilt and that is cause for celebration, or at least the consumption of candy.

EXAMINING STUDENT WRITING

1. Does Prestwich follow a logical plan of organization? Suggest how the organization could be improved.

2. Do you think further details are needed? If so, suggest which paragraphs need more detail.

3. Prestwich's thesis is in the form of a question. Is this format effective or would a statement be more effective? Give reasons for your answer.

4. Do you think the notion of cultural guilt is adequately explained?

ESL Tip

In the United States, *Halloween* is a holiday for fun—for dressing in costume, going trick-or-treating for candy, having parties, and telling scary stories about ghosts and skeletons. Halloween is sometimes compared to the Hispanic holiday called The Day of the Dead, but the origins, customs, and purpose of these two holidays differ. Halloween is not a time for remembering dead relatives. The United States has two other holidays for that purpose—Memorial Day and Veterans Day (a holiday that honors all who served in the military, the living and the dead).

Paragraph Writing Scenarios

Friends and Family

1. Think of a good friend with whom you once had a major argument. Write a paragraph explaining what that argument was about and how you got over it.

2. Write a paragraph describing a relative other than your parents who you were close to as a child.

Classes and Campus Life

1. Think about the teachers you have this year. Write a paragraph comparing two of them. What are the main differences in their styles of teaching?

2. If there is a campus store, write a paragraph about the things you regularly would buy there or would not buy there. If there is not a store on your campus, write a paragraph explaining why you think your school should add one.

Working Students

1. Write an imaginary letter to your boss explaining what you would do to improve your workplace.

2. Write a paragraph explaining why you deserve a raise.

Communities and Cultures

1. People often form ideas about a culture without knowing anyone from that culture. Describe one incorrect idea, misconception, or stereotype that people have about a culture.

2. People live in a variety of communities. Choosing from urban, suburban, rural, or small-town neighborhoods, write a paragraph describing the one you'd most like to live in and why.

Writing Success Tip 13

How to Write a Summary

In many college courses, you will be asked to write a summary of a reading. A summary is a very short restatement of the ideas and major supporting details. It does not include all information in the reading. The following tips will help you gather and organize the material you need to write a clear summary:

1. **Be sure you understand the reading and have identified the writer's major points.**

2. **Reread the material and underline each major idea, or draw a revision map of the reading.**

3. **Write one sentence that states the writer's overall concern or most important idea.** To do this, ask yourself, "What one topic is the material about?" Then ask, "What point is the writer trying to make about that topic?" This sentence will be the topic sentence of your summary.

4. **Be sure to use your own words rather than those of the author.**

5. **Review the major supporting information that you underlined.** Select key details to include in your summary. The amount of detail you include will depend on your purpose for writing the summary.

6. **Present ideas in the summary in the same order in which they appear in the reading.**

7. **If the writer presents a clear opinion on, or expresses an attitude toward, the subject matter, include it in your summary.**

WRITING ABOUT A READING

THINKING BEFORE READING

The following reading, "A Brother's Murder," explains how a man feels about the circumstances surrounding the death of his street-smart, younger brother. As you read this selection, notice that Brent Staples uses specific details to make his essay vivid and real. Also notice that he arranges his details logically, mainly using the time-sequence pattern.

1. Preview the reading using the steps provided in Chapter 2, p. 38.

2. Connect the reading to your own experience by answering the following questions:

    a. If you grew up in a neighborhood filled with crime, run-down buildings, and hopelessness, would you remain part of the community or move away from it?

    b. What could you say or do to help a relative or friend headed for trouble?

READING
A Brother's Murder
Brent Staples

1   It has been more than two years since my telephone rang with the news that my younger brother Blake—just 22 years old—had been murdered. The young man who killed him was only 24. Wearing a ski mask, he emerged from a car, fired six times at close range with a massive .44 Magnum, then fled. The two had once been inseparable friends. A senseless rivalry—beginning, I think, with an argument over a girlfriend—escalated from **posturing**, to threats, to violence, to murder. The way the two were living, death could have come to either of them from anywhere. In fact, the assailant had already survived multiple gunshot wounds from an incident much like the one in which my brother lost his life.

posturing
putting on an attitude, posing

2   I left the East Coast after college, spent the mid- and late-1970s in Chicago as a graduate student, taught for a time, then became a journalist. Within 10 years of leaving my hometown, I was overeducated and "upwardly mobile," ensconced on a quiet, tree-lined street where voices raised in anger were scarcely ever heard. The telephone, like some grim **umbilical**, kept me connected to the old world with news of deaths, imprisonings, and misfortune. I felt emotionally beaten up. Perhaps to protect myself, I added a psychological dimension to the physical distance I had already achieved. I rarely visited my hometown. I shut it out.

umbilical
connecting cord, similar to the cord which joins a baby to the placenta in the womb

3   As I fled the past, so Blake embraced it. On Christmas of 1983, I traveled from Chicago to a black section of Roanoke, Virginia, where he then lived. The desolate public housing projects, the hopeless, idle young men crashing against one another—these reminded me of the embittered town we'd grown up in. It was a place where once I would have been comfortable, or at least sure of myself. Now, hearing of my brother's forays into crime, his scrapes with police and street thugs, I was scared, unsteady on foreign terrain.

4   I saw that Blake's romance with the street life and the hustler image had flowered dangerously. One evening that late December, standing in some Roanoke dive among drug dealers and grim, hair-trigger losers, I told him I feared for his life. He had affected the image of the tough he wanted to be. But behind the dark glasses and the **swagger**, I glimpsed the baby-faced toddler I'd once watched over. I nearly wept. I wanted desperately for him to live.

swagger
boastful show of fearlessness

Immortal
unable to die

The young think themselves **immortal**, and a dangerous light shone in his eyes as he spoke laughingly, of making fools of the policemen who had raided his apartment looking for drugs. He cried out as I took his right hand. A line of stitches lay between the thumb and index finger. Kickback from a shotgun, he explained, nothing serious. Gunplay had become part of his life.

5   I lacked the language simply to say: Thousands have lived this for you and died. I fought the urge to lift him bodily and shake him. This place and the way you are living smells of death to me, I said. Take some time away, I said. Let's go downtown tomorrow and buy a plane ticket anywhere, take a bus trip, anything to get away and cool things off. He took my alarm casually. We arranged to meet the following night—an appointment he would not keep. We embraced as though through glass. I drove away.

recurrent
returning, repeating

6   As I stood in my apartment in Chicago holding the receiver that evening in February 1984, I felt as though part of my soul had been cut away. I questioned myself then, and I still do. Did I not reach back soon or earnestly enough for him? For weeks I awoke crying from a **recurrent** dream in which I chased him, urgently trying to get him to read a document I had, as though reading it would protect him from what had happened in waking life. His eyes shining like black diamonds, he smiled and danced just beyond my grasp. When I reached for him, I caught only the space where he had been.

—From *Bearing Witness*

GETTING READY TO WRITE

Reviewing the Reading

1. How and why did Blake, Staples's younger brother, die?
2. Why was Staples so worried about Blake?
3. Describe Staples's attempts to help Blake when he visited him in 1983 in Roanoke, Virginia.
4. What effects did Blake's death have on Staples?

Examining the Reading Using an Idea Map

Review the reading by completing the missing parts of the idea map shown on the next page.

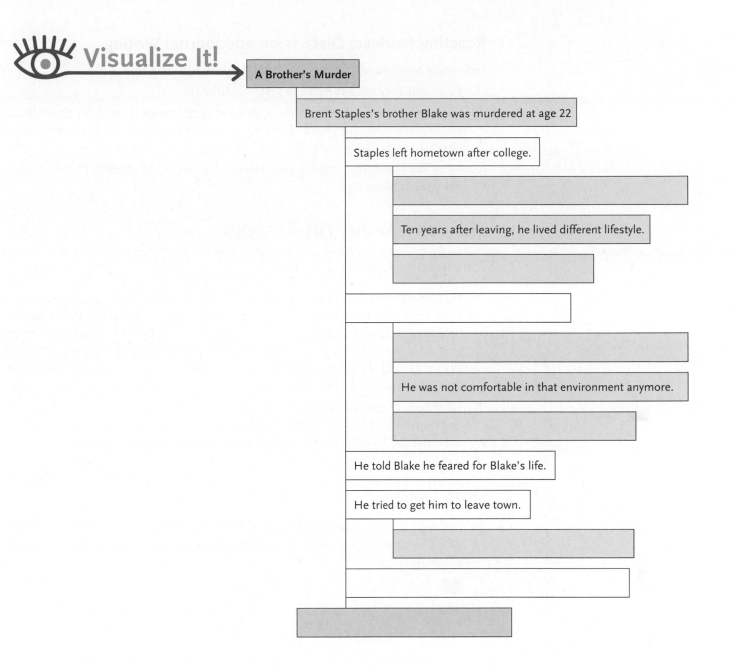

Visualize It!

A Brother's Murder

Brent Staples's brother Blake was murdered at age 22

Staples left hometown after college.

Ten years after leaving, he lived different lifestyle.

He was not comfortable in that environment anymore.

He told Blake he feared for Blake's life.

He tried to get him to leave town.

Strengthening Your Vocabulary

Part A: Using the word's context, word parts, or a dictionary, write a brief definition of each of the following words or phrases as it is used in the reading.

1. rivalry (paragraph 1) _____

2. escalated (paragraph 1) _____

3. ensconced (paragraph 2) _____

4. desolate (paragraph 3) _____

5. forays (paragraph 3) _____

6. terrain (paragraph 3) _____

Part B: Choose one of the words above and draw a word map (see p. 84) of it.

Reacting to Ideas: Discussion and Journal Writing

Get ready to write about the reading by discussing the following:

1. Why did Brent Staples rarely visit his hometown?

2. Staples wonders whether he could have done more to protect and rescue his brother. Do you think there was more he could or should have done? Explain.

3. Why do you think Staples keeps dreaming about his brother? What does his dream mean?

WRITING ABOUT THE READING

Paragraph Options

1. Staples describes embracing his brother as if through glass. This description and others throughout the reading suggest that Staples and his brother could not communicate well, although they seemed to care about one another. Write a paragraph describing your relationship with someone you had difficulty communicating with or your relationship with someone you could communicate with easily.

2. Members of the same family often are very different, and sometimes the opposite of each other. Write a paragraph explaining how you are either very similar to or very different from a member of your family.

Essay Option

3. Staples's brother lost his life to the violence of street crime. Write an essay describing what you feel can or should be done to avoid such a tragic waste of life.

Revision Checklist

Paragraph Development

1. Is the topic manageable (neither too broad nor too narrow)?

2. Is the paragraph written with the reader in mind?

3. Does the topic sentence identify the topic?

4. Does the topic sentence make a point about the topic?

5. Does each sentence support the topic sentence?

6. Is there sufficient detail?

7. Is there a sentence at the end that brings the paragraph to a close?

Sentence Development

8. Are there any sentence fragments, run-on sentences, or comma splices?

9. Are ideas combined to produce more effective sentences?

10. Are adjectives and adverbs used to make the sentences vivid and interesting?

11. Are relative clauses and prepositional phrases like *-ing* phrases used to add detail?

12. Are pronouns used correctly and consistently?

CHAPTER REVIEW AND PRACTICE

CHAPTER REVIEW

To review and check your recall of the chapter, select the phrase from the box below that best fits in each of the following sentences. Keep in mind that each phrase may be used more than once.

least/most	spatial	time-sequence

1. "The following steps should be taken before you turn on your new computer. First, make sure it is plugged in. Next, turn on all peripherals." This is an example of a _____ paragraph.

2. *To the east, beside, on the other side*, and *beneath* are all examples of _____ arrangement transitions.

3. "Talk about a disaster! It was bad enough that the dress I wanted to wear had a stain. The bus came late, and I spilled coffee on my application. To make things even worse, I sneezed on the interviewer!" The writer chose to tell this story using a _____ arrangement.

4. The following is an example of a _____ map:

    How to Bake a Cake

    a. butter pan

    b. preheat oven

    c. assemble, measure, and combine ingredients

    d. pour batter into pan and place pan in oven

    e. bake

5. "The model is wearing a lovely ensemble that begins with a chic scarf knotted at the neck. Below it, the notched collar of the jacket adds a tailored look. This look is further enhanced by the trim belt at the waist." The announcer described the outfit using _____ arrangement.

(continued)

6. In a _____ arrangement, ideas are organized according to a particular quality, such as importance.

7. *During, later, first,* and *at last* are all examples of _____ transitions.

8. To supply descriptive details according to their physical relationship to each other is to use _____ arrangement.

9. *Best of all, moreover, especially,* and *in addition* are all examples of _____ transitions.

10. The _____ arrangement is used to present information in the order in which it occurred.

EDITING PRACTICE

The following paragraph lacks transitions to connect its details. Revise it by adding transitional words or phrases where useful.

Registering a used car with the Department of Motor Vehicles requires several steps. You should be sure you have proper proof of ownership. You must have the previous owner's signature on the "transfer of ownership" stub of his or her registration or on an ownership certificate to show that you purchased the car. You also need a receipt for the amount you paid for the car. You must provide proof that the vehicle is insured. You need to obtain forms from your insurance company showing you have the required amount of insurance. You must have the car inspected if the old inspection sticker has expired. Take the previous owner's registration form or ownership certificate, insurance forms, and proof of inspection to the Department of Motor Vehicles office. Here, you will fill out a new registration form and pay sales tax and a registration fee. Then you will be issued a temporary registration. Within two weeks, you will receive your official vehicle registration in the mail.

INTERNET ACTIVITIES

1. Details, Details

Explore the online collections of photographs from the George Eastman House.

http://www.geh.org/

Choose five photographs to evaluate. Discuss the types of details that the museum provides for each photograph. Then create a list of details that more fully describes each picture.

2. Sensory Details

You can add depth to your descriptions with sensory details. This Web page from St. Cloud State compares general and specific sentences.

http://leo.stcloudstate.edu/acadwrite/sensorydetails.html

For each type of deail listed, write your own set of general and speclfic sentences.

3. MyWritingLab

Visit this site to get more help with developing, arranging, and connecting details in paragraphs.

http://www.mywritinglab.com

Click on the Study Plan tab, then on "Paragraph Basics and Development," and then on "Developing, Arranging, and Connecting Details."

14 Using Methods of Organization

In this chapter you will learn to:

1. Use nine methods of paragraph development: narration, description, example, definition, comparison and contrast, classification, process, cause and effect, and argument.

2. Use transitions to connect your ideas.

WRITE ABOUT IT!

Study the photograph above and then write a paragraph about it.

You could have developed your paragraph in a number of ways. For example, perhaps you told a story about a child enjoying an ice cream sundae. If so, you used a method of development called **narration** (discussed in Section A of this chapter). If your paragraph described the delicious taste, texture, or flavors of the ice cream, you used a method of development called **description** (Section B of this chapter). There are other possible ways to write a paragraph about ice cream, using different methods of development. In this chapter you will learn the different methods for developing and organizing a paragraph.

WRITING

Methods of Organization

Separate sections of this chapter are devoted to each of the following methods of development:

Section A: Narration	Tells a story that involves ice cream
Section B: Description	Describes the taste, texture, or flavor of ice cream
Section C: Example	Gives examples of kinds of ice cream (soft serve, premium, ice cream bars)
Section D: Definition	Defines what ice cream is to someone unfamiliar with it
Section E: Comparison and Contrast	Compares different flavors of ice cream
Section F: Classification	Explains the different types of ice cream (fat free, sugar free, etc.)
Section G: Process	Explains how ice cream is made or explains how to make an ice cream sundae
Section H: Cause and Effect	Explains why people enjoy ice cream
Section I: Argument	Makes the case that ice cream should be on every restaurant menu

Each of these methods of development produces an entirely different paragraph. The method you use depends on what you want to say and how you want to say it. For example, if you wanted your readers to visualize or imagine something, you might use description. If you wanted your readers to understand how something works, you would use process. If you wanted to convince your readers of something, you would use argument. The method you choose, then, should suit your purpose for writing. The nine methods of development described in this chapter offer you a wide range of choices for developing and organizing your writing. By learning to use each of them, you will develop a variety of new approaches to paragraph writing.

A: Narration

What Is Narration?

The technique of <u>making a point</u> by telling a story is called **narration**. Narration is *not* simply listing a series of events—"this happened, then that happened." Narration shapes and interprets events to make a point. Notice the difference between the two paragraphs below.

ESL Tip

Make a point means to "express the idea that a story or anecdote exemplifies." A common conversational question in English is "What's your point?" It means "Why are you telling me this? What's the idea behind it?"

Paragraph 1: Series of Events

Last Sunday we visited the National Zoo in Washington, D.C. As we entered, we decided to see the panda bear, the elephants, and the giraffes. All were outside enjoying the springlike weather. Then we visited the bat cave. I was amazed at how closely bats pack together in a small space. Finally, we went into the monkey house. There we spent time watching the giant apes watch us.

Paragraph 2: Narrative

Last Sunday's visit to the National Zoo in Washington, D.C., was a lesson to me about animals in captivity. First we visited the panda, the elephants, and the giraffes. All seemed slow moving and locked into a dull routine—pacing around their yards. Then we watched the seals. Their trainer had them perform stunts for their food; they would never do these stunts in the wild. Finally, we stopped at the monkey house, where sad, old apes stared at us and watched kids point at them. The animals did not seem happy or content with their lives.

The first paragraph retells events in the order in which they happened, but with no shaping of the story. The second paragraph, a narrative, also presents events in the order in which they happened, but uses these events to make a point: animals kept in captivity are unhappy. Thus, all details and events work together to support that point. You can visualize a narrative paragraph as follows. Study the model and the map for paragraph 2.

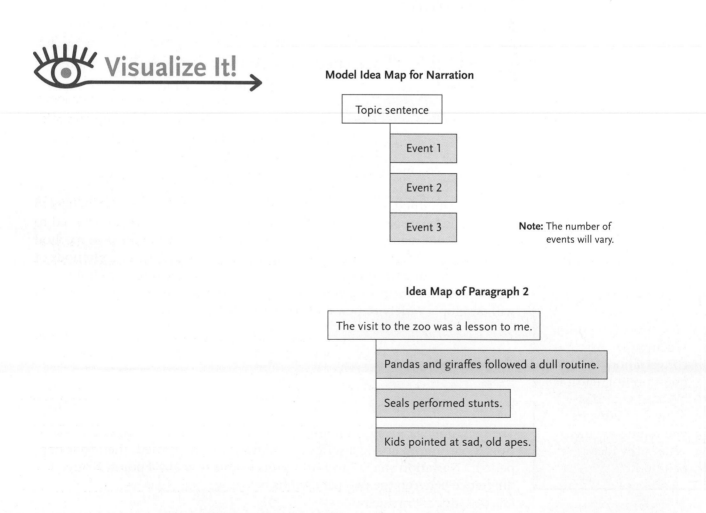

Visualize It!

Model Idea Map for Narration

Topic sentence

Event 1

Event 2

Event 3

Note: The number of events will vary.

Idea Map of Paragraph 2

The visit to the zoo was a lesson to me.

Pandas and giraffes followed a dull routine.

Seals performed stunts.

Kids pointed at sad, old apes.

How to Develop a Narrative Paragraph

Developing a narrative paragraph involves writing a topic sentence and presenting sufficient details to support it.

Write a Clear Topic Sentence

Your topic sentence should accomplish two things:

1. **It should identify your topic.**
2. **It should reveal your attitude toward your topic.**

For example, suppose you are writing about visiting a zoo. Your topic sentence could take your narrative in a variety of directions, each of which would reveal a very different attitude toward the experience.

- During my recent visit to the zoo, I was saddened by the animals' behavior in captivity.
- A recent visit to the zoo gave my children a lesson in geography.
- My recent visit to the zoo taught me more about human nature than about animals.

Examine It!

Directions: The following paragraph uses the narrative method of development. Study its annotations to discover how the writer supports the topic sentence and organizes her ideas.

Author establishes the importance of the narrative

Topic sentence

Description of events

Final comment reveals McPherson's mental state

I can't eat. I can't sleep. And I certainly can't study. I stare at a single paragraph for a quarter of an hour but can't absorb it. How can I, when behind the words, on the white background of the paper, I'm watching an endless loop of my parents' deaths? Watching as their cream-colored Buick flies through the guardrail and over the side of the bridge to avoid old Mr. McPherson's red truck? Old Mr. McPherson, who confessed as he was led from the scene that he wasn't entirely sure what side of the road he should have been on and thinks that maybe he hit the gas instead of the brake? Old Mr. McPherson, who showed up at church one legendary Easter without trousers?

—Gruen, *Water for Elephants*, p. 21

EXERCISE A-1

Writing in Progress

Directions: Complete three of the following topic sentences by adding information that describes an experience you have had related to the topic.

EXAMPLE   My first job *was an experience I would rather forget.*

1. Holidays _____

2. A frightening event _____

3. My first day on campus _____

4. Cell phones _____

5. My advisor/instructor _____

Include Sufficient Details

A narrative paragraph should include enough detail to support your topic sentence and allow your reader to understand fully the experience you are writing about. Be sure you have answered most of the following questions:

- *What* events occurred?
- *Where* did they happen?
- *When* did they happen?
- *Who* was involved?
- *Why* did they happen?
- *How* did they happen?

EXERCISE A-2

Writing in Progress

Directions: Using one of the topic sentences you wrote in Exercise A-1, brainstorm a list of relevant and sufficient details to support it.

How to Organize a Narrative Paragraph

The events in a narrative are usually arranged in the order in which they happened. This method of organization is called **time-sequence arrangement** (see Chapter 13, p. 348, for a discussion of this method). Transitions are especially important in narrative paragraphs because they identify and separate events from one another. Useful transitions are shown below.

ESL Tip

For a comparison of *during* and *while,* see the ESL Tip on p. 349.

Narration: Useful Transitions			
first	then	in the beginning	next
second	later	after	during
third	at last	following	after that
finally			while

EXERCISE A-3

Writing in Progress

Directions: Using the topic sentence you wrote in Exercise A-1, and the relevant and sufficient details you generated in Exercise A-2, present your details in time-sequence order, using transitions as needed.

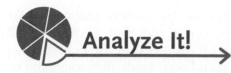

Analyze It!

Directions: The paragraph in the left column is a professional example of a narrative paragraph. Read the paragraph and then complete the idea map below.

Foxy came over early in the evening of July 3 to help Dayton load Babe into the back of the pickup for her ride to the rodeo. Fencing had been fixed to the sides of the bed, which was pulled against the open gate of the corral. A runway made of thick boards covered with a piece of shag carpet was rigged to the tailgate. I watched from the open window while Dayton spread the flat bottom of the truck with fresh hay, then waited while Foxy rustled and spooked Babe. It took awhile. She raced by the ramp, flicking her tail and shaking her head, kicking dust into Foxy's new rodeo clothes. Her hooves struck the ground hard as hammers, and she shook the bit, flapping the rope out of Foxy's reach. Finally, as if she knew what she was doing, she charged into the truck so fast that Dayton backed against the cab and waved his arms to ward her off, but the next minute, she had lowered her head to chew some hay, her heaving sides the only sign she was excited.

—Dorris, *A Yellow Raft in Blue Water*, pp. 276–277

Idea Map

Topic Sentence
| Babe was being loaded into a pickup truck to go to the rodeo. |

Event 1

Event 2

Event 3

Event 4

Event 5
| Babe settled down and chewed hay. |

B: Description

What Is Description?

Descriptive writing uses words and phrases that appeal to the senses—taste, touch, smell, sight, hearing. Descriptive writing helps your reader imagine an object, person, place, or experience. The details you use should also leave your reader with an overall impression of what you are describing. Here is a sample descriptive paragraph written by a student, Ted Sawchuck. Notice how he makes you feel as if you are in the kitchen with him as he prepares chili.

My favorite chili recipe requires a trip to the grocery store and a day to hang around the kitchen stirring, but it is well worth the expense and time. Canned, shiny red kidney beans and fat, great white northern beans simmer in the big pot, while ground beef and kielbasa sizzle and spit in a cast-iron skillet. Raw white onions bring tears to one's eyes, and they are quickly chopped. Plump yellow and orange peppers are chopped to add fiber and flavor, while six cloves of garlic, smashed, make simmering all day a necessity. When it cooks, this chili makes the whole house smell mouthwateringly good. When eaten, chunks of kielbasa stand out in a spicy, garlicky sauce with small nuggets of ground beef.

Notice that this paragraph describes tastes, smells, sounds, and colors. You even learn how it feels to chop an onion. Notice, too, that all of the details directly support an overall impression that is expressed in the first sentence. You can visualize a descriptive paragraph as follows. Study the model and the map for Ted's paragraph.

 **Visualize It!**

Model Idea Map for Description

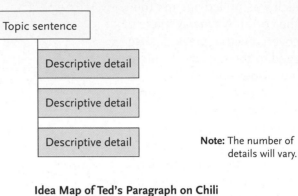

Topic sentence

Descriptive detail

Descriptive detail

Descriptive detail

Note: The number of details will vary.

Idea Map of Ted's Paragraph on Chili

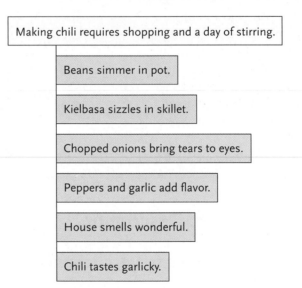

Making chili requires shopping and a day of stirring.

Beans simmer in pot.

Kielbasa sizzles in skillet.

Chopped onions bring tears to eyes.

Peppers and garlic add flavor.

House smells wonderful.

Chili tastes garlicky.

How to Develop a Descriptive Paragraph

A descriptive paragraph has three key features, an overall impression, sensory details, and descriptive language.

1. **Create an overall impression.** The **overall impression** is the *one* central idea you want to present to your reader. It is the single, main point that all of your details prove or support. For example, if you are writing a paragraph about your math instructor's sense of humor, then all of your details should be about amusing things he or she has said or done. Your overall impression should be expressed in your topic sentence, usually at the beginning of the paragraph. Notice that each of the following topic sentences expresses a different overall impression of Niagara Falls:

   a. Niagara Falls is stunningly beautiful and majestic.

b. The beauty of Niagara Falls is hidden by its tourist-oriented, commercial surroundings.

c. Niagara Falls would be beautiful to visit if I could be there alone, without the crowds of tourists.

Your overall impression is often your first reaction to a topic. Suppose you are writing about your college snack bar. Think of a word or two that sums up how you feel about it. Is it noisy? Smelly? Relaxing? Messy? You could develop any one of these descriptive words into a paragraph. For example, your topic sentence might be:

The snack bar is a noisy place that I try to avoid.

The details that follow would then describe the noise—the clatter of plates, loud conversations, chairs scraping the floor, and music blaring.

 **Examine It!**

Directions: The following paragraph, about the eruption of Mount St. Helens, a volcano in Washington state, uses the descriptive method of development. Notice how each of the highlighted words and phrases helps you visualize the eruption.

The slumping north face of the mountain produced the greatest landslide witnessed in recorded history; about of 2.75 km³ (0.67 mi³) of rock, ice, and trapped air, all fluidized with steam, surged at speeds approaching 250 kmph (155 mph). Landslide materials traveled for 21 km (13 mi) into the valley, blanketing the forest, covering a lake, filling the rivers below. The eruption continued with intensity for 9 hours, first clearing out old rock from the throat of the volcano and then blasting new material.

—Christopherson, *Geosystems*, p. 368

EXERCISE B-1

Writing in Progress

Directions: Brainstorm a list of words that sum up your reaction to each of the following topics. Then develop each list of words into a topic sentence that expresses an overall impression and could lead to a descriptive paragraph.

TOPIC   A parent or guardian

REACTION   Dad: loving, accepting, smart, helpful, calm, generous

TOPIC SENTENCE   My whole life, my father has been generous and helpful in the way he let me be myself.

1. TOPIC   A library, gym, or other public place that you have used

REACTION   _____

TOPIC SENTENCE   _____

                 _____

                 _____

2. TOPIC   A part-time job, past or present

    REACTION   _____

    TOPIC SENTENCE   _____

    _____

    _____

3. TOPIC   A small shop or a shopkeeper familiar to you

    REACTION   _____

    TOPIC SENTENCE   _____

    _____

    _____

    _____

4. TOPIC   A music video, movie, or song

    REACTION   _____

    TOPIC SENTENCE   _____

    _____

    _____

5. TOPIC   A person in the news

    REACTION   _____

    TOPIC SENTENCE   _____

    _____

    _____

    _____

2. **Include sensory details.** Sensory details appeal to your senses—your sense of touch, taste, sight, sound, and smell. Try to imagine your topic—the person, place, thing, or experience. Depending on what your topic is, write down what it makes you see, hear, smell, taste, or feel.

EXERCISE B-2

Writing in Progress

Directions: Using one of the topic sentences you wrote in Exercise B-1, brainstorm details that support the overall impression it conveys.

3. **Use descriptive language.** Descriptive language uses words that help your readers imagine your topic and make it exciting and vivid to them. Consider the following sentences. The first is dull and lifeless; the second describes what the writer sees and feels.

NONDESCRIPTIVE   The beach was crowded with people.

DESCRIPTIVE   The beach was overrun with teenage bodies wearing neon Lycra suits and slicked with sweet-smelling oil.

Making your details more descriptive is not difficult. Use the guidelines below.

NEED TO KNOW

Using Descriptive Details

1. **Use verbs that help your reader picture the action.**

   NONDESCRIPTIVE   The boy walked down the beach.

   DESCRIPTIVE   The boy ambled down the beach.

2. **Use exact names.**   Include the names of people, places, brands, animals, flowers, stores, streets, products—whatever will make your description more precise.

   NONDESCRIPTIVE   Kevin parked his car near the deserted beach.

   DESCRIPTIVE   Kevin parked his maroon Saturn convertible at Burke's Garage next to the deserted beach.

3. **Use adjectives to describe.**   Adjectives are words that describe nouns. Place them before or after nouns to add detail.

   NONDESCRIPTIVE   The beach was deserted.

   DESCRIPTIVE   The remote, rocky, windswept beach was deserted.

4. **Use words that appeal to the senses.**   Use words that convey touch, taste, smell, sound, and sight.

   NONDESCRIPTIVE   I saw big waves roll on the beach.

   DESCRIPTIVE   Immense black waves rammed the shore, releasing with each crash the salty, fishy smell of the deep ocean.

How to Organize a Descriptive Paragraph

Among the common methods of ordering details in descriptive writing are

- **Spatial arrangement.**   You organize details according to their physical location (see Chapter 13, p. 350, for a discussion of this method). For example, you could describe a favorite newsstand by arranging your details from right to left or from front to back.

- **Least/most arrangement.**   You organize details in increasing or decreasing order, according to some quality or characteristic, such as importance. (See Chapter 13, p. 352, for a discussion of this method.) Suppose your overall impression of a person is that she is disorganized. You might start with some minor traits (she can never find a pen) and move to more serious and important characteristics of disorganization (she misses classes and forgets appointments).

Whatever method you choose to arrange your details, you will want to use good transitional words and phrases between details.

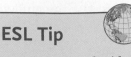

ESL Tip

Don't confuse *beside* with *besides*. *Beside* means "next to." *Besides* means "in addition."

Primarily means "mainly" or "most important." *Secondarily* means "next most important" or "not as important."

Description: Useful Transitions

SPATIAL	LEAST/MOST
above, below, inside, outside, beside	first, second, primarily, secondarily
next to, facing, nearby, to the right, to the left, in front of, across	most important, also important

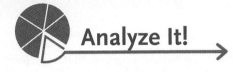

Analyze It!

Directions: The paragraph on the left is a professional example of a descriptive paragraph. For each part of the house listed below, list several descriptive words that help you visualize its appearance.

The earth by the front door was worn flat, smoothed by the dumping and drying of dishwater. Shingles were blown off the roof in an irregular pattern that reminded me of notes on a music sheet, and tan cardboard replaced glass in a pane of the attic window. The house and the land had been through so many seasons, shared so much rain and sun, so much expanding and shrinking with heat and cold, that the seams between them were all but gone. Now the walls rose from the ground like the sides of a short, square hill, dug out by the wind and exposed.

—Dorris, *A Yellow Raft in Blue Water*, p. 251

Roof: _____

_____

Attic window: _____

_____

Walls: _____

_____

_____

EXERCISE B-3

Writing in Progress

Directions: Using the details you developed in Exercise B-2, write a paragraph. Assume that your reader is unfamiliar with what you are describing. Use descriptive language and organize your paragraph using a spatial or least/most arrangement, and use transitions as needed.

C: Example

What Is an Example?

An **example** is a specific instance or situation that explains a general idea or statement. Apples and grapes are examples of fruit. Martin Luther King Day and Thanksgiving Day are examples of national holidays. Here are a few sample general statements along with specific examples that illustrate them:

GENERAL STATEMENT	EXAMPLES
1. I had an exciting day.	a. My sister had her first baby.
	b. I got a bonus check at work.
	c. I reached my goal of 20 laps in the pool.
2. Joe has annoying habits.	a. He interrupts me when I am talking.
	b. He is often late and makes no apologies.
	c. He talks with his mouth full.

ESL Tip

Note the use of third-person singular verbs for Joe's habits, what he does regularly (*interrupts, is, talks*).

Here is a sample paragraph written by Annie Lockhart that uses examples to explain the general idea of superstitious beliefs:

> Superstition affects many people on a daily basis. For example, some people think it is very unlucky if a black cat crosses their path, so they go to great lengths to avoid one. Also, according to another superstitious belief, walking under a ladder brings bad luck. Putting shoes on a bed is thought to be a sign that a death will occur in the family. People tend either to take superstitions very seriously or to reject them out of hand as fanciful imagination; regardless, they play an important part in our culture.

Notice that the paragraph gives three examples of superstitions. You can visualize an example paragraph as follows. Study the model and the map for the paragraph on superstitions.

 Visualize It!

Model Idea Map for Example

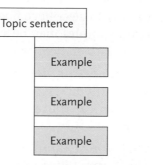

Topic sentence

Example

Example

Example

Note: The number of examples will vary.

Idea Map for Annie's Paragraph on Superstition

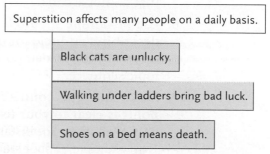

Superstition affects many people on a daily basis.

Black cats are unlucky.

Walking under ladders bring bad luck.

Shoes on a bed means death.

How to Develop an Example Paragraph

Developing an example paragraph involves writing a topic sentence and selecting appropriate examples to support it.

Write a Topic Sentence

Your topic sentence should accomplish two things:

1. **It should identify your topic.**
2. **It should make a general statement that the examples support.**

   Here are a few examples of topic sentences. Can you predict the types of examples each paragraph would contain?

- Consumers often purchase brand names they have seen advertised in the media.
- Advertisers use attention-getting devices to make a lasting impression in the minds of their consumers.
- Some teenagers are obsessed with instant messaging, using it to the extreme and forsaking other forms of communication.

Choose Appropriate Examples

Make sure the examples you choose directly support your topic sentence. Use the following guidelines in choosing examples:

1. **Choose clear examples.** Do not choose an example that is complicated or has too many parts; your readers may not be able to see the connection to your topic sentence clearly.

2. **Use a sufficient number of examples to make your point understandable.** The number you need depends on the complexity of the topic and your readers' familiarity with it. One example is sufficient only if it is well developed. The more difficult and unfamiliar the topic, the more examples you will need. For instance, if you are writing about how purchasing books at the college bookstore can be viewed as an exercise in patience, two examples may be sufficient. However, if you are writing about religious intolerance, you probably will need more than two examples.

3. **Include examples that your readers are familiar with and understand.** If you choose an example that is out of the realm of your readers' experience, the example will not help them understand your main point.

4. **Vary your examples.** If you are giving several examples, choose a wide range from different times, places, people, etc.

5. **Choose typical examples.** Avoid outrageous or exaggerated examples that do not accurately represent the situation you are discussing.

6. **Each example should be as specific and vivid as possible, accurately describing an incident or situation.** Include as much detail as is necessary for your readers to understand how the situation illustrates your topic sentence.

7. **Make sure the connection between your example and your main point is clear to your readers.** If the connection is not obvious, include an explanation. For instance, if it is not clear that poor time management is an example of poor study habits, explain how the two relate.

Examine It!

Directions: The following paragraph is a good model of an example paragraph. Study its annotations to discover how the writers use examples to develop their paragraph.

Alternative Energy Sources

Topic sentence   New technologies are helping to make alternative sources of energy cost effective. In Pennsylvania and Connecticut, *for example*, the

Example 1 (new technology)   waste from landfills is loaded into furnaces and burned to generate electricity for thousands of homes. Natural sources of energy, *such as* the sun and the wind, are also becoming more attractive. The electric-

Example 2 (wind power)   ity produced by 300 wind turbines in northern California, *for instance*, has resulted in a savings of approximately 60,000 barrels of oil per year. Solar energy also has many applications, from pocket calculators

Example 3 (applications)   to public telephones to entire homes, and is even used in spacecraft, where conventional power is unavailable.

—adapted from Bergman and Renwick, *Introduction to Geography*, p. 343, and Carnes and Garraty, *The American Nation*, p. 916

EXERCISE C-1

Writing in Progress

Directions: Select one of the topics listed below, narrow it, and write a topic sentence for it. Then brainstorm a list of examples that support it.

1. The behavior of professional athletes
2. The value of travel or a vacation
3. People's eating habits
4. Television commercials
5. Restaurant dining

How to Organize an Example Paragraph

Be sure to arrange your examples logically. You might arrange them from most to least important or least to most important (see Chapter 13, p. 352 and section B of this chapter, p. 375). You might also arrange them chronologically, in order of time, if the examples are events in the past. For example, if you are reporting on how early educational experiences influenced you, you might begin with the earliest situation and progress to the most recent.

Regardless of the order you use, be sure to connect your examples with transitional words and phrases like those shown below.

Example: Useful Transitions		
for example	for instance	to illustrate
one example	another example	
also		

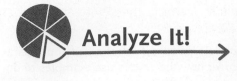

Analyze It!

Directions: The following paragraph is a good model of an example paragraph. Read the paragraph and highlight each example in one color of marker. Using a different color of marker, highlight the sentences that the examples support.

Controlling Information and Using Technology

To maintain their positions of power, elites try to control information. Fear is a favorite tactic of dictators. To muffle criticism, they imprison, torture, and kill reporters who dare to criticize their regime. Under Saddam Hussein, the penalty for telling a joke about Hussein was having your tongue cut out. Lacking such power, the ruling elites of democracies rely on more covert means. The new technology is another tool for the elite. Telephones can be turned into microphones even when they are off the hook. Machines can read the entire contents of a computer in a second, without leaving evidence that they have done so. Security cameras—"Tiny Brothers"—have sprouted almost everywhere. Face-recognition systems can scan a crowd of thousands, instantly matching the scans with digitized files of individuals. With these devices, the elite can monitor citizens' activities without anyone knowing that they are being observed. Dictatorships have few checks on how they employ such technology, but in democracies, checks and balances, such as requiring court orders for search and seizure, at least partially curb their abuse. The threat of bypassing such restraints on power are always present, as with the Homeland Security laws.

—Henslin, *Sociology*, p. 249

EXERCISE C-2

Writing in Progress

Directions: Using the topic sentence and examples you generated in Exercise C-1, write an example paragraph. Present your details in a logical order, using transitions as needed.

D: Definition

What Is Definition?

A **definition** is an explanation of what something is. It has three essential parts:

1. The term being defined
2. The group, or category, to which the term belongs
3. Its distinguishing characteristics

Suppose you had to define the term *cheetah*. If you said it was a cat, then you would be stating the group to which it belongs. **Group** means the general category of which something is a part. If you said a cheetah lives in Africa and southwest Asia, has black-spotted fur, is long-legged, and is the fastest animal on land, you would be giving some of its distinguishing characteristics. **Distinguishing characteristics** are those details that allow you to tell an item apart from others in its same group. The details about the cheetah's fur, long legs, and speed enable a reader to distinguish it from other large cats in Africa and southwest Asia. Here are a few more examples:

TERM	GROUP	DISTINGUISHING CHARACTERISTICS
opal	gemstone	greenish blue colors
comedian	entertainer	makes people laugh
fear	emotion	occurs when a person feels threatened or in danger

Here is a sample definition paragraph written by a student, Ted Sawchuck.

Sushi is a Japanese food consisting of small cakes of cooked rice wrapped in seaweed. While it is commonly thought of as raw fish on rice, it is actually any preparation of vinegared rice. Sushi can also take the form of conical hand rolls and the more popular sushi roll. The roll is topped or stuffed with slices of raw or cooked fish, egg, or vegetables. Slices of raw fish served by themselves are commonly mistaken for sushi but are properly referred to as *sashimi*.

In the paragraph above, the term being defined is *sushi*. Its group is Japanese food, and its distinguishing characteristics are detailed. You can visualize a definition paragraph as follows. Study the model and the map for the paragraph on sushi shown below.

Visualize It!

Model Idea Map for Definition

Topic sentence (term and general class)

Distinguishing characteristic

Distinguishing characteristic

Distinguishing characteristic

Note: The number of characteristics will vary.

Idea Map of Ted's Paragraph on Sushi

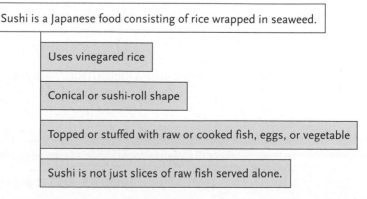

Sushi is a Japanese food consisting of rice wrapped in seaweed.

Uses vinegared rice

Conical or sushi-roll shape

Topped or stuffed with raw or cooked fish, eggs, or vegetable

Sushi is not just slices of raw fish served alone.

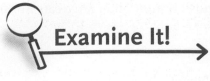

Examine It!

Directions: The following paragraph is a good model of a definition paragraph. Study the annotations to discover how the writers define the term *nervous system*.

The Nervous System

Topic sentence

First distinguishing feature

Second distinguishing feature

Third distinguishing feature

Example

    The **nervous system,** the master controlling and communicating system of the body, has three overlapping functions. (1) It uses millions of sensory receptors to monitor changes occurring both inside and outside the body. These changes are called stimuli and the gathered information is called *sensory input.* (2) It processes and interprets the sensory input and decides what should be done at each moment—a process called *integration.* (3) It causes a response by activating our muscles or glands; the response is called *motor output.* An example will illustrate how these functions work together. When you are driving and see a red light ahead (sensory input), your nervous system integrates this information (red light means "stop"), and your foot goes for the brake (motor output).

—Marieb, *Anatomy and Physiology,* p. 387

EXERCISE D-1

ESL Tip

A *role model* is someone a person admires and wants to imitate in some way. Young people benefit from having role models as examples of good and/or successful behavior. Parents, other relatives, and teachers often serve as role models.

Directions: For each term listed below, give the group it belongs to and at least two of its distinguishing characteristics.

TERM	GROUP	DISTINGUISHING CHARACTERISTIC
1. baseball	_____	_____
2. a role model	_____	_____
3. blogging	_____	_____
4. terrorism	_____	_____
5. facial expressions	_____	_____

How to Develop a Definition Paragraph

Developing a definition paragraph involves writing a topic sentence and adding explanatory details.

Write a Topic Sentence

The topic sentence of a definition paragraph should accomplish two things:

1. **It should identify the term you are explaining.**
2. **It should place the term in a general group. It may also provide one or more distinguishing characteristics.**

In the topic sentence below, the term being defined is *psychiatry*, the general group is "a branch of medicine," and its distinguishing feature is that it "deals with mental and emotional disorders."

Psychiatry is a branch of medicine that deals with mental and emotional disorders.

EXERCISE D-2

Writing in Progress

Directions: Write a topic sentence that includes a group and a distinguishing characteristic for each of the following items:

1. shirt _____

2. horror _____

3. hip-hop _____

4. age discrimination _____

5. ballroom dancing _____

Add Explanatory Details

Your topic sentence will usually *not* be sufficient to give your reader a complete understanding of the term you are defining. You will need to explain it further in one or more of the following ways:

1. **Give examples.** Examples can make a definition more vivid and interesting to your reader. (To learn more about using examples, see section C of this chapter, p. 376.)

2. **Break the term into subcategories.** Breaking your subject down into subcategories helps to organize your definition. For example, you might explain the term *discrimination* by listing some of its types: racial, gender, and age.

3. **Explain what the term is not.** To bring the meaning of a term into focus for your reader, it is sometimes helpful to give counterexamples, or to discuss in what ways the term means something different from what one might expect. Notice that Sawchuck does this in the paragraph on sushi.

4. **Trace the term's meaning over time.** If the term has changed or expanded in meaning over time, it may be useful to trace this development as a way of explaining the term's current meaning.

5. **Compare an unfamiliar term to one that is familiar to your readers.** If you are writing about rugby, you might compare it to football, a more familiar sport. Be sure to make the connection clear to your readers by pointing out characteristics that the two sports share.

How to Organize a Definition Paragraph

You should logically arrange the distinguishing characteristics of a term. You might arrange them from most to least familiar or from more to less obvious, for example. Be sure to use strong transitional words and phrases to help your readers follow your presentation of ideas, guiding them from one distinguishing characteristic to another. Useful transitional words and phrases are shown below.

Definition: Useful Transitions			
can be defined as	means	is	
one	a second	another	also

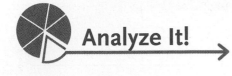 **Analyze It!**

Directions: The paragraph on the left is a good model of a paragraph that uses definition as a method of development. Complete the outline below using information given in the paragraph.

What Is a Tale?

The name *tale* is sometimes applied to any story, whether short or long, true or fictitious. But defined in a more limited sense, a **tale** is a story, usually short, that sets forth strange and wonderful events in more or less bare summary, without detailed character-drawing. *Tale* implies a story in which the goal is to reveal something marvelous rather than to reveal the character of someone. In the English folk tale "Jack and the Beanstalk," for instance, we take away a more vivid impression of the miraculous beanstalk and the giant who dwells at its top than of Jack's mind or personality.

—adapted from Kennedy and Gioia, *Literature*, p. 7

I. Tale

A. Often defined as _____.

_____

B. In a more limited sense, it has specific characteristics.

1. It is usually _____.

2. It describes events _____ form.

3. Its goal is to _____, rather than to reveal someone's character.

a. Example: _____:
the _____ is memorable, but Jack's personality is not.

Directions: Select one of the topic sentences you wrote for Exercise D-2. Write a paragraph defining that topic, using transitions as needed.

E: Comparison and Contrast

What Are Comparison and Contrast?

Comparison and contrast are two ways of organizing information about two or more subjects. **Comparison** focuses on similarities; **contrast** focuses on differences. When writing paragraphs, it is often best to focus either on similarities or on differences, instead of trying to cover both in a short piece of writing. Essay-length pieces can focus on both similarities and differences, but it is often easier to concentrate on one or the other. Here is a sample contrast paragraph written by Ted Sawchuck:

> Every time I go out for Mexican food, I have to choose between tacos de carne asada and tacos al pastor—they are tasty, but different. The tacos de carne asada are three small tortillas stuffed with chopped steak, served with a dish each of cilantro, onion, tomato, and fiery salsa. The tacos al pastor are similar, but chorizo is added to the chopped steak. While the tacos al pastor are a little greasier, they also have more spice and heat. Tacos de carne asada are drier with less flavor, but there's more room to add the vegetables, and that often makes for more dynamic flavor possibilities.

In this paragraph, Sawchuck discusses the differences between two types of tacos. He examines their ingredients, their spiciness, and their overall flavor. You can visualize a comparison or contrast paragraph as follows. Study the models and the map for Ted's paragraph.

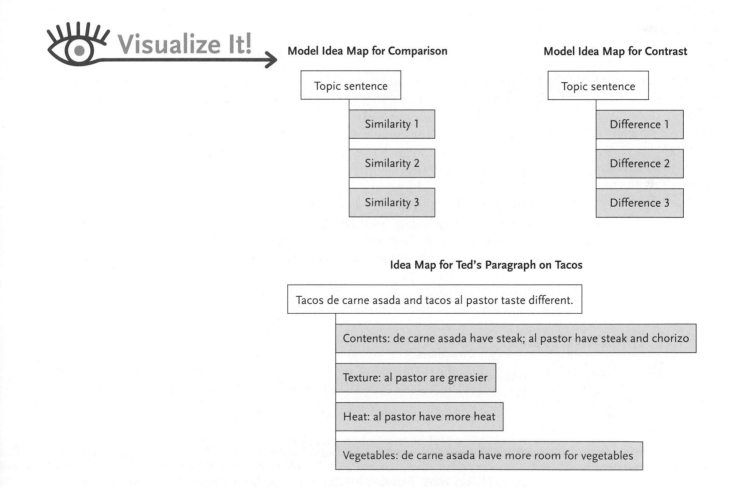

Visualize It!

Model Idea Map for Comparison

Topic sentence

Similarity 1

Similarity 2

Similarity 3

Model Idea Map for Contrast

Topic sentence

Difference 1

Difference 2

Difference 3

Idea Map for Ted's Paragraph on Tacos

Tacos de carne asada and tacos al pastor taste different.

Contents: de carne asada have steak; al pastor have steak and chorizo

Texture: al pastor are greasier

Heat: al pastor have more heat

Vegetables: de carne asada have more room for vegetables

How to Develop a Comparison or Contrast Paragraph

Developing a comparison or contrast paragraph involves writing a topic sentence and developing points of comparison or contrast.

Write a Topic Sentence

Your topic sentence should do two things:

1. **It should identify the two subjects that you will compare or contrast.**
2. **It should state whether you will focus on similarities, differences, or both.**

Here are a few sample topic sentences that meet the requirements above:

- Judaism is one of the smallest of the world's religions; Hinduism is one of the largest.
- Neither Judaism nor Hinduism limits worship to a single location, although both hold services in temples.
- Unlike Hinduism, Judaism teaches belief in only one God.

Be sure to avoid topic sentences that announce what you plan to do. Here's an example: "I'll compare network news and local news and show why I prefer local news."

Develop Points of Comparison or Contrast

The first thing you have to decide in writing a comparison or contrast paragraph is on what bases you will compare your two subjects. These bases are called **points of comparison** or **contrast**. Suppose you are comparing two different jobs that you have held. Points of comparison could be your salary, work schedule, required tasks, responsibilities, relationships with other employees, relationship with your boss, and so forth. The points of comparison you choose should depend on what you want your paragraph to show—your purpose for writing. If your purpose is to show what you learned from the jobs, then you might compare the tasks you completed and your responsibilities. If you want to make a case that working conditions in entry level jobs are poor, then you might use responsibilities, work schedule, and relationship with your boss as points of comparison.

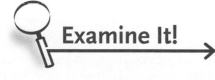 Examine It!

Directions: The following paragraph is a good model of a comparison and contrast paragraph. Study the annotations to discover how the writer explains the differences between two types of tumors.

Malignant and Benign Tumors

Topic sentence

Difference #1

Not all tumors are **malignant** (cancerous); in fact, more are **benign** (noncancerous). Benign and malignant tumors differ in several key ways. Benign tumors are generally composed of ordinary-looking cells enclosed in a fibrous shell or capsule that prevents their spreading to other body areas. Malignant tumors, in contrast, are usually not enclosed in a protective capsule and can therefore spread to other organs. Unlike benign tumors, which merely expand to take over a given space, malignant cells invade surrounding tissue, emitting clawlike protrusions that disrupt chemical processes within healthy cells.

Difference #2

—adapted from Donatelle, *Health: The Basics*, p. 324

EXERCISE E-1
Writing in Progress

Directions: For two of the topics below, brainstorm lists of similarities or differences. Review your lists and choose points of comparison. Then write topic sentences for them.

1. Two special places
2. Two favorite pastimes
3. Two styles of dress
4. Two cars
5. Two public figures
6. Two sports
7. Two college classes
8. Two relatives

How to Organize a Comparison or Contrast Paragraph

Once you have identified similarities or differences and drafted a topic sentence, you are ready to organize your paragraph. There are two ways you can organize a comparison or contrast paragraph:

- subject by subject
- point by point

Subject-by-Subject Organization

In the **subject-by-subject method**, you write first about one of your subjects, covering it completely, and then about the other, covering it completely. Ideally, you cover the same points of comparison or contrast for both and in the same order. With subject-by-subject organization, you begin by discussing your first job—its salary, working conditions, and responsibilities. Then you discuss your second job—its salary, working conditions, and responsibilities. You can visualize the arrangement with the idea map shown on p. 388.

To develop each subject, focus on the same kinds of details and discuss the same points of comparison in the same order. Organize your points within each topic, using a most-to-least or least-to-most arrangement.

Visualize It!

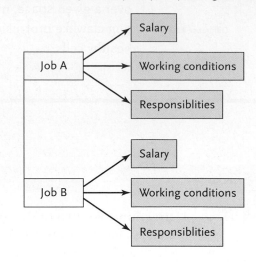

Model Idea Map for Subject-by-Subject Organization

Analyze It!

Directions: The paragraph on the left is a good model of a paragraph that uses comparison and contrast as a method of development. Complete the map below using information given in the paragraph.

Types of Leaders

Groups have two types of leaders (Bales 1950, 1953; Cartwright and Zander 1968). The first is easy to recognize. This person, called an **instrumental leader** (or *task-oriented leader*), tries to keep the group moving toward its goals. These leaders try to keep group members from getting sidetracked, reminding them of what they are trying to accomplish. The **expressive leader** (or *socioemotional leader*), in contrast, usually is not recognized as a leader, but he or she certainly is one. This person is likely to crack jokes, to offer sympathy, or to do other things that help to lift the group's morale. Both type of leadership are essential: the one to keep the group on track, the other to increase harmony and minimize conflicts.

—Henslin, *Sociology*, p. 169

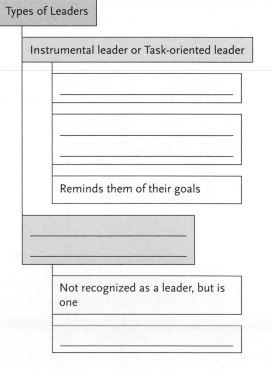

EXERCISE E-2

Writing in Progress

Directions: Using the subject-by-subject method of organization, write a comparison or contrast paragraph on one of the topics you worked with in Exercise E-1.

Point-by-Point Organization

In the **point-by-point method of organization**, you discuss both of your subjects together for each point of comparison or contrast. For the paragraph on jobs, you would write about the salary for Job A and Job B, and then you would write about working conditions for Job A and Job B, and so on.

You can visualize the organization this way:

Model Idea Map for Point-by-Point Organization

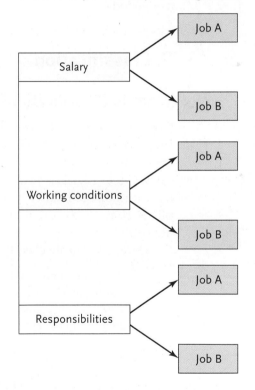

When using this organization, maintain consistency by discussing the same subject first for each point. (For example, always discuss Job A first and Job B second for each point.)

If your paragraph focuses only on similarities or only on differences, arrange your points in a least-to-most or most-to-least pattern.

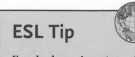

ESL Tip

For help using *transitional words and phrases* when writing comparison or contrast pieces, see the ESL Guide, E.1., "Transitional Words and Phrases: Transitions for Contrast" (p. 642 and p. 644).

<u>Transitions</u> are particularly important in comparison and contrast writing. Because you are discussing two subjects and covering similar points for each, your readers can easily become confused. Useful transitions are shown below.

Comparison and Contrast Useful Transitions	
To show similarities	likewise, similarly, in the same way, too, also
To show differences	however, on the contrary, unlike, on the other hand, but, although

EXERCISE E-3

Writing in Progress

Directions: Review the paragraph you wrote for Exercise E-2. Add transitions, as needed.

F: Classification

What Is Classification?

Classification explains a subject by identifying and describing its types or categories. For instance, a good way to discuss medical personnel is to arrange them into categories: doctors, nurse practitioners, physician's assistants, nurses, technicians, and nurse's aides. If you wanted to explain who makes up your college faculty, you could classify the faculty members by the disciplines they teach (or, alternatively, by age, level of skill, race, or some other factor).

Here is a sample classification paragraph written by Elsie Hunter:

> If you are interested in entering your pedigreed pet in the upcoming cat show, make sure you check with the Cat Fanciers' Association first. The CFA, sponsor of the show, has strict rules regarding eligibility. You must enter your cat in the right category. Only cats in the Championship Class, the Provisional Class, or the Miscellaneous Class will be allowed to participate. The first category in every cat show is the Championship Class. There are 37 pedigreed breeds eligible for showing in this class, some of which may sound familiar, such as the Abyssinian, the Maine Coon, the Siamese, and the Russian Blue. The Provisional Class allows only three breeds; the American Bobtail, a breed that looks like a wildcat but acts like a pussycat; the LaPerm, a curly-haired cutie that's descended from early American barn cats; and the semi-longhaired Siberian, a breed that was first imported from Russia in 1990. The Miscellaneous Class allows only one breed—the big Ragamuffin with its silky, rabbitlike coat. So, before you rush out and pay the entry fee, make sure you have something fancy enough for the Cat Fanciers' Association.

This paragraph explains the eligibility for a cat show by describing the three categories of cats allowed to enter the show.

You can visualize the process of classification as follows. Study the model and the map for Elsie's paragraph below.

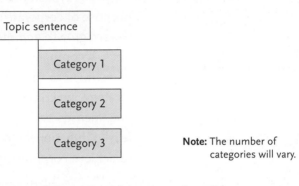

Model Idea Map for Classification

Topic sentence

Category 1

Category 2

Category 3

Note: The number of categories will vary.

Idea Map for Elsie's Paragraph on Cats

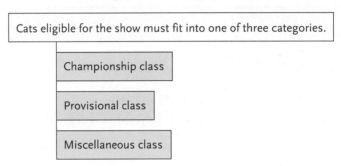

Cats eligible for the show must fit into one of three categories.

Championship class

Provisional class

Miscellaneous class

How to Develop a Classification Paragraph

Developing a classification paragraph involves deciding on a basis of classification for the subject you are discussing, writing a topic sentence, and explaining each subgroup.

Decide on What Basis to Classify Information

To write a paper using classification, you must first decide on a basis for breaking your subject into subgroups. Suppose you are given an assignment to write about some aspect of campus life. You decide to classify the campus services into groups. You could classify them by benefit, location, or type of facility, depending on what you wanted the focus of your writing to be.

The best way to plan your classification paragraph is to find a good general topic and then brainstorm different ways to break it into subgroups or categories.

Examine It!

Directions: The following paragraph is a good model of a classification paragraph. Study the annotations to discover how the writers classify strategies used by companies.

Company Strategies

Topic sentence

Category 1

Category 2

Category 3

Three types of strategy are usually considered by a company. The purpose of **corporate strategy** is to determine the firm's overall attitude toward growth and the way it will manage its businesses or product lines. A company may decide to *grow* by increasing its activities or investment or to *retrench* by reducing them. **Business** (or **competitive**) **strategy**, which takes place at the level of the business unit or product line, focuses on improving the company's competitive position. At the level of **functional strategy**, managers in specific areas decide how best to achieve corporate goals by being as productive as possible.

—adapted from Ebert and Griffin, *Business Essentials*, p. 117

EXERCISE F-1

Directions: For each of the following topics, brainstorm to discover different ways you might classify them.

1. TOPIC Crimes

   WAYS TO CLASSIFY _____

   _____

   _____

2. TOPIC Movies

   WAYS TO CLASSIFY _____

   _____

   _____

3. TOPIC Web sites

   WAYS TO CLASSIFY _____

   _____

   _____

Most topics can be classified in a number of different ways. Stores can be classified by types of merchandise, prices, size, or customer service provided, for example. Use the following tips for choosing an appropriate basis of classification:

- **Consider your audience.** Choose a basis of classification that will interest them. Classifying stores by size may not be as interesting as classifying them by merchandise, for example.

- **Choose a basis that is uncomplicated.** If you choose a basis that is complicated or lengthy, your topic may be difficult to write about. Categorizing stores by prices may be unwieldy, since there are thousands of products sold at various prices.

- **Choose a basis with which you are familiar.** While it is possible to classify stores by the types of customer service they provide, you may have to do some research or learn more about available services in order to write about them.

EXERCISE F-2

Writing in Progress

Directions: Choose one of the following topics. Brainstorm a list of possible ways to classify the topic.

1. Professional athletes or their fans

2. Bad drivers

3. Diets

4. Cell phone users

5. Friends

Write a Topic Sentence

Once you have chosen a way to classify a topic and have identified the subgroups you will use, you are ready to write a topic sentence. Your topic sentence should accomplish two things:

1. **It should identify your topic.**

2. **It should indicate how you will classify items within your topic.**

The topic sentence may also mention the number of subgroups you will use. Here are a few examples:

- Three relatively new types of family structures are single-parent families, blended families, and families without children.

- Since working as a waiter, I've discovered that there are three main types of customer complaints.

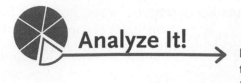 Analyze It!

Directions: The paragraph in the left column is a good model of a paragraph that uses classification as a method of development. Complete the chart on the right using information given in the paragraph.

Types of Burns

Burns are classified according to their severity (depth) as first-, second-, or third-degree burns. In **first-degree burns,** only the epidermis is damaged. The area becomes red and swollen. Except for temporary discomfort, first-degree burns are not usually serious and generally heal in two to three days without any special attention. **Second-degree burns** involve injury to the epidermis and the upper region of the dermis. The skin is red and painful, and *blisters* appear. Because sufficient numbers of epithelial cells are still present, regrowth (regeneration) of the epithelium can occur. Ordinarily, no permanent scars result if care is taken to prevent infection. **Third-degree burns** destroy the entire thickness of the skin. The burned area appears blanched (gray-white) or blackened, and because the nerve endings in the area are destroyed, the burned area is not painful. In third-degree burns, regeneration is not possible, and skin grafting must be done to cover the underlying exposed tissues.

—Marieb, *Essentials of Human Anatomy and Physiology,* p. 124

Characteristic	First-Degree Burns	Second-Degree Burns	Third-Degree Burns
Appearance	_____ _____	_____	_____ _____
Degree of Skin Damage	_____ _____	_____ _____ _____	_____
Healing Properties	_____ _____	_____ _____ _____	_____ _____ _____

EXERCISE F-3

Writing in Progress

Directions: For one of the topics in Exercise F-2, write a topic sentence that identifies the topic and explains your method of classification.

Explain Each Subgroup

The details in your paragraph should explain and provide further information about each subgroup. Depending on your topic and/or your audience, it may be necessary to define each subgroup. If possible, provide an equal amount of detail for each subgroup. If you define or offer an example for one subgroup, you should do the same for each of the others.

How to Organize a Classification Paragraph

The order in which you present your categories depends on your topic. Possible ways to organize the categories include from familiar to unfamiliar, from oldest to newest, or from simpler to more complex. Be sure to use transitions to signal your readers that you are moving from one category to another. Useful transitions are shown below.

Classification: Useful Transitions		
first	second	third
one	another	also
in addition	then	last

EXERCISE F-4
Writing in Progress

Directions: For the topic sentence you wrote in Exercise F-3, write a classification paragraph. Be sure to identify and explain each group. Use transitions, as needed.

G: Process

What Is Process?

A **process** is a series of steps or actions that one follows in a particular order to accomplish something. When you assemble a toy, bake a cake, rebuild an engine, or put up a tent, you do things in a specific order. A **process paragraph** explains the steps to follow in completing a process. The steps are given in the order in which they are done. Here is sample process paragraph. In it, the student writer, Ted Sawchuck, explains how copyediting is done at his college's student newspaper.

> The Fourth Estate's copyediting process is not very complicated. First, articles are submitted in electronic format and are read by Merren, the copy editor. Next, she makes changes and ensures all the articles are in their proper place. Then, section editors have a day to read the stories for their sections and make changes. Finally, all articles, photographs, cartoons, and anything else to be included in the upcoming issue is read and fact-checked by the editor-in-chief.

In this paragraph the writer identifies four steps. Notice that they are presented in the order in which they happen. You can visualize a process paragraph as follows. Study the model and the map on the following page for the paragraph above.

There are two types of process paragraphs—a "how-to" paragraph and a "how-it-works" paragraph:

- A **"how-to" paragraph explains how something is done.** For example, it may explain how to change a flat tire, aid a choking victim, or locate a reference source in the library.

- A **"how-it-works" paragraph explains how something operates or happens.** For example, it may explain the operation of a pump, how the human body regulates temperature, or how children acquire speech.

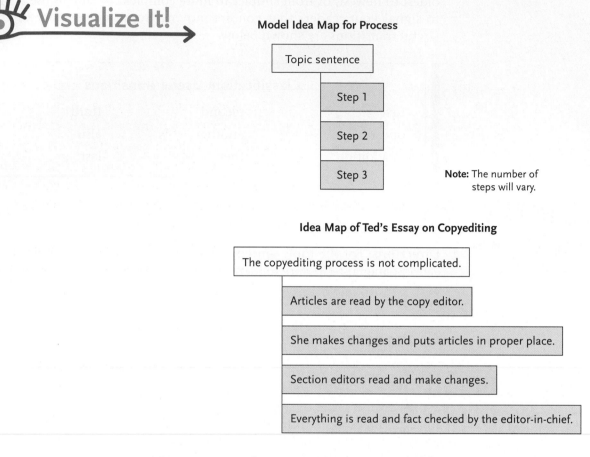

Visualize It!

Model Idea Map for Process

Topic sentence

Step 1

Step 2

Step 3

Note: The number of steps will vary.

Idea Map of Ted's Essay on Copyediting

The copyediting process is not complicated.

Articles are read by the copy editor.

She makes changes and puts articles in proper place.

Section editors read and make changes.

Everything is read and fact checked by the editor-in-chief.

How to Develop a Process Paragraph

Developing a process paragraph involves writing a topic sentence and explaining each step clearly and thoroughly.

Write a Topic Sentence

For a process paragraph, your topic sentence should accomplish two things:

1. **It should identify the process or procedure.**
2. **It should explain to your reader why familiarity with it is useful, interesting, or important (*why* he or she should learn about the process).** Your topic sentence should state a goal, offer a reason, or indicate what can be accomplished by using the process.

Here are a few examples of topic sentences that contain both of these important elements:

- Reading maps, a vital skill if you are taking vacations by car, is a simple process, except for the final refolding.
- Because reading is an essential skill, all parents should know how to interest their children in recreational reading.
- To locate information on the Internet, you must know how to use a search engine.

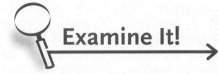

Examine It!

Directions: The following paragraph is a good model of a classification paragraph. Study the annotations to discover how the writers classify strategies used by companies.

Heading announces topic	**The Digestive Process**
Step 1: stretching of wall Step 2: gastric juices	The digestive process involves three basic steps. As food enters and fills the stomach, its wall begins to stretch. At the same time the gastric juices are being secreted. Then the three muscle layers of the stomach
Step 3: pummelling and compression	wall become active. They compress and pummel the food, breaking it apart physically, all the while continuously mixing the food with the enzyme-containing gastric juice so that the semifluid chyme is formed.
Comparison to something familiar helps reader understand three steps	The process looks something like the preparation of a cake mix, in which the floury mixture is repeatedly folded on itself and mixed with the liquid until it reaches uniform texture.

—Marieb, *Essentials of Human Anatomy and Physiology*, p. 487

EXERCISE G-1

Writing in Progress

Directions: Write a topic sentence for one of the topics listed below:

1. How to have an exciting vacation
2. How to cure an illness
3. How to shop on the Internet
4. How to build or repair _____
5. How _____ works

Explain the Steps

Use the following tips when explaining each step in a process:

1. **Include only essential, necessary steps.** Avoid comments, opinions, and unnecessary information because they may confuse your reader.

2. **Assume that your reader is unfamiliar with your topic** (unless you know otherwise). Be sure to define unfamiliar terms and describe clearly any technical or specialized tools, procedures, or objects.

3. **Use a consistent point of view.** Use either the first person ("I") or the second person ("you") throughout. Don't switch between them.

4. **List needed equipment.** For how-to paragraphs, tell your readers what they will need to complete the process. For a how-to paragraph on making chili, list the ingredients, for example.

5. **Identify pitfalls and problems.** Alert your readers about potential problems and places where confusion or error may occur. For instance, warn your chili-making readers to add chili peppers gradually and to taste the chili frequently along the way.

How to Organize a Process Paragraph

Process paragraphs should be organized sequentially according to the order in which the steps are done or occur. It is usually a good idea to place your topic sentence first. Placing it in this position provides your reader with a purpose for reading. Be sure to use transitional words and phrases to signal your readers that you are moving from one step to another. Useful transitions are listed below.

Process: Useful Transitions		
first	then	next
second	later	after
third	while	following
after	finally	afterward
before		

 **Analyze It!**

Directions: The paragraph in the left column is a good model of a paragraph that uses process as a method of development. In the right column, list the steps in the method of loci process using information given in the paragraph.

The Method of Loci

The *method of loci* is a memory device that can be used when you want to remember a list of items such as a grocery list or when you give a speech or a class report and need to make your points in order without using notes. The word *loci* (pronounced "LOH-sye") is the plural form of *locus*, which means "location" or "place." Here's how to use the method of loci. Select any familiar place—your home, for example—and simply associate the items to be remembered with locations there. Progress in an orderly fashion. For example, visualize the first item or idea you want to remember in its place on the driveway, the second in the garage, the third at the front door, and so on, until you have associated each item you want to remember with a specific location. You may find it helpful to conjure up oversized images of the items that you place at each location. When you want to recall the items, take an imaginary walk starting at the first place—the first item will pop into your mind. When you think of the second place, the second item will come to mind, and so on.
—Wood, et al., *Mastering the World of Psychology,* p. 181

List the steps involved in the method of loci memory device.

Step 1: _____

_____

Step 2: _____

Step 3: _____

_____

Step 4: _____

_____

EXERCISE G-2
Writing in Progress

Directions: Revise the draft you wrote for Exercise G-1. Check transitional words and phrases and add more, if necessary, to make your ideas clearer.

H: Cause and Effect

What Are Cause and Effect?

Causes are explanations of why things happen. **Effects** are explanations of what happens as a result of an action or event. Each day we face situations that require cause-and-effect analysis. Some are daily events; others mark important life decisions. Why won't my car start? Why didn't I get my student loan check? What will happen if I skip class today? How will my family react if I decide to get married? Here is a sample cause-and-effect paragraph. The student writer, Ted Sawchuck, discusses what can go wrong when preparing guacamole.

> Adding too many ingredients to guacamole will ruin the delicate flavor created by the interplay between fatty avocado, spicy peppers, and sweet tomatoes. Adding yogurt, for example, dilutes the dip to an almost souplike consistency and ruins the flavor. Dumping in salsa overpowers the delicate avocado so that you don't know what you are eating. Another common error, adding too much salt, masks the luxurious flavor of the avocado found in the best guacamole.

In this paragraph the student writer identifies three causes and three effects. You can visualize a cause-and-effect paragraph as follows. Study the model and the map for Ted's paragraph.

Model Idea Map for Cause and Effect

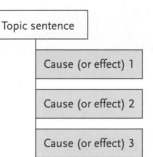

Topic sentence

Cause (or effect) 1

Cause (or effect) 2

Cause (or effect) 3

Note: The number of causes or effects will vary.

Idea Map of Ted's Paragraph on Guacamole

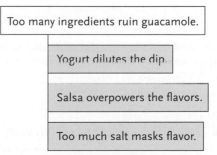

Too many ingredients ruin guacamole.

Yogurt dilutes the dip.

Salsa overpowers the flavors.

Too much salt masks flavor.

How to Develop a Cause-and-Effect Paragraph

Developing a cause and effect paragraph involves distinguishing between causes and effects, writing a topic sentence, and providing relevant and sufficient details.

Distinguish Between Cause and Effect

How can you distinguish between causes and effects? To determine causes, ask:

"Why did this happen?"

To identify effects, ask:

"What happened because of this?"

Let's consider an everyday situation: you lost your set of keys, so you are locked out of your apartment. This is a simple case in which one cause produces one effect. You can diagram this situation as follows:

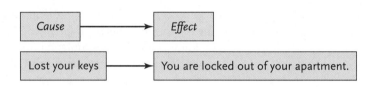

Most situations, however, are much more complicated than the one shown above. Sometimes cause and effect work like a chain reaction: one cause triggers an effect, which in turn becomes the cause of another effect. In a chain reaction, each event in a series influences the next, as shown in the following example:

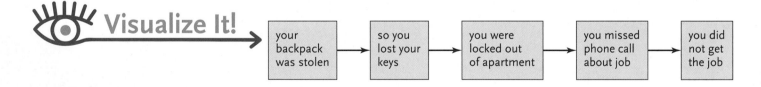

At other times, many causes may contribute to a single effect, as shown in the following diagram.

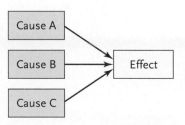

For example, there may be several reasons why you decided to become a veterinarian:

 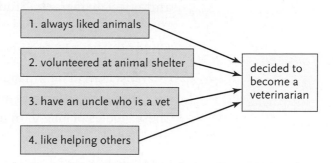

At other times, a single cause can have multiple effects, as shown below:

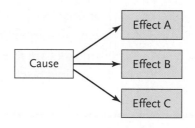

Suppose, for example, you decide to take a second part-time job:

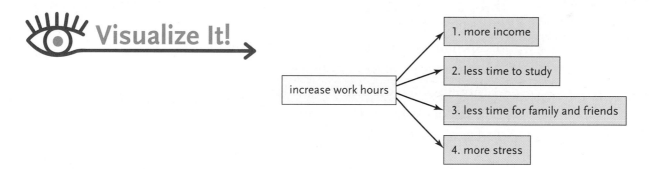

When analyzing a cause-and-effect situation that you plan to write about, ask yourself the following questions:

1. What are the causes? What are the effects? (To help answer these questions, draw a diagram of the situation.)

2. Which should be emphasized—cause or effect?

3. Are there single or multiple causes? Single or multiple effects?

4. Is a chain reaction involved?

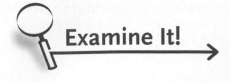

Examine It!

Directions: The following paragraph is a good model of a cause-and-effect paragraph. Study the annotations to discover how the writers explain the effects of marijuana.

Chronic Use of Marijuana

Most current information about chronic marijuana use comes from countries such as Jamaica and Costa Rica, where the drug is not illegal. **[Effect #1]** These studies of long-term users (for 10 or more years) indicate that marijuana causes lung damage comparable to that caused by tobacco **[Effect #2]** smoking. Indeed, smoking a single joint may be as bad for the lungs as smoking three tobacco cigarettes. Other risks associated with marijuana include suppression of the immune system, blood pressure changes, and impaired memory function. Recent studies suggest that **[Effect #3]** pregnant women who smoke marijuana are at a higher risk for stillbirth or miscarriage and for delivering low–birth weight babies and babies with abnormalities of the nervous system. Babies born to marijuana smokers are five times more likely to have features similar to those exhibited by children with fetal alcohol syndrome.

—Donatelle, *Access to Health*, p. 436

EXERCISE H-1

Writing in Progress

Directions: Identify possible causes and effects for three of the following situations:

1. Spending too much time surfing the Internet
2. Academic cheating or dishonesty
3. An important decision you made
4. The popularity of cell phones
5. Earning good grades

Write a Topic Sentence

To write effective topic sentences for cause-and-effect paragraphs, do the following:

1. **Clarify the cause-and-effect relationship.** Before you write, carefully identify the causes and the effects. If you are uncertain, divide a sheet of paper into two columns. Label one column "Causes" and the other "Effects." Brainstorm about your topic, placing your ideas in the appropriate column.

2. **Decide whether to emphasize causes or effects.** In a single paragraph, it is best to focus on either causes or effects—not both. For example, suppose you are writing about students who work two part-time jobs. You need to

decide whether to discuss why they work two jobs (causes) or what happens to students who work two jobs (effects). Your topic sentence should indicate whether you are going to emphasize causes or effects. (In essays, you may consider both causes and effects.)

3. **Determine whether the events are related or independent.** Analyze the causes or effects to discover if they occurred as part of a chain reaction or are not related to one another. Your topic sentence should suggest the type of relationship you are writing about. If you are writing about a chain of events, your topic sentence should reflect this—for example, "A series of events led up to my brother's decision to join the military." If the causes or effects are independent, then your sentence should indicate that—for example, "Young men and women join the military for a number of different reasons."

Analyze It!

Directions: The paragraph in the left column is a good model of a paragraph that uses cause and effect as a method of development. Read it and then complete the outline in the right column using information given in the paragraph.

Risk Factors for Ulcers

Although ulcers are commonly associated with stress, they can be brought on by other risk factors. Chronic use of aspirin and other nonsteroidal anti-inflammatory drugs increases the risk of ulcer because these agents suppress the secretion of both mucus and bicarbonate, which normally protect the lining of the GI tract from the effects of acid and pepsin. The risk of ulcer is also increased by chronic alchol use or the leakage of bile from the duodenum into the stomach, both of which can disrupt the mucus barrier. Surprisingly, ulcers are usually not associated with abnormally high rates of stomach-acid secretion; more often than not, acid secretion is normal or even below normal in most people with ulcers.

—adapted from Germann and Stanfield,
Principles of Human Physiology, p. 622

A. List four causes of ulcers.

1. _____

_____

2. _____

_____

3. _____

_____

4. _____

_____

EXERCISE H-2

Writing in Progress

Directions: For one of the topics you chose in Exercise H-1, decide whether you will focus on causes or effects. Then write a topic sentence for a paragraph that will explain either causes *or* effects.

Provide Relevant and Sufficient Details

Each cause or effect you describe must be relevant to the situation introduced in your topic sentence. Each cause or reason requires explanation, particularly if it is *not* obvious. Jot down a list of the causes or reasons you plan to include. This process may help you think of additional ones and will give you a chance to consider how to explain or support each cause or reason. You might decide to eliminate one or to combine several.

How to Organize a Cause-and-Effect Paragraph

There are several ways to arrange the details in a cause-and-effect paragraph. The method you choose depends on your purpose in writing, as well as on your topic. Suppose you are writing a paragraph about the effects of a hurricane on a coastal town. Several different arrangements of details are possible:

1. **Chronological** A chronological organization arranges your details in the order in which situations or events happened. For example, the order in which damage occurs during the course of a hurricane would become the order in which you present your details about the event. This arrangement is similar to the arrangement you learned in section A of this chapter, "Narration," p. 370. A chronological arrangement works for situations and events that occurred in a specific order.

2. **Order of importance** In an order-of-importance organization, the details are arranged from least to most important or from most to least important. In describing the effects of a hurricane, you could discuss the most severe damage first and then describe lesser damage. Alternatively, you could build up to the most important damage for dramatic effect.

3. **Spatial** Spatial arrangement of details uses physical or geographical position as a means of organization. In recounting the hurricane damage, you could start by describing damage to the beach and then work toward the center of town.

4. **Categorical** This method of arrangement divides the topic into parts or categories. Using this arrangement to describe hurricane damage, you could recount what the storm did to businesses, roads, city services, and homes.

Because cause-and-effect relationships can be complicated, be sure to use transitional words and phrases to signal your reader which are causes and which are effects. Useful transitions are shown below.

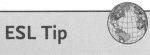

ESL Tip

For help with *cause-and-effect transitions*, see the ESL Guide, E.4., "Transitions for Reasons or Purpose," and E.5., "Transitions for Results" (pp. 645–646).

Cause and Effect: Useful Transitions	
FOR CAUSES	FOR EFFECTS
because, due to, one cause is . . . , another is . . . , since, for, first, second	consequently, as a result, thus, resulted in, one result is . . . , another is . . . , therefore

EXERCISE H-3
Writing in Progress

Directions: Write a paragraph developing the topic sentence you wrote for Exercise H-2. Be sure to include relevant and sufficient details. Organize your paragraph according to one of the methods described above.

I: Argument

What Is Argument?

An **argument** is a line of reasoning intended to persuade the reader or listener to agree with a particular viewpoint or to take a particular action. An argument presents reasons and evidence for accepting a belief or position or for taking a specific action. For example, you might argue that testing cosmetic products on animals is wrong, or that a traffic signal should be installed at the end of your street. An argument has three essential parts:

- **An issue** This is the problem or controversy that the argument addresses. It is also the topic of an argument paragraph. Gun control legislation is an example of an issue.

- **A position** A position is the particular point of view a writer has on an issue. There are always at least two points of view on an issue—pro and con. For example, you may be for or against gun control. You may favor or oppose lowering the legal drinking age.

- **Support** Support consists of the details that demonstrate your position is correct and should be accepted. There are three types of support: reasons, evidence, and emotional appeals.

Here is a sample argument paragraph:

> I strongly urge residents to vote "NO" on a referendum to withdraw funding for the proposed renovation of the Potwine town soccer fields. The town's other available fields are at capacity, and the number of children trying out for soccer is still growing. There are now more than 2,000 children between the ages of 6 and 13 playing on recreational and travel soccer teams. Meanwhile, the number of fields the college is willing to let us use has been reduced from 19 to 2. We are now having to rent fields in neighboring towns to accommodate all of the teams playing on Saturday afternoons! Opponents of the renovation always cite money as an obstacle. In fact, the money to fix the fields has been sitting in a Community Preservation Act fund for more than 15 years. Let the upcoming election be the final one, and make it one for the children—our own and the generations to come. Vote NO.

In this paragraph, the issue is the renovation of soccer fields. The writer's claim is that the renovation is necessary. The paragraph then offers reasons for the renovation.

Study the model and the map for this paragraph on the following page.

 Visualize It!

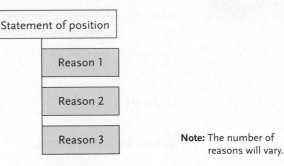

Model Idea Map for Argument

Statement of position

Reason 1

Reason 2

Reason 3

Note: The number of reasons will vary.

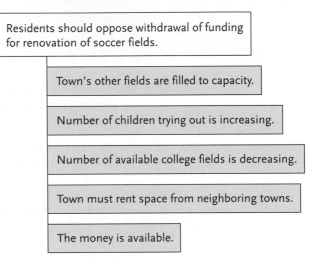

Idea Map of Paragraph on Soccer Fields

Residents should oppose withdrawal of funding for renovation of soccer fields.

Town's other fields are filled to capacity.

Number of children trying out is increasing.

Number of available college fields is decreasing.

Town must rent space from neighboring towns.

The money is available.

How to Develop an Argument Paragraph

Developing an argument paragraph involves writing a topic sentence, supporting your position with reasons and evidence, and addressing opposing viewpoints.

Write a Topic Sentence

Your topic sentence should do the following:

1. **Identify the issue.**
2. **State your position on the issue.**

The following topic sentence makes it clear that the writer will argue against the use of animals for medical research:

> The testing of cosmetics on animals should be outlawed because it is cruel, unnecessary, and disrespectful of animals' place in the chain of life.

Notice that this thesis identifies the issue and makes it clear that the writer opposes animal testing. It also suggests the three major reasons she will present: (1) it is cruel, (2) it is unnecessary, and (3) it is disrespectful. You do not always have to include the major points of your argument in your topic sentence statement, but including them does help the reader know what to expect. This topic sentence also makes clear what action the author thinks is appropriate: using animals in medical research should be outlawed.

ESL Tip

For help using modal verbs, see the ESL Guide, A.2., "Verbs: Modal Auxiliaries" (p. 627).

Here are a few more topic sentences. Notice that they use the verbs *must*, *would*, and *should*.

- If we expect industries to be environmentally responsible, then we should provide tax breaks to help cover their costs.

- It would be a mistake to assume sexual discrimination has been eliminated or even reduced significantly over the decade.

- The number of women on our college's Board of Trustees must be increased.

Examine It!

Directions: The following paragraph is a good model of an argument paragraph. Study the annotations to discover how the writer argues that animals should be used in medical research.

Heading announces the issue

Animals Should Be Used in Medical Research

Topic sentence: States a position

Reason 1

    Laboratory animal research is fundamental to medical progress. Vaccines for devastating human diseases like polio and smallpox and equally serious animal diseases like rabies, feline leukemia, and distemper were all developed through the use of research animals.

Reason 2

The discovery, development, and refinement of drugs that could arrest, control, or eliminate such human diseases as AIDS, cancer, and heart disease all require the use of laboratory animals whose physiological mechanisms are similar to humans. I have only noted above a few of the many examples where animals have been used in

Reason 3

human and veterinary medical research. It's also important to note that studies in behavior, ecology, physiology, and genetics all require the use of animals, in some capacity, to produce valid and meaningful knowledge about life on this planet.

—Donald W. Tuff, "Animals and Research" from *NEA Higher Education Advocate*

EXERCISE I-1

Writing in Progress

Directions: For three of the following issues, take a position and write a topic sentence.

1. Professional athletes' salaries
2. Drug testing in the workplace
3. Using cell phones while driving
4. Mandatory counseling for drug addicts
5. Buying American-made products
6. Adopting shelter animals
7. A topic of your choice

Support Your Position

There are two primary types of support that you can use to explain why your position should be accepted:

- **Reasons** Reasons are general statements that back up a position. Here are a few reasons to support an argument in favor of parental Internet controls:

  The Internet contains sites that are not appropriate for children.

  The Internet is a place where sexual predators can find victims.

  No one else polices the Internet, so parents must do so.

- **Evidence** The most common types of evidence are facts and statistics, quotations from authorities, examples, and personal experience.

Use a Variety of Evidence

Facts and Statistics

When including facts and statistics, be sure to do the following:

1. **Obtain statistics from reliable online or print sources.** These include databases, almanacs, encyclopedias, articles in reputable journals and magazines, or other trustworthy reference materials from your library.

2. **Use up-to-date information, preferably from the past year or two.** Outdated statistics may be incorrect or misleading.

3. **Make sure you define terms and units of measurement.** For example, if you say that 60 percent of adults regularly play the lottery, you should define what "regularly" means.

Quotations from Authorities

You can also support your position by using expert or authoritative statements of opinion or conclusions. Experts or authorities are those who have studied a subject extensively, conducted research on it, or written widely about it. For example, if you are writing an essay calling for stricter preschool-monitoring requirements to prevent child abuse, the opinion of a psychiatrist who works extensively with abused children would provide convincing support.

Examples

Examples are specific situations that illustrate a point. Refer to section C of this chapter for a review of how to use them as supporting details. In a persuasive essay, your examples must represent your position and should illustrate as many aspects of your position as possible. Suppose your position is that a particular television show should be cancelled because it contains excessive use of inappropriate language. The evidence you choose to support this position should be specific examples of the language used.

Personal Experience

If you are knowledgeable about a subject, your personal experiences can be convincing evidence. for example, if you were writing an essay supporting the position that being a child in a single-parent household encourages a teenager or young adult to mature earlier, you could discuss your own experiences with assuming new responsibilities.

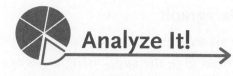

Analyze It!

Directions: The paragraph in the left column is a good model of a paragraph that uses argument as a method of development. Complete the map in the right column using information given in the paragraph.

Animals Should Not Be Used in Medical Research

I cannot accept the argument that research on animals is necessary to discover "cures" for humans. Many diseases and medications react very differently in animals than they do in humans. Aspirin, for example, is toxic to cats, and there are few diseases directly transmittable from cats to humans. I particularly abhor the "research" conducted for cosmetic purposes. The Draise test—where substances are introduced into the eyes of rabbits and then examined to see if ulcers, lesions or other observable reactions take place—is archaic and inefficient. Other alternatives exist that are more accurate and do not cause unnecessary suffering to our fellow creatures. Household products are also tested needlessly on animals using the LD-50 test. Animals, in many cases puppies, are force-fed these toxic chemicals to determine the dosage at which exactly 50 percent of them die. These tests are not necessary and do not give very useful information.

—Adapted from Molina, "Animals and Research"
from *NEA Higher Education Advocate*

Statement of position: _____

_____

Reason 1: _____

_____

Reason 2: _____

_____

Reason 3: _____

_____

EXERCISE I-2

Writing in Progress

Directions: Generate reasons and evidence to support one of the topic sentences you wrote for Exercise I-1.

Address Opposing Viewpoints

An opposing viewpoint is the position that is the opposite of the one you take. It is effective to recognize opposing viewpoints because it builds your credibility and shows that you are open minded. For example, suppose you are arguing that children should wear uniforms to school. You could also recognize or acknowledge that opponents believe uniforms stifle creativity and individuality. You may also decide to refute, or argue against, opposing viewpoints. *Refute* means "to present evidence that a statement is wrong." You could refute, the notion that uniforms stifle individuality by stating that children will find more useful and important ways of expressing their individuality if uniforms are required. Think of refutation as a process of finding weaknesses in your opponent's argument.

How to Organize an Argument Paragraph

There are two common ways to organize an argument paragraph.

1. **Place the topic sentence first and then give the supporting evidence and reasons.**

2. **Give your evidence and reasons first and conclude with the topic sentence.**

Because argumentation is complex, be sure to use transitional words and phrases to guide your reader from one reason or piece of evidence to another. Useful transitions are shown below.

Argument: Useful Transitions	
one reason	another reason
a second reason	therefore
furthermore	because

EXERCISE I-3

Directions: Using the reasons and evidence you generated in Exercise I-2, write an argument paragraph. Be sure to recognize and/or refute opposing viewpoints.

A STUDENT ESSAY

The Writer

Darlene Gallardo is a college student who lives near the U.S.–Mexican border.

The Writing Task

In this essay, which was published in *Hispanic* magazine, Gallardo shares her thoughts on her Mexican heritage and relates her experience with folklorico (Mexican folk dancing). As you read the essay, notice both the sequence of events and her use of descriptive language.

What My Culture Means to Me
Darlene Gallardo

Defines term used in the title

Thesis statement

1   *Culture* is a term used to define a person's way of life. Cultures differ from one part of the world to another. Most people accept the culture in which they were brought up and are proud of it, as I am. Others, on the other hand, are not. I consider myself lucky to live in a border city. This way I am exposed to two different cultures, American and Mexican.

Topic sentence

Descriptive details

2   When I was about five and a half years old, my parents enrolled me in dance classes. Walking into class with my older sister on our first day, I was amazed at what I saw. I had never seen Mexican folklorico dance before. The dance was very graceful and full of expression. I did not quite understand why the girls were wearing high shoes and long, heavy skirts. As I grew older, I learned what folklorico was and why costumes were important. This was one of the few symbols of the Mexican culture.

Topic sentence

Descriptive details

3   Folklorico dancing brings joy to those who watch it. It is performed with great passion. The stomping of the feet accompanied by the dancers' yells sends chills down your spine. The reactions and compliments given to me by the audience after a performance give me a feeling I try to hold on to until the next performance.

4   I have been dancing for fourteen years with various groups. When I started high school, I decided to take time off and concentrate on school. This was a hard choice to make, but in my heart of hearts I knew school came first. During high school, I would go to many performances given by folklorico groups. It was all too strange for me. Now I was in the audience. Watching the dancers

Descriptive details

perform made me want to get up there and dance. That is why I joined Ballet Folklorico Paso Del Norte in February of 1993.

5   Our practices are long and hard, and we have performances every weekend and sometimes on weekdays. There are times when we perform three to four times a day. To me it's worth it. The group has been presented many awards and has been invited to many cities. Last summer we were invited to perform in Oklahoma. It was a very emotional experience for everyone. People came up and took photographs with us. Many had never seen this type of dancing before. I couldn't help but wonder if the Mexican culture was lost.

Topic sentence

Topic sentence

6   I was very honored to think that I had presented something to the people that they enjoyed and would remember forever. It made me realize that when I am dancing, I am not just dancing for myself but for people of different races and backgrounds. It also brought to my attention that the Mexican culture is not lost; it just isn't acknowledged as much. There are many Hispanics who are very successful and proud, and many who are waiting for an opportunity.

Conclusion explains the importance of dancing

7   I have just now completed my first year of college at the University of Texas at El Paso. I'm still dancing and plan to do so for as long as I can. I never thought that a simple thing like dancing would be an important symbol of my background. I am trying to pass this down to younger generations by teaching folklorico at a community center. My advice to young Hispanics is to never deny where you come from. I know I will become successful. The confidence that I have within me comes from being proud to be who I am.

EXAMINING STUDENT WRITING

1. Evaluate Gallardo's thesis statement. How could it be revised?

2. Does the essay follow a logical plan? Describe its organization.

3. Evaluate the effectiveness of the title, introduction, and conclusion.

4. Underline four examples of the use of descriptive language. In which paragraphs of the essay do you think more description could have been included?

Paragraph Writing Scenarios

Friends and Family

1. Write a paragraph defining friendship.

2. Choose a parent or close family member whom you admire. Write a paragraph giving examples that demonstrate this person's admirable characteristics.

Classes and Campus Life

1. Write a paragraph classifying the types of problems that may lead to dropping out of college.

2. Write a paragraph explaining how you studied for a particular exam.

Working Students

1. Write a paragraph describing an employer or supervisor for whom you have worked. Be sure to create an overall impression about this person.

2. Write a paragraph comparing or contrasting two co-workers.

Communities and Cultures

1. Write a paragraph about a tradition that you value. Write a narrative paragraph that details the events related to the tradition.

2. Choose a community to which you belong. Write a paragraph about an activity that you share with other members. Be sure to explain why you chose to participate.

Writing Success Tip 14

Avoiding Plagiarism and Citing Sources

Plagiarism is using another person's words or ideas without giving that person credit. (*Plagiarism* comes from a Latin word meaning "to kidnap.") An author's writing is considered legal property. To take an author's words or ideas and use them as your own is dishonest. To avoid plagiarism, keep in mind the following points:

1. **It is not necessary to credit information that is common knowledge—the major facts of history, for example—or information that is available in many reference books.**

2. **You should credit unique ideas, little-known facts, interpretations of facts, and unique wording.**

3. **If you copy in your notes a phrase, sentence, or paragraph from a source, always put quotation marks around it.** Then you'll never make the mistake of presenting it as your own. Following the quotation, indicate the title of the source and the author's name.

4. **When taking notes on someone else's unique ideas, place brackets around your notes to indicate that the information was taken from a source.** In your notes, include information on the source.

To learn how to credit the sources you use, see Chapter 15, Writing Success Tip 15, "How to Credit Sources," p. 436.

WRITING ABOUT A READING

THINKING BEFORE READING

In this selection from *Newsweek* magazine, Leticia Salais writes about how she changed her mind and decided to embrace her native language in "Saying 'Adios' to Spanglish." As you read, pay attention to the organization of the essay and to the reasons Salais gives for her decision.

1. Preview the reading, using the steps discussed in Chapter 2, p. 38.

2. Connect the reading to your own experience by answering the following questions:

   a. Has your ethnic background or cultural heritage played an important role in your own life?

   b. When you were younger, did you want to change anything about the circumstances in which you grew up?

adios
Spanish for good-bye

Spanglish
an informal language that combines Spanish and English

READING

SAYING 'ADIOS' TO SPANGLISH

Growing up, I wanted nothing to do with my heritage. My kids made me see how wrong that was.

Leticia Salais

1   *Niños, vengan a comer.* My 18-month-old son pops out from behind the couch and runs to his high chair. My 7-year-old has no idea what I just said. He yells out from the same hiding spot: "What did you say?" My older son does not suffer from hearing loss. He is simply not bilingual like his brother, and did not understand that I was telling him to come eat.

2   Growing up in the poorest neighborhoods of El Paso, Texas, I did everything I could to escape the poverty and the color of my skin. I ran around with kids from the west side of town who came from more-affluent families and usually didn't speak a word of Spanish. I spoke Spanish well enough, but I pretended not to understand it and would not speak a word of it. In school, I refused to speak Spanish even with my Hispanic friends. I wanted nothing to do with it. While they joined Chicano clubs, all I wanted to do was be in the English literacy club. Even at home, the only person to whom I spoke Spanish was my mom, and that's only because she wouldn't have understood me otherwise.

Anglo
a white American of non-Hispanic descent

3   After I got married and moved to Tucson, Ariz., I thought I was in heaven. Though I was actually in the minority, I felt right at home with my **Anglo** neighbors. When I got pregnant with my first son, I decided that English would be his first language and, if I could help it, his only language. I never spoke a word of Spanish around him, and when his grandparents asked why he did not understand what they were saying, I made excuses. He understands but he's very shy. He understands the language but he refuses to speak it. In reality, I didn't want him to speak it at all.

4   In a land of opportunity, I soon realized I had made a big mistake. I was denying my son one of the greatest gifts I had to offer: the ability to be bilingual. I saw the need for interpreters on a daily basis in the health field where I worked. Even trips to the grocery store often turned into an opportunity to help someone who could not understand English or vice versa.

telenovelas
Spanish soap operas on television

5   In the nursing home where I worked, I met a wonderful group of Spanish-speaking individuals, whom I bonded with right away. I longed to speak like they did, enunciating the words correctly as they rolled off their tongues. It sounded like music to me. I started watching Spanish **telenovelas** and listening to Spanish morning shows on the radio just to improve my vocabulary. I heard words that had never been uttered around me growing up in a border town where people spoke a mixture of Spanish and English. A co-worker from Peru had the most eloquent way of speaking in a language that I recognized as Spanish yet could not fully comprehend. Did I also cheat myself of being bilingual?

6   Today I can take any English word and, like magic, easily find its Spanish equivalent. I now live a life that is fully bilingual. I hunger for foreign movies from Spain and the interior of Mexico just to challenge myself by trying to guess

what all the words mean. I even surprise my mom when she doesn't understand what I'm saying. I know she is proud that I no longer speak Spanglish, and I am no longer embarrassed to speak Spanish in public. I see it as a secret language my husband and I share when we don't want those around us to understand what we are saying. I quickly offer the use of my gift when I see someone struggling to speak English or to understand Spanish, and I quietly say a prayer of thanks that I am not in his or her shoes. I feel empowered and blessed that I can understand a conversation in another language and quickly translate it in my head.

7   My second son has benefited from my bilingual tongue. I speak only Spanish to him while my husband speaks only English; I am proud to say that his first language was Spanish. My 7-year-old, on the other hand, still has a way to go. I'm embarrassed that I foolishly kept my beautiful native language from him. I hope I have not done irreversible damage. A couple of years ago, I began speaking to him only in Spanish, but I had not yet heard him utter a complete sentence back.

8   Then, as if my prayers were answered, from behind the couch, I heard a tiny voice exclaim, *Ven, mira esto*. It was my older son instructing his little brother to come look at what he was doing. Maybe I won't be his first bilingual teacher, but it looks like he's already learning from another expert—his bilingual brother. Maybe it's not too late after all.

GETTING READY TO WRITE

Reviewing the Reading

1. Where did the author grow up?

   _____

2. List three examples of how the author tried to escape her heritage while she was growing up.

   _____

   _____

   _____

3. How did the author feel about her first son learning Spanish?

   _____

4. How did the author improve her Spanish?

   _____

5. How did the author and her husband teach their second son to be bilingual?

   _____

Examining the Reading Using An Idea Map

Review the reading by completing the missing parts of the idea map shown below.

Visualize It!

> Saying 'Adios' to Spanglish

> After years of trying to get away from her heritage, Salais came to see her native language as a gift to share with her children and others.

> Growing up in a border town, Salais wanted to escape poverty, the color of her skin, and her Spanish language.

> Salais got married and moved to Tucson, Arizona.

> _____ .

> She realized her mistake in denying her son the ability to be bilingual.

> _____ .

> Salais is now fully bilingual.

> _____
> _____ .

> _____ .

Strengthening Your Vocabulary

Part A: Using the word's context, word parts, or a dictionary, write a brief definition of each of the following words or phrases as it is used in the reading.

1. bilingual (paragraph 1) _____
2. affluent (paragraph 2) _____
3. bonded (paragraph 5) _____
4. enunciating (paragraph 5) _____
5. eloquent (paragraph 5) _____
6. empowered (paragraph 6) _____
7. irreversible (paragraph 7) _____

Part B: Choose one of the words above and draw a word map (see p. 84) of it.

Reacting to Ideas: Discussion and Journal Writing

Get ready to write about the reading by discussing the following:

1. What is the author's purpose for writing this article?

2. Why did the author think she was "in heaven" when she moved to Arizona?

3. Why did the author feel like she had to make excuses about her son not speaking Spanish? Why was the author's mother proud when her daughter no longer spoke Spanglish?

4. How did the author come to view her bilingual ability as a gift? In what ways does she share her gift outside of her family?

WRITING ABOUT THE READING

Paragraph Options

1. Write a paragraph describing your own ethnic background or cultural heritage.

2. The author described her efforts to escape the circumstances in which she grew up. Were there any aspects of your childhood that you wanted to escape or change? Write a paragraph explaining your answer.

3. Having children caused the author to have a change of heart about speaking Spanish. Think of a time when you had a significant change of heart, and write a paragraph about your experience.

Essay Options

4. The author views her ability to speak two languages as a gift she can give to her children. Write an essay describing a "gift" you would like to pass on to your children. It may be the ability to speak another language, a tradition from your own childhood, or a personal quality such as your sense of humor or love of sports. Be sure to explain why you would choose this particular gift, for example, how would it benefit your child?

5. The author describes several advantages to being bilingual. Write an essay identifying the ones in the article as well as any other benefits you can think of. If you are able to speak more than one language, include examples from your own experience. For example, have you ever been able to assist someone else because of your ability to speak another language?

6. What cultural or ethnic background did each of your parents come from? How did those influences emerge in the family in which you grew up? Write an essay about how your parents' separate experiences in their own families affected the family they formed together.

Revision Checklist

Paragraph Development

1. Is the topic manageable (neither too broad nor too narrow)?
2. Is the paragraph written with the reader in mind?
3. Does the topic sentence identify the topic?
4. Does the topic sentence make a point about the topic?
5. Does each sentence support the topic sentence?
6. Is there sufficient detail?
7. Is there a sentence at the end that brings the paragraph to a close?

Sentence Development

8. Are there any sentence fragments, run-on sentences, or comma splices?
9. Are ideas combined to produce more effective sentences?
10. Are adjectives and adverbs used to make the sentences vivid and interesting?
11. Are relative clauses and prepositional phrases like *-ing* phrases used to add detail?
12. Are pronouns used correctly and consistently?

CHAPTER REVIEW AND PRACTICE

CHAPTER REVIEW

To review and check your recall of the chapter, match each term in Column A with its meaning in Column B and write the letter of the correct definition in the space provided.

COLUMN A

_____ 1. Classification

_____ 2. Definition

_____ 3. Process

_____ 4. Narration

_____ 5. Description

_____ 6. Example

_____ 7. Cause and effect

_____ 8. Argument

_____ 9. Comparison and contrast

COLUMN B

a. focuses on similarities and differences

b. describes the order in which things are done or how they work

c. takes a position on an issue

d. presents, supports an impression with sensory details

e. makes a point by telling a story

f. explains by giving situations that illustrate the topic sentence

g. explains why things happen or explains what happens as a result of an action

h. explains a term by giving its class and distinguishing characteristics

i. explains by dividing something into groups or categories

 ## EDITING PRACTICE

The following informative paragraph comparing two types of skis is not organized logically. Revise this paragraph so that its main idea is developed logically.

Cross-country skis and downhill skis are different in many aspects. Cross-country skis are intended for gliding over fairly level terrain. Unlike cross-country skis, downhill skis have steel edges and their bindings keep the entire boot

(continued)

clamped to the ski. Downhill skis are broader and heavier, and they have a flatter bottom. Cross-country skis are lightweight and very narrow, and their bottoms are curved so the skis do not lie flat on the snow. Downhill skis are meant for skiing down steep slopes using frequent turns. The bindings on cross-country skis do not keep the heel clamped down, since the long, running strides used in cross-country skiing depend on free movement of the heel.

INTERNET ACTIVITIES

1. Online Narratives

Visit this Web page from the Voices of Civil Rights project to read some featured stories.

http://www.voicesofcivilrights.org/voices3.html

Choose one to evaluate. Write a list of key words and phrases that you found interesting and significant.

2. Processes Explained

Explore science topics at the How Stuff Works Web site.

http://science.howstuffworks.com/

Write the steps that explain one concept described here.

3. Homeless Youth

Skim this information on the City of Seattle Web site about homeless youth.

http://www.newavenues.org/3myths

Write a paragraph summarizing the causes and effects described here.

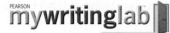

4. MyWritingLab

Visit this site to get more help with using methods of organization.

http://www.mywritinglab.com

Click on the Study Plan tab, then on "Paragraph Basics and Development," and then on "Narration," "Description," "Example," "Definition," "Comparison and Contrast," "Classification," "Process," "Cause and Effect," and "Argument."

15 Revising Underdeveloped Paragraphs

WRITE ABOUT IT!

Write a sentence describing the garden in the first photograph. No doubt you had trouble doing so. Now write a sentence describing the garden in the second photograph. How do your descriptions differ?

Many ineffective paragraphs are like the first photograph above. They do not provide enough information and leave the reader frustrated and confused. In this chapter you will learn how to recognize common paragraph problems and how to revise and fix them.

WRITING

Revising Ineffective Topic Sentences

Your topic sentence is the most important sentence in the paragraph. It promises what the remainder of the paragraph will deliver. A weak topic sentence usually produces a weak paragraph. Your topic sentence will be weak if it (1) lacks a viewpoint or attitude, (2) is too broad, or (3) is too narrow.

Topic Sentences That Lack a Point of View

A topic sentence should identify your topic *and* express an attitude or viewpoint. It must make a point about the topic.

If your topic is the old roller coaster at Starland Park, it is not enough to make a general statement of fact in your topic sentence.

LACKS POINT OF VIEW   There is an old roller coaster at Starland Park.

Your reader would rightly ask in this case, "So what?" A topic sentence needs to tell the reader what is important or interesting about your topic. It should state the point you are going to make in the rest of the paragraph. For every topic, you can find many points to make in a topic sentence. For example:

EXPRESSES POINT OF VIEW   The old roller coaster at Starland Park is unsafe and should be torn down.

The old roller coaster at Starland Park no longer seems as frightening as it did when I was young.

Three types of people go on the old roller coaster at Starland Park: the brave, the scared, and the stupid.

If you write a topic sentence that does not express a viewpoint, you will find you have very little or nothing to write about in the remainder of the paragraph. Look at these topic sentences:

LACKS POINT OF VIEW   Pete works at the YMCA.

EXPRESSES POINT OF VIEW   Pete got over his shyness by working at the YMCA.

If you used the first topic sentence, "Pete works at the YMCA," what else could you include in your paragraph? If you instead used the second topic sentence, you would have something to write about. You could describe Pete before and after he began working at the YMCA, discuss positive aspects of the job, or give examples of friends Pete has made through his work.

Notice how the following topic sentences have been revised to express a point of view.

LACKS POINT OF VIEW   Mark plays soccer.

REVISED   Mark's true personality comes out when he plays soccer. [Details can explain Mark's personality as revealed by his soccer game.]

LACKS POINT OF VIEW	Professor Cooke teaches accounting.
REVISED	Professor Cooke makes accounting practical. [Details can describe how Professor Cooke makes accounting skills relevant to everyday life.]
LACKS POINT OF VIEW	I read newspapers.
REVISED	I recommend reading newspapers from back to front. [Details can give reasons why this method is best.]

The following suggestions will help you revise your topic sentence if you discover that it lacks a point of view:

1. **Use brainstorming, freewriting, or branching.** Try to generate more ideas about your topic. Study your results to discover a way to approach your topic.

2. **Ask yourself questions about your topic sentence.** Specifically, ask "Why?" "How?" "So what?" or "Why is this important?" Answering your own questions will give you ideas for revising your topic sentence.

EXERCISE 15-1

Directions: The following topic sentences lack a point of view. Revise each to express an interesting view on the topic.

| SENTENCE | I took a biology exam today. |
| REVISED | The biology exam that I took today contained a number of surprises. |

1. I am taking a math course this semester.

   REVISED _____

   _____

2. I purchased a video camera last week.

   REVISED _____

   _____

3. Soft rock was playing in the dentist's office.

   REVISED _____

   _____

4. Sam has three televisions and four radios in his household.

   REVISED _____

   _____

5. There is one tree on the street where I live.

   REVISED _____

6. Many people wear headphones on their way to work.

REVISED _____

_____

7. Our sociology professor will give us three exams.

REVISED _____

_____

8. The first hurricane of the season is predicted to strike land tomorrow.

REVISED _____

_____

9. My four-year-old son has learned the alphabet.

REVISED _____

_____

10. Juanita enrolled her son in a day-care center.

REVISED _____

_____

Topic Sentences That Are Too Broad

Some topic sentences express a point of view, but they are too broad in scope.

TOO BROAD   The death penalty is a crime against humanity.

This statement cannot be supported in a single paragraph. Lengthy essays, even entire books, have been written to argue this opinion.

A broad topic sentence promises more than you can reasonably deliver in a single paragraph. It leads to writing that is vague and rambling. With a broad topic sentence, you will end up with too many facts and ideas to cover or too many generalities (general statements) that do not sufficiently explain your topic sentence. In the following example, note the broad topic sentence and its effects on paragraph development.

Sample Paragraph

> All kinds of violent crimes in the world today seem to be getting worse. Sometimes I wonder how people could possibly bring themselves to do such horrible things. One problem may be the violent acts shown on television programs. Some people think crime has a lot to do with horror movies and television programs. We have no heroes to identify with other than criminals. News reporting of crimes is too "real"; it shows too much. Kids watch these programs without their parents and don't know what to make of them. Parents should spend time with their children and supervise their play.

The topic sentence above promises more than a good paragraph can reasonably deliver: to discuss all violent crimes in the world today and their worsening nature. If you reread the paragraph, you will see that in the supporting sentences the author wanders from topic to topic. She first mentions violence on television, then moves to lack of heroes. Next she discusses news reporting that is too graphic, then switches to children watching programs alone. Finally, she ends with parental supervision of children. Each point about possible causes of violence or ways to prevent it seems underdeveloped.

An effective topic sentence needs to be more focused. For example, the topic sentence for a paragraph about crime might focus on one type of crime in one city and one reason for its increase.

FOCUSED   Home burglaries are increasing in Owensville because of increased drug usage.

Another effective topic sentence for a paragraph on crime could focus on one possible cause of rising violence in the workplace.

FOCUSED   The mass layoffs in the past few years have led to more criminal acts by desperate, unemployed workers.

The topic sentence of the following paragraph is also too broad.

Sample Paragraph

> People often forget the spirit and value of life and concentrate on worldly goods. These people buy things for show—nice cars, nice clothes, nice houses. These people are scraping their pennies together just to live well. They do not realize that things not from the store are just as nice. Their health, their families, and the people they care about are far more important than money. You can be rich and poor at the same time.

Because the topic was too broad, the writer continued to use general statements throughout the paragraph and to repeat the same or similar ideas. A more effective approach might be to select one worldly good and show how it affects one person.

FOCUSED   My sister is so concerned with dressing stylishly that she ignores everyone around her.

Now the writer can explain how an emphasis on clothing detracts from her sister's relationship with others.

Another effective topic sentence might focus the paragraph on not taking good health for granted:

FOCUSED   I used to think I could buy my way to happiness, but that was before I lost my good health.

The following suggestions will help you revise your topic sentence if you discover that it is too broad:

1. **Narrow your topic.** A topic that is too broad often produces a topic sentence that is too broad. Narrow your topic by subdividing it into smaller topics. Continue subdividing until you produce a topic that is manageable in a single paragraph.

2. **Rewrite your topic sentence to focus on one aspect or part of your topic.** Ask yourself, "What is the part of this topic that really interests me or that I care most about? What do I know most about the topic and have the most to say about?" Then focus on *that* aspect of the topic.

3. **Apply your topic sentence to a specific time and place.** Ask yourself, "How does this broad topic that I'd like to write about relate to some

particular time and place that I know about? How can I make the general topic come alive by using a well-defined example?"

4. **Consider using one of your supporting sentences as a topic sentence.** Reread your paragraph; look for a detail that could be developed or expanded.

EXERCISE 15-2
Writing in Progress

Directions: Turn each of the following broad topic sentences into a well-focused topic sentence that could lead to an effective paragraph. Remember that your topic sentence must also include a point of view. Then compare your answers with your classmates' answers to see the variety of effective topic sentences that can come from a broad one.

TOO BROAD   Hunting is a worthwhile and beneficial sport.

FOCUSED   Hunting deer in overpopulated areas is beneficial to the herd.

1. I would like to become more creative.

   REVISED   _____

   _____

2. Brazil is a beautiful country.

   REVISED   _____

   _____

3. Pollution is a big problem.

   REVISED   _____

   _____

4. The space program is amazing.

   REVISED   _____

   _____

5. It is very important to learn Japanese.

   REVISED   _____

   _____

6. We must protect the environment.

   REVISED   _____

   _____

7. Lani is a good mother.

   REVISED _____

   _____

8. The book was interesting.

   REVISED _____

   _____

9. Lots of magazines are published.

   REVISED _____

   _____

10. Honesty is important.

   REVISED _____

   _____

Topic Sentences That Are Too Narrow

If your topic sentence is too narrow, you will realize it right away because you won't have enough to write about to complete your paragraph. Topic sentences that are too narrow also frequently lack a point of view.

TOO NARROW	My birdfeeder attracts yellow songbirds.
REVISED	Watching the different birds at our feeder is a pleasant diversion enjoyed by our entire family, including our cat.
TOO NARROW	My math instructor looks at his watch frequently.
REVISED	My math instructor has a number of nervous habits that detract from his lecture presentations.

The following suggestions will help you revise your topic sentence when it is too narrow:

1. **Broaden your topic to include a wider group or range of items or ideas.** For example, do not write about one nervous habit; write about several. Look for patterns and trends that could form the basis of a new, broader topic sentence.

2. **Broaden your topic so that it takes in both causes and effects or makes comparisons or contrasts.** For example, do not write only about how fast an instructor lectures. Also write about the effect of his lecture speed on students trying to take notes, or contrast that instructor with others who have different lecture styles.

3. **Brainstorm and research; try to develop a more general point from your narrower one.** Ask yourself, "What does this narrow point mean? What are its larger implications?" Suppose you've written the following topic sentence:

   I wanted to buy a CD this week, but it was not in my budget.

   You could expand this idea to discuss the importance or value of making and following a weekly budget.

> ## NEED TO KNOW
> ### Topic Sentences
>
> Ineffective paragraphs may frustrate, confuse, or bore your reader. **A weak topic sentence may**
>
> - lack a point of view or attitude toward the topic.
> - be too broad.
> - be too narrow.
>
> **To revise a topic sentence that lacks a point of view**
>
> - use brainstorming, freewriting, or branching.
> - ask yourself questions about your topic sentence to focus on a particular viewpoint.
>
> **To narrow a topic sentence that is too broad, consider**
>
> - narrowing your topic.
> - rewriting your topic sentence to focus on one aspect of your topic.
> - applying your topic sentence to a specific time and place.
> - using one of your supporting sentences as a topic sentence.
>
> **To broaden a topic sentence that is too narrow, consider**
>
> - broadening your topic to make it more inclusive.
> - broadening your topic to consider causes and effects or to make comparisons or contrasts.
> - brainstorming and researching to develop a more general point.

EXERCISE 15-3

Directions: Turn each of the following narrow topic sentences into a broader, well-focused topic sentence that could lead to an effective paragraph. Remember that your topic sentence must also include a point of view. Then compare your answers with your classmates' answers to see the variety of effective topic sentences that can come from a narrow one.

TOO NARROW Football players wear protective helmets.

REVISED Football players wear several types of protective equipment to guard against injuries.

1. I planted a tomato plant in my garden.

    REVISED _____

    _____

2. The cafeteria served hot dogs and beans for lunch.

   REVISED _____

   _____

3. Orlando sings in a low key.

   REVISED _____

4. Suzanne bought a stapler for her desk.

   REVISED _____

   _____

5. Koala bears are really marsupials, not bears.

   REVISED _____

   _____

6. On our vacation, we stopped at a small town called Boothbay Harbor.

   REVISED _____

   _____

7. Homemade bread contains no preservatives.

   REVISED _____

8. At Halloween, the girl dressed as a witch.

   REVISED _____

   _____

9. The comedian told a joke about dental floss.

   REVISED _____

   _____

10. We had a family portrait taken for Christmas.

    REVISED _____

    _____

Revising Paragraphs to Add Supporting Details

The details in a paragraph should give your reader sufficient information to make your topic sentence believable. Paragraphs that lack necessary detail are called **underdeveloped paragraphs.** Underdeveloped paragraphs lack supporting sentences to prove or explain the point made in the topic sentence. As you read the following student paragraph, keep the topic sentence in mind and consider whether the rest of the sentences support it.

ESL Tip

An *impatient* person has trouble waiting and becomes angry or irritated by delay. *Impatient* is an adjective; *impatience* is the noun. The endings on these words are common adjective and noun endings. *Im-* is the negative prefix usually used with a word that begins with *p* or *m*.

Sample Student Paragraph

I am a very impatient person, and my impatience interferes with how easily I can get through a day. If I ask for something, I want it immediately. If I'm going somewhere and I'm ready and somebody else isn't, I get very upset. I hate driving behind someone who drives slowly when I cannot pass. I think that annoys me the most, and it never happens unless I am in a hurry. If I were less impatient, I would probably feel more relaxed and less pressured.

This paragraph begins with a topic sentence that is focused (it is neither too broad nor too narrow) and that includes a point of view. It promises to explain how the writer's impatience makes it difficult for him to get through a day. However, the rest of the paragraph does not fulfill this promise. Instead, the writer gives two very general examples of his impatience: (1) wanting something and (2) waiting for someone. The third example, driving behind a slow driver, is a little more specific, but it is not developed well. The last sentence suggests, but does not explain, that the writer's impatience makes him feel tense and pressured.

Taking into account the need for more supporting detail, the author revised his paragraph as follows:

Revised Paragraph

I am a very impatient person, and my impatience interferes with how easily I can get through a day. For example, when I decide to buy something, such as a new CD, I *have* to have it right away—that day. I usually drop everything and run to the store. Of course, I shortchange myself on studying, and that hurts my grades. My impatience hurts me, too, when I'm waiting for someone, which I hate to do. If my friend Alex and I agree to meet at noon to work on his car, I get annoyed if he's even five minutes late. Then I usually end up saying something nasty or sarcastic like "Well, where *were* you?" which I regret later. Perhaps I am most impatient when I'm behind the steering wheel. If I get behind a slow driver, I get annoyed and start honking and beeping my horn. I know this might fluster the other driver, and afterwards I feel guilty. I've tried talking to myself to calm down; sometimes it works, so I hope I'm overcoming this bad trait.

Did you notice that the writer became much more specific in the revised version? He gave an example of something he wanted—a CD—and he described his actions and their consequences. The example of waiting for someone was provided by the incident involving his friend Alex. Finally, the writer explained the driving example in more detail and stated its consequences. With the extra details and supporting examples, the paragraph is more interesting and effective.

The following suggestions will help you revise an underdeveloped paragraph:

1. **Analyze your paragraph sentence by sentence.** If a sentence does not add new, specific information to your paragraph, delete it or add to it so that it becomes relevant.

2. **Think of specific situations, facts, or examples that illustrate or support your topic.** Often you can make a general sentence more specific.

3. **Brainstorm, freewrite, or branch.** To come up with additional details or examples to use in your paragraph, try some prewriting techniques. If necessary, start fresh with a new approach and new set of ideas.

4. **Reexamine your topic sentence.** If you are having trouble generating details, your topic sentence may be the problem. Consider changing the approach.

   EXAMPLE   Rainy days make me feel depressed.

   REVISED   Rainy days, although depressing, give me a chance to catch up on household chores.

5. **Consider changing your topic.** If a paragraph remains troublesome, look for a new topic and start over.

EXERCISE 15-4

Directions: The following paragraph is poorly developed. What suggestions would you make to the writer to improve the paragraph? Write them in the space provided. Be specific. Which sentences are weak? How could each be improved?

I am attending college to improve myself. By attending college, I am getting an education to improve the skills that I'll need for a good career in broadcasting. Then, after a successful career, I'll be able to get the things that I need to be happy in my life. People will also respect me more.

_____

_____

_____

_____

_____

EXERCISE 15-5

Directions: Evaluate the following paragraph by answering the questions that follow it.

One of the best ways to keep people happy and occupied is to entertain them. Every day people are being entertained, whether it is by a friend for a split second or by a Broadway play for several hours. Entertainment is probably one of the nation's biggest businesses. Entertainment has come a long way from the past; it has gone from plays in the park to films in eight-screen movie theaters.

1. Evaluate the topic sentence. What is wrong with it? How could it be revised?

   _____

   _____

2. Write a more effective topic sentence on the topic of entertainment.

   _____

   _____

3. Evaluate the supporting details. What is wrong with them?

   _____

   _____

   What should the writer do to develop her paragraph?

   _____

   _____

4. Use the topic sentence you wrote in question 2 above to develop a paragraph about entertainment.

   _____

   _____

   _____

   _____

   _____

   _____

   _____

EXERCISE 15-6

Writing in Progress

Directions: Develop one of the topic sentences you wrote in Exercise 15-2 into a paragraph that uses good supporting details. Then, draw an idea map of your paragraph, and revise your paragraph as needed.

NEED TO KNOW

Adding Supporting Details

To revise an underdeveloped paragraph,

- analyze your paragraph sentence by sentence.
- think of specific situations, facts, or examples that illustrate or support your main point
- use brainstorming, freewriting, or branching.
- reexamine your topic sentence.
- consider changing your topic.

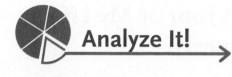

Analyze It!

Directions: The topic sentence in the left column is ineffective because it is too broad. In the right column, rewrite the topic sentence to be more specific. Then rewrite the paragraph so that it contains concrete details that support the topic sentence.

There are a wide variety of books available for leisure reading. Many people find that thrillers—novels that have an exciting plot—make great "escape" literature. Thrillers are usually easy to read. Thrillers sometimes overlap with mysteries, another popular genre. Then there are science fiction and romances, too. When choosing a book for leisure reading, a person should consider the difficulty level of the book. Some people find it relaxing to read nineteenth-century novels, but other readers are frustrated by the unfamiliar language and slow action. It is not always easy to find the perfect book, but the library offers helpful resources for the determined leisure reader.

Topic Sentence: _____

_____

_____

_____

_____

_____

_____

_____

_____

A STUDENT ESSAY

The Writer

Fidel Sanchez is a student at Richard J. Daley College in Chicago, Illinois.

The Writing Task

Sanchez wrote this essay for a writing class. His instructor encouraged him to

enter his essay in a writing contest sponsored by Longman Publishers, the publisher of this book. Sanchez's essay was selected from among hundreds of essays as a good model essay. As you read, notice that each of Sanchez's paragraphs is well developed.

The Worst and Best Jobs of My Life
Fidel Sanchez

Title suggests the thesis

Thesis statement

Topic sentence

Sanchez inserts details about the job

Reasons why job was necessary

Topic sentence

Topic sentence

Details about the second job

Conclusion

Sanchez realizes the importance of wise career planning

1   Depending on what job you choose, that choice can greatly influence your life either positively or negatively. Jobs have the power to give you a feeling of hope, meaning, accomplishment, and fulfillment or to leave you feeling broken, devastated, depressed, with a sense of hopelessness that never seems to go away. I have had two jobs in my life that have greatly affected me; one job made me feel important and useful, while the other job made me feel the exactly the opposite.

2   The first job I had was as a teacher's clerical assistant in high school. The credit hours were essential if I were to graduate so I took the job. I would help my teacher, Ms. Witherspoon, with the hordes of student papers that came her way. She would decorate them with soul-crushing F's or award-winning A's, along with little tidbits on how to do better next time. I would then leisurely type in all the information about each student's poor or near perfect academic performance into the computer. Correcting the piles of homework assignments and multiple-choice tests was time consuming because she had so many students, but this task became easier once I had all the answers in my head. That line of work made me feel important, and, furthermore, I knew what I was doing, and I felt I was making a difference.

3   Now, my second job was the exact opposite of the first. I wanted to go to college, and my parents wanted to help me by paying my tuition. However my parents, due to medical reasons, could not work, so it became my responsibility to support them and to earn money for college. I started to search for job openings around my neighborhood. Finally, I found employment at a company called Sun Optics; there I would make a fair amount of money.

4   The company made glasses for people with visual problems. I thought the job would be exhilarating since I was trying something new in my life. I would receive clear, see-through bags of frames along with an ophthalmologist's description of what the customer wanted for his or her glasses. Then I would put them on a specified colored tray with a round circular piece of plastic that soon would become lenses. My first day on the job was atrocious. Nearly cutting my finger as I tried to dull the sharp edges of freshly cut lenses did not impress my boss. Learning how to heat plastic frames with burning hot sand in order to put in the lens was challenging, too. Sometimes the job required a little something extra like drilling a hole in the lens. My employers were supposed to teach me how to do these extra things, but they never did. When I talked to them about it all they did was bellow at me and make hostile remarks.

5   I was more of a liability than an asset as I continued to work for Sun Optics. Dread came over me as I would get up every morning to go to work. This anxiety left me the day my parents told me they could start working again, so I was able to quit this job and start college. The thought that I might have to face unpleasant jobs later in life made me realize that I had better start making good, sensible, and well-thought-out choices about what I want to do with my life and

what career I want. We're all employees of an enterprise called life, so it's up to me to choose a career that will make this enterprise enjoyable and rewarding.

EXAMINING STUDENT WRITING

1. What is Sanchez's purpose for writing the essay?
2. How is the essay organized?
3. Highlight the transitions that move the reader from one topic to another.
4. What additional details could Sanchez have provided?

Paragraph Writing Scenarios

Friends and Family

1. Write a paragraph about someone in the past who encouraged you to do your best and how they would feel about you now.

2. Write a paragraph that begins "My friends would say my best feature is. . ."

Classes and Campus Life

1. Which would you like to do more, get a job or go on to get another degree?

2. Students have different learning styles. Some learn best from lectures, others by reading, and still others by doing hands-on experiments. Write a paragraph explaining how you learn best.

Working Students

1. Imagine a friend was stealing from your workplace. Would you tell your boss about it, even if it meant losing that friend? Why or why not?

2. Write a paragraph about how your current job does or does not have anything in common with the career you'd like to pursue in the future.

Communities and Cultures

1. Which would best describe the role you play in your community: peacemaker, troublemaker, or the one who stays out of the way?

2. Choose a holiday that is important in your culture and describe how it is typically celebrated.

> ## Writing Success Tip 15
>
> ### How to Credit Sources
>
> In Writing Success Tip 14 (p. 413), you learned how to avoid plagiarism—taking someone else's ideas or wording and presenting them as your own. The problem is easily avoided by being sure to give credit to the sources you use. When you do use someone else's words or ideas, you must indicate from where and whom you took the information.
>
> 1. **Be sure to record complete information on each source you use.** On a 3-by-5-inch index card, in a computer file, or on a photocopy of the source materials you have found, write the source's title and author and the page number of the quotation or other information you want to use. If the source is a book, include the publisher and the year and place of publication. If the source is a magazine article, include the volume and issue numbers and the beginning and ending page numbers of the article. For Internet sources, include the author's name, the title, the date of publication, the site's URL, and the date you accessed the site.
>
> 2. **In your paper, use the documentation style that your instructor specifies.** Two common documentation methods are the MLA (Modern Language Association) style and the APA (American Psychological Association) style. With both styles, you place a brief reference to the source within your paper, giving the author, the title, and the page number for the material you used. You then give complete information on your sources in a list of references at the end of your paper.
>
> 3. **To obtain further information about MLA and APA styles, consult the most recent edition of the *MLA Handbook for Writers of Research Papers* or *the Publication Manual of the American Psychological Association.* Your library or bookstore will have copies. You can also find** summaries of these styles in some writing handbooks or online.

WRITING ABOUT A READING

THINKING BEFORE READING

Jerry Adler, senior editor for *Newsweek* magazine, writes about the relationship between education and smoking in "The Working-Class Smoker," which first appeared in the magazine's health section. As you read, identify the author's topic, his thesis, and the types of details he includes to support his point.

1. Preview the reading, using the steps discussed in Chapter 2, p. 38.

2. Connect the reading to your own experience by answering the following questions:

    a. Are you a smoker? Why or why not?

    b. Why do people continue to smoke even though they know it is harmful?

READING
THE WORKING-CLASS SMOKER

Jerry Adler

1   Michael Bloomberg, the billionaire mayor of New York City, is a fanatical opponent of smoking, and if you had his life, you'd want to live as long as possible, too. Things might look different to, say, a waitress at a roadside chain restaurant, like the ones Barbara Ehrenreich described in "Nickel and Dimed" (2001), who smoke out of "defiant self-nurturance," because "work is what you do for others; smoking is what you do for yourself." Don't they know that cigarettes are bad for them? Yes. That message has reached "well over 90 percent" of the population, according to Harvard economist David Cutler. Although smoking has declined steeply in the United States from its peak in the early 1950s, when nearly half of all adults smoked (compared with about 21 percent today), it is proving remarkably intransigent at the bottom of the **socioeconomic** ladder. As of 2006, 35 percent of Americans with a ninth- to 11th-grade education—like the ones Ehrenreich wrote about—smoked. The figure for Americans with a graduate degree—like Bloomberg, a Harvard M.B.A.—was 7 percent.

socioeconomic
involving both social and economic factors

2   Those figures, in turn, help explain the discouraging statistic that Cutler and two coauthors reported in a recent issue of the journal *Health Affairs:* that increases in life expectancy in recent decades have been concentrated almost entirely among better-educated Americans. To put it concretely, says Ellen Meara, an assistant professor of health-care policy at Harvard Medical School, if you were 25 in 1990 with a high school diploma or less, your life expectancy was 49.6 years more, to 74.6. If you had attended college at all, even without graduating, you could expect to live more than five years longer, to 80. In 2000, a 25-year-old with any college experience had a life expectancy of 81.6, an improvement of a year and a half. The other group was stuck exactly where it had been 10 years before, a finding that Cutler described as "harsh."

3   Life is unfair in many ways, and the better educated and better paid have some obvious advantages, including better access to health care. But why should a voluntary decision not to smoke be among them? Is it willpower? Actually, the defining

Increases in life expectancy in recent decades have left behind those who didn't go to college.

characteristic of the people Ehrenreich wrote about was how hard they worked, every bit as hard as, say, a college-educated journalist.

targeting
aiming sales and marketing efforts at a particular group of people

4   No one knows for sure. Some public-health experts blame tobacco companies for "**targeting**" low-income and minority neighborhoods with billboards and store promotions—but surely that's a case of going where their remaining customers are. No doubt they'd be happy to sell cigarettes to people who shop at health-food stores if they could. So researchers look for psychological explanations. They suggest that blue-collar workers who smoke choose present gratification over future benefits. But there's also evidence that attending college by itself encourages healthy behavior; when community colleges open in rural areas, enrolling local youths who otherwise would have gone into the work force, smoking goes down.

5   Perhaps there's a clue in a bit of unpublished research by Cutler on a related question: why does seat-belt use go up with education? Anyone can understand the danger of flying through the windshield in a collision. But some data suggest that the less education you have, the likelier you are to agree with the statement "It doesn't matter if I wear a seat belt, because if it's my time to die, I'll die."

6   So for anyone reading this who never got beyond high school, here's a bit of free advice: it does matter. Life is uncertain, but that's no reason to surrender to fate. You don't need a Harvard M.B.A. to understand that.

GETTING READY TO WRITE

Reviewing the Reading

1. According to the selection, what is the percentage of
   a. people who know smoking is bad for them? _____
   b. adults who smoked in the 1950s? _____
   c. adults who smoke today? _____
   d. Americans with a ninth- to 11th-grade education who smoke?
      _____
   e. Americans with a graduate degree who smoke? _____

2. Explain how the life expectancy of a 25-year-old changed from 1990 to 2000, depending on level of education.

   _____

   _____

3. What was the defining characteristic of the people Barbara Ehrenreich wrote about in *Nickel and Dimed*? _____

4. Cite at least two reasons given in the article for why less-educated Americans are more likely to smoke. _____

   _____

   _____

Examining the Reading Using an Idea Map

Examine the reading by completing the missing parts of the idea map on the following page.

 **Visualize It!** →

> **The Working-Class Smoker**
>
> People with less education are more likely to smoke than those with college experience.
>
> > Most people know smoking is bad for them.
> >
> > _____
> > _____
> > _____.
> >
> > Increases in life expectancy are concentrated among better-educated Americans.
> >
> > _____
> > _____.
> >
> > _____
> > _____.
> >
> > _____.
> >
> > Seat-belt use goes up with education.
>
> Concludes with advice: _____
> _____.

Strengthening Your Vocabulary

Part A: Using the word's context, word parts, or a dictionary, write a brief definition of each of the following words or phrases as it is used in the reading.

1. fanatical (paragraph 1) _____

   _____

2. self-nurturance (paragraph 1) _____

   _____

3. intransigent (paragraph 1) _____

4. concretely (paragraph 2) _____

5. harsh (paragraph 2) _____

6. gratification (paragraph 4) _____

Part B: Choose one of the words above and draw a word map (see p. 84) of it.

Reacting to Ideas: Discussion and Journal Writing

Get ready to write about the reading by discussing the following:

1. What is meant by the phrase "defiant self-nurturance" in the first paragraph?

2. Why does the author compare a waitress to the mayor of New York City?

3. If "well over 90 percent" of the population knows that smoking is bad for them, why do you think people still choose to smoke?

4. Explain the purpose of the photograph included with the selection. Is the photograph effective?

5. Consider whether your own experience supports the conclusions described in the article. For example, among your family members, are those with college experience less likely to smoke than those with a high school diploma or less?

WRITING ABOUT THE READING

Paragraph Options

1. Replace the underlined words in the following quote from paragraph 1 so that the statement reflects your own philosophy: "<u>Work</u> is what you do for others; <u>smoking</u> is what you do for yourself." Write a paragraph explaining your revised statement.

2. Imagine that someone you care about has made the statement in paragraph 5: "It doesn't matter if I wear a seat belt, because if it's my time to die, I'll die." Write a paragraph presenting your response.

3. How would you describe the author's attitude toward his subject? Write a paragraph using examples from the reading to support your answer.

Essay Options

4. Think of a situation in which you chose present gratification over future benefits or delayed gratification over immediate benefits. Write an essay describing your choice and its consequences. Do you wish you had made a different decision at the time?

5. According to the selection, simply attending college (even without graduating) improves life expectancy and encourages healthy behavior. What evidence from your own experience supports or refutes those claims? Write an essay describing your observations.

Revision Checklist

Paragraph Development

1. Is the topic manageable (neither too broad nor too narrow)?
2. Is the paragraph written with the reader in mind?
3. Does the topic sentence identify the topic?
4. Does the topic sentence make a point about the topic?
5. Does each sentence support the topic sentence?
6. Is there sufficient detail?
7. Is there a sentence at the end that brings the paragraph to a close?

Sentence Development

8. Are there any sentence fragments, run-on sentences, or comma splices?
9. Are ideas combined to produce more effective sentences?
10. Are adjectives and adverbs used to make the sentences vivid and interesting?
11. Are relative clauses and prepositional phrases like *-ing* phrases used to add detail?
12. Are pronouns used correctly and consistently?

CHAPTER REVIEW AND PRACTICE

CHAPTER REVIEW

> To review and check your recall of the chapter, select the word or phrase from the box below that best completes each of the following sentences. Not all of the words and phrases will be used.
>
> | | | | | |
> |---|---|---|---|---|
> | too narrow | too broad | time sequence | point of view | place |
> | questions | answers | causes and effects | sentence | paragraph |
>
> 1. A topic sentence should express a _____.
>
> 2. A topic sentence that covers too much information is _____.
>
> 3. To revise a topic sentence that lacks a point of view, ask yourself questions _____.
>
> 4. A topic sentence is _____ if you discover you do not have enough to write about.
>
> 5. One way to revise a topic sentence that is too narrow is to consider _____ or comparisons and contrasts.
>
> 6. One way to revise a topic sentence that is too broad is to limit your topic to a specific time or _____.
>
> 7. One way to revise an underdeveloped paragraph is to analyze each _____ to determine what it contributes to the paragraph.

 ## EDITING PRACTICE

This paragraph is skimpy and underdeveloped. Revise it by adding details.

> In our family, Thanksgiving Day is one of the most important holidays of the year. Last year our large extended family, including children as well as adults, gathered at a relative's farmhouse in New Hampshire. People started arriving the day before Thanksgiving. It was a cold day. Everyone helped complete a multitude of chores. The next morning, preparations for the big dinner began in earnest.

First we stuffed the turkey. While the turkey was roasting in the oven, we

prepared a number of side dishes and dessert. When Thanksgiving dinner was

finally served, the food itself seemed less important than the simple fact of being

together. For that, we gave thanks.

INTERNET ACTIVITIES

1. Analyzing Paragraphs

Find a newspaper or magazine article with at least five substantial paragraphs. Then use this outline from an instructor at Dakota State University.

http://www.homepages.dsu.edu/moosen/format_for_outline.htm

Identify the topic sentences in the article. Evaluate how well the author developed the paragraphs and used topic sentences.

2. Cohesion

Use these guidelines provided by the School of Literature and Language at Louisiana Tech University when revising your next essay. They will help you find and correct problems with your paragraphs.

http://garts.latech.edu/owl/revise/coherence.htm

3. MyWritingLab

Visit this site to get more help with revising paragraphs.

http://www.mywritinglab.com

Click on the Study Plan tab, then on "Paragraph Basics and Development," and then on "Revising Paragraphs."

16 Using an Idea Map to Spot Revision Problems

In this chapter you will learn to:

1. Use an idea map to identify problems in your paragraphs.

2. Use an idea map to correct the problems you identify.

WRITE ABOUT IT!

How many shots do you suppose it takes to get the perfect photograph for an advertisement? Write a list of the factors a photographer might consider in choosing the right photograph.

Photographers take many shots to get just the right one. As a writer, you need to take many "shots" at a paragraph or essay to get it right. That is, you need to write several drafts before the paragraph or essay says what you want it to say.

Some students find revision a troublesome step because it is difficult for them to see what is wrong with their own work. After working hard on a first draft, it is tempting to say to yourself that you've done a great job and to think, "This is fine." Other times, you may think you have explained and supported an idea clearly when actually you have not. In other words, you may be blind to your own paper's weaknesses. Almost all writing, however, needs and benefits from revision. An idea map can help you spot weaknesses and discover what you may not have done as well as you thought.

An idea map will show how each of your ideas fits with and relates to all of the other ideas in a paragraph or essay. When you draw an idea map, you reduce your ideas to a skeleton form that allows you to see and analyze them more easily.

In this chapter you will learn how to use an idea map to (1) discover problems in a paragraph and (2) guide your revision. This chapter will discuss five questions to ask that will help you identify weaknesses in your writing, and it will suggest ways to revise your paragraphs to correct each weakness.

1. **Does the paragraph stray from the topic?**
2. **Does every detail belong?**
3. **Are the details arranged and developed logically?**
4. **Is the paragraph balanced?**
5. **Is the paragraph repetitious?**

WRITING

Does the Paragraph Stray from the Topic?

When you are writing a first draft of a paragraph, it is easy to drift away from the topic. As you write, one idea triggers another, and that idea another, and eventually you end up with ideas that have little or nothing to do with your original topic, as in the following first-draft student paragraph.

Sample Student Paragraph

One Example of Toxic Waste

The disposal of toxic waste has caused serious health hazards. Love Canal is one of the many toxic dump sites that have caused serious health problems. This dump site in particular was used by a large number of nearby industries. The canal was named after a man named Love. Love Canal, in my opinion, was an eye-opener on the subject of toxic dump sites. It took about ten years to clean the dump site up to a livable condition. Many people living near Love Canal developed cancers. There were many miscarriages and birth defects. This dump site might have caused irreversible damage to our environment, so I am glad it has been cleaned up.

The following idea map shows the topic sentence of the paragraph and, underneath it, the supporting details that directly relate to the topic sentence. All the unrelated details are in a list to the right of the map. Note that the concluding sentence is also included in the map, since it is an important part of the paragraph.

Visualize It!

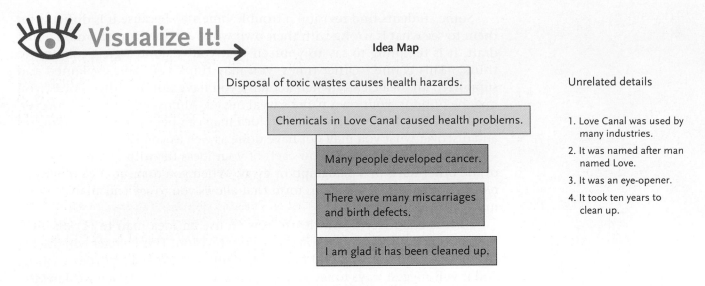

Idea Map

Disposal of toxic wastes causes health hazards.

Chemicals in Love Canal caused health problems.

Many people developed cancer.

There were many miscarriages and birth defects.

I am glad it has been cleaned up.

Unrelated details

1. Love Canal was used by many industries.
2. It was named after man named Love.
3. It was an eye-opener.
4. It took ten years to clean up.

In this paragraph the author began by supporting her topic sentence with the example of Love Canal. However, she began to drift when she explained how Love Canal was named. To revise this paragraph, the author could include more detailed information about Love Canal health hazards or examples of other disposal sites and their health hazards.

You can use an idea map to spot where you begin to drift away from your topic. To do this, take the last idea in the map and compare it with your topic sentence.

Last idea ⟷ Topic sentence

Does the last idea directly support your topic sentence? If not, you may have drifted from your topic. Check the second-to-last detail, going through the same comparison process. Working backward, you'll see where you started to drift. This is the point at which to begin revising.

What to Do If You Stray Off Topic

Use the following suggestions to revise your paragraph if it strays from your topic:

1. **Locate the last sentence that does relate to your topic, and begin your revision there.** What could you say next that *would* relate to the topic?

2. **Consider expanding your existing ideas.** If, after two or three details, you have strayed from your topic, consider expanding the details you have, rather than searching for additional details.

3. **Reread your brainstorming, freewriting, or branching to find more details.** Look for additional ideas that support your topic. Do more brainstorming, if necessary.

4. **Consider changing your topic.** Drifting from your topic is not always a loss. Sometimes by drifting you discover a more interesting topic than your original one. If you decide to change topics, revise your entire paragraph. Begin by rewriting your topic sentence.

EXERCISE 16-1

Directions: Read the following first-draft paragraph. Then draw an idea map that includes the topic sentence, only those details that support the topic sentence, and the concluding sentence. List the unrelated details to the side of the map, as in the example on p. 446. Identify where the writer began to stray from the topic, and make specific suggestions for revising this paragraph.

> Junk food lacks nutrition and is high in calories. Junk food can be anything from candy and potato chips to ice cream and desserts. All of these are high in calories. But they are so tasty that they are addictive. Once a person is addicted to junk food, it is very hard to break the addiction. To break the habit, one must give up any form of sugar. And I have not gone back to my old lifestyle in over two weeks. So it is possible to break an addiction, but I still have the craving.

EXERCISE 16-2

Writing in Progress

Directions: Write a paragraph on one of the following topics. Then draw an idea map of it. Use the same procedure you used in Exercise 16-1. If you have strayed from your topic, revise your paragraph using the suggestions given above.

1. A memorable sight, sound, or meal
2. City language or country language
3. Trends in TV ads
4. A crowd you have watched or been a part of
5. The way that a certain friendship developed

Does Every Detail Belong?

Every detail in a paragraph must directly support the topic sentence or one of the other details. Unrelated information should not be included, a mistake one student made in the following first-draft paragraph.

Sample Student Paragraph

> In a world where stress is an everyday occurrence, many people relieve stress through entertainment. There are many ways to entertain ourselves and relieve stress. Many people watch movies to take their minds off day-to-day problems. However, going to the movies costs a lot of money. Due to the cost, some people rent movies at video stores. Playing sports is another stress reliever. Exercise always helps to give people a positive attitude and keeps them in shape. Racquetball really keeps you in shape because it is such a fast game. A third form of entertainment is going out with friends. With friends, people can talk about their problems and feel better about them. But some friends always talk and never listen, and such conversation creates stress instead of relieving it. So if you are under stress, be sure to reserve some time for entertainment.

The following idea map shows that this writer included four unrelated details:

 Visualize It!

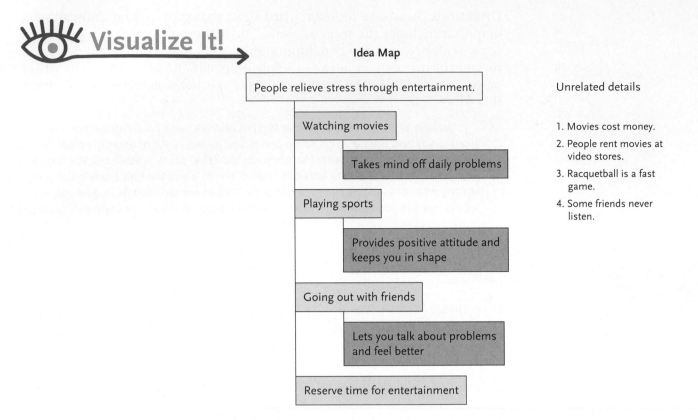

Idea Map

People relieve stress through entertainment.

Watching movies

Takes mind off daily problems

Playing sports

Provides positive attitude and keeps you in shape

Going out with friends

Lets you talk about problems and feel better

Reserve time for entertainment

Unrelated details

1. Movies cost money.
2. People rent movies at video stores.
3. Racquetball is a fast game.
4. Some friends never listen.

To spot unrelated details, draw an idea map. To decide whether a detail is unrelated, ask, "Does this detail directly explain the topic sentence or one of the other details?" If you are not sure, ask, "What happens if I take this out?" If meaning is lost or if confusion occurs, the detail is important. Include it in your map. If you can make your point just as well without the detail, mark it "unrelated."

In the sample student paragraph on p. 447, the high cost of movies and the low-cost alternative of renting videos do not directly explain how or why movies are entertaining. The racquetball detail does not explain how exercise relieves stress. The detail about friends not listening does not explain how talking to friends is helpful in reducing stress.

Making Sure Every Detail Belongs

The following suggestions will help you use supporting details more effectively:

1. **Add explanations to make the connections between your ideas clearer.** Often a detail may not seem to relate to the topic because you have not explained *how* it relates. For example, health-care insurance may seem to have little to do with the prevention of breast cancer deaths until you explain that mammograms, which are paid for by some health-care plans, can prevent deaths.

2. **Add transitions.** Transitions make it clearer to your reader how one detail relates to another.

3. **Add new details.** If you've deleted several <u>nonessential</u> details, your paragraph may be too sketchy. Return to the prewriting step to generate more details you can include.

ESL Tip

Nonessential means "not necessary." It's correct to say *nonessential* or *inessential*. Either prefix can be used.

EXERCISE 16-3

Directions: Read the following paragraph and draw an idea map of it. Underline any unrelated details and list them to the side of your map. What steps should the writer take to revise this paragraph?

> Your credit rating is a valuable thing that you should protect and watch over. A credit rating is a record of your loans, credit card charges, and repayment history. If you pay a bill late or miss a payment, that information becomes part of your credit rating. It is, therefore, important to pay bills promptly. Some people just don't keep track of dates; some don't even know what date it is today. Errors can occur in your credit rating. Someone else's mistakes can be put on your record, for example. Why these credit-rating companies can't take more time and become more accurate is beyond my understanding. It is worthwhile to get a copy of your credit report and check it for errors. Time spent caring for your credit rating will be time well spent.

EXERCISE 16-4

Writing in Progress

Directions: Study the paragraph and the idea map you drew for Exercise 16-2. Check for unrelated details. If you find any, revise your paragraph using the suggestions given above.

Are the Details Arranged and Developed Logically?

Details in a paragraph should follow some logical order. As you write a first draft, you are often more concerned with expressing your ideas than with presenting them in the correct order. As you revise, however, you should make sure you have followed a logical arrangement. Chapter 13 discusses various methods of arranging and developing details. The following Need to Know box reviews these arrangements:

NEED TO KNOW

Methods of Arranging and Developing Details

Method	Description
1. Time sequence	Arranges details in the order in which they happen.
2. Spatial	Arranges details according to their physical location.
3. Least/most	Arranges details from least to most or from most to least, according to some quality or characteristic.

Chapter 14 discusses several methods of organizing and presenting material. The following Need to Know box on the next page reviews these arrangements:

NEED TO KNOW

Methods of Organizing and Presenting Material

Method	Description
1. Narration	Arranges events in the order in which they occurred.
2. Description	Arranges descriptive details spatially or uses the least/most arrangement.
3. Example	Explains by giving situations that illustrate a general idea or statement.
4. Definition	Explains by giving a subject's category or distinguishing characteristics.
5. Comparison and contrast	Explains an idea by comparing or contrasting it with another, usually more familiar, idea.
6. Classification	Explains by identifying types or categories.
7. Process	Arranges steps in the order in which they are to be completed.
8. Cause and effect	Explains why something happened or what happened as a result of a particular action.
9. Argument	Takes a position on an issue.

ESL Tip

Haphazard means "lacking organization." It has negative connotations, suggesting that the activity should have been better planned.

Your ideas need a logical arrangement to make them easy to follow. Poor organization creates misunderstanding and confusion. After drafting the following paragraph, a student drew an idea map that showed her organization was haphazard.

Sample Student Paragraph

When I was pregnant with my son, I wondered if life would ever be normal again. There were the nights I couldn't sleep because of all the kicking and the baby moving up to my lungs so I couldn't breathe. That was when I really had it! Each month I got bigger and bigger, and after a while I was so big I couldn't bend over or see my feet. Then there was the morning sickness. I don't know why they call it that because you're sick all the time for the first two months. Then there were all those doctor visits during which she told me, "Not for another week or two." Of course, when I realized my clothes didn't fit, I broke down and cried. But all of a sudden everything started up, and I was at the hospital delivering the baby two weeks early, and it's like it happened so fast and it was all over, and I had the most beautiful baby in my arms and I knew it was worth all that pain and suffering.

An idea map lets you see quickly when a paragraph has no organization or when an idea is out of order. This student's map showed that her paragraph did not present the events of her pregnancy in the most logical arrangement:

Visualize It!

Idea Map

When I was pregnant, I wondered if life would ever be normal.

Couldn't sleep—baby kicking, breathing difficult

Got bigger and bigger

Morning sickness

Doctor: "Not for another week"

Clothes didn't fit

Birth

time sequence. She therefore reorganized the events in the order in which they happened and revised her paragraph as follows:

Revised Paragraph

When I was pregnant with my son, I wondered if life would ever be normal again. First there was the morning sickness. I don't know why they call it that because I was sick all the time for the first two months. Of course, when I realized my clothes didn't fit, I broke down and cried. Each month I got bigger and bigger, and finally I was so big I couldn't bend over or see my feet. Then there were the nights I couldn't sleep because of all the kicking and the baby moving up to my lungs so I couldn't breathe. That was when I really had it. Finally, there were all those doctor visits during which she told me, "Not for another week or two." But all of a sudden everything started to happen, and I was at the hospital delivering the baby two weeks early. Everything happened so fast. It was all over, and I had the most beautiful baby in my arms. Then I knew it was worth all that pain and suffering.

Arranging and Developing Details Logically

The following suggestions will help you revise your paragraph if it lacks organization:

1. **Review the methods of arranging and developing details and of organizing and presenting material** (see the Need to Know boxes on pp. 449–500). Will one of those arrangements work? If so, number the ideas in your idea map according to the arrangement you choose. Then begin revising your paragraph.

   If you find one or more details out of logical order in your paragraph, do the following:

   - **Number the details in your idea map to indicate the correct order, and revise your paragraph accordingly.**

   - **Reread your revised paragraph and draw another idea map.**

   - **Look to see if you've omitted necessary details.** After you have placed your details in a logical order, you are more likely to recognize gaps.

2. **Look at your topic sentence again.** If you are working with a revised arrangement of supporting details, you may need to revise your topic sentence to reflect that arrangement.

3. **Check whether additional details are needed.** Suppose, for example, you are writing about an exciting experience, and you decide to use the time-sequence arrangement. Once you make that decision, you may need to add details to enable your reader to understand exactly how the experience happened.

4. **Add transitions.** Transitions help make your organization obvious and easy to follow.

EXERCISE 16-5

Directions: Read the following student paragraph, and draw an idea map of it. Evaluate the arrangement of ideas. What revisions would you suggest?

> The minimum wage is not an easily resolved problem; it has both advantages and disadvantages. Its primary advantage is that it does guarantee workers a minimum wage. It prevents the economic abuse of workers. Employers cannot take advantage of workers by paying them less than the minimum. Its primary disadvantage is that the minimum wage is not sufficient for older workers with families to support. For younger workers, such as teenagers, however, this minimum is fine. It provides them with spending money and some economic freedom from their parents. Another disadvantage is that as long as people, such as a teenagers, are willing to work for the minimum, employers don't need to pay a higher wage. Thus, the minimum wage prevents experienced workers from getting more money. But the minimum wage does help our economy by requiring a certain level of income per worker.

EXERCISE 16-6

Writing in Progress

Directions: Review the paragraph and idea map you produced for Exercise 16-2. Evaluate the logical arrangement of your points and details, and revise if needed.

Is the Paragraph Balanced?

An effective paragraph achieves a balance among its points. That is, each idea receives an appropriate amount of supporting detail and emphasis. The following student paragraph lacks balance, as its idea map on the following page shows.

Sample Student Paragraph

Waiting

Waiting is very annoying, exhausting, and time consuming. Waiting to buy books at the college store is an example of a very long and tiresome task. I need to buy books, and so does everyone else. This causes the lines to be very long. Most of the time I find myself leaning against the wall daydreaming. Sometimes I will even leave the line and hope to come back when the store isn't extremely busy. But that never works because everyone else seems to get the same idea. So I finally realize that I just have to wait. Another experience is waiting for a ride home from school or work. My ride always seems to be the last car to pull up in the parking lot. When I am waiting for my ride, I often wonder what it would be like to own a car or if I will ever make it home. Waiting in line at a fast-food restaurant is also annoying because, if it is fast, I shouldn't have to wait. Waiting for an elevator is also no fun. Waiting just seems to be a part of life, so I might as well accept it.

Visualize It!

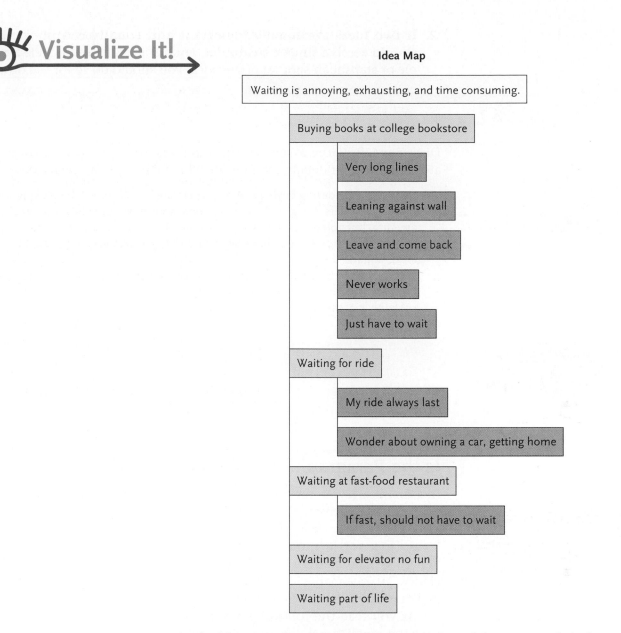

Idea Map

Waiting is annoying, exhausting, and time consuming.

Buying books at college bookstore

Very long lines

Leaning against wall

Leave and come back

Never works

Just have to wait

Waiting for ride

My ride always last

Wonder about owning a car, getting home

Waiting at fast-food restaurant

If fast, should not have to wait

Waiting for elevator no fun

Waiting part of life

As the idea map above shows, a major portion of the paragraph is devoted to waiting in line to buy books. The second example, waiting for a ride, is not as thoroughly explained. The third example, waiting at a fast-food restaurant, is treated in even less detail, and the fourth, waiting for an elevator, has the least detail. To revise, the writer should expand the treatment of waiting for rides, fast food, and elevators, and perhaps decrease the treatment of the bookstore experience. An alternative solution would be for the writer to expand the bookstore experience and eliminate the other examples. In this case, a new topic sentence would be needed.

Making Sure Your Paragraph Is Balanced

The following suggestions will help you revise your paragraph for balance:

1. **Not every point or example must have the *same* amount of explanation.** For example, more complicated ideas require more explanation than simpler, more obvious ones. When you are using a least/most arrangement, the more important details may need more coverage than the less important ones.

2. **If two ideas are equally important and equally complicated, they should receive similar treatment.** For instance, if you include an example or statistic in support of one idea, you should do so for the other.

EXERCISE 16-7

Directions: Read the following paragraph, and draw an idea map of if. Evaluate the balance of details and indicate where more details are needed.

> I am considering buying a puppy. There are four breeds I am looking at: golden retrievers, beagles, Newfoundlands, and cocker spaniels. Cocker spaniels are cute, but golden retrievers are cute *and* intelligent. Golden retrievers are very gentle with children, and I have two sons. They are also very loyal. But they have a lot of fur, and they shed, unlike beagles, which have short fur. Newfoundlands are very large, and they have dark-colored fur that would show up on my rug. Newfoundlands also drool a lot. My apartment is small, so a Newfoundland is probably just too big, furry, and clumsy.

EXERCISE 16-8

Writing in Progress

Directions: Review your paragraph and idea map for Exercise 16-2. Evaluate the balance of details, and revise if necessary.

Is the Paragraph Repetitious?

In a first draft, you may express the same idea more than once, each time in a slightly different way. As you are writing a first draft, repetitive statements may help you stay on track. They keep you writing and help generate new ideas. However, it is important to eliminate repetition at the revision stage. Repetitive statements add nothing to your paragraph. They detract from its clarity. An idea map will bring repetition to your attention quickly because it makes it easy to spot two or more very similar items.

As you read the following first-draft student paragraph, see if you can spot the repetitive statements. Then notice how the idea map on the next page clearly identifies the repetition.

Sample Student Paragraph

> Chemical waste dumping is an environmental concern that must be dealt with, not ignored. The big companies care nothing about the environment. They would just as soon dump waste in our backyards as not. This has finally become a big issue and is being dealt with by forcing the companies to clean up their own messes. It is incredible that large companies have the nerve to dump just about anywhere. The penalty should be steep. When the companies are caught, they should be forced to clean up their messes.

The idea map shows that points 1, 2, and 4 say nearly the same thing—that big companies don't care about the environment and dump waste nearly anywhere. Because there is so much repetition, the paragraph lacks development. To revise, the writer first needs to eliminate the repetitious statements. Then she needs to generate more ideas that support her topic sentence and explain why or how chemical waste dumping must be dealt with.

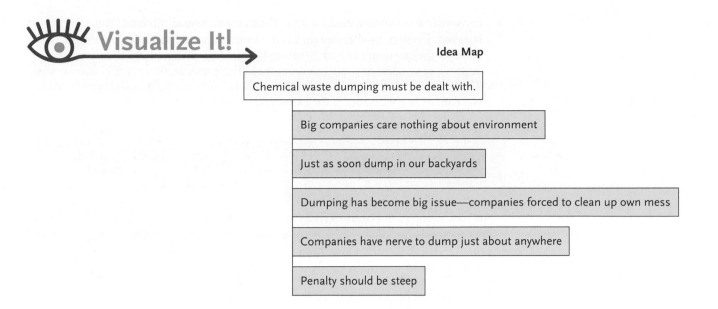

Visualize It!

Idea Map

Chemical waste dumping must be dealt with.

Big companies care nothing about environment

Just as soon dump in our backyards

Dumping has become big issue—companies forced to clean up own mess

Companies have nerve to dump just about anywhere

Penalty should be steep

How to Avoid Repetition

The following suggestions will help you revise a paragraph with repetitive ideas:

1. **Try to combine ideas.** Select the best elements and wording of each idea and use them to produce a revised sentence. Add more detail if needed.

2. **Review places where you make deletions.** When you delete a repetitious statement, check to see whether the sentence before and the sentence after the deletion connect. Often a transition will be needed to help the paragraph flow easily.

3. **Decide whether additional details are needed.** Often we write repetitious statements when we don't know what else to say. Thus, repetition often signals lack of development. Refer to Chapter 15 for specific suggestions on revising underdeveloped paragraphs.

4. **Watch for statements that are only slightly more general or specific than one another.** For example, although the first sentence below is general and the second is more specific, they repeat the same idea.

   Ringing telephones can be distracting. The telephone that rang constantly throughout the evening distracted me.

To make the second sentence a specific example of the idea in the first sentence, rather than just a repetition of it, the writer would need to add specific details about how the telephone ringing throughout the evening was a distraction.

EXERCISE 16-9

Directions: Read the following paragraph and underline all repetitive statements. Make suggestions for revision.

Children misbehaving is an annoying problem in our society. I used to work as a waiter at Denny's, and I have seen many incidences in which parents allow their children to misbehave. I have seen many situations that you would just not believe. Once I served a table at which the parents allowed their four-year-old to make his toy spider crawl up and down my pants as I tried to serve the food. The parents just laughed. Children have grown up being rewarded for their actions, regardless of whether they are good or bad. Whether the child does something the parents approve of or whether it is something they disapprove of, they react in similar ways. This is why a lot of toddlers and children continue to misbehave. Being rewarded will cause the child to act in the same way to get the same reward.

NEED TO KNOW

Using Idea Maps

An idea map is a visual display of the ideas in your paragraph. It allows you to see how ideas relate to one another and to identify weaknesses in your writing. You can use idea maps to answer the following five questions that will help you revise your paragraphs:

- Does the paragraph stray from the topic?

- Does every detail belong?

- Are the details arranged and developed logically?

- Is the paragraph balanced?

- Is the paragraph repetitious?

EXERCISE 16-10

Writing in Progress

Directions: Review your paragraph and idea map for Exercise 16-2. Identify and revise any repetitive statements.

 **Analyze It!**

Directions: The following paragraph strays from its topic and includes details that do not belong. Revise the paragraph by deleting all sentences that do not directly support the thesis.

Do you have trouble getting out of the house on time in the morning? If you are not a naturally well-organized person, you may need to overcompensate by being super organized in the morning. A detailed checklist can help you accomplish the seemingly impossible goal of leaving home exactly when you are supposed to. It is especially difficult to leave on time if you are tired or feeling lazy. When making such a checklist, most people find it helpful to backtrack to the previous evening. Do you have clean clothes for the next day, or do you need to do a load of laundry? Are your materials for school or work neatly assembled, or is there a landslide of papers covering your desk? Do you need to pack a lunch? You get the picture. In your checklist, include tasks to complete the night before as well as a precise sequence of morning tasks with realistic estimates of the time required for each task. If you have children, help them make checklists to keep track of homework assignments. Child development experts stress the importance of predictable structure in children's lives. If you live with a friend or spouse, make sure to divide all chores in an equitable way. Often one person tends to be neater than the other, so you may need to make compromises, but having an explicit agreement about household responsibilities can help prevent resentment and conflict at home.

A STUDENT ESSAY

The Student Writer

Zoë Cole is a student athlete majoring in elementary education.

The Writing Task

Zoë Cole was taking a writing class and was asked to write an essay about a childhood experience.

She chose to write about her experiences playing soccer. Cole's first draft is shown below along with the idea map she drew to help her revise. Study the first draft, her idea map, and the section titled "Evaluating the Idea Map" before you read her final draft.

Sports and Life
Zoë Cole

First Draft

1   I started playing soccer when I was four. Most of the girls in my preschool were playing, and two of their dads were the coaches, Danny and Chuck. The first time I played soccer I didn't know anything about it, except that it looked like it was fun. I didn't know about winning and losing, except in Candyland, the first board game I ever played. I just had a good time chasing the ball and trying to kick it. So I was surprised when some of the other girls on my team started talking about "Oh, we lost. It's not fair."

2   When I was seven we moved. I got on a town team, and some of the girls were good. They had been playing together for three years and I was the new kid. Some of them already thought they were stars. One of them, Emma, was a bully. She thought she was better than the rest of us. But Annie, whose dad was one of the coaches, was really nice. I didn't understand why Emma was mean, especially since she wasn't as good as Annie.

3   In fact, this early experience playing soccer was my first lesson in how different people can be. I realized that not all of my friends were nice all the time. I also realized that someone could be nice one-on-one but not so nice on a team. Like Emma, who was fun to play with at home but who just got meaner and more bossy during games. That wasn't true of Annie: she was nice all the time. If I had to give an example of a bad sport, it would be Emma. Unlike Annie, she never stopped telling us what to do and pointing out our mistakes. And if we lost, she threw a fit. It made the other kids not like her, which only made her worse. I haven't stayed in touch with Emma, but I've met people like her and I usually avoid them. I don't like being criticized or blamed when things go wrong, especially by someone who has room for improvement herself!

4   Despite some of the unpleasant players, I did enjoy the game. I enjoyed the competition, but I also just liked being outside with other kids. It was also a break in the routine of my very traditional household. Dinner at 6, bath at 8, bed at 8:30. My parents were always there to watch me play, which made me feel important. My older brother, who was also a soccer player, thought I wasn't very good, but I didn't care.

5   Annie is still my friend. Eighteen years have gone by since we met at recreation league, and she's still the same easygoing person. She was never bossy or critical like Emma, and she played really well, too. Some of the other girls were nice and would compliment you after a good play, like saying "good try" if you missed, but Annie never said much. She just grinned. She looked cute when she did it, because she had one tooth missing in the front. She grinned at you when you kicked in a goal and she grinned at you when you missed the ball completely. She never got upset and would do her silly victory dance even when we lost. She was first on line to slap hands with the other team. And she's still like that. Whether things are going really well or bad, I can always count on that Annie grin. You could say Annie is a trustworthy player, but she's more than that because she's like that when there's not a game. She's just Annie and she's everyone's friend and if she doesn't like you, she keeps it to herself.

6   There were other girls on the team who were sort of in between Annie and Emma. A couple of them were like, really insecure and neurotic and thought that everything they did mattered, good or bad. They wouldn't pass when someone was clear, but would try and take the ball alone down to the goal and then get upset when the other team took it away. They thought it was more about *them* and not the team. Some of them didn't go on playing and by high school a few had quit completely. One who didn't quit should have, because she was always scared of getting hurt. She would only go after the ball if other people on the team were there first.

7   Me, I still love soccer, but I am a different type of player than all of those whom I have described. I may not be as good as Annie, but I always play hard and try my best. I never walk away from the field feeling like I should have done something I didn't do. And I care about my teammates and the opposing players, too. I guess that's what life is all about; trying your best. If you do, you'll never let yourself down.

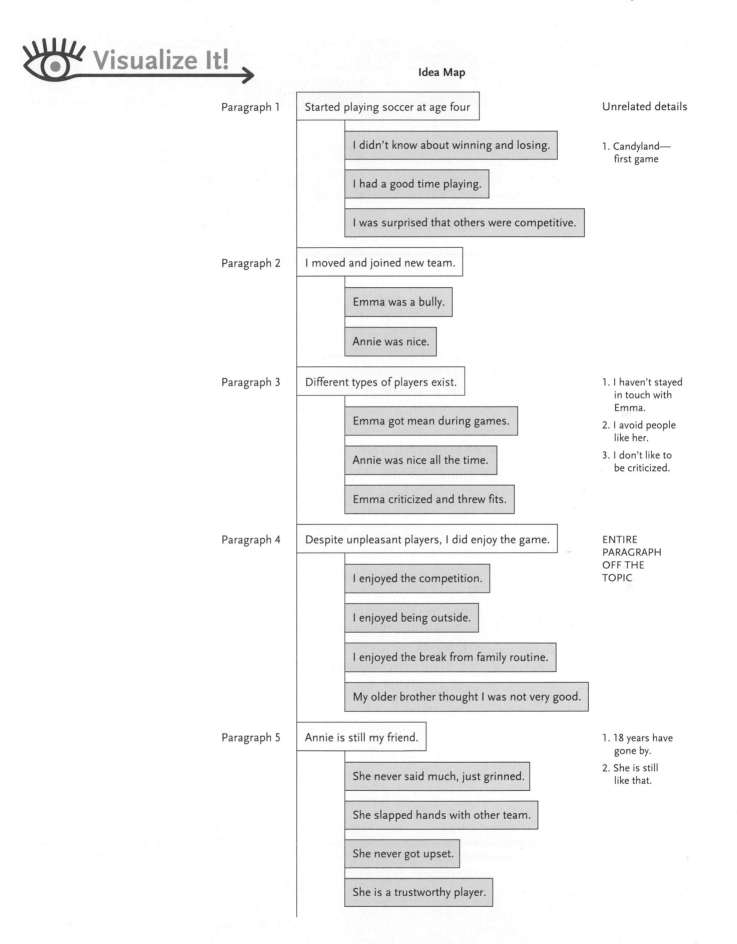

Visualize It!

Idea Map

Paragraph 1 — Started playing soccer at age four

I didn't know about winning and losing.

I had a good time playing.

I was surprised that others were competitive.

Unrelated details

1. Candyland— first game

Paragraph 2 — I moved and joined new team.

Emma was a bully.

Annie was nice.

Paragraph 3 — Different types of players exist.

Emma got mean during games.

Annie was nice all the time.

Emma criticized and threw fits.

1. I haven't stayed in touch with Emma.
2. I avoid people like her.
3. I don't like to be criticized.

Paragraph 4 — Despite unpleasant players, I did enjoy the game.

I enjoyed the competition.

I enjoyed being outside.

I enjoyed the break from family routine.

My older brother thought I was not very good.

ENTIRE PARAGRAPH OFF THE TOPIC

Paragraph 5 — Annie is still my friend.

She never said much, just grinned.

She slapped hands with other team.

She never got upset.

She is a trustworthy player.

1. 18 years have gone by.
2. She is still like that.

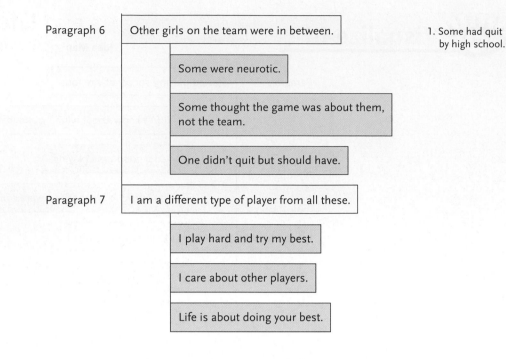

EVALUATING THE IDEA MAP

Zoë studied her idea map and realized the following:

1. She jumped from player to player, instead of concentrating on one at a time.

2. She also felt the essay was a story about individual people but did not make any points about them.

3. For the topic of paragraph 3, she had written, "Many different types of players did exist." She decided to make this statement her thesis. She decided to use specific players as examples of types of players instead of writing about the players as topics themselves. She created names for her categories.

4. She decided to include herself as an example of a Team Player.

5. She realized she needed to include an example of the insecure player in paragraph 6.

6. She eliminated paragraph 4, since it was not about types of players.

7. In all of the paragraphs, she eliminated the unrelated details that she identified.

Sports and Life
Zoë Cole

Final Draft

Introduction: background
information

Thesis statement

Topic sentence

Example: Kayla

Topic sentence

Example: Emma

Topic sentence

Example: Annie

1   When I was four years old, I began playing soccer on my neighborhood recreation team. I took to the sport right away and continued to play for the next sixteen years, both on school teams and with independent and increasingly more competitive travel leagues. From these years of experience, I have come to recognize that there are four basic types of athletes, each with a different attitude about being part of a team. To make it simple, I've given each of these types a name: the Insecure Player, the Poor Sport, the Trustworthy Player, and the Team Player. No matter what the game, I believe you'll find one of each of these types on every team, field, court, or blacktop. I'll use my own girls' soccer team as an example.

2   I'd have to put my friend Kayla in the first category, which is the Insecure Player group. Kayla worried so much about her ability that she had trouble connecting with the rest of the team. She rarely stayed in position, but would charge at the ball no matter where it went. Some people accused her of being a "hot dog," but I knew how insecure she felt. Because she was afraid of letting the team down, she overcompensated, trying to make plays that weren't hers to make in order to prove her worth on the team. When the play failed, or we lost a game, Kayla would slink off, ashamed and too embarrassed to face the rest of the team. No matter how many times the coach would tell her she wasn't solely responsible for whatever went wrong, she couldn't let up. In trying too hard, she upset the balance of the team and continued to feel awful. I put her in the category of Insecure Player because she never could step back and see herself as only one part of the team.

3   Another type of player is the Poor Sport. Emma was a good example of a Poor Sport. She was a good player—one of the best we had, in fact—but, nonetheless, she had a negative effect on the team. She was quick to yell at other players during games when they made a mistake or neglected to do something *she* thought they should have done. No matter how many times the coach told Emma to stop, she didn't, becoming in effect the team bully. She took this bad attitude a step further, letting everyone know who she deemed worthy of being her friend and ostracizing those whose abilities she considered inferior. If we lost a game, she was the first to point out whose responsibility it was, reciting a list of bad plays and who made them. Never mind that we were only ten years old; Emma was already the ultimate Poor Sport.

4   Then there is the Trustworthy Player—the one you can always count on. Annie was a completely neutral player who never let her emotions show. She showed up on time, said little, and played hard. She was consistent, strong, and unafraid. When Annie played defense, no one worried; we knew she wouldn't let the ball get by. When we won, she smiled. When we lost, she shrugged.

There was no celebration and no mourning by Annie. She was like an efficient machine, always on, never distracted. This attitude carried over into her everyday life, and we have remained friends. She is still as steady as she was at ten, and I appreciate her reliable, calm presence.

Topic sentence   5   And finally there is the Team Player. This type of player puts the team first

Example: the writer herself   and herself second. I am a good example of a Team Player. I stopped playing soccer in college but never lost my love of the game. I also never forgot I was part of a team. Sure, I liked to win, but I knew that we were only human. Exhaustion, illness, and injury all contributed to how we played. And there were simply teams who were better. Maybe they had better coaching, maybe they practiced more, maybe they were older; there were just times when we were beaten, fair and square. But I never felt down or angry. I loved the game so much that I was able to admire a competitor who showed heart and skill on the field—even as she was contributing to our defeat!

Conclusion: comments on   6   I've tried to carry this understanding of sportsmanship with me throughout

the value of sports   my adult life. Playing on a team helped me understand people better— especially myself. I find that my early exposure to teamwork has made me a good collaborator and therefore more valuable at work. Sure, I hate to lose. But I think losing has a lot to do with attitude. As long as you always play your best or work your hardest, you never really lose.

EXAMINING STUDENT WRITING

1. What was the most important revision that Cole made?

2. Evaluate the title. Could she have chosen a more descriptive title?

3. Do you think it was effective for Cole to use herself as a example of one of the categories?

4. What other revisions do you feel are needed?

Paragraph Writing Scenarios

Friends and Family

1. Write a paragraph that begins "The most important thing I learned from my mother is . . . "

2. Write about an event that stands out in the history of your family.

Classes and Campus Life

1. Which of the "Three R's" (Reading, Writing and Arithmetic) is the most difficult for you? What are you doing to make it easier?

2. Do you think race should be considered in awarding financial aid? Why or why not?

Working Students

1. Write a paragraph that begins "When I go to bed at night, I worry about . . ."

2. Write an imaginary job description that fits you perfectly.

Communities and Cultures

1. What is a typical weekend activity you enjoy doing with a group?

2. Write a paragraph about what you would miss most about your present community if you had to move away.

Writing Success Tip 16

Writing Application Letters

When you send your **résumé** (a list of your qualifications for a job) to a prospective employer, you should include a letter of application (also known as a cover letter) with it. Your letter introduces you and interests the employer in you. Employers pay careful attention to cover letters because they reveal much about an applicant's personality, style, and writing ability. Use the following tips to write a confident, convincing, and effective cover letter.

1. **Length** Your letter should be no more than one page long.

2. **Typing** Type your letter using standard letter format.

3. **Address and salutation** Address the letter to an individual rather than a company or department. Make a phone call, if necessary, to discover who is in charge of employment interviews. Use a standard salutation, such as "Dear Mr. _____ :" or "Dear Ms. _____ :."

4. **First paragraph** The first paragraph should capture your reader's attention and state your purpose for writing. If someone has referred you to the company, mention his or her name. Indicate exactly the position for which you are applying. Try to show that you know something about the company.

5. **Gimmicks** Avoid gimmicks and cute beginnings; they are seldom effective.

6. **Body** Highlight your qualifications in one or two paragraphs. Explain how you can contribute to the company.

7. **Last paragraph** End your letter by requesting an interview. Indicate when you are available, and be sure to include your telephone number, and e-mail address if you have one.

8. **Closing** Use a standard closing, such as "Yours truly" or "Sincerely." Then include your full name, leaving enough space above it for your signature.

9. **Revise and proofread** Be sure your letter is convincing, effective, and correct. Be sure it is free of errors in grammar, punctuation, and spelling. Ask someone else to read it before you send it.

ESL Tip

Ms. is an abbreviation (short form) that can be used to address a woman when you don't know whether she's married. Many women in business use *Ms.* rather than *Miss* or *Mrs.;* they consider their marital status irrelevant in the workplace. The pronunciation of *Ms.* rhymes with *his*.

WRITING ABOUT A READING

The following reading, "You Can't Be Thin Enough: Body Images and the Mass Media," is from the book *Sociology: A Down-to-Earth Approach to Core Concepts,* by James M. Henslin. As you read, notice the variety of evidence that the author includes to support his thesis.

1. Preview the reading, using the steps discussed in Chapter 2, p. 38.

2. Connect the reading to your own experience by answering the following questions:

   a. How would you describe the ideal body type?

   b. Are most people content or dissatisfied with their body type? Why?

READING
YOU CAN'T BE THIN ENOUGH: BODY IMAGES AND THE MASS MEDIA

James M. Henslin

1   *An ad for Kellogg's Special K cereal shows an 18-month-old girl wearing nothing but a diaper. She has a worried look on her face. A bubble caption over her head has her asking, "Do I look fat?" (Krane et al. 2001)*

2   When you stand before a mirror, do you like what you see? To make your body more attractive, do you watch your weight or work out? You have ideas about what you should look like. Where did you get them?

3   TV and magazine ads keep pounding home the message that our bodies aren't good enough, that we've got to improve them. The way to improve them, of course, is to buy the advertised products: hair extensions for women, hairpieces for men, hair transplants, padded bras, diet programs, anti-aging products, and exercise equipment. Muscular hulks show off machines that magically produce "six-pack abs" and incredible biceps—in just a few minutes a day. Female movie stars effortlessly go through their own tough workouts without even breaking into a sweat. Women and men get the feeling that attractive members of the opposite sex will flock to them if they purchase that wonder-working workout machine.

4   Although we try to shrug off such messages, knowing that they are designed to sell products, the messages still get our attention. They penetrate our thinking and feelings, helping to shape ideal images of how we "ought" to look. Those models so attractively clothed and coiffed as they walk down the runway, could they be any thinner? For women, the message is clear: You can't be thin enough. The men's message is also clear: You can't be muscular enough.

5   Woman or man, your body isn't good enough. It sags where it should be firm. It bulges where it should be smooth. It sticks out where it shouldn't, and it doesn't stick out enough where it should.

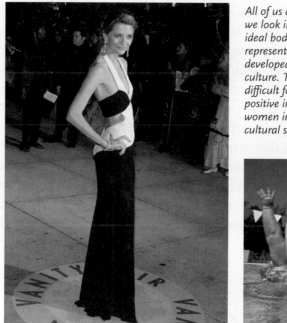

All of us contrast the reality we see when we look in the mirror with our culture's ideal body types. Mischa Barton represents an ideal body type that has developed in some parts of Western culture. These cultural images make it difficult for larger people to maintain positive images of their bodies. These women in Florida have struggled against cultural stereotypes.

6   And—no matter what your weight is—it's too much. You've got to be thinner. Exercise takes time, and getting in shape is painful. Once you do get in shape, if you slack off it seems to take only a few days for your body to sag into its previous slothful, drab appearance. You can't let up, you can't exercise enough, and you can't diet enough.

7   But who can continue at such a torrid pace, striving for what are unrealistic cultural ideals? A few people, of course, but not many. So liposuction is appealing. Just lie there, put up with a little discomfort, and the doctor will vacuum the fat right out of your body. Surgeons can transform flat breasts into super breasts overnight. They can lower receding hairlines and smooth furrowed brows. They remove lumps with their magical tummy tucks, and can take off a decade with their rejuvenating skin peels, face lifts, and Botox injections.

8   With impossibly shaped models at *Victoria's Secret* and skinny models showing off the latest fashions in *Vogue* and *Seventeen*, half of U.S. adolescent girls feel fat and count calories. Some teens even call the plastic surgeon. Anxious lest their child violate peer ideals and trail behind in her race for popularity, parents foot the bill. Some parents pay $25,000 just to give their daughters a flatter tummy.

9   With peer pressure to alter the body already intense, surgeons keep stoking the fire. A sample ad: "No Ifs, Ands or Butts. You Can Change Your Bottom Line in Hours!" Some surgeons even offer gift certificates—so you can give your loved ones liposuction or Botox injections along with their greeting card.

10   The thinness craze has moved to the East. Glossy magazines in Japan and China are filled with skinny models and crammed with ads touting diet pills and diet teas. In China, where famine used to abound, a little extra padding was valued as a sign of good health. Today, the obsession is thinness. Not-so-subtle ads scream that fat is bad. Some teas come with a package of diet pills. Weight-loss machines, with electrodes attached to acupuncture pressure points, not only reduce fat but also build breasts—or so the advertisers claim.

11   Not limited by our rules, advertisers in Japan and China push a soap that supposedly "sucks up fat through the skin's pores." What a dream product!

liposuction

a surgical procedure in which fat is removed from under the skin by means of suction

Botox

a cosmetic form of botulinum toxin that temporarily paralyzes the muscles that cause wrinkles, making the skin appear smoother

After all, even though our TV models smile as they go through their paces, those exercise machines do look like a lot of hard work.

12   Then there is the other bottom line: Attractiveness does pay off. U.S. economists studied physical attractiveness and earnings. The result? "Good-looking" men and women earn the most, "average-looking" men and women earn more than "plain" people, and the "ugly" earn the least. In Europe, too, the more attractive workers earn more. Then there is that potent cash advantage that "attractive" women have: They attract and marry higher-earning men.

13   More popularity *and* more money? Maybe you can't be thin enough after all. Maybe those exercise machines are a good investment. If only we could catch up with the Japanese and develop a soap that would suck the fat right out of our pores. You can practically hear the **jingle** now.

jingle
a catchy song used in advertising

GETTING READY TO WRITE

Reviewing the Reading

1. According to the reading, what message is sent by TV and magazine ads?

    _____

2. How is the men's message different from the women's message?

    _____

3. What statistic is cited for how many adolescent girls in the United States feel fat and count calories? _____

4. In addition to the United States, what other countries are described as having an obsession with thinness? _____

5. List two financial advantages associated with physical attractiveness.

    _____

    _____

Examining the Reading Using An Idea Map

Review the reading by completing the missing parts of the idea map shown on the following page.

Visualize It!

You Can't Be Thin Enough: Body Images and the Mass Media

TV and magazine ads send the message that our bodies aren't good enough and we've got to improve them.

_____
_____

The messages penetrate our thinking and feelings, shaping ideal images of how we "ought" to look.

Women should be thinner; men should be more muscular.

_____
_____

Unrealistic cultural ideals make liposuction, cosmetic surgery, and other procedures appealing.

_____

Attractiveness pays off financially.

_____
_____
_____

Concluding reference to the title and to the Japanese fat-sucking soap.

Strengthening Your Vocabulary

Part A: Using the word's context, word parts, or a dictionary, write a brief definition of each of the following words or phrases as it is used in the reading.

1. penetrate (paragraph 4) _____

2. coiffed (paragraph 4) _____

3. slothful (paragraph 6) _____

4. torrid (paragraph 7) _____

5. receding (paragraph 7) _____

6. furrowed (paragraph 7) _____

7. rejuvenating (paragraph 7) _____

8. violate (paragraph 8) _____

9. potent (paragraph 12) _____

Part B: Choose one of the words above and draw a word map (see p. 84) of it.

Reacting to Ideas: Discussion and Journal Writing

Get ready to write about the reading by discussing the following:

1. Discuss Western culture's ideal body types. How do these "ideal" bodies affect your own body image?

2. Why did the author begin this selection with the description of a cereal ad?

3. What is the purpose of the photographs included with the selection?

4. Would you consider cosmetic surgery or any of the other procedures described in the article? Why or why not?

5. Discuss the last paragraph of the reading. What do you think the author is revealing about his attitude toward the subject?

WRITING ABOUT THE READING

Paragraph Options

1. Write a paragraph answering the first question posed in paragraph 2: "When you stand before a mirror, do you like what you see?"

2. Who or what shapes or influences your ideas about what you should look like? Write a paragraph explaining your answer.

3. What is your opinion of teenagers having cosmetic surgery as described in the reading? Write a paragraph explaining your answer.

Essay Options

4. Look through a popular magazine and study the ads it contains. Identify several that send the message that "our bodies aren't good enough," and choose two to write about in an essay. Describe the product being marketed and the ideal body type featured in the ad. Be sure to evaluate the effectiveness of each ad.

5. Choose a TV program to analyze. What body images are portrayed on the show? How realistic are these images? Is there evidence of cultural stereotypes on the show? Pay particular attention to the commercials that air during the show. What products are being advertised? What body images are featured in the commercials? Write an essay describing your observations.

Revision Checklist

Paragraph Development

1. Is the topic manageable (neither too broad nor too narrow)?
2. Is the paragraph written with the reader in mind?
3. Does the topic sentence identify the topic?
4. Does the topic sentence make a point about the topic?
5. Does each sentence support the topic sentence?
6. Is there sufficient detail?
7. Is there a sentence at the end that brings the paragraph to a close?

Sentence Development

8. Are there any sentence fragments, run-on sentences, or comma splices?
9. Are ideas combined to produce more effective sentences?
10. Are adjectives and adverbs used to make the sentences vivid and interesting?
11. Are relative clauses and prepositional phrases like *-ing* phrases used to add detail?
12. Are pronouns used correctly and consistently?

CHAPTER REVIEW AND PRACTICE

CHAPTER REVIEW

To review and check your recall of the chapter, select the word or phrase from the box below that best completes each of the following sentences. Not all of the words and phrases will be used.

logically	unrelated	forward	idea map	repetitive
strayed	backwards	sequentially	balanced	

1. A(n) _____ can help you spot weaknesses in your writing.

2. When your paragraph has little or nothing to do with your original topic, you have _____ from the topic.

3. When drawing an idea map, list _____ details to the right of the map.

4. To identify where you drifted from your topic, read your paragraph _____, and compare each idea with your topic sentence.

5. You should arrange details in a paragraph _____.

6. A paragraph is _____ if each idea receives an appropriate amount of detail and emphasis.

7. A paragraph that contains information that is stated more than once is _____.

EDITING PRACTICE

Paragraph 1

The following first draft of a student's paragraph has a number of problems in paragraph development and organization. Draw an idea map for this paragraph, and then revise the paragraph using the map.

Students attend my college for financial, social, and academic reasons. The college I attend is a community college, and most of the students still live at home. Attending a community college gives them the opportunity to experiment for a couple of years before they decide about careers. Also, it is a state school, so the cost of tuition is more reasonable than it might be in a private college.

The college is located in a beautiful setting in the countryside on the site of a former landscape nursery. Since the students commute to school and the student body is small, it is easy to get to know a lot of people. The commute takes most students less than 30 minutes. Most of the students come from a few local high schools, so there is not a long period of social adjustment. My college has an excellent reputation because of our sports teams that are usually in contention for a state title. Many of the students who attend my college are either committed to a particular vocational program, or they have not yet made up their minds about a career.

Paragraph 2

The following paragraph is underdeveloped. Draw an idea map and revise the paragraph by expanding on and adding details in order to support its main point.

The average American worker is worse off today than at any time in the past decade. There are fewer good jobs now. Living expenses and taxes have increased. Workers' salaries have declined. More families need both spouses to work. Clearly, we are worse off today.

INTERNET ACTIVITIES

1. Eliminating Wordiness

Read over these tips for eliminating wordiness in your writing from Purdue University; then complete the exercise on the second Web site.

http://owl.english.purdue.edu/handouts/general/gl_concise.html

http://owl.english.purdue.edu/handouts/general/gl_conciseEX1.html

2. Revision

Print out this revision checklist created by the Writing Center at Wilkes University. Use it to revise your next essay. Try applying these questions to an article in a magazine or newspaper. How well did the author revise his or her work?

http://www.wilkes.edu/pages/782.asp

3. MyWritingLab

Visit this site to get more help with using idea maps.

http://www.mywritinglab.com

Click on the Study Plan tab and then on "Essay Basics, Development, and Common Problems" for a review of essay writing strategies.

17

Essay Basics and Development

In this chapter you will learn to:

1. Structure an essay.

2. Write effective thesis statements.

3. Support your thesis with evidence.

4. Write effective titles, introductions, and conclusions.

WRITE ABOUT IT!

The photograph above shows a building under construction. Write a sentence explaining how constructing a building is similar to the task of writing.

Your sentence probably included the idea that writing is a work in progress; it is a series of steps. In this chapter you will learn how to write essays. You will learn how to structure an essay, write an effective thesis statement, support your thesis with evidence, and write effective introductions, conclusions, and titles.

WRITING

An Overview of the Essay

If you can write a paragraph, you can write an essay. The structure is similar, and they have similar parts. A paragraph expresses one main idea, called the **topic**, and is made up of several sentences that support that idea. The main idea is expressed in a sentence called the **topic sentence**. An essay also expresses one key idea, called the **thesis**. This is expressed in a sentence called the **thesis statement.** The chart below shows how the parts of the paragraph are very much like the parts of an essay.

ESL Tip

The prefix *trans-* means "across" or "from one place to another." A transitional sentence carries the reader from the idea before it to the idea that follows it, making the connection between them easier to understand.

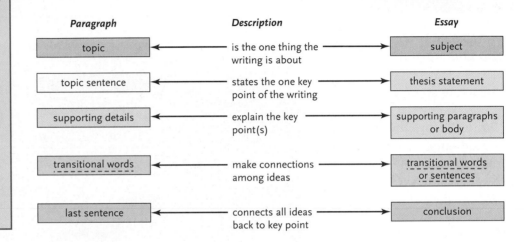

Paragraph	Description	Essay
topic	is the one thing the writing is about	subject
topic sentence	states the one key point of the writing	thesis statement
supporting details	explain the key point(s)	supporting paragraphs or body
transitional words	make connections among ideas	transitional words or sentences
last sentence	connects all ideas back to key point	conclusion

The Structure of an Essay

Think of the organization of an essay as modeling the organization of a paragraph, with one idea being explained by supporting details. Because an essay is usually at least three paragraphs long, and often more, it needs an opening paragraph, called the **introduction,** that focuses the reader and provides necessary background information before the thesis is presented. The paragraphs that support the thesis are called the **body** of the essay. Due to length and complexity, an essay also needs a final paragraph, called the **conclusion,** to draw the ideas discussed together and bring it to an end. You can visualize the organization of an essay as shown on the following page.

Planning Your Essay

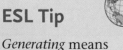

ESL Tip

Generating means "producing or creating."

An essay requires more time spent in planning and organization than does a single paragraph, although the process is the same. It involves selecting an appropriate topic and generating ideas. The topic for an essay should be broader than for a single paragraph. For more information on broadening or narrowing topics, see Chapter 18, pp. 499–502. To generate ideas for an essay, use the techniques you learned in Chapter 11 for generating ideas for paragraphs.

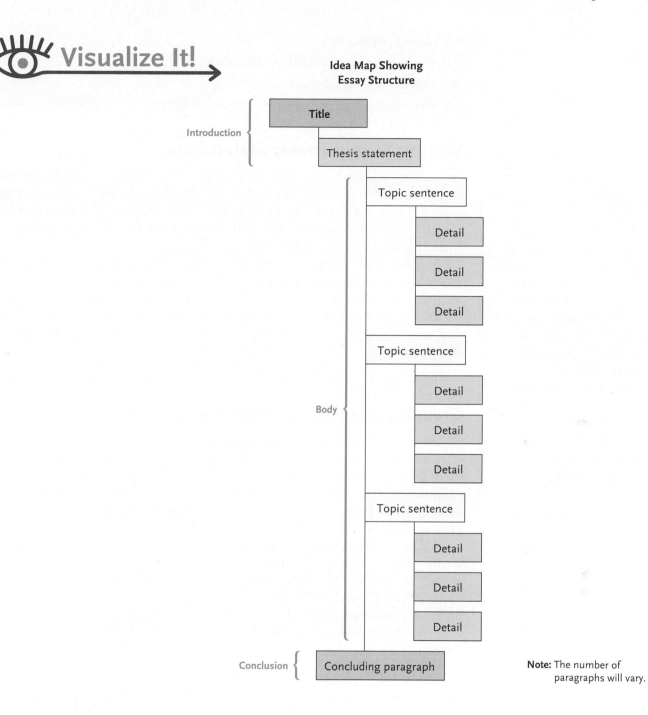

Visualize It!

Idea Map Showing Essay Structure

Introduction
- Title
- Thesis statement

Body
- Topic sentence
  - Detail
  - Detail
  - Detail
- Topic sentence
  - Detail
  - Detail
  - Detail
- Topic sentence
  - Detail
  - Detail
  - Detail

Conclusion
- Concluding paragraph

Note: The number of paragraphs will vary.

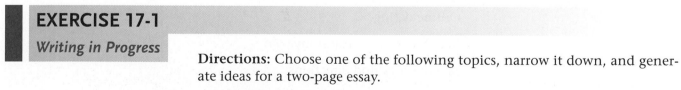

EXERCISE 17-1

Writing in Progress

Directions: Choose one of the following topics, narrow it down, and generate ideas for a two-page essay.

1. Organic or health foods
2. Natural disasters
3. Predictable or unpredictable behaviors
4. Teenage fads or fashions
5. Controlling stress

6. Valued possessions

7. An unfortunate accident or circumstance

8. A technological advance

Writing Strong Thesis Statements

ESL Tip

In an ESL dictionary, you'll find many meanings of the word *sound* as a verb, noun, and adjective. Here, it is an adjective meaning "good or correct." To broaden your vocabulary, read though all the dictionary definitions of *sound*, including the idiomatic expressions. Take notes on some meanings that are new to you.

To develop a sound essay, you must begin with a well-focused thesis statement. A **thesis statement** tells your reader what your essay is about and gives clues to how the essay will unfold. The thesis statement should not only identify your topic but also express the main point about your topic that you will explain or prove in your essay.

Some students think they should be able to just sit down and write a thesis statement. But a thesis statement rarely springs fully formed into a writer's mind: it evolves and, in fact, may change significantly during the process of prewriting, grouping ideas, drafting, and revising. The next section will show you how to draft a thesis statement and how to polish it into a focused statement.

Grouping Your Ideas to Discover a Thesis Statement

The first step in developing a thesis statement is to generate ideas to write about. Use one of the four prewriting methods you have studied: (1) free-writing, (2) brainstorming, (3) questioning, and (4) branching. Refer to p. 298 of Chapter 11, "Planning and Organizing," for a review of these strategies. Once you have ideas to work with, the next step is to group or connect your ideas to form a thesis. Let's see how one student produced a thesis following these steps.

Markella Tsoukalas was majoring in psychology. The instructor in her writing course assigned a short (one-to-two-page) essay on the effects of technology on modern life. After brainstorming a list of various technologies including cell phones, DVD players, and video games, she decided to write about computers and specifically about the Internet. She then did a second brainstorming about uses and effects of the Internet. She came up with the following list.

Instant messaging

Research for college papers

Online dating

Match.com and eHarmony.com

Mapquest to find directions

Chat rooms

Meet new friends

College Web site

E-mail—socializing with friends

MySpace

Google to find the answer to anything

Online profiles

Accuracy of online profiles

Markella's next step in writing her essay was to select usable ideas and try to group or organize them logically. In the brainstorming list above, Markella saw three main groups of ideas: communicating, socializing, and online dating. She sorted her list into categories:

Communicating: instant messaging, chat rooms, completing assignments

Socializing: MySpace, online profiles, friending new people

Online Dating: Match.com, eHarmony.com

Once Markella had grouped her ideas into these categories, she could write a thesis statement:

> The Internet has become an excellent means of communicating, socializing, and meeting potential dates.

This thesis statement identifies her topic—the Internet—and suggests three ways in which it has affected her life. You can see how this thesis statement grew out of her idea groupings. Furthermore, this thesis statement gives her readers clues as to how she will organize the essay. A reader knows from this preview which uses she will discuss and in what order.

How to Group Ideas

How do you know which ideas to group? Look for connections and relationships among ideas that you generate during prewriting. Here are some suggestions:

1. **Look for categories.** Try to discover how you can classify and subdivide your ideas. Think of categories as titles or slots in which you can place ideas. Look for a general term that is broad enough to cover several of your ideas. For example, Markella broke down the many uses of the Internet into communicating, socializing, and online dating. Suppose you were writing a paper on favoritism. You could break down the topic by a category, such as place.

   SAMPLE THESIS STATEMENT   Whether it's practiced in the workplace, in a classroom, or on Capitol Hill, favoritism is unfair.

2. **Try organizing your ideas chronologically.** Group your ideas according to the clock or calendar.

   SAMPLE THESIS STATEMENT   From the ancient Mayans to King Henry VIII's court to present day Congress, personal relationships have always played a role in professional achievement.

3. **Look for similarities and differences.** When working with two or more topics, see if you can approach them by looking at how similar or different they are.

   SAMPLE THESIS STATEMENT   The two great pioneers of psychotherapy, Freud and Jung, agreed on the concept of the libido but completely disagreed on other issues.

4. **Separate your ideas into causes and effects or problems and solutions.** You can often analyze events and issues in this way.

> SAMPLE THESIS STATEMENT   The phrase "it takes a village to raise a child" means that birth parents alone do not determine what an individual will grow up to be.

5. **Divide your ideas into advantages and disadvantages, or pros and cons.** When you are evaluating a proposal, product, or service, this approach may work.

> SAMPLE THESIS STATEMENT   Deciding on a major before starting college can either help a student stay focused and on track or keep him or her from discovering new interests.

6. **Consider several different ways to approach your topic or organize and develop your ideas.** As you consider what your thesis statement is going to be, push yourself to see your topic from a number of different angles or from a fresh perspective.

For example, Markella could have examined her brainstorming list and decided to focus only on the Internet as an information source, looking more deeply into search engines and informational Web sites. In other words, within every topic lie many possible thesis statements.

Guidelines for Writing Thesis Statements

A thesis statement should explain what your essay is about, and it should also give your readers clues to its organization. Think of your thesis statement as a promise; it promises your reader what your paper will deliver. Here are some guidelines to follow for writing an effective thesis statement:

1. **It should state the main point of your essay.** It should not focus on details; it should give an overview of your approach to your topic.

> TOO DETAILED   Because babies don't know anything about the world around them, parents should allow them to touch toys and other objects.

> REVISED   Because babies don't know anything about the world around them when they are born, they need to spend lots of time touching, holding, and exploring the everyday things we take for granted.

2. **It should assert an idea about your topic.** Your thesis should express a viewpoint or state an approach to the topic.

> LACKS AN ASSERTION   Advertisers promote beer during football games.

> REVISED   One of the reasons you see so many beer ads during ball games is that men buy more beer than women.

3. **It should be as specific and detailed as possible.** For this reason, it is important to review and rework your thesis *after* you have written and revised drafts.

> TOO GENERAL   You need to take a lot of clothes with you when you go camping.

REVISED   Because the weather can change so quickly in the Adiron-
               dacks, it is important to pack clothing that will protect
               you from both sun and rain.

4. **It may suggest the organization of your essay.** Mentioning key points
   that will be discussed in the essay is one way to do this. The order in
   which you mention them should be the same as the order in which you
   discuss them in your essay.

DOES NOT SUGGEST   Learning to read is important for your whole life.
ORGANIZATION

REVISED   Literacy is a necessary tool for academic,
                     professional, and personal success.

5. **It should not be a direct announcement.** Do not begin with phrases
   such as "In this paper I will . . ." or "My assignment was to discuss . . ."

DIRECT ANNOUNCEMENT   What I am going to write about is how working
                        out can make you better at your job.

REVISED   Exercise can dramatically improve the per-
                        formance of everyone, from front office to
                        assembly-line workers.

6. **It should offer a fresh, interesting, and original perspective on the
   topic.** A thesis statement can follow the guidelines discussed above, but,
   if it seems dull or predictable, it needs more work.

PREDICTABLE   Complex carbohydrates are good for you.

REVISED   Diets that call for cutting out carbohydrates completely are
                overlooking the tremendous health benefits of whole
                grains.

EXERCISE 17-2
Writing in Progress

Directions: Using the topic you chose and the ideas you generated about it
in Exercise 17-1, develop a thesis statement.

Supporting Your Thesis with Substantial Evidence

Every essay you write should offer substantial evidence in support of your
thesis statement. This evidence makes up the body of your essay. **Evidence**
can consist of personal experience, anecdotes (stories that illustrate a point),
examples, reasons, descriptions, facts, statistics, and quotations (taken from
sources).

Many students have trouble locating concrete, specific evidence to support their theses. Though prewriting yields plenty of good ideas and helps
you focus your thesis, prewriting ideas may not always provide sufficient evidence. Often you need to brainstorm again for additional ideas. At other
times, you may need to consult one or more sources to obtain further information on your topic (see Writing Success Tip 14, Avoiding Plagiarism and
Citing Sources, p. 413).

The table below lists ways to support a thesis statement and gives an example of how Markella could use each in her essay on different ways to use the Internet.

TABLE 17-1   WAYS TO ADD EVIDENCE

Topic: The Internet's Impact

Support Your Thesis by	Example
Telling a story (narration)	Relate a story about a couple who met using an online dating service.
Adding descriptive detail (description)	Give details about one person's MySpace profile.
Giving an example	Give an example of types of personal likes and dislikes that are included in one person's online profile.
Giving a definition	Explain the meaning of the term "friendship status."
Making comparisons	Compare two online dating sites.
Making distinctions (contrast)	Compare instant messaging with face-to-face conversations.
Discussing types or kinds (classification)	Discuss the types of information that can be found on the Internet.
Explaining how something works (process)	Explain how to register on MySpace.
Giving reasons (causes)	Explain what factors contribute to the popularity of chat rooms.
Analyzing effects	Explain why online profiles can be misleading.

The table offers a variety of ways Markella could add evidence to her essay, but she would not need to use all of them. Instead, she should choose the one that is the most appropriate for her audience and purpose. Markella could also use different types of evidence in combination. For example, she could *describe* a particular online dating site and *tell a story* that illustrates its use.

Use the following guidelines in selecting evidence to support your thesis:

1. **Be sure your evidence is relevant.** That is, it must directly support or explain your thesis.

2. **Make your evidence as specific as possible.** Help your readers see the point you are making by offering detailed, concrete information. For example, if you are explaining the dangers of driving while intoxicated, include details that make that danger seem immediate: victims' names and injuries, types of vehicle damage, statistics on the loss of life, and so on.

3. **Be sure your information is accurate.** It may be necessary to check facts, verify stories you have heard, and ask questions of individuals who may have provided information.

4. **Locate sources that provide evidence.** Because you may not know enough about your topic and lack personal experience, you may be unable to provide strong evidence. When this happens, locate several sources on your topic.

5. **Be sure to document any information that you borrow from other sources.** Consult Writing Success Tip 14, p. 413, for information on citing sources.

EXERCISE 17-3
Writing in Progress

Directions: Write a first draft of an essay for the thesis statement you wrote in Exercise 17-2. Support your thesis statement with at least three types of evidence.

 Analyze It!

Directions: Below is the brainstorming one student did on the topic of space exploration. Study the brainstorming and use the key below to identify and group the ideas into three sets of related ideas that could be used in an essay. Choose one of the topics, create a topic sentence, and list the ideas you would use in the order you would use them.

Space Exploration

what if Columbus and other explorers hadn't taken the risk to explore new worlds?

space travel inspires younger generation

space travel a luxury when poverty, famine, and war on Earth

recent Gallup poll shows 71% of Americans support the space program

why not just use robots—why risk human lives?

achievements of Hubble telescope, International Space Station, humans on moon

national trauma from shuttle disasters

space shuttle Challenger and Columbia deaths

basic scientific research often leads to unexpected practical applications

exploring space could involve discoveries that solve energy crisis and other problems

natural resources on other planets

NASA-developed technologies (led to laptop computers, solar power cells)

no matter how advanced the technology, human error will always cause problems

satellite enabled telephone and TV communications, global navigation, weather forecast

adverse health effects of weightlessness (bone loss, muscle damage, loss red blood cells)

is it worth it to go to the moon?

travel to other planets takes too long

astronauts vulnerable to cosmic radiation

V = value of space program R = Risks of space program D = disadvantages of space program

A Student Essay

The Writer

Markella Tsoukalas is a student at Fairleigh Dickinson University in Teaneck, New Jersey. She is a junior and is majoring in business management with a concentration in human resources.

The Writing Task

Now let's take a look at how Markella developed her essay on the impact of the Internet. As you read her draft, notice in particular the types of evidence she uses and how her thesis statement promises what her essay delivers.

Interest-catching title

You Looked Better on MySpace
Markella Tsoukalas

1   The Internet has revolutionized America's way of communicating and of meeting new and interesting people. When the Internet was first introduced to American society, only the rich and famous had access to it because only they could afford computers; now, the majority of U.S. households have computer

Thesis statement

and Internet access. The Internet has become an excellent means of communicating, socializing, and meeting one's soul mate.

Topic sentence

2   When I first got Internet access, I was obsessed with the instant messaging and chat rooms. They were new ways of communicating with my friends

Personal experience or evidence

without worrying about increasing the phone bill. My parents thought it was the best thing ever invented because I wasn't going out as much with my friends, which meant that I wasn't spending as much money. There was no need for them to be worrying constantly about where I was and if I was okay. For about a year, I was glued to the computer because I was fascinated with all the different techniques and programs that were available. Now I socialize on the Internet at a more moderate level and use it for school-related assignments and finding needed information, as well.

3   I went to the mall on a busy Saturday, and, as usual, it was packed. While walking around, I must have seen about ten people wearing shirts saying "You looked better on MySpace." (MySpace is a site created for people who want to meet and socialize with others who share common interests.) I giggled to myself and was in shock that people had the boldness to wear a shirt like that in

Topic sentence

public. However, the logo does emphasize the popularity of MySpace and suggests the problems of online profiles. Each user creates a profile detailing his or her likes and dislikes, and posts a picture, if desired. If the user sees some-

Explanation of how MySpace works

one attractive on MySpace, a simple request is sent requesting friendship status. MySpace allows people to socialize with people they know and with people they have just met. MySpace offers a safe way of meeting people without face-to-face encounters.

Topic sentence

4   There is a soul mate for every person in the world, but it is harder for some than others to find that special person. Match.com and eHarmony.com were created for those "hard to find" soul mates. Like MySpace, when a user creates a profile that includes a list of the user's interests, the user is matched with

Details about online dating sites

someone who is perceived to have similar interests. A major advantage of both of the sites is that they allow the matched couple to get to know one another before meeting in person, if they choose. The couple can decide if there is sufficient mutual connection for a face-to-face meeting. There have been many relationships made through Match.com and eHarmony.com; some have led to marriage. They are great sites to try out if you are having troubles in the love department.

Conclusion: Markella recaps three main points and comments on how each has affected her

5   I am fortunate that the Internet has found its way into my life. It's one of the most convenient sources for communication and information sharing. Socializing on the Internet has put me in touch with people from all different countries. As for finding a soul mate, I'll leave you guessing on that one. Overall, as the Internet continues to expand throughout the world, our experiences will also expand.

Making Connections Among Your Ideas Clear

To produce a well-written essay, be sure to make it clear how your ideas relate to one another. There are several ways to do this:

1. **Use transitional words and phrases.** The transitional words and phrases that you learned in Chapter 14 for connecting ideas are helpful for making your essay flow smoothly and communicate clearly. Table 17-2 lists useful transitions for each method of organization. Notice the use of these transitional words and phrases in Markella's essay: *when, now, where,* and *however.*

ESL Tip

For several pages of information about *transitions,* see the ESL Guide, E., "Transitional Words and Phrases" (p. 642).

TABLE 17-2   USEFUL TRANSITIONAL WORDS AND PHRASES

Method of Development	Transitional Words and Phrases
Most-Least/Least-Most	most important, above all, especially, particularly important, less important
Spatial	above, below, behind, beside, next to, inside, outside, to the west (north, etc.), beneath, near, nearby, next to
Time Sequence	first, next, now, before, during, after, eventually, finally, at last, later, meanwhile, soon, then, suddenly, currently, after, afterward, after a while, as soon as, until
Narration/Process	first, second, then, later, in the beginning, when, after, following, next, during, again, after that, at last, finally
Description	see Spatial and Most-Least/Least-Most above
Example	for example, for instance, to illustrate, in one case
Definition	means, can be defined as, refers to, is
Classification	one, another, second, third
Comparison	likewise, similarly, in the same way, too, also
Contrast	however, on the contrary, unlike, on the other hand, although, even though, but, in contrast, yet
Cause and Effect	because, consequently, since, as a result, for this reason, therefore, thus

2. **Write a transitional sentence.** This sentence is usually the first sentence in the paragraph. It might come before the topic sentence or it might *be* the topic sentence. Its purpose is to link the paragraph in which it appears with the paragraph before it. Sometimes it comes at the end of the paragraph and links the paragraph to the following one.

3. **Repeat key words.** Repeating key words from either the thesis statement or the preceding paragraph helps your reader see connections among ideas. In Markella's essay, notice the repetition of key words and phrases such as *Internet* and *MySpace*.

EXERCISE 17-4
Writing in Progress

Directions: Review the draft you wrote for Exercise 17-3. Analyze how effectively you have connected your ideas. Add key words or transitional words, phrases, or sentences, as needed.

Writing the Introduction, Conclusion, and Title

The introduction, conclusion, and title each serve a specific function. Each strengthens your essay and helps your reader better understand your ideas.

Writing the Introduction

An introductory paragraph has three main purposes.

1. **It presents your thesis statement.**

2. **It interests your reader in your topic.**

3. **It provides any necessary background information.**

Although your introductory paragraph appears first in your essay, it does *not* need to be written first. In fact, it is sometimes best to write it last, after you have developed your ideas, written your thesis statement, and drafted your essay.

We have already discussed writing thesis statements earlier in the chapter (see p. 476). Here are some suggestions on how to interest your reader in your topic:

TABLE 17-3 WAYS TO INTEREST YOUR READER	
Technique	Example
Ask a provocative or controversial question	How would you feel if the job you had counted on suddenly fell through?
State a startling fact or statistic	Last year, the United States government spent a whopping billion dollars a day on interest on the national debt.
Begin with a story or an anecdote	The day Liam Blake left his parka on the bus was the first day of what would become the worst snowstorm the city had ever seen.
Use a quotation	Robert Frost wrote "Two roads diverged in a wood, and I—/I took the one less traveled by,/And that has made all the difference."
State a little-known fact, a myth, or a misconception	What was Harry S. Truman's middle name? Stephen? Samuel? Simpson? Actually, it's just plain "S." There was a family dispute over whether to name him for his paternal or maternal grandfather, an argument that was settled by simply using the common initial "S."

A straightforward, dramatic thesis statement can also capture your reader's interest, as in the following example:

> The first day I walked into Mr. Albierto's advanced calculus class, I knew I had made a huge mistake.

An introduction should also provide the reader with any necessary background information. Consider what information your reader needs to understand your essay. You may, for example, need to define the term *genetic engineering* for a paper on that topic. At other times, you might need to provide a brief history or give an overview of a controversial issue.

Now reread the introduction to Markella's essay on p. 482. How does she introduce her topic?

EXERCISE 17-5
Writing in Progress

Directions: Revise the introduction to the essay you wrote for Exercise 17-3.

Writing the Conclusion

The final paragraph of your essay has two functions: It should reemphasize your thesis statement and draw the essay to a close. It should not be a direct announcement, such as "This essay has been about . . ." or "In this paper I hoped to show that . . ."

It's usually best to revise your essay at least once *before* working on the conclusion. During your first or second revision, you often make numerous changes in both content and organization, which may, in turn, affect your conclusion.

Here are a few effective ways to write a conclusion. Choose one that will work for your essay.

1. **Look ahead.** Project into the future and consider outcomes or effects.

2. **Return to your thesis.** If your essay is written to prove a point or convince your reader of the need for action, it may be effective to end with a sentence that recalls your main point or calls for action. If you choose this way to conclude, be sure not to merely repeat your first paragraph. Be sure to reflect on the thoughts you developed in the body of your essay.

3. **Summarize key points.** Especially for longer essays, briefly review your key supporting ideas. Notice how Markella's concluding paragraph touches upon each of her three main points: communication, socializing, and dating online.

If you have trouble writing your conclusion, it's probably a tip-off that you need to work further on your thesis or organization.

EXERCISE 17-6

Directions: Write or revise a conclusion for the essay you wrote for Exercise 17-3.

Selecting a Title

Although the title appears first in your essay, it is often the last thing you should write. The title should identify the topic in an interesting way, and it may also suggest the focus. To select a title, reread your final draft, paying particular attention to your thesis statement and your overall method of development. Here are a few examples of effective titles:

"Which Way Is Up?" (for an essay on mountain climbing)

"A Hare Raising Tale" (for an essay on taking care of rabbits)

"Topping Your Bottom Line" (for an essay on how to increase profitability)

To write accurate and interesting titles, try the following tips:

1. **Write a question that your essay answers.** For example: "What Are the Signs That It's Safe to Approach a Strange Dog?"

2. **Use key words that appear in your thesis statement.** If your thesis statement is "Diets rich in lean beef can help teenagers maintain higher levels of useable iron," your title could be "Lean Beef Is Good for Teens."

3. **Use brainstorming techniques to generate options.** Don't necessarily go with the first title that pops into your mind. If in doubt, try out some options on friends to see which is most effective.

EXERCISE 17-7

Writing in Progress

Directions: Come up with a good title for the essay you wrote for Exercise 17-3.

Essay Writing Scenarios

Friends and Family

1. Describe a family item you would save in the event of a natural disaster. Whose was it, and why is it special to you?

2. Write an essay that begins "The best vacation my family ever took together was . . ."

Classes and Campus Life

1. Mark Twain wrote, "The person who *does* not read good books has no advantage over the person who *can't* read them." Write a short essay explaining what you think he meant.

2. Where do you do your best work, in class discussions or alone on a computer? Why?

Working Students

1. Explain which you'd prefer, a job in which you deal with people or with things.

2. Describe something you do in your daily life that you would never do at work.

Communities and Cultures

1. Community leaders can be elected officials or ordinary citizens. Write an essay about one person who makes (or has made) a difference in your community.

2. Describe one thing you did as a teenager to fit in with a particular group.

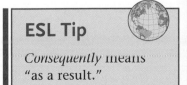

ESL Tip

Consequently means "as a result."

Writing Success Tip 17

Writing Essay Exam Answers

You can master the art of writing good essay-exam answers. The following suggestions and strategies will help:

1. **Read the directions carefully.** They may, for example, tell you to answer only two out of four questions.

2. **Plan your time.** For example, if you have to answer two essay questions in a 50-minute class session, give yourself 20 to 25 minutes for each one.

3. **Answer the easiest question first.** Doing so may take you less time than you budgeted, and consequently, you can spend additional time on harder questions.

4. **Analyze each question.** Look for words that tell you what to write about and how to organize your answer. If an exam question says, "Trace the history of advertising in the United States," the word *trace* tells you to organize your essay using a time-sequence arrangement. The question also identifies and focuses the topic—the history of advertising.

5. **Plan your answer.** On the back of the exam or on a separate sheet of paper that you will not turn in, jot down ideas you will include in your essay. Arrange your ideas to follow the method of development suggested in the question.

6. **Write your thesis statement.** A thesis statement is like a topic sentence. It announces what your essay will be about. Thesis statements in essay-exam answers should be simple and straightforward. Start by rewording the question.

SAMPLE ESSAY QUESTION	SAMPLE THESIS STATEMENT
Describe the psychological factors that may affect a person's decision to change jobs.	There are five psychological factors that may affect a person's decision to change jobs.
Define and give an example of age discrimination.	Age discrimination takes place whenever people are mistreated or unfairly judged simply because of how old they are.

7. **Present adequate supporting details.** Write a separate paragraph for each major supporting detail. Begin each paragraph with a topic sentence that introduces each new point. Each paragraph should provide relevant and sufficient support for the topic sentence.

8. **Proofread your answer.** Be sure to leave enough time to proofread your answer. Check for errors in spelling, punctuation, and grammar.

9. **If you run out of time . . .** If you run out of time before you have finished answering the last question, don't panic. Take the last minute or two to make a list or outline of the other points you planned to cover. Some instructors will give you partial credit for this outline.

WRITING ABOUT A READING

THINKING BEFORE READING

Originally published in the *New York Times*, this reading, "Calling in Late," deals with the behavior changes brought about by the use of cell phones. Author Kate Zernike explains how punctuality has lost its importance since people can easily call and explain that they will be late. As you read, notice how the author states and supports a thesis.

1. Preview the readings, using the steps discussed in Chapter 2, p. 38.

2. Connect the reading to your own experience by answering the following questions:

   a. Do you have a cell phone? What do you use it for?

   b. How do you feel about punctuality? Is it important for you and your friends to be on time?

READING

CALLING IN LATE

Kate Zernike

crutch
something you rely on for support

chronically
occuring habitually or repeatedly

focus groups
small groups asked for feedback on a specific issue

1   Restauranteurs, hairstylists and friends and family of the unpunctual have suspected it for several years. Now research is providing some evidence: as cell phones have become more prevalent, with more than half of Americans now wireless, so too has lateness. Phones have enabled more people to fall behind schedule, and have provided a new **crutch** for the **chronically** tardy. "I don't know how my friends stayed my friends before I had a cell phone," David Goldin said.

2   Researchers who study the effect of cell phones on society talk of a nation living in "soft time"—a bubble in which expectations of where and when to meet shift constantly because people expect others to be constantly reachable. Eight-thirty is still 8 o'clock as long as your voice arrives on time—or even a few minutes after—to advise that you will not be wherever you are supposed to be at the appointed hour. "We're seeing a swing toward people calling us three and four times to say, 'We're going to be late,'" said Jimmy Bradley, the owner of three restaurants in Manhattan. "Instead of making a reservation and planning your day around it, it seems as though more and more people don't really plan anything."

3   James E. Katz, a professor of communication at Rutgers University, has studied the behavior of thousands of cell phone users in surveys, in **focus groups** and in observational research, and he argues in two recent books, "Perpetual Contact" and "Machines That Become Us," that the cell phone has changed the nature of time and relationships. "It has erased the meaning of late," he said. "Just by calling and changing the plan, you're able to change being late to being on time."

4   The Context-Based Research Group, a consulting firm in Baltimore made up mostly of anthropologists, surveyed 144 cell phone users in seven cities around the world in 2000 and again in 2002, asking them to document their lives in diaries and photographs. In the United States, the researchers looked at San Francisco and New York City, finding that some forms of bad cell phone etiquette had declined—in 2002, for example, people were less likely to share the dripping details of their personal lives with the 60 other riders on the bus. But they said that more people reported being late or being victimized by others who were, blaming cell phones for the behavior.

5   Arriving late for a dinner reservation is only the beginning. Career coaches say they now must explicitly instruct job applicants not to call ahead to say they will be late for an interview. Day care centers say parents who used to be on time regularly phone to say they will be late picking up their children, and psychotherapists report that more people are showing up late for appointments—wasting time at $3 a minute. Phyllis F. Cohen, a psychoanalyst in New York, said one patient routinely calls from a cab to say she is 10 blocks away. She begins her therapy on the phone, but hangs up when she reaches the elevator for fear of being overheard. (As for the cabbies, Dr. Cohen said, "She's convinced they don't understand English.") "It's the people who were chronically late before," Dr. Cohen said. "Now they have a way of easing the conscience a bit and getting some time in. I view it as simply another form of resistance that we didn't have before."

6   To some, the flexibility provided by cell phones has improved social relations and reduced the stresses of lives that are increasingly busy. "It adds another layer of refinement to our coordination," said Leysia Palen, a professor of computer science at the University of Colorado at Boulder who has studied behavior among new cell phone users. "You don't have to rely on the agreed-upon time from the day before, and you can give people information about why you're doing it. It allows for more fluidity, more forgiveness, because there's this explanation of why you're late."

7   Ken Li, who had arrived 15 minutes late—O.K., he admitted, it was 23—to meet a friend at Schiller's on Wednesday, could only agree. "Before, you had to go to a spot and stay there all night," he said. "Now it's just like, 'Hey, where are you?' It gives you the freedom to go bumping around." He explained his lateness by saying he had to take a shower. "I could have gotten in the shower earlier," he said. "But it didn't seem urgent. And I'm calling her to tell her." Indeed, when he finally discovered his friend, Charade Woo, waiting with her phone at the bar, she seemed unruffled. "He did the polite thing," she said.

8   To others, there is a distinct downside, what Dr. Katz of Rutgers calls "the unbearable tentativeness of being." Or, as Chase Taylor, a personal trainer, put it, "the '-ish' thing"—as in "Meet me at 6-ish." "The window spreads open longer if you know you can call," said Mr. Taylor, who works at Equinox Fitness Clubs in New York. "If they didn't have a phone, they'd be more apt to just get there. It's nice that you're letting me know so I don't have to wait, but I'm still waiting anyway."

9   The extreme consequence of leaving everything to the last, wireless, minute is the **dissolution** of any plan at all. Last New Year, Daryl Levinson and several

dissolution
breakdown; destruction

friends decided to meet, but didn't specify an exact time. Instead they checked in periodically–after the first drink, after dinner, after the first party. "It was never quite convenient to meet, so we kept putting it off, until eventually it got to be too late," said Mr. Levinson, a law professor at New York University. "We just gave up and went home."

10   The investigators at Context-Based Research concluded that the United States has become more like Brazil, where time has been **spongy** for generations. (In Brazil, on the other hand, people who used to just arrive late now complain that they have to call and explain.) "The cell phone is positioned as something making you more spontaneous, more efficient," said Robbie Blinkoff, the principal anthropologist at the firm. "If you turn that on its head, it's also about allowing you to be more lazy."

spongy
soft, indefinite

11   Carol Page, who is the founder of Cellmanners.com, a cell phone etiquette site, described an e-mail message she received from a 16-year-old boy whose mother had called him from her cell phone to say she would be late picking him up from soccer practice. Was there some emergency? A flat tire? No: she had stopped along the way to look at some pottery. "It's become 'Since I have a cell phone, I can **dawdle** more,' " Ms. Page said.

dawdle
take more time than necessary to do something or get somewhere

12   Dr. Katz said the subjects of his observations never considered themselves late if they called to alert the people they were meeting. "They say they are being more considerate of the other person by asking permission to be late," he said. But ultimately, researchers say, being late is a way of exercising power. "You think you're doing a good thing," Dr. Blinkoff said. "But in reality you're saying, 'I'm more important than you—my time is more important than yours is.' There's this sense that if you're late, you must be really busy, and if you're really busy, you must be a really important person." That can damage relationships. In a survey of 1,425 people nationwide by Dr. Katz in 2000, 14 percent said bad cell phone manners, including tardiness, had hurt a close relationship. "It gnaws away at someone's self-esteem if they're being told they're the next-most-important thing to that bargain sweater," he said.

13   Slowly, people are fighting hard against soft time. Some day care centers are beginning to charge steep fees when parents arrive late to claim their children. Restaurants are increasingly refusing to seat people who are waiting for stragglers, or not taking reservations at all. Most radically, perhaps, some people are announcing that they have thrown away their phones; their friends will simply have to make plans and stick to them.

14   "It was an excuse for people to be late," said Chris Ohanesian, a 40-year-old currency broker in Manhattan who finally tossed his cell phone out the window of his car while driving six months ago. "It's funny," he said, not looking amused, "Within the week I threw it out, people started showing up on time. I started showing up on time. Punctuality all of a sudden increased in my life."

15   The Botanic Gardens Children's Center in Cambridge, Mass., has noticed that fewer parents are running late this year, perhaps because the penalty for the first 15 minutes has risen to $25, from $10, and a charge of $40 for a half-hour has been imposed. "My feeling is, if you can be here consistently at 10 past 6, you can be here consistently at 6," said Kathleen Parrish, the director.

16   Mr. Bradley, the New York restaurateur, decided not to take reservations when he opened his latest restaurant, Mermaid Inn, in the East Village, because so few people were honoring them. "We saw it as a way to work through the trend, as opposed to being a victim of the trend," he said. So far, people seem to be filling the restaurant anyway.

17   As for Mr. Ohanesian, he eventually got a new cell phone. But only because his wife was pregnant. And he gave the number only to her and the doctors.

18   The baby? She arrived a week early.

GETTING READY TO WRITE

Reviewing the Reading

1. How are cell phones enabling more and more people to be late?

2. What types of businesses are seeing a change in their clients' behavior due to cell phones?

3. Not everyone in the article thinks that cell phone behavior is a problem. List these opposing viewpoints.

4. Define the phrase "soft time." Cite an example from the reading that illustrates this term.

5. How are some people and businesses responding to what they perceive as negative behavior involving cell phones and punctuality?

6. What is special about Chris Ohanesian? Why do you think the author included his story?

Examining the Reading Using an Idea Map

Review the reading by completing the missing parts of the idea map shown on the following page.

Visualize It!

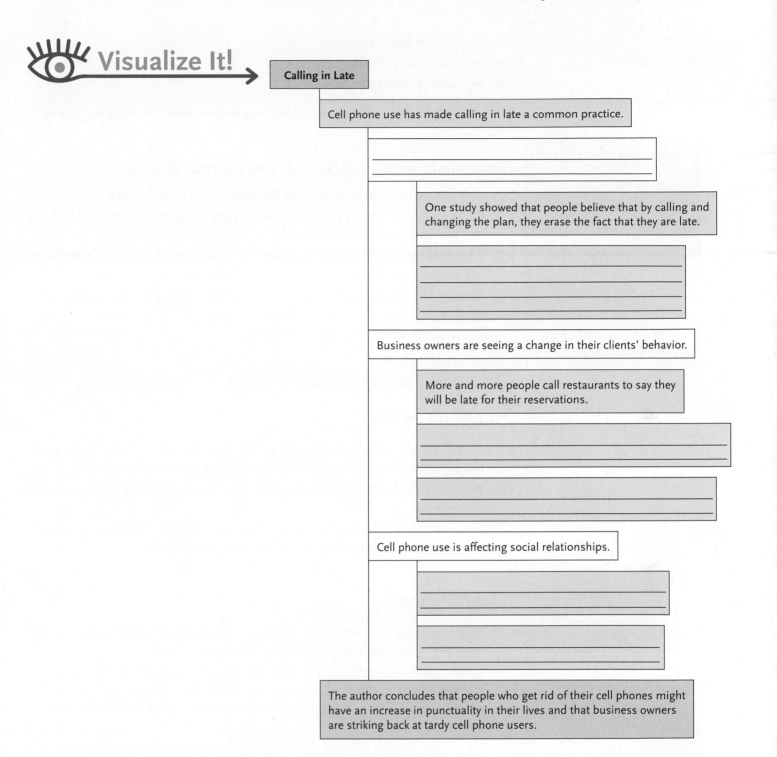

Calling in Late

Cell phone use has made calling in late a common practice.

_____
_____

One study showed that people believe that by calling and changing the plan, they erase the fact that they are late.

_____
_____
_____

Business owners are seeing a change in their clients' behavior.

More and more people call restaurants to say they will be late for their reservations.

_____
_____
_____

_____
_____

Cell phone use is affecting social relationships.

_____
_____
_____

_____
_____

The author concludes that people who get rid of their cell phones might have an increase in punctuality in their lives and that business owners are striking back at tardy cell phone users.

Strengthening Your Vocabulary

Part A: Using the word's context, word parts, or a dictionary, write a brief definition of each of the following words or phrases as it is used in the reading.

1. prevalent (paragraph 1) _____

2. refinement (paragraph 6) _____

3. fluidity (paragraph 6) _____

4. tentativeness (paragraph 8) _____

5. dissolution (paragraph 9) _____

6. spontaneous (paragraph 10) _____

7. imposed (paragraph 15) _____

Part B: Choose one of the words above and draw a word map (see p. 84) of it.

(see p. 84)

ESL Tip

Critical has many meanings, so, when you hear or read this word, be careful to interpret it correctly. Here, it means "very important" (because something bad might happen if you are late).

Reacting to Ideas: Discussion and Journal Writing

Get ready to write about the reading by discussing the following:

1. Discuss the use of cell phones. Should people use them in public places such as libraries and restaurants?

2. Write about a time when you overheard someone's private or personal cell phone conversation. What was your reaction?

3. Discuss the issue of punctuality. When is it <u>critical</u> to you that you be on time?

WRITING ABOUT THE READING

Paragraph Options

1. Write a paragraph about cell phone etiquette. What is the most important thing people should keep in mind when using their cell phones?

2. Write a paragraph about a time when you felt annoyed by someone's cell phone use.

3. Not everyone uses a cell phone on a regular basis. Write a paragraph about one reason someone might not want a cell phone.

Essay Options

ESL Tip

Free is another word with multiple meanings. (One ESL dictionary lists 25 meanings just as an adjective!) Here, *free* means "without."

4. Write an essay that addresses cell phone etiquette. Point out some of the negative behaviors and suggest ways to improve them.

5. Some places are becoming cell phone <u>free</u>. Write a letter urging a place of business or a public institution to either allow or ban cell phones in their facilities. Be sure to present reasons and examples to support your position.

6. Take a few days to observe the cell phone use of people around you. Then organize the behaviors you witness into categories. Use this information to write an essay that describes typical cell phone behavior.

Revision Checklist

Paragraph Development

1. Is the topic manageable (neither too broad nor too narrow)?
2. Is the paragraph written with the reader in mind?
3. Does the topic sentence identify the topic?
4. Does the topic sentence make a point about the topic?
5. Does each sentence support the topic sentence?
6. Is there sufficient detail?
7. Is there a sentence at the end that brings the paragraph to a close?

Sentence Development

8. Are there any sentence fragments, run-on sentences, or comma splices?
9. Are ideas combined to produce more effective sentences?
10. Are adjectives and adverbs used to make the sentences vivid and interesting?
11. Are relative clauses and prepositional phrases like *-ing* phrases used to add detail?
12. Are pronouns used correctly and consistently?

CHAPTER REVIEW AND PRACTICE

CHAPTER REVIEW

To review and check your recall of the chapter, select the word or phrase from the box below that best fits in each of the following sentences. Keep in mind that not all words or phrases will be used.

direct announcements	paragraph	relevant	reemphasize
essay	group	interest	
topic	identify	main point	
delete	generate ideas	redirect	

1. One function of a thesis statement is to identify the _____.

2. You should _____ about your topic before writing your thesis statement.

(continued)

3. An essay is similar to a _____ in structure.

4. One way to discover a thesis statement is to _____ your ideas generated by brainstorming or freewriting.

5. In writing thesis statements, you should avoid _____.

6. A thesis statement expresses the _____ of your essay.

7. Evidence that supports the thesis should be _____ and specific.

8. One function of an introduction is to _____ your reader.

9. The conclusion should _____ your thesis.

10. The title of an essay should _____ the topic of the essay.

EDITING PRACTICE

The following paragraph lacks transitions to connect its details. Revise it by adding transitional words or phrases where useful.

Anyone who has been to a professional hockey game has a right to be disgusted. It is especially true if you have attended one in the past five years. Players are permitted to bash each other on the ice. They are allowed to get away with it. Sometimes players are encouraged to do this. Often they are encouraged by their coaches or other players. People are starting to object to paying good money to attend a game. This is especially true when most of what you get to see is a street fight. Hockey is a contact sport. It is understandable that arguments will break out among players. This causes tempers to flare. It is unfair to subject fans to a dramatic show of violence. Most of the fans have paid good money to watch the game, not the fights. The National Hockey League should fine and suspend players. They should do this each time they get into a fight. If they did this, soon the players would be playing hockey with appropriate sportsmanlike conduct instead of fighting.

INTERNET ACTIVITIES

1. Introductions, Conclusions, and Titles

Review this information about introductions, conclusions, and titles from the writing center at George Mason University. Evaluate your own work using these guidelines. Try rewriting the titles of a few essays you have already written.

http://www.gmu.edu/departments/writingcenter/handouts/introcon.html

2. Transitions

Study this Web site about transitions. Exchange papers with a peer and then analyze them for the use of transitions. Are transitions overused or underused? Does the paper include transitional sentences as well as transitional phrases? Give constructive criticism and consider revising your paper based on the suggestions you receive.

http://studentsuccess.asu.edu/files/shared/tempe/tipsheets/Transitions.doc

3. MyWritingLab

Visit this site to get an overview of essay basics and development.

http://www.mywritinglab.com

Click on the Study Plan tab, then on "Essay Basics, Development, and Common Problems," and then on "The Structure of the Essay," "Writing Strong Thesis Statements," and "Writing the Introduction, Conclusion, and Title."

18 Avoiding Common Problems in Essays

WRITE ABOUT IT!

It is easy to spot what is wrong with a photo. Write a sentence explaining what you notice in this one. Once you know what to look for, it is also easy to spot errors and areas that need improvement in your essays. Even the best writers run into problems; it is not uncommon for writers to make several starts and numerous revisions before they are satisfied with what they have written. Sometimes they even scrap what they have written and start afresh. In this chapter you will learn how to identify and fix five key problems you may encounter in writing essays. Specifically, you will learn to identify and fix topics that are too broad or too narrow, ineffective thesis statements, underdeveloped essays, and disorganized essays. You will also learn to use revision maps to evaluate your essays.

WRITING

Problem #1: The Topic Is Too Broad

One common mistake in writing an essay is choosing a topic that is too broad. No matter how hard you work, if you begin with a topic that is too broad, you will not be able to produce a successful essay. If your topic is too broad, there will be too much information to include, and you will not be able to cover all the important points with the right amount of detail.

Suppose you are taking a sociology class and have been asked to write a two-page paper on your impression of campus life so far. If you just wrote down the title "Campus Life" and started writing, you would find that you had too much to say and probably would not know where to start. Should you write about your classes, meeting new friends, adjusting to differences between high school and college, or managing living arrangements? Here are a few more examples of topics that are too broad:

- Pollution (Choose one type and focus on causes or effects.)
- Vacations (Choose one trip, and focus on one aspect of the trip, such as meeting new people.)
- Movies (Choose one movie, and concentrate on one feature, such as character development, plot, or humor.)

How to Identify the Problem

Here are the symptoms of a topic that is too broad:

1. **You have too much to say.** If it seems as if you could go on and on about the topic, it is probably too broad.

2. **You feel overwhelmed.** If you feel the topic is too difficult or the task of writing about it is unmanageable, you may have too much to write about. Another possibility is that you have chosen a topic about which you do not know enough.

3. **You are not making progress.** If you feel stuck, your topic may be too broad. It also may be too narrow (see Problem #2 below).

4. **You are writing general statements and not explaining them.** Having too much to cover forces you to make broad, sweeping statements that you cannot explain in sufficient depth.

How to Narrow a Broad Topic

One way to narrow a topic that is too broad is to divide it into subtopics using the topic-narrowing techniques shown in Chapter 11, p. 295. Then choose one subtopic and use it to develop new ideas for your essay.

Another way to limit a broad topic is to answer questions that will limit it. Here are six questions that are useful in limiting your topic to a particular place, time, kind, or type:

1. **Who?**
2. **What?**
3. **When?**
4. **Where?**
5. **Why?**
6. **How?**

Suppose your topic is job hunting. You realize it is too broad and apply the questions below.

Topic: Job Hunting	
QUESTIONS	EXAMPLES
Who?	Who can help me with job hunting? (This question limits the topic to people and agencies that offer assistance.)
What?	What type of job am I seeking? (This question limits the topic to a specific occupation.)
When?	When is the best time to job hunt? (This question limits the topic to a particular time frame, such as right after graduation.)
Where?	Where is the best place to find job listings? (This question limits the topic to one source of job listings, such as the Internet.)
Why?	Why is it important to network with friends and family? (This question limits the topic to one way to search for jobs.)
How?	How should I prepare my resumé? (This question limits the topic to one aspect of job hunting.)

ESL Tip

Don't confuse the noun *résumé* with the verb *resume*. A *résumé* is an outline of a person's educational background, work experience, and skills. *Resume* means "start doing something again after an interruption." **Note:** Accent marks are rare in English, but they are used in a few words picked up from other languages.

EXERCISE 18-1

Directions: Narrow three of the following topics to one aspect that is manageable in a two-page essay.

1. Athletics
2. Public education
3. The military
4. The change of seasons
5. Television programming

6. Crime

7. Principles to live by

8. Children's toys

Problem #2: The Topic Is Too Narrow

Another common mistake is to choose a topic that is too narrow. If you decide to write about the effects of the failure of Canada geese to migrate from western New York during the winter, you will probably run out of ideas, unless you are prepared to do extensive library or Internet research. Instead, broaden your topic to the migration patterns of Canada geese. Here are a few more examples of topics that are too narrow:

- The history of corn mazes in the Ohio River valley
- Shopping on eBay for designer handbags
- The attitude of a nasty receptionist at the veterinarian's office

How to Identify the Problem

Here are the symptoms of a topic that is too narrow:

1. **After a paragraph or two, you have nothing left to say.** If you run out of ideas and keep repeating yourself, your topic is probably too narrow.

2. **Your topic does not seem important.** If your topic seems insignificant, it probably is. One reason it may be insignificant is that it focuses on facts rather than ideas.

3. **You are making little or no progress.** A lack of progress may signal a lack of information.

4. **Your essay is too factual.** If you find you are focusing on small details, your topic may be too narrow.

How to Broaden a Narrow Topic

To broaden a topic that is too narrow, try to extend it to cover more situations or circumstances. If your topic is the price advantage of shopping for your chemistry textbook on the Internet, broaden it to include various other benefits of Internet shopping for textbooks. Discuss price, but also consider convenience and free shipping. Do not limit yourself to one type of textbook. Specifically, to broaden a topic that is too narrow:

1. **Think of other situations, events, or circumstances that illustrate the same idea.**

2. **Think of a larger concept that includes your topic.**

EXERCISE 18-2

Directions: Broaden three of the following topics to ones that are manageable in a two-page essay.

1. A groom who wore sneakers to his formal wedding

2. Materials needed for _____ (a craft or hobby)

3. Your parents' attitude toward crime
4. Your local high school's dress code that prohibits short skirts
5. An annoying advertisement
6. A friend's pet peeve
7. A child's first word
8. Missing a deadline for a college psychology paper

Problem #3: The Thesis Statement Needs Revision

The best time to evaluate and, if necessary, revise your thesis statement is after you have written a first draft. At that time you can see if your essay delivers what your thesis promises. If it does not, it needs revision, or you need to refocus your essay.

How to Identify the Problem

Here are the characteristics of a weak thesis statement:

1. **The essay does not explain and support the thesis.**
2. **The thesis statement does not cover all the topics included in the essay.**
3. **The thesis statement is vague or unclear.**
4. **The thesis statement makes a direct announcement.**

How to Revise Your Thesis Statement

When evaluating your thesis statement, ask the following questions:

1. **Does my essay develop and explain my thesis statement?** As you write an essay, its focus and direction may change. Revise your thesis statement to reflect any changes. If you discover that you drifted away from your original thesis and you want to maintain it, work on revising so that your paper delivers what your thesis statement promises.

2. **Is my thesis statement broad enough to cover all the points I made in the essay?** As you develop your first draft, you may find that one idea leads naturally to another. Both must be covered by the thesis statement. For example, suppose your thesis statement is "Because of the number of patients our clinic sees in a day, the need for nurse practitioners has increased dramatically." If, in your essay, you discuss lab technicians and interns as well as nurses, then you need to broaden your thesis statement.

3. **Does my thesis statement use vague or unclear words that do not clearly focus the topic?** For example, in the thesis statement "Physical therapy can help bursitis," the word *help* is vague and does not suggest how your essay will approach the topic. Instead, if your paper discusses the effectiveness of physical therapy, this approach should be reflected in your thesis: "When it comes to chronic bursitis, deep tissue massage by a trained physical therapist can be very effective."

EXERCISE 18-3

Directions: Identify what is wrong with each of the following thesis statements, and revise each to make it more effective.

1. Most people like to dance.
2. Call the doctor when you're sick.
3. Everyone should read the newspaper.
4. It's important to keep your receipts.
5. Driving in snow is dangerous.

EXERCISE 18-4

Writing in Progress

Directions: Choose one of the topics you worked with from Exercise 18-1 or 18-2. Generate ideas about the topic and write a tentative thesis statement.

Problem #4: The Essay Is Underdeveloped

An underdeveloped essay is one that lacks sufficient information and evidence to support the thesis.

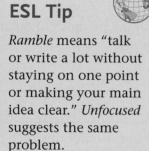

ESL Tip

Ramble means "talk or write a lot without staying on one point or making your main idea clear." *Unfocused* suggests the same problem.

How to Identify the Problem

Here are the characteristics of an underdeveloped essay:

1. **The essay seems to ramble or is <u>unfocused</u>.**
2. **The essay repeats information or says the same thing in slightly different ways.**
3. **The essay makes general statements but does not support them.**
4. **The essay lacks facts, examples, comparisons, or reasons.**

How to Revise an Underdeveloped Essay

Use the following suggestions to revise an underdeveloped essay:

1. **Delete sentences that are repetitious and add nothing to the essay.** If you find you have little or nothing left, do additional brainstorming, freewriting, or branching to discover new ideas. If this technique does not work, consider changing your topic to one about which you have more to say.
2. **Make sure your topic is not too broad or too narrow.** If it is, use the suggestions for topic revision given earlier in the chapter on p. 499 and p. 501.
3. **Go through your essay sentence by sentence and highlight any ideas that you could further develop and explain.** Develop these ideas into separate paragraphs.
4. **Make sure each topic sentence is clear and specific.** Then add details to each paragraph that make it sharp and convincing.

EXERCISE 18-5

Writing in Progress

Directions: Using the thesis statement you wrote in Exercise 18-4, write an essay. Then evaluate and revise it, if necessary, using the suggestions given above.

Problem #5: The Essay Is Disorganized

A disorganized essay is one that does not follow a logical method of development. A disorganized essay makes it difficult for your readers to follow your train of thought. If readers must struggle to follow your ideas, they may stop reading or lose their concentration. In fact, as they struggle to follow your thinking, they may miss important information or misinterpret what you are saying.

How to Identify the Problem

Use the following questions to help you evaluate the organization of your essay:

1. **Does every paragraph in the essay support or explain your thesis statement?**
2. **Do you avoid straying from your topic?**
3. **Does each detail in each paragraph explain the topic sentence?**
4. **Do you make it clear how one idea relates to another by using transitions?**

How to Revise Disorganized Essays

To improve the organization of your essay, use one of the methods of organization discussed in Chapter 14. Here is a brief review:

METHOD OF ORGANIZATION	PURPOSE
Narration	Presents events in the order in which they happened
Description	Gives descriptive, sensory details
Example	Explains a situation or idea by giving circumstances that illustrate it
Definition	Explains the meaning of a term by giving its class and distinguishing characteristics
Comparison and Contrast	Focuses on similarities and differences
Classification	Explains by organizing a topic into groups or categories
Process	Describes the order in which things are done
Cause and Effect	Explains why things happen or what happens as a result of something else
Argument	Gives reasons to support a claim

Once you have chosen and used a method of development, be sure to use appropriate transitions to connect your ideas.

Another way to spot and correct organizational problems is to draw an idea or revision map as discussed below. Using a map will help you visualize the progression of your ideas graphically and see which ideas fit and which do not.

EXERCISE 18-6
Writing in Progress

Directions: Evaluate the organization of the essay you wrote in Exercise 18-5. Revise it using the suggestions given above.

Using Maps to Guide Your Revision

In Chapter 16, "Using an Idea Map to Spot Revision Problems," you learned to draw revision maps to evaluate paragraphs. The same strategy works well for essays, too. A revision map will help you evaluate the overall flow of your ideas as well as the effectiveness of individual paragraphs.

To draw an essay revision map, begin by listing your title at the top of the page. Write your thesis statement underneath it, and then list the topic of each paragraph. Next, work through each paragraph, recording your ideas in abbreviated form. Then write the key words of your conclusion. If you find details that do not support the topic sentence, record those details to the right of the map. Use the model on p. 506 as a guide.

When you've completed your revision map, conduct the following tests:

1. **Read your thesis statement along with your first topic sentence.** Does the topic sentence clearly support your thesis? If not, revise it to make the relationship clearer. Repeat this step for each topic sentence.

2. **Read your topic sentences, one after the other, without reading the corresponding details.** Is there a logical connection between them? Have you arranged them in the most effective way? If not, revise to make the connection clearer or to improve your organization.

3. **Examine each individual paragraph.** Are there enough relevant, specific details to support the topic sentence?

4. **Read your introduction and then look at your topic sentences.** Does the essay deliver what the introduction promises?

5. **Read your thesis statement and then your conclusion.** Are they compatible and consistent? Does the conclusion agree with and support the thesis statement?

EXERCISE 18-7
Writing In Progress

Directions: Draw a revision map of the essay you wrote and revised in Exercises 18-5 and 18-6. Make further revisions as needed.

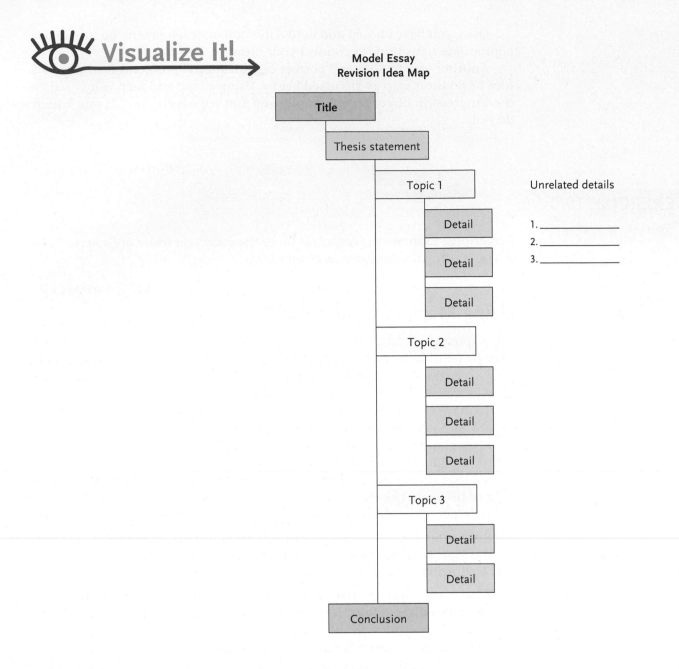

Visualize It!

Model Essay Revision Idea Map

Seeking Further Help

If the suggestions offered in this chapter do not help you solve a problem with a particular essay, be sure to use the following resources:

- **Your classmates.** Ask a classmate to read your essay and make comments and suggestions.

- **Your instructor.** Visit your instructor during office hours. Take a draft of your paper with you and have specific questions in mind.

- **The Writing Lab.** Many campuses have a writing lab where students can get help with papers. Take your draft with you and ask for feedback and revision ideas.

Analyze It!

Directions: A student wrote the following outline for an essay on American beauty pageants. Study the outline and identify what is wrong with it. Cross out details that do not support the thesis statement or do not belong where they are placed in the outline. You may add new details, if needed.

Essay Title: "Women's Beauty Pageants in the United States"

I. Introduction
   A. History of U.S. beauty pageants
   1. Miss America Pageant
   2. International Beauty Pageants
   3. Miss USA Pageant

   B. Thesis statement: Woman's beauty pageants are unfair to women and unhealthy for their participants.

II. Body of Essay
   A. Drawbacks outweigh benefits
   1. Such entertainment is harmful to women
   2. Not best way to support charities and worthy causes

   B. Contest rules
   1. Swimsuit and evening gown competition
   2. Age limitations
   3. Talent contests
   4. Men not similarly judged on their looks

   C. Pageants create biased, unfair standards of beauty
   1. Western standards of beauty are used
   2. Racial and ethnic groups not widely represented
   3. Talent and congeniality carry little weight in judging

   D. Contest sponsors
   1. Commercial advertisers
   2. Other types of promoters

   E. Pageants are degrading for women
   1. Create "cattle show" mentality
   2. Undermine the goals and progress of women's rights

   F. Pageants promote physically unhealthy practices
   1. Pressure to become thin creates health problems
      a. Anorexia
      b. Other eating disorders
      c. liposuction
   2. Little emphasis on women's intelligence, talent, character, skills

III. Conclusion
   A. Surprising that beauty pageants are still so popular worldwide
   B. Women should not support these pageants.

A STUDENT ESSAY

The Writer

Anna Majerczyk is a student at Triton College, where she is studying to become a dental hygienist.

The Writing Task

For her writing class, Anna was asked to write an essay about an experience that changed her life. As you read, notice how she introduces, develops, and supports her thesis statement.

My Big Deal Knee Surgery
Anna Majerczyk

Interesting, catchy title

Background on her knee surgery

1   A few years ago while playing volleyball, I dislocated my knee for the first time. After I had my cast removed, and after nine months of not walking, the doctors told me I had to be careful or it might happen again. I was very careful but it still recurred. In June 2004, I was sitting Indian-style playing with my nephew on the floor. When I got up, my kneecap popped out. For four months I went to doctors for tests, and, finally, my orthopedist said that I must have knee surgery. I was not scared at all because I have had surgery before, so I knew

Thesis statement

what to expect. I was sure that this time would be the same thing—not a big deal—but it was not.

Topic sentence

Details make situation real

2   October 19, 2004, the day of my surgery, was a crazy day. I went to sleep at midnight and I woke up at 2 in the morning shaking like gelatin, and I could not control it. I was really scared, counting how many hours I had left before surgery. Different weird thoughts went through my head. At 6 in the morning I took a shower and kept myself busy trying to forget I was supposed to be at the hospital at 8:30 A.M. I took my parents with me, because after surgery I would not be able to drive. We left at 7:30 A.M. My mom was driving the car, and driving me crazy. She was driving very fast and nervously; we were yelling at each other for no reason.

Topic sentence

Author reveals her feelings

3   Finally, when we got to the hospital, my parents and I went to building D for outpatient same-day surgery. The lady at the front desk checked my name on the list and then told me to take an elevator to the second floor. When we got to the second floor, there was another front desk, and another lady asking the same questions. When we were standing by the desk, one of the nurses opened the door. I saw doctors, nurses, and patients on the beds. It scared me so much that I said to my parents with tears in my eyes, "I am not going anywhere; let's go home!" But I knew that I had no choice if I wanted to walk normally again. The lady at the desk showed me which way to go. We went to the third front desk. The nurse told me the number of my bed and to change my clothes.

Topic sentence

Detailed description of events

4   I was very nervous and scared as a parade of people entered the room. First came the priest, who blessed me. Then came a nurse, with papers to sign. Then came another nurse, who took my temperature and checked my blood pressure. A third nurse came and gave me an antibiotic; a fourth nurse gave me IV fluids, and a fifth nurse came with health insurance forms. Then the doctor came to make a notation on my knee, just to be sure that he would operate on the correct knee. Right after the doctor came the anesthesiologist to discuss the best type of anesthesia for me. The most nerve-racking part was when everyone who was working around me kept asking me how I was doing that day. How was I supposed to feel before surgery? I knew that they were trying to be nice, but that question sounded ridiculous. At 11:00 A.M., they wheeled me to the operating room. All I remember is that it was cold and silent. I moved from my bed to the operating table, and the nurses connected me to the monitors. In a second, I felt dizzy; they had put me to sleep.

Topic sentence

5   I woke up in the recovery room with a nurse sitting next to me. I took off the oxygen mask. I told the nurse that I was dirty, but I wanted to say that I was thirsty. She said that I could not have anything to drink, but she gave me a wet towel to moisten my lips. Also, I was expecting a lot of pain, but I did not feel any.

Topic sentence

6   After 15 minutes, the same nurse took me to my mom. We spent an additional three hours there with nurses, the doctor, and the physical therapist. The nurses told me what to expect after surgery and what not to. The doctor explained the operation he had performed on my knee, and the physical therapist showed me how to walk with crutches. When my mom and I were ready to go home, the fire alarm went off. The hospital employees stopped us. We could smell that there was something burning in the hospital. After firefighters checked the hospital, we were finally able to go home.

7   One week after surgery I went for my first physical therapy session. For the first time after surgery, my bandage was changed and I got a look at my knee. It looked very nice with three little holes. At the same time, without a reason, I was getting hotter and weaker, with shortness of breath. People around me did not know what was going on and started yelling. My arms felt numb. "There is something wrong with her heart," someone said. I felt like I was dying. My whole life flashed in front of my eyes. I do not remember how I got to the emergency room. I spent four hours sitting in a wheelchair in the waiting room. Another five hours were spent on tests. After looking into my medical history, the ER doctor checked me for blood clots. He diagnosed that I had experienced a panic attack, and I went home with medication to calm me down.

Topic sentence

Conclusion: she reflects on the experience

8   Consequently, the whole knee surgery experience changed my entire outlook on life. During the five weeks of walking with crutches, I realized how difficult handicapped life could be. I had problems with opening doors, walking up and down the stairs, carrying things, and engaging in activities that I thought were easy before my surgery. After the panic attack, it took me a while to get better. Now I am scared of everything. When there is too much commotion around me, I feel a shortness of breath, and I think I am having another panic attack. I struggle with this on a daily basis. The moral of the story is be careful when you play with babies; you may be the one who needs a babysitter!

EXAMINING STUDENT WRITING

1. How did Majerczyk organize her essay?

2. Highlight several transitional words and phrases that Majerczyk uses to connect her ideas.

3. Highlight three places where Majerczyk uses descriptive details effectively.

4. Evaluate Majerczyk's use of dialogue. What does it contribute to the essay?

5. Examine Majerczyk's last sentence. Is this an effective conclusion?

Essay Writing Scenarios

Friends and Family

1. Compare the jobs your grandparents held with those your parents hold. How has the level and type of job changed over time? What does this change suggest about family growth and change?

2. Write an essay about where you preferred to play as a child; at a park or playground, in a backyard, on a street, at a friend's house, etc.

Classes and Campus Life

1. What kind of person is attracted to your major? Describe the qualities someone should have if he or she is interested in this field.

2. Write an essay about something you did really well in high school.

Working Students

1. Many students work and attend college at the same time. What skills does it take to balance school and work?

2. Write an essay about what you will look for in your next job. How will it be different from the job you have currently?

Communities and Cultures

1. Traditionally, men and women have had very different roles in different cultures. Write an essay about one thing that only women used to do in your culture that men now also do, or vice versa.

2. People do many things to show off their status in a community. Describe one thing that people buy, drive, or wear to show that they are important.

Writing Success Tip 18

Taking Writing Competency Tests

Some colleges require students to pass competency tests in writing. Competency tests are designed so that you will not be placed in courses that are too difficult or too easy. Think of them as readiness tests. Try your best, but don't be upset if you don't score at the required level. It is best to be certain you have the skills you need before tackling more difficult courses.

Preparing for Competency Tests

If your test requires that you write an essay, follow these suggestions:

1. **Study your error log** (see Writing Success Tip 4 on p. 116). If you haven't kept an error log, review papers your instructor has marked to identify your most common errors. Make a list of these common errors. As you revise and proofread your competency test answers, mentally check for each of these errors.

2. **Construct a mental revision checklist before you go into the exam.** Use the final revision checklist in this book as a guide (see p. 516). If time permits, jot your checklist down on scrap paper during the exam and use it to revise your essay.

3. **If your test is timed, plan how to divide your time.** Estimate how much time you will need for each step in the writing process. To find out, gauge your time on a practice test. Wear a watch to the exam, and check periodically to keep yourself on schedule.

4. **Take a practice test.** Ask a classmate to make up a topic or question for you to write about. It should be the same type of question that will be on the test. Give yourself the same time limit that the test will have. Then ask your classmate to evaluate your essay.

Taking Competency Tests

1. **If you are given a choice of topics to write about, choose the one about which you know the most.** One of the most common mistakes students make on competency tests is failing to support their ideas with specific details. If you are familiar with a topic, you will be able to supply details more easily.

2. **If none of the topics seems familiar, spend a minute or two generating ideas on each topic before choosing one.** You will quickly see which will be the best choice.

3. **As you've learned throughout this book, be sure to follow the writing process step by step.** Generate and organize your ideas before you write. If time permits, revise your essay, using your mental revision checklist, and proofread, checking for common errors.

ESL Tip

The nouns *competency* and *competence* mean "the ability to do something well enough for it to be acceptable." The adjective is *competent*.

WRITING ABOUT A READING

ESL Tip

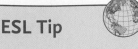

Here, *engage in bashing* means to *bash* ("find fault with, criticize, say bad things about"). In this phrase, *engage* means "to participate in or do some activity." The *opposite* sex refers to the sex that the speaker, writer, or person being discussed is not.

THINKING BEFORE READING

Notable humorist Dave Barry wrote this piece, "From Now On, Let Women Kill Their Own Spiders," for a column in the *Miami Herald*. In it, Barry deals with one of his favorite topics—the behavioral differences between men and women. As you read, pay attention to the author's use of humor as well as the organization of the essay.

1. Preview the reading, using the steps discussed in Chapter 2, p. 38.

2. Connect the reading to your own experience by answering the following questions:

   a. Do you think communication problems exist between men and women?

   b. Why do people <u>engage in bashing</u> the <u>opposite sex</u>?

READING

FROM NOW ON, LET WOMEN KILL THEIR OWN SPIDERS

Dave Barry

1   From time to time I receive letters from a certain group of individuals that I will describe, for want of a better term, as "women." I have such a letter here, from a Susie Walker of North Augusta, S.C., who asks the following question: "Why do men open a drawer and say, 'Where is the spatula?' instead of, you know, looking for it?"

2   This question expresses a commonly held (by women) negative stereotype about guys of the male gender, which is that they cannot find things around the house, especially things in the kitchen. Many women believe that if you want to hide something from a man, all you have to do is put it in plain sight in the refrigerator, and he will never, ever find it, as evidenced by the fact that a man can open a refrigerator containing 463 pounds of assorted meats, poultry, cold cuts, condiments, vegetables, frozen dinners, snack foods, desserts, etc., and ask with no irony whatsoever, "Do we have anything to eat?"

snide
sarcastic in a mean way

generalizations
general statements made by observing a number of particular instances

Riverdance
a dance group specializing in Irish dancing

3   Now I could respond to this stereotype in a **snide** manner by making **generalizations** about women. I could ask, for example, how come your average woman prepares for virtually every upcoming event in her life, including dental appointments, by buying new shoes, even if she already owns as many pairs as the entire **Riverdance** troupe. I could point out that, if there were no women, there would be no such thing as Leonardo DiCaprio. I could ask why a woman would walk up to a perfectly innocent man who is minding his own business watching basketball and demand to know if a certain pair of pants makes her butt look too big, and then, no matter what he answers, get mad

at him. I could ask why, according to the best scientific estimates, 93 percent of the nation's severely limited bathroom-storage space is taken up by decades-old, mostly empty tubes labeled "moisturizer." I could point out that, to judge from the covers of countless women's magazines, the two topics most interesting to women are (1) Why men are all disgusting pigs, and (2) How to attract men.

4   Yes, I could raise these issues in response to the question asked by Susie Walker of North Augusta, S.C., regarding the man who was asking where the spatula was. I could even ask WHY this particular man might be looking for the spatula. Could it be that he needs a spatula to kill a spider, because, while he was innocently watching basketball and minding his own business, a member of another major gender—a gender that refuses to personally kill spiders but wants them all dead—DEMANDED that he kill the spider, which nine times out of ten turns out to be a male spider that was minding its own business? Do you realize how many men arrive in hospital emergency rooms every year, sometimes still gripping their spatulas, suffering from painful spider-inflicted injuries? I don't have the exact statistics right here, but I bet they are chilling.

5   As I say, I could raise these issues and resort to the kind of negativity indulged in by Susie Walker of North Augusta, S.C. But I choose not to. I choose, instead, to address her question seriously, in hopes that, by improving the communication between the genders, all human beings—both men and women, together—will come to a better understanding of how **dense** women can be sometimes.

dense
thick-headed, slow-witted

6   I say this because there is an excellent reason why a man would open the spatula drawer and, without looking for the spatula, ask where the spatula is: The man does not have TIME to look for the spatula. Why? Because he is busy thinking. Men are almost always thinking. When you look at a man who appears to be merely scratching himself, rest assured that inside his head, his brain is humming like a high-powered computer, processing millions of pieces of information and producing important insights such as, "This feels good!"

7   We should be grateful that men think so much, because over the years they have thought up countless inventions that have made life better for all people, everywhere. The shot clock in basketball is one example. Another one is underwear-eating bacteria. I found out about this thanks to the many alert readers who sent me an article from *New Scientist* magazine stating that Russian scientists—and you KNOW these are guy scientists—are trying to solve the problem of waste disposal aboard spacecraft, by "designing a cocktail of bacteria to digest astronauts' cotton and paper underpants." Is that great, or what? I am picturing a utopian future wherein, when a man's briefs get dirty, they will simply dissolve from his body, thereby freeing him from the chore of dealing with his soiled underwear via the labor-intensive, time-consuming method he now uses, namely, dropping them on the floor.

harping
talking tiresomely and repetitively about a topic

8   I'm not saying that guys have solved all the world's problems. I'm just saying that there ARE solutions out there, and if, instead of **harping** endlessly about spatulas, we allow guys to use their mental talents to look for these solutions, in time, they will find them. Unless they are in the refrigerator.

GETTING READY TO WRITE

Reviewing the Reading

1. Why does Barry begin his essay by mentioning spatulas? How does he refer back to this later in the essay?
2. Identify the stereotypical behaviors that Barry addresses.
3. Why does Barry mention the bacteria-eating underwear?

Examining the Reading Using an Idea Map

Review the reading by filling in the missing parts of the idea map below.

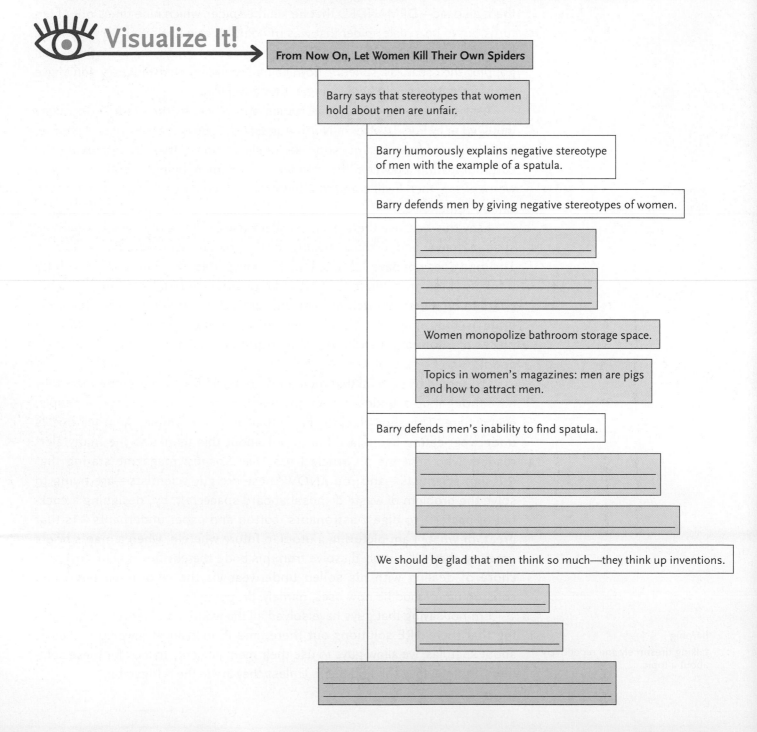

Visualize It!

From Now On, Let Women Kill Their Own Spiders

Barry says that stereotypes that women hold about men are unfair.

Barry humorously explains negative stereotype of men with the example of a spatula.

Barry defends men by giving negative stereotypes of women.

_____

_____

Women monopolize bathroom storage space.

Topics in women's magazines: men are pigs and how to attract men.

Barry defends men's inability to find spatula.

_____

_____

We should be glad that men think so much—they think up inventions.

_____

_____

_____

Strengthening Your Vocabulary

Part A: Using the word's context, word parts, or a dictionary, write a brief definition of each of the following words or phrases as it is used in the reading.

1. irony (paragraph 2) _____

   _____

2. virtually (paragraph 3) _____

   _____

3. indulged (paragraph 5) _____

   _____

4. utopian (paragraph 7) _____

   _____

Part B: Choose one of the words above and draw a word map (see p. 84) of it.

Reacting to Ideas: Discussion and Journal Writing

Get ready to write about the reading by discussing the following:

1. Discuss the way we treat boys and girls differently. How do we reinforce stereotypes (such as females are afraid of spiders) that continue into adulthood?

2. Discuss Dave Barry's writing. Do you think he is funny? What kind of humor do you find entertaining these days?

3. Write about a time when you did something that <u>baffled</u> a member of the opposite sex.

> ### ESL Tip
>
> *Baffled* means "puzzled" or "confused." The assignment is to write about a time when a member of the opposite sex (a female if you're a man or a male if you're a woman) didn't understand your behavior.

WRITING ABOUT THE READING

Paragraph Options

1. Write a paragraph describing a situation you witnessed in which a member of one sex commented unfairly about a member of the opposite sex.

2. Some women think that men have a hard time finding things that are in plain sight. Write a paragraph about a time when you witnessed this stereotypical behavior or about a time in which this stereotype proved to be false.

3. Barry claims that men are always thinking about solutions to problems. Write a paragraph agreeing or disagreeing with this opinion.

Essay Options

4. Write an essay about stereotypes. Choose one stereotype, define it, and give some examples that illustrate it. Be sure to explain how believing in stereotypes can be harmful.

5. Try your hand at humorous writing. Pick a topic of current interest in the news and write an opinion essay about it using wit, sarcasm, irony, and/or ridicule.

6. Not all men and not all women have the kinds of communication problems that Barry describes. Write an essay about the positive ways in which men and women can function together in a work, school, social, or political situation.

Revision Checklist

Paragraph Development

1. Is the topic manageable (neither too broad nor too narrow)?
2. Is the paragraph written with the reader in mind?
3. Does the topic sentence identify the topic?
4. Does the topic sentence make a point about the topic?
5. Does each sentence support the topic sentence?
6. Is there sufficient detail?
7. Is there a sentence at the end that brings the paragraph to a close?

Sentence Development

8. Are there any sentence fragments, run-on sentences, or comma splices?
9. Are ideas combined to produce more effective sentences?
10. Are adjectives and adverbs used to make the sentences vivid and interesting?
11. Are relative clauses and prepositional phrases like -*ing* phrases used to add detail?
12. Are pronouns used correctly and consistently?

CHAPTER REVIEW AND PRACTICE

CHAPTER REVIEW

To review and check your recall of the chapter, match each item in Column A with its meaning in Column B and write the letter of the meaning in the space provided.

COLUMN A

_____ 1. Underdeveloped essay

_____ 2. Broad topic

_____ 3. Narrow topic

_____ 4. Disorganized essay

_____ 5. Revision map

_____ 6. Ineffective thesis statement

_____ 7. Vague thesis statement

_____ 8. An essay that repeats the same information over and over

_____ 9. Asking the questions Who?, What?, When?, Where?, Why?, and How?

_____ 10. Thinking of other situations or events that illustrate your topic

COLUMN B

a. An essay that does not follow a logical train of thought

b. An essay in which the topic is too narrow

c. Method for broadening a topic

d. An essay that does not support and explain its thesis

e. One that does not cover all the points made in the essay

f. A topic that covers too much

g. Ways to narrow a topic that is too broad

h. A topic that is too specific or detailed

i. A diagram that helps you evaluate and improve your essay

j. One that does not suggest how the essay will approach the topic

EDITING PRACTICE

Paragraph 1

The following narrative paragraph is weak because it lacks focus and only retells events. Revise it by fleshing out the details and focusing them so they make a point.

> Last summer my family took a trip to the Canadian Rockies. We flew to Chicago and then to Calgary. Then we took a train into the mountains. We stopped at Banff first. The next part of the trip was long and very scenic. We crossed a number of rivers, rode along riverbanks, and went through tunnels. At the end of the first day, we stayed in Kamloops, British Columbia. The next day, we traveled down the mountains to Vancouver and arrived there in the afternoon. We were tired, but we had fun.

Paragraph 2

The following paragraph contains a weak topic sentence. Revise this sentence to make it stronger.

> It is good to study history. First, studying history gives you a new way of looking at your own life. When you learn about the past, you begin to see that your lifetime is only part of a larger picture. Second, history can help you understand problems better. You begin to see why the world is as it is and what events caused it to be this way. Finally, history allows you to think of yourself in a different way. In looking at everything that has happened before us, we as individuals seem small and unimportant.

INTERNET ACTIVITIES

1. Thesis Statements

Try this quiz from El Paso Community College on evaluating a thesis statement.

http://www.epcc.edu/Student/Tutorial/Writingcenter/Handouts/paragraph essaystructure/essaystructure/Quizzes/thesisquiz.htm

Create your own quiz for a peer to complete. How does an exercise like this help you to develop your thesis writing skills?

2. Common Problems

Study this information from Illinois Valley Community College on how to avoid common problems with writing papers. Write five paragraphs. Each one should summarize one of the problems.

http://www.ivcc.edu/eng1002/handout_research_paper_problems.htm

3. MyWritingLab

Visit this site for more information and practice on revising essays.

http://www.mywritinglab.com

Click on the Study Plan tab, then on "Essay Basics, Development, and Common Problems," and then on "Revising the Essay."

PART VII

A Multicultural Reader

WRITING ABOUT A READING

THINKING BEFORE READING

The following reading, "The Beautiful Laughing Sisters—An Arrival Story," is from the book *The Middle of Everywhere: Helping Refugees Enter the American Culture* by Mary Pipher. Pipher is a well-known author and psychologist with a special interest in the influence of culture on mental health. In this selection, Pipher describes the experience of a family of refugees whose difficult journey has brought them to a new life in America.

1. Preview the reading using the steps described in Chapter 2, page 38.

2. Connect the reading to your own experience by answering the following questions:

   a. What do you know about how your family or ancestors came to America?

   b. Have you or has someone you know immigrated to the United States? Why did you or did he or she leave home?

READING

THE BEAUTIFUL LAUGHING SISTERS— AN ARRIVAL STORY

Mary Pipher

cultural broker
someone who helps people from other countires learn the customs of their new country

1   One of the best ways to understand the refugee experience is to befriend a family of new arrivals and observe their experiences in our country for the first year. That first year is the hardest. Everything is new and strange, and obstacles appear like the stars appear at dusk, in an uncountable array. This story is about a family I met during their first month in our country. I became their friend and **cultural broker** and in the process learned a great deal about the refugee experience, and about us Americans.

2   On a fall day I met Shireen and Meena, who had come to this country from Pakistan. The Kurdish sisters were slender young women with alert expressions. They wore blue jeans and clunky high-heeled shoes. Shireen was taller and bolder, Meena was smaller and more soft-spoken. Their English was limited and heavily accented. (I later learned it was their sixth language after Kurdish, Arabic, Farsi, Urdu, and Hindi.)* They communicated with each other via small quick gestures and eye movements. Although they laughed easily, they watched to see that the other was okay at all times.

---

*These languages, in addition to many others, are spoken in the Middle Eastern countries of Iran, Iraq, India, and Palestine.

3   Shireen was the youngest and the only one of the six sisters who was eligible for high school. Meena, who was twenty-one, walked the ten blocks from their apartment to meet Shireen at school on a bitterly cold day. Shireen told the family story. Meena occasionally interrupted her answers with a reminder, an amendment, or laughter.

4   Shireen was born in Baghdad in 1979, the last of ten children. Their mother, Zeenat, had been a village girl who entered an arranged marriage at fourteen. Although their father had been well educated, Zeenat couldn't read or write in any language. The family was prosperous and "Europeanized," as Shireen put it. She said, "Before our father was in trouble, we lived just like you. Baghdad was a big city. In our group of friends, men and women were treated as equals. Our older sisters went to movies and read foreign newspapers. Our father went to cocktail parties at the embassies."

5   However, their father had opposed Saddam Hussein, and from the time of Shireen's birth, his life was in danger. After Hussein came to power, terrible things happened to families like theirs. One family of eleven was taken to jail by his security forces and tortured to death. Prisoners were often fed rice mixed with glass so that they would quietly bleed to death in their cells. Girls were raped and impregnated by the security police. Afterward, they were murdered or killed themselves.

6   It was a hideous time. Schoolteachers tried to get children to betray their parents. One night the police broke into the family's house. They tore up the beds, bookcases, and the kitchen, and they took their Western clothes and tapes. After that night, all of the family except for one married sister made a daring escape into Iran.

7   Meena said, "It was a long time ago but I can see everything today." There was no legal way to go north, so they walked through Kurdistan at night and slept under bushes in the day. They found a guide who made his living escorting **Kurds** over the mountains. Twice they crossed rivers near flood stage. Entire families had been swept away by the waters and one of the sisters almost drowned when she fell off her horse. The trails were steep and narrow and another sister fell and broke her leg. Meena was in a bag slung over the guide's horse for three days. She remembered how stiff she felt in the bag, and Shireen remembered screaming, "I want my mama."

8   This was in the 1980s. While this was happening I was a psychologist building my private practice and a young mother taking my kids to *Sesame Street Live* and **Vacation Village on Lake Okoboji**. I was dancing to the music of my husband's band, Sour Mash, listening to Van Morrison and Jackson Browne and reading P. D. James and Anne Tyler. Could my life have been happening on the same planet?

9   The family made it to a refugee camp in Iran. It was a miserable place with smelly tents and almost no supplies. Shireen said this was rough on her older siblings who had led lives of luxury. She and Meena adjusted more quickly. The sisters studied in an Iranian school for refugees.

10   They endured this makeshift camp for one very bad year. The Iranians insisted that all the women in the camp wear heavy scarves and robes and conform to strict rules. The soldiers in the camp shouted at them if they wore even

Kurds
a people of the Middle East whose homeland is in the mountainous regions of Iraq, Iran, and Turkey

Vacation Village on Lake Okoboji
a family resort in northwestern Iowa

a little lipstick. Shireen once saw a young girl wearing makeup stopped by a guard who rubbed it off her face. He had put ground glass in the tissue so that her cheeks bled afterward.

11 They decided to get out of Iran and traveled the only direction they could, east into Pakistan. They walked all the way with nothing to drink except salty water that made them even thirstier. I asked how long the trip took and Shireen said three days. Meena quickly corrected her: "Ten years."

12 Once in Pakistan they were settled by a relief agency in a border town called Quetta, where strangers were not welcome. The family lived in a small house with electricity that worked only sporadically. The stress of all the moves broke the family apart. The men left the women and the family has never reunited.

13 Single women in Quetta couldn't leave home unescorted and the sisters had no men to escort them. Only their mother, Zeenat, dared go out to look for food. As Meena put it, "She took good care of us and now we will take care of her."

14 The sisters almost never left the hut, but when they did, they wore robes as thick and heavy as black carpets. Meena demonstrated how hard it was to walk in these clothes and how she often fell down. Even properly dressed, they were chased by local men. When they rode the bus to buy vegetables, they were harassed.

15 Without their heroic mother, they couldn't have survived. For weeks at a time, the family was trapped inside the hut. At night the locals would break their windows with stones and taunt the sisters with threats of rape. Meena interrupted to say that every house in the village but theirs had weapons. Shireen said incredulously, "There were no laws in that place. Guns were laws."

16 One night some men broke into their hut and took what little money and jewelry they had left. They had been sleeping and woke to see guns flashing around them. The next day they reported the break-in to the police. Shireen said, "The police told us to get our own guns." Meena said, "We were nothing to them. The police slapped and pushed us. We were afraid to provoke them."

17 During the time they were there, the Pakistanis tested a nuclear bomb nearby and they all got sick. An older sister had seizures from the stress of their lives. Shireen said defiantly, "It was hard, but we got used to hard."

18 Still, the young women laughed as they told me about the black robes and the men with guns. Their laughter was a complicated mixture of anxiety, embarrassment, and relief that it was over. It was perhaps also an attempt to distance themselves from that time and place.

19 They'd studied English in the hut and made plans for their future in America or Europe. Shireen said, "I always knew that we would escape that place."

20 In Quetta the family waited ten years for papers that would allow them to immigrate. Shireen looked at me and said, "I lost my teenage years there—all my teenage years."

21 Finally, in frustration, the family went on a hunger strike. They told the relief workers they would not eat until they were allowed to leave Quetta. After a few days, the agency paperwork was delivered and the family was permitted to board a train for Islamabad.

22 In Islamabad they lived in a small apartment with no air conditioning. Every morning they would soak their curtains in water to try to cool their rooms. It was dusty and polluted and they got typhoid fever and heat sickness. They had

a year of interviews and waiting before papers arrived that allowed them to leave for America. Still, it was a year of hope. Zeenat picked up cans along the roads to make money. One sister ran a beauty parlor from their home. They all watched American television, studied English, and dreamed of a good future.

Lincoln
the capital of Nebraska

23   Finally they flew to America—Islamabad to Karachi to Amsterdam to New York to St. Louis to **Lincoln**. Shireen said, "We came in at night. There were lights spread out over the dark land. Lincoln looked beautiful."

24   We talked about their adjustment to Lincoln. Five of the sisters had found work. They didn't have enough money though, and they didn't like the cold. Meena needed three root canals and Zeenat had many missing teeth and needed bridgework, false teeth, everything really. Still, they were enjoying the sense of possibilities unfolding. Shireen put it this way, "In America, we have rights." She pronounced "rights" as if it were a sacred word.

25   Meena mentioned that traffic here was more orderly and less dangerous than in Pakistan. The girls loved American clothes and makeup. Two of their sisters wanted to design clothes. Another was already learning to do American hairstyles so that she could work in a beauty shop. Meena wanted to be a nurse and Shireen a model or flight attendant. She said, "I have traveled so much against my will. Now I would like to see the world in a good way."

26   Shireen said that it was scary to go to the high school. Fortunately, her study of English in Pakistan made it easy for her to learn Nebraska English. She liked her teachers but said the American students mostly ignored her, especially when they heard her thick accent.

27   I was struck by the resilience of these sisters. In all the awful places they had been, they'd found ways to survive and even joke about their troubles. These young women used their intelligence to survive. Had they lived different lives, they would probably have been doctors and astrophysicists. Since they'd been in Lincoln, they'd been happy. Shireen said, "Of course we have problems, but they are easy problems."

28   I gave the sisters a ride home in my old Honda. They invited me in for tea, but I didn't have time. Instead I wrote out my phone number and told them to call if I could help in any way.

29   When I said good-bye, I had no idea how soon and how intensely I would become involved in the lives of this family. Two weeks later Shireen called to ask about an art course advertised on a book of matches. It promised a college degree for thirty-five dollars. I said, "Don't do it." A couple of weeks later she called again. This time she had seen an ad for models. She wondered if she should pay and enter the modeling contest. Again I advised, "Don't do it." I was embarrassed to tell her that we Americans lie to people to make money. Before I hung up, we chatted for a while.

30   I wanted to make sure they learned about the good things in our city. Advertisers would direct them to the bars, the malls, and anything that cost money. I told them about what I loved: the parks and prairies, the lakes and sunsets, the sculpture garden, and the free concerts. I lent them books with Georgia O'Keefe paintings and pictures of our national parks.

31   For a while I was so involved with the lives of the sisters that Zeenat told me that her daughters were now my daughters. I was touched that she was

willing to give her daughters away so that they could advance. I tactfully suggested we could share her daughters, but that she would always be the real mother.

GETTING READY TO WRITE

Reviewing the Reading

1. How many languages do the sisters speak? List them.
2. Where did the family come from originally? Describe their life before they immigrated.
3. Why was the family in danger in Baghdad?
4. What was life like in the Iranian refugee camp?
5. Why did the family go on a hunger strike in Quetta (Pakistan)? What was the result?

Examining the Reading Using an Idea Map

Draw a map of the reading using the guidelines on p. 47.

Strengthening Your Vocabulary

Part A: Using the word's context, word parts, or a dictionary, write a brief definition of each of the following words or phrases as it is used in the reading.

1. array (paragraph 1) _____

   _____

2. amendment (paragraph 3) _____

   _____

3. makeshift (paragraph 10) _____

   _____

4. sporadically (paragraph 12) _____

   _____

5. harassed (paragraph 14) _____

   _____

6. resilience (paragraph 27) _____

   _____

Part B: Choose one of the words above and draw a word map (see p. 84) of it.

Reacting to Ideas: Discussion and Journal Writing

Get ready to write about the reading by discussing the following:

1. Do you agree that befriending a family of new arrivals is one of the best ways to understand the refugee experience? What do you think the author learned "about us Americans" (paragraph 1)?

2. The author compares her own life with the refugee family's experience during the same time period (paragraph 8). Why did she include this information in the essay?

3. Why was the family's time in Islamabad "a year of hope" (paragraph 22)?

4. What is the author's purpose in writing this article? Consider what she wants you to do or think after reading this essay.

5. Describe the author's tone throughout the essay. How does she reveal her feelings toward her subject?

WRITING ABOUT THE READING

Paragraph Options

1. Somehow, the girls were able to laugh when describing some of their hardships. Think of a time when you were dealing with an unpleasant or difficult situation, and write a paragraph explaining whether you were able to find any humor in the situation afterward.

2. The author says that Shireen pronounced the word *rights* as if it were sacred (paragraph 24). Do you consider that word sacred as well? Write a paragraph explaining your answer.

3. The girls' mother, Zeenat, is described as *heroic* (paragraph 15). Write a paragraph in which you imagine what qualities she has that make her heroic, based on what you know about her from the reading.

Essay Options

4. What is the "arrival story" for your own family? Write an essay describing how your ancestors (or perhaps your own family) left their country of origin and arrived in America. Explain their reasons for leaving home; for example, did they flee persecution as did the family in the reading? Were they seeking jobs or other opportunities unavailable in their home country? If necessary, interview older family members for information about your family's history for this essay.

5. The author explains how she wanted the family to see the good things in their new city. Imagine that you are acting as a cultural broker, and write an essay describing what you would do to introduce a new arrival to your own city and country. What "good things" would you want to share about where you live? What would you want to warn a refugee about? Explain where you would take him or her to experience a taste of the place where you live.

6. The sisters seem to have embraced certain aspects of American culture, including clothes and makeup. What other aspects of American culture do you think will present opportunities and challenges for the sisters? Write an essay explaining your answer.

WRITING ABOUT A READING

THINKING BEFORE READING

The following reading, "The Struggle to Be an All-American Girl," uses adjectives and adverbs effectively to bring vividness and realism to the events of the author's childhood story.

1. Preview the reading, using the steps described in Chapter 2, page 38.

2. Connect the reading to your own experience by answering the following questions:

   a. Think about your family heritage or ethnic background. What is your attitude toward it?

   b. Consider your childhood education. Do you have mostly positive or mostly negative memories?

READING

THE STRUGGLE TO BE AN
ALL-AMERICAN GIRL

Elizabeth Wong

1   It's still there, the Chinese school on Yale Street where my brother and I used to go. Despite the new coat of paint and the high wire fence, the school I knew ten years ago remains remarkably, stoically the same.

2   Every day at 5 P.M., instead of playing with our fourth- and fifth-grade friends or sneaking out to the empty lot to hunt ghosts and animal bones, my brother and I had to go to Chinese school. No amount of kicking, screaming, or pleading could dissuade my mother, who was solidly determined to have us learn the language of our heritage.

3   Forcibly, she walked us the seven long, hilly blocks from our home to school, depositing our defiant tearful faces before the stern principal. My only memory of him is that he swayed on his heels like a palm tree, and he always clasped his impatient twitching hands behind his back. I recognized him as a repressed maniacal child killer, and knew that if we ever saw his hands we'd be in big trouble.

4   We all sat in little chairs in an empty auditorium. The room smelled like Chinese medicine, an imported faraway mustiness, like ancient mothballs or dirty closets. I hated that smell. I favored crisp new scents, like the soft French perfume that my American teacher wore in public school.

5   There was a stage far to the right, flanked by an American flag and the flag of the Nationalist Republic of China, which was also red, white and blue but not as pretty.

kowtow
kneel, touching forehead to ground

ideographs
symbols representing ideas or objects

6   Although the emphasis at the school was mainly language—speaking, reading, writing—the lessons always began with an exercise in politeness. With the entrance of the teacher, the best student would tap a bell and everyone would get up, **kowtow**, and chant, "Sing san ho," the phonetic for "How are you, teacher?"

7   Being 10 years old, I had better things to learn than **ideographs** copied painstakingly in lines that ran right to left from the tip of a *moc but,* a real ink pen that had to be held in an awkward way if blotches were to be avoided. After all, I could do the multiplication tables, name the satellites of Mars, and write reports on *Little Women* and *Black Beauty.* Nancy Drew, my favorite book heroine, never spoke Chinese.

8   The language was a source of embarrassment. More times than not, I had tried to disassociate myself from the nagging loud voice that followed me wherever I wandered in the nearby American supermarket outside Chinatown. The voice belonged to my grandmother, a fragile woman in her seventies who could outshout the best of the street vendors. Her humor was raunchy; her Chinese rhythmless, patternless. It was quick; it was loud; it was unbeautiful. It was not like the quiet, lilting romance of French or the gentle refinement of the American South. Chinese sounded pedestrian. It sounded public.

9   In Chinatown, the comings and going of hundreds of Chinese on their daily tasks sounded chaotic and frenzied. I did not want to be thought of as mad, as talking gibberish. When I spoke English, people nodded at me, smiled sweetly, said encouraging words. Even the people in my culture would cluck and say that I'd do well in life. "My, doesn't she move her lips fast," they would say, meaning that I'd be able to keep up with the world outside Chinatown.

10   My brother was even more fanatical than I about speaking English. He was especially hard on my mother, criticizing her, often cruelly, for her pidgin speech—smatterings of Chinese scattered like chop suey in her conversation. "It's not 'What it is,' Mom," he'd say in exasperation. "It's 'What *is* it, what *is* it!'" Sometimes Mom might leave out an occasional "the" or "a," or perhaps a verb of being. He would stop her in mid-sentence: "Say it again, Mom. Say it right." When he tripped over his own tongue, he'd blame it on her: "See, Mom, it's all your fault. You set a bad example."

11   What infuriated my mother most was when my brother cornered her on her consonants, especially "r." My father had played a cruel joke on Mom by assigning her an American name that her tongue wouldn't allow her to say. No matter how hard she tried, "Ruth" always ended up "Luth" or "Roof."

12   After two years of writing with a *moc but* and reciting words with multiples of meanings, I finally was granted a cultural divorce. I was permitted to stop Chinese school.

13   I though of myself as multicultural. I preferred tacos to egg rolls; I enjoyed **Cinco de Mayo** more than Chinese New Year.

14   At last, I was one of you; I wasn't one of them.

15   Sadly, I still am.

Cinco de Mayo
Mexican holiday celebrating the defeat of Napoleon III in the Battle of Puebla

GETTING READY TO WRITE

Reviewing the Reading

1. At the end of the essay, Wong says, "At last, I was one of you; I wasn't one of them." To whom do the *you* and the *them* refer?

2. Summarize Wong's attitude toward her Chinese heritage.

3. Why do you think Wong's mother insisted she attend Chinese school?

Examining the Reading Using an Idea Map

Draw a map of the reading using the guidelines on p. 47.

Strengthening Your Vocabulary

Part A: Using the word's context, word parts, or a dictionary, write a brief definition of each of the following words or phrases as it is used in the reading.

1. stoically (paragraph 1) _____

_____

2. dissuade (paragraph 2) _____

_____

3. repressed (paragraph 3)_____

_____

4. maniacal (paragraph 3)_____

_____

5. disassociate (paragraph 8) _____

_____

6. chaotic (paragraph 9) _____

_____

7. frenzied (paragraph 9) _____

_____

Part B: Choose one of the words above and draw a word map (see p. 84) of it.

Reacting to and Discussing Ideas

Get ready to write about the reading by discussing the following:

1. Why do you think Wong's brother criticized his mother's inability to speak English?

2. Why does Wong say she prefers tacos to egg rolls?

3. Explain the meaning of the title of the essay.

WRITING ABOUT THE READING

Paragraph Options

1. Wong was embarrassed by her Chinese heritage. Write a paragraph describing a situation in which you were proud of or embarrassed by your heritage or by the cultural behavior of a member of your family.

2. Write a paragraph in which you describe a family tradition. Use plenty of adjectives and adverbs in your description.

Essay Options

3. Wong states that Nancy Drew, the main character in an American mystery novel series, was her heroine. Write an essay describing a person, real or fictional, whom you admire. Be sure to describe the specific characteristics that make this person your hero or heroine.

4. Clearly, Wong and her brother viewed their heritage from a different perspective than that of their parents and grandparents. Write an essay in which you evaluate generational differences within your own family. Choose one topic or issue, and consider how different your family's generations view the matter.

■

WRITING ABOUT A READING

THINKING BEFORE READING

The following reading, "Are Latinos Different?" was written by Sandra Márquez, a Los Angeles–based journalist. In this article, which appeared on HispanicMagazine.com in October 2003, Márquez addresses the health differences between Hispanics and non-Hispanic whites in the United States, as well as the implications for medical research.

1. Preview the reading using the steps described in Chapter 2, page 38.

2. Connect the reading to your own experience by answering the following questions:

    a. What is racial or ethnic profiling?

    b. Do health issues vary among different ethnic groups?

READING
ARE LATINOS DIFFERENT?

Sandra Márquez

taboo
forbidden

1   Profiling, the practice of compiling data for the purpose of making generalizations about a particular race or ethnic group, is considered **taboo**, or at least politically incorrect, when it comes to criminal behavior or traffic stops. In terms of science, most anyone who received a U.S. public school education was taught that, despite different skin colors, all human bodies were created equally. There was no genetic difference among races.

2   So why the growing trend toward "medical profiling"? Why the need to do medical research that specifically looks at health patterns of Hispanics? The answer is simple, according to Dr. David Hayes-Bautista, director of the Center for the Study of Latino Health and Culture at the University of California Los Angeles. The more than 38 million Latinos living in the United States represent an "**epidemiological paradox.**" Despite popular conceptions, Latinos live longer and have a lower incidence of heart attacks, the leading forms of cancer and stroke than the general public.

epidemiological
referring to the branch of medicine that studies the causes, distribution, and control of diseases in populations

paradox
a statement that seems contradictory but is true

cultura
culture

3   The difference isn't a genetic one, according to the doctor. His research on the topic has convinced him that the generally good health of Hispanics is rooted in **cultura**. And by studying Latino health patterns, he believes that the general public will benefit.

4   "Although Latino populations may generally be described as low-income and low-education with little access to care, Latino health outcomes are generally far better than those of non-Hispanic whites," Hayes-Bautista writes in *Latinos: Remaking America*, published in 2002 by Harvard University and the University of California Press. "This paradox has been observed in so many Latino populations in so many regions over so many years that its existence cries out to be explained," states Hayes-Bautista.

5   The flip side of his research also merits further inquiry. Hispanics have a high incidence of diabetes—64 percent higher than white Americans—AIDS and cirrhosis of the liver, the latter of which is higher among Hispanics than any other group. Recent studies looking specifically at Hispanic health patterns have been conducted by the American Cancer Society, the American Heart Association and the National Alliance of State and Territorial AIDS Directors.

6   The Cancer Society study found that Hispanics are less likely than white Americans to develop and die from lung, breast, prostate and colon cancer—while being more prone to the less common cancer of the cervix, liver and gall bladder. The Heart Association study found that Type 2 diabetes has reached epidemic proportions among Hispanics. And the AIDS study found that Hispanics, who comprise 13 percent of the U.S. population, account for 20 percent of those living with AIDS.

7   But the issue of medical profiling is not without controversy. The debate is reflected in a California ballot measure to be decided Oct. 7. Proposition 54,

dubbed the Racial Privacy Act, would bar state officials from gathering data on race and ethnicity. The initiative's website (www.racialprivacy.org) claims the measure is a step toward creating a "colorblind society." "As the most ethnically diverse state in the Union, California has the most to gain by compelling its government to treat all citizens equally and without regard to race. The latest U.S. Census divides Americans into a whopping 126 different ethnic/racial categories. How many categories should Californians put up with?" it asks.

8 Although Proposition 54's backers say the new law would include an exemption for medical research, prominent groups such as Kaiser Permanente and the California Health Association, appear unconvinced and have opposed the measure.

9 Oscar Cisneros, a policy analyst for the Latino Issues Forum, a public policy and advocacy institute in San Francisco, said the medical research exemption would only apply to clinical settings. If approved, he said the measure would make it harder for public health officials who rely on government data to tailor messages to specific risk groups. It would also have implications for tracking a public health threat such as SARS, which originated in China, Cisneros says "It's not like they force people to reveal their race," Cisneros says of government demographic data. "It's all voluntary information that allows them to get a better picture of what is really going on."

10 Lorenzo Abundiz, 50, a retired Santa Ana, California, firefighter who was told he had just weeks to live after being diagnosed with a rare form of sarcoma cancer five years ago, said he would like to see medical research focus on one thing—finding a cure for all cancers. "Cancer has no preference. It will get everyone: black, white, Mexican. It will nail you. I want to see where everybody bonds together, like cancer survivors like me, and says, 'Let's find a cure,' " says Abundiz, who in July underwent a CAT scan indicating he was in full remission.

11 Abundiz received a state firefighter medal of valor for rescuing two fellow firefighters from a tire shop fire by single-handedly lifting a 500-pound wall without wearing protective breathing gear. He has also been lauded for rescuing pets from burning homes and in June 2001, he married his sweetheart, Peggy, in New York's Times Square in front of millions of viewers on ABC's Good Morning America. He believes toxic exposure on the job made him susceptible to cancer. Nonetheless, it does run in his family. His father died of prostate cancer. He credits the love of his wife, a vegetarian diet, and learning to live more with nature by "letting butterflies land on my fingers and seeing God in nature" for his survival.

12 Dr. Hayes-Bautista says a "Latino norm" is apparent in all of his medical research. He believes "something that Latinos do each day," explains Hispanic health patterns and further study could lead to a reduction of heart disease, cancer and strokes in the population at large. "At the larger level, it has to be culture, which would include what people eat. It probably has to include family or social networks, and it [even] might have something to do with spirituality, the mind-body connection," he says.

GETTING READY TO WRITE

Reviewing the Reading

1. Define the term "profiling."

2. Briefly compare Latinos with non-Hispanic whites on the following health issues discussed in the article. (The first one is done for you.)

   a. length of life: _____

   b. heart attacks: _____

   c. diabetes: _____

   d. AIDS: _____

   e. cirrhosis of the liver: _____

   f. lung, breast, prostate, and colon cancer: _____

   _____

3. What does Dr. Hayes-Bautista believe is at the root of Hispanics' generally good health?

4. What is the purpose of California's Proposition 54?

5. Why was Lorenzo Abundiz awarded a medal of valor?

6. What does Lorenzo Abundiz believe made him susceptible to cancer?

Examining the Reading Using an Idea Map

Draw a map of the reading using the guidelines on p. 47.

Strengthening Your Vocabulary

Part A: Using the word's context, word parts, or a dictionary, write a brief definition of each of the following words or phrases as it is used in the reading.

1. epidemic (paragraph 6) _____

   _____

2. controversy (paragraph 7) _____

   _____

3. exemption (paragraph 8) _____

   _____

4. remission (paragraph 10) _____

   _____

5. valor (paragraph 11) _____

   _____

6. lauded (paragraph 11) _____

   _____

7. susceptible (paragraph 11) _____

_____

Part B: Choose one of the words above and draw a word map (see p. 84) of it.

Reacting to Ideas: Discussion and Journal Writing

Get ready to write about the reading by discussing the following:

1. What is controversial about medical profiling?

2. Why does the good health of Hispanics present a paradox?

3. Explain what is meant by the phrase, "a colorblind society" (paragraph 7).

4. Evaluate the quality of the supporting evidence in this article. What sources does the author draw upon for information? How credible are they?

WRITING ABOUT THE READING

Paragraph Options

1. Why do you think the author wrote about Lorenzo Abundiz in this article? Write a paragraph explaining who he is and why his story is significant.

2. Have you ever felt that you were stereotyped—or even profiled—based on some aspect of your identity (for example, age, ethnicity, or gender)? Write a paragraph describing your experience.

3. Do you think Proposition 54 should have been passed (it wasn't)? Write a paragraph explaining why or why not.

Essay Options

4. In the context of Dr. Hayes-Bautista's research, *culture* includes what people eat, their family or social networks, and spirituality. Write an essay describing these aspects of your culture, and how they could affect your own health. Feel free to include other aspects of your culture that may be relevant to your health.

5. In addition to medical profiling, many other medical issues provoke debate and/or controversy. Choose an issue, such as stem-cell research or medicinal marijuana, and write an essay taking a stand on one side of the issue. Be sure to include evidence to support your argument and to persuade your readers to accept your point of view.

6. According to the article, supporters of Proposition 54 object to the U.S. census's "whopping 126 different ethnic/racial categories" for Americans. How do you feel about being asked to place yourself in a particular category? Write an essay describing your response to requests for personal information about yourself, whether in a national census or on a college application or some other type of form. Are you ever concerned about how the information will be used?

WRITING ABOUT A READING

THINKING BEFORE READING

The following reading, "Light Skin Versus Dark," was written by Pulitzer Prize–winning journalist Charisse Jones, co-author of the American Book Award–winning *Shifting: The Double Lives of Black Women in America*. In this essay, which first appeared in *Glamour* magazine, Jones describes her experiences with an especially painful form of racism.

1. Preview the reading using the steps described in Chapter 2, page 38.
2. Connect the reading to your own experience by answering the following questions:
   a. How would you define racism?
   b. What instances of bias, in the form of racism, ageism, or sexism, have you experienced?
   c. What are the physical qualities that make a person beautiful?

READING
LIGHT SKIN VERSUS DARK

Charisse Jones

1   I'll never forget the day I was supposed to meet him. We had only spoken on the phone. But we got along so well, we couldn't wait to meet face-to-face. I took the bus from my high school to his for our blind date. While I nervously waited for him outside the school, one of his buddies came along, looked me over, and remarked that I was going to be a problem, because his friend didn't like dating anybody darker than himself.

2   When my mystery man—who was not especially good-looking—finally saw me, he took one look, uttered a hurried hello, then disappeared with his smirking friends. I had apparently been pronounced ugly on arrival and dismissed.

3   That happened nearly fifteen years ago. I'm thirty now, and the hurt and humiliation have long since faded. But the memory still lingers, reinforced in later years by other situations in which my skin color was judged by other African Americans—for example, at a cocktail party or a nightclub where light-skinned black women got all the attention.

4   A racist encounter hurts badly. But it does not equal the pain of "colorism"—being rejected by your own people because your skin is colored cocoa and not cream, ebony and not olive. On our scale of beauty, it is often the high yellows—in the **lexicon** of black America, those with light skin—whose looks reap the most attention. Traditionally, if someone was described that way, there was no need to say that person was good-looking. It was a given that light

lexicon
vocabulary; terminology

was lovely. It was those of us with plain brown eyes and darker skin hues who had to prove ourselves.

5   I was twelve, and in my first year of junior high school in San Francisco, when I discovered dark brown was not supposed to be beautiful. At that age, boys suddenly became important, and so did your looks. But by that time—the late 1970s—black kids no longer believed in that sixties **mantra**, "Black is beautiful." Light skin, green eyes, and long, wavy hair were once again synonymous with beauty.

mantra
a frequently repeated word or phrase, sometimes used as a motto or prayer

6   Colorism—and its subtext of self-hatred—began during slavery on plantations where white masters often favored the lighter-skinned blacks, many of whom were their own children. But though it began with whites, black people have kept colorism alive. In the past, many black sororities, fraternities, and other social organizations have been notorious for accepting only light-skinned members. Yes, some blacks have criticized their lighter-skinned peers. But most often in our history, a light complexion had been a passport to special treatment by both whites *and* blacks.

7   Some social circles are still defined by hue. Some African Americans, dark and light, prefer light-skinned mates so they can have a "pretty baby." And skin-lightening creams still sell, though they are now advertised as good for making blemishes fade rather than for lightening whole complexions.

8   In my family, color was never discussed, even though our spectrum was broad—my brother was very light; my sister and I, much darker. But in junior high, I learned in a matter of weeks what had apparently been drummed into the heads of my black peers for most of their lives.

9   Realizing how crazy it all was, I became defiant, challenging friends when they made silly remarks. Still, there was no escaping the distinctions of color.

10   In my life, I have received a litany of twisted compliments from fellow blacks. "You're the prettiest dark-skinned girl I have ever seen" is one; "You're pretty for a dark girl" is another.

11   A light-complexioned girlfriend once remarked to me that dark-skinned people often don't take the time to groom themselves. As a journalist, I once interviewed a prominent black lawmaker who was light-skinned. He drew me into the shade of a tree while we talked because, he said, "I'm sure you don't want to get any darker."

12   Though some black people—like film-maker Spike Lee in his movie *School Daze*—have tried to provoke debate about colorism, it remains a painful topic many blacks would rather not confront. Yet there has been progress. In this age of Afrocentrism, many blacks revel in the nuances of the African American rainbow. Natural hairstyles and dreadlocks are in, and Theresa Randle, star of the hit film *Bad Boys*, is only one of several darker-skinned actresses noted for their beauty.

13   That gives me hope. People have told me that color biases among blacks run too deep ever to be eradicated. But I tell them that is the kind of attitude that allows colorism to persist. Meanwhile, I do what I can. When I notice that a friend dates only light-skinned women, I comment on it. If I hear that a movie follows the tired old scenario in which a light-skinned beauty is the love interest while a darker-skinned woman is the comic **foil**, the butt of "ugly" jokes, I don't go see it. Others can do the same.

foil
one who is used as a contrast to enhance the distinctive characteristics of another

14   There is only so much blacks can do about racism, because we need the cooperation of others to make it go away. But healing ourselves is within our control.

15   At least we can try. As a people we face enough pain without inflicting our own wounds. I believe any people that could survive slavery, that could disprove the lies that pronounced them less than human, can also teach its children that black is beautiful in all of its shades.

16   Loving ourselves should be an easy thing to do.

GETTING READY TO WRITE

Reviewing the Reading

1. Define the term colorism.

2. According to the author, where and why did colorism originate?

3. How old was the author when she first noticed the connection between skin color and beauty?

4. What film addresses the topic of colorism?

5. How does the author confront instances of colorism in her life today?

Examining the Reading Using an Idea Map

Draw a map of the reading using the guidelines on p. 47.

Strengthening Your Vocabulary

Part A: Using the word's context, word parts, or a dictionary, write a brief definition of each of the following words or phrases as it is used in the reading.

1. synonymous (paragraph 5) _____

_____

2. subtext (paragraph 6) _____

_____

3. notorious (paragraph 6) _____

_____

4. spectrum (paragraph 8) _____

_____

5. litany (paragraph 10) _____

_____

6. nuances (paragraph 12) _____

_____

7. eradicated (paragraph 13) _____

_____

Part B: Choose one of the words above and draw a word map (see p. 84) of it.

Reacting to Ideas: Discussion and Journal Writing

Get ready to write about the reading by discussing the following:

1. The author contrasts her own lack of awareness with "what had apparently been drummed into the heads of my black peers for most of their lives" (paragraph 8). Do you think her perception was accurate? Why or why not?

2. How have the author's earlier impressions of color bias been reinforced as an adult?

3. What does Jones mean when she refers to colorism's "subtext of self-hatred" (paragraph 6)?

4. Who do you think is the intended audience for this essay? Do you think it was written primarily for blacks or whites? Women or men?

WRITING ABOUT THE READING

Paragraph Options

1. The author states, "There is only so much blacks can do about racism, because we need the cooperation of others to make it go away" (paragraph 14). Write a paragraph explaining this statement and discussing why colorism is different.

2. Do you think the author believes that colorism can be eliminated? Do you believe it can? Write a paragraph explaining your answers.

3. "Light Skin Versus Dark" is an example of persuasive writing. What is the author trying to convince the reader to think or to do? Write a paragraph summarizing her basic argument and explaining why you accept or reject it.

Essay Options

4. This reading examines some of the perceptions of beauty among African Americans. What is your own standard of beauty? How did you form your ideas about what is beautiful? Consider how your definition of beauty may contrast with that of people from other races or ethnic backgrounds. Also think about those who are different from you in other ways, such as age, gender, or socioeconomic status. Write an essay exploring different definitions of beauty.

5. Jones says that she became defiant in response to finding out about "the distinctions of color" in junior high. Think of a time in your life when you learned a difficult truth or had an unpleasant revelation. How did

you respond? Write an essay describing the situation and your response. If it has continued to be an issue in your life, as colorism has for Jones, explain how you choose to respond to it today.

6. Despite the efforts of Spike Lee and others, the author says that colorism continues to be "a painful topic many blacks would rather not confront." Choose another topic that you believe people find difficult to confront and write an essay in which you provoke debate. Be sure to define the issue and describe how you hope to contribute to an understanding of (or solution to) the issue.

WRITING ABOUT A READING

THINKING BEFORE READING

The following reading, "Thank You, M'am," was written by Langston Hughes in 1958. Hughes was a distinguished and prolific writer who made an important contribution to the Harlem Renaissance (a period following Word War I during which African-American writers produced a sizable body of literature) through his poetry, prose, and drama. In this short story, Hughes tells of a woman and a boy brought together by a failed attempt at purse snatching.

1. Preview the reading using the steps described in Chapter 2, page 38.

2. Connect the reading to your own experience by answering the following questions:

   a. Have you or someone you know ever been the victim of a theft? How did you or your acquaintance react?

   b. Would you be willing to help someone who had tried to do you harm?

READING

THANK YOU, M'AM

Langston Hughes

She was a large woman with a large purse that had everything in it but a hammer and nails. It had a long strap, and she carried it slung across her shoulder. It was about eleven o'clock at night, dark, and she was walking alone, when a boy ran up behind her and tried to snatch her purse. The strap broke with the sudden single tug the boy gave it from behind. But the boy's weight and the weight of the purse combined caused him to lose his balance. Instead of taking off full blast as he had hoped, the boy fell on his back on the sidewalk and his legs flew up. The large woman simply turned around and kicked him right square in his blue-jeaned **sitter**. Then she reached down, picked the boy up by his shirt front, and shook him until his teeth rattled.

After that the woman said, "Pick up my pocketbook, boy, and give it here."

She still held him tightly. But she bent down enough to permit him to stoop and pick up her purse. Then she said, "Now ain't you ashamed of yourself?"

Firmly gripped by his shirt front, the boy said, "Yes'm."

5   The woman said, "What did you want to do it for?"

The boy said, "I didn't aim to."

She said, "You a lie!"

By that time two or three people passed, stopped, turned to look, and some stood watching.

"If I turn you loose, will you run?" asked the woman.

10   "Yes'm," said the boy.

"Then I won't turn you loose," said the woman. She did not release him.

"Lady, I'm sorry," whispered the boy.

"Um-hum! Your face is dirty. I got a great mind to wash your face for you. Ain't you got nobody home to tell you to wash your face?"

"No'm," said the boy.

15   "Then it will get washed this evening," said the large woman, starting up the street, dragging the frightened boy behind her.

He looked as if he were fourteen or fifteen, frail and willow-wild, in tennis shoes and blue jeans.

The woman said, "You ought to be my son. I would teach you right from wrong. Least I can do right now is to wash your face. Are you hungry?"

"No'm," said the being-dragged boy. "I just want you to turn me loose."

"Was I bothering *you* when I turned that corner?" asked the woman.

20   "No'm."

"But you put yourself in contact with *me*," said the woman. "If you think that that contact is not going to last a while, you got another thought coming. When I get through with you, sir, you are going to remember Mrs. Luella Bates Washington Jones."

Sweat popped out on the boy's face and he began to struggle. Mrs. Jones stopped, jerked him around in front of her, put a **half nelson** about his neck, and continued to drag him up the street. When she got to her door, she dragged the boy inside, down a hall, and into a large kitchenette-furnished room at the rear of the house. She switched on the light and left the door open. The boy could hear other roomers laughing and talking in the large house. Some of their doors were open, too, so he knew he and the woman were not alone. The woman still had him by the neck in the middle of her room.

She said, "What is your name?"

"Roger," answered the boy.

25   "Then, Roger, you go to that sink and wash your face," said the woman, whereupon she turned him loose—at last. Roger looked at the door—looked at the woman—looked at the door—*and went to the sink.*

"Let the water run until it gets warm," she said. "Here's a clean towel."

"You gonna take me to jail?" asked the boy, bending over the sink.

"Not with that face, I would not take you nowhere," said the woman. "Here I am trying to get home to cook me a bite to eat, and you snatch my pocketbook! Maybe you ain't been to your supper either, late as it be. Have you?"

"There's nobody home at my house," said the boy.

30   "Then we'll eat," said the woman. "I believe you're hungry—or been hungry—to try to snatch my pocketbook!"

"I want a pair of blue suede shoes," said the boy.

"Well, you didn't have to snatch *my* pocketbook to get some suede shoes," said Mrs. Luella Bates Washington Jones. "You could of asked me."

"M'am?"

The water dripping from his face, the boy looked at her. There was a long pause. A very long pause. After he had dried his face, and not knowing what else to do, dried it again, the boy turned around, wondering what next. The door was open. He could make a dash for it down the hall. He could run, run, run, *run*!

35   The woman was sitting on the daybed. After a while she said, "I were young once and I wanted things I could not get."

There was another long pause. The boy's mouth opened. Then he frowned, not knowing he frowned.

The woman said, "Um-hum! You thought I was going to say *but,* didn't you? You thought I was going to say, *but I didn't snatch people's pocketbooks.* Well, I wasn't going to say that." Pause. Silence. "I have done things, too, which I would not tell you, son—neither tell God, if He didn't already know. Everybody's got something in common. So you set down while I fix us something to eat. You might run that comb through your hair so you will look presentable."

In another corner of the room behind a screen was a gas plate and an icebox. Mrs. Jones got up and went behind the screen. The woman did not watch the boy to see if he was going to run now, nor did she watch her purse, which she left behind her on the daybed. But the boy took care to sit on the far side of the room, away from the purse, where he thought she could easily see him out of the corner of her eye if she wanted to. He did not trust the woman *not* to trust him. And he did not want to be mistrusted now.

"Do you need somebody to go to the store," asked the boy, "maybe to get some milk or something?"

40   "Don't believe I do," said the woman, "unless you just want sweet milk yourself. I was going to make cocoa out of this canned milk I got here."

"That will be fine," said the boy.

She heated some lima beans and ham she had in the icebox, made the cocoa, and set the table. The woman did not ask the boy anything about where he lived, or his folks, or anything else that would embarrass him. Instead, as they ate, she told him about her job in a hotel beauty shop that stayed open late, what the work was like, and how all kinds of women came in and out, blondes, redheads, and Spanish. Then she cut him a half of her ten-cent cake.

"Eat some more, son," she said.

When they were finished eating, she got up and said, "Now here, take this ten dollars and buy yourself some blue suede shoes. And next time, do not make the mistake of latching onto *my* pocketbook *nor nobody else's*—because shoes got by devilish ways will burn your feet. I got to get my rest now. But from here on in, son, I hope you will behave yourself."

45   She led him down the hall to the front door and opened it. "Good night! Behave yourself, boy!" she said, looking out into the street as he went down the steps.

The boy wanted to say something other than, "Thank you, m'am," to Mrs. Luella Bates Washington Jones, but although his lips moved, he couldn't even say that as he turned at the foot of the barren stoop and looked up at the large woman in the door. Then she shut the door.

GETTING READY TO WRITE

Reviewing the Reading

1. Why did the boy try to steal the woman's purse? What did he want to buy?
2. What did the boy do once the woman "turned him loose" at her apartment?
3. Where did the woman work?
4. Explain the title of the story.

Examining the Reading Using an Idea Map

Draw a map of the reading using the guidelines on p. 47.

Strengthening Your Vocabulary

Part A: Using the word's context, word parts, or a dictionary, write a brief definition of each of the following words or phrases as it is used in the reading.

1. slung (paragraph 1) _____

   _____

2. frail (paragraph 16) _____

   _____

3. barren (paragraph 46) _____

   _____

Part B: Choose one of the words above and draw a word map (see p. 84) of it.

Reacting to Ideas: Discussion and Journal Writing

Get ready to write about the reading by discussing the following:

1. In what time period does this story take place? What clues are given about the story's setting (time and place)?

2. Why didn't the boy run when he had the chance?

3. What does the woman mean when she says, "Everybody's got something in common" (paragraph 37)?

4. How does Hughes's choice of words and language contribute to the story?

5. Why do you think the woman acted as she did? What inferences can you make about her?

WRITING ABOUT THE READING

Paragraph Options

1. How do you picture Mrs. Luella Bates Washington Jones? How do you picture Roger? Using the details and descriptions in the short story, and any inferences you can make from the characters' conversations, write a paragraph describing each character. Feel free to speculate about each character's family and other aspects of their lives.

2. How did the boy's feelings change during the course of the story? Write a paragraph identifying the emotions that you think he experienced as the story progressed. Be sure to explain what caused his feelings to change.

3. Mrs. Jones says that "shoes got by devilish ways will burn your feet" (paragraph 44). Write a paragraph explaining what she means.

Essay Options

4. Write an essay imagining what happens after the end of this story. How will the events of that night affect both characters? Will the boy "behave" because of how the woman treated him? Will the woman become part of the boy's life or will the two characters go their separate ways? Feel free to add details and take the story wherever you want it to go.

5. In this story, the woman responded in ways that were unexpected but ultimately generous. Think of an incident when your own reaction (or someone else's) took you by surprise, leading to unexpected consequences. Write an essay describing the incident, the surprising reaction, and the consequences.

WRITING ABOUT A READING

THINKING BEFORE READING

The following reading is taken from the textbook *Sociology: A Down-to-Earth Approach* by James M. Henslin. The chapter in which this reading appeared deals with cultural diversity. Notice how the author uses research and references to popular culture to illustrate his points.

1. Preview the reading, using the steps discussed in Chapter 2, p. 38.

2. Connect the reading to your own experience by answering the following questions:

   a. What do you know about Tiger Woods?

   b. With what ethnic group(s) do you identify?

READING

TIGER WOODS AND THE EMERGING MULTIRACIAL IDENTITY: MAPPING NEW ETHNIC TERRAIN

James M. Henslin

1   Tiger Woods, perhaps the top golfer of all time, calls himself Cablinasian. Woods invented this term as a boy to try to explain to himself just who he was—a combination of Caucasian, Black, Indian, and Asian (Leland and Beals 1997; Hall 2001). Woods wants to embrace both sides of his family. To be known by a racial-ethnic identity that applies to just one of his parents is to deny the other parent.

2   Like many of us, Tiger Woods' heritage is difficult to specify. Analysts who like to quantify ethnic heritage put Woods at one-quarter Thai, one-quarter Chinese, one-quarter white, an eighth Native American, and an eighth African American. From this chapter, you know how ridiculous such computations are, but the sociological question is why many consider Tiger Woods an African American. The U.S. racial scene is indeed complex, but a good part of the reason is simply that this is the label the media chose. "Everyone has to fit somewhere" seems to be our attitude. If they don't, we grow uncomfortable. And for Tiger Woods, the media chose African American.

3   The United States once had a firm "color line"—a barrier between racial-ethnic groups that you didn't dare cross, especially in dating or marriage. This invisible barrier has broken down, and today such marriages are common (*Statistical Abstract* 2002: Table 47). Several campuses have interracial student organizations. Harvard has two, one just for students who have one African American parent (Leland and Beals 1997).

terrain
territory

4   As we march into unfamiliar ethnic **terrain**, our classifications are bursting at the seams. Kwame Anthony Appiah, of Harvard's Philosophy and Afro-American

Tiger Woods, after making one of his marvelous shots, this one at Great Britain's Open Championship at St. George's in Sandwich, UK.

Studies Departments, says, "My mother is English; my father is Ghanaian. My sisters are married to a Nigerian and a Norwegian. I have nephews who range from blond-haired kids to very black kids. They are all first cousins. Now according to the American scheme of things, they're all black—even the guy with blond hair who skis in Oslo" (Wright 1994).

5   The U.S. census, which is taken every ten years, used to make everyone choose from Caucasian, Negro, Indian, and Oriental. Everyone was sliced and diced and packed into one of these restrictive classifications. After years of complaints, the list was expanded. In the 2000 census, everyone had to declare that they were or were not "Spanish/Hispanic/Latino." Then they had to mark "one or more races" that they "consider themselves to be." They could choose from White; Black, African American, or Negro; American Indian or Alaska Native; Asian Indian, Chinese, Filipino, Japanese, Korean, Vietnamese, Native Hawaiian, Guamanian or **Chamorro**, Samoan, or other Pacific Islander. Finally, if these didn't do it, you could check a box called "Some Other Race" and then write whatever you wanted.

Chamorro
the original ethnic group of the Northern Mariana Islands in the North Pacific Ocean

6   Perhaps the census should list Cablinasian. Of course there should be GASH for the German-African-Swedish-Hispanic Americans, BITE for those of Botswanian-Indonesian-Turkish-English descent, and STUDY for the Swedish-Turkish-Uruguan-Danish-Yugoslavian Americans. These terms make as much sense as the categories we currently use.

GETTING READY TO WRITE

Reviewing the Reading

1. Describe Tiger Woods's ethnic heritage. Why is it of interest?
2. How have "color lines" been crossed in this country?
3. How has the U.S. census changed in its reporting for ethnicity?
4. What is the author's attitude toward the census classification?

Examining the Reading Using an Idea Map

Draw a map of the reading using the guidelines on p. 47.

Strengthening Your Vocabulary

Part A: Using the word's context, word parts, or a dictionary, write a brief definition of each of the following words or phrases as it is used in the reading.

1. embrace (paragraph 1) _____

   _____

2. heritage (paragraph 2) _____

   _____

3. barriers (paragraph 3) _____

   _____

4. interracial (paragraph 3) _____

   _____

5. estrictive (paragraph 5) _____

   _____

Part B: Choose one of the words above and draw a word map (see p. 84) of it.

Reacting to Ideas: Discussion and Journal Writing

Get ready to write about the reading by discussing the following:

1. Did you know that Tiger Woods has such a diverse heritage? How does the media portray his ethnic background?
2. Many people are interested in the ethnic backgrounds of famous people. Do you think ethnic background affects celebrity status and popularity?
3. Discuss the ways in which our society has come to embrace people of diverse heritages. In what areas do we still need to improve?

WRITING ABOUT THE READING

Paragraph Options

1. Invent a term similar to Woods's "Cablinasian" that describes your ethnic background. Write a paragraph explaining what your term means.

2. Write a paragraph about a sports figure that you admire. What makes this person worth your interest?

3. The author provides examples from the U.S. census. Write a paragraph expressing your opinion of the census classifications.

Essay Options

4. The author states that the "U.S. racial scene is complex." Write an essay that explains what this phrase means. Be sure to include examples to support your ideas.

5. Some people believe that we should be "colorblind" in our approach to diverse groups, while others believe it is important to embrace and celebrate the differences between people. Write an essay about which idea you think is the better way to deal with multiculturalism.

6. Write an essay describing a way in which your college recognizes and encourages diversity. Your audience is made up of high school seniors from a variety of ethnic backgrounds.

P A R T   V I I I

Reviewing the Basics

GUIDE TO REVIEWING THE BASICS

OVERVIEW

Most of us know how to communicate in our own language. When we talk or write, we put our thoughts into words and, by and large, we make ourselves understood. But many of us do not know the specific terms and rules of grammar. Grammar is a system that describes how language is put together. Grammar must be learned, almost as if it is a foreign language.

Why is it important to study grammar, to understand grammatical terms like *verb, participle,* and *gerund* and concepts like *agreement* and *subordination?* There are several good reasons. Knowing grammar will allow you to

- **recognize an error in your writing and correct it.** Your papers will read more smoothly and communicate more effectively when they are error free.

- **understand the comments of your teachers and peers.** People who read and critique your writing may point out a "fragment" or a "dangling modifier." You will be able to revise and correct the problems.

- **write with more impact.** Grammatically correct sentences are signs of clear thinking. Your readers will get your message without distraction or confusion.

As you will see in this section, "Reviewing the Basics," the different areas of grammatical study are highly interconnected. The sections on parts of speech, sentences, punctuation, mechanics, and spelling fit together into a logical whole. To recognize and correct a run-on sentence, for example, you need to know both sentence structure *and* punctuation. To avoid errors in capitalization, you need to know parts of speech *and* mechanics. If grammar is to do you any good, your knowledge of it must be thorough. As you review the following "basics," be alert to the interconnections that make language study so interesting.

Grammatical terms and rules demand your serious attention. Mastering them will pay handsome dividends: error-free papers, clear thinking, and effective writing.

A Understanding the Parts of Speech

The eight parts of speech are **nouns**, **pronouns**, **verbs**, **adjectives**, **adverbs**, **conjunctions**, **prepositions**, and **interjections**. Each word in a sentence functions as one of these parts of speech. Being able to identify the parts of speech in sentences allows you to analyze and improve your writing and to understand grammatical principles discussed later in this section.

It is important to keep in mind that *how* a word functions in a sentence determines *what* part of speech it is. Thus, the same word can be a noun, a verb, or an adjective, depending on how it is used.

NOUN

He needed some blue wallpaper.

VERB

He will wallpaper the hall.

ADJECTIVE

He went to a wallpaper store.

A.1 NOUNS

A **noun** names a person, place, thing, or idea.

People	*woman, winner, Maria Alvarez*
Places	*mall, hill, Indiana*
Things	*lamp, ship, air*
Ideas	*goodness, perfection, harmony*

The form of many nouns changes to express **number** (**singular** for one, **plural** for more than one): *one bird, two birds; one child, five children*. Most nouns can also be made **possessive** to show ownership by the addition of *-'s: city's, Norma's*.

Sometimes a noun is used to modify another noun:

NOUN MODIFYING DIPLOMA

Her goal had always been to earn a college diploma.

Nouns are classified as **proper, common, collective, concrete, abstract, count,** and **noncount.**

1. **Proper nouns** name specific people, places, or things and are always cap-italized: *Martin Luther King, Jr.; East Lansing; Ford Taurus.* Days of the week and months are considered proper nouns and are capitalized.

PROPER NOUN   PROPER NOUN   PROPER NOUN

In September Allen will attend Loyola University.

2. **Common nouns** name one or more of a general class or type of person, place, thing, or idea and are not capitalized: *president, city, car, wisdom.*

COMMON NOUN   COMMON NOUN   COMMON NOUN   COMMON NOUN

Next fall the students will enter college to receive an education.

3. **Collective nouns** name a whole group or collection of people, places, or things: *committee, team, jury.* They are usually singular in form.

COLLECTIVE NOUN   COLLECTIVE NOUN

The flock of mallards is flying over the herd of bison.

4. **Concrete nouns** name tangible things that can be tasted, seen, touched, smelled, or heard: *sandwich, radio, pen.*

CONCRETE NOUN   CONCRETE NOUN

The frozen pizza was stuck in the freezer.

5. **Abstract nouns** name ideas, qualities, beliefs, and conditions: *honesty, goodness, poverty.* Use a singular verb with an abstract noun.

ABSTRACT NOUNS   ABSTRACT NOUN

Their marriage was based on love, honor, and trust.

ABSTRACT NOUN

Poverty is a major problem in the United States.

SINGULAR VERB

6. **Count nouns** name items that can be counted. Count nouns can be made plural, usually by adding *-s* or *-es: one river, three rivers; one box, ten boxes.* Some count nouns form their plural in an irregular way: *man, men; goose, geese.*

COUNT NOUN   COUNT NOUN   COUNT NOUN

The salespeople put the invoices in their files.

7. **Noncount nouns** name ideas or qualities that cannot be counted. Noncount nouns almost always have no plural form: *air, knowledge, unhappiness.*

NONCOUNT NOUN   NONCOUNT NOUN

As the rain pounded on the windows, she tried to find the courage to walk home from work.

A.2 PRONOUNS

A **pronoun** is a word that substitutes for or refers to a noun or another pronoun. The noun or pronoun to which a pronoun refers is called the pronoun's **antecedent**. A pronoun must agree with its antecedent in person, number, and gender (these terms are discussed later in this section).

> After the <u>campers</u> discovered the <u>cave</u>, <u>they</u> mapped <u>it</u> for the next <u>group</u>, <u>which</u> was arriving next week. [The pronoun *they* refers to its antecedent, *campers;* the pronoun *it* refers to its antecedent, *cave;* the pronoun *which* refers to its antecedent, *group.*]

The eight kinds of pronouns are **personal, demonstrative, reflexive, intensive, interrogative, relative, indefinite**, and **reciprocal**.

1. **Personal pronouns** take the place of nouns or pronouns that name people or things. A personal pronoun changes form to indicate **person, gender, number**, and **case**.

   Person is the grammatical term used to distinguish the speaker (**first person:** *I, we*); the person spoken to (**second person:** *you*); and the person or thing spoken about (**third person:** *he, she, it, they*). **Gender** is the term used to classify pronouns as **masculine** (*he, him*); **feminine** (*she, her*); or **neuter** (*it*). **Number** classifies pronouns as **singular** (one) or **plural** (more than one). Some personal pronouns also function as adjectives modifying nouns (*our house*).

PERSON	SINGULAR	PLURAL
First person	I, me, my, mine	we, us, our, ours
Second person	you, your, yours	you, your, yours
Third person		
Masculine	he, him, his	
Feminine	she, her, hers	they, them, their, theirs
Neuter	it, its	

1ST PERSON SINGULAR · 1ST PERSON SINGULAR (PRONOUN/ADJECTIVE) · 1ST PERSON SINGULAR (PRONOUN/ADJECTIVE) · 3RD PERSON SINGULAR · 3RD PERSON PLURAL

I called my manager about my new clients. She wanted to know as soon as they placed their first orders. "Your new clients are important to us," she said.

3RD PERSON PLURAL (PRONOUN/ADJECTIVE) · 2ND PERSON SINGULAR (PRONOUN/ADJECTIVE) · 3RD PERSON SINGULAR

A pronoun's **case** is determined by its function as a subject (**subjective** or **nominative case**) or an object (**objective case**) in a sentence. A pronoun that shows ownership is in the **possessive case**.

2. **Demonstrative pronouns** refer to particular people or things. The demonstrative pronouns are *this* and *that* (singular) and *these* and *those* (plural). (*This, that, these,* and *those* can also be demonstrative adjectives when they modify a noun.)

> This is more thorough than that.

> The red shuttle buses stop here. These go to the airport every hour.

3. **Reflexive pronouns** indicate that the subject performs actions to, for, or upon itself. Reflexive pronouns end in *-self* or *-selves.*

> We excused ourselves from the table and left.

PERSON	SINGULAR	PLURAL
First person	myself	ourselves
Second person	yourself	yourselves
Third person	himself	
	herself	themselves
	itself	

4. An **intensive pronoun** emphasizes the word that comes before it in a sentence. Like reflexive pronouns, intensive pronouns end in *-self* or *-selves.*

> The filmmaker herself could not explain the ending.

> They themselves repaired the copy machine.

Note: A reflexive or intensive pronoun should not be used as a subject of a sentence. An antecedent for the reflexive pronoun must appear in the same sentence.

> INCORRECT   Myself create colorful sculpture.

> CORRECT   I myself create colorful sculpture.

5. **Interrogative pronouns** are used to introduce questions: *who, whom, whoever, whomever, what, which, whose.* The correct use of *who* and *whom* depends on the role the interrogative pronoun plays in a sentence or clause. When the pronoun functions as the subject of the sentence or clause, use *who.* When the pronoun functions as an object in the sentence or clause, use *whom.*

> What happened?

> Which is your street?

> Who wrote *Ragtime?* [*Who* is the subject of the sentence.]

> Whom should I notify? [*Whom* is the object of the verb *notify: I should notify whom?*]

6. **Relative pronouns** relate groups of words to nouns or other pronouns and often introduce adjective clauses or noun clauses (see p. 587). The relative pronouns are *who, whom, whoever, whomever,* and *whose* (referring to people) and *that, what, whatever,* and *which* (referring to things).

> In 1836 Charles Dickens met John Forster, who became his friend and biographer.

> We read some articles that were written by former astronauts.

7. **Indefinite pronouns** are pronouns without specific antecedents. They refer to people, places, or things in general.

> <u>Someone</u> has been rearranging my papers.

> <u>Many</u> knew the woman, but <u>few</u> could say they knew her well.

Here are some frequently used indefinite pronouns:

	SINGULAR	PLURAL
another	nobody	all
anybody	none	both
anyone	no one	few
anything	nothing	many
each	one	more
either	other	most
everybody	somebody	others
everyone	someone	several
everything	something	some
neither		

8. **The reciprocal pronouns** *each other* and *one another* indicate a mutual relationship between two or more parts of a plural antecedent.

> Bernie and Sharon congratulated <u>each other</u> on their high grades.

EXERCISE 1

Directions: In each of the following sentences (a) circle each noun and (b) underline each pronoun.

EXAMPLE   When <u>we</u> finished the (project), <u>our</u> (manager) celebrated by ordering (pizza) for <u>everyone</u> in the (office).

1. I know the course will be challenging, but I will do whatever it takes to succeed.

2. The blue whale can weigh up to 150 tons; its heart alone weighs as much as a car.

3. Victor and his co-workers collaborated on the report, but he wrote the final version himself.

4. Whoever calls to identify the song playing on the radio will win a free CD.

5. My son and daughter both love sports: his favorite sport is basketball, and hers is baseball.

6. Anybody who owns a car can save a small fortune on repairs by taking a basic course in automotive mechanics.

7. Whose leftover food is making the refrigerator smell bad?

8. Kayla is president of a club that promotes environmental awareness and encourages students to use their bikes instead of cars.

9. During the horror movie, my friend and I kept screaming and grabbing each other.

10. This is a busy time of year, but that is no excuse for skipping your workout.

A.3 VERBS

Verbs express action or state of being. A grammatically complete sentence has at least one verb in it.

There are three kinds of verbs: **action verbs**, **linking verbs**, and **helping verbs** (also known as **auxiliary verbs**).

1. **Action verbs** express physical and mental activities.

    Mr. Royce <u>dashed</u> for the bus.

    The incinerator <u>burns</u> garbage at high temperatures.

    I <u>think</u> that seat is taken.

    The programmer <u>worked</u> until 3:00 A.M.

    Action verbs are either **transitive** or **intransitive**. The action of a **transitive verb** is directed toward someone or something, called the **direct object** of the verb. Direct objects receive the action of the verb. Transitive verbs require direct objects to complete the meaning of the sentence.

    | | TRANSITIVE | DIRECT |
    | SUBJECT | VERB | OBJECT |

    Amalia <u>made</u> clocks.

    An **intransitive verb** does not need a direct object to complete the meaning of the sentence.

    | | INTRANSITIVE |
    | SUBJECT | VERB |

    The traffic <u>stopped</u>.

    Some verbs can be both transitive and intransitive, depending on their meaning and use in a sentence.

    INTRANSITIVE   The traffic <u>stopped</u>. [No direct object.]

                                            DIRECT OBJECT
    TRANSITIVE   The driver <u>stopped</u> the <u>bus</u> at the corner.

2. A **linking verb** expresses a state of being or a condition. A linking verb connects a noun or pronoun to words that describe the noun or pronoun.

Common linking verbs are forms of the verb *be* (*is, are, was, were, being, been*), *become, feel, grow, look, remain, seem, smell, sound, stay,* and *taste*.

Their child <u>grew</u> tall.

The office <u>looks</u> messy.

Mr. Davenport <u>is</u> our accountant.

3. **A helping (auxiliary) verb** helps another verb, called the **main verb**, to convey when the action occurred (through verb tense) and to form questions. One or more helping verbs and the main verb together form a **verb phrase.** Some helping verbs, called **modals,** are always helping verbs:

    can, could   shall, should
    may, might   will, would
    must, ought to

The other helping verbs can sometimes function as main verbs as well:

    am, are, be, been, being, did, do, does
    had, has, have
    is, was, were

The verb *be* is a very irregular verb, with eight forms instead of the usual five: *am, is, are, be, being, been, was, were.*

HELPING   MAIN
VERB   VERB

The store <u>will</u> <u>close</u> early on holidays.

HELPING   MAIN
VERB   VERB

<u>Will</u> the store <u>close</u> early on New Year's Eve?

Forms of the Verb

All verbs except *be* have five forms: the **base form** (or dictionary form), the **past tense,** the **past participle,** the **present participle,** and the **-s form.** The first three forms are called the verb's **principal parts.** The infinitive consists of *to* plus a base form: *to go, to study, to talk.* For **regular verbs,** the past tense and past participle are formed by adding *-d* or *-ed* to the base form. **Irregular verbs** follow no set pattern to form their past tense and past participle.

TENSE	REGULAR	IRREGULAR
Infinitive	work	eat
Past tense	worked	ate
Past participle	worked	eaten
Present participle	working	eating
-s form	works	eats

Verbs change form to agree with their subjects in person and number (see p. 274); to express the time of their action (**tense**); to express whether the action is a fact, command, or wish (**mood**); and to indicate whether the subject is the doer or the receiver of the action (**voice**).

Principal Parts of Irregular Verbs

Consult the following list and your dictionary for the principal parts of irregular verbs.

BASE FORM	PAST TENSE	PAST PARTICIPLE
be	was, were	been
become	became	become
begin	began	begun
bite	bit	bitten
blow	blew	blown
burst	burst	burst
catch	caught	caught
choose	chose	chosen
come	came	come
dive	dived, dove	dived
do	did	done
draw	drew	drawn
drive	drove	driven
eat	ate	eaten
fall	fell	fallen
find	found	found
fling	flung	flung
fly	flew	flown
get	got	gotten
give	gave	given
go	went	gone
grow	grew	grown
have	had	had
know	knew	known
lay	laid	laid
lead	led	led
leave	left	left
lie	lay	lain
lose	lost	lost
ride	rode	ridden
ring	rang	rung
rise	rose	risen
say	said	said
set	set	set
sit	sat	sat
speak	spoke	spoken
swear	swore	sworn
swim	swam	swum
tear	tore	torn
tell	told	told
throw	threw	thrown
wear	wore	worn
write	wrote	written

Tense

The **tenses** of a verb express time. They convey whether an action, process, or event takes place in the present, past, or future.

The three **simple tenses** are **present, past,** and **future.** The **simple present** tense is the base form of the verb (and the *-s* form of third-person singular subjects; see p. 264); the **simple past** tense is the past-tense form; and the **simple future** tense consists of the helping verb *will* plus the base form.

The **perfect tenses,** which indicate completed action, are **present perfect, past perfect,** and **future perfect.** They are formed by adding the helping verbs *have* (or *has*), *had,* or *will have* to the past participle.

In addition to the simple and perfect tenses, there are six progressive tenses. The **simple progressive tenses** are the **present progressive,** the **past progressive,** and the **future progressive.** The progressive tenses are used for continuing actions or actions in progress. These progressive tenses are formed by adding the present, past, and future forms of the verb *be* to the present participle. The **perfect progressive tenses** are the **present perfect progressive,** the **past perfect progressive,** and the **future perfect progressive.** They are formed by adding the present perfect, past perfect, and future perfect forms of the verb *be* to the present participle.

The following chart shows all the tenses for a regular verb and an irregular verb in the first person. (For more on tenses, see p. 264.)

TENSE	REGULAR	IRREGULAR
Simple present	I talk	I go
Simple past	I talked	I went
Simple future	I will talk	I will go
Present perfect	I have talked	I have gone
Past perfect	I had talked	I had gone
Future perfect	I will have talked	I will have gone
Present progressive	I am talking	I am going
Past progressive	I was talking	I was going
Future progressive	I will be talking	I will be going
Present perfect progressive	I have been talking	I have been going
Past perfect progressive	I had been talking	I had been going
Future perfect progressive	I will have been talking	I will have been going

Mood

The mood of a verb indicates the writer's attitude toward the action. There are three moods in English: **indicative**, **imperative**, and **subjunctive**.

The **indicative mood** is used for ordinary statements of fact or questions.

The light <u>flashed</u> on and off all night.

<u>Did</u> you <u>check</u> the batteries?

The **imperative mood** is used for commands, suggestions, or directions. The subject of a verb in the imperative mood is *you*, though it is not always included.

<u>Stop</u> shouting!

<u>Come</u> to New York for a visit.

<u>Turn</u> right at the next corner.

The **subjunctive mood** is used for wishes, requirements, recommendations, and statements contrary to fact. For statements contrary to fact or for wishes, the past tense of the verb is used. For the verb *be,* only the past-tense form *were* is used.

If I <u>had</u> a million dollars, I'd take a trip around the world.

If my supervisor <u>were</u> promoted, I would be eligible for her job.

To express suggestions, recommendations, or requirements, the infinitive form is often used.

I recommend that the houses <u>be</u> sold after the landscaping is done.

The registrar required that Maureen <u>pay</u> her bill before attending class.

Voice

Transitive verbs (those that take objects) may be in either the active voice or the passive voice (see p. 272). In an **active-voice** sentence, the subject performs the action described by the verb; that is, the subject is the actor. In a **passive-voice** sentence, the subject is the receiver of the action. The passive voice of a verb is formed by using an appropriate form of the helping verb *be* and the past participle of the main verb.

SUBJECT   ACTIVE
IS ACTOR   VOICE
Dr. Hillel <u>delivered</u> the report on global warming.

SUBJECT IS RECEIVER   PASSIVE VOICE
The report on global warming <u>was delivered</u> by Dr. Hillel.

EXERCISE 2

Directions: Revise the following sentences, changing each verb from the present tense to the tense indicated.

EXAMPLE   I <u>check</u> the inventory of office supplies.

PAST TENSE   *I checked the inventory of office supplies.*

1. They <u>explain</u> the problem to the computer technician.

    SIMPLE FUTURE _____

2. Kwan <u>reads</u> fairy tales to his daughter.

    PRESENT PROGRESSIVE _____

3. I <u>sell</u> the most product replacement plans.

    PAST PERFECT _____

4. The carefree days of summer <u>come</u> to an end.

    FUTURE PROGRESSIVE _____

5. Scientists <u>detect</u> evidence of liquid water on one of Saturn's moons.

    PRESENT PERFECT _____

6. Robert <u>laughs</u> at his cat's attempt to catch a fly.

    PAST PROGRESSIVE _____

7. I <u>complete</u> my degree requirements in May.

    FUTURE PERFECT _____

8. Darren <u>prepares</u> his final presentation for the course.

    PAST PERFECT PROGRESSIVE _____

9. The campus singing groups <u>rehearse</u> for two months.

    FUTURE PERFECT PROGRESSIVE _____

10. Emily and Teresa <u>play</u> soccer on the weekends.

    PRESENT PERFECT PROGRESSIVE _____

A.4 ADJECTIVES

Adjectives modify nouns and pronouns. That is, they describe, identify, qualify, or limit the meaning of nouns and pronouns. An adjective answers the question *Which one? What kind?* or *How many?* about the word it modifies.

WHICH ONE?   The <u>twisted</u>, <u>torn</u> umbrella was of no use to its owner.

WHAT KIND?   The <u>spotted</u> owl has caused <u>heated</u> arguments in the Northwest.

HOW MANY?   <u>Many</u> customers waited for <u>four</u> days for telephone service to be restored.

In form, adjectives can be **positive** (implying no comparison), **comparative** (comparing two items), or **superlative** (comparing three or more items). (See p. 185 for more on the forms of adjectives.)

POSITIVE

The computer is <u>fast</u>.

COMPARATIVE

Your computer is <u>faster</u> than mine.

SUPERLATIVE

This is the <u>fastest</u> computer I have ever used.

There are two general categories of adjectives. **Descriptive adjectives** name a quality of the person, place, thing, or idea they describe: *mysterious man, green pond, healthy complexion*. **Limiting adjectives** narrow the scope of the person, place, or thing they describe: *my computer, this tool, second try*.

Descriptive Adjectives

A **regular** (or **attributive**) adjective appears next to (usually before) the word it modifies. Several adjectives can modify the same word.

The <u>enthusiastic</u> <u>new</u> hairstylist gave <u>short</u>, <u>lopsided</u> haircuts.

The <u>wealthy</u> dealer bought an <u>immense</u> <u>blue</u> vase.

Sometimes nouns function as adjectives modifying other nouns: *tree house, hamburger bun*.

A **predicate adjective** follows a linking verb and modifies or describes the subject of the sentence or clause (see p. 576; see p. 585 on clauses).

PREDICATE ADJECTIVE

The meeting was <u>long</u>. [Modifies the subject, *meeting*.]

Limiting Adjectives

1. The **definite article**, *the,* and the **indefinite articles,** *a* and *an,* are classified as adjectives. *A* and *an* are used when it is not important to specify a particular noun or when the object named is not known to the reader (*A radish adds color to a salad*). *The* is used when it is important to specify one or more of a particular noun or when the object named is known to the reader or has already been mentioned (*The radishes from the garden are on the table*).

    A squirrel visited the feeder that I just built. The squirrel tried to eat some bird food.

2. When the possessive pronouns *my, your, his, her, its, our,* and *their* are used as modifiers before nouns, they are considered **possessive adjectives.**

    Your friend borrowed my laptop for his trip.

3. When the demonstrative pronouns *this, that, these,* and *those* are used as modifiers before nouns, they are called **demonstrative adjectives.** *This* and *these* modify nouns close to the writer; *that* and *those* modify nouns more distant from the writer.

    Buy these formatted disks, not those unformatted ones.

    This freshman course is a prerequisite for those advanced courses.

4. **Cardinal adjectives** are words used in counting: *one, two, twenty,* and so on.

    I read four biographies of Jack Kerouac and seven articles about his work.

5. **Ordinal adjectives** note position in a series.

    The first biography was too sketchy, whereas the second one was too detailed.

6. **Indefinite adjectives** provide nonspecific, general information about the quantities and amounts of the nouns they modify. Some common indefinite adjectives are *another, any, enough, few, less, little, many, more, much, several,* and *some.*

    Several people asked me if I had enough blankets or if I wanted the thermostat turned up a few degrees.

7. The **interrogative adjectives** *what, which,* and *whose* modify nouns and pronouns used in questions.

    Which radio station do you like? Whose music do you prefer?

8. The words *which* and *what,* along with *whichever* and *whatever,* are **relative adjectives** when they modify nouns and introduce subordinate clauses.

    She couldn't decide which job she wanted to take.

9. **Proper adjectives** are adjectives derived from proper nouns: *Spain* (noun), *Spanish* (adjective); *Freud* (noun), *Freudian* (adjective). Most proper adjectives are capitalized.

    Shakespeare lived in Elizabethan England.

    The speaker used many French expressions.

EXERCISE 3

Directions: Revise each of the following sentences by adding at least three adjectives.

EXAMPLE   My jacket provided little protection from the wind.

REVISED   *My flimsy jacket provided little protection from the bitter,*
gusting wind.

1. The aroma of freshly baked bread greeted us as we entered the farmhouse.

_____

_____

2. Marvin's goal is to establish a preschool program that will meet the needs of children.

_____

_____

3. The barking of my neighbor's dog kept me awake for most of the night.

_____

_____

4. In the lab, students must follow rules about the use of equipment and materials.

_____

_____

5. I could hear my friend's laugh rising above the voices of other people at the reception.

_____

_____

6. A customer service representative must have communication skills and a patient personality.

_____

_____

7. My daughter constructs buildings out of blocks to house her collection of toy animals.

_____

_____

8. The painting that Akiko exhibited at the student art show was a success.

_____

_____

9. The lights of the aurora borealis created a display in the night sky.

_____

_____

10. As a volunteer at the local animal shelter, Susan solicits donations and helps find owners for the pets.

_____

_____

A.5 ADVERBS

Adverbs modify verbs, adjectives, other adverbs, or entire sentences or clauses (see p. 585 on clauses). Like adjectives, adverbs describe, qualify, or limit the meaning of the words they modify.

An adverb answers the question *How? When? Where? How often?* or *To what extent?* about the word it modifies.

HOW?	Cheryl moved <u>awkwardly</u> because of her stiff neck.
WHEN?	I arrived <u>yesterday</u>.
WHERE?	They searched <u>everywhere</u>.
HOW OFTEN?	He telephoned <u>repeatedly</u>.
TO WHAT EXTENT?	Simon was <u>rather</u> slow to answer his e-mail.

Many adverbs end in *-ly* (*lazily, happily*), but some adverbs do not (*fast, here, much, well, rather, everywhere, never, so*), and some words that end in *-ly* are not adverbs (*lively, friendly, lonely*). Like all other parts of speech, an adverb may be best identified by examining its function within a sentence.

I <u>quickly</u> skimmed the book. [Modifies the verb *skimmed*]

<u>Very</u> angry customers crowded the service desk. [Modifies the adjective *angry*]

He was injured <u>quite</u> seriously. [Modifies the adverb *seriously*]

<u>Apparently</u>, the job was bungled. [Modifies the whole sentence]

Like adjectives, adverbs have three forms: **positive** (does not suggest any comparison), **comparative** (compares two actions or conditions), and **superlative** (compares three or more actions or conditions; see also p. 185).

POSITIVE POSITIVE

Andy rose early and crept downstairs quietly.

COMPARATIVE COMPARATIVE

Jim rose earlier than Andy and crept downstairs more quietly.

SUPERLATIVE

Bill rose the earliest of anyone in the house and crept downstairs most quietly.

SUPERLATIVE

Some adverbs, called **conjunctive adverbs** (or **adverbial conjunctions**)—such as *however, therefore,* and *besides*—connect the ideas of one sentence or clause to those of a previous sentence or clause. They can appear anywhere in a sentence. (See p. 155 for how to punctuate sentences containing conjunctive adverbs.)

CONJUNCTIVE ADVERB

James did not want to go to the library on Saturday; however, he knew the books were overdue.

The sporting-goods store was crowded because of the sale. Leila, therefore, was asked to work extra hours.

CONJUNCTIVE ADVERB

Some common conjunctive adverbs are listed below, including several phrases that function as conjunctive adverbs.

accordingly	for example	meanwhile	otherwise
also	further	moreover	similarly
anyway	furthermore	namely	still
as a result	hence	nevertheless	then
at the same time	however	next	thereafter
besides	incidentally	nonetheless	therefore
certainly	indeed	now	thus
consequently	instead	on the contrary	undoubtedly
finally	likewise	on the other hand	

EXERCISE 4

Directions: Write a sentence using each of the following comparative or superlative adverbs.

EXAMPLE   earlier: The library is open until 5:00 on weekdays, but it closes earlier on weekends.

1. fastest: _____

_____

2. less carefully: _____

_____

3. most cheaply: _____

_____

4. higher: _____

_____

5. best: _____

_____

6. more generously: _____

_____

7. hardest: _____

_____

8. closer: _____

_____

9. least efficiently: _____

_____

10. better: _____

_____

A.6 CONJUNCTIONS

Conjunctions connect words, phrases, and clauses. There are three kinds of conjunctions: **coordinating**, **correlative**, and **subordinating**. **Coordinating** and **correlative conjunctions** connect words, phrases, or clauses of equal grammatical rank. (A **phrase** is a group of related words lacking a subject, a predicate, or both. A **clause** is a group of words containing a subject and a predicate; see pp. 573 and 574.)

1. The **coordinating conjunctions** are *and, but, nor, or, for, so,* and *yet.* These words must connect words or word groups of the same kind. Therefore, two nouns may be connected by *and,* but a noun and a clause cannot be. *For* and *so* can connect only independent clauses.

COORDINATING

NOUN   CONJUNCTION   NOUN

We studied the novels of Toni Morrison and Alice Walker.

COORDINATING
CONJUNCTION

VERB | VERB

The copilot successfully flew <u>and</u> landed the disabled plane.

COORDINATING INDEPENDENT
INDEPENDENT CLAUSE CONJUNCTION CLAUSE

The carpentry course sounded interesting, <u>so</u> Meg enrolled.

COORDINATING SUBORDINATE
INDEPENDENT CLAUSE CONJUNCTION CLAUSE

We hoped that the mail would come soon <u>and</u> that it would contain
our bonus check.

2. **Correlative conjunctions** are pairs of words that link and relate grammatically equivalent parts of a sentence. Some common correlative conjunctions are *either/or, neither/nor, both/and, not/but, not only/but also,* and
whether/or. Correlative conjunctions are always used in pairs.

CORRELATIVE CONJUNCTIONS

<u>Either</u> the electricity was off, <u>or</u> the bulb had burned out.

3. **Subordinating conjunctions** connect dependent, or subordinate, clauses
to independent clauses (see p. 105). Some common subordinating conjunctions are *although, because, if, since, until, when, where,* and *while.*

SUBORDINATING CONJUNCTION

<u>Although</u> the movie got bad reviews, it drew big crowds.

SUBORDINATING CONJUNCTION

She received a lot of mail <u>because</u> she was a reliable correspondent.

A.7 PREPOSITIONS

A **preposition** links and relates its **object** (a noun or a pronoun) to the rest of
the sentence. Prepositions often show relationships of time, place, direction,
and manner.

PREPOSITION   OBJECT OF PREPOSITION

I walked <u>around</u> the <u>block</u>.

PREPOSITION   OBJECT OF PREPOSITION

She called <u>during</u> our <u>meeting</u>.

COMMON PREPOSITIONS				
along	besides	from	past	up
among	between	in	since	upon
around	beyond	near	through	with
at	by	off	till	within
before	despite	on	to	without
behind	down	onto	toward	
below	during	out	under	
beneath	except	outside	underneath	
beside	for	over	until	

Some prepositions consist of more than one word; they are called **phrasal prepositions** or **compound prepositions**.

PHRASAL PREPOSITION   OBJECT OF PREPOSITION

According to our records, you have enough credits to graduate.

PHRASAL PREPOSITION   OBJECT OF PREPOSITION

We decided to make the trip in spite of the snowstorm.

COMMON COMPOUND PREPOSITIONS		
according to	in addition to	on account of
aside from	in front of	out of
as of	in place of	prior to
as well as	in regard to	with regard to
because of	in spite of	with respect to
by means of	instead of	

The object of the preposition often has modifiers.

Not a sound came from the child's room except a gentle snoring.

Sometimes a preposition has more than one object (a **compound object**).

The laundromat was between campus and home.

Usually the preposition comes before its object. In interrogative sentences, however, the preposition sometimes follows its object.

OBJECT OF PREPOSITION   PREPOSITION

What did your supervisor ask you about?

The preposition, the object or objects of the preposition, and the object's modifiers all form a **prepositional phrase**.

PREPOSITIONAL PHRASE

The scientist conducted her experiment throughout the afternoon and early evening.

There may be many prepositional phrases in a sentence.

PREPOSITIONAL PHRASE   PREPOSITIONAL PHRASE

The water from the open hydrant flowed into the street.

The noisy kennel was underneath the beauty salon, despite the complaints of customers.

Alongside the weedy railroad tracks, an old hotel with faded grandeur stood near the abandoned brick station on the edge of town.

Prepositional phrases frequently function as adjectives or adverbs. If a prepositional phrase modifies a noun or pronoun, it functions as an adjective. If it modifies a verb, adjective, or adverb, it functions as an adverb.

The auditorium inside the conference center has a special sound system. [Adjective modifying the noun *auditorium*]

The doctor looked cheerfully at the patient and handed the lab results across the desk. [Adverbs modifying the verbs *looked* and *handed*]

EXERCISE 5

Directions: Expand each of the following sentences by adding a prepositional phrase in the blank.

EXAMPLE   Hummingbirds sip nectar ~~from flowers~~.

1. The meteorologist predicts that the heat wave will continue _____ .

2. _____ , Kate sat in the front row and took careful notes.

3. I cautiously stepped _____ to keep my new shoes dry.

4. The batter hit the ball so hard that it flew _____ .

5. If you misplace your house key, use the extra key located _____ .

6. The orchestra conductor walked _____ and raised his baton.

7. My daughter always hides _____ when we play hide and seek.

8. When Sofia walks _____ , she often picks up seashells.

9. Our manager said the report must be completed _____ .

10. When Jamal opened the door, the cat ran _____ and escaped outside.

A.8 INTERJECTIONS

Interjections are words that express emotion or surprise. They are followed by an exclamation point, comma, or period, depending on whether they stand alone or serve as part or all of a sentence. Interjections are used in speech more than in writing.

<u>Wow</u>! What an announcement!

<u>So</u>, was that lost letter ever found?

<u>Well</u>, I'd better be going.

B Understanding the Parts of Sentences

A **sentence** is a group of words that expresses a complete thought about something or someone. A sentence must contain a **subject** and a **predicate**.

Subject	*Predicate*
Telephones	ring.
Cecilia	laughed.
Time	will tell.

Depending on their purpose and punctuation, sentences are **declarative, interrogative, exclamatory,** or **imperative.**

A **declarative sentence** makes a statement. It ends with a period.

SUBJECT PREDICATE
The snow fell steadily.

An **interrogative sentence** asks a question. It ends with a question mark (?).

SUBJECT   PREDICATE
Who called?

An **exclamatory sentence** conveys strong emotion. It ends with an exclamation point (!).

SUBJECT   PREDICATE
Your photograph is in the company newsletter!

An **imperative sentence** gives an order or makes a request. It ends with either a period or an exclamation point, depending on how mild or strong the command or request is. In an imperative sentence, the subject is *you,* but this often is not included.

PREDICATE
Get me a fire extinguisher now! [The subject *you* is understood: (*You*) get me a fire extinguisher now!]

B.1 SUBJECTS

The **subject** of a sentence is whom or what the sentence is about. It is who or what performs or receives the action expressed in the predicate. The subject is often a **noun**, a word that names a person, place, thing, or idea.

> Julia worked on her math homework.

> The rose bushes must be watered.

> Honesty is the best policy.

The subject of a sentence can also be a **pronoun**, a word that refers to or substitutes for a noun.

> She revised the memo three times.

> I will attend the sales meeting.

> Although the ink spilled, it did not go on my shirt.

The subject of a sentence can also be a group of words used as a noun.

> Reading e-mail from friends is my idea of a good time.

Simple Versus Complete Subjects

The **simple subject** is the noun or pronoun that names what the sentence is about. It does not include any **modifiers**—that is, words that describe, identify, qualify, or limit the meaning of the noun or pronoun.

> SIMPLE SUBJECT
> The bright red concert poster caught everyone's eye.

> SIMPLE SUBJECT
> High-speed computers have revolutionized the banking industry.

When the subject of a sentence is a proper noun (the name of a particular person, place, or thing), the entire name is considered the simple subject.

> SIMPLE SUBJECT
> Martin Luther King, Jr., was a famous leader.

The simple subject of an imperative sentence is *you*.

> SIMPLE SUBJECT
> [You] Remember to bring the sales brochures.

The **complete subject** is the simple subject plus its modifiers.

> COMPLETE SUBJECT
> SIMPLE SUBJECT
> The sleek, black limousine waited outside the church.

COMPLETE SUBJECT

Fondly remembered as a gifted songwriter, fiddle player, and storyteller, Quintin Lotus Dickey lived in a cabin in Paoli, Indiana.

SIMPLE SUBJECT

Compound Subjects

Some sentences contain two or more subjects joined with a coordinating conjunction (*and, but, nor, or, for, so, yet*). Those subjects together form a **compound subject.**

COMPOUND SUBJECT

Maria and I completed the marathon.

COMPOUND SUBJECT

The computer, the printer, and the DVD player were not usable during the blackout.

B.2 PREDICATES

The **predicate** indicates what the subject does, what happened to the subject, or what is being said about the subject. The predicate must include a **verb**, a word or group of words that expresses an action or a state of being (for example, *run, invent, build, know, will decide, become*).

Joy swam sixty laps.

The thunderstorm replenished the reservoir.

Sometimes the verb consists of only one word, as in the previous examples. Often, however, the main verb is accompanied by a **helping verb** (see p. 557).

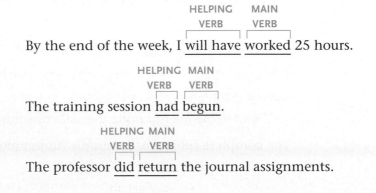

HELPING   MAIN
VERB   VERB

By the end of the week, I will have worked 25 hours.

HELPING MAIN
VERB   VERB

The training session had begun.

HELPING MAIN
VERB   VERB

The professor did return the journal assignments.

Simple Versus Complete Predicates

The **simple predicate** is the main verb plus its helping verbs (together known as the **verb phrase**). The simple predicate does not include any modifiers.

SIMPLE PREDICATE

The proctor hastily collected the blue books.

SIMPLE PREDICATE

The moderator had introduced the next speaker.

The **complete predicate** consists of the simple predicate, its modifiers, and any complements (words that complete the meaning of the verb; see p. 576). In general, the complete predicate includes everything in the sentence except the complete subject.

COMPLETE PREDICATE

SIMPLE PREDICATE

The music sounds better from the back of the room.

COMPLETE PREDICATE

SIMPLE PREDICATE

Bill decided to change the name of his company to something less controversial and confusing.

Compound Predicates

Some sentences have two or more predicates joined by a coordinating conjunction (*and, but, nor*). These predicates together form a **compound predicate**.

COMPOUND PREDICATE

Marcia unlocked her bicycle and rode away.

COMPOUND PREDICATE

The supermarket owner will survey his customers and order the specialized foods they desire.

EXERCISE 6

Directions: Underline the simple or compound subject and circle the simple or compound predicate in each of the following sentences.

EXAMPLE   Elizabeth Cady Stanton (championed) women's rights.

1. The coffee in the staff lounge tastes even worse than vending-machine coffee!

2. Of all the pediatricians in the clinic, Dr. Alvarez has the gentlest beside manner.

3. Students in the nursing program and staff of the local hospital are organizing a community health fair.

4. In their reviews of the new Italian restaurant, food critics praised the linguini with clam sauce and raved about the lobster ravioli.

5. By the end of next year, I will have repaid most of my student loans.

6. For many film stars of the 1940s, singing and dancing were essential job skills.

7. Kenji and his friend jog for thirty minutes most mornings and lift weights at least twice a week.

8. Last spring my sister took a criminal justice course and audited a sociology course.

9. Many well-known actors and other media celebrities made appearances at the political fund-raiser.

10. The art of modern sculptor Claes Oldenburg includes giant replicas of small, mundane objects such as a button or a lipstick.

B.3 COMPLEMENTS

A **complement** is a word or group of words used to complete the meaning of a subject or object. There are four kinds of complements: **subject complements**, which follow linking verbs; **direct objects** and **indirect objects**, which follow transitive verbs (verbs that take an object); and **object complements**, which follow direct objects.

Linking Verbs and Subject Complements

A linking verb (such as *be, become, seem, feel, taste*) links the subject to a **subject complement**, a noun or adjective that renames or describes the subject. (See p. 556 for more about linking verbs.) Nouns that function as complements are called **predicate nominatives** or **predicate nouns**. Adjectives that function as complements are called **predicate adjectives.**

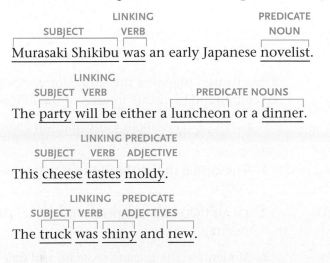

Direct Objects

A **direct object** is a noun or pronoun that receives the action of a transitive verb (see p. 556). A direct object answers the question *What?* or *Whom?*

TRANSITIVE VERB   DIRECT OBJECT

The pharmacist helped us. [The pharmacist helped *whom?*]

TRANSITIVE VERB   DIRECT OBJECTS

Jillian borrowed a bicycle and a visor. [Jillian borrowed *what?*]

Indirect Objects

An **indirect object** is a noun or pronoun that receives the action of the verb indirectly. Indirect objects name the person or thing *to whom* or *for whom* something is done.

TRANSITIVE   INDIRECT   DIRECT
VERB   OBJECT   OBJECT

The computer technician gave me the bill. [He gave the bill *to whom?*]

TRANSITIVE VERB   INDIRECT OBJECTS   DIRECT OBJECTS

Eric bought his wife and son some sandwiches and milk. [He bought food *for whom?*]

Object Complements

An **object complement** is a noun or adjective that modifies (describes) or re-names the direct object. Object complements appear with verbs like *name, find, think, elect, appoint, choose,* and *consider.*

DIRECT OBJECT   NOUN AS OBJECT COMPLEMENT

We appointed Dean our representative. [*Representative* renames the direct object, *Dean.*]

DIRECT OBJECT   ADJECTIVE AS OBJECT COMPLEMENT

The judge found the defendant innocent of the charges. [*Innocent* modi-fies the direct object, *defendant.*]

B.4 BASIC SENTENCE PATTERNS

There are five basic sentence patterns in English. They are built with combi-nations of subjects, predicates, and complements. The order of these ele-ments within a sentence may change, or a sentence may become long and complicated when modifiers, phrases, or clauses are added. Nonetheless, one of five basic patterns stands at the heart of every sentence.

PATTERN 1

Subject	+	Predicate
I		shivered.
Cynthia		swam.

PATTERN 2

Subject	+	Predicate	+	Direct Object
Anthony		ordered		a new desk.
We		wanted		freedom.

PATTERN 3

Subject	+	Predicate	+	Subject Complement
The woman		was		a welder.
Our course		is		interesting.

PATTERN 4

Subject	+	Predicate	+	Indirect Object	+	Direct Object
My friend		loaned		me		a laptop.
The company		sent		employees		a questionnaire.

PATTERN 5

Subject	+	Predicate	+	Direct Object	+	Object Complement
I		consider		her singing		exceptional.
Lampwick		called		Jiminy Cricket		a beetle.

EXERCISE 7

Directions: Complete each sentence with a word or words that will function as the type of complement indicated.

EXAMPLE   The students elected Liang <u>president of the Student Senate.</u>
                                                    object complement

1. These gardenias smell so _____ that they are making me sneeze.
                                predicate adjective

2. Matt checked the _____ of the previous meeting to verify that the
                         direct object

   committee had reached agreement on the issue.

3. When my kids were young, I always sang _____ lullabies at bedtime.
                                              indirect object

4. Some fans were not impressed by the band's latest CD, but I found the new songs _____ and _____.
   object complements

5. My grandparents have been _____ for 50 years, and they are still in love.
   predicate adjective

6. Caitlin e-mailed her _____ a map showing the location of her new apartment.
   indirect object

7. As I spend more time with my co-worker, we are becoming closer _____.
   predicate noun

8. When Damian walked across the stage to receive his diploma, he seemed very _____ and _____.
   predicate adjectives

9. Latoya and her business partner are planning to open a new _____.
   direct object

10. The professor warned students that keeping up with the assigned reading in this course could be a _____.
    predicate noun

B.5 EXPANDING THE SENTENCE WITH ADJECTIVES AND ADVERBS

A sentence may consist of just a subject and a verb.

Linda studied.

Rumors circulated.

Most sentences, however, contain additional information about the subject and the verb. Information is commonly added in three ways:

- **by using adjectives and adverbs**
- **by using phrases** (groups of words that lack either a subject or a predicate or both)
- **by using clauses** (groups of words that contain both a subject and a predicate)

Using Adjectives and Adverbs to Expand Your Sentences

Adjectives are words used to modify or describe nouns and pronouns (see p. 562). Adjectives answer questions about nouns and pronouns such as

Which one? What kind? How many? Using adjectives is one way to add detail and information to sentences.

WITHOUT ADJECTIVES   Dogs barked at cats.

WITH ADJECTIVES   Our <u>three</u> <u>large</u>, <u>brown</u> dogs barked at <u>the</u> <u>two</u> <u>terrified</u> <u>spotted</u> cats.

Note: Sometimes nouns and participles are used as adjectives (see p. 582 on participles).

NOUN USED AS ADJECTIVE

People are rediscovering the <u>milk</u> bottle.

PRESENT PARTICIPLE   PAST PARTICIPLE
USED AS ADJECTIVE   USED AS ADJECTIVE

Mrs. Simon had a <u>swimming</u> pool with a <u>broken</u> drain.

Adverbs add information to sentences by modifying or describing verbs, adjectives, or other adverbs (see p. 565). An adverb usually answers the question *How? When? Where? How often?* or *To what extent?*

WITHOUT ADVERBS   I will clean.

The audience applauded.

WITH ADVERBS   I will clean <u>very</u> <u>thoroughly</u> <u>tomorrow</u>.

The audience applauded <u>loudly</u> and <u>enthusiastically</u>.

B.6 EXPANDING THE SENTENCE WITH PHRASES

A **phrase** is a group of related words that lacks a subject, a predicate, or both. A phrase cannot stand alone as a sentence. Phrases can appear at the beginning, middle, or end of a sentence.

WITHOUT PHRASES   I noticed the stain.

Sal researched the topic.

Manuela arose.

WITH PHRASES   <u>Upon entering the room</u>, I noticed the stain <u>on the expensive carpet</u>.

<u>At the local aquarium</u>, Sal researched the topic <u>of shark attacks</u>.

<u>An amateur astronomer</u>, Manuela arose <u>in the middle of the night to observe the lunar eclipse</u> but, <u>after waiting ten minutes in the cold</u>, gave up.

There are eight kinds of phrases: **noun; verb; prepositional;** three kinds of **verbal phrases (participial, gerund, and infinitive); appositive;** and **absolute.**

Noun and Verb Phrases

A noun plus its modifiers is a **noun phrase** (*red shoes, the quiet house*). A main verb plus its helping verb is a **verb phrase** (*had been exploring, is sleeping;* see p. 557 on helping verbs.)

Prepositional Phrases

A **prepositional phrase** consists of a preposition (for example, *in, above, with, at, behind*), an object of the preposition (a noun or pronoun), and any modifiers of the object. (See p. 569 for a list of common prepositions.) A prepositional phrase functions like an adjective (modifying a noun or pronoun) or an adverb (modifying a verb, adjective, or adverb). You can use prepositional phrases to tell more about people, places, objects, or actions. A prepositional phrase usually adds information about time, place, direction, manner, or degree.

As Adjectives

The woman with the briefcase is giving a presentation on meditation techniques.

Both of the telephones behind the partition were ringing.

As Adverbs

The fire drill occurred in the morning.

I was curious about the new human resources director.

The conference speaker came from Australia.

With horror, the crowd watched the rhinoceros's tether stretch to the breaking point.

A prepositional phrase can function as part of the complete subject or as part of the complete predicate but should not be confused with the simple subject or simple predicate.

COMPLETE SUBJECT | COMPLETE PREDICATE

SIMPLE SUBJECT   PREPOSITIONAL PHRASE   SIMPLE PREDICATE

The red leather-bound volumes on the dusty shelf were filled with obscure facts.

PREPOSITIONAL PHRASE

COMPLETE PREDICATE

SIMPLE PREDICATE   PREPOSITIONAL PHRASE

Pat ducked quickly behind the potted fern.

Verbal Phrases

A **verbal** is a verb form that cannot function as the main verb of a sentence. The three kinds of verbals are **participles**, **gerunds**, and **infinitives**. A **verbal phrase** consists of a verbal and its modifiers.

Participles and Participial Phrases

All verbs have two participles: present and past. The **present participle** is formed by adding *-ing* to the infinitive form (*walking, riding, being*). The **past participle** of regular verbs is formed by adding *-d* or *-ed* to the infinitive form (*walked, baked*). The past participle of irregular verbs has no set pattern (*ridden, been*). (See p. 558 for a list of common irregular verbs and their past participles.) Both the present participle and the past participle can function as adjectives modifying nouns and pronouns.

PAST PARTICIPLE   PRESENT PARTICIPLE
AS ADJECTIVE   AS ADJECTIVE

Irritated, Martha circled the confusing traffic rotary once again.

A **participial phrase** consists of a participle and any of its modifiers.

PARTICIPIAL PHRASE

PARTICIPLE

We listened for Isabella climbing the rickety stairs.

PARTICIPIAL PHRASE

PARTICIPLE

Disillusioned with the whole system, Kay sat down to think.

PARTICIPIAL PHRASE

PARTICIPLE

The singer, having caught a bad cold, canceled his performance.

Gerunds and Gerund Phrases

A **gerund** is the present participle (the *-ing* form) of the verb used as a noun.

Shoveling is good exercise.

Rex enjoyed gardening.

A **gerund phrase** consists of a gerund and its modifiers. A gerund phrase, like a gerund, is used as a noun and can therefore function in a sentence as a subject, a direct or indirect object, an object of a preposition, a subject complement, or an appositive.

GERUND PHRASE

Photocopying the report took longer than Alice anticipated. [Subject]

GERUND PHRASE

The director considered making another monster movie. [Direct object]

GERUND PHRASE

She gave running three miles daily credit for her health. [Indirect object]

GERUND PHRASE

Before learning Greek, Omar spoke only English. [Object of the preposition]

GERUND PHRASE

Her business is designing collapsible furniture. [Subject complement]

GERUND PHRASE

Wayne's trick, memorizing license plates, has come in handy. [Appositive]

Infinitives and Infinitive Phrases

The **infinitive** is the base form of the verb as it appears in the dictionary preceded by the word *to*. An **infinitive phrase** consists of the word *to* plus the infinitive and any modifiers. An infinitive phrase can function as a noun, an adjective, or an adverb. When it is used as a noun, an infinitive phrase can be a subject, object, complement, or appositive.

INFINITIVE PHRASE

To love one's enemies is a noble goal. [Noun used as subject]

INFINITIVE PHRASE

The season to sell bulbs is the fall. [Adjective modifying *season*]

INFINITIVE PHRASE

The chess club met to practice for the state championship. [Adverb modifying *met*]

Sometimes the *to* in an infinitive phrase is not used.

Frank helped us learn the new accounting procedure. [The *to* before *learn* is understood.]

Note: Do not confuse infinitive phrases with prepositional phrases beginning with the preposition *to*. In an infinitive phrase, *to* is followed by a verb; in a prepositional phrase, *to* is followed by a noun or pronoun, or an adjective and a noun.

Appositive Phrases

An **appositive** is a noun that explains, restates, or adds new information about another noun. An **appositive phrase** consists of an appositive and its modifiers. (See p. 594 for punctuation of appositive phrases.)

APPOSITIVE

Claude Monet completed the painting *Water Lilies* around 1903. [Adds information about the noun *painting*]

APPOSITIVE PHRASE

APPOSITIVE

Francis, my neighbor with a large workshop, lent me a wrench. [Adds information about the noun *Francis*]

Absolute Phrases

An **absolute phrase** consists of a noun or pronoun and any modifiers followed by a participle or a participial phrase (see p. 595). An absolute phrase modifies an entire sentence, not any particular word within the sentence. It can appear anywhere in a sentence and is set off from the rest of the sentence with a comma or commas. There may be more than one absolute phrase in a sentence.

ABSOLUTE PHRASE

The winter being over, the geese returned.

ABSOLUTE PHRASE

Senator Arden began his speech, his voice rising to be heard over the loud applause.

ABSOLUTE PHRASE

A vacancy having occurred, the hotel manager called the first name on the reservations waiting list.

EXERCISE 8

Directions: Expand each of the following sentences by adding adjectives, adverbs, and/or phrases (prepositional, verbal, appositive, or absolute).

EXAMPLE   Mike and Chen studied.

EXPANDED   *The day before the exam, Mike and Chen studied*

together for three hours without a single break.

1. I hung a poster. _____

_____

2. The squirrel snatched a seed. _____

_____

3. Thomas invited Monica. _____

_____

4. Midori demonstrated. _____

_____

5. I am working. _____

_____

6. Tyrell included graphs. _____

_____

7. Canoeing was an experience. _____

_____

8. The leader scheduled a meeting. _____

_____

9. Angelina helped her grandfather. _____

_____

10. I walked. _____

_____

B.7 EXPANDING THE SENTENCE WITH CLAUSES

A **clause** is a group of words that contains a subject and a predicate. A clause is either **independent** (also called **main**) or **dependent** (also called **subordinate**).

An **independent clause** can stand alone as a grammatically complete sentence.

INDEPENDENT CLAUSE   INDEPENDENT CLAUSE

SUBJECT PREDICATE   SUBJECT PREDICATE

The alarm sounded, and I awoke.

INDEPENDENT CLAUSE · INDEPENDENT CLAUSE

SUBJECT · PREDICATE · SUBJECT · PREDICATE

The scientist worried. The experiment might fail.

INDEPENDENT CLAUSE · INDEPENDENT CLAUSE

SUBJECT · PREDICATE · SUBJECT · PREDICATE

He bandaged his ankle. It had been sprained.

A **dependent clause** has a subject and a predicate, but it cannot stand alone as a grammatically complete sentence because it does not express a complete thought. Most dependent clauses begin with either a **subordinating conjunction** or a **relative pronoun**. These words connect the dependent clause to an independent clause.

SUBORDINATING

CONJUNCTION · SUBJECT · PREDICATE

because the alarm sounded

SUBORDINATING

CONJUNCTION · SUBJECT · PREDICATE

that the experiment might fail

RELATIVE PRONOUN

(SUBJECT) · PREDICATE

which had been sprained

These clauses do not express complete thoughts and therefore cannot stand alone as sentences. When joined to independent clauses, however, dependent clauses function as adjectives, adverbs, and nouns and are known as **adjective** (or **relative**) **clauses**, **adverb clauses**, and **noun clauses**. Noun clauses can function as subjects, objects, or complements.

Common Subordinating Conjunctions		
after	inasmuch as	that
although	in case that	though
as	in order that	unless
as far as	insofar as	until
as if	in that	when
as soon as	now that	whenever
as though	once	where
because	provided that	wherever
before	rather than	whether
even if	since	while
even though	so that	why
how	supposing that	
if	than	
Relative Pronouns		
that	which	
what	who (whose, whom)	
whatever	whoever (whomever)	

Adjective Clause

DEPENDENT CLAUSE

He bandaged his ankle, which had been sprained. [Modifies *ankle*]

Adverb Clause

DEPENDENT CLAUSE

Because the alarm sounded, I awoke. [Modifies *awoke*]

Noun Clause

DEPENDENT CLAUSE

The scientist worried that the experiment might fail. [Direct object of *worried*]

Sometimes the relative pronoun or subordinating conjunction is implied or understood rather than stated. Also, a dependent clause may contain an implied predicate. When a dependent clause is missing an element that can clearly be supplied from the context of the sentence, it is called an **elliptical clause.**

ELLIPTICAL CLAUSE

The circus is more entertaining than television [is]. [*Is* is the understood predicate in the elliptical dependent clause.]

ELLIPTICAL CLAUSE

Canadian history is among the subjects [that] the book discusses. [*That* is the understood relative pronoun in the elliptical dependent clause.]

Relative pronouns are generally the subject or object in their clauses. *Who* and *whoever* change to *whom* and *whomever* when they function as objects.

B.8 BASIC SENTENCE CLASSIFICATIONS

Depending on its structure, a sentence can be classified as one of four basic types: **simple, compound, complex,** or **compound-complex.**

Simple Sentences

A **simple sentence** has one independent (main) clause and no dependent (subordinate) clauses (see p. 105). A simple sentence contains at least one subject and one predicate. It may have a compound subject, a compound predicate, and various phrases, but it has only one clause.

SUBJECT PREDICATE

Sap rises.

SUBJECT   COMPOUND PREDICATE

In the spring the sap rises in the maple trees and is boiled to make a thick, delicious syrup.

Compound Sentences

A **compound sentence** has at least two independent clauses and no dependent clauses (see p. 149). The two independent clauses are usually joined with a comma and a coordinating conjunction (*and, but, nor, or, for, so, yet*). Sometimes the two clauses are joined with a semicolon and no coordinating conjunction or with a semicolon and a conjunctive adverb like *nonetheless* or *still* followed by a comma. (See p. 566 on conjunctive adverbs and p. 155 on punctuation.)

INDEPENDENT CLAUSE

Reading a novel by Henry James is not like reading a thriller, but with patience the rewards are greater.

INDEPENDENT CLAUSE

INDEPENDENT CLAUSE   INDEPENDENT CLAUSE

I set out to explore the North River near home; I ended up at Charlie's Clam Bar.

INDEPENDENT CLAUSE

Complex Sentences

A **complex sentence** has one independent clause and one or more dependent clauses (see p. 149). The clauses are joined by subordinating conjunctions or relative pronouns (see p. 110).

INDEPENDENT CLAUSE   DEPENDENT CLAUSE

We tried to find topics to talk about while we waited for the bus.

INDEPENDENT CLAUSE   DEPENDENT CLAUSE

The receptionist greeted me warmly as I entered the office because I hadn't seen her in a long time.

DEPENDENT CLAUSE

Compound-Complex Sentences

A **compound-complex sentence** contains two or more independent clauses and one or more dependent clauses (see p. 150).

DEPENDENT CLAUSE   INDEPENDENT CLAUSE

If students work part-time, they must plan their studies carefully, and they must limit their social lives.

INDEPENDENT CLAUSE

INDEPENDENT CLAUSE   INDEPENDENT CLAUSE   INDEPENDENT CLAUSE

It was mid-March, and the pond had begun to melt; I walked toward it expectantly as I wondered if I could go skating one last time.

DEPENDENT CLAUSE   DEPENDENT CLAUSE

EXERCISE 9

Directions: Combine each of the following pairs of sentences into a single sentence by forming independent and/or dependent clauses. You may need to add, change, or delete words.

EXAMPLE   **a.** The sandals were not selling well.

            b. The store marked down the price of the sandals.

COMBINED   *The sandals were not selling well, so the store marked down the price.*

1. **a.** Alicia is good at making minor plumbing repairs.

   b. Alicia does not attempt to fix electrical problems.

   _____

   _____

2. **a.** My brother, an excellent gourmet cook, tried a new dessert recipe.

   b. The new dessert recipe was a total disaster.

   _____

   _____

3. **a.** Yuan previewed the course syllabus online.

   b. Yuan decided to take a different course instead.

   _____

   _____

4. **a.** First the clay tiles must be thoroughly dried in the sun.

    b. Then the clay tiles are fired in the kiln.

    _____

5. **a.** Only a few people signed up for the summer course.

    b. The summer course has been canceled.

    _____

6. **a.** Ezra, the host of the potluck barbecue, will grill hamburgers and veggie dogs.

    b. Each guest will bring beer or a side dish.

    _____

    _____

7. **a.** Rachel is enrolled in the local community college.

    b. Rachel is studying to become an emergency medical technician.

    _____

    _____

8. **a.** Keisha will babysit her sister's kids on Saturday.

    b. Keisha will take the kids to the park.

    _____

9. **a.** The Meals On Wheels program is looking for volunteers to deliver meals.

    b. The volunteers must use their own cars to deliver the meals.

    _____

    _____

10. **a.** Some students study best late at night.

    b. Other students do their best studying in the morning.

    _____

    _____

Using Punctuation Correctly

C.1 END PUNCTUATION

When to Use Periods

Use a period in the following situations:

1. **To end a sentence unless it is a question or an exclamation.**

   We washed the car even though we knew a thunderstorm was imminent.

Note: Use a period to end a sentence that states an indirect question or indirectly quotes someone's words or thoughts.

   INCORRECT   Margaret wondered if she would be on time?

   CORRECT   Margaret wondered if she would be on time.

2. **To punctuate many abbreviations.**

   M.D.   B.A.   P.M.   B.C.   Mr.   Ms.

Do not use periods in acronyms, such as *NATO* and *AIDS,* or in abbreviations for most organizations, such as *NBC* and *NAACP.*

Note: If a sentence ends with an abbreviation, the sentence has only one period, not two.

   The train was due to arrive at 7:00 P.M.

When to Use Question Marks

Use question marks after direct questions.

   How long can a coral snake grow?

If a quotation ends in a question mark, place the question mark within the closing quotation marks.

   She asked the grocer, "How old is this cheese?"

If a quotation is included in a sentence that asks a question, the question mark goes after the closing quotation mark.

   Did you say Margaret said, "I will not come"?

591

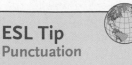
Note: Use a period, not a question mark, after an indirect question.

She asked the grocer how old the cheese was.

When to Use Exclamation Points

Use an exclamation point at the end of a sentence that expresses particular emphasis, excitement, or urgency. Use exclamation points sparingly, however, especially in academic writing.

What a beautiful day it is!   Dial 911 right now!

C.2 COMMAS

The comma is used to separate parts of a sentence from one another. If you omit a comma when it is needed, you risk making a clear and direct sentence confusing.

When to Use Commas

Use a comma in the following situations:

1. **Before a coordinating conjunction that joins two independent clauses** (see p. 125).

   Terry had planned to leave work early, but he was delayed.

2. **To separate a dependent (subordinate) clause from an independent clause when the dependent clause comes first in the sentence** (see p. 159).

   After I left the library, I went to the computer lab.

3. **To separate introductory words and phrases from the rest of the sentence.**

   Unfortunately, I forgot my umbrella.

   To pass the baton, I will need to locate my teammate.

   Exuberant over their victory, the football-team members carried the quarterback on their shoulders.

4. **To separate a nonrestrictive phrase or clause from the rest of a sentence.** A **nonrestrictive** phrase or clause is added to a sentence but does not change the sentence's basic meaning.

   To determine whether an element is nonrestrictive, read the sentence without the element. If the meaning of the sentence does not essentially change, then the commas are *necessary*.

   My sister, who is a mail carrier, is afraid of dogs. [The essential meaning of this sentence does not change if we read the sentence without the subordinate clause: *My sister is afraid of dogs.* Therefore, commas are needed.]

Mail carriers who have been bitten by dogs are afraid of them. [If we read this sentence without the subordinate clause, its meaning changes considerably: *Mail carriers are afraid of (dogs)*. It seems to say that *all* mail carriers are afraid of dogs. In this case, adding commas is not correct.]

5. **To separate three or more items in a series.**

   Note: A comma is *not* used *after* the last item in the series.

   I plan to take math, psychology, and writing next semester.

6. **To separate coordinate adjectives: two or more adjectives that are not joined by a coordinating conjunction and that equally modify the same noun or pronoun.**

   The thirsty, hungry children returned from a day at the beach.

   To determine if a comma is needed between two adjectives, use the following test. Insert the word *and* between the two adjectives. Also try reversing the order of the two adjectives. If the phrase makes sense in either case, a comma is needed. If the phrase does not make sense, do not use a comma.

   The tired, angry child fell asleep. [*The tired and angry child* makes sense; so does *The angry, tired child*. Consequently, the comma is needed.]

   Sarah is an excellent psychology student. [*Sarah is an excellent and psychology student* does not make sense, nor does *Sarah is a psychology, excellent student*. A comma is therefore not needed.]

7. **To separate parenthetical expressions from the clauses they modify.** Parenthetical expressions are added pieces of information that are not essential to the meaning of the sentence.

   Most students, I imagine, can get jobs on campus.

8. **To separate a transition from the clause it modifies.**

   In addition, I will revise the bylaws.

9. **To separate a quotation from the words that introduce or explain it.**

   Note: The comma goes *inside* the closing quotation marks.

   "Shopping," Barbara explained, "is a form of relaxation for me."

   Barbara explained, "Shopping is a form of relaxation for me."

10. **To separate dates, place names, and long numbers.**

    October 10, 1981, is my birthday.

    Dayton, Ohio, was the first stop on the tour.

    Participants numbered 1,777,716.

11. **To separate phrases expressing contrast**

    Sam's good nature, not his wealth, explains his popularity.

EXERCISE 10

Directions: Revise each of the following sentences by adding commas where needed.

EXAMPLE   If you feel like seeing a movie tonight, give me a call.

1. According to the American Red Cross Hurricane Katrina and Hurricane Rita destroyed more than 350,000 homes.

2. Many fans who attended the rock concert thought the band sounded great but some were disappointed that the concert was so short.

3. "If you're feeling brave " said Lin "we could ski down the black-diamond trail."

4. Diego met with his academic advisor who is the chair of the computer science department to discuss career options.

5. When I switched to a vegan diet I quit eating meat fish eggs and milk.

6. During Ben's performance review the manager commended him for his positive respectful interactions with patrons.

7. Tonight as you may recall is your night to do the dishes.

8. Volunteering for Habitat for Humanity has been a pleasure not a burden.

9. I don't have time to go swimming right now; besides it looks like it's going to rain.

10. Shauna is planning to visit her friend in Washington D.C. when the cherry blossoms bloom.

C.3 UNNECESSARY COMMAS

It is as important to know where *not* to place commas as it is to know where to place them. The following rules explain where it is incorrect to place them:

1. **Do not place a comma between a subject and its verb, between a verb and its complement, or between an adjective and the word it modifies.**

INCORRECT   The stunning, imaginative, and intriguing, painting, became the hit of the show.

CORRECT   The stunning, imaginative, and intriguing painting became the hit of the show.

2. **Do not place a comma between two verbs, subjects, or complements used as compounds.**

COMPOUND VERB

INCORRECT   Sue <u>called</u>, and <u>asked</u> me to come by her office.

CORRECT   Sue called and asked me to come by her office.

3. **Do not place a comma before a coordinating conjunction joining two dependent clauses.**

DEPENDENT CLAUSE

INCORRECT   The city planner examined blueprints <u>that the park designer had submitted</u>, and <u>that the budget officer had approved.</u>

DEPENDENT CLAUSE

CORRECT   The city planner examined blueprints that the park designer had submitted and that the budget officer had approved.

4. **Do not place commas around restrictive clauses, phrases, or appositives.** Restrictive clauses, phrases, and appositives are modifiers that are essential to the meaning of the sentence.

INCORRECT   The girl, <u>who grew up down the block</u>, became my lifelong friend.

CORRECT   The girl who grew up down the block became my lifelong friend.

5. **Do not place a comma before the word *than* in a comparison or after the words *like* and *such* as in an introduction to a list.**

INCORRECT   Some snails, <u>such as</u>, the Oahu tree snail, have more colorful shells, <u>than</u> other snails.

CORRECT   Some snails, such as the Oahu tree snail, have more colorful shells than other snails.

6. **Do not place a comma next to a period, a question mark, an exclamation point, a dash, or an opening parenthesis.**

INCORRECT   "When will you come back?," Dillon's son asked him.

CORRECT   "When will you come back?" Dillon's son asked him.

INCORRECT   The bachelor button, (also known as the cornflower) grows well in ordinary garden soil.

CORRECT   The bachelor button (also known as the cornflower) grows well in ordinary garden soil.

7. **Do not place a comma between cumulative adjectives.** Cumulative adjectives, unlike coordinate adjectives (see p. 593), cannot be joined by *and* or rearranged.

INCORRECT   The light, yellow, rose blossom was a pleasant birthday surprise. [*The light and yellow and rose blossom* does not make sense, so the commas are incorrect.]

CORRECT   The light yellow rose blossom was a pleasant birthday surprise.

C.4 COLONS AND SEMICOLONS

When to Use a Colon

A colon follows an independent clause and usually signals that the clause is to be explained or elaborated on. Use a colon in the following situations:

1. **To introduce items in a series after an independent clause.** The series can consist of words, phrases, or clauses.

   I am wearing three popular colors: magenta, black, and white.

2. **To signal a list or a statement introduced by an independent clause ending with *the following* or *as follows*.**

   The directions are as follows: take Main Street to Oak Avenue and then turn left.

3. **To introduce a quotation that follows an introductory independent clause.**

   My brother made his point quite clear: "Never borrow my car without asking me first!"

4. **To introduce an explanation.**

   Mathematics is enjoyable: it requires a high degree of accuracy and peak concentration.

5. **To separate titles and subtitles of books.**

   Biology: A Study of Life

Note: A colon must always follow an independent clause. It should not be used in the middle of a clause.

   INCORRECT   My favorite colors are: red, pink, and green.

   CORRECT   My favorite colors are red, pink, and green.

When to Use a Semicolon

Use a semicolon in the following situations:

1. **To separate two closely related independent clauses not connected by a coordinating conjunction** (see p. 127).

   Sam had a 99 average in math; he earned an A in the course.

2. **To separate two independent clauses joined by a conjunctive adverb** (see p. 156).

   Margaret earned an A on her term paper; consequently, she was exempt from the final exam.

3. **To separate independent clauses joined with a coordinating conjunction if the clauses are very long or if they contain numerous commas.**

   By late afternoon, having tried on every pair of black checked pants in the mall, Marsha was tired and cranky; but she still had not found what she needed to complete her outfit for the play.

4. **To separate items in a series if the items are lengthy or contain commas.**

   The soap opera characters include Marianne Loundsberry, the heroine; Ellen and Sarah, her children; Barry, her ex-husband; and Louise, her best friend.

5. **To correct a comma splice or run-on sentence** (see pp. 127, 136).

EXERCISE 11

Directions: Correct each of the following sentences by placing colons and semicolons where necessary. Delete any incorrect punctuation.

> EXAMPLE   Even when I'm busy, I try to make time for my three favorite hobbies: reading, gardening, and biking.

1. When Kyoko plans a hike, she makes sure her backpack contains the following items;water, power bars, sunscreen, bug repellent, a windbreaker, and a cell phone.

2. Mark Twain said it best,"The difference between the almost right word and the right word . . . 'tis the difference between the lightning-bug and the lightning.'"

3. Consider this amazing fact,the superheated air, that surrounds a bolt of lightning, is about four times hotter than the surface of the sun.

4. I couldn't have made it through college without coffee; in fact, if I were writing a memoir about that period, the title would probably be "College, The Coffee Years."

5. The classic movie, *Casablanca*, had a stellar cast; Humphrey Bogart, who played the role of Rick,Ingrid Bergman, who played Ilsa,and Claude Rains, who played Louis.

6. It is certainly reassuring when a pediatrician tells you not to worry about your sick child,however, you also need to trust your own instincts and advocate for your child.

7. Any decent job should provide: a fair salary, reasonable working hours, and a safe work environment,these elements are nonnegotiable.

8. When I was a child, my grandfather gave me clear instructions for picking strawberries,pick the berries that are bright red, but leave the light, red berries.

9. The last thing Jasper needed was responsibility for another pet, nevertheless, the large, dark, pleading, eyes of the abandoned puppy, proved irresistible.

10. For my son's birthday, his two cousins, and several children from the neighborhood joined us for a picnic in the park, everyone had a great time.

C.5 DASHES, PARENTHESES, HYPHENS, APOSTROPHES, QUOTATION MARKS

Dashes (—)

The dash is used to (1) separate nonessential elements from the main part of the sentence, (2) create a stronger separation, or interruption, than commas or parentheses, and (3) emphasize an idea, create a dramatic effect, or indicate a sudden change in thought.

> My sister—the friendliest person I know—will visit me this weekend.

> My brother's most striking quality is his ability to make money—or so I thought until I heard of his bankruptcy.

Do not leave spaces between the dash and the words it separates.

Parentheses ( )

Parentheses are used in pairs to separate extra or nonessential information that often amplifies, clarifies, or acts as an aside to the main point. Unlike dashes, parentheses de-emphasize information.

> Some large breeds of dogs (golden retrievers and Newfoundlands) are susceptible to hip deformities.

> The prize was dinner for two (maximum value, $50.00) at a restaurant of one's choice.

Hyphens (-)

Hyphens have the following primary uses:

1. **To split a word when dividing it between two lines of writing or typing** (see p. 605).

2. **To join two or more words that function as a unit, either as a noun or as a noun modifier.**

mother-in-law	single-parent families
twenty-year-old	school-age children
state-of-the-art sound system	

Apostrophes (')

Use apostrophes in the following situations:

1. **To show ownership or possession.** When the person, place, or thing doing the possessing is a singular noun, add -'s to the end of it, regardless of what its final letter is.

The man's DVD player	John Keats's poetry
Aretha's best friend	

- With plural nouns that end in -s, add only an apostrophe to the end of the word.

the twins' bedroom	postal workers' hours
teachers' salaries	

With plural nouns that do not end in -s, add -'s.

children's books	men's slacks

- Do not use an apostrophe with the possessive adjective *its.*

INCORRECT   It's frame is damaged.

CORRECT   Its frame is damaged.

2. **To indicate omission of one or more letters in a word or number.** Contractions are used in informal writing but usually not in formal academic writing.

it's [it is]	hasn't [has not]
doesn't [does not]	'57 Ford [1957 Ford]
you're [you are]	class of '89 [class of 1989]

Quotation Marks (" ")

Quotation marks separate a direct quotation from the sentence that contains it. Here are some rules to follow in using quotation marks.

1. **Quotation marks are always used in pairs.**

   Note: A comma or period goes at the end of the quotation, inside the quotation marks.

   Marge declared, "I never expected Peter to give me a watch for Christmas."

   "I never expected Peter to give me a watch for Christmas," Marge declared.

2. **Use single quotation marks for a quotation within a quotation.**

My literature professor said, "Byron's line 'She walks in beauty like the night' is one of his most sensual."

Note: When quoting long prose passages of more than four typed lines, do not use quotation marks. Instead, set off the quotation from the rest of the text by indenting each line ten spaces from the left margin. This format is called a **block quotation.**

The opening lines of the Declaration of Independence establish the purpose of the document:

> When in the Course of human events it becomes necessary for one people to dissolve the political bonds which have connected them with another, and to assume among the powers of the earth, the separate and equal station to which the Laws of Nature and of Nature's God entitle them, a decent respect to the opinions of mankind requires that they should declare the causes which impel them to the separation.

3. **Use quotation marks to indicate titles of songs, short stories, poems, reports, articles, and essays.** Books, movies, plays, operas, paintings, statues, and the names of television series are italicized.

"Rappaccini's Daughter" (short story)

60 Minutes (television series)

"The Road Not Taken" (poem)
Huckleberry Finn (book)

4. **Colons, semicolons, exclamation points, and question marks, when not part of the quoted material, go outside of the quotation marks.**

What did George mean when he said, "People in glass houses shouldn't throw stones"?

EXERCISE 12

Directions: To the following sentences, add dashes, apostrophes, parentheses, hyphens, and quotation marks where necessary.

EXAMPLE   All faculty members' e-mail addresses are listed in the college directory.

1. Whenever my friend has a personal problem, he just buys another self help book.

2. What famous play includes the line, I have always relied on the kindness of strangers ?

3. If a movie is rated PG parental guidance suggested , I preview it myself to make sure that it s appropriate for my eight year old son.

4. When asked to identify the greatest rock song of all time, the music critic replied, That's easy the song Stairway to Heaven by the band Led Zeppelin.

5. Answering customers questions about computer products is Aaron s responsibility.

6. One of Maya Angelou s most beloved poems is I Know Why the Caged Bird Sings; equally inspirational is her poem I Rise.

7. Be careful if you see the horse s ears flattened against its head, as this may mean that the horse is about to kick.

8. If you can wait a minute, said Serena, I d be happy to check that price for you.

9. Alfred Hitchcock s film *Psycho*   possibly the greatest horror movie of all time   has terrified generations of viewers since its release in 1960.

10. The professor assigned two more Hemingway stories, in addition to My Old Man : Hills Like White Elephants and A Clean Well-Lighted Place.

D Managing Mechanics and Spelling

D.1 CAPITALIZATION

In general, capital letters are used to mark the beginning of a sentence, to mark the beginning of a quotation, and to identify proper nouns. Here are some guidelines on capitalization:

What to Capitalize	*Example*
1. First word in every sentence	Prewriting is useful.
2. First word in a direct quotation	Sarah commented, "That exam was difficult!"
3. Names of people and animals, including the pronoun *I*	Aladdin Clarence Thomas Spot
4. Names of specific places, cities, states, nations, geographic areas or regions	New Orleans the Southwest Lake Erie
5. Government and public offices, departments, buildings	Williamsville Library House of Representatives
6. Names of social, political, business, sporting, cultural organizations	Boy Scouts Buffalo Bills
7. Names of months, days of the week, holidays	August Tuesday Halloween
8. In titles of works: the first word following a colon, the first and last words, and all other words except articles, prepositions, and conjunctions	*Biology: A Study of Life* "Once More to the Lake"
9. Races, nationalities, languages	African-American, Italian, English

10. Religions, religious figures, sacred books	Hindu, Hinduism, God, Allah, the Bible
11. Names of products	Tide, Buick
12. Personal titles when they come right before a name	Professor Rodriguez Senator Hatch
13. Major historic events	World War I
14. Specific course titles	History 201, Introduction to Psychology

EXERCISE 13

Directions: Capitalize words as necessary in the following sentences.

EXAMPLE   Henry Thoreau said, "t̲o regret deeply is to live afresh."

1. Artist Georgia O'Keeffe lived for many years in new mexico, painting images that captured the stark beauty of the american southwest.

2. I haven't completed my paper for professor Stern yet, so I will have to finish writing it over the thanksgiving break.

3. On april 9, 1865, the american civil war drew to a close when confederate general Robert E. Lee surrendered at appomattox court house.

4. The springfield city library now offers free access to wireless internet service.

5. The first five books of the old testament of the bible form the sacred jewish text of the pentateuch.

6. Science is not my strongest subject, so I took the course physics for poets to fulfill my science requirement.

7. Baseball legend Jackie Robinson, who played for the brooklyn dodgers, told the story of his life in the book *I never had it made: an autobiography of Jackie Robinson.*

8. The great salt lake, located in northern utah, is much saltier than the pacific ocean; the salty water makes swimmers unusually buoyant, so they float very easily.

9. The novel *all quiet on the western front* tells the story of a young soldier's experience during world war I.

10. My daughter refuses to eat anything but kellogg's frosted flakes for breakfast; while she eats, she studies the picture of tony the tiger on the cereal box.

D.2 ABBREVIATIONS

An abbreviation is a shortened form of a word or phrase that is used to represent the whole word or phrase. The following is a list of common acceptable abbreviations:

What to Abbreviate	*Example*
1. Some titles before or after people's names	Mr. Ling Samuel Rosen, M.D. *but* Professor Ashe
2. Names of familiar organizations, corporations, countries	CIA, IBM, VISTA, USA
3. Time references preceded or followed by a number	7:00 A.M. 3:00 P.M. A.D. 1973
4. Latin terms when used in footnotes, references, or parentheses	i.e. [*id est*, "that is"] et al. [*et alii*, "and others"]

Here is a list of things that are usually *not* abbreviated in a paragraph or essay:

What Not to Abbreviate	*Example* Incorrect	Correct
1. Units of measurement	thirty in.	thirty inches
2. Geographic or other place names when used in sentences	N.Y. Elm St.	New York Elm Street
3. Parts of written works when used in sentences	Ch. 3	Chapter 3
4. Names of days, months, holidays	Tues.	Tuesday
5. Names of subject areas	psych.	psychology

EXERCISE 14

Directions: Correct the inappropriate use of abbreviations in the following sentences. If a sentence contains no errors, write "C" beside it.

EXAMPLE   The tiny lizard is only about four ~~cm~~ long.

centimeters
_____

_____ 1. Homer Hickam, a boy known for building homemade rockets during the 1950s, became a NASA engineer as an adult.

_____ 2. A great sprinter, Susan is expected to win the fifty-yd. dash.

_____ 3. Spicy foods—e.g., hot peppers—sometimes disagree with me.

_____ 4. My English lit. class meets Tues. and Th. at 2:00.

_____   5. Some convicted criminals have been freed from prison after DNA testing proved they were innocent.

_____

_____   6. The co. I work for is located on Walnut St. in Phila.

_____

_____   7. I stayed up until 3:00 A.M to finish reading the final chap. of this exciting novel.

_____

_____   8. The *Aeneid,* Virgil's epic poem about the founding of Rome, was written about 30 B.C.E.

_____

_____   9. During Aug., the heat in TX can be brutal.

_____

_____   10. Prof. Jenkins has a very engaging lecture style.

_____

D.3 HYPHENATION AND WORD DIVISION

On occasion you may want to divide and hyphenate a word on one line and continue it on the next. Here are some guidelines for dividing words.

1. **Divide words only when necessary.** Frequent word divisions make a paper difficult to read.

2. **Divide words between syllables.** Consult a dictionary if you are unsure how to break a word into syllables.

   di-vi-sion   pro-tect

3. **Do not divide one-syllable words.**

4. **Do not divide a word so that a single letter is left at the end of a line.**

   INCORRECT   a-typical

   CORRECT   atyp-ical

5. **Do not divide a word so that fewer than three letters begin the new line.**

   INCORRECT   visu-al

   CORRECT   vi-sual

   INCORRECT   caus-al [This word cannot be divided at all.]

6. **Divide compound words only between the words.**

some-thing   any-one

7. **Divide words that are already hyphenated only at the hyphen.**

ex-policeman

EXERCISE 15

Directions: Insert a diagonal (/) mark where each word should be divided. Write "N" in the margin if the word should not be divided.

EXAMPLE   fic/tion

_____ 1. crashing   _____ 6. elite

_____ 2. splurge   _____ 7. unsteady

_____ 3. cross-reference   _____ 8. sandpaper

_____ 4. amorphous   _____ 9. x-ray

_____ 5. glory   _____ 10. property

D.4 NUMBERS

Numbers can be written as numerals (600) or words (six hundred). Here are some guidelines for when to use numerals and when to use words:

When to Use Numerals	Example
1. Numbers that are spelled with more than two words	375 students
2. Days and years	August 10, 1993
3. Decimals, percentages, fractions	56.7 59 percent 1¾ cups
4. Exact times	9:27 A.M.
5. Pages, chapters, volumes; acts and lines from plays	chapter 12 volume 4
6. Addresses	122 Peach Street
7. Exact amounts of money	$5.60
8. Scores and statistics	23–6 5 of every 12

When to Use Words	Example
1. Numbers that begin sentences	Two hundred ten students attended the lecture.
2. Numbers of one or two words	sixty students, two hundred women

EXERCISE 16

Directions: Correct the misuse of numbers in the following sentences. If a sentence contains no errors, write "C" next to it.

EXAMPLE I planned to read fifty pages last night, but I only made it to page ~~forty-two.~~ 42

_____ 1. When we rehearse Act 6 of the play, I keep messing up line sixteen.

_____ 2. Beat one and three-quarters cups of sugar into the softened butter.

_____ 3. In 2007 a Gallup survey showed that roughly seven out of ten Americans own a dog or a cat.

_____ 4. Lola ran the race in fourteen point three seconds.

_____ 5. 46 percent of Americans have used the Internet, e-mail, or text messaging to participate in the political process.

_____ 6. The world's population is expected to reach almost nine billion by the year 2042.

_____ 7. According to the syllabus, we need to read chapters seven and eight by next week.

_____ 8. Jian's daughter proudly reported that she had saved two dollars and twenty-seven cents in her piggy bank.

_____ 9. On weekdays, I always set my alarm for 7:10 A.M., but I generally hit the snooze bar and sleep for another 15 or 20 minutes.

_____ 10. When I was ten years old, my goal was to read every volume of the encyclopedia, but I only finished part of volume 1.

D.5 SUGGESTIONS FOR IMPROVING SPELLING

Correct spelling is important in a well-written paragraph or essay. The following suggestions will help you submit papers without misspellings:

1. **Do not worry about spelling as you write your first draft.** Checking a word in a dictionary at this point will interrupt your flow of ideas. If you do not know how a word is spelled, spell it the way it sounds. Circle or underline the word so you remember to check it later.

2. **Keep a list of words you commonly misspell.** This list can be part of your error log.

3. **Every time you catch an error or find a misspelled word on a paper returned by your instructor, add it to your list.**

4. **Study your list.** Ask a friend to quiz you on the words. Eliminate words from the list after you have passed several quizzes on them.

5. **Develop a spelling awareness.** You'll find that your spelling will improve just by your being aware that spelling is important. When you encounter a new word, notice how it is spelled and practice writing it.

6. **Pronounce words you are having difficulty spelling.** Pronounce each syllable distinctly.

7. **Review basic spelling rules.** Your college library or learning lab may have manuals, workbooks, or computer programs that cover basic rules and provide guided practice.

8. **Be sure to have a dictionary readily available when you write.**

9. **Read your final draft through once, checking only for spelling errors.** Look at each word carefully, and check the spelling of those words of which you are uncertain.

D.6 SIX USEFUL SPELLING RULES

The following six rules focus on common spelling trouble spots:

1. **Is it *ei* or *ie*?**

   Rule: Use *i* before *e*, except after *c* or when the syllable is pronounced *ay* as in the word *weigh*.

   > EXAMPLE   *i* before *e:* bel<u>ie</u>ve, n<u>ie</u>ce
   >
   > except after *c:* rec<u>ei</u>ve, conc<u>ei</u>ve
   >
   > or when pronounced *ay:* n<u>ei</u>ghbor, sl<u>ei</u>gh

Exceptions:	either	neither	foreign	forfeit
	height	leisure	seize	weird

2. **When adding an ending, do you keep or drop the final *e*?**

   Rules: **a.** Keep the final *e* when adding an ending that begins with a consonant. (Vowels are *a, e, i, o, u,* and sometimes *y;* all other letters are consonants.)

   > hope → hope<u>ful</u>   aware → aware<u>ness</u>
   > live → live<u>ly</u>   force → force<u>ful</u>

   b. Drop the final *e* when adding an ending that begins with a vowel.

   > hope → hop<u>ing</u>   file → fil<u>ing</u>
   > note → not<u>able</u>   write → writ<u>ing</u>

Exceptions:	argument	truly	changeable
	awful	manageable	courageous
	judgment	noticeable	outrageous
	acknowledgment		

3. **When adding an ending, do you keep the final *y*, change it to *i*, or drop it?**

    Rules: **a.** Keep the *y* if the letter before the *y* is a vowel.

    >   del<u>ay</u> → del<u>ay</u>ing   b<u>uy</u> → b<u>uy</u>ing   pr<u>ey</u> → pr<u>ey</u>ed

    b. Change the *y* to *i* if the letter before the *y* is a consonant, but keep the *y* for the *-ing* ending.

    >   defy → def<u>i</u>ance   marr<u>y</u> → marr<u>i</u>ed
    >   → def<u>y</u>ing   → marr<u>y</u>ing

4. **When adding an ending to a one-syllable word, when do you double the final letter if it is a consonant?**

    Rules: **a.** In one-syllable words, double the final consonant when a single vowel comes before it.

    >   dr<u>op</u> → dr<u>op</u>ped   sh<u>op</u> → sh<u>op</u>ped   p<u>it</u> → p<u>it</u>ted

    b. In one-syllable words, *don't* double the final consonant when two vowels or a consonant comes before it.

    >   rep<u>air</u> → rep<u>air</u>able   s<u>ound</u> → s<u>ound</u>ed
    >   r<u>eal</u> → r<u>eal</u>ize

5. **When adding an ending to a word with more than one syllable, when do you double the final letter if it is a consonant?**

    Rules: **a.** In multisyllable words, double the final consonant when a single vowel comes before it *and* the stress falls on the last syllable. (Vowels are *a, e, i, o, u,* and sometimes *y.* All other letters are consonants.)

    >   beg<u>in</u>´ → beg<u>in</u>ning   transm<u>it</u>´ → transm<u>it</u>ted
    >   rep<u>el</u>´ → rep<u>el</u>ling

    b. In multisyllable words, do *not* double the final consonant (a) when a vowel comes before it *and* (b) the stress is not on the last syllable once the new ending is added.

    >   refer → reference

    >   admit → admitance

6. **To form a plural, do you add *-s* or *-es*?**

    Rules: **a.** For most nouns, add *-s.*

    >   cat → cat<u>s</u>   house → house<u>s</u>

    b. Add *-es* to words that end in *-o* if the *-o* is preceded by a consonant.

    >   her<u>o</u> → her<u>oes</u>   potat<u>o</u> → potat<u>oes</u>

    Exceptions: zoos, radios, ratios, and other words ending with two vowels.

    c. Add *-es* to words ending in *-ch, -sh, -ss, -x,* or *-z.*

    >   chur<u>ch</u> → chur<u>ches</u>   fo<u>x</u> → fo<u>xes</u>   di<u>sh</u> → di<u>shes</u>

Commonly Misused Words and Phrases

This list is intended as a guide to words and phrases that often are confusing. If the word or phrase you seek is not here, check in a good dictionary.

a, an Use *an* before words that begin with a vowel sound (the vowels are *a, e, i, o,* and *u*) or a silent *h: an airplane, an honor.* Use *a* before words that begin with a consonant sound: *a book, a house.*

a while, awhile *A while* is a phrase containing an article and a noun; *awhile* is an adverb meaning "for some time." *A while* can be used following a preposition, such as *for: Wait here for a while. Awhile* is used to modify a verb: *We need to rest awhile.*

accept, except *Accept* is a verb that means "receive"; *She accepted the gift gratefully. Except* is usually a preposition meaning "other than," "but," or "excluding": *Everyone has left except me.*

advice, advise *Advice* is a noun: *He gave me his best advice about health insurance. Advise* is a verb: *I can only advise you about it.*

affect, effect *Affect* is almost always a verb meaning "influence": *Smoking affects one's health. Effect* can be either a verb or a noun. In its usual use, as a noun, it means "result": *The drug has several side effects.* When *effect* is used as a verb, it means "cause" or "bring about": *The committee was able to effect a change in the law.*

all ready, already *All ready* means "completely prepared." *Already* means "by this time" or "previously."

all right, alright Although the form *alright* is often used, most authorities regard it as a misspelling of *all right.*

all together, altogether *All together* means "as a group" or "in unison": *The workers presented their grievance all together to the supervisor. Altogether* is an adverb that means "completely" or "entirely": *His answer was not altogether acceptable.*

allusion, illusion An *allusion* is an indirect reference or a hint: *Her allusions about his weight embarrassed him.* An *illusion* is a false idea or appearance: *Cosmetic surgery is intended to create the illusion of youth.*

almost, most See *most, almost.*

alot, lots, lots of *Alot* should be written only as two words: *a lot.* It is an informal substitute for *many* or *much,* as are *lots* and *lots of.* You should avoid all three in formal writing.

among, between   See *between, among.*

amount of, number of   Use *amount of* to refer to quantities that cannot be counted: *A large amount of milk had been left in the refrigerator.* Use *number of* with quantities that can be counted: *A large number of eggs had been left in the carton.*

and/or   Avoid using *and/or* unless your writing is of a technical, business, or legal nature. Remember that in these types of writing *and/or* indicates *three* options: one *or* the other *or* both.

anybody, any body; anyone, any one   *Anybody* and *anyone* are indefinite pronouns that mean "any person at all": *Does anybody (anyone) have change for a dollar? Any body* consists of a noun modified by the adjective *any: Is any body of government responsible for this injustice? Any one,* the pronoun *one* modified by *any,* refers to a certain person or thing in a group: *You may choose any one of the desserts with your entree.*

anyone, any body   See *anybody, any body; anyone, any one.*

anyplace, anywhere   *Anyplace* is informal for *anywhere* and should be avoided in formal writing.

anyways, anywheres, nowheres; anyway, anywhere, nowhere.   Use *anyway, anywhere,* and *nowhere* rather than the forms ending in *-s.*

as   Using *as* instead of *because, since* or *while* can lead to confusion: *The ball game was canceled as it started raining.* Here, *as* could mean either "because" or "when." Avoid using *as* rather than *whether* or *who:*

We are not sure ~~as~~ we can be there. *whether*

She is the person ~~as~~ interrupted my lunch hour. *who*

as, as if, as though, like   See *like, as if, as though.*

bad, badly   *Bad* is an adjective; *badly* is an adverb. *Badly* should be used to modify verbs: *They sang quite badly. Bad* can be used to modify nouns or pronouns: *The bad behavior irritated the child's hostess.* In addition, *bad* should be used after linking verbs, such as *am, is, become, feel,* or *seem: She felt bad last night.*

being as, being that   Use *because* or *since* rather than these expressions. Besides being informal, they can make sentences awkward.

Between, among   Use *between* when referring to two things or people: *My wife and I divide the household chores between us.* Use *among* for three or more things or people: *The vote was evenly divided among the four candidates.*

bring, take   Use *bring* to describe the movement of an object toward you: *Bring me the newspaper, please.* Use *take* when the movement is away from you: *Will you take these letters to the mailbox?*

can, may   In formal writing you should make a distinction between *can* and *may. Can* refers to the ability to do something: *He can run a mile in less than five minutes. May* indicates permission: *You may choose whichever CD you want.*

censor, censure   *Censor* as a verb means "edit or ban from the public for moral or political reasons": *The school board voted not to censor the high school reading lists but to recommend novels with literary merit.* The verb *censure* means "criticize or condemn publicly": *The member of Congress was censured because of questionable fund-raising practices.*

complement, compliment   *Complement* is a verb meaning "complete, add to, or go with": *They make a good couple; their personalities <u>complement</u> each other. Compliment* as a verb means "praise or flatter": *I must <u>compliment</u> you on your quick wit.* As a noun it means "flattering remark": *You should not regard his <u>compliments</u> as sincere.*

conscience, conscious   *Conscience* is a noun meaning "sense of moral right or wrong": *His <u>conscience</u> required him to return the lost wallet. Conscious* is an adjective meaning "alert, aware, awake": *Were you <u>conscious</u> of the change in temperature?*

continual, continuous   *Continual* means "happening regularly": *<u>Continual</u> calls by telemarketers are a nuisance. Continuous* means "happening for a long period of time without interruption": *The car alarm made a <u>continuous</u>, high-pitched noise.*

could have, could of   See *of, have.*

data   *Data,* the plural form of the Latin noun *datum,* means "facts or information." *Data* is often accepted as either a plural or a singular noun: *These data <u>are</u> conclusive. This data <u>is</u> conclusive.* Though technically correct, the singular form *datum* is rarely used.

different from, different than   *Different from* is the preferred expression: *Today is <u>different from</u> yesterday.* However, when *different from* leads to an awkward construction, *different than* is becoming acceptable: *Today Cheryl is <u>different than</u> she was last month* (avoids *from what she last month*).

disinterested, uninterested   *Disinterested* means "objective or impartial": *The dispute was mediated by a <u>disinterested</u> party. Uninterested* means "not interested": *She was so <u>uninterested</u> in the football game that she nearly fell asleep.*

doesn't, don't   *Don't* is the contraction for *do not,* not for *does not: We <u>don't</u> want it.*

She ~~don't~~ ^{doesn't} have any.

due to   The phrase *due to* should be used only when it functions as a predicate adjective after a linking verb (usually a form of *be*): *His ill health was <u>due to</u> his poor diet.* It should not be used as a preposition meaning "because of" or "on account of":

The ball game was canceled ~~due to~~ ^{because of} bad weather.

effect, affect   See *affect, effect.*

elicit, illicit   *Elicit* is a verb meaning "draw out" or "bring to light": *The police were unable to <u>elicit</u> any information from the accomplice. Illicit* is an adjective meaning "illegal": *The suspect had <u>illicit</u> drugs on his person.*

emigrate, immigrate   See *immigrate, emigrate.*

etc.   This is the abbreviation for the Latin *et cetera,* meaning "and so on." Ending a list with *etc.* is acceptable in informal writing and in some technical writing and business reporting. However, in formal writing it is preferable to end a list with an example or with *and so on.*

everyday, everyday   *Everyday* is an adjective that means "ordinary" or "usual": *They decided to use their <u>everyday</u> dishes for the party. Every day,* an adjective and a noun, means "occurring on a daily basis": *<u>Every day</u>, he walks the dog in the morning.*

explicit, implicit   *Explicit* is an adjective that means "clearly stated": *I left explicit instructions for the worker.* *Implicit* means "indirectly stated or implied": *The fact that he didn't object indicated his implicit approval of the arrangement.*

farther, further   When referring to distance, use *farther*: *He lives farther from work than she does.* When you mean "additional," use *further*: *Upon further consideration, I accept the position.*

fewer, less   *Fewer* refers to items that can be counted: *There are fewer people here today than yesterday.* *Less* refers to a general amount that cannot be counted: *We have less orange juice than I thought.*

firstly, secondly, thirdly   Use *first, second, third* instead, to avoid sounding pretentious and needing to add *-ly* to remaining numbers in a list.

further, farther   See *farther, further.*

get   *Get* is a verb used in many slang and colloquial expressions. Avoid the following uses.

That really g̶o̶t̶ ̶t̶o̶ me. *(annoyed (moved))*   We've g̶o̶t̶ ̶t̶o̶ go now. *(must)*

I g̶o̶t̶ ̶b̶a̶c̶k̶ ̶a̶t̶ her. *(took revenge on)*   Don't g̶e̶t̶ sick. *(become)*

G̶e̶t̶ ̶moving o̶n̶ that. *(Start doing)*   We g̶o̶t̶ ̶t̶o̶ the party late. *(arrived at)*

We g̶o̶t̶ ̶d̶o̶n̶e̶ early. *(finished)*

good, well   *Good* is an adjective: *I enjoy a good workout.* It should not be used as an adverb. *Well* should be used instead:

We ate g̶o̶o̶d̶ on our vacation. *(well)*

Well can also be an adjective when used with verbs expressing feeling or state of being: *She feels well today.*

got to   See *get.*

hanged, hung   *Hanged* is the past tense and past participle form of the verb *hang*, meaning "execute": *He was hanged as a traitor.* *Hung* is the past tense and past participle form of the verb *hang* in all its other meanings: *We hung the picture above the fireplace.*

have, of   See *of, have.*

have got to   See *get.*

he/she, his/her; he or she, his or her   At one time, it was permissible to use *he* to mean *he or she.* Now, this is seldom appropriate. Use *he or she* and *his or her*, rather than *he/she, his/her*, when referring to a person whose gender is unknown: *Everyone must learn to walk before he or she runs.* If using these or other "double" pronouns becomes awkward, revise your sentence by using the plural pronoun or by refocusing the sentence.

When you meet e̶a̶c̶h̶ ̶g̶u̶e̶s̶t̶, ask h̶i̶m̶ ̶t̶o̶ ̶h̶e̶r̶ to show h̶i̶s̶ ̶o̶r̶ ̶h̶e̶r̶ ID c̶a̶r̶d̶. *(guests) (them) (their) (cards)*

When you meet each guest, ask to see an ID card.

hisself *Hisself* is nonstandard. Use *himself*.

hung, hanged See *hanged, hung*.

if, whether Use *if* when expressing a condition: *If I leave early, I can beat the rush hour traffic.* Use *whether* when expressing an alternative: *I don't know whether to stay or to leave.*

illicit, elicit See *elicit, illicit*.

illusion, allusion See *allusion, illusion*.

immigrate, emigrate *Immigrate (to)* means "come to a country": *They recently immigrated to the United States. Emigrate (from)* means "leave a country": *They emigrated from Mexico for economic reasons.*

implicit, explicit See *explicit, implicit*.

imply, infer Speakers or writers *imply*. They suggest or hint at something: *He implied that he was unhappy with my work.* Listeners or readers *infer* by drawing conclusions from what they have read, heard, or seen: *I inferred that I need to become more conscientious.*

in, into, in to Use *in* to indicate position or location: *Your book is in the drawer.* Use *into* to show movement: *They were led into a winding corridor.* Sometimes *in* and *to* are used close together as separate words: *They gave in to our requests.*

in regard to, in regards to *In regards to* confuses two other phrases—*in regard to* and *as regards*. Use either of the last two or use *regarding: In regard to (as regards; regarding) your last phone call, I will arrive in time for the 2:30 meeting.*

infer, imply See *imply, infer*.

irregardless, regardless *Irregardless* is nonstandard. Use *regardless* instead.

is when, is where *When* and *where* are often used incorrectly in sentences that define. Using just *is* or rewording your sentence can correct this faulty construction:

> A touchdown ~~is when~~ you cross your opponent's goal line with
> is scored when
>
> the ball in your possession.

> A touchdown ~~is when you cross~~ your opponent's goal line with
> is crossing
>
> the ball in your possession.

> Art history ~~is where you study~~ the world's great art treasures.
> is the study of

Its, it's *Its* is the possessive case form of the pronoun *it*; no apostrophes are used to show possession with personal pronouns (*his, hers, its, theirs*). *The poodle scratched its ear. It's* is the contraction for *it is: It's time for a change.*

Kind, sort, type These words are singular and should be used with singular modifiers and verbs: *This kind of book is expensive.* They should be used in their plural forms with plural modifiers and verbs: *These types of pens work best* Using *a* following *type of, kind of,* or *sort of* is incorrect:

What type of ~~a~~ dog is that?

Also, omitting *of* is nonstandard:

I can't guess what type _∧ car that is.
                   of

Kind of, sort of   Avoid using *kind of* or *sort of* in formal speech or writing to mean "somewhat" or "rather":

            rather
The movie was ~~kind of~~ scary.
             ∧

              somewhat
The traffic was ~~sort of~~ slow this morning.
              ∧

lay, lie   *Lay* is a transitive verb meaning "put or place." Its principal parts are *lay, laid, laid: Lay your bag here. She laid her bag here. She has laid her bag here every day. Lie* is an intransitive verb meaning "recline or be situated." Its principal parts are *lie, lay, lain: Lie down for a while. He lay down for a while. He has lain down every few hours.*

leave, let   *Leave* is a verb that means "depart," "exit," or "let be": *We will leave the room, so that you can be left alone. Let* means "permit or allow": *They would not let me go.*

less, fewer   See *fewer, less.*

like, as, as if, as though   *Like* is a preposition and should be used only with a noun or a noun phrase: *You look like your mother.* Do not use *like* as a conjunction to introduce subordinate clauses. Use *as, as if,* or *as though.*

     as
Do ~~like~~ I tell you.
   ∧

         as if (as though)
She looks ~~like~~ she is ready to fall asleep.
       ∧

loose, lose   *Loose* is an adjective meaning "not tight" or "not attached securely": *A loose brick fell into the fireplace. Lose* is a verb that means "misplace" or "not win": *Don't lose your way in the woods. They will lose the game unless they score soon.*

lots, lots of   See *alot, lots, lots of.*

may, can   See *can, may.*

may be, maybe   *Maybe* is a verb phrase: *The train may be late this morning. Maybe* is an adverb meaning "perhaps" or "possibly": *Maybe we can have lunch together tomorrow.*

may have, may of   See *of, have.*

media, medium   *Media* is the plural form of *medium: Of all the broadcast media, television is the medium that reaches most households.*

might have, might of   See *of, have.*

most, almost   *Most* should not be used in place of *almost.* When you mean "nearly," use *almost;* when you mean "the greatest number or quantity" use *most: She gets most of her exercise by walking to work almost every day.*

nowhere, nowheres   See *anyways, anywheres, nowheres.*

number of, amount of   See *amount of, number of.*

of, have   *Of* is spelled the way the contraction *'ve,* for *have,* sounds. Always write *could have, may have, might have, should have,* and *would have.*

off, off of   Use *off* or *from* instead of *off of:*

The poodle jumped off ~~of~~ the bed as I entered the room.

OK, O.K., okay   All three of these spellings are acceptable in informal writing, but they should be avoided in formal writing or speech.

percent (per cent), percentage   *Percent* should be used with a specific number: *Less than 40 percent of the class passed the exam. Percentage* is used when no number is referred to: *A large percentage of adults cannot program a VCR.*

plus   *Plus* is used as a preposition meaning "in addition to." *His skill plus his compassion made him a fine surgeon.* It should not be used as a conjunction in place of *and.*

He is very skillful, ~~plus~~ _{and} he is compassionate.

principal, principle   The noun *principal* can mean "sum of money (excluding interest)" or "important person in an organization": *At any time, you can pay the principal on this loan. The high school principal distributed the awards.* As an adjective, *principal* means "most important": *His principal concern was their safety. Principle* is a noun meaning "rule or standard": *The principles stated in the Constitution guide our democracy.*

raise, rise   *Raise* is a transitive verb meaning "lift." Its principal parts are *raise, raised,* and *raised: Raise the flag at sunrise. He raised the, flag at sunrise. They have raised the flag at sunrise for years. Rise* is an intransitive verb meaning "go higher" or "get to one's feet." Its principal parts are *rise, rose,* and *risen: I rise early on weekends. The sun gradually rose in the sky. The bread dough has already risen.*

real, really   *Real* is an adjective meaning "genuine" or "actual": *He found a real gold coin. Really* is an adverb meaning "very or extremely": *He is really proud of his discovery.*

reason is because, reason is that   Use *that* rather than *because* in formal speech and writing:

The reason I am late is ~~because~~ _{that} my car broke down.

regardless, irregardless   See *irregardless, regardless.*

set, sit   *Set* is a transitive verb meaning "put or place." Its principal parts are *set, set, set: Please set the pitcher on the table. I set it on the counter, instead. I will set it on the table later. Sit* is an intransitive verb meaning "be seated." Its principal parts are *sit, sat,* and *sat: I sit in the front row. He sat behind me. They have sat for too long.*

shall, will   *Shall* was once preferred for use with *I* or *we* and for expressing determination. Today, *will* and *shall* are practically in terchangeable for these instances, so *will* is acceptable for expressing future time with *be,* in all uses. *Shall* is now used primarily in polite questions: *Shall we dance?*

should have, should of   See *of, have.*

sometime, some time, sometimes   *Sometime* is an adverb meaning "at an unspecified point in the future": *We'll see that movie sometime.* *Some time* is an adjective (*some*) and a noun (*time*), and as a phrase it means "a period of time": *We'll find some time for that later.* *Sometimes* is an adverb meaning "now and then": *Sometimes recreation must be viewed as important.*

sort   See *kind, sort, type.*

sort of   See *kind of, sort of.*

stationary, stationery   *Stationary* is an adjective meaning "not moving": *Attach the birdhouse to a stationary object, such as a tree. Stationery* is a noun meaning "writing paper": *She sent a note on her personal stationery.*

suppose to, use to, supposed to, used to   *Suppose to* and *use to* are nonstandard and unacceptable substitutes for *supposed to* and *used to.*

sure, surely   *Sure* is an adjective: *She was sure she was correct. Surely* is an adverb: *She is surely correct.*

sure and, try and, sure to, try to   *Sure to* and *try to* are the correct forms.

take, bring   See *bring, take.*

than, then   *Than* is a conjunction that is used to make a comparison: *That is larger than I thought. Then* is an adverb used to indicate time: *Let's finish this first and then have dinner.*

that, which, who   Frequently, there is confusion about these relative pronouns. *That* refers to persons, animals, and things; *which* refers to animals and things; and *who* (and *whom*) refer to persons. To keep the distinctions clear, follow these guidelines.

1. Use *who* (*whom*) when referring to persons: *He is the one who won the contest.*

2. Use *which* for animals and things when it introduces nonrestrictive clauses: *My Sony Walkman, which I bought at Wal-Mart, works perfectly.*

3. Use *that* for animals and things when introducing restrictive relative clauses: *Everything that I did was misunderstood.*

their, there, they're   *Their* is a possessive pronoun: *They gave their tickets to the usher. There* is an adverb indicating place: *Put the chair over there, please. They're* is the contraction of *they are: They're going to be disappointed.*

theirself, theirselves, themself, themselves   *Theirself, theirselves,* and *themselves* are nonstandard substitutes for *themselves: They built the boat by themselves.*

these kind(s), these sort(s), these type(s)   See *kind, sort, type.*

to, too, two   *To* is either a preposition indicating direction or part of an infinitive: *I'm going to the store to buy groceries. Too* is an adverb meaning "also" or "more than enough": *She is too thin to be healthy. Can I come too? Two* is a number: *I'll be home in two hours.*

toward, towards   These words are interchangeable, but *toward* is preferred in American English. Use consistently whichever form you choose.

try and, try to   See *sure and, try and, sure to, try to.*

type   See *kind, sort, type.*

use to, used to   See *suppose to, use to, supposed to, used to.*

wait for, wait on   *Wait for* means "await" or "pause in expectation": *Wait for me at the bus stop. Wait on* means "serve" or "act as a waiter": *The restaurant owner <u>waited on us</u>.*

way, ways   *Ways* is a colloquial substitute for *way.* In formal writing and speech, use *way:*

> We have a long ~~ways~~ to go.
> ^{way}

well, good   See *good, well.*

whether, if   See *if, whether.*

which, who, that   See *that, which, who.*

who's, whose   *Who's* is the contraction of *who is*: *<u>Who's</u> knocking on the door? Whose* is the possessive form of *who*: *<u>Whose</u> car is that? Naomi is the one <u>whose</u> mother is the famous writer.*

will, shall   See *shall, will.*

would have, would of   See *of, have.*

your, you're   *Your* is a possessive pronoun: *<u>Your</u> apology is accepted. You're* is the contraction of *you are*: *<u>You're</u> welcome to join us for dinner.*

PART IX

ESL Guide for Nonnative Speakers of English

ESL GUIDE FOR NONNATIVE SPEAKERS OF ENGLISH

TO THE STUDENT

A cartoon once showed two apprehensive cats walking into a classroom. The sign on the door read, "Barking 101." Perhaps you felt a little like one of those nervous cats when you first entered a classroom to study English. Perhaps you wondered whether you were trying to do the impossible. But you were determined. After all, English is the most widely spoken language in the world, and it is the language of international business, technology, travel, sports, and entertainment. In short, it's an extremely useful language for work and for fun.

By now, you've reached a certain comfort level with English, a significant achievement. But now, the bar is higher. Your goal is to write correct, coherent, college-level English. This textbook and *ESL Guide* are designed to help you reach that goal. However, the book can do the job only in combination with your time and effort.

"How does one eat an elephant?" an old joke asks. The answer is "One bite at a time." You cannot master a language in a month or even in a year, but you can speed up the ongoing process of improving your English skills by these methods:

1. **Use and study English daily, as many hours a day as you can.** Read it and speak it with friends. Study vocabulary. (Perhaps set a goal of learning four new words a day.) Seek out opportunities to hear and use English by going to museums, libraries, and English-language movies. Use the Internet to do practice exercises and communicate with other ESL students around the world. (See the list of Web sites at the end of this guide.)

2. **Trust your ear—but not always.** You've been using English a long time, so sometimes what sounds right to you is right, even if you don't understand why. However, also realize that, if you have been speaking English mostly with people who are also nonnative speakers, you may have "fossilized" errors. In other words, what sounds right to you, because you've heard it so much, may actually be wrong. Ask your friends who are native English speakers to correct your errors in grammar and word usage.

3. **Keep in mind that writing isn't speaking.** When you speak, you often use incomplete sentences, and that's fine, but, in writing, you should use complete sentences. When you speak, intonation helps to convey your meaning; in writing, punctuation is needed to do that. Writing (especially academic writing) is more formal; it is not the place for slang.

4. **Learn to self-correct.** Listen to your own speech, and try to catch errors. Reread the writing you do for school (and not just for your English class). Reread it several times, each time looking for a different type of error or weakness. Writing is a process. A good piece of writing rarely comes from one draft.

5. **Remember that all four language skills—speaking, listening, reading, and writing—are interrelated.** If you work hard on one of these skills, that is likely to improve your skills in the other three areas as well. In particular, if you read a lot of published writing in English, you will see how people who know the language well construct sentences, paragraphs, and entire pieces of writing. This will improve your writing.

6. **English has the largest vocabulary of any language, and it is also a highly idiomatic language; don't depend upon your bilingual dictionary to answer all your questions about it.** You should also have an ESL dictionary. It defines words in the simplest vocabulary possible, shows you how to use words in sentences, provides definitions of idioms, explains the differences between similar words that are often confused, and does much more.

You are one of about 1.5 billion speakers of English, a truly global language. Your efforts to improve your English skills will surely enrich your life.

A | Verbs

A.1 ACTIVE-VOICE VERB TENSES AND RELATED FORMS

Ways to Write About the Present

1. **Simple present tense.** Use the simple present tense for (1) actions that happen repeatedly and (2) continuing actions expressed with nonaction verbs. (See section A.3. in this Guide for a list of these verbs.) The affirmative form of the simple present is only one word. It uses the infinitive except when the subject is third-person singular. Then the verb must end in *-s.*

   How can a third-person singular subject be recognized? Remember that first person means the speaker or writer: *I* or *we.* Second person means the listener or reader: *you.* Third person includes everyone and everything else. *Singular* means "one."

   Use the third-person singular verb form with the following subjects:

AN UNCOUNTABLE NOUN	That <u>music sounds</u> beautiful. My <u>homework is</u> difficult.
SOME ABSTRACT NOUNS	Is <u>happiness</u> an achievable goal? Is this <u>transportation</u> safe?
A GERUND	<u>Being</u> late for work <u>isn't</u> a good idea. <u>Having</u> a good job <u>is</u> important.
A COLLECTIVE NOUN	My <u>family enjoys</u> picnics.

   Singular collective nouns usually take a singular verb.

   To make a third-person singular verb, add *-s* or *-es* to the infinitive. Add *-es* if the verb ends in *ch, sh, s, x,* or *z* (*I wash, she washes*). If the verb ends in a consonant + *-y*, change the *-y* to *-i* and add *-es* (*I try/he tries*).

AFFIRMATIVE	<u>I want</u> a used car. <u>Carlos fixes</u> cars. <u>Carlos has</u> his own repair shop.

(*Note:* The verb *have* has an irregular third-person singular form: *has.*)

For most questions, use *do* except for third-person singular, which uses *does:*

> Why <u>do you need</u> a car?
>
> Why <u>does a car need</u> gas?

For questions with a question word or phrase as the subject, don't use a helping verb.

> <u>Who needs</u> a car?
>
> <u>How many Americans own</u> cars?

For negative sentences, use *don't* (or *do not*) for all subjects except third-person singular. Use *doesn't* (or *does not*) for third-person singular. Don't put an *-s* or *-es* on the main verb.

NEGATIVE   <u>Horses don't have</u> toes.
            <u>My dog doesn't have</u> long ears.

When *have* is the main verb, Americans use a helping verb. They don't say, "My dog hasn't long ears."

When using the verb *be*, use *am, is,* or, *are* for affirmative. Use *am not, isn't,* or *aren't* for negative. For questions with *be*, put the correct form of *be* before the subject.

> <u>Are you</u> a new student here? <u>Am I</u> in this class? <u>Is this book</u> yours?

2. **Present continuous tense.** Use *am, is,* or *are* + _____*ing.* Use this tense for actions happening at this moment or during a time period not yet ended. It can also be used for future when a future time expression is stated or implied.

AFFIRMATIVE   <u>I am painting</u> my living room this week.
              <u>We're sitting</u> in class right now.

QUESTIONS   <u>Are you enjoying</u> this flight?
              <u>How many people are flying</u> on this plane?

NEGATIVE   <u>I'm not writing</u> my essay tonight.
              <u>Joe and I aren't playing</u> tennis tomorrow.

When an Action or Condition Continues from Past to Present

1. **Present perfect tense.** Use *has* for third-person singular, *have* for all other subjects. Then add the past participle of the main verb. The past participle may be irregular.

2. **Present perfect continuous tense.** Use *has been* for third-person singular, *have been* for all other subjects. Then add the *-ing* form (the present participle) of the main verb.

Use these two tenses for actions or conditions that started in the past and continue into the present. For nonaction verbs, such as *like* and *want,* which cannot be used in a continuous tense, use present perfect. For many sentences, you can use either tense.

AFFIRMATIVE	I have spoken English for many years. I have been speaking English since I was a child.
QUESTIONS	How long have you been speaking English? Who has been teaching you? Have you ever been to England? (meaning "at any time in your life")
NEGATIVE	My brother hasn't learned any English yet. My sisters haven't either.

Note: For indefinite past uses of the present perfect, see the following section on past tenses.

Ways to Write About the Past

1. **Simple past tense.** Regular verbs end in *-ed*; irregular verbs have other forms. Use this tense to write about past actions, especially those that occurred only once. Use *did* in most questions and negatives. Use the infinitive of the main verb with *did* or *didn't*.

AFFIRMATIVE	I went to a movie last Saturday. I walked all the way there.
QUESTIONS	Did you like the movie? Who went with you?
NEGATIVE	I didn't like the movie. I didn't go with anyone.

   When using the verb *be*, use *was* for singular and *were* for plural. The verb after *you* is always plural.

   > Why were you late? (This might be asked of one person or more than one.)

   > The trains weren't on time this morning.

2. **Past continuous tense.** Use *was* or *were* + _____*ing*. Use this tense to write about actions that continued for a period of time.

   > I was doing homework all evening, so I missed a good TV show.

   Use this tense when a longer, earlier action is interrupted by a shorter action:

   > They were driving too fast when the accident happened.

   Use the past continuous after *while*; use the simple past after *when*.

AFFIRMATIVE	While I was driving on the highway, another car hit mine.
QUESTIONS	Were you listening to the radio when the accident happened? Who was driving when the accident happened?
NEGATIVE	I was driving, but I wasn't driving fast at all.

3. **Present perfect tense.** Use *have* or *has* + the past participle. This tense (or the simple past) can be used to write about a past action if the sentence doesn't tell *when* it happened. Don't use it with *ago* phrases or *when* clauses

because these tell a definite past time. Present perfect is often used to tell about repeated past actions. Use *has* with third-person singular subjects.

AFFIRMATIVE   I've visited your country many times.
My brother has been there, too.

QUESTIONS   What countries have you visited?
Who has traveled with you?

NEGATIVE   I haven't visited any South American countries yet.

4. **Past perfect tense.** Use *had* + the past participle. Use this tense when there are two past actions in the same sentence. Put the earlier action in past perfect and the later one in simple past. (*Note:* If there is a word such as *before* or *after* that clarifies which action occurred first, you can use the simple past tense for both verbs.)

AFFIRMATIVE   I had already studied English before I came to the
United States.

QUESTION   Had you thought about leaving home for a long time
before you left?

NEGATIVE   I hadn't spoken a word of English before I arrived here.

5. **Past perfect continuous tense.** Use *had been* + _____*ing.* Use this tense when a sentence has two past actions, and the earlier one continued for a while.

AFFIRMATIVE   I had been living in Paris for many years before I came here.

QUESTIONS   Who(m) had you been living with before you got your
own apartment?

NEGATIVE   I hadn't been sharing an apartment with anybody until
I came to the United States.

6. **The form *used to* is followed by an infinitive (base form) verb with no ending.** Use this verb form to write about something that was true in the past but isn't anymore. *Used to* tells about actions that happened many times or conditions that lasted a long time.

AFFIRMATIVE   I used to live in South America, but now I live in
North America.

Ways to Write About the Future

1. **Simple future tense.** Use *will* or *shall* + the infinitive verb form. Use the simple future for something that will happen very soon, for promises, and for formal speech or writing.

Salesman to customer: "I'll get those shoes for you right away."

I'm sorry my essay is late. I'll turn it in by Monday.

Our economy will be in trouble if inflation continues.

Note: When the verb in the main clause is in the future, the verb in a subordinating time clause is in the present tense. If it's a third-person-singular verb, it must end in *-s.*

AFFIRMATIVE	When Boris <u>comes</u> to visit Chicago, <u>we'll go</u> sightseeing.
QUESTIONS	Who <u>will come</u> with him? Where <u>will</u> he <u>stay</u>?
NEGATIVE	He <u>won't stay</u> in my apartment. It's too small. (*will not = won't*)

2. **Use the present tense of *be* + *going to* + the infinitive of the main verb to talk about general plans**, especially in casual conversation. Contractions are usually used.

AFFIRMATIVE	<u>I'm going to be</u> at work until 10 o'clock tonight.
QUESTIONS	When <u>are you going to quit</u> that terrible job?
NEGATIVE	<u>I'm not going to leave</u> my current job until I find another one.

3. **Future continuous tense.** Use *will be* + the present participle (the *-ing* form) of the main verb. Use this tense to write about continuing actions in the future.

AFFIRMATIVE	The plane <u>will be arriving</u> late, but my uncle <u>will be waiting</u> for me.
QUESTIONS	<u>Will you be staying</u> with your uncle? <u>Will you be paying</u> him rent?
NEGATIVE	<u>I won't be paying</u> him any rent until I find a job.

4. **Present tenses for future actions.** You can use either of the present tenses to talk about the future if there is a time expression or some other indication of future meaning.

> John <u>is coming</u> to Los Angeles <u>soon</u>.
>
> His plane <u>arrives</u> next Monday at noon.

5. **Future perfect.** Use *will have* + the past participle. Use this tense to write about an action that is now in the future but will be in the past when a stated future time comes.

> By next summer, I <u>will have finished</u> two years of college.

6. **Future perfect continuous.** Use *will have been* + the present participle. This tense is also used for future actions that will, at some later time, be past.

> I <u>will have been attending</u> this school for four years by the time I graduate.

A.2 MODAL AUXILIARIES

"Modals are really strange and confusing," one ESL student remarked. It's true. These ten little words are used to convey a great many different meanings such as ability, possibility, permission, opportunity, advice, obligation, necessity, a promise, a request, an offer, an inference—or the negative of any of these. The following chart lists uses and examples.

MODALS	USES	SAMPLE SENTENCES
will/would/ shall	future	I'll go with you to the movie.
	a promise	We'll help you tomorrow.
	subjunctive	I would help you if I had time.
	wants	I'd like some coffee, please.
	future, first person	We shall win this election!
can/could	present ability	Joe can swim very well.
	suggestion	We could go to a movie or watch TV.
	past (in)ability	I couldn't swim when I was a child.
	past opportunity not taken	We could have gone swimming, but we played tennis instead.
may/might	possibility	He may (might) be in New York City.
	past possibility	He may (might) have gone to New York City.
should/ ought to	advice	You should quit smoking.
	obligation	I should visit my sick aunt.
	past mistake	I shouldn't have eaten six hot dogs.
must	necessity	You must pay taxes.
	inference	Joe isn't home. He must be at the library.
	inference about the past	He must have gone to the library. (He probably went to the library.)

Note: When writing about the past, don't use *must* for the meaning of necessity. Use *had to*:

I had to go to the doctor yesterday because I felt very sick.

Modals and Contractions

1. The only modals that have contractions are

   would = 'd (the same contraction as is used for *had*): *I'd, he'd, they'd,* etc.

   will = 'll: *I'll, she'll, we'll,* etc.

2. The irregular contraction for *will not* is *won't.*

3. Most modals can be contracted with *not (can't, couldn't shouldn't,* etc.), but Americans rarely contract *may, ought,* or *shall* with *not.*

4. When speaking, people may say, "John'll be here soon." However, in a piece of writing, don't contract a noun and a verb. Write "John will be here soon." or "He'll be here soon."

A Few Rules for Using Modals

1. **Never put an ending on a modal verb.** Unlike most other auxiliary (helping) verbs, modal verbs do not have endings that tell person or tense.

2. **Never put an ending on the verb immediately after a modal.** Use the infinitive.

3. **Note that the modal verb phrase is the same for both present and future.**

   I <u>can help</u> you <u>now</u>. (or) I <u>can help</u> you <u>tomorrow</u>.

4. **Don't use *to* after a modal except for *ought to*.**

   She <u>ought to get</u> a dog.

   She <u>should get</u> a dog.

5. **Use *shall* only with *I* or *we*.** *Shall* is usually used for more serious matters and/or in more formal situations. Americans don't use it much except for offers such as "Shall I get you some coffee?" or suggestions such as "Shall we go now?"

Why Are Modals Confusing?

The main reason modals are confusing is that most of them have more than one meaning.

1. ***Could* + an infinitive verb has two meanings.**

   FUTURE   We could <u>buy</u> a car <u>next month</u>.

   PAST   I <u>couldn't speak</u> English <u>last year</u>.

2. ***Could have* + a past participle has two meanings.**

   PAST OPPORTUNITY NOT TAKEN   We could <u>have bought</u> a big house, but we liked this one.

   A PAST POSSIBILITY   "Why wasn't Joe at his sister's birthday party last Saturday?"
   "We're not sure. He could <u>have been</u> out of town that day."

   Could is the only modal that has both a two-word and a three-word form for talking about the past. The negative uses of these forms also have different meanings.

   LACK OF ABILITY   I <u>couldn't go</u> to my friend's house last night because I had to study.

   IMPOSSIBILITY   You couldn't <u>have seen</u> me at Lisa's party. I wasn't there.

3. ***Should have* plus a past participle refers to a past mistake.** It has a negative meaning. It means the subject didn't do something and regrets not doing it. On the other hand, *shouldn't have* plus a past participle means the subject did something and regrets that.

   I <u>shouldn't have bought</u> a motorcycle last year.

   I <u>should have gotten</u> a car instead.

4. ***May* can mean permission or possibility (or the negatives of these).**

   PERMISSION   You <u>may not bring</u> your gun on the airplane.

   POSSIBILITY   You <u>may get</u> into trouble if you try.

5. **Many other expressions have the same meanings as modal phrases:**

<u>You may not smoke</u> on the airplane. / <u>You're not allowed to smoke</u> on the airplane.

<u>I must go</u> home soon. / <u>I have to go</u> home soon.

<u>You shouldn't drink</u> any more beer. / <u>You'd better not drink</u> any more beer.

<u>You can't drive</u> without a license. / <u>You're not supposed to drive</u> without a license.

<u>I would rather have tea</u> than coffee. / <u>I prefer tea</u> to coffee.

A.3 NONACTION VERBS

Some verbs listed in the following chart are never, or usually not, used in continuous tenses.

Verbs Not Usually Used in Continuous Tenses
Sensory perception: *see, hear, taste, smell*
I <u>see</u> our teacher, Dr. Franklin, over there.
Mental activity: *believe, forget, mean, know, think, recognize, remember, understand*
I <u>believe</u> he saw me, too.
Ownership/possession: *belong, have, own, possess*
He <u>owns</u> a boat, but he <u>doesn't have</u> a car.
Feelings/opinions/attitudes: *appreciate, dislike, hate, love, need, prefer, seem, want*
Dr. Franklin <u>loves</u> his five dogs, but he <u>dislikes</u> all other animals.
Other: *cost*
Textbooks <u>cost</u> a lot of money these days.

A.4 PASSIVE VOICE

How to Make Passive Voice Tenses

1. **In active voice sentences,** the subject performs the action of the verb.

<u>People speak</u> English all over the world.

<u>No one has seen</u> him for a week.

In passive voice sentences, the subject does not do the action; something happens to the subject.

<u>English is spoken</u> all over the world.

He <u>hasn't been seen</u> for a week.

2. **Of the 12 active voice tenses, eight are used in passive.** To make a passive verb, put the verb *be* in the tense you want, and then add the past participle (see chart).

Eight Passive Voice Tenses	
TENSE	EXAMPLE
Simple present	Every four years, a president <u>is elected</u> in the United States.
Present continuous	<u>Is</u> a president <u>being elected</u> this year?
Present perfect	Sometimes the same candidate <u>has been elected</u> to serve two terms.
Simple past	Franklin Roosevelt <u>was elected</u> president four times from 1932 to 1944.
Past continuous	Was your family living in the United States when those elections <u>were being held</u>?
Past perfect	President Roosevelt <u>had</u> recently <u>been elected</u> for his fourth term when he died in April 1945.
Simple future	The next president election <u>won't be held</u> until 2012.
Future perfect	By December 2012, another presidential election <u>will have been held</u>.

3. **Passive sentences can also be made with modals.**
   For the present or future, use a modal + *be* + the past participle.

   The dog <u>should be fed</u>. (This is advice. The poor dog is hungry.)

   For the past, use a modal + *have been* + the past participle:

   The dog <u>should have been fed</u>. (He wasn't fed. That was a mistake.)

4. **There are only two continuous tenses used in passive, present and past.** To make these tenses, use *being*. Use *am/is/are being* for present and *was/were being* for past.

   The injured player <u>was being carried</u> from the field when the ambulance came.

5. **Make a passive tense negative by making the first verb negative.**

   My dog <u>won't be fed</u> again until seven o'clock.

   He <u>hasn't been fed</u> since breakfast.

6. **Make questions with the passive voice the usual way: put the first helping verb before the subject.**

   <u>Why won't your dog be fed</u> sooner?

   <u>Is your cat being fed</u> right now?

When to Use Passive Voice

Most writing should be in the active voice, but there are times when the passive voice is the better choice. Here are the main reasons for using the passive voice.

1. **The doer of the action is unknown.**

   This house <u>was built</u> 50 years ago.

2. **The doer of the action isn't important.**

   Q: Is this bread fresh?

   A: It <u>was baked</u> this morning. (It doesn't matter who baked it.)

3. **The person or people who did the action are obvious.**

   I <u>was born</u> in April.

   You don't need to say, "My mother bore me in April." or "My mother gave birth to me in April." Everyone knows that your mother did it.

4. **The speaker does not want to mention the source of certain information.**

   I <u>was told</u> that John and Louise are getting divorced.

5. **Passive is often used to talk or write about the creation of a work of art.**

   War and Peace <u>was written</u> by Tolstoy.

   Use *by* before the doer of the action in passive.

6. **Passive is often used to avoid a vague *you, they,* or *someone*.**

   The store <u>will be remodeled</u> next month.

   Not   They will remodel the store next month.

   Papers <u>can be typed</u> in the computer lab.

   Not   You can type a paper in the computer lab.

7. **Passive is often used in scientific and other scholarly writing.**

   Five explosive chemicals <u>were put</u> into the test tube before the lab blew up.

B Nouns

B.1 PLURAL FORMS OF REGULAR NOUNS

Section A.1 (p. 551) in "Reviewing the Basics" covers the seven categories of nouns. "Avoiding Subject-Verb Agreement Errors" in Chapter 10 (pp. 274–277) provides explanation and practice with subject-verb agreement. Section D.2 (p. 602) reviews which nouns need to be capitalized. Here is a chart of spelling rules for plural nouns.

Spelling Rules for Plural Nouns	
1. Make most nouns plural by adding -s.	*school/schools, desk/desks*
2. When the singular form ends in *ch*, *sh*, *s*, *x*, or *z*, add -*es*.	*tax/taxes, watch/watches*
3. When the singular ends in *f* or *fe*, change it to -*ves*.	*knife/knives, shelf/shelves* exceptions: *chiefs, roofs*
4. When the singular ends in a consonant + *y*, change *y* to *i*, then add -*es*. If it ends in a vowel + *y*, just add -*s*.	*city/cities, toy/toys*
5. When the singular ends in a consonant + *o*, add -*es*. When it ends in a vowel + *o*, just add -*s*.	*tomato/tomatoes, hero/heroes, studio/studios, ratio/ratios, radio/radios* **musical exceptions**: *solos, pianos, cellos, sopranos*

B.2 PLURAL FORMS OF IRREGULAR NOUNS

Nouns that do not form their plurals by adding *-s* or *-es* are called **irregular nouns**. Here are some examples.

1. **Some common irregular plurals:**

   foot/feet   tooth/teeth   child/children   woman/women   man/men

2. **Some academic irregular plurals:**

   alumnus/alumni   analysis/analyses   crisis/crises   datum/data

   hypothesis/hypotheses   parenthesis/parentheses   thesis/theses

3. **Some words with both a regular and an irregular plural:**

   person/people or *persons*

   appendix/appendices or *appendixes   medium/media* or *mediums*

   memorandum/memoranda or *memorandums   syllabus/syllabi* or *syllabuses*

4. **Some words with only one form for singular and plural:**

   deer, fish, sheep

5. **Some words with a plural form only:**

   pants, glasses (for eyes), *clothes, groceries*

6. **Some words that look plural but can be singular:**

   news (always singular) *series means*

B.3 POSSESSIVE FORMS OF NOUNS

To make a noun possessive, do the following:

1. **Add an apostrophe + -*s* to all singular nouns and to plural irregular nouns.**

   Columbus's ships   the library's book collection   the children's home

2. **Add just an apostrophe to nouns that are plural and regular (end in -*s*).**

   the students' desks   the professors' office   two cities' museums

For more explanation and examples, see "Reviewing the Basics," C.5, "Apostrophes" (p. 599).

B.4 GERUNDS AND INFINITIVES

Gerunds and infinitives are called *verbals* because they are words made from verbs. However, they function as nouns in a sentence. A *gerund* is the same form as a present participle, the verb used to make continuous tenses; it is the infinitive + *-ing* (*waiting, running,* etc.). An *infinitive* is the base form of a verb, usually preceded by *to* (*to wait, to run,* etc.).

Common Uses of Gerunds and Infinitives

1. As subjects of clauses, either a gerund or an infinitive can be used. The gerund is used more often.

   <u>Studying</u> is hard work.
   <u>To study</u> is hard work.
   <u>Raising</u> children is difficult.
   (*Raising* is the subject, not *children*, so the verb is singular.)

2. As objects of prepositions, only gerunds (not infinitives) can be used. Use a gerund even after the preposition *to*.

   Maria is interested <u>in starting</u> her own business. She's looking forward <u>to being</u> her own boss.

3. When using a verbal as the object of a verb, sometimes you need a gerund, sometimes an infinitive; sometimes either one is okay.

   Maria <u>wants to start</u> her own business. She <u>will enjoy being</u> her own boss. She <u>likes being</u> (or <u>to be</u>) the boss.

Try to learn the common verbs that take only gerunds as direct objects if the direct object is a verbal. (The list includes *admit, avoid, consider, delay, deny, dislike, enjoy, miss, practice, suggest,* and many more.) Once you know these, you can safely use the full infinitive (with *to*) for most others. For a longer list of verbs followed by gerunds and other information about gerund and infinitive constructions, go online to the first Web site listed in section G of this *ESL Guide*.

C Pronouns

Several sections of this book provide explanations and practice with pronoun usage. To review pronouns, read the "Using Pronouns Clearly and Correctly" section in Chapter 9 (pp. 231–238) and Section A.2 in *Reviewing the Basics* (pp. 553–556).

C.1 PERSONAL PRONOUNS

The following chart shows the uses of personal pronouns:

	Personal Pronouns			
SUBJECT PRONOUNS	OBJECT PRONOUNS	POSSESSIVE PRONOUNS (AS ADJECTIVES)	POSSESSIVE PRONOUNS	REFLEXIVE PRONOUNS
I	me	my	mine	myself
you	you	your	yours	yourself (-ves)
he	him	his	his	himself
she	her	her	hers	herself
it	it	its	—	itself
we	us	our	ours	ourselves
they	them	their	theirs	themselves

Subject Pronouns

1. Use a subject pronoun (*I, we,* etc.) as the subject of a clause and after a linking verb.

     They (*not* Them) are nice.

     It is he. (*not* him)

2. **When using a compound subject, use subject pronouns.**

   Tom and I (*not* me) are working on this project together.

3. **When using pronouns in compound subjects, it's polite for the speaker or writer to refer to himself or herself last and to the listener or reader first.**

   You and they (*not* They and you) can meet with Bill and me on Friday.

4. **Remember that *you* takes a plural verb even when referring to only one person.**

Object Pronouns

1. **Use object pronouns after a verb.**

   Please help them do this research.

2. **Use object pronouns after a preposition.**

   The professor gave our graded papers to us.

Pronouns Used as Possessive Adjectives

1. **Use the possessive adjective pronouns before a noun.** For example, use *our* and *my* not *us* and *mine*.

   Dr. Nguyen called our pharmacy to give my prescription to the pharmacist.

2. **Be careful about spelling!** Don't confuse *his* with *he's* (*he is*), *your* with *you're* (*you are*), or *their* with *they're* (*they are*) or *there*.

Possessive Pronouns Used as Pronouns

1. **These forms are not used before a noun. They replace the noun.**

   These books aren't Juanita's. They're mine. (*not* mine books).

2. **Compare these forms with the ones used as possessive adjectives.** Note that, except for *mine*, the forms used as pronouns all end in *-s*. Only *his* is the same in both forms.

Reflexive Pronouns

Reflexive pronouns have two main uses.

1. **They are used when the subject did, does, or will do something to himself or herself.**

   I hurt myself. *but* My dog hurt me.

2. **They are used for emphasis.**

   The chancellor herself visited our class. (She didn't send someone else.)

Note: Reflexive pronouns have a singular and a plural form for the second person. To one person say, "Did you hurt yourself?" To more than one, say "Did you hurt yourselves?"

C.2 INDEFINITE PRONOUNS

Study the list of indefinite pronouns in "Reviewing the Basics," A.2. "Pronouns" (p. 555). Use a singular verb with all pronouns listed in the singular columns, even if they refer to several people or things.

<u>Everything is</u> ready, and <u>everyone is</u> here.

D | Adjectives and Adverbs

To read about types of adjectives, see "Reviewing the Basics," A.4, "Adjectives" (p. 562). To review the comparative and superlative patterns and irregular adjectives and adverbs, see Chapter 7 (pp. 185–190). For samples of comparisons of equality using *as . . . as,* look in the *ESL Guide* E.2, "Transitional Words and Phrases: Transitions of Equality, Addition, and Similarity" (p. 644).

D.1 SOME GRAMMATICAL REMINDERS

1. *Well* is usually an adverb, but it is also used as an adjective to mean "healthy."

2. *Much* is used in questions and negative statements but not in affirmative statements.

    Does he have <u>much</u> money?

    Yes, he has a <u>lot of</u> (a <u>great deal of</u>) money.

3. **Which form should you use—an adjective or an adverb?** If the word describes a noun or pronoun, use an adjective. If it describes a verb, adjective, or another adverb, use an adverb. If it tells *how* something is, was, or will be done, use an adverb.

    She is a <u>quick</u> runner.   *but*   She runs <u>quickly</u>.

4. **Most adjectives can be made into adverbs by adding -ly.** However, some words can be adjectives or adverbs, for example, *hard* and *fast*.

    ADJECTIVE   Carlos <u>is a hard worker</u>.

    ADVERB   He <u>works hard</u>.

    Don't use *hardly* as an adverb for *hard*. *Hardly* means "almost not at all."

    He has <u>hardly</u> any money. (He has almost no money.)

5. Note these spelling changes when making comparative and superlative forms:

Y TO I   healthy, healthier, healthiest

DOUBLING   big, bigger, biggest

To review doubling rules, see "Reviewing the Basics," D.6, "Six Useful Spelling Rules," #4–5 (p. 607).

D.2 RELATIVE (ADJECTIVE) CLAUSES

1. **A relative (adjective) clause, like all clauses, has a subject and verb.** However, a relative clause isn't a complete sentence; it's a dependent clause, so it must be attached to a main idea.

   The huge statue that stands in New York Harbor is called the Statue of Liberty.

2. **A relative clause can be introduced by one of these words:** *who, whom, that, which, whose, whoever, whomever, when,* or *where.*

3. **With restrictive clauses, which identify or limit the meaning of the subject, no commas are used.**

4. **With nonrestrictive clauses, which do not identify or limit the meaning of the subject, commas are used before the clause begins and also at the end—unless the clause comes at the end of a sentence.** See examples of restrictive and nonrestrictive clauses in the following chart.

When to Use *Who, That,* and *Which*	
Use *who* . . .	to talk about a person or people (singular or plural): I know the name of the man *who* designed the Statue of Liberty.
Use *that* . . .	to talk about a person, animal, or thing (singular or plural) for restrictive clauses only (the ones without commas): The day *that* the statue was unveiled there was a big celebration.
Use *which* . . .	to talk about things and animals only; generally, for nonrestrictive clauses: Liberty's right arm, *which* is high in the air, holds a torch.

5. **An adjective clause describes a noun or, occasionally, a pronoun.** It must be placed immediately after the word it describes. Otherwise, the sentence might be confusing.

    INCORRECT   Liberty is in New York Harbor, <u>which was built by Frederic Bartholdi</u>.

    CORRECT   Liberty, <u>which was built by Frederic Bartholdi</u>, is in New York Harbor.

    (The statue, not the harbor, was built by Bartholdi.)

6. ***Whose* is the possessive form of *who*.** It is used to indicate a relationship or ownership. The usual pattern is a noun, *whose*, another noun.

    <u>The woman whose poem</u> is written on Liberty's pedestal is Emma Lazarus.

7. **Warning! Don't use *what* to begin an adjective clause.** *What* is used to introduce noun clauses. Noun clauses answer the question *who* or *what* about the verb.

    NOUN CLAUSE   Lydia asked <u>what material the statue was made of</u>. "Copper," a guide said.

8. **What's the difference between *who* and *whom*?** *Who* is a subject pronoun, like *I* and *they*; *whom* is an object pronoun, like *me* and *them*. Americans seldom use *whom* in informal speaking or writing, but it is appropriate in serious speeches and academic writing. Use *whom* as the object of a verb or a preposition.

    WHO AS A SUBJECT   Bartholdi is the man <u>who</u> designed the Statue of Liberty.

    WHOM AS THE OBJECT OF THE VERB USED   The woman <u>whom</u> Bartholdi used as the model for the face was probably his mother.

    WHOM AS THE OBJECT OF A PREPOSITION   The guide <u>whom</u> Lydia spoke to was very polite.

    OR

    The guide to <u>whom</u> Lydia spoke was very polite.

Transitional Words and Phrases

Transitions are words and phrases used within sentences, between sentences, or between paragraphs to help readers understand how one idea relates to the next.

E.1 TRANSITIONS FOR CONTRAST

There are several ways to express an idea that ends with a surprising result or condition.

Coordinating Conjunctions (*but* and *yet*)

1. *Yet*, which often means "up to now," is also a synonym for *but*. When using *but* or *yet* as a coordinating conjunction (connecting two complete ideas that could be separate sentences), place a comma before the transition.

   I like coffee, <u>but</u> I never drink it. (or) I like coffee, <u>yet</u> I never drink it.

2. **Do not use a comma after a coordinating conjunction if the idea that follows is not a complete thought.** To be a complete thought, the clause must have a subject, verb, and complete idea.

   NO COMMAS   I like <u>dogs but</u> not cats.
                   We saw <u>tigers but</u> didn't see elephants at the zoo.

   There is no subject after *but* in the examples above.

   COMMAS   I like <u>dogs, but I</u> don't like cats.
              We saw the <u>tigers, but we</u> didn't see elephants.

   I is the subject after *but* in the first example. *We* is the subject after *but* in the second example.

Subordinating Conjunctions (*although, even though, though,* and *while*)

1. *Although, even though,* and *though* all mean the same and are grammatically the same. Note that *although* is one word, but *even though* is two words. *While,* which is often used to connect two actions happening at the same time, is also a contrast word meaning *but.* Never write clauses that begin with subordinating conjunctions as complete sentences.

   INCORRECT   Even though Joe is in debt. He bought his wife a diamond necklace.

2. Also, put the more important idea in the main (independent) clause and the less important idea in the subordinate (dependent) clause.

   INCORRECT   Even though Joe bought his wife a diamond necklace, he is in debt.

3. Sentences with subordinating conjunctions are reversible. Either clause can come first.

   CORRECT   Even though Joe is in debt, he bought his wife a diamond necklace.

   CORRECT   Joe bought his wife a diamond necklace even though he's in debt.

Conjunctive Adverbs (*however, nevertheless, still,* and *nonetheless*)

When using one of these contrast words, place a semicolon before the transitional word and a comma after it, or use a period before the conjunctive adverb and a comma after it.

   INCORRECT   She loved the necklace, however, she returned it.

   CORRECT   She loved the necklace; however, she returned it.

Warning: The other contrast conjunctive adverbs have a more limited meaning than *however.* Use *nevertheless, still,* or *nonetheless* when the first clause states a truth and the second clause (which usually has the same subject) states a surprising fact about that truth.

   Joe is very smart; nevertheless, (*or* however) he doesn't get good grades.

   Joe is a good student; however, (*not* nevertheless) his brother isn't.

Phrases That Indicate Contrast

Write a subject and verb after *in spite of the fact that.*

   In spite of the fact that it's raining, I want to take a walk.

Don't use a subject and verb after *despite.*

   Despite the rain, I want to take a walk.

E.2 TRANSITIONS FOR EQUALITY, ADDITION, AND SIMILARITY

Some Patterns for Discussing Things, Places, or People That Are the Same or Similar

1. Use helping verbs to complete comparisons with short forms.

   New York City has a lot of skyscrapers, and *so does* Chicago.

   New York City has a lot of skyscrapers, and Chicago *does, too.*

2. Use a noun (not an adjective) after *the same.*

   He is the same height as his father. (*not* the same tall).

   New York's skyscrapers are not the same style as Chicago's.

3. Use *similarly* or *likewise* between two complete ideas.

   Chicago has a lot of skyscrapers; similarly (*or* likewise), New York City is famous for its skyscrapers. (You can use a period or a semicolon between the clauses.)

4. Use *like* before a noun (or an adjective and a noun). Use *alike* after a verb.

   Chicago, like New York City, has a lot of skyscrapers.

   Chicago and New York City are alike (*or* the same) in this way: both have skyscrapers.

Word Pairs to Discuss Similarities

Both Orville Wright and his brother Wilbur worked on the invention of the airplane.

Neither Orville nor Wilbur is alive today. (Note the singular verb with *neither*.)

Not only did Thomas Edison perfect the electric light bulb, but he also invented the phonograph.

Words to Use to Add Similar Things, Places, or People

1. **Use the coordinating conjunction *and*.** Use a comma when *and* connects two complete ideas.

   Edison was a famous inventor, and so was Alexander Graham Bell.

2. **Use the conjunctive adverbs *besides, moreover, furthermore,* and *also*.** (Don't confuse *besides* with *beside*, which means "next to.")

   Tourists can visit Edison's home in New Jersey; besides, his home in Florida is open to the public.

3. **Use the phrases *in addition* and *in addition to*.**

> <u>In addition to</u> my home phone, I also have an office phone, a cell phone, an e-mail account, and a fax machine. Why couldn't you get in touch with me?

> I have three phone numbers; <u>in addition</u>, I have three e-mail accounts.

E.3 TRANSITIONS FOR TIME

1. **One action happened, happens, or will happen after another action.**

   Any of these—*when, as soon as, once,* or *after*—can be inserted into the blank below:

   > I'll get a full-time job _____ I finish school.

   As soon as means "immediately after."

   Then or *next* can be inserted after a semicolon or a period but not after a comma.

   INCORRECT   I'll finish school, <u>then</u> I'll get a full-time job.

   CORRECT   I'll finish school; <u>then,</u> I'll get a full-time job. (OR)
                I'll finish school, <u>and then</u> I'll get a full-time job.

2. **Two actions happened, happen, or will happen at the same time.**

   > <u>While I was watching TV</u>, my roommate was studying. (complex sentence)

   > I was watching TV; <u>meanwhile</u>, my roommate was studying. (compound sentence)

3. **An action continued, continues, or will continue up to a stated time. Then the first action ends.**

   > I'll wait here <u>until Linette arrives</u>.

4. **An action continued from a stated time in the past up to the present.**

   > I've been waiting for Linette <u>since noon</u>.

5. **An action will happen if something else doesn't happen (or vice versa).**

   > I'll eat lunch alone <u>unless Linette arrives</u>.

   > I won't eat lunch alone <u>unless Linette never arrives</u>.

E.4 TRANSITIONS FOR REASONS OR PURPOSE

1. **Use a subject and verb after *because* but not after *because of*.**

   > I took a Canadian Rockies tour <u>because I wanted</u> to see the beautiful scenery.

My brother couldn't go with me <u>because of his job</u> (or) <u>because he had to work</u>.

2. **Either *so* or *so that* can be used before a reason or a purpose.**

We went to the International Peace Park <u>so that we could see the mountains and glaciers</u>.

3. **Before a purpose or reason, an infinitive or *in order* + an infinitive can also be used.**

We took a cruise on Waterton Lake <u>to look</u> for mountain goats and other wild animals.

We went to Banff <u>in order to see</u> this picturesque town beloved by skiers.

E.5 TRANSITIONS FOR RESULTS

1. Use the coordinating conjunction *so* preceded by a comma to express a result.

We didn't have much rain during the trip, <u>so</u> our trip was very nice.

2. In the following sentence, you can put any of these in the blank: *therefore, consequently*, or *as a result*.

I enjoyed my Canadian trip; _____, I'm taking another one next summer.

F

Conditional Statements and Subjunctive Verb Forms

If statements are of two main types: (1) those about a possibility and (2) those about something that cannot possibly happen (or have happened), at least not within the stated time period. Both types are reversible; the *if* clause can come first or second.

Possibility: Past, Present, and Future

1. **Some statements express uncertainty about the past.**

    Julia's children probably cried all morning <u>if their trip was cancelled</u>.

    (The speaker doesn't know if their trip was cancelled or not.)

2. **Some statements express uncertainty about what's happening in the present.**

    <u>If it's raining in L.A. now</u>, Julia and the children may be at home.

3. **Some statements express uncertainty about the future.** These are about what might happen under certain circumstances.

    <u>If it stops raining soon</u>, Julia and the children will go to Disney World.

    Other ways to express uncertainty about the future are the following:

    If my car starts, I'll go out. <u>If not</u>, I'll stay home.

    I'll go out <u>unless</u> my car doesn't start. I won't go out <u>unless</u> my car starts.

    If my car starts, I'll go out; <u>otherwise</u>, I'll stay home.

Impossibility: Subjunctive Statements

In these subjunctive sentences, the speaker or writer is imagining that things would be different if something impossible could (or did) happen.

1. **Present unreal, active voice.**

>   If cars <u>had</u> wings, they <u>could fly</u>. (They don't have wings, so they can't fly.)

    The verb in the *if* clause is past; the main clause verb is a modal + an infinitive.

2. **Present unreal with the verb *be*.**

>   <u>If I were</u> taller, I <u>might be</u> a basketball player. (I'm not tall enough for basketball.)

    The verb in the *if* clause is *were* with all subjects; the main clause verb begins with a modal.

3. **Past unreal, active voice.**

>   If no one <u>had invented</u> cars or airplanes, the air <u>would have remained</u> unpolluted.

>   (We have cars and airplanes, so we have polluted air.)

    The *if* clause verb is past perfect; the main clause verb is a modal + *have* + a past participle.

F.2 ADDITIONAL USES OF THE SUBJUNCTIVE

1. **Statements with *wish* are usually about something impossible.** Clauses beginning *I wish* use a past tense verb to tell about the present and past perfect to tell about the past:

    PRESENT   I wish I <u>could go</u> to Disneyland this year, but I don't have enough money.

    PAST   I wish I <u>hadn't bought</u> a car; then, I <u>would have had</u> enough money for a vacation.

2. **Subjunctive forms are used in some statements about recommendations and requirements.** See "Reviewing the Basics," A.3, "Verbs" (under "Mood") p. 560.

G Web Sites for ESL Students

The Internet offers a wealth of free Web sites for practicing all four English skills—listening, reading, speaking, and writing. Listed below are just a few of the sites that offer grammar explanations and quizzes (with answers), games, reading materials, sites for communicating with ESL and EFL students from around the world, and much more. Some of the sites listed below are linking sites; they direct users to other ESL sites for activities.

The Owl at Purdue: http://owl.english.purdue.edu/owl/resource/627/04

ESLoop: http://www.esloop.org

Dave's ESL Café: http://www.eslcafe.com

ESL Independent Study Lab: http://www.lclark.edu/~krauss/toppicks/toppicks.html

TTESL/TEFL/TESOL/ESL/EFL/ESOL Links: http://iteslj.org/links

Guide to Grammar and Writing: http://grammar.ccc.commnet.edu/grammar

Note: Sometimes online addresses change. If a site is unreachable via the URL, type its name into Google to get a link to it.

There are also ESL dictionaries online. The *Longman Dictionary of Contemporary English Online* (http://www.ldoceonline.com) has an 88,000-word vocabulary and gives sample phrases to show how words are used. It's an excellent reference tool.

Credits

Photo Credits

Page 1, left to right: Simon Jarratt/Corbis; Digital Vision/Veer; Blend Images/Veer; **6, right:** Javier Pierini/Corbis; **17:** David Hanover/Getty Images; **36, top:** David Rae Morris/Reuters/Landov; **36, bottom:** Steven Prezant/Corbis; **37, left to right:** Frank Siteman/PhotoEdit Inc.; Peter M. Fisher/Corbis; **89:** C. J. Burton; **94:** Courtesy Mutual America Life Insurance Company and MCS Advertising, Ltd.; **123:** Digital Vision/Alamy; **141:** Mark Leibowitz/ Masterfile; **148:** Javier Perini/Corbis; **174:** Don Klumpp/Getty Images; **176:** © The New Yorker Collection 1983 Jack Ziegler from cartoonbank.com. All Rights Reserved.; **194:** Anne Senstad; **201:** Don Farrall/Getty Images; **219:** Ryan Pyle/Corbis; **225:** AP Images Alessandro Trovati; **230:** Digital Vision/Getty Images; **257:** Dave Kaup/AFP/Getty Images; **263:** PhotoAlto/Veer; **286:** George Waldman; **292:** Janine Wiedel Photolibrary/Alamy; **294:** © The New Yorker Collection 1976 George Booth from cartoonbank.com. All Rights Reserved.; **310:** Robbie McClaren; **315:** Courtesy Newman's Own and Gotham Advertising; **320:** The Advertising Archives; **337:** Susie Macnelly/Tribune Media Services; **344:** Topham/The Image Works; **366:** Jeffrey Coolidge/ Getty Images; **421:** Andrea Jones/ Garden Exposures Photo Library; **437:** Simon Reuterskiold/ Alamy; **444:** Niall McDiarmid/Alamy; **465, left:** Allstar Picture Library/Alamy; **465, right:** Mark Richards/ PhotoEdit Inc.; **473:** Brian F. Peterson/Corbis; **498:** Matthias Clamer/Getty Images; **545:** AFP/Getty Images.

Text Credits

Chapter 1

Page 24: James M. Henslin, *Sociology: A Down-To-Earth Approach*, Sixth Edition, pp. 380–381. Boston: Allyn and Bacon, 2003.

Chapter 2

Page 39: From Saul Kassin, *Psychology*, Fourth Edition, pp. 244–245. Copyright © 2004. Adapted by permission of Pearson Education, Inc., Upper Saddle River, NJ, and by permission of the author.; **Page 51:** Dave Ropeik, "What Really Scares Us" from *Parade Magazine*, March 30, 2003. Reprinted by permission of the author.

Chapter 3

Page 58: From Audesirk/Audesirk/Byers, *Biology: Life on Earth*, Eighth Edition, p. 381, Fig 19–12. Copyright © 2008 by Pearson Education, Inc. Reprinted by permission.; **Page 60:** Dictionary entry "drink." Copyright © 2006 by Houghton Mifflin Harcourt Publishing Company. Reproduced by permission from *The American Heritage Dictionary of the English Language, Fourth Edition.*; **Page 62:** Dictionary entry "green." Copyright © 2006 by Houghton Mifflin Harcourt Publishing Company. Reproduced by permission from *The American Heritage Dictionary of the English Language, Fourth Edition.*; **Page 63:** Dictionary entry "oblique." Copyright © 2006 by Houghton Mifflin Harcourt Publishing Company. Reproduced by permission from *The American Heritage Dictionary of the English Language, Fourth Edition.*; **Page 65:** Barbara Miller, *Anthropology*, Second Edition, p. 484. Boston: Pearson/Allyn and Bacon, 2008.; **Page 66:** Thesaurus entry "explain." Copyright

© 2004 by Houghton Mifflin Harcourt Publishing Company. Reproduced by permission from *The American Heritage College Thesaurus, First Edition.*; **Page 70:** H.L. Capron, *Computers: Tools for an Information Age*, Fifth Edition. Reading, MA: Addison-Wesley, 1998.; **Page 82:** Curtis, Byer, and Shainberg, *Living Well: Health in Your Hands*, p. 360. New York: HarperCollins College Publishers, 1995.; **Page 82:** Joseph A. DeVito, *Messages: Building Interpersonal Communication Skills*, Third Edition, pp. 22–23. New York: HarperCollins College Publishers, 1996.; **Page 82:** Curtis, Byer, and Shainberg, *Living Well: Health in Your Hands*, p. 67. New York: HarperCollins College Publishers, 1995.; **Page 83:** Robert A. Wallace, *Biology: The World of Life*, Sixth Edition, p. 834. New York: Addison Wesley Educational Publishers, 1992.; **Page 89:** Jeffrey Kluger, "The Buzz on Caffeine," *Time* Magazine, December 14, 2004. Copyright TIME, Inc. Reprinted by permission. TIME is a registered trademark if Time Inc. All rights reserved.

Chapter 4

Page 118: Cynthia Audet, "Scar" from *The Sun* (January 2003). Also appeared in *The Utne Reader*, May-June 2003. Copyright © 2003 by Cynthia Audet. Reprinted by permission of the author.

Chapter 5

Page 140: "Back to School: Students Must Be Prepared to Use Debt Wisely" from *Card News*, August 20, 2003, p. 1. Reprinted/adapted by permission of Online Financial Innovations.

Chapter 6

Page 167: David Bardeen, "Not Close Enough for Comfort" from *The New York Times Magazine*, February 29, 2004. Copyright © 2004 by David Bardeen. Reprinted by permission of the author.

Chapter 7

Page 191: Gentry Carlson, "The Longest Day." Reprinted by permission of the author.; **Page 194:** Anthony Swofford, "The Homecoming, and Then the Hard Part." From *Newsweek*, May 31, 2004. © 2004 Newsweek, Inc. All rights reserved. Used by permission and protected by the Copyright Laws of the United States. The printing, copying, redistribution, or retransmission of the Material without express written permission is prohibited. www.newsweek.com.

Chapter 8

Page 220: Kim Hyo-Joo, "English, Friend or Foe?" Reprinted by permission of the author.; **Page 223:** Lance Armstrong, "Before and After" from *It's Not About the Bike*. Copyright © 2000 by Lance Armstrong. Used by permission of G.P. Putnam's Sons, a division of Penguin Group (USA) Inc.

Chapter 9

Page 252: Kelly Bajier, "Rebuilding a Dream." Reprinted by permission of the author.; **Page 256:** Lornet Turnball, "Sudanese Describes How He Became a Slave at 7: Activist Wants World to Know Practice Continues," *The Seattle Times*, April 8, 2004, p. B2. Reprinted by permission of The Seattle Times.

Chapter 10

Page 281: Rachel Goodman, "The Places in My Life." Reprinted by permission of the author.; **Page 285:** Paul Duke, "If ER Nurses Crash, Will Patients Follow?" From *Newsweek*, February 2, 2004. © 2004 Newsweek, Inc. All rights reserved. Used by permission and protected by the Copyright Laws of the United States. The printing, copying, redistribution, or retransmission of the Material without express written permission is prohibited. www.newsweek.com.

Chapter 11

Page 306: Ebtisam Abusamak, "Am I a Conformist?" Reprinted by permission of the author.; **Page 309:** Christie Scotty, "Can I Get You Some Manners with That?" From *Newsweek*, October 18, 2004. © 2004 Newsweek, Inc. All rights reserved. Used by permission and protected by the Copyright Laws of the United States. The printing, copying, redistribution, or retransmission of the Material without express written permission is prohibited. www. newsweek.com.

Chapter 12

Page 332: Rachel Goodman, "Beautiful Words + Beautiful Images = One Beautiful Advertisement." Reprinted by permission of the author.; **Page 336:** From James M. Henslin, *Sociology: A Down-to-Earth Approach Core Concepts*, Third Edition, p. 303. © 2009 James M. Henslin. Reproduced by permission of Pearson Education, Inc.

Chapter 13

Page 355: Maya Preswich, adapted from "Halloween Fun Without Cultural Guilt," *The Daily Northwestern*, October 30, 1997. Reprinted by permission of The Daily Northwestern.; **Page 359:** Brent Staples, "A Brother's Murder," as appeared in *The New York Times Magazine* (About Men column), March 30, 1986, p. 72. Reprinted by permission of The New York Times Syndication Sales Corporation.

Chapter 14

Page 369: Sara Gruen, *Water for Elephants*, p. 21. Chapel Hill, NC: Algonquin Books of Chapel Hill, 2006.; **Page 371:** Michael Dorris, *A Yellow Raft in Blue Water*, p. 251. New York: Henry Holt and Company, 1987.; **Page 373:** Robert W. Christopherson, *Geosystems: An Introduction to Physical Geography*, Fourth Edition, p. 368. Upper Saddle River, NJ: Prentice-Hall, 2000.; **Page 379:** Bergman and Renwick, *Introduction to Geography*, Second Edition, p. 356. Upper saddle River, NJ: Prentice-Hall, 2002. Carnes and Garraty, *The American Nation*, Tenth Edition, p. 916. New York: Longman, 2000.; **Page 380:** James M. Henslin, *Sociology: A Down-To-Earth Approach*, Ninth Edition, p. 249. Boston: Pearson/Allyn and Bacon, 2008.; **Page 382:** Elaine Marieb, *Human Anatomy & Physiology*, Fifth Edition, p. 387. San Francisco: Benjamin Cummings, 2001.; **Page 384:** X.J. Kennedy and Dana Gioia, *Literature: An Introduction to Fiction, Poetry, and Drama*, Third Compact Edition, p. 7. New York: Longman, 2003.; **Page 386:** Rebecca J. Donatelle, *Health: The Basics*, Fifth Edition, p. 324. San Francisco: Benjamin Cummings, 2003.; **Page 388:** James M. Henslin, *Sociology: A Down-To-Earth Approach*, Ninth Edition, p. 169. Boston: Pearson/ Allyn and Bacon, 2008.; **Page 392:** Ronald J. Ebert and Ricky W. Griffin, *Business Essentials*, Fourth Edition, p 117. Upper Saddle River, NJ: Prentice Hall, 2003.; **Page 394:** Elaine Marieb, *Essentials of Human Anatomy & Physiology*, Ninth Edition, p. 124. San Francisco: Pearson/Benjamin Cummings, 2009.; **Page 395:** Paragraph by Ted Sawchuck. Reprinted by permission of the author.; **Page 397:** Elaine Marieb, *Essentials of Human Anatomy & Physiology*, Ninth Edition, p. 487. San Francisco: Pearson/Benjamin Cummings, 2009.; **Page 398:** Wood, Wood, and Boyd, *Mastering the World of Psychology*, Third Edition, p. 181. Boston: Pearson/Allyn and Bacon, 2008.; **Page 399:** Paragraph by Ted Sawchuck. Reprinted by permission of the author.; **Page 402:** Rebecca J. Donatelle, *Health: The Basics*, Eighth Edition, p. 205. San Francisco: Pearson/ Benjamin Cummings, 2009.; **Page 403:** William J. Germann and Cindy Stanfield, *Principles of Physiology*, First Edition, p. 622. San Francisco:

Benjamin Cummings, 2002.; **Page 407:** Donald W. Tuff, "Animals and Research," *NEA Higher Education Advocate*, Volume X, Number 5, March 1994.; **Page 409:** Angela Molina, "Animals and Research," *NEA Higher Education Advocate*, Volume X, Number 5, March 1994.; **Page 411:** Darlene Gallardo, "What My Culture Means to Me," *Hispanic Magazine*, June 1996. Reprinted by permission of Televisa Publishing.; **Page 414:** Leticia Salais, "Saying 'Adios' to Spanglish." From *Newsweek*, December 17, 2007. © 2007 Newsweek, Inc. All rights reserved. Used by permission and protected by the Copyright Laws of the United States. The printing, copying, redistribution, or retransmission of the Material without express written permission is prohibited. www.newsweek.com.

Chapter 15

Page 434: Fidel Sanchez, "The Worst and Best Jobs of My Life." Reprinted by permission of the author.; **Page 437:** Jerry Adler, "The Working-Class Smoker." From *Newsweek*, March 31, 2008. © 2008 Newsweek, Inc. All rights reserved. Used by permission and protected by the Copyright Laws of the United States. The printing, copying, redistribution, or retransmission of the Material without express written permission is prohibited. www.newsweek.com.

Chapter 16

Page 457: Zoë Cole, "Sports and Life." Reprinted by permission of the author.; **Page 464:** From James M. Henslin, *Sociology: A Down-to-Earth Approach Core Concepts*, Third Edition, pp. 116–117. © 2009 James M. Henslin. Reproduced by permission of Pearson Education, Inc.

Chapter 17

Page 482: Markella Tsoukalas, "You Looked Better on My Space." Reprinted by permission of the author.; **Page 489:** Kate Zernike, "Calling in Late" from *The New York Times*, October 26, 2003. © 2003 The New York Times. All rights reserved. Used by permission and protected by the Copyright Laws of the United States. The printing, copying, redistribution, or retransmission of the Material without express written permission is prohibited. www.nytimes.com.

Chapter 18

Page 508: Anna Majerczyk, "My Big Deal Knee Surgery." Reprinted by permission of the author.; **Page 512:** Dave Barry, "From Now On, Let Women Kill Their Own Spiders" from *Dave Barry Is Not Taking This Sitting Down* by Dave Barry. © 2000 by Dave Barry. Used by permission of Crown Publishers, a division of Random House, Inc.

Multicultural Reader

Page 522: Mary Pipher, excerpt from "The Beautiful Laughing Sisters-An Arrival Story" from *The Middle of Everywhere*. Copyright © 2002 by Mary Pipher. Reprinted by permission of Houghton Mifflin Harcourt Publishing Company. This material may not be reproduced in any form or by any means without the prior written permission of the publisher.; **Page 528:** Elizabeth Wong, "The Struggle to Be an All-American Girl," originally appeared in *The Los Angeles Times*, September 7, 1980. © 1980 by Elizabeth Wong. Reprinted by permission of the author.; **Page 532:** Sandra Márquez, "Are Latinos Different?" *Hispanic Magazine*, October 2003. Reprinted by permission of Televisa Publishing.; **Page 536:** Charisse Jones, "Light Skin Versus Dark," as first appeared in *Glamour Magazine*, 1995. Reprinted by permission of the author.; **Page 540:** Langston Hughes, "Thank You Ma'm" from *Short Stories* by Langston Hughes. Copyright © 1996 by Ramona Bass and Arnold Rampersad. Reprinted by permission of Hill and Wang, a division of Farrar, Straus and Giroux, LLC.; **Page 545:** James M. Henslin, "Tiger Woods and the Emerging Multiracial Identity: Mapping New Ethnic Terrain" from *Sociology: A Down-to-Earth Approach Core Concepts*, p. 253. © 2009 by James M. Henslin. Reproduced by permission of Pearson Education, Inc.

Index